The PROPER STUDY of MAN

The PROPER STUDY of MAN

Perspectives on the Social Sciences

JAMES FADIMAN

Stanford University

THE MACMILLAN COMPANY, *New York*

The Macmillan Company
866 Third Avenue, New York,
New York 10022

Collier-Macmillan Canada, Ltd.,
Toronto, Ontario

Library of Congress catalog card number:
74-120341
First Printing

Preface

This book of readings can be used as a supplement to any course in social science, psychology, sociology, or anthropology that deals with understanding human experience.

The parts are arranged so that there is a progression of related ideas. Core concepts are presented in Part I, with more specialized areas following. It is anticipated that most instructors will not assign all of the readings. It is hoped, however, that they will include in their assignments several articles that they personally assume might be least useful, factual, or appropriate. I have found that students have benefited from my negative preferences or biases about social science as well as from my positive choices.

The sections in this book have been chosen to highlight each other, to encourage discussion, debate, and the development of critical ability. Students can and should develop the acuity to discover flaws in reasoning, statistics, methodology, and the like. It is equally important that they develop the capacity to evaluate findings or ideas in any of the social sciences with some realization of the possible errors and the potential validity of the author's conclusions.

There is no particular emphasis on "classic papers" nor on the "most famous authors," although both are present to some extent. I have tried to build a collection that will encourage students to think more clearly about social science and the problem areas it encompasses.

It may be useful to discuss the format of this book for it differs somewhat from more conventional readers. The articles in each section are intended to raise basic issues that no amount of factual information can ever resolve. For example, the first section on values suggests that values are simultaneously central to behavior, relatively parochial, necessary, variable, highly personal, fixed, and mutable. There is no simple approach to understanding values nor is there a list of desirable or undesirable values included. The various points of view serve as disturbing, unsettling, and perhaps revealing attempts to grapple with values in their actual complexity. I suggest that, in using any subsection, the instructor have his students read all selections. The student will benefit most from the reflection of one selection upon another.

The word *perspectives* in the subtitle of this book is also repeated in the individual readings. They do not present a unified point of view nor are they intended to be biased toward any particular social science. I operate on the assumption that we are an improvable race, that we are different from animals in certain critical ways, and that we will survive. Thus my choice of readings may be more hopeful and humanistic than another teacher's. The critical notion, however, is that a student can gain more perspective on his world, his culture, his family, himself, and his core perceptions by using this book. If this collection furthers such a change, the remainder of the student's education will be more relevant and meaningful. Although this volume may be of limited use for a student planning a career in social science, through reading it he may find it easier to decide if he indeed seeks such a career and why.

The major topics chosen are not a random subset of headings, but form a progression. Part I, "Our Immediate World," deals with some of the fundamental aspects of our interpersonal existence: how we perceive, the effects of values on perception, and the effects of the family constellation on our values. This section touches close to our biological core. Whatever your theory of man, whatever your occupation, whatever your future plans, your immediate world must be grasped before you can understand more complex social environments.

Part II, "The World of Learning," moves from this core to the area where students and teachers are most directly involved on a day-to-day basis. Teaching, education, and creativity, the three "muses" of learning, are related yet separable, connected, yet distinct. A clearer look at these three areas allows a better synthesis.

Part III, "The Inner World," exposes and discusses the spectrum of possibilities for the individual within a culture, whose breadth can be perceived and confronted as one emerges from the learning environment. Mental illness, with its bewildering mosaic of light and shade, is distinct from the ruddy optimistic determinism of mental health. The dividing line between illness and health, the approved and the disapproved, the acceptable and unacceptable, is always being redrawn. Deviance is in the eye of the beholder. Psychedelics, whatever their eventual cultural effect, suggest views of the inner world that cut across all previous definitions of well-unwell, sane-insane, real-unreal. Normal and altered states of consciousness are the stuff of the inner world.

Part IV, "America and the Social System," moves from the inner world to our cultural environment. Like fish in water, we find it easy to overlook the space in which we move and set up our lives. I have used commentaries from different historical periods to look at certain underlying American propensities that have formed our culture. Contemporary questions of law and order, differences in opportunity, and the impact of specific institutions are classic issues in every democracy. Some of the interactive effects of these issues are presented.

Part V, "Perspectives on the Future," opens up the view of social science toward the future. The science of alternate futures, still without a Latin or

Greek suffix to designate it, is a social science combining the skills and intuition of a dozen disciplines and applying them to the task of developing intricate and detailed predictions of patterns of things to come. The selections here are intended to provide an awareness of the necessity for interweaving the humanism of social science with the pragmatic utilitarian thrust of the technology of tomorrow.

Thus this book progresses from a view of "the personal core," and educational process to a look at individual life styles, a consideration of the American environment, and, finally, to a glimpse of the shape of things to come. Obviously, the use you make of this book will be your own to decide. I have demonstrated how the book developed for me, and outlined one way of reading through it.

J. F.

Los Altos Hills, California

Contents

PART II *The World of Learning* 89

PART III *The Inner World* 171

To the Student

The purpose of this book is to introduce you to a series of both respectable and unsettling ideas and points of view that may be helpful in grasping whatever factual or value-free material you are attempting to learn. We cannot easily escape from our culture, our inner life, our education, or our family background (although we can with sufficient discipline transcend them). It is helpful to consider as meaningfully as possible the ideas, the prejudices, the speculations, the use of numbers, logic, metaphor, and persuasion employed by the many capable authors in this book to convince you about a host of notions. To agree or disagree is easy and requires no wisdom. Understanding why you take a stand and what are the implications of your point of view require a different quality and level of understanding.

To introduce you more fully to social science as a living science, all of the selections in this book deal directly with people. There are many fine studies on animals as well, but I could not, in all conscience, include them in a book that suggests avenues for human understanding. The word *perspectives* in the subtitle implies that this book is not filled with representative, average, or normal slices of social sciences. Instead, it focuses on relevant issues considered by different men of varied backgrounds and points of view. The writings included are useful in understanding contemporary man in contemporary culture.

In addition to this broad goal, the selections were made for the following purposes:

1. Understanding these readings should allow you to seek more effectively for answers to fundamental questions, including:

Who am I?

What am I doing here?

What is going on?

2. Evaluating these readings should allow you to realize that within the social sciences there are tools, methods, suggestions, even discoveries or explanations, that can help you answer these questions.

To further these purposes, I had two criteria other than appropriateness of the subject matter. The first was that the selection be well-written. (The sad truth about important but poorly written articles is that one rarely reads enough of them to grasp their importance.) The second criterion was that the articles should not be overtechnical. It is a problem in social science that the more technical articles have the shortest half-life. The methods of doing and publishing research change so swiftly that it is a rare study that is read ten years after it first appears. Fundamental issues about human behavior should be more durable than their 1940, 1950, or 1960 package.

Social science still suffers from the pomposity of a young discipline. As we learn more, we can become more restrained, more sensible. Until then enjoy this book for what it is.

J. F.

PART I *Our Immediate World*

This is where it starts. Immediate perception is that kind of awareness you experience when you get up in the morning and look into a mirror. You *know* that the reflection is you; no doubts, no questions, no pondering or introspective anxiety. You simply know.

There is a large body of evidence suggesting that many of the ideas, attitudes, and "facts" that give us a similar kind of gut response are modifiable, trainable, and teachable and subject to distortion and error. In this section you can explore some of the complexities that become evident when you lift the top off the obvious, the mundane, the most banal of our perceptions.

What is natural? The urge to reproduce, the tendency to war, the love of beauty, the male as dominant? All can be questioned. What is obvious? The universe is expanding; the earth is flat; life is an accident; humans are frightened of the dark. All of those ideas are or have been stated as truths. What causes what? Rain helps the crops grow; your sun is in Gemini thus you are likely to be fickle; $E=mc^2$. Those notions deal with current models of causality, but all can be questioned.

The first place to deal with these and related issues is in your immediate personal world. How we begin to see and grasp the world is critical to understanding how we then behave in relation to our view of the world.

SECTION A *Perception*

Things are seldom what they seem. The way we describe an event is one way of changing our memory and understanding of that event. Because we tend to obtain our picture of the world through our use of language, it is critical to appreciate how central our language is to our beliefs. The way we order the world determines many of our values and limits our capacity to observe new experiences.

The problem raised in these articles is that we are not able to see with simple, direct perception, but only through the various personal and cultural filters we use to simplify the world around us.

The error we make is that we think we know something until we are forced to look closely. When you read the short "haunted swing" article, consider that *even knowing the illusion makes it no less real.* Social scientists are supposed to be able to remain detached, strictly objective, as they observe interpersonal situations, personality manifestations, and cultural events. It is harder to do than it appears to be.

1

Cultural and Developmental Factors in Perception

Wayne Dennis

In the research literature on perception, one finds that the majority of investigators in this field have been interested in perception as it occurs in dark rooms and at exposure times of fractions of a second. The stimuli perceived usually are geometrical figures, numbers, letters, or words. The subjects, of course, are university students. The factors studied most commonly are stimulus factors. Psychologists in the past have been more interested in spatial relations than in social relations, more concerned with sensory interaction than with interaction between persons. . . .

Many of the approaches which have contributed most to the study of social

From Robert Blake, Glenn Ramsey (eds.), *Perception: An Approach to Personality*, copyright © 1951, The Ronald Press Company, New York. This selection is abridged from pp. 148–154, 169. Reprinted by permission of the publisher.

factors in perception are usually classified under other headings. Studies of suggestion, including hypnotism, have made several contributions. Investigations of emotional expression throw light upon social influences in perception as well as upon emotion. Projective techniques, of course, must deal with perception as well as with personality. Some important lines of evidence are historical and anthropological rather than experimental. In reviewing studies of social factors in perception, the writer will feel free to draw upon sources such as these, to which our books on perception seldom make reference.

It should be understood that, in developing his own topic, the present writer recognizes that he is dealing with only one of the factors which influence the perceptual processes. Structural determinants, chemical determinants, linguistic determinants all are present, but these topics are covered in other Chapters. While convinced of the importance of his topic, the present writer does not wish to be understood as championing a cause. If this Chapter neglects other factors, it is because that is expected. An adequate approach to problems in perception will require that all factors be considered in proper proportion. The plan of this symposium shows that the persons responsible for its organization were fully aware that a many-sided attack upon perceptual processes is demanded and that scientific partisanship is to be avoided.

Definition of "Perception"

To prevent misunderstanding, it is necessary to indicate first in what sense the word *perception* is used in this Chapter. It will be used to refer to an experience which is occasioned by the stimulation of sense organs. That is, perceptions are to be distinguished from memory images, reveries, trains of association, and hallucinations because these are not directly caused by stimulation.

A perception requires the presence of a stimulus. However, it is generally agreed that an experience which is occasioned by a stimulus is influenced not only by the immediate stimulus but also by the reinstatement of the effects of previous stimuli. If this were not so, we would speak of sensation rather than of perception. A stimulus not only elicits direct sensory effects but also arouses images and feelings which are fused with the more direct effects of the stimulus. The direct sensory effects are followed not only by immediate supplements to the stimulus but also by a whole chain of associations, memories, daydreams, reasoning, etc. The more distant of these, as indicated above, are not called perceptions. Ordinarily only the interpretation of the stimulus is called perception. The present writer believes, however, that the demarcation between perception and subsequent experiences must be an arbitrary one, and a precise distinction will not be attempted.

It should not be inferred from the preceding discussion that a stimulus appears as if out of the blue. That, of course, is erroneous. A stimulus breaks in upon a pre-existing experience which acts in part to determine whether or not the stimulus will be perceived and, if so, how it will be perceived. Thus, perception is not the result of a succession of discrete impingements from the outside world, but rather it is a continuous tuning-in, amplification, suppression, and interpretation.

Cultural Factors in Perception

HISTORICAL AND ANTHROPOLOGICAL EVIDENCE

As indicated previously, the experimental evidence for social influence in perception is slight, but the historical and anthropological evidence is great. Let us first take some instances from the recent past of our own society. Not many decades ago the use of lipstick and of cigarettes by the feminine sex was restricted to a certain group of professional women. Today no such restriction exists. It is almost certain that a woman wearing lipstick and smoking a cigarette not only arouses attitudes different today from formerly but that she is perceived differently. Within the same era of change, to choose a different example, the qualities perceived in a man with a full beard have doubtless altered considerably. We know that Wundt, William James, and G. Stanley Hall, bearded as they were, were perceived as unaffected, whereas it does not seem at all likely that these traits would be attributed to a psychologist of today who appeared in the same type of facial adornment.

Such simple examples of the influence of the social milieu upon the perception of personality traits could be multiplied endlessly. In certain Far Eastern areas, the woman who appears with a veil is perceived as conventional and modest; here the woman who appears with one may be judged to be alluring, probably intentionally alluring. What is heard in the South as normal speech is diagnosed as dialect in the North and vice versa. What is understood in Texas as a simple statement of fact is often interpreted elsewhere as unconscionable exaggeration. Turning to anthropological literature, we note that an illness which is seen in one society as a sign of supernatural favor is seen in another group as proof of sorcery. What is an omen of good luck in one culture forebodes ill in another. Old people are endowed with wisdom and power in the minds of one tribe, but by a second group they are despised and shunned. The sun itself is perceived variously as baleful and beneficent, moonlight may be eerie or romantic, and the same shooting star may have different significances, depending upon him who sees it.

Malinowski (8, 9) has shown that even the perception of resemblance in facial features is affected by culture, the Trobriand Islanders steadfastly refusing to see resemblances among maternal kinsmen but noting and perhaps exaggerating resemblances in the paternal line.

Among the few instances of traditional psychological research conducted among primitive groups, there is one (12) which is concerned with the Müller-Lyer illusion. The staff of the Torres Straits expedition in 1898 found that certain native groups were much less subject to the illusion than were European subjects. One hypothesis which was advanced to account for this relative immunity to the illusion was that the natives' use of spears, the heads of which resembled part of the Müller-Lyer figure, might have had some effect upon their responses to the test figure. Whatever the interpretation of this observation, the Torres Straits expedition deserves mention for including not only this illusion, but also many other perceptual tests in their research schedule, an inclusion which has not been duplicated by modern anthropological field workers.

Experimental Evidence

Studies of Set and Suggestion. As indicated previously, some of the experimental evidence regarding the effects of another person or of a group of persons upon an individual's perception comes from studies of set and of suggestion (2, 3).

Thus there is experimental evidence that what a person sees in a complex situation are the aspects of it to which he has been instructed to attend. For instance, if told to observe what follows certain stimuli, he does not perceive nearly as well what it is that precedes them. The control of experience by another person extends even to perceiving objects which are not present. This may seem to be a self-contradiction in the terms in which we have defined perception, but let us nevertheless, discuss such extreme cases.

We are familiar with the warmth illusion (4, 5), in which the subject reports an experience of warmth even though no heat has been applied to the apparatus, and a similar phenomenon in which an electric shock is reported in connection with a piece of equipment which has been disconnected from the electric circuit. A group suggestion demonstration has been reported by Slosson (14), who opened a vial of distilled water before a college chemistry class, telling the class that the vial contained a powerful odor. He asked the members of the class to hold up their hands as they smelled the odor. A wave of hands went up, starting with the foremost rows and spreading to the back. At least three fourths of the class perceived odor. The experiment had to be discontinued at the end of a minute because some of those in the front seats were being unpleasantly affected and were about to leave the room.

If it is objected that the subjects mentioned in the preceding experiments did not really have the experiences which they claimed but were giving reports merely to please the experimenter or to avoid punishment, more convincing evidence is provided by the study of Perky (11), which was done in Titchener's laboratory. Perky's subjects, several of whom were psychologists experienced in introspection, were, under certain conditions, unable to distinguish between visual stimuli and subjective visual images which were aroused by the instructions.

As an area intermediate between anthropological evidence and experimental evidence, the studies of Bartlett (1) may be mentioned. He investigated the reproduction by subjects of stories and pictures alien to their own culture. Bartlett found that reproduction was characteristically modified toward the familiar. Unfortunately for our purposes, Bartlett did not determine how much of this distortion occurred in perception and how much took place in the interval between perception and reproduction. Still other studies could be cited relevant to our present topic, but they would serve merely as further illustrations of an already evident point.

Among the recent writers who have stressed the social factors in perception is Ichheiser (7). He has proposed several types of false perception of the qualities of other persons. For instance, he proposes that what is true of a small segment of an individual's behavior is frequently assumed to be a general trait of that person. Again he proposes that a situational factor, such as unemployment, is often seen as due to personal qualities, a type of figure-and-ground effect in social perception. His monograph is full of fruitful hypotheses, although to be sure they are presented as obvious facts rather than as theories. Ichheiser presents no data; he scarcely suggests that data are needed to prove his views.

Thus in regard to social factors in perception we are at this point: no one seems to doubt that our perception of objects in the inanimate world, and particularly the meaning of these objects, is determined by culture. Our interpretation of persons likewise is admittedly influenced by our own group membership. While we recognize these influences when they are pointed out to us, they seem to play little part in our systematic accounts of personality. We assume that the general citizen's perception of the world is affected by his church, his vocation, his party, his lodge, and his newspaper, but we have not taken the trouble to study these influences. We assume that we as psychologists are somewhat more "scientific" and impartial in our perceptions than is the average man, but evidence on this point is similarly lacking.

Perceptual Errors in Psychologists. It is difficult to know where to begin in considering a topic in which the chief principle seems so obvious and yet for which there are so few adequate supporting investigations. However, it seems best to begin at home. So long as we as psychologists assume that we are relatively free of errors, prejudices, or preconceptions, we are less likely to develop effective demonstrations of the fallibility of perception. Let us see, therefore, whether there is evidence that we have not yet attained the objectivity and sophistication which we desire. In pursuing this aim, we shall review some instances in which psychologists have failed to recognize the role of social influences upon perception in their own professional subject matter.

Hypnosis. In this area, the field of hypnosis (6) provides some pretty examples of the fact that an observer's beliefs concerning psychological phenomena will determine what he perceives and, even further, what phenomena are actually produced.

Hypnotic phenomena were first believed to be due to a special form of energy, animal magnetism. This belief resulted in a person's experiencing magnetism and in exhibiting the expected behavior. When hypnosis was believed by Mesmer (10) to lead to crises, the crises were produced. For hypnotists who believed otherwise, the crises did not occur. When hypnosis was believed by Charcot to go through certain stages, the appropriate stages were exhibited by his subjects. When subjects knew nothing of these stages, they behaved differently. When conceptions changed, the phenomena changed. Gradually the hypnotists found that they had been under the control of their own suggestions no less than had their subjects. Today it is very generally agreed that hypnotism is scarcely to be distinguished from any other control of one person by another in situations in which no resistance, suspicion, or antagonism is aroused in the subject. One could cite experiments showing that results comparable to hypnosis can be obtained without any use of the concepts or the pattern of hypnosis. In general, Hull's extensive experiments (6) show little difference between so-called hypnotic and waking suggestion.

Infant Emotions. For a second example of the fallibility of perceptions, let us consider a study by a behaviorist, who might be expected to perceive data with little admixture of cultural influences. All of us are familiar with the views of Watson on emotions in infancy. Watson (15), in part on the basis of general observation and no doubt in part on other bases, became convinced that certain stimuli elicited distinctive results in the infant. Specifically, he proposed that loud sounds and falling elicited a pattern called fear and that restraint of movements was followed by a pattern called anger. Both of these were alleged to be distinguishable from the effects of hunger and of pain. These views were published by Watson not as theories but as facts based upon observation, and this was the beginning of a subculture in American psychology. The views were very widely disseminated and were accepted uncritically.

Sherman (13) took movies of infants stimulated in the ways indicated above and exhibited them to graduate students in psychology, to medical students, and to nurses. Apparently all these students had been indoctrinated with Watson's views, for their judgments concerning the response patterns which followed each stimulus corresponded closely to those of Watson. When, however, Sherman removed from the movie the frames which revealed the stimuli which were used, there was little agreement as to the patterns of response. In other words, Watson and the student subjects had been seeing what they expected to see. A better demonstration of social influences in the interpretation of human behavior could scarcely be devised. It should be especially important for us to know that the supposedly "hard-boiled" behaviorists were subject to distortion in their observation of behavior. One would expect persons engaged in psychological research to be particularly aware of the extent to which their "objective" data may be of their own creation. . . .

REFERENCES

1. Bartlett, F. C. *Remembering*. Cambridge: Cambridge University Press, 1932.
2. Binet, A. *La suggestibilité*. Paris: Schleicher Freres, 1900.

3. Bird, C. Suggestion and Suggestibility. *Psychol. Bull.,* 1939, *36*, 264–83.
4. Brown, W. Individual and sex differences in suggestibility. *Univ. Calif. Publ. Psychol.,* 1916, *2*, 291–430.
5. Heron, W. T. The group demonstration of illusory warmth as demonstrative of the phenomenon of suggestion. *J. abnorm. soc. Psychol.,* 1927, *22*, 341–44.
6. Hull, C. L. *Hypnosis and suggestibility.* New York: Appleton-Century-Crofts, Inc., 1933.
7. Ichheiser, G. Misunderstandings in human relations. *Amer. J. Sociol.,* 1949, *55*, Sept., Part 2.
8. Malinowski, B. The psychology of sex and the foundations of kinship in primitive societies. *Psyche,* London, 1923–24, *4*, 98–129.
9. ______. Psychoanalysis and anthropology. *Psyche,* London, 1923–24, *4*, 293–333.
10. Mesmer, F. A. *Mémoire sur la découverte du magnétisme animal.* Paris, 1779. Trans. G. Frankau, *Mesmerism.* London: Macdonald & Co., Ltd., 1948.
11. Perky, C. W. An experimental study of imagination. *Amer. J. Psychol.,* 1910, *21*, 422–52.
12. Seligman, C. G. The vision of the natives of British Guinea. In *Report of the Cambridge anthropological expedition to Torres Straits,* 1901, ed. A. C. Haddon. Cambridge University Press, Vol. II.
13. Sherman, M. The differentiation of emotional responses in infants. I. Judgments of emotional responses from motion picture views and from actual observation. *J. comp. Psychol.,* 1927, *7*, 265–84.
14. Slosson, E. E. A classroom demonstration of suggestion. *Psychol. Rev.,* 1899, *6*, 407–8.
15. Watson, J. B., & Morgan, J. J. B. Emotional reactions and psychological experimentation. *Amer. J. Physcol.,* 1917, *28*, 163–74.

2

Universal Ethical Principles

Ralph Linton

The problem of whether there are universally applicable ethical principles has been debated by philosophers for centuries, but recent world developments make it of much more than academic interest. . . .

All human societies are composed of members of the same mammalian species. . . . Every culture has to provide for the same basic physiological and psychological needs of individuals. Moreover, the organization, operation, and perpetuation of societies involve the same basic problems whether the society is in Australia, Africa, or Arkansas. Children have to be produced fed, sheltered, and trained. The diversified activities by which the various members of a society contribute to the well-being of the whole have to be assigned to individuals who must, in turn, be reimbursed for their services. Leadership in communal activities has to be provided and disputes have to be settled or at least circumscribed before they can disrupt the community.

Each of these things can be done in any one of several different ways, but all of them have to be done if the society is to survive. Moreover, the actual range of variation seems to be strictly delimited. As the social scientist's acquaintance with a large number of cultures improves, he cannot fail to be more impressed with their similarities than with their differences. This is especially the case where his acquaintance extends to continuous first-hand contact with the societies involved. Any individual who is willing to observe and imitate can orient himself in any human society. A Cortez or a Pizarro, confronted by a complex civilization most of whose overt behavior patterns were completely alien to his experience could still grasp the social and political picture and apply the same principles of statecraft which he would have used in Europe. . . .

One of the first requirements of a scientific approach to the problem of universal ethical principles is a clear delimitation of the frame of reference within which the comparative studies are to be made. *It must be stressed that the significant units are societies, not individuals.* . . .

Not only is the society the unit for ethical studies but *ethical systems function only in terms of in-groups.* Since the structure of societies is reminiscent of those Chinese sweetmeat boxes filled with smaller fitted boxes which contain still smaller ones, it is often difficult to determine the limits of the group which ethical systems apply. Thus every society contains a number of family groups, which are organized into communities. The communities are, in turn, organized into larger units, tribes at the "primitive" level, which may form part of still larger groupings such as confederacies or states established by conquest. Lastly, the concept of social membership may be extended to include the whole of mankind, as in some Messianic religions, or even, on the basis of a pantheistic philosophy, to include the whole of nature. Needless to say, at this point the emotional affects on which ethics depends for behavioral expression become so diluted that ethical concepts are rarely applied in practice. . . .

It seems that in spite of the common social phenomenon of groups within groups the same ethical system applies to all forms of social interaction within the society. In general, the smaller and more closely knit the unit within the society, the greater the emphasis on ethical considerations in the dealings of the unit's members with each other. Thus all societies reprehend unethical behavior between the members of nuclear families, i.e., parents and children, more severely than any other sort. Next in importance come more distant kindred and members of the same village, the relative emphasis differing with the culture. Ethical rules apply with still less vigor to dealings with members of other communities within the society and with least vigor to interaction with socially marginal individuals such as foreign traders or tolerated refugees. With these last two groups, length of association seems to be the most important factor: the longer the association, the stronger the tendency to recognize ethical principles in social interaction. . . .

To conclude, it seems probable that the extent to which ethical standards are recognized and adhered to in the social interactions of individuals is primarily a function (in the mathematical sense) of the closeness and continuity of association between the individuals involved. This might be explained in psychological terms of identification, but it can also be explained in terms of practical, informal sanctions. To cheat or abuse a person with whom you have to go on interacting afterward is much more likely to bring reprisals than is the same sort of behavior toward a comparative stranger. An excellent example of this principle is seen in the different patterns of treatment of field slaves and house slaves in all slave-holding societies. House slaves are always dealt with more leniently but a much higher level of honesty is expected from them. . . .

To return to the problem of universal ethical principles, ethical relativists seem to be particularly intrigued by the differences in the patterns of sex behavior approved in different societies. In fact, many of them seem to follow our own colloquial practice of making "morals" and "sex behavior" equivalent. Different societies do differ more in their attitudes toward sex than in any other activity within the field of ethics, but all of them have very definite rules governing sex behavior, and these rules have much in common. Thus all societies prohibit incest and punish it with great vigor. The same holds for rape, although there may be differences in the exact definition of this offense. The main differences in sexual mores lie in attitudes toward premaritial chastity and toward exclusive possession of spouses.

Many societies do not expect pre-marital chastity from either boys or girls. Their attitude toward adolescent affairs is much like our own amused tolerance of "puppy love." Thanks to the period of adolescent sterility, such affairs rarely result in pregnancy, so have little implication for the society as a whole. Nearly all societies frown on promiscuity, in the sense of entertaining a large number of partners. In most "primitive" societies the extension of incest taboos to remote relatives, and the comparatively small size of the adolescent group, limit the possibilities severely. In all societies which permit pre-marital affairs, it is taken for granted that they will result in the formation of permanent matings and the establishment of new nuclear families.

With one or two doubtful exceptions, marriage is a universal institution. Moreover, the lifelong union of spouses is everywhere the ideal no matter how easy and frequent separations may be in practice. The rights and duties between parents, between parents and offspring, and between children of the same parents are always culturally defined and enforced by ethical sanctions. Thus each parent must make certain contributions toward the economic life of the family. Loyalty to the spouse is expected in most societies and those which permit exceptions limit these to situations in which there is a conflict between the claims of one spouse and those of the other spouse's kindred.

The marriage relation always limits the sex activities of both parties. Although sex relations with more than one individual may be permitted, the available partners and the conditions under which they may enjoy a spouse's favors are always culturally established and ethically sanctioned. Even in polygynous and polyandrous societies, the rights of plural wives or husbands are clearly defined. Thus in many polygynous societies, each wife is entitled to her husband's company for one day in turn. For a husband to spend another wife's day with a favorite is regarded as adultery and more severely reprehended than ordinary adultery, since it strikes at the very roots of the family system.

Permitted sex relations by married people outside marriage are found in about the same number of societies and frequently in the same societies as those which permit pre-marital experimentation. However, the possible partners are socially designated and the affairs are arranged in such a way as to avoid either disruption of the family unit or ego injury to the spouse. Thus in wife-lending the borrower is, with few exceptions, either a close relative, such as a younger brother, or a friend who does not live in the same community. In either case the man who receives the favor is expected to reciprocate in kind when he is able to do so. Conversely, the wife may have sexual rights in some of the husband's male relatives, but culture patterns establish which ones and the arrangement is thoroughly understood at the time of the marriage.

Both permitted adolescent love-making and permitted non-monogamous sex behavior in marriage reflect a lowered evaluation of sex per se. Where the sexual act is regarded as a normal, pleasurable exercise, like eating, and where parentage is a matter of social ascription rather than biological relationship, the claims of kinship or even friendship are given precedence over those of exclusive possession. At the same time, practically all societies recognize adultery as unethical and punish the offenders. The same man who will lend his wife to a friend or brother will be roused to fury if she goes to another man without his permission.

Turning to the rights and duties between parents and children, the only point at which sex enters is in the almost universal prohibition of sex relations between parent and offspring. As far as known, no society permits sex relations between mother and son while only two or three permit it between father and daughter, and even in these it is limited to royal or sacerdotal groups. The comparative study of other parent-child relations is complicated by the fact that societies differ greatly in the emphasis they place on the nuclear family. In several matrilineal societies, what are ordinarily the paternal functions are shifted from a woman's husband to her brother. In such cases the ethical obligations between a child and his maternal uncle are practically the same as those between a child and his father in patrilineal societies.

In all societies the parents are expected to care for and train children while the children in turn will care for them in old age. In connection with the training, different societies permit differing disciplinary techniques which vary greatly in severity. However, no society approves sadistic behavior on the part of a parent or any sort of discipline which results in permament injury. With few exceptions, children are expected to accord both parents respect and obedience. Violence against a parent is a major crime in nearly all societies. Since the care and training of children is the primary function of the family as an institution, failure of either side to live up to its obligations in the parent-child relationship is severely reprehended. Supernatural sanctions are invoked more frequently here than in any other type of social interaction.

The obligations between siblings show more variation than those between parents and offspring. In all cases, some degree of loyalty and mutual assistance is prescribed, but the extent of these claims differs enormously in different societies. The rivalry of half-siblings is recognized and allowed for in the ethical systems of most polygynous societies but violence, treachery, and deceit are disapproved. Even in monogamous societies there is always some conflict between the claims of the sibling group and those of the new nuclear families established by its members' marriages. Various societies lay stress on one or the other of these groups as the focus for individual loyalties. Patterns vary from societies which expect the wife to sever all relations with her siblings at marriage to those which regard spouses as only peripherally attached to the functional family. This is, in such cases, a group of real or classificatory siblings. The most nearly universal regulation governing sibling interaction is the prohibition of sex relations, but even here the exceptions are much more numerous than for the parent-child incest rule.

In addition to its basic function of child-rearing, the family is normally an economic unit for both production and consumption. This pattern tends to break down under modern urban conditions, but throughout most of the world ethical sanctions are invoked to ensure that each family member contributes to the family economy and also receives an adequate return for his services. In cases where some member seems to receive a disproportionate share of the family income, investigation usually shows that this share is not used for personal benefit but is disbursed to increase the family prestige.

Lastly, the family everywhere is expected to support its members' interests and to present a united front to outsiders. Particular members may be sacrificed for the good of the whole, but to side with another family against one's own is everywhere regarded as wrong. The only cases in which it might be adjudged right for a man to ignore the interest of his own family are those in which there is a clash between this and the interest of some larger social unit to which the family belongs. In such cases of conflicting loyalties, some cultures prescribe that the family be favored, some the larger group. The significant point is that loyalty to any social unit to which the individual belongs is always regarded as a virtue, disloyalty as a vice.

So much for the ethical patterns governing sex behavior and family life. It can be seen that the similarities far outweigh the differences. The same seems to hold true for another aspect of culture, i.e., property, although here also there is considerable difference in the behavior patterns which implement the common values. To understand the ethical values involved, it is necessary to give a brief description of property concepts in general.

All societies recognize personal property in tools, utensils, ornaments, and so forth. The only exceptions are a few completely communistic societies established by sophisticated individuals as a part of religious movements, and no society of this sort has ever had a long duration. The concept of personal property is easily explained in terms of the individual's identification with objects he has made or habitually uses. Similar identification can often be seen in domestic animals. Products of hunting and food gathering, domestic animals and crops, either garnered or in the field, are universally owned by either individuals or the smallest family groupings operating as organized economic units. The principle involved seems to be that the products of skill or labor belong to the individual or group which has exercised these qualities. Private ownership of means of production is mainly a phenomenon of civilization, especially modern mechanized civilization, but it is not unknown in simpler societies. Individuals, families, or even corporate groups often own such productive appliances as canoes or nets and permit others to use them for a fee.

With respect to land or other irreplaceable natural resources all societies retain the right of eminent domain. The differences lie in the point at which the society recognizes a threat to its well-being and takes over. However, subject to this right, there is a universal tendency toward individual or family ownership of land or resources which possess continuing value. Even at the simplest levels of technological development, family hunting territories are usual in regions where game is non-migratory. More advanced societies recognize ownership of such resources as winter pasture, fishing places, and improved land. With respect to the last, it is a general rule that crops belong to the individuals or groups who have planted them, but the land itself reverts to the society's common holding when it is no longer in use. Most societies have, in addition to individual holdings, waste land of little value whose products can be exploited by any society member.

There are no economically equalitarian societies. Even among nomadic food gatherers the good hunter with a clever wife has more food, better equipment, and more ornaments. Among food-raising peoples the inequalities in wealth may be striking. It is not uncommon in such societies to have natural resources preempted by wealthy families to such a degree that poor individuals are almost excluded from access to them. However, all societies have culturally recognized patterns for the care of the poor or unfortunate. Extension of family ties and disgrace attaching to failure to care for relatives are usually enough to provide food and shelter at a survival level. Charity, as distinct from the fulfillment of family obligations, is also common. In fact, in most uncivilized societies the main incentive for the accumulation of property seems to be the desire to disburse the surplus at public functions, thus acquiring prestige. The principal alternative to this practice is the destruction or interment of surplus property at funerals but this form of ostentatious waste is highly developed in only a few cultures.

Societies living under conditions that preclude any large accumulation of property nearly all have patterns for sharing food and lending surplus tools and weapons. This is quite different from genuine communal ownership, since the owner of the things shared gains prestige and expects reciprocal favors. Under such conditions theft becomes ridiculous and is so regarded. It is said that the Eskimos do not punish thieves but whenever a thief's name is mentioned everybody laughs. In societies where accumulation is possible, theft is everywhere regarded as a crime and is severely punished. Actually, it is rare in most uncivilized communities. This may be due less to ethical considerations than to the ease with which objects which are not mass-produced can be recognized. Only a kleptomaniac would steal something which he could not use or profitably dispose of without immediate detection. It is worth noting in this connection that with the introduction of money into uncivilized societies both hoarding and theft of money usually appear even though attitudes toward theft of other types of property remain unchanged.

All societies recognize economic obligations of the sort involved in exchange of goods and services and the individual who fails to live up to them is punished simply but effectively by exclusion from future exchanges. Attitudes with respect to sharp practices show more diversity but each society defines the areas in which such practices are permitted and usually has rules as to what techniques are or are not permissible. Thus the Yankee of the horse-trading era regarded it as quite legitimate to hide the faults of a horse as long as he could do so without a direct lie. The trading was regarded as a sport, a battle of wits waged according to mutually recognized rules. However, once the parties agreed that it was a trade, neither side could withdraw without complete loss of reputation. . . .

Attitudes toward lying differ greatly in various societies. The North European is almost unique in regarding verbal truth as an ethical value per se. Most societies regard lying as quite permissible under most circumstances and ability to detect the truth regardless of what is said as a legitimate test of intelligence. The judgments of Solomon brought him great credit but it is not recorded that the litigants were embarrassed at being caught in untruth. However, all societies demand truth in at least certain areas of personal interaction, and a great many of them seek to insure it by invoking supernatural sanctions, i.e., oaths.

Attitudes on offenses against the person appear highly variable at first sight. It would seem that the only offense which is universally reprehended is killing or maiming without justification. All societies recognize and punish the crime of murder as distinct from justifiable homicide, but their definitions of murder differ considerably. Some of the complications disappear when it is recognized that many societies place ego injury through insult on a par with bodily injury. Such injury justifies physical retaliation, often by culturally delimited techniques, as in the *code duello*. However, it is only with the development of government in the modern sense that the problem of preventing physical aggression can be solved. Where blood revenge is a culture pattern, it may serve as a deterrent to initial acts of violence, but once the act has been committed the consequences are an increasing number of violent acts. The most effective technique for preventing violence in the absence of centralized authority is the institution of *wergild* by which the offender has to pay a fine so heavy that he can rarely meet it without the assistance of his relatives. The knowledge that they will have to part with property if one of the kindred maims or kills a member of another kin group insures that they will do their best to prevent the crime from taking place.

It is interesting to note that no society has successfully solved the problem of preventing psychic aggression. The practice of malevolent magic must not be classed under that head since, to societies which believe in it, it ranks as a form of physical attack. Most societies distinguish between justifiable and unjustifiable use of malevolent magic and punish the latter with great severity, since the insidious nature of the magician's attack makes him a potential threat to the whole community. Psychic aggression either directly through curses or indirectly through slander is actionable in many societies. However, the form which such aggression takes varies greatly from one society to another. Many factors are involved in an individual's insult reaction. Even in Europe where the *code duello* had been elaborated for generations, courts of honor had to be convened to pass on doubtful cases of insult.

Information is now available on a large number of cultures which are so widely distributed in time and space that they provide an adequate sample for comparative studies. There is no society on record which does not have an ethical system. Apparent exceptions are due to the observer's failure to recognize the social limits within which the system is expected to apply. By an ethical system we mean definite ideas regarding what constitutes right or wrong behavior in most situations involving social interaction with a high degree of consistency in the values which these ideas reflect. Whether the society's members consciously generalize from their specific judgments of right and wrong to an abstract ethical system is a different matter. However, a certain amount of generalization is inevitable. There must be agreement on general principles governing the interaction of individuals since the actual situations which may arise are extremely variable. Even in our own law courts, after thousands of years of accumulated experience, every year produces cases for which there are no precedents.

The values reflected in ethical systems seem to be much the same everywhere. However, the relative importance attached to particular values differs considerably from one society to another and even at different points in the history of the same society. Thus one society may attach great importance to chastity per se and organize wide areas of behavior about it while another regards it as secondary to such a value as hospitality. Contrast the British attitudes toward sex during the Regency with those of a generation later under Queen Victoria. Again, human life may be held so cheap relative to honor that no man is counted as really adult until he has fought a duel, or so dear that killing under any circumstances is punished by death or exile. The important point is that in spite of such variations in the value hierarchy, there is no society which does not have adverse attitudes toward killing society members or in which sexual selectivity is not approved.

Among the values involved in ethical systems, that of insuring the perpetuation and successful functioning of the society always takes first place. Acts which threaten the group are condemned and punished with greater severity than those which threaten only individuals. Note our own attitudes toward treason and toward murder. All societies also recognize that there is a point beyond which the interests of the individual must be made subordinate to those of the state. Note the universality of property regulations comparable to our own right of eminent domain. Within the limits set by the priority given to a society's needs, all ethical systems also seek to provide for the physical and psychological needs of individuals. All societies guard persons in the marriage relationship from both physical deprivation and ego injury by recognizing and enforcing their mutual rights and duties. They also provide a high degree of security in all the other relationships within the family group by approving all forms of cooperation and condemning acts which threaten family solidarity. The recognition of personal property militates against both actual deprivation and ego injury while all societies have developed techniques for the distribution of economic surplus to those who are in want. Violence, allowing for the cultural differences in definition of that term, is everywhere condemned and techniques are present to prevent its outbreak and minimize its consequences. This list could be extended considerably in terms of less fundamental values which are common to a very large proportion of the world's cultures if not to all.

The resemblances in ethical concepts so far outweigh the differences that a sound basis for mutual understanding between groups of different cultures is already in existence. The present difficulties seem to stem from two main sources: the first is that societies which share the same values often differ considerably in the relative importance which they attach to them. To judge from historic evidence on the changes which have taken place in various cultures, such differences are by no means insurmountable. A greater difficulty lies in the age-old tendency of every society's members to assume that ethical systems apply only within their own tribe or nation. This attitude is difficult to overcome but the modern world is witnessing a rapid expansion of social horizons. When people learn to think of themselves as members of a single world society, it will be easy for them to agree on a single ethical system.

3

Language, Thought, and Reality

Benjamin L. Whorf

Every normal person in the world, past infancy in years, can and does talk. By virtue of that fact, every person—civilized or uncivilized—carries through life certain naïve but deeply rooted ideas about talking and its relation to thinking. Because of their firm connection with speech habits that have become unconscious and automatic, these notions tend to be rather intolerant of opposition. They are by no means entirely personal and haphazard; their basis is definitely systematic, so that we are justified in calling them a system of natural logic—a term that seems to me preferable to the term common sense, often used for the same thing.

According to natural logic, the fact that every person has talked fluently since infancy makes every man his own authority on the process by which he formulates and communicates. He has merely to consult a common substratum of logic or reason which he and eveyone else is supposed to possess. Natural logic says that talking is merely an incidental process concerned strictly with communication, not with formulation of ideas. Talking, or the use of language, is supposed only to "express" what is essentially already formulated nonlinguistically. Formulation is an independent process, called thought or thinking, and is supposed to be largely indifferent to the nature of particular languages. Languages have grammars, which are assumed to be merely norms of conventional and social correctness, but the use of language is supposed to be guided not so much by them as by correct, rational, or intelligent THINKING.

Thought, in this view, does not depend on grammar but on laws of logic or reason which are supposed to be the same for all observers of the universe—to represent a rationale in the universe that can be "found" independently by all intelligent observers, whether they speak Chinese or Choctaw. In our own culture, the formulations of mathematics and of formal logic have acquired the reputation of dealing with this order of things: i.e., with the realm and laws of pure thought. Natural logic holds that different languages are essentially parallel methods for expressing this one-and-the-same rationale of thought and, hence, differ really in but minor ways which may seem important only because they are seen at close range. It holds that mathematics, symbolic logic, philosophy, and so on are systems contrasted with language which deal directly with this realm of thought, not that they are themselves specialized extensions of language. . .

When linguists became able to examine critically and scientifically a large number of languages of widely different patterns, their base of reference was expanded; they

Reprinted from *Language, Thought, and Reality: Selected Writings of Benjamin Lee Whorf* (John B. Carroll, ed.), by permission of The M.I.T. Press, Cambridge, Massachusetts.

experienced an interruption of phenomena hitherto held universal, and a whole new order of significances came into their ken. It was found that the background linguistic system (in other words, the grammar) of each language is not merely a reproducing instrument for voicing ideas but rather is itself the shaper of ideas, the program and guide for the individual's mental activity, for his analysis of impressions, for his synthesis of his mental stock in trade. Formulation of ideas is not an independent process, strictly rational in the old sense, but is part of a particular grammar, and differs, from slightly to greatly, between different grammars. We dissect nature along lines laid down by our native languages. The categories and types that we isolate from the world of phenomena we do not find there because they stare every observer in the face; on the contrary, the world is presented in a kaleidoscopic flux of impressions which has to be organized by our minds—and this means largely by the linguistic systems in our minds. We cut nature up, organize it into concepts, and ascribe significances as we do, largely because we are parties to an agreement to organize it in this way—an agreement that holds throughout our speech community and is codified in the patterns of our language. The agreement is, of course, an implicit and unstated one, BUT ITS TERMS ARE ABSOLUTELY OBLIGATORY; we cannot talk at all except by subscribing to the organization and classification of data which the agreement decrees.

This fact is very significant for modern science, for it means that no individual is free to describe nature with absolute impartiality but is constrained to certain modes of interpretation even while he thinks himself most free. The person most nearly free in such respects would be a linguist familiar with many widely different linguistic systems. As yet no linguist is in any such position. We are thus introduced to a new principle of relativity, which holds that all observers are not led by the same physical evidence to the same picture of the universe, unless their linguistic backgrounds are similar, or can in some way be calibrated. . . .

When Semitic, Chinese, Tibetan, or African languages are contrasted with our own, the divergence in analysis of the world becomes more apparent; and, when we bring in the native languages of the Americas, where speech communities for many millenniums have gone their ways independently of each other and of the Old World, the fact that languages dissect nature in many different ways becomes patent. The relativity of all conceptual systems, ours included, and their dependence upon language stand revealed. That American Indians speaking only their native tongues are never called upon to act as scientific observers is in no wise to the point. To exclude the evidence which their languages offer as to what the human mind can do is like expecting botanists to study nothing but food plants and hothouse roses and then tell us what the plant world is liked!

Let us consider a few examples. In English we divide most of our words into two classes, which have different grammatical and logical properties. Class 1 we call nouns, e.g., 'house, man'; class 2, verbs, e.g., 'hit, run.' Many words of one class can act secondarily as of the other class, e.g., 'a hit, a run,' or 'to man (the boat),' but, on the primary level, the division between the classes is absolute. Our language thus gives us bipolar division of nature. But nature herself is not thus polarized. If it be said that 'strike, turn, run,' are verbs because they denote temporary or short-lasting events, i.e., actions, why then is 'fist' a noun? It also is a temporary event. Why are 'lightning, spark, wave, eddy, pulsation, flame, storm, phase, cycle, spasm, noise, emotion' nouns? They are temporary events. If 'man' and 'house' are nouns because they are long-lasting and stable events, i.e., things, what then are 'keep, adhere, extend, project, continue, persist, grow, dwell,' and so on doing among the verbs? If it be objected that 'possess, adhere' are verbs because they are stable relationships rather than stable precepts, why then should 'equilibrium, pressure, current, peace, group, nation, society, tribe, sister,' or any kinship term be among the nouns? It will be found that an "event" to US means "what our language classes as a verb" or something analogized therefrom. And it will be found that it is not possible to define 'event, thing, object, relationship,' and so on, from nature, but that to define them always involves a circuitous return to the grammatical categories of the definer's language.

In the Hopi language, 'lightning, wave, flame, meteor, puff of smoke, pulsation' are verbs—events of necessarily brief duration cannot be anything but verbs. 'Cloud' and 'storm' are at about the lower limit of duration for nouns. Hopi, you see, actually has a classification of events (or linguistic isolates) by duration type, something strange to our modes of thought. On the other hand, in Nootka, a language of Vancouver Island, all words seem to us to be verbs, but really there are no classes 1 and 2; we have, as it were, a monistic view of nature that gives us only one class of word for all kinds of events. 'A house occurs' or 'it houses' is the way of saying 'house,' exactly like 'a flame occurs' or 'it burns.' These terms seem to us like verbs because they are inflected for durational and temporal nuances, so that the suffixes of the word for house event make it mean long-lasting house, temporary house, future house, house that used to be, what started out to be a house, and so on. . .

One significant contribution to science from the linguistic point of view may be the greater development of our sense of perspective. We shall no longer be able to see a few recent dialects of the Indo-European family, and the rationalizing techniques elaborated from their patterns, as the apex of the evolution of the human mind, nor their present wide spread as due to any survival from fitness or to anything but a few events of history—events that could be called fortunate only from the parochial point of view of the favored parties. They, and our own thought processes with them, can no longer be envisioned as spanning the gamut of reason and knowledge but only as one constellation in a galactic expanse. A fair realization of the incredible degree of diversity of linguistic system that ranges over the globe leaves one with an inescapable feeling that the human spirit is inconceivably old; that the few thousand years of history covered by our written records are no more than the thickness of a pencil mark on the scale that measures our past experience on this planet; that the events of these recent millenniums spell nothing in any evolutionary wise, that the race has taken no sudden spurt, achieved no commanding synthesis during recent millenniums, but has only played a little with a few of the linguistic formulations and views of nature bequeathed from an inexpressibly longer past. Yet neither this feeling nor the sense of precarious dependence of all we know upon linguistic tools which themselves are largely unknown need be discouraging to science but should, rather, foster that humility which accompanies the true scientific spirit, and thus forbid that arrogance of the mind which hinders real scientific curiosity and detachment.

4

Sight, Sound, and the Fury

Marshall McLuhan

On his recent visit to America, Roy Campbell mentioned that when Dylan Thomas had discovered he could read poetry on the radio, this discovery transformed his later poetry for the better. Thomas discovered a new dimension in his language when he established a new relation with the public.

Until Gutenberg, poetic publication meant the reading or singing of one's poems to a small audience. When poetry began to exist primarily on the printed page, in the seventeenth century, there occurred that strange mixture of sight and sound later known as "metaphysical poetry" which has so much in common with modern poetry.

American colonization began when the only culture available to most men was that of the printed book. European culture was then, as now, as much an affair of music, painting, sculpture, and communication as it was of literature. So that to this day North Americans associate culture mainly with books. But, paradoxically, it is in North America that the new media of sight and sound have had the greatest popular sway. Is it precisely because we make the widest separation between culture and our new media that we are unable to see the new media as serious culture? Have four centuries of book-culture hypnotized us into such concentration on the content of books and the new media that we cannot see that the very form of any medium of communication is as important as anything that it conveys?

Ireland is perhaps the only part of the English-speaking world where the oral tradition of culture has strongly persisted in spite of the printed page. And Ireland has given us Wilde, Shaw, Yeats, Synge, and Joyce in recent years—all of them masters of the magic of the spoken word. A Ballynooley farmer who returned to Ireland from America said to his neighbor: "In three years I didn't meet a man who could sing a ballad, let alone compose one on his feet."

The printed page was itself a highly specialized (and spatialized) form of communication. In 1500 A.D. it was revolutionary. And Erasmus was perhaps the first to grasp the fact that the revolution was going to occur above all in the classroom. He devoted himself to the production of textbooks and to the setting up of grammar schools. The printed book soon liquidated two thousand years of manuscript culture. It created the solitary student. It set up the rule of private interpretation against public disputation. It established the divorce between "literature and life." It created a new and highly

Reprinted from *Commonweal,* Vol. 60 (1954), pp. 168–97, by permission of the publisher.

abstract culture because it was itself a mechanized form of culture. Today, when the textbook has yielded to the classroom project and the classroom as social workshop and discussion group, it is easier for us to notice what was going on in 1500. Today we know that the turn to the visual on one hand, that is, to photography, and to the auditory media of radio and public address systems on the other hand, has created a totally new environment for the educational process.

André Malraux has recently popularized the notion of the art revolution of our time in his *Museum without Walls.* His theme is that the picture book today can embrace a greater range of art than any museum. By bringing such a range of art within portable compass, however, it has changed even the painter's approach to painting. Again, it is not just a question of message, image, or content. The picture-book as a museum without walls has for the artist a new technical meaning, just as for the spectator, pictorial communication means a large but unconscious shift in his ways of thought and feeling.

We have long been accustomed to the notion that a person's beliefs shape and color his existence. They provide the windows which frame, and through which he views, all events. We are less accustomed to the notion that the shapes of a technological environment are also idea-windows. Every shape (gimmick or metropolis), every situation planned and realized by man's factive intelligence, is a window which reveals or distorts reality. Today, when power technology has taken over the entire global environment to be manipulated as the material of art, nature has disappeared with nature-poetry. And the effectiveness of the classroom has diminished with the decline of the monopoly of book-culture. If Erasmus saw the classroom as the new stage for the drama of the printing press, we can see today that the new situation for young and old alike is classrooms without walls. The entire urban environment has become aggressively pedagogic. Everybody and everything has a message to declare, a line to plug.

This is the time of transition from the commercial age, when it was the production and distribution of commodities which occupied the ingenuity of men. Today we have moved from the production of packaged goods to the packaging of information. Formerly we invaded foreign markets with goods. Today we invade whole cultures with packaged information, entertainment, and ideas. In view of the instantaneous global scope of the new media of sight and sound, even the newspaper is slow. But the press ousted the book in the nineteenth century because the book arrived too late. The newspaper page was not a mere enlargement of the book page. It was, like the movie, a new collective art form.

To retrace some of this ground, it will help to recall that in the *Phaedrus,* Plato argued that the new arrival of writing would revolutionize culture for the worse. He suggested that it would substitute reminiscence for thought and mechanical learning for the true dialectic of the living quest for truth by discourse and conversation. It was as if he foresaw the library of Alexandria and the unending exegesis upon previous exegesis of the scholiasts and grammarians.

It would seem that the great virtue of writing is its power to arrest the swift process of thought for steady contemplation and analysis. Writing is the translation of the audible into the visual. In large measure it is the spatialization of thought. Yet writing on papyrus and parchment fostered a very different set of mental habits from those who associate with print and books. In the first place, silent reading was unknown until the macadamized, streamlined surfaces of the printed page arrived to permit swift traverse of the eye alone. In the second place, difficulty of access to manuscripts impelled students to memorize so far as possible everything they read. This led to encyclopedism, but also to having on tap in oral discourse one's entire erudition.

The child at school in the Middle Ages had first to make his own copies of texts from dictation. He had next to compile his own grammar and lexicon and commonplace book. The arrival of plenty of cheap, uniform, printed texts changed all this. The mechanization of writing by means of the assembly line of movable type speedily expanded the range of available reading and just as quickly reduced the habit of oral discourse as a way of learning. During the sixteenth century, however, a degree of equilibrium persisted between oral and written learning which we associate with the special excellence of Elizabethan drama, sermon, and poetry.

In the reverse direction, much of the vivid energy of American speech and writing in the twentieth century is the result of the movement away from book-culture toward oral communication. This nonliterary direction of speech has been felt to a much smaller degree in England and in Europe during the same period. Radio in particular has encouraged the return to the panel discussion and the round table. But the spontaneous move toward the seminar and class discussion as learning process has been helped by press and photography too, in so far as these have challenged the monopoly of the book.

Above all, the habits of the business community in demanding conference and discussion as the swift way of establishing insight into method and procedure in various specialized branches of business—these have prompted the new reliance on speech as a means of discovery. It is significant, for example, that the atomic physicists found that only by daily, face-to-face association could they get on with their tasks during the past war.

It has long been a truism that changes in material culture cause shifts in the patterns of the entire culture. The ancient road made possible armies and empires and destroyed the isolated city states of Greece. But the road depended in the first place on writing. Behind the imperial command of great land areas stood the written word in easily transportable form. In the nineteenth century, the newspapers, especially after the telegraph, paid for new roads and faster transport by land and sea. The press altered the forms of government and the telegraph brought secret diplomacy to an end. When events in Egypt or Russia, London, Paris, or New York were known everywhere at once, the time for secret negotiation was reduced to hours and minutes. And the great national populations of the world, alerted and emotionalized by the press, could confront one another immediately for a showdown.

Printing had from the first fostered nationalism because the vernaculars with their large reading publics were more profitable to commercial publishers than Latin. The press has pushed this nationalism to its ultimate point. There it remains. But photography and movies, like music and painting, are international in their power of appeal. The power of pictures to leap over national frontiers and prejudices is well-known, for good and ill.

One aspect of the press deserves special comment in this same respect. The contents of newspapers, their messages and information, have steadily promoted nationalism. But the form of the newspaper page is powerfully intercultural and international. The unformulated message of an assembly of news items from every quarter of the globe is that the world today is one city. All war is civil war. All suffering is our own. So that regardless of the political line, or the time or the place, the mere format of the press exerts a single pressure. Basic acceptance of this fact is recorded in the steady weakening of interest in political parties everywhere.

From the point of view of its format, the press as a daily cross-section of the globe is a mirror of the technological instruments of communication. It is the popular daily book, the great collective poem, the universal entertainment of our age. As such it has modified poetic techniques and in turn has already been modified by the newer media of movie, radio, and television. These present revolutions in communication as radical as printing itself. In fact, they are "magic casements opening on the foam of perilous seas," on which few of us have yet ventured in thought, art or living. If Erasmus was the first to size up and exploit the printing press as a new force in art and education, James Joyce was the first to seize upon newspaper, radio, movie, and television to set up his "verbivocovisual" drama in *Finnegans Wake*. Pound and Eliot are, in comparison with Joyce, timid devotees of the book as art form. But most of the difficulties which the ordinary person encounters with the poetry of Pound and Eliot disappear if it is viewed as a historical newsreel of persons, myths, ideas, and events with thematic musical score built in. Joyce had a much greater trust of language and reality than Pound or Eliot. By contrast they give their language and reality the Hollywood glamor treatment. Joyce is closer to a De Sica film with its awareness of the intimate riches of the most ordinary scenes and situations.

But the reader who approaches Pound, Eliot, and Joyce alike as exploiters of the cinematic aspects of language will arrive at appreciation more quickly than the one who unconsciously tries to make sense of them by reducing their use of the new media of communication to the abstract linear forms of the book page.

The basic fact to keep in mind about the movie camera and projector is their resemblance to the process of human cognition. That is the real source of their magical, transforming power. The camera rolls up the external world on a spool. It does this by rapid still shots. The projector unwinds this spool as a kind of magic carpet which conveys the enchanted spectator anywhere in the world in an instant. The camera records and analyzes the daylight world with more than human intensity because of the forty-five degree angle of the camera eye. The projector reveals this daylight world on a dark screen where it becomes a dream world.

The wonderful resemblance in all this to human cognition extends at least this far: in cognition we have to interiorize the exterior world. We have to recreate in the medium of our senses and inner faculties the drama of existence. This is the work of the *logos poietikos*, the agent intellect. In speech we utter that drama which we have analogously recreated within us. In speech we make or *poet* the world even as we may say that the movie parrots the world. Languages themselves are thus the greatest of all works of art. They are the collective hymns to existence. For in cognition itself is the whole of the poetic process. But the artist differs from most men in his power to arrest and then reverse the stages of human apprehension. He learns how to embody the stages of cognition (Aristotle's "plot") in an exterior work which can be held up for contemplation.

Even in this respect the movie resembles the cognitive process since the daylight world which the camera rolls up on the spool is reversed and projected to become the magical dream world of the audience. But all media of communication share something of this cognitive character which only a Thomist vision of existence and cognition dare do justice to.

Television, for example, differs from the movie in the immediacy with which it picks up and renders back the visible. The TV camera is like the microphone in relation to the voice, The movie has no such immediacy of pickup and feedback. As we begin to look into the inevitably cognitive character of the various media we soon get over the jitters that come from exclusive concern with any one form of communication.

In his *Theory of the Film*, Bela Balazs

notes how "the discovery of printing gradually rendered illegible the faces of men. So much could be read from paper that the method of conveying meaning by facial expression fell into desuetude. Victor Hugo wrote once that the printed book took over the part played by the cathedral in the Middle Ages and became the carrier of the spirit of the people. But the thousands of books tore the one spirit . . . into thousands of opinions . . . tore the church into a thousand books. The visible spirit was thus turned into a legible spirit and visual culture into a culture of concepts."

Before printing, a reader was one who discerned and probed riddles. After printing, it meant one who scanned, who skipped along the macadamized surfaces of print. Today at the end of that process we have come to equate reading skill with speed and distraction rather than wisdom. But print, the mechanization of writing, was succeeded in the nineteenth century by photography and then by the mechanization of human gesture in the movie. This was followed by the mechanization of speech in telephone, phonograph and radio. In the talkies, and finally with TV, came the mechanization of the totality of human expression, of voice, gesture, and human figure in action.

Each of these steps in the mechanization of human expression was comparable in its scope to the revolution brought about by the mechanization of writing itself. The changes in the ways of human association, social and political, were telescoped in time and so hidden from casual observers.

If there is a truism in the history of human communication it is that any innovation in the external means of communication brings in its train shock on shock of social change. One effect of writing was to make possible cities, roads, armies, and empires. The letters of the alphabet were indeed the dragon's teeth. The printed book not only fostered nationalism but made it possible to bring the world of the past into every study. The newspaper is a daily book which brings a slice of all the cultures of the world under our eyes every day. To this extent it reverses the tendency of the printing press to accentuate merely national culture. Pictorial journalism and reportage tend strongly in the same international direction. But is this true of radio? Radio has strengthened the oral habit of communication and extended it, via the panel and round table, to serious learning. Yet radio seems to be a form which also strengthens the national culture. Merely oral societies, for example, are the ultimate in national exclusiveness.

A group of us recently performed an experiment with a large group of students. We divided them into four sections and assigned each section to a separate communication channel. Each section got the identical lecture simultaneously, but one read it, one heard it as a regular lecture in a studio, one heard it on radio and one heard and saw it as a TV broadcast. Immediately afterwards we administered a quiz to determine apprehension and understanding of this new and difficult material. The TV section came out on top, then the radio section, then the studio, and reading sections at the bottom. This was a totally unexpected result and it is too soon to generalize; but it is quite certain that the so-called mass media are not necessarily ordained to be channels of popular entertainment only.

It is "desirable" in thinking about the new media that we should recall that buildings are mass communications and that the first mechanical medium was print from movable type. In fact, the discovery of movable type was the ancestor of all assembly lines, and it would be foolish to overlook the impact of the technological form involved in print on the psychological life of readers. To overlook this would be as unrealistic as to ignore rhythm and tempo in music. Likewise it is only common sense to recognize that the general situation created by a communicative channel and its audience is a large part of that in which and by which the individuals commune.

The encoded message cannot be regarded as a mere capsule or pellet produced at one point and consumed at another. Communication is communication all along the line.

One might illustrate from sports. The best brand of football played before fifty people would lack something of the power to communicate. The large, enthusiastic crowd is necessary to represent the community at large, just as the players enact a drama which externalizes certain motivations and tensions in the communal life which would not otherwise be visible or available for audience participation. In India huge crowds assemble to experience *darshan*, which they consider to occur when they are massed in the presence of a visible manifestation of their collective life.

The new media do something similar for us in the West. Movies, radio, and TV establish certain personalities on a new plane of existence. They exist not so much in themselves but as types of collective life felt and perceived through a mass medium. L'il Abner, Bob Hope, Donald Duck, and Marilyn Monroe become points of collective awareness and communication for an entire society. And as technology increasingly undertakes to submit the entire planet as well as the contents of consciousness to the purposes of man's factive intelligence, it behooves us to consider the whole process of magical transformation involved in the media acutely and extensively.

From this point of view it should be obvious, for example, that the framers of the Hollywood morality code were operating with a very inadequate set of perceptions and concepts about the nature of the movie medium. Modern discussions of censorship, in the same way, are helplessly tied to conceptions borrowed from book-culture alone. And the defenders of book-culture have seldom given any thought to any of the media as art forms, the book least of all. The result is that their "defense" might as well be staged on an abandoned movie lot for all the effect it has on the actual situation.

When I wrote *The Mechanical Bride* some years ago I did not realize that I was attempting a defense of book-culture against the new media. I can now see that I was trying to bring some of the critical awareness fostered by literary training to bear on the new media of sight and sound. My strategy was wrong, because my obsession with literary values blinded me to much that was actually happening for good and ill. What we have to defend today is not the values developed in any particular culture or by any one mode of communication. Modern technology presumes to attempt a total transformation of man and his environment. This calls in turn for an inspection and defense of all human values. And so far as merely human aid goes, the citadel of this defense must be located in analytical awareness of the nature of the creative process involved in human cognition. For it is in this citadel that science and technology have already established themselves in their manipulation of the new media.

5

The "Haunted Swing" Illusion

R. W. Wood

I was much interested this summer in the curious sensations produced by a purely optical illusion, known as the "Haunted Swing," at the Midwinter Fair in San Francisco. On entering the building we found ourselves in a spacious cubical room, furnished with a sofa, table, chairs, etc., a massive iron safe, and a piano, together with other minor articles. But the most conspicuous object was the huge swing, capable of holding forty or more persons, which hung in the centre, suspended from an iron cylinder which passed through the centre of the room. We took our seats and the swing was put in motion, the arc gradually increasing in amplitude until each oscillation carried us apparently into the upper corners of the room. Each vibration of the swing caused those peculiar "empty" sensations within which one feels in an elevator; and as we rushed backwards toward the top of the room there was a distinct feeling of "leaning forward," if I can so describe it—such as one always experiences in a backward swing, and an involuntary clutching at the seats to keep from being pitched out. We were then told to hold on tightly as the swing was going clear over, and, sure enough, so it did, though the illusion was not so perfect as the high oscillations.

The device was worked in the following way: The swing proper was practically at rest, merely being joggled a trifle, while the room itself was put in motion, the furniture being fastened down to the floor, so that it could be turned completely over. The illusion was good, though the absence of centrifugal force, and the fact that the swing did not move with uniform acceleration as it descended, would indicate to a careful observer that he was not swinging freely. The curious and interesting feature however, was, that even though the action was fully understood, as it was in my case, it was impossible to quench the sensations of "goneness within" with each apparent rush of the swing. The minute the eyes were shut the sensations vanished instantly. Many persons were actually made sick by the illusion. I have met a number of gentlemen who said they could scarcely walk out of the building from dizziness and nausea. I myself experienced no sensations of dizziness, being accustomed to heights and to rapid motion; but the sensation before described was always present (and I visited the place several times), though I tried to suppress it and reason against it.

Reprinted from the *Psychological Review* Vol. 2 (1892), pp. 277–278, by permission of the American Psychological Association.

SECTION B *The Effects of Values*

There was a time when science was supposed to be "value-free," which meant that scientists, at least when hard at work, were purely objective, interested only in truth, and disinterested in the effects or applications of their work. In other words they were reputed to be capable of operating differently from the rest of us, but such was never true.

Scientific values are a special subset of values that direct attention and intention to specific areas of human concern. In addition there are overriding values concerning which scientific methods are good and which are not, which branches of science are valid and which are invalid or inappropriate. Eventually, the word *scientism* was coined to denote a set of rigid mental attitudes characteristic of scientists.

At this writing the situation in science is improving. We are increasingly aware that we all hold certain ideas as basic and universal. However, it is also evident that what I consider basic ideas may be contrary to yours. The articles in this section bring out some of the effects of recognizing and developing different basic concepts of the world.

I have read and reread Florence Kluckhohn's article through the years and each time I am reminded of the limits of my own world-view. She presents data that illustrate ways of seeing the universe that are fully as valid as my own. Dorothy Lee questions the problem of values at a deeper level; for what, after all, is ultimate? These two papers should give the student the mind-stretching needed to try his own ideas while considering John Gillin's article on American values. This article can be challenged on a number of minor points because America has undergone some modification in its basic value structure since it first appeared. Yet it looks as if the underlying fabric remains as he saw it. My values differ from those he calls typical and, as a Californian, I have to be careful to isolate them from the more typical American values. The short final statement by Jacob Bronowski is typical of the new scientists who have faced the values question directly.

In spite of our successful ways of describing them, values remain personal, subjective, elusive, and resistant to change. Knowing facts is not enough; knowing the values we place on facts allows us to understand the effects new facts can have on new decisions.

6

Dominant and Variant Value Orientations

Florence Rockwood Kluckhohn

For all those concerned with the lives of individuals and the problems which arise in those lives there has long been a question —even an argument—as to how much the individual is a product of his biological heritage and how much the result of environmental forces. That either a strictly biological or an over-simply formulated environmental theory of human behavior is absurdly one-sided most of us have long ago accepted. Yet most of us also know that we are really only at the beginning of the time-consuming and arduous process from which we hope to derive an understanding of that infinitely complicated interplay of biological, psychological, social, and other factors which create the personality and character structure of individuals. We still display a tendency to concentrate on certain factors and exclude others. Some are too much given to interpretations in strictly psychological terms, some too eager to use only the conceptual lenses provided by the sociologist, the anthropologist, or the economist, and others equally zealous with still other approaches.

Today the awareness is growing—rapidly growing—that anything like a full understanding of the concrete situations in which we see individuals requires a use of the explanatory concepts of more than one discipline and requires their use in other ways than an occasional "borrowing" to account for the extraneous. The goal of an integration of our several approaches to a study of human behavior and social situations is clearly before us and recognized as a goal, yet no one can rightly claim that we are close to achieving it.

One specific example of this growing interest in the multiple rather than the unitary approach to individual and social problems is found in the current and frequent linkage of the terms "culture" and "personality." The practical reflection of this we find in the frequent queries of many in the fields of education, social work, colonial administration, and industry as to what a knowledge of cultural factors offers them for a better understanding of the situations and the individuals with which they must deal. Even clinical psychologists and psychiatrists, whose theories have necessarily centered upon the psychological processes of the individual, are asking what the effect of varying cultural patterns upon the actions and motives of individuals may be.

Reprinted from *Personality in Nature, Society, and Culture,* Clyde K. Kluckhohn, Henry A. Murray, and David M. Schneider, eds. (2nd ed., New York: Alfred A. Knopf, 1953), by permission of the author. A fuller version of the theory appears in *Variations in Value Orientations* by Florence Rockwood Kluckhohn and Fred L. Strodtbeck (New York: Harper & Row, 1961).

Some real progress has been made, especially in the last decade or so, in bringing together psychological and socio-cultural theories. For those interested in a very brief sketch of the history of this development we would recommend Dr. Ralph Linton's introduction to Dr. Abram Kardiner's *The Psychological Frontiers of Society* (1).

Illustrative of the kind of conceptual integration which has to date been achieved, Linton points to the concept of "basic personality" which he himself and Dr. Kardiner developed in their collaborative work. Basic personality, he states, is a configuration involving several different elements. It rests upon the following postulates:

1. That the individual's early experiences exert a lasting effect upon his personality, especially upon the development of his projective system.
2. That similar experiences will tend to produce similar personality configurations in the individuals who are subjected to them.
3. That the techniques which the members of any society employ in the care and rearing of children are culturally patterned and will tend to be similar, although never identical, for various families within the society.
4. That the culturally patterned techniques for the care and rearing of children differ from one society to another.

If these postulates are correct, and they seem to be supported by a wealth of evidence, it follows:

1. That the members of any given society will have many elements of early experience in common.
2. That as a result of this they will have many elements of personality in common.
3. That since the early experience of individuals differs from one society to another, the personality norms for various societies will also differ.

The *basic personality type* for any society is that personality configuration which is shared by the bulk of the society's members as a result of the early experiences which they have in common. It does not correspond to the total personality of the individual but rather to the projective systems or, in different phraseology, the value-attitude systems which are basic to the individual's personality configuration. Thus the same basic personality type may be reflected in many different forms of behavior and may enter into many different total personality configurations. (1, pp. vi–viii)

The studies of various other anthropologists and the collaborative work many of them have done with psychologists, psychiatrists, and sociologists have gone far in demonstrating many of the relationships between individual desires and group experiences—between culture and personality. Yet, for all of the valuable insights produced and the considerable progress thus far achieved, there have been some severe and—in the opinion of the writer—justified criticisms of many of the facile conclusions drawn by some anthropologists. Especially in some of the recent interpretations of so-called national character structure, one notes a repeated tendency to derive highly generalized and far sweeping conclusions from a few specific items of culture content. Sociologists and psychologists alike have cavilled at the apparent ignoring of interaction processes by some anthropologists and at the too deterministic effects often claimed for cultural factors.

Much of the difficulty in all attempts to use the cultural anthropologists' concepts and data arise from an absence of a systematic theory of cultural variation and from the tendency of most anthropologists to rely too much upon mere empirical generalizations. The most casual observer is aware that the customs of different societies vary. He knows, too, that the behavior patterns of individuals within a given society are often markedly different. Indeed, when dealing with variation at this level one cannot but be acutely conscious of the wide range of "individual differences." But it is not this plethora of specific content which is of the most critical importance if the aim is to understand better the relationship of cultural factors to either the structuring of social groups or the personalities of the individuals who comprise the social groups. It is rather the generalized meanings or values which should be the major, or at least the first, concern.

Specific patterns of behavior insofar as they are influenced by cultural factors (and few are not so influenced) are the concrete expressions reflecting generalized meanings or values. And to the extent that the individual personality is a product of training in a particular cultural tradition it is also at the generalized value level that one finds the most significant differences.

As Gregory Bateson has remarked: "The human individual is endlessly simplifying organizing, and generalizing his own view of his own environment; he constantly imposes his own constructions and meanings; these constructions and meanings (are) characteristic of one culture as over against another (2)." Or, as Clyde Kluckhohn has stated: "There is a 'philosophy' behind the way of life of every individual and of every relatively homogeneous group at any given point in their histories (3)."

The writer agrees with these and many similar statements made by other anthropologists which emphasize the importance of "value orientations" in the lives of individuals and groups of individuals (4). There is in many of them, however, too much stress—implied when not actually stated—upon the unitary character of value orientations. Variation for the same individual when he is playing different roles and variation between whole groups of persons within a single society are not adequately accounted for. More important still, the emphasis upon the uniqueness of the variable value systems of different societies ignores the fact of the universality of human problems and the correlate fact that human societies have found for some problems approximately the same answers. Yet certainly it is only within a frame of reference which deals with universals that variation can be understood. Without it, it is not possible to deal systematically with either the problem of similarity and difference as between the value systems of different societies or the question of variant values within societies.

Human behavior mirrors at all times an intricate blend of the universal and the variable. The universals and variations are of many kinds. All human beings have many and significant biological similarities as members of a particular species—*homo sapiens*—yet variability within the species is great. We frequently note both the similarities and differences which are psychological.

The problem of the dominant and variant in cultural patterning can, of course, be approached in different ways. Precisely which way will depend upon the specific type of investigation being made. The aim of the approach of this paper is a conceptual scheme which will permit a systematic ordering of cultural value orientations within the framework of common human—universal—problems. It is only when we have delineated the central types of value orientations and the ranges of possible variability in them that we can make systematic comparisons of either single orientations or the total *value orientation profiles* of whole societies or parts of societies.

The first fundamental assumption upon which the conceptual scheme is based is: *There is a limited number of basic human problems for which all peoples at all times and in all places must find some solution.* The five common human problems tentatively singled out as those of key importance can be stated in the form of questions:

1. What are the *innate predispositions of* man? (Basic human nature)
2. What is the relation of *man to nature*?
3. What is the significant *time* dimension?

TABLE 1. Human Problems and Type Solutions

Innate Predispositions:	Evil (mutable or immutable)	Neither good nor bad (mutable or immutable)	Good (mutable or immutable)
Man's Relation to Nature:	Man subjugated to nature	Man in nature	Man over nature
Time Dimension:	Past	Present	Future
Valued Personality Type:	Being	Being-in-Becoming	Doing
Modality of Relationship:	Lineal	Collateral	Individualistic

4. What is the valued *personality type*?
5. What is the dominant modality of the *relationship of man to other men*?

The problems as stated in these questions are regarded as constant; they arise inevitably out of the human situation. The solutions found for them are variable but not limitlessly so. It is the second major assumption of the conceptual scheme that *the variability in solutions is variability within a range of possible solutions.* The limits of variability suggested as a testable conceptualization are the three point ranges for each of the main orientations given in the Table. Nothing mystical is claimed for the number *three*, but as will be seen in the following explanations, such a breakdown seems, in almost all cases, to be both logically adequate and empirically sound.

To the question of what innate human nature is, there are the three logical divisions of evil, neither good nor evil (or mixed), and good. And such, in fact, seem to be the distinctions which have been made by societies. Variation within this range is, of course, possible. Human nature can be regarded as evil and unalterable or evil and perfectible. It can be good and unalterable or good and corruptible. It can be viewed as neither good nor evil and treated as invariant or as subject to influence. This kind of variability, however, falls within the basic threefold classification and is probably a result of the relationship of the human-nature orientation to other orientations.

Illustrations of these differences in the definition of innate predispositions are easily found. We have only to look about us to recognize that there is considerable variability in our present day American conception of human nature. The orientation we inherited from Puritan ancestors, and still strong in many of us, is that human nature is basically evil but perfectible. Constant control and discipline of the self are essential if any real goodness is to be achieved and maintained, and the danger of regression is always present. But some in our society today—perhaps a growing number—are inclined to the more tolerant view that human nature is a mixture of the good and the bad. These would say that control and effort are certainly needed, but lapses can be understood and need not always be severely condemned. Such a definition of basic human nature would appear to be a somewhat more common one among the peoples of the world—both literate and nonliterate—than the view we have held in our own historical past. Whether there are any total societies given to the definition of human nature as *immutably good* is to be doubted. The position is, however, a possible one and should be found ever present as an alternative definition within societies.

The three-point range of variation in the *man-nature* relationship—that of Man Subjugated to Nature, Man in Nature, and Man Over Nature—is too well known from the work of philosophers and culture historians to need a detailed explanation. Mere illustration will demonstrate the differences.

Spanish-American culture as I have

known it in the American-Southwest illustrates well the Man Subjugated to Nature position. To the typical Spanish-American sheep-raiser in that region there is little or nothing which can be done if a storm comes to damage his range lands or destroy his flocks. He simply accepts the inevitable as the inevitable. His attitude toward illness and death is the same fatalistic attitude. "If it is the Lord's will that I die I shall die" is the way he expresses it. Many a Spanish-American has been known to refuse the help of any doctor because of this attitude.

Another way of phrasing the *man-nature* relationship is to regard all natural forces and man himself as one harmonious whole. One is but an extension of the other, and both are needed to make the whole. Such was the attitude frequently found as the dominant one in China in the past centuries.

A third way of viewing this relationship is that of Man Against—or Over—Nature. According to this view, which is clearly the one characteristic of Americans, natural forces are something to be overcome and put to the use of human beings. We span our rivers with bridges, blast through our mountains to make tunnels, make lakes where none existed, and do a thousand and one other things to exploit nature and make it serve our human needs. In general this means that we have an orientation to life which is that of overcoming obstacles. And it is difficult for us to understand the kind of people who accept the obstacle and give in to it or even the people who stress the harmonious oneness of man and nature.

The possible cultural phrasings of the *man in time* problem breaks easily into the three point range of Past, Present and Future. Far too little attention has been given to this problem and its phrasings. Meaningful cultural differences have been lost sight of in the too sweeping and too generalized view that folk peoples have no time sense, and no need of one, whereas urbanized and industrial peoples must have one. Whether days are regarded as sunrise to sundown wholes or as split into hours and minutes, and whether or not a clock is deemed a useful culture object are not the critically important criteria for a consideration of the orientation to time.

Spengler had quite another order of fact in mind than this when he made, in his quite profound discussion of "time" in the *Decline of the West*, this emphatic and categorical statement: "It is by the meaning that it intuitively attaches to time that one culture is differentiated from another (5)." Time and Destiny were what were being related in Spengler's conception. For the most part his concern was with the twofold division of orientations into those which were the timeless a-historic present and the ultra-historical projection into the future. Always on the plane of the macroscopic and concerned with directionality as a cyclical unfolding, he apparently did not feel a need to deal with the problem of the traditionalistic or past orientation which was so important a part of Max Weber's treatment of moral authority. The threefold division proposed for the cultural orientation schema has, therefore, its similarity to Spengler's conception in the distinction between a timeless, traditionless, future-ignoring present and a realizable future. It differs in that it also differentiates from these an orientation which looks to the traditions of the past either as something to be maintained or as something to be recaptured. There is in the conception as here phrased an aspect of the orientation which is relative to the standards and norms of authority which is not explicitly included in Spengler's conception.

Obviously all societies at all times must deal with all the three time-problems. All have some conception of the past, all have a present, and all give some kind of attention to the future time-dimension. They differ, however, in their emphasis on past, present, or future at a given period, and a very great deal can be told about the particular society or part of a society being studied, much about the direction of change within it can be predicted, with a knowledge of where that emphasis is.

Illustrations of these different emphases are also easily found. Spanish-Americans, whom we have described as having the attitude that man is a victim of natural forces, are also a people who emphasize present time. They pay little attention to what has happened in the past, and regard the future as a vague and most unpredictable period. Planning for the future or hoping that the future will be better than either present or past simply is not their way of life. In dealing with Spanish-Americans one must always take into account the fact that they have quite a different time sense from our own. Too often, we, who are in the habit of making definite appointments for two or five o'clock and expect to keep and have them kept, are baffled by the Spanish-Americans to whom two or five o'clock means little or nothing. For an appointment made for two o'clock he may arrive at any time between one and five o'clock, or, most likely, he will not arrive at all. Something else which interests him more may well have turned up to absorb his attention.

China of past generations, and to some extent still, was a society which put its main emphasis upon past time. Ancestor worship and a strong family tradition were both expressions of this Past Time orientation. So also was the Chinese attitude that nothing new ever happened in the present or would happen in the future. It had all happened before in the far distant past. Thus it was that the proud American who thought he was showing some Chinese a steamboat for the first time was quickly put in his place by the remark: "Our ancestors had such a boat two thousand years ago." Many modern European countries also tended to stress the past. Even England—insofar as it has been dominated by an aristocracy and traditionalism—has voiced this emphasis. Indeed, one of the chief differences between ourselves and the English is to be found in our somewhat varying attitudes toward time. We have difficulty in understanding the respect the English have for tradition, and they do not appreciate our disregard for it.

Americans, more than most people of the world, place emphasis upon the future—a future which we anticipate to be "bigger and better." This does not mean we have no regard for the past or fail to give thought to the present. But it certainly is true that no current generation of Americans ever wants to be called "old-fashioned." We do not consider the ways of the past to be good just because they are past, and we are seldom content with the present. This makes of us a people who place a high value on change.

The fourth of the common human problems is called the *Valued Personality Type*. The range of variation in this case yields the Being, the Being-in-Becoming, and the Doing orientations. Since it is assumed that all the orientations are an aspect of the action and motivational systems of the individual personalities, *Valued Personality Type* is not the happiest of terms for designating this particular range of them. For the time being, however, we shall retain the term.

These orientations have been derived for the most part from the distinction long made by philosophers between Being and Becoming. Indeed, to a marked degree, the three-way distinction is in accord with the classification of personality components made by the philosopher Charles Morris—the Dionysian, the Apollonian, and the Promethean. The abstractly conceived component which he labels the *Dionysian*—the personality component type which releases and indulges existing desires—is somewhat what is meant by the Being orientation. His *Apollonian* component—the component type that is self-contained and controls itself through a meditation and detachment that bring understanding—is to some extent the

Being-in-Becoming. His active, striving *Promethean* component is similar to the Doing orientation (6).

The accordance is, however, far from complete. As used in this schema the terms Being and Becoming, now made into the three-point range of Being, Being-in-Becoming, and Doing, are much more narrowly defined than has been the custom of philosophers. Furthermore, the view here is that these orientations vary independently relative to those which deal with the relation of man to nature, to time and innate predispositions. The tendency of the philosophers, writing with different aims, has been to treat these several types of orientations as relatively undifferentiated clusters.

The essence of the Being orientation is that it stresses the spontaneous expression of what is conceived to be "given" in the personality. The orientation is, as compared with the Being-in-Becoming or Doing, essentially *non*developmental. It might even be phrased as a spontaneous expression of impulses and desires; yet care must be taken not to make this interpretation a too literal one. In no society, as Clyde Kluckhohn has commented, does one ever find a one-to-one relationship between the desired and the desirable. The concrete behavior of individuals in complex situations and the moral codes governing that behavior usually reflect all the orientations simultaneously. A stress upon the "isness" of the personality and a spontaneous expression of that "isness" is not pure license as we can easily see if we turn our attention to a society or segments of a society in which the Being orientation is dominant. Mexican society, for example, is clearly one in which the Being orientation is dominant. Their wide-range patterning of *Fiesta* activities alone shows this. Yet never in the *Fiesta* or other patterns of spontaneity is there pure impulse gratification. The value demands of other of the orientations—the relational orientation, the conception of human nature as being good and evil and in need of control and others—all make for codes which restrain individuals in very definite ways.

The Being-in-Becoming orientation shares with the Being a great concern with what the human being is rather than what he can accomplish, but here the similarity ends. In the Being-in-Becoming orientation the idea of development so little stressed in the Being orientation is paramount.

Erich Fromm's conception of "the spontaneous activity of the total integrated personality" is close to the Being-in-Becoming type. "By activity," he states, "we do not mean 'doing something' but rather the quality of the creative activity which can operate in one's emotional, intellectual, and sensuous experiences and in one's will as well. One premise of this spontaneity is the acceptance of the total personality and the elimination of the split between reason and nature (7)." A less favorably prejudiced and, for our purposes, a more accurately limited statement would be: the Being-in-Becoming orientation emphasizes self-realization—self-development—of all aspects of the self as an integrated whole.

The Doing orientation is so characteristically the one dominantly stressed in American society that there is little need for an extensive definition. Its most distinguishing feature is its demand for action in the sense of accomplishment and in accord with standards which are conceived as being external to the acting individual. Self-judgment as well as the judgment of others is largely by means of measurable accomplishment through action. What does the individual do, what can he, or will he, accomplish are almost always primary questions in our scale of appraisal of persons. "Getting things done" and finding ways "to do something" about any and all situations are stock American phrases. Erich Fromm also recognizes this orientation as separable from what he defines in his concept of spontaneity and which we have called the Being-in-Becoming, but he seems to view it as mainly compulsive. With this I cannot agree. Many persons in our society who follow patterns in accord with the Doing orientation are compulsive; many are not. Conformity, which is essential in all societies, whatever the arrangement of their orientations, should not be so much and so often confounded with compulsiveness.

The fifth and last of the common human problems treated in this conceptual scheme is the definition of man's relation to other men. This orientation, the *relational*, has three sub-divisions: the Lineal, the Collateral, and the Individualistic.

Sociologists have long used various types of dichotomies to differentiate homogeneous folk societies from the more complex urban societies. *Gemeinschaft-gesellschaft*, traditionalistic—rational-legal, mechanical-organic solidarity, or simply rural-urban—are the most familiar of the several paired terms. Anthropologists, who have for the most part studied *gemeinschaft* or folk peoples, have frequently in their analyses of kinship structure or social organization made much of the difference between lineage and a lateral extension of relationships.

The distinctions being made here obviously owe much to the concepts used in both these fields, but they are not identical with those of either field. The Lineal, Collateral, and Individualistic relational principles are analytical elements in total relational systems and are not to be confused with categories descriptive of concrete systems.

It is in the nature of the case that all societies—all groups—must give some attention to all three principles. Individual autonomy cannot be and is not ignored by the most extreme type of *gemeinschaft* society. Collaterality is found in all societies. The individual is not a human being outside a group and one kind of group emphasis is that put upon laterally extended relationships. These are the immediate relationships in time and place. All societies must also pay some attention to the fact that individuals are biologically and culturally related to each other through time. This is to say that there is always a Lineal principle in relationships which is derived from age and generational differences and cultural tradition. The fundamental question is always that of emphasis.

There will always be variability in the primacy and nature of goals according to which of the three principles is stressed. If the individualistic principle is dominant and the other two interpreted in terms of it —as is the case in the United States—individual goals will have primacy over the goals of either the Collateral or Lineal group. When the Collateral principle is dominant, the goals—or welfare—of the laterally extended group have primacy for all individuals. The group in this case is viewed as being moderately independent of other similar groups and the question of continuity through time is not critical. Where the Lineal principle is most heavily stressed it is again group goals which are of primary concern to individuals, but there is the additional factor that an important one of those goals is continuity through time. Both continuity and ordered positional succession are of great importance, when Lineality dominates the *relational* system. Spanish-American society has been, until recently, one with a relatively strong Lineal stress, combined with a strong second order Collaterality.

How continuity and ordered positional succession are achieved in a Lineal *relational* system is separate from the principle as such. It does in fact seem to be the case that the most successful way of maintaining a stress on Lineality is through mechanisms which are either actual hereditary ones based upon biological relatedness or ones which are assimilated to a kinship system. The English, for example, maintained such an emphasis into the present time by consistently moving successful members of its more individualistic middle class into the established peerage system. Other societies have found other but similar mechanisms.

Thus far in the discussion of the major orientations the aim has been to show that different societies make different selections among possible solutions of common human problems. They raise to dominant position some one of the alternative principles. However, at no time has it been stated or implied that any society will or can ignore any of the dimensions. On the contrary, it is a fundamental proposition of this conceptual approach that all dimensions of all orientations *not only are but must be* present at all times in the pattern structure of every society.

However important it is to know what is dominant in a society at a given time, we shall not go far toward the understanding of the dynamics of that society without paying careful heed to the variant orientations. That there be individuals and whole groups of individuals who live in accordance with patterns which express variant rather than the dominantly stressed orientations is, it is maintained, essential to the maintenance of the society. *Variant values, are, therefore, not only permitted but actually required.* It has been the mistake of many in the social sciences, and of many in the field of practical affairs as well, to treat all behavior and certain aspects of motivation which do not accord with the dominant values as some kind of deviance. It is urged that we cease to confuse the deviant who by his behavior calls down the sanctions of his group with the variant who is accepted and frequently required as far as the total social system is concerned. This is especially true in a society such as ours, where beneath the surface of what has so often been called our compulsive conformity, there lies a wide range of variation. The dynamic interplay of the dominant and the variant is one of the outstanding features of American society, but as yet it has been little analyzed or understood.

Illustrations of variant value orientations, whether of individuals or whole groups, are numerous. Let us look at these three kinds: *ethnic difference* of which the United States has had, and still has, so much; *class difference; role difference* as it is seen in the role of the American woman.

The usual tendency of most observers has been either to view all ethnic groups as one undifferentiated whole or, with a concern for understanding better the problems of particular groups, to seek out the quite specific ways in which they differ. Attention is given to the kind of parental authority and to the attitude they have toward women, or perhaps we delve into the type of child-training patterns they follow. These specific patterns are, of course, important; but it is obvious that knowing them all is in most cases impossible. Furthermore, when there is no general framework within which to consider the specific differences noted, there develops so frequently a tendency to attribute too much to single items of cultural content.

We could know many such concrete patterns followed by the Spanish-Americans in the Southwest and still not know why after one hundred years within the borders of the United States their way of life has changed so little until very recently. We can know and have known many such patterns and yet are forced to admit that understanding between Anglo-Americans and Spanish-Americans is not, even now, very great.

When, however, we look to fundamental differences in value orientations we are led quickly to this proposition: The slow rate of assimilation of Spanish-Americans (and more recent Mexican immigrants), and the low level of understanding as well, are in large part attributable to a wide disparity in *all* the major orientations of Anglo-Americans and Spanish-Americans.

Illustrations of most of the Spanish-American orientations have already been given singly. Let us now take them as a whole system and again quickly compare them to the system of orientations dominantly stressed in American society. Where the Anglo-American stresses Individualism, the Spanish-American puts his primary emphasis upon a combination of the Lineal and the Collateral. The semi-feudal *patron-peon* system of Mexicans, both in the United

States and in Mexico, has neither permitted nor required very much independent behavior of most people. Or, to phrase this another way, whereas the Anglo-American is quite systematically trained for independent behavior, the Spanish-American or Mexican is trained for dependence.

The American dominant *time* orientation has been noted to be Future, that of the Spanish-Americans, Present. We show a vague awareness of this difference when we so often refer to Mexicans in general as being a *mañana* people. Yet how very much bound by our own cultural values we are when we interpret *mañana* to mean that a Mexican will always put off until tomorrow what should be done today. Tomorrow in a highly specific sense is meaningless to the Spanish-American or Mexican. He lives in a timeless present, and as one Mexican scholar phrased it: "The Mexican never puts off until tomorrow what can be done *only* today."

Consider, too, the vast difference between the Spanish-American Being orientation and the American emphasis upon Doing or accomplishing. Doing things in the name of accomplishment is not usual Spanish-American behavior. That which "is" is in large part taken for granted and considered as something to be enjoyed rather than altered.

Our own and the Spanish-Americans' definition of the *man-nature* relationship are likewise poles apart. We set out to conquer, overcome, and exploit nature; they accept the environment with a philosophical calm bordering on the fatalistic. And seldom in Spanish-American culture does one find evidence of our own historical view of human nature as Evil but Perfectible. Their view would appear to be much more that of human nature as a mixture of the Good and Bad.

With such differences as these it is not a cause for wonder that Anglo-American educators, social workers, politicians, and a host of others have been both deeply frustrated and quite unsuccessful in their many attempts either to alter rapidly the Spanish-American way of life or adjust Anglo-American values to it. Nor is it strange that the understanding between Anglo- and Spanish-Americans in an area (New Mexico and Arizona) where each group constitutes approximately a half of the total population has been inadequate throughout a whole century.

This highly dramatic and most extreme illustration of cultural variation within our own borders tells us a great deal if only we look at it in terms of major value orientations instead of always considering particular and specific bits of behavior. The specific to be very meaningful, we repeat, must be viewed as an item in the wider context of value orientations.

Generalizing this conception to all such groups as the Spanish-American we would first hypothesize that *the rate and degree of assimilation of any ethnic group into general dominant American culture will in large part depend upon the degree of goodness of fit of the group's own basic value orientations with those of dominant American culture.*

Class differences have greatly concerned American social scientists in the last two decades. The best known studies of the class structure of the United States are those of W. Lloyd Warner and his associates, but there are also many others with different points of view and in which conclusions very different from those of the Warner group are reached. From all the studies we have learned much that Americans have been unwilling to admit or discuss in past years. We know that there are great differences between the classes in attitudes toward education and politics, in association memberships, in family life, in occupational interests and opportunities, in reading habits, in recreational interests, and a host of other things.

Yet in spite of all the differences observed and recorded, there is a tendency in all the studies to assume that all the variation is variation on the same value theme—the so-called American Creed. What is remarked is that the behavior and attitudes of some classes are harmoniously in tune with the generalized creed, whereas those of other classes are off in pitch and limited in range. That the value themes themselves might be different is seldom suggested.

But according to the conceptual scheme of the dominant and variant in cultural orientations, it is assumed at the start that then is a dominant class—in the case of the United States, the middle class—in which adherence to dominant values is marked, but also that there are other classes which hold to variant values in much of what they do and believe. As I have suggested elsewhere, the observed behavior of an upper class in an old and declining community shows an adherence to lineality rather than individualism, to past time more than future, and to Being or Being-in-Becoming rather than to Doing personalities. Also in some parts of the lower class—a class so heterogeneous and diffuse that it should be "classes" and not just "class"—Present Time and Being orientations are often combined with either Individualism or Collaterality.

There has not been sufficient work done to date to state with certainty that this different approach will provide a more accurate knowledge and appraisal of class differences. One study now in progress—a study of the occupational aspirations of a large group of high school boys in a metropolitan community—shows some promise of demonstrating the existence of value orientation differences between classes and segments of classes (8). In another study just completed by Dr. Charles McArthur it has been shown that, on the average, public and private school boys give predictably different responses to the pictures in the Murray and Morgan Thematic Apperception Test (9). For example, on the assumption that in a public school boys are predominantly middle class and hence Future Time and Doing oriented, while private school boys—especially those of certain selected schools—are predominantly upper class with Past Time and either a Being or Being-in-Becoming orientation, these two predictions were made as to the variability of responses to the first picture of the test (a small boy is seated before a table on which there lies a violin; the subject is asked to invent a story about him):

1. That more public school boys (now students in a large university) will tell stories to the violin picture in which the parent demands work from the child.
2. That more private school boys will tell violin stories in which the music lesson-is seen by the child as a way to create beauty and/or express or develop himself.

These predictions, and twelve others similar in type but different in content, were borne out by McArthur's data. And, as he himself said: "They constituted a neat demonstration that the attitudes of individuals, as measured by one of the psychologist's best projective tests of personality, can be predicted from a knowledge of the person's sub-cultural orientations profile."

The role of the woman in the United States is as little understood for its variant character as are some of the differences in social classes. Although it is frequently stated that the feminine role is poorly defined and full of contradictions, it has not been noted that the behavior expected of women in the wife-mother role is relative to value orientations which are markedly different from the dominant American values that are so well expressed in the man's occupational role.

In his occupational role the man—ideally at least—is expected to be autonomous and independent, whereas from the woman as a wife and mother we all expect a subordination of individualistic goals to those of the family as a group. Man's occupational role is also an action-oriented one which expresses well the Doing orientation, while in woman's role it is expected that much more attention will be given to all those things intellectual, aesthetic, and moral which busy men so often define as the nice but non-essential embroidery of American life. It is, in other words, more of the Being-in-Becoming orientation that women are supposed to adhere to. As for the *Time* orientation it is again man's role which most fully expresses American's dominant *future* emphasis. For the most part, daughters and wives are limited to a vicarious participation in the goals of future promise. The glory which comes from mounting success is largely a man's glory, the light from which is, for women, merely reflective.

Differences such as these are both considerable and troublesome in a society which theoretically stands for an equality of the sexes. When one studies carefully the history of the feminine role it becomes very clear that a central issue for many years has been woman's demand for the right to participate more fully in all those activities in which *dominant* American values are expressed.

In recent years the issue has become the more acute because of the kind of education the women of today receive. Girls are no longer trained in markedly different ways or for different things than boys are. Throughout childhood and youth the girl child goes to school with boys and is taught very much as they are taught. From babyhood on, she learns the ways of being independent and autonomous, and she is expected to know how to look after herself all through adolescence and beyond—forever if need be. The hope is expressed, of course, that she will not have to remain independent and will not, therefore, need to use much of what she has learned. Instead, and this is the truly great problem, she is expected, upon her marriage, or certainly after children are born, to give her attention to all those things which are defined as feminine and for which she has not been well trained at all. It is not to be wondered that the strains in the feminine role are numerous and make for serious personality difficulties in many women.

In other instances of variant roles the strains are fewer. The man who chooses to be a withdrawn scholar or an artist may often be made to feel that he is outside the main stream of life, but it is doubtful that he is subject to as many doubts about the value of what he does as are many women. In the main this is because he is creative, whereas the intellectual and aesthetic interests of women have been, to date, chiefly appreciative.

There is, of course, much more value variation within our own or any other social system than these few illustrations indicate. The varying roles any individual plays at different times and places may be, and often are, different in the value orientations they express. No individual any more than any whole society can live always in all situations in accord with patterns which allow for expression of only a single dimension of the orientations. One can also note many shifts of emphasis in the range of one orientation or another as between the different historical time periods of a social system. Indeed, whatever the type of problem or the situation one may choose for study, variations in value orientations are certain to be found. Thus we repeat: If a knowledge of major cultural value orientations is essential to the understanding of social situations and individual personalities (and I would say it certainly is), it is also necessary to know the variant value orientations and their relation to the dominant ones.

REFERENCES

1. Kardiner, Abram: *The Psychological Frontiers of Society* (New York, Columbia University Press, 1945).
2. Bateson, Gregory: "Cultural Determinants of Personality," in J. McV. Hunt (ed.): *Personality and the Behavior Disorders* (New York, Ronald Press, 1944), Vol. 2, p. 273.

3. Kluckhohn, Clyde: "Values and Value Orientations in the Theory of Action," in Talcott Parsons and Edward A. Shils (eds.): *Toward a General Theory of Action* (Cambridge, Harvard University Press, 1951), p. 409.
4. Kluckhohn, Ibid., p. 411, defines value orientation as follows: "a generalized and organized conception, influencing behavior, of nature, of man's place in it, of man's relation to man, and of the desirable and non-desirable as they may relate to man-environment and interhuman relations."
5. Spengler, Oswald: *The Decline of the West,* tr. Charles F. Atkinson (New York, Knopf, 1926–8).
6. Morris, Charles: *Paths of Life* (New York, Harpers, 1942), esp. chap. II.
7. Fromm, Erich: *Escape from Freedom* (New York, Farrar and Rhinehart, 1941).
8. This project is sponsored by the Harvard University Laboratory of Social Relations and is under the direction of Professors Samuel A. Stouffer and Talcott Parsons and the writer.
9. McArthur, Charles: Cultural Values as Determinants of Imaginal Productions, unpublished Ph.D. thesis, Harvard University, 1952.

7

Are Basic Needs Ultimate?

Dorothy Lee

The purpose of this paper is to urge a re-examination of the premise which so many of us implicitly hold that culture is a group of patterned means for the satisfaction of a list of human needs. This is, of course, not a new issue either with psychologists or anthropologists. The concept of an inventory of basic needs rose to fill the vacuum created when the behaviorists banished the old list of instincts. Yet, in spite of dissatisfaction with this, many of us continue to think of cultural behavior in terms of some form of the stimulus-response principle. Anthropologists borrowed the principle from psychology, without first testing it against ethnographic material, so that often, when the psychologist uses anthropological material, he gets his own back again in new form, and receives no new insights. There are two assumptions involved here: (1) the premise that action occurs in answer to a need or a lack; and (2) the premise that there is a list. In recent years, anthropologists, influenced by the new psychology, have often substituted *drives* or *impulses* or *adjustive responses* for the old term *needs*, but the concept of the list remains with us. We hold this side by side with the conflicting conception of culture as a totality,

Dorothy Lee, "Are Basic Needs Ultimate?" *Journal of Abnormal and Social Psychology,* Vol. 43, 1948, pp. 361-395.

of personality as organismic, as well as with adherence to psychosomatic principles. We deplore the presentation of culture as a list of traits, yet we are ready to define culture as an answer to a list of needs.

This definition of culture has proved a strain. When we found that the original list of basic needs or drives was inadequate, we, like the psychologists, tried to solve the difficulty by adding on a list of social and psychic needs; and, from here on, I use the term *need* in a broad sense, to cover the stimulus-response phrasing of behavior. When the list proved faulty, all we had to do was to add to the list. We have now such needs as that for novelty, for escape from reality, for security, for emotional response. We have primary needs, or drives, and secondary needs, and we have secondary needs playing the role of primary needs. The endless process of adding and correcting is not an adequate improvement; neither does the occasional substitution of a "totality of needs" for a "list of needs" get at the root of the trouble. Where so much elaboration and revision is necessary, I suspect that the original unit itself must be at fault; we must have a radical change.

In applying the list of needs to different cultures, we found that modification was necessary. It was apparent that the need for food of a member of American society is far greater than that of the members of most other societies. Curiously enough, we also find that though a laborer on a New Guinea plantation needs a minimum diet of seven pounds of yams, plus a stated amount of meat, an Arapesh in his own hamlet, working in his fields, climbing up and down steep mountain sides, working hard at ceremonials, can live a meaningful life and procreate healthy children on three pounds of yams a day, and almost no meat.

Is further modification necessary here, or is there another factor at work? Faced with data of this sort, we have been tempted to apply a utilitarian calculus. We have said that when the Arapesh gardens inefficiently in company with his brother-in-law, and when he plants his fruit tree on someone else's distant land, he multiplies his exertions and minimizes his subsistence so as to achieve a maximum of social warmth. But is he really filling two distinct needs, slighting one at the expense of the other? When he takes his pig to another hamlet, and asks someone else's wife to feed and bring it up, what need exactly is he satisfying? And is this need greater than the general human need for food? And does its satisfaction supply a substitute for caloric intake? These questions are nonsense, but we do run into them if we carry the premise of a list of needs far enough.

The assumption of a list of needs was put under its greatest strain, I think, during the recent war. We had assumed that "the role of . . . needs in human behavior is that of first causes." Then how could we explain the behavior of certain small nations, who chose freely to lose necessary food, shelter, security, etc., rather than join the Axis? Why did whole nations court physical annihilation rather than subscribe to Axis doctrines? Why did fathers and husbands and daughters expose their beloved families to danger of torture or death by joining the underground? In this country, why did millions of people who had adequate food and shelter and "security" choose to jeopardize their lives? We can say, of course, that they were satisfying their need for emotional response, in this case the approval of others. One anthropologist did express it in this way. But why was it this particular course of action which was sure to bring them the approval of others? And how could these needs have been the cause of behavior whose goal was neither individual nor group survival?

To my mind, this means that either needs are not the cause of all behavior, or that the list of needs provides an inadequate unit for assessing human behavior.

I am not saying that there are no needs; rather, that if there are needs, they are derivative not basic. If, for example, physical survival was held as the ultimate goal in some society, it would probably be found to give rise to those needs which have been stated to be basic to human survival; but I know of no culture where human physical survival has been shown, rather than unquestioningly assumed by social scientists, to be the ultimate goal.

I believe that it is value, not a series of needs, which is at the basis of human behavior. The main difference between the two lies in the conception of the good which underlies them. The premise that man acts so as to satisfy needs presupposes a negative conception of the good as amelioration or the correction of an undesirable state. According to this view, man acts to relieve tension; good is the removal of evil and welfare the correction of ills; satisfaction is the meeting of a need; good functioning comes from adjustment, survival from adaptation; peace is the resolution of conflict; fear, of the supernatural or of adverse public opinion, is the incentive to good conduct; the happy individual is the well-adjusted individual.

Perhaps this view of what constitutes the good is natural and applicable in a culture which also holds that man was born in sin, whether in Biblical or in psychoanalytic terms. But should we, who believe that other cultures should be assessed according to their own categories and premises, impose upon them our own unexamined conception of the good, and thus always see them as striving to remove or avoid ills? It seems to me that, when we do not take this negative view of the good for granted, other cultures often appear to be maintaining "justment" rather than striving to attain adjustment. For example, for the Hopi, the good is present and positive. An individual is "born in hopiness," so to speak, and strives throughout life to maintain and enhance this hopiness. There is no external reward for being good, as this is taken for granted. It is evil which is external and intrusive, making a man kahopi, or unhopi; that is, un-peaceful, ungood.

In my opinion, the motivation underlying Hopi behavior is *value*. To the Hopi, there is value in acting as a Hopi within a Hopi situation; there is satisfaction in the situation itself, not in the solution of it or the resolution of tension. I speak of value, but rather than define it I shall indicate what I mean by presenting value situations. I want to point out that the notion of value is incompatible with that of a list of needs, or adjustive responses, or drives; so that, wherever it is held, the list must go.

Now, if we substitute the notion of value for that of needs, we are no longer troubled with the difficulty of trying to assess a totality in terms of an aggregate, since value is total and is to be found in a total situation. When we listen to a symphony, we get satisfaction from a whole, not from eighteen thousand notes and a series of arrangements. I can give you an inventory of my daughter, her three teeth, her seventeen pounds, her inability to sit up yet, her mixed smell, her bald head; is it this which causes my behavior when I rush joyfully home to her as soon as I leave my office?

Again, we find that the Hopi like to eat corn; would we be justified in assuming that a Hopi would therefore find it good to work for wages so as to earn money to buy corn to satisfy his hunger? To the Hopi, corn is not nutrition; it is a totality, a way of life. Something of this sort is exemplified in the story which Talayesva tells of the Mexican trader who offered to sell salt to the Hopi group who were starting out on a highly ceremonial Salt Expedition. Within its context this offer to relieve the group of the hardships and dangers of the religious journey sounds ridiculous. The Hopi were not just going to get salt to season their dishes. To them, the journey was part of the process of growing corn and of maintaining harmonious interrelations with nature and what we call the divine. It was the Hopi Way, containing Hopi value. Yet even an ethnographer, dealing with Hopi culture in terms of basic needs, views the Salt Expedition as the trader did, and classifies it under *Secondary Economic Activities.*

So also with our earlier example of the Arapesh. Their eating is not a distinct act satisfying a single need. Food to the Arapesh is good; it incorporates intensive social intercourse; it is the medium of intimacy and identification with others, the symbol of human relations which to them are the primary good. It satisfies the total individual. When we analyze the mouthful of yams into so much nutrition plus so much social warmth, that is exactly what we are doing and no more; we do not find these distinctions or elements—we create them. What we find are aspects of a total situation without independent existence. Our impulse is to break up the situation because we are culturally trained to comprehend a totality only after we break it up into familiar phrasings. But in this way we miss the value inherent in it, since it disappears with analysis, and cannot be recreated synthetically afterwards. Having created a series of elements, we then find no difficulty in motivating them according to a series of needs.

If needs are inborn and discrete, we should find them as such in the earliest situations of an individual's life. Yet take the Tikopia or the Kwoma infant, held and suckled without demand in the mothers' encircling arms. He knows no food apart from society, has no need for emotional response since his society is emotionally continuous with himself; he certainly feels no need for security. He participates in a total situation. Even in our own culture, the rare happy child has no need for emotional response or approval or security or escape from reality or novelty. If we say that the reason that he has no need for these things is that he does have them already, we would be begging the question. I believe, rather, that these terms or notions are irrelevant when satisfaction is viewed in terms of positive present value, and value itself as inherent in a total situation.

On the other hand, it is possible to see needs as arising out of the basic value of a culture. In our own culture, the value of individualism is axiomatically assumed. How else would it be possible for us to pluck twenty infants, newly severed from complete unity with their mothers, out of all social and emotional context, and classify them as twenty atoms on the basis of a similarity of age? On this assumption of individualism, a mother has need for individual self-expression. She has to have time for and by herself; and since she values individualism, the mother in our culture usually does have this need for a private life.

We also believe that a newborn infant must become individuated, must be taught physical and emotional self-dependence; we assume, in fact, that he has a separate identity which he must be helped to recognize. We believe that he has distinct rights, and sociologists urge us to reconcile the needs of the child to those of the adults in the family, on the assumption, of course, that needs and ends are individual, not social. Now, in maintaining our individual integrity and in passing on our value of individualism to the infant, we create needs for food, for security, for emotional response, phrasing these as distinct and separate. We force the infant to go hungry, and we see suckling as merely a matter of nutrition, so that we can then feel free to substitute a bottle for the breast and a mechanical bottle-holder for the mother's arms; thus we ensure privacy for the mother and teach the child self-dependence. We create needs in the infant by withholding affection and then presenting it as a series of approvals for an inventory of achievements or attributes. On the assumption that there is no emotional continuum, we withdraw ourselves, thus forcing the child to strive for emotional response and security. And thus, though habituation and teaching, the mother reproduces in the child her own needs, in this case the need for privacy which inevitably brings with it related needs.

Now the child grows up needing time to himself, a room of his own, freedom of choice, freedom to plan his own time and his own life. He will brook no interference and no encroachment. He will spend his wealth installing private bathrooms in his house, buying a private car, a private yacht, private woods and a private beach, which he will then people with his privately chosen society. The need for privacy is an imperative one in our society, recognized by official bodies of our government. And it is part of a system which stems from and expresses our basic value.

In other cultures, we find other systems, maintaining other values. The Arapesh, with their value of the social, created a wide gap between ownership and possession, which they could then bridge with a multitude of human relations. They plant their trees in someone else's hamlet, they rear pigs owned by someone else, they eat yams planted by someone else. The Ontong-Javanese, for whom also the good is social, value the sharing of the details of everyday living. They have created a system, very confusing to an American student, whereby a man is a member of at least three ownership groups, determined along different principles, which are engaged cooperatively in productive activities; and of two large households, one determined along matrilineal lines, one along patrilineal lines. Thus, an Ontong-Javanese man spends part of the year with his wife's sisters and their families, sharing with them the intimate details of daily life, and the rest of the year on an outlying island, with his brothers and their families. The poor man is the man who has no share in an outlying island, who must eat and sleep only in a household composed of his immediate family and his mother's kin, when unmarried; and who must spend the whole year with his wife's kin, when married. He has the same amount and kind of food to eat as his wealthy neighbors, but not as many coconuts to give away; he has shelter as adequate as that of the wealthy, but not as much of the shared living which is the Ontong-Javanese good.

In speaking of these other cultures, I have not used the term *need.* I could have said, for example, that the Ontong-Javanese needs a large house, to include many maternally related families. But I think this would have been merely an exercise in analysis. On the other hand, when I spoke of our own culture, I was forced to do it in terms of needs, since I have been trained to categorize my own experience in these terms. But even here, these are not basic needs, but rather part of a system expressing our basic value; and were we able to break away from our substantival or formal basis of categorizing, I think we should find these to be aspects or stresses or functions, without independent existence. Culture is not, I think, "a response to the total needs of a society"; but rather a system which stems from and expresses something had, the basic values of society.

REFERENCES

ALLPORT, GORDON. *Personality.* New York: H. Holt & Company, 1937.

BEAGLEHOLE, E. *Notes on Hopi Economic Life.* Yale University Publications in Anthropology, no. 15. New Haven: Yale University Press, 1937.

FIRTH, RAYMOND. *We, The Tikopia.* New York: American Book Company, 1936.

GILLIN, J. "Cultural Adjustment." *American Anthropology, 46*:429–447 (1944).

HOGBIN, I. *Law and Order in Polynesia,* New York: Harcourt, Brace and Company, Inc., 1934.

KARDINER, A. *The Individual and His Society.* New York: Columbia University Press, 1939.

KLUCKHOHN, CLYDE and KELLY, W. H. "The Concept of Culture." In Linton, R. (ed.) *The Science of Man in the World Crisis.* New York: Columbia University Press, 1945.
LEWIN, K. *A Dynamic Theory of Personality.* New York: McGraw-Hill Book Company, 1935.
LINTON, R. *The Study of Man.* New York: D. Appleton-Century Company, Inc., 1936.
______. *The Cultural Basis of Personality.* New York: D. Appleton-Century Company, Inc., 1945.
MEAD, MARGARET. *Sex and Temperament in Three Primitive Societies.* New York: William Morrow & Company, Inc., 1935.
______. "The Arapesh of New Guinea." In Mead, M. (ed.) *Cooperation and Competition Among Primitive Peoples.* New York: McGraw-Hill Book Company, 1937.
______. *The Mountain Arapesh: I. An Importing Culture.* Anthropological Papers of the American Museum of Natural History, 36: pt. 3 (1938).
MURDOCK, G. P. "The Science of Culture." *American Anthropology, 34*:200–215 (1932).
MURRAY, H. A. *Explorations in Personality.* New York: Oxford University Press, 1938.
PARSONS, E. C., ed. *A Pueblo Indian Journal,* 1920–1921. (American Anthropological Association Memoirs, no. 32). Menasha, Wisconsin, 1925.
SIMMONS, LEO W. *Sun Chief.* New Haven: Yale University Press, 1942.
WATSON, J. B. *Psychology from the Standpoint of a Behaviorist.* Philadelphia: J. B. Lippincott Company, 1919.
______. *Psychological Care of Infant and Child.* New York: W. W. Norton & Company, Inc., 1928.
WHITE, L. "Energy and Evolution of Culture." *American Anthropology, 45*:335–356 (1943).
WHITING, J. *Becoming a Kwoma.* New Haven: Yale University Press, 1941.
WISSLER, C. *Introduction to Social Anthropology.* New York: H. Holt & Company, 1929.

8

National and Regional Cultural Values in the United States

John Gillin

The following partial list of values is offered as being dominant in United States culture as a whole. Space is lacking for documentation or discussion of numerous corollaries and variations.

1. Personal output of energy is regarded as a good thing in its own right, whether in earning a living, in recreation, or in other endeavors. It does not necessarily mean "manual labor," but does imply "keeping busy" and "hard work." Personal effort is necessary to the solution of all problems. "Laziness" is bad.

2. Pragmatic ingenuity is valued and is

Reprinted by permission of The University of North Carolina Press from John Gillin, "National and Regional Cultural Values in the United States," *Social Forces,* XXXIV (December, 1955), pp. 107–13.

expected to be applied not only to materialistic problems, but to all problems, including social and personal maladjustment. Conversely, low rating is given to the passive contemplation of "unsolved mysteries" for sheer aesthetic or other "impractical" reasons. It should be noted that *thrift* is a value probably to be included under this heading.

3. Mechanistic world view: the universe and any discrete aspect of it are wholes consisting of parts that work together, well or badly, as the case may be, and this image is of course, valued as the correct one. Through pragmatic ingenuity and energy man may discover and manipulate these mechanical relations. (a) Practically all features of life experience are seen in the image of material things, which are regarded either as parts or as mechanically interrelated mechanisms; this concept includes time as a thing, also "personality," "group relations," etc. (b) Precise measurement is highly valued, not only for material objects, but also for time, "intelligence" of the individual, interpersonal interactions, etc. The idea is that in a mechanistic scheme the component parts must "fit" and therefore must be of exactly the correct size. "Adjustment" in this sense means essentially the same thing. Great value is placed upon money, not only as an economic instrument, but also because of its usefulness in "measuring" many intangibles, such as social status, influence, etc. (c) Cleanliness and orderliness may also be seen as subsidiary values of a mechanistic world view. Machines do not work well if dirty and if the parts are out of place; neither do individuals or social groups. (d) Science is appreciated so long as it is applied in such a way as to "make things work better." Pure science or curiosity for its own sake is each regarded as dubious in the general culture.

4. Mobility of the person, whether with respect to physical or social position, rates high. One is reminded of the mechanical interchangeability of adjustment of parts, because whether one moves to a strange locality or to a higher social stratum great emphasis is put upon "fitting into" the new situation, unless one goes outside the boundaries of the nation.

5. Change and novelty are values in themselves within a restricted area of the culture, such as styles of consumer goods, amusements, and vacations. Such things are supposed to give the average American a "thrill," i.e., relief from the ennui of routine. Changes in basic social institutions or in the general value system, however, are usually viewed as "radical" when first proposed.

6. Optimism, as contrasted with fatalism or melancholy, is valued. Any problem can be solved if suitable energy and ingenuity are applied to it. Furthermore, God, insofar as he represents a general cultural formulation, will help, because he approves of these methods. When God is looking the other way, about the only thing that can block success is bad luck. But if one keeps at the job and uses his head, the "breaks are bound to come his way."

7. Individualism, always highly praised, has some aspects more or less peculiar to the American system. Among them are the following. (a) Ideally each person should have an equal opportunity economically, socially, and politically at the start of his adult life. Officially this is supposed to be guaranteed by the refusal to recognize hereditary economic and social classes, by universal free education, by universal adult suffrage, and the right to hold public office open to all native-born citizens. These rights are supposed to be upheld regardless of race, creed, or color. Given such equal opportunity the individual's success in winning the rewards provided by the culture depends upon his following or applying the appropriate values of the system, especially energy and ingenuity. (b) Freedom or liberty for the individual is prized and is formally guaranteed by such legal formulations as the Bill of Rights. Liberty is regarded as freedom from

unnecessary frustrations and interferences, many of which are explicitly spelled out. What freedom is *for*, on the other hand, is much less clear. Officially, it is described as "the pursuit of happiness," but the system of values contains neither a general nor a specific definition of "happiness" as a state of affairs. (c) Self-reliance and initiative are expected of individuals; Americans are supposed to be "self-starting." Courage in the face of obstacles is also involved, and the individual is borne up by adherence to the general value of optimism. (d) Status achieved "through one's own efforts" is valued. Although high status carries with it many perquisites, it does not, according to the pattern, confer the right to treat persons of lower status openly as "inferiors," implying that their less fortunate position is due to failure to apply the values of the system. Other persons may make such comparisons, but not the occupant of high status. (e) Achievement requires a certain competitiveness in the individual, and competiveness is also a general value of the culture, expected not only of individuals but also of groups.

The individualistic values are tempered by the worth placed on (f) generosity and (g) social conformity. The ideal individual is generous and takes an interest in other members of his group or society, in the weak, the unfortunate, the underdogs. In modern America, acting, at least, in conformity with this value wins more rewards than crass "selfishness." Outward conformity to the opinions of others has a certain value in relation to the individual. Although some observers hold that conformity in thoughts and "feelings" is also a part of the value system, this writer postulates that it is not—yet. (h) However, individuals are expected to have consciences; that is, the values of the cultural system are supposed to be internalized in persons and the internal punishment of guilt sanctions deviations from them. In common parlance an individual with a well developed conscience or super-ego who acts in accordance is a man or woman of "character."

8. Competitiveness has already been mentioned in connection with individualism. Most observers, as well as native defenders, of the system hold that it is a general value permeating almost all parts of the culture. It is institutionalized among business organizations, but also appears among religious sects, certain social classes, groups of scholars, and so on. Conversely anything which tends to stifle competition, such as economic monopoly or inherited perquisites, is regarded unfavorably.

9. In the American system competitiveness is tempered by the value of "fair play," probably borrowed from British culture.

10. Cooperation in the common welfare is another value that mitigates competitiveness. It is manifested by a great variety of voluntaristic groups and organizations, all of which are oriented at least toward the common welfare of their members and often toward that of the whole society. Voluntary charitable contributions in which all are expected to participate, controlled neither by church nor state, are characteristic of the society.

11. Honesty or frankness in human relations has high value ideally, while dissimulation is "bad."

12. Prestige as manifested in respect or deference given by others is highly valued. No space is available to discuss the numerous forms of prestige, but it should be remarked that, contrary to some superficial observations, it is not exclusively a matter of high social position or large financial resources. It is held in the system that prestige and respect *can* be achieved by any member of the society, and that, strictly speaking, all prestige *must* be achieved or "earned."

13. Power or the ability, by some means or other, (a) to influence or control other persons or groups is an American value. In the system, however, power exerted over

other persons through force is given a low rating. The ideally "best" type of power is that achieved and maintained by "moral" suasion and influence. (b) Power over material things, including other animals, and over the forces of nature, is a basic value and is sought without limit.

14. Recreation is a "right" for Americans, but from the ideal point of view, is defined somewhat literally. This is to say that, although recreation is doing something one is not required to do (in distinction to "work"), whatever is done should recreate one, it should "be good for you." Thus recreation is to be distinguished from mere pleasure; only certain pleasures are also recreational. Activities that run counter to the major values are bad, regardless of how pleasurable they may be. Needless to say numerous members of the society do not behave entirely consistently with this value pair.

15. Efficiency is another ideal value sometimes, of course, not followed. In line with the mechanistic world view it is held that all things should operate to the full extent of their inherent capacities and at the lowest cost in whatever terms. This applies not only to machines, but also to social organizations and personalities. One of the virtues of pragmatic ingenuity is that by its application the efficiency of anything can be increased. With respect to the population as a whole, as well as the individual organism, good health, both physical and mental, is valued, not only because it is pleasant but also because it is efficient.

16. Love is a state of interpersonal relations that practically all Americans cherish. It is generally regarded as a satisfying feeling state which may be enjoyed by the individual either actively or passively. The "best" kind of love, however, is reciprocal. Although one hears most about love of the romantic kind, nevertheless the non-sexual love of the family and friendship types is highly prized. Whether between the sexes, in the family or in friendship, love means essentially a sort of intimate relationship in which most thoughts or feelings of individual advantage are submerged in one's regard for the loved person or persons.

17. Inner-regulated morality is believed to be one of the virtues of the system. In the general culture it is thought that all individuals should have a "conscience" and should "feel guilty" when doing "wrong." In other words, the value system is supposed to be supported and maintained in conduct by an inner mechanism in each individual whose sanctions are internal rather than external. This is believed by many to be one of the bases of the American type of democracy. As American society has grown in size and complexity, doubts have arisen as to the effectiveness of this mechanism, supported by evidence of crime, delinquency, and other forms of "social disorganization." And there is, as Riesman has pointed out, some reason to question whether inner-regulated morality can still be regarded as a basic value of the system.

It will be noticed that no place is given in the above list to values of a "spiritual" or transcendental type. Foreign observers frequently ask: Is there nothing Americans value beyond these? What are the ultimate goals of existence? Does not life and the universe have some "higher" meaning? And so on. With the decline in this century of general acceptance in America of the traditional theological answers to such questions, the average person as well as those who speak for the nation find it difficult to provide positive formulations that have meaning to others not reared in the United States value system. This writer believes that convincing evidence can be produced that, buried in the American culture, certain values of a spiritual and transcendental nature do exist, of which few Americans are consciously aware and which, therefore, they are unable to make explicit. This is not the place to attempt a demonstration and formulation. It does seem to be true that the culture has so developed during the past fifty years as to set up defenses, one might say, against overt consideration of the "soul," "the absolute," and the like. Not the least of such defenses is American humor, which in addition to serving as a social sanction and tension-reducer, also acts as a deflector of serious attempts to discuss submerged values that have become unfashionable.

Since any culture is in part a set of customary adaptations to natural environment and resources, it is to be expected in a territory of the size and geographical diversity of the continental United States that a considerable variation in adaptive and exploitative aspects of culture will occur. Despite the efficiency of transportation and communication which has made the United States the most culturally homogeneous nation of its size in history, there is every reason to expect some continued diversity in the cultural aspects of materialistic adaptation and exploitation of natural resources. These diversities will not be listed here, nor can we discuss the values attached to them. Whether such factors, together with variety in historical backgrounds, will continue to have a controlling effect on basic regional value systems is a matter for further investigation.

Here I shall venture to set down only a tentative check list of regional cultural values that may serve to stimulate further research. Perhaps it is necessary to emphasize that no judgment of relative worth of the various regional values is made or implied. Where nothing is said about a certain value of the national culture it will be assumed that the regional culture conforms to the national standard.

1. NORTHEAST. (a) *Special emphases.* Hard work and thrift are still given special emphasis in rural subcultures. Hereditary status is more firmly established than in the country as a whole. Power over persons and groups, including those in other parts of the nation is emphasized, and is more explicitly justified, especially in cosmopolitan centers like Boston and New York. Change and novelty are played down in rural areas, rated high in New York metropolitan area. Very strong differences are shown between metropolitan and rural values in general. (b) *Special values.* Seaboard cities tend to be internationally "minded" and to blend European values into the system rather than rejecting them outright.

2. SOUTHEAST. (a) *Special emphases.* Protestant morality is especially strong. Non-commercial recreations of the "folk" type are well developed. Family relations are strong and include extended kin group. Status and power tend to be based on kinship connections more than in any other region with the exception of Back Bay Boston. Hard work is necessary for most, but little valued as a good in itself. Pragmatic ingenuity, and the corollaries of the mechanistic world view, especially cleanliness and orderliness, are rated lower than in the country as a whole. Mobility of the person is a necessary evil rather than a positive good. Change and optimism for their own sakes rate low. Freedom for the individual from outside (non-Southern) interference is highest of the individualistic values. General competitiveness is restrained by the power and kinship systems. (b) *Special values.* Doctrine of white supremacy and resulting race-castes. Idealization of women in the image of the "lady." Violence as a solution of interpersonal and intergroup problems. Regional cultural chauvinism resulting in attitude that the Southeast can solve its problems if outsiders will not interfere, that it is a special region with a culture uniquely fitted to it, and that "the rest of the country is against us."

3. MIDDLE STATES. This region is often described as the "most typical" of the United States. (a) *Special emphases.* Outward symbols of prestige and power are devalued and emphasis is placed on "democratic leveling." Much of Middle

Western suspicion of "Easterners" and "foreigners" may be connected with the notion that money is supposed to be an instrument for work but not for the gaining of (financial) power. Optimism is strong, especially in the form of community "boosting." Conformity to community norms is rated high by various observers. Honesty and outspokenness are especially valued and the notion is often expressed that "Easterners are crooks," and "foreigners, frankly, are inferior." All the other national values are, in general, strongly held. (b) *Special values.* "Isolationism," if it may be called a value, is the feature of the Middle States most often cited. The basic notion seems to be that the United States is quite capable of "going it alone" without becoming entangled in international affairs.

4. SOUTHWEST. This region, lying along the border with Mexico was, of course, formerly a part of that country. It also contains a large area originally settled by the Mormons, as well as other areas (mostly in eastern Texas) settled from the Southeast. (a) *Special emphases.* Although the personal application of energy is highly regarded, manual labor, such as work in the fields, is denigrated for Americans and often considered to be the proper function of Mexicans and Negroes. Whether this is a heritage from Mexico or is connected with the fact that much of the region was originally exploited by cattle and sheep raising on the open range (a type of work that does not require "manual labor") remains to be determined. The original distinction between the horseman and the field worker has led to a degree of classification of the population, although the value of equality of opportunity is strongly held, at least for white "Americans." If we are to believe the publicity, the recent oil millionaires have substituted the Cadillac for the horse as a symbol of status. Physical mobility, whether by horse or mechanical means, has always been highly valued. Optimism is high and perhaps "luck" and "taking a chance" are valued more than in the country as a whole. With respect to measurement, bigness seems to have a certain value in its own right, often said to be associated with a world view conditioned by "wide open spaces." (b) *Special values.* A certain romantic and nostalgic value is given to Spanish-Mexican culture, as evidenced to some extent in architecture, costume, Catholic fiestas, and popular music. Otherwise it is difficult to find much Mexican influence in the value system of the culture. Likewise a sentimental value is given to the image of the old days of the "open range," celebrated in roundups, rodeos, and "covered wagon days" of ceremonial significance. Of course, the cult of the "Old Southwest" has been spread nationally through the mass media of communication mainly for the consumption of moppets of the male sex.

5. NORTHWEST. (a) *Special emphases.* Although originally settled by a fairly homogeneous North European Protestant stock from the Southeast and New England, the region has lately received large increments of newcomers with Catholic European backgrounds. Frugality and hard work have been traditionally highly valued in this region, and optimism would probably be rated lower than the national level, partly because of the comparative harshness of nature. In fact, during ruinous periods of drouth in the Dakotas, for instance, it has seemed that the regional culture contained a certain fatalism. The former open range country culture shares some of the "horse culture" values of the Southwest.

6. FAR WEST. (a) *Special emphases.* Outstanding, perhaps, is optimism. This is the region of "progress unlimited." As someone has said, the Far West is the melting pot of elements from all over the United States, rather than from the Old World. Consequently family ties count for comparatively little, and the emphasis on social and physical mobility is strong.

Conformity for the individual probably is lowest of any region, and is reflected in great freedom and informality in dress and interpersonal relations. Recreation in the form of "outdoor living" receives special emphasis and there is a more conscious attempt to blur the line between work and play than elsewhere. The Far West has a special focus on cooperation for the public welfare in the unusually high emphasis placed on development of water and other natural resources. As a whole Far Westerners are perhaps less bound by Puritan consciences than residents of other regions. There is high tolerance for eccentricity and flamboyant expressions of individualism. Change and novelty are valued in many ways for themselves. It is difficult to say that the Far West has developed special values, but, as indicated, its regional subculture has given a special "twist" to many of the universal American values.

9

The Conscience of a Scientist

Dr. Jacob Bronowski

When W. C. Röntgen won the first Nobel prize in 1901, he was the model of what the public expected a scientist to be: paternal, full-bearded, and remote, perhaps something of a laboratory dreamer (had he discovered X-rays by accident?) and certainly a benefactor to mankind. There was no shadow in the picture; if the public that day thought any figure sinister, it was not that of the scientist but of Alfred Nobel.

The picture of the scientist in the public mind has darkened since then. One cause, of course, has been the death-dealing part played by science in two wars. But more deeply, the public is troubled by the growing entry of science into all policy, which it cannot stem and does not know how to guide.

So the public has come to ask, more and more, what principles guide the scientist himself. Does he indeed acknowledge any principles? Or is he a machine that thumps out the facts, neutral, inhuman, and at bottom irresponsible!

These questions have shaken scientists as well, and have made them look afresh at their own activity. The first illumination that has come from this is in seeing that science must indeed be judged as an activity. The nature of science lies not in the facts that it discovers, but in the process by which they are discovered.

Of course the facts, any facts, are ethically neutral; but they cannot be discovered (and tested, and organized in theories) unless the process is guided by a strong ethic. Scientists must agree that they want to uncover *the truth*, and every means that they devise must serve this end. There is therefore no distinction in science between ends and means: the means must

From *The Sciences,* December 1967; © The New York Academy of Sciences, 1967; reprinted by permission.

be as truthful in detail, a matter of absolute trust between man and man, as the end itself.

To help discover the truth is a communal task, which lays a common charge on every member of the community of scientists. It is a false distinction to say (as laymen sometimes say) that science can tell us *what is* but not *what we ought to do*. For if the end of science is to reach the truth, then it follows that as scientists we *ought* to act in such a way that what *is* true can be verified to be so.

Science has succeeded as a method by putting this principle into practice. It has organized the society of scientists so that their actions follow the principle naturally. In effect, the society of scientists honors a set of values which are designed to reach the truth by open argument.

The first of these practical values is independence; for without that there can be no progress to truth—no argument is possible, and no experimental test is convincing. The natural ground for independence is originality, and that is another value in science. Both values are expressed in dissent, and it is therefore necessary that science should safeguard dissent by giving a special value to all forms of freedom: free enquiry, free thought, and free speech. Thus one of the values of science is tolerance, not as a mark of indifference to the views of others, but as a mark of equal respect for them.

It seems strange in this modern analysis of science to come upon such underlying values as tolerance, freedom, and respect. They point to the finding at the center of this study, which is that science is a human and social activity. It cannot be conceived as the work of a machine, or even of one man. The pursuit of truth in the full sense (in the full senses) of science is an argument in a community of equals. That cannot be separated from the confronting values which give tone and tension to the community: among them independence and freedom, tolerance and justice, dissent and respect. In a society in which these human values did not exist, science would have to invent them to make its practice possible.

Those who fear (and rightly fear) the destructive uses of science sometimes plead that scientists should censor such discoveries, or even put a moratorium on all discovery now. They have despaired of making statesmen honor the human values, and they ask scientists to act in their place not for one nation but for mankind.

Why are scientists reluctant to play the benevolent despot in this way? The answer, we see, lies in the whole tradition of science. In its essence, it is a democratic and not a dictatorial process. It moves by open argument to free agreement, and to break with that method is for most scientists a breach of faith.

More, it is a breach with the values which have given science its unique power. Free inquiry, free speech, open publication have been the conditions for the success of science, and it could not grow now without them. Scientists are afraid of any plan that would suspend these in order to meet some present threat, however grave it may seem at the time; for they fear that the damage to the free tradition would be done once for all. The destructive uses of science (and of ignorance too) are a menace to man's values. But the values which have fostered science are also human, and their interruption would be a loss which scientists fear for all mankind.

SECTION C *The Family— Durable and Flexible*

In spite of a great deal of effective and ineffective rebellion against our families, it is still very difficult to grow up without one. The rise and proliferation of communes, microcommunities where children are raised conjointly, may change this. The rebirth of the concept of the tribe may offer radical solutions to problems that exist in the contemporary family. However, in the near future, it is probable that we will continue to see the family in its present form. It will be better if we understand some of the dynamics of this institution before looking at larger social units.

There is a theory in India that one is born into the family that can teach him most of the things he must learn. This theory suggests that whatever difficulties, sufferings, joys, opportunities, and confusions arise from one's family have been selected for his personal development. The upsetting aspect of this notion is that it removes responsibility from parents. That is, they are doing what they were programmed to do by nature. It places much more responsibility on the children in that they deserve what they are getting.

In the West we presuppose the opposite theory. The family lays its heavy hand on the unformed, malleable child. We are all, therefore, a result of this molding from the top.

In either case we are what we have been brought up to be. This section explores some of the basic parameters of this process.

The Russian revolution brought with it massive social experiments. Nicholas S. Timasheff chronicles the rise and fall of one of them. Its failure is a sobering reflection on the underlying forces that maintain the Western family unit. Other articles deal with family units more similar to our own. John Sirjamaki looks at the relationships between values, perceptions, and social institutions. Talcott Parsons, in a fairly complex article, suggests profound results that arise from our particular cultural configuration. Our family is far more than a home, but far less than a total culture. The article by James S. Plant extends beyond the single family and discusses the effects of one modern cultural artifact—crowding. The effects of crowding are not well understood. Neither do we have any firm idea of the effects of pollution, malnutrition, easy access to information via television, and a host of other variables that affect the modern family. It is easy to speculate, more difficult to predict.

This section ends with Horace Miner's classic study of the Nacirema, a strange and disturbing culture whose peculiar view of the world is so different from our own.

10

The Attempt to Abolish the Family in Russia

Nicholas S. Timasheff

In their attempts to create a new culture, the revolutionists always meet resistance. This resistance is displayed by individuals, but they resist because they have been molded by mighty institutions through which social structure and culture are perpetuated. In modern society, these pillar of society are the family, the school, and the church. From the standpoint of the revolutionists, two of them, the family and the church, are hopeless, for it is their very nature to preserve tradition. But the school might perhaps be transformed into an instrument of cultural revolution.

Hence, for those who are eager to endow a nation with a new culture, a definite program of action follows: they must loosen the family ties; they must destroy or at least weaken the church; and they must transform the school into an accelerator of cultural revolution. This was the natural program of the Communists while they performed their Great Experiment.

With respect to the family, the destructive attitude is sometimes denied by pro-Communist writers outside of Russia.[1] The reason is obvious; the value of the family is beyond question, say, in this country, and a regime which is hostile to it cannot count on many sympathizers, But in 1919, an authoritative representative of the regime said: "The family has ceased to be a necessity, both for its members and for the State." A few years later, another high dignitary declared that the Communists had to undermine the family, "this formidable stronghold of all the turpitudes of the old regime."[2] And acts were still more conclusive than words.

The family, which was to be destroyed, was of the patriarchal type. In old Russia, marriage was a religious institution. Only religious marriage and divorce were recognized, so that the rules of the corresponding religious communities were exclusively applied. The superiority of the husband over the wife was legally recognized, but there was no joint property of the consorts.[3] The wife received the husband's last name, but the Russians emphasized that, in contradistinction to

[1] See, for instance, Nathan Berman, "Juvenile Delinquency in the Soviet Union," *American Journal of Sociology*, March, 1937.

[2] A. Kollontay, "The Family and the Communist State" (Russian; 1919), p. 8; N. Bukharin, *Proceedings of the XIII Congress of the Communist Party* (Russian; 1924), p. 545.

[3] Cf. John Hazard in "Law and the Soviet Family," *Wisconsin Law Review*, 1939, p. 245.

the West, their women never were addressed as "Mrs. John Doe'; their first names had to be used. Parental authority was strong; up to the age of twenty-one, children needed parental consent for marriage and quite a few other significant acts. Naturally, the institution of inheritance existed. Thus, the strong family structure prevailed; this was especially the case among the peasants and the lower-middle class, whereas among the upper classes, the intellectuals, and the workers there was a well-expressed tendency to weaken the family ties.

This stronghold of the old order, this instrument of culture tradition, was attacked by the Communists from the very start of their rule.[4] The general tendency was to destroy the stable character of marital relations and make marriage as easily soluble as possible. Naturally, marriage was liberated from all bonds with religion: after a certain date, church weddings ceased to be accorded any legal effect. Instead of going to church, the prospective consorts had to apply for "registration" of their marriage to local boards established for that purpose. Measures were taken to deprive the registration of the character of an impressive ceremony. The boards were usually located in some dark and abject room of an office building, and no words about the significance of marriage were uttered by the officials.

The most drastic change concerned divorce: in contradistinction to the old law which made it so difficult, the decrees of December 17 and 18, 1917, permitted every consort to declare that he wanted his marriage to be canceled. No reasons were to be given to the board. Receiving the application, it had to grant the cancellation immediately if there was mutual consent; if this was not the case, divorce was to be granted by the court, but this was a meaningless formality, since the court had to do it at the request of each consort, even if the other one opposed it. If one of the consorts was absent, he or she was notified by a postcard.

In addition to this, incest, bigamy, and adultery were dropped from the list of criminal offenses. Abortion was explicitly permitted by the decree of November 20, 1920, provided that it was performed by an approved physician in a state hospital. Under these conditions, the physician had to accede to requests for abortion even if no valid reasons could be established. Under war communism, inheritance ceased to exist.

When marriage can be canceled by means of a postcard, when there is no distinction between legitimacy and illegitimacy, when inheritance is unknown, parental authority is naturally weakened, and this effect was one of the purposes of the measures described. In official propaganda, the idea was persistently emphasized that children had to obey their parents only insofar as the parents complied loyally with the directions of those in power. This signified, among other things, that unless they wanted to risk placing themselves in a dangerous position, parents could not oppose the propaganda of the Marxist doctrine, including atheism, to which the children were exposed at school. There they were taught to do their best to re-educate their parents in the Communist spirit and denounce them to the authorities if they displayed a marked counter-revolutionary attitude. Numerous family tragedies evolved on that basis, the state backing the children against the parents. Time and again the idea was publicly discussed as to whether family education ought not to be abolished and replaced by education in state institutions. Reluctantly, the idea was rejected as impractical, at least for the period of transition.

[4] First by the decree of December 17 and 18, 1917, later on consolidated and expanded by the Family Code of October 22, 1918.

During the NEP,[5] a partial restoration of the family could be expected, if the Marxist doctrine were correct and monogamy and the strong family were the counterpart of the individualistic manner of production. There was actually one almost unavoidable concession; this was the restoration of inheritance. But in contrast with the Marxist scheme, the attack on the family was rather strengthened. A new Family Code was prepared in 1925, and the draft was submitted to an informal discussion. Voices from the countryside were unfavorable, but this did not stop the government, and the new code was enacted as of January 1, 1927. The main innovation was the introduction of the institution of "the non-registered marriage," legally equal to the registered one. This meant that courts and boards were obliged to consider every union of a man and woman as marriage provided that at least one of the following conditions were present: (1) durable cohabitation; (2) common menage; (3) declaration of the relationship before third persons, or (4) mutual support and common education of the children. The unforeseen effect was the legalization of bigamy: applying the new law, the Supreme Court prescribed the division of the estate of a deceased man between his registered and nonregistered wife.[6]

The period of the Second Socialist Offensive was characterized by additional efforts to uproot the traditional structure of the family. The labor law of the period made it obligatory to accept any job imposed on the individual, and often husband and wife were assigned work in different towns. To the complaint of a teacher that she was artificially separated from her husband, the Labor Board replied that divorce was easy and that she probably could find another husband in the place of her occupation. In Stalingrad, it was decided to create "socialist suburbs" consisting of houses without apartments for family life, replaced by single rooms, refectories, and nurseries. The plan fell through because nobody but bachelors agreed to live in such suburbs.

The antifamily policy was crowned by partial success: around 1930, on the average, family ties were substantially weaker than they had been before the revolution. But this partial success was more than balanced by a number of detrimental effects unforeseen by the promoters of the Communist experiment. About 1934, these detrimental effects were found to endanger the very stability of the new society and its capacity to stand the test of war. Let us review these effects.

1. The abuse of the freedom of divorce and abortion resulted in an ominous decrease of the birth rate. No natality figures have ever been published for the crucial years, but in 1937, the population proved to be 13 million behind expectation, so that around 1934, the deficit must already have been large. To what extent this was due to the freedoms just mentioned cannot be established. But the following figures speak for themselves: in 1934, in the medical institutions of the city of Moscow, 57 thousand children were born, but 154 thousand abortions were performed; in 1935 already under changing conditions, the figures were 70 thousand, and 155 thousand. As to divorce, the frequency of which also pushes down the birth rate, the following figures were reported from Moscow: in 1934, in 100 marriages there were 37 divorces, and in the first half of 1935, there were 38.3 divorces.[7]

2. The dissolution of family ties especially of the parent-child relations threatened to produce a wholesale dissolution of community ties, with rapidly increasing juvenile delinquency as the main symptom. In 1935, the Soviet papers were full of information

[5] New Economic Policy.

[6] Decision of the Supreme Court of the RSFSR, reported in *Sudebnaya Praktika,* 1929, No. 20.

[7] *Izvestia,* July 7, 1935.

and indignation about the rise of hooliganism, i.e., of crimes in which the sadistic joy of inflicting pain on somebody or destroying something of value was paramount. Everywhere, wrote the papers, gangs invaded workingmen's dwellings, ransacked them, and destroyed or spoiled what they did not take away; if somebody dared to resist, he was mercilessly killed. In trains, the hooligans sang obscene songs; to prolong the fun, they did not permit travelers to alight at their destinations if they had not finished singing. Sometimes the schools were besieged by neglected children; other times gangs beat the teachers and attacked women, or regularly fought against one another.

3. Finally, the magnificent slogans of the liberation of sex and the emancipation of women proved to have worked in favor of the strong and reckless, and against the weak and shy. Millions of girls saw their lives ruined by Don Juans in Communist garb, and millions of children had never known parental homes.

The disintegration of the family did not disturb the Communists, since this was precisely what they wanted to achieve, but they were disturbed by quite a few collateral effects of the disorganization. The unfavorable trend of the population figures threatened to undermine both the labor supply and the strength of the nation at arms—for wars to be waged by the next generation. In the specific circumstances of 1934, the waste of human energy in juvenile delinquency, the combat against it, and love affairs, and the accumulation of unfavorable attitudes among the victims of the new family order—or perhaps disorder is the correct word?—could no longer be tolerated: they undermined the strength of the nation for the war which was straight ahead. The unfavorable development had to be stopped, and to achieve this the government had no other choice but to re-enforce that pillar of society which is the family. These were the main lines of development:

1. Contrary to the teachings of the previous years, young people were instructed to consider marriage "as the most serious affair in life," since in principle it should be a union for life. Statements such as follow, which never could have appeared in the course of the Communist experiment, now daily adorned the Soviet papers and magazines: "There are people who dare to assert that the Revolution destroys the family; this is entirely wrong: the family is an especially important phase of social relations in socialist society. . . . One of the basic rules of Communist morals is that of strengthening the family. . . . The right to divorce is not a right to sexual laxity. A poor husband and father cannot be a good citizen. People who abuse the freedom of divorce should be punished." And actually, in 1935, the Soviet government started to prosecute men for rape who "changed their wives as gloves," registering a marriage one day and divorce the next. *Pravda* told the following story:

Engineer P. seduced a girl by promising to marry her. When symptoms of pregnancy appeared, the girl reminded him of his promise. His reply was: "Look, dear, you are the seventh girl in my life to whom the same unpleasant thing has occurred. Here is a letter from another woman who is also bearing a child of mine. Could I marry her, too?" The girl insisted, but the engineer terminated the discussion by saying: "Forget about marriage. Do as you like. Here is money to pay for an abortion." Having told the story, the paper added: "This man should be tried, and his trial ought to be a 'demonstrative trial.'"[8]

In the official journal of the Commissariat of Justice these amazing statements may be found:

The State cannot exist without the family. Marriage is a positive value for the

[8] *Pravda,* June 4 and 26, 1935; *Molodaya Gvardiya,* 1935, No. 1.

Socialist Soviet State only if the partners see in it a lifelong union. So-called free love is a bourgeois invention and has nothing in common with the principles of conduct of a Soviet citizen. Moreover, marriage receives its full value for the State only if there is progeny, and the consorts experience the highest happiness of parenthood.[9]

To inculcate the rediscovered value of marriage into the minds of the younger generation, not only the negative method of deterrence by trials and producing indignation by well-chosen stories was used, but also the positive method of glorifying marriage by well-staged ceremonies; perhaps one could speak of "demonstrative marriage." Here is a story from, *Izvestia.* The people involved are a *kolhoz* brigadier, V., and the first parachutist among *kolhoz* girls, B. The scene is Northern Caucasus, one of Russia's granaries.

The romance lasted about two years. In the beginning, V. hated B. He did his best to organize a shock brigade,[10] but she preferred dancing and diverted the energy of youth towards that futility. When V. saw that he was unable to discourage that attraction he joined the movement, even started helping young people organize dances and athletic performances, and in return was helped by them in work. Then suddenly, when B. made her first jump, V. decided that life without her would be valueless, and proposed to her. She accepted. The secretaries of the regional and local party organizations decided to sponsor the marriage. Stimulated by them, the collective farm took over all preparations and decorated the village beautifully for the great day. The people's commissar for agriculture was invited to come. He could not accept, but congratulated the young people by wire and offered them a magnificent gift, a phonograph and a set of records.

The story is continued in *Pravda.* Early in the morning guests started arriving. Among them were leaders of the party, the Soviets, and the economic organizations, as well as the champion of the girl parachutists of the Union. About noon, a score of airplanes appeared in the sky. The betrothed were offered a ride, after which they were enthusiastically acclaimed by the crowd. About five o'clock, 800 guests were invited to dinner. Tables were overloaded with mutton, hams, ducks, chickens, pies, and other dishes. After a while the regional party secretary rose and made a speech congratulating the V.'s on their marriage, the most serious step in their lives. He expressed the hope that they would live in perfect unity and procreate an abundant Bolshevik progeny. The 800 present rose and drank to the health of the newlyweds. The people danced and rejoiced far into the night.[11]

Was not this an invitation to millions of young people to reconsider those ideas about marriage which, until quite recently, they were taught as belonging to the very essence of the doctrine? To re-enforce the new ideas, very simple, but probably very effective symbolic means were used. The registration offices ceased to be filthy places. Now, young people found them clean, comfortable, well furnished; the officers became polite, friendly, underlining the seriousness of the act. Marriage certificates started being issued on decent paper, no longer on wrapping paper, as was the case previously. For a small additional sum, the newlyweds could receive a marriage certificate designed by artists.[12] Then, in the fall of 1936, wedding rings started being sold in Soviet shops.[13] Since these rings are used in church weddings, this novelty could be interpreted as an invitation, on the part of the government, to have the civil marriage

[9] *Sotsialisticheskaya Zakonnost,* 1939, No. 2.
[10] A group of workers pledged to work substantially faster and better than required by regulations.
[11] *Izvestia,* September 9, 1935; *Pravda,* September 11, 1935.
[12] *Izvestia,* July 7, 1937; *Krasyaya Gazeta,* November 4, 1934.
[13] *New York Times*, November 18, 1936.

or registration, re-enforced and made almost indissoluble by the church.

2. The freedom of divorce was first curtailed and then almost abolished. The first phase appears in the law of June 27, 1936, which introduced a number of inhibitions. It calls for the summoning of both parties when a divorce is to be registered.

Moreover, according to the law of September 28, 1935, the fact of divorce must be marked in the passports and birth certificates of the consorts. Commenting on this regulation, *Izvestia* expressed the hope that before marrying a "fluttering scoundrel," a girl would ask him to produce his papers and then perhaps renounce the honor of becoming his thirtieth bride.[14]

Finally, the fee for divorce which previously had been rather nominal was substantially raised; instead of three rubles one had to pay 50 rubles for the first divorce, 150 for the second, and 300 for the third and each subsequent divorce.

The effect of the antidivorce drive may be measured by the following figures: in the course of the second half of the year 1936, the number of divorces in the Ukraine was 10,992, against 35,458 in the second half of 1935;[15] in other words, it decreased more than three times.

The second phase appears in the decree of July 8, 1944.

Prospective applicants for divorce will henceforth be obliged to state their reasons and satisfy the courts that these reasons are serious and valid. Both parties must appear personally before a lower court which hears all the evidence and then seeks to determine if it cannot effect a reconciliation. If this is believed impossible, the petition can be carried to a higher court. Witnesses must be heard in both courts. The court fees have been raised to 2,000 rubles.

It is probable that the courts, obeying the government's directions, will demand very good reasons and irrefutable evidence to grant a divorce, In consequence, obtaining a divorce in Russia will probably become more difficult than in many states of this country.

Moreover, the decree of July 8, 1944, abolished the institution of "unregistered marriage" introduced in 1926. Now, only "registered marriage" is legally recognized; as a corollary, the "bourgeois" distinction between legitimate and illegitimate children has reappeared in Soviet law. In addition to this, "the research of paternity" has been explicitly forbidden, so that illegitimate children and their mothers will receive no alimony. Very definitely, this will prove a mighty deterrent to extra-marital relations, insofar as girls are concerned.

3. The freedom to dispose of unborn children through abortions no longer exists. Early in 1935 a campaign against abortion was started. Articles began to appear in Soviet papers written by high medical authorities explaining the harm which abortion, especially repeated abortion, inflicts on women.[16] Praising maternity, these authorities declared that the longing for children had suddenly reappeared among the women of the Soviet Union—a manner of saying that now Stalin wanted them to bear as many children as possible. Trials resulting in severe sentences finished the careers of persons operating clandestine "abortaria"; their very emergence disclosed that, without change in the law, Soviet hospitals no longer performed abortion at the simple request of the pregnant woman. Finally a draft law prohibiting abortion was published and offered for public discussion. Numerous objections were raised, mainly based on intolerable dwelling conditions. Nevertheless, the law of June 27, 1936, abolished the freedom of abortion which had been considered one of the highest achievements of Communism by many pro-Communists.

Repealing the notorious law of Novem-

[14] *Izvestia,* February 12, 1937.
[15] *New York Times*, July 11, 1944.
[16] For instance, by Arkhangelski, member of the Academy of Sciences, *Izvestia,* June 5, 1935.

ber 20, 1920, the new law prohibited abortion in all cases except where there was danger of life or health of the pregnant woman or danger of hereditary transmission of serious sickness. As in the former law, only medical men were permitted to perform the operation. Pressure exerted on a woman to induce her into abortion was declared a crime punishable by two years in prison. To make more childbearing possible, the law promised a large extension of the network of maternity hospitals, day nurseries, and kindergartens. Maternity grants were increased, and special allowances were promised to mothers of six or more children.[17]

4. The peculiar parent-child relationship which had obtained under the Communist experiment, and which granted superiority to the children, was reversed to one which is considered normal in the world; once more, children have to recognize the authority of their parents. Obviously, the change could not be effected through legal enactment, and the method of persuasion through propaganda was used exactly in the same manner as it was used to stabilize marriage. Statements like these could be found almost daily on the pages of Soviet papers, beginning with the spring of 1935:

> Young people should respect their elders, especially their parents. . . . The respect and care of parents is an essential part of the Comsomol[18] morals. . . . One must respect and love his parents, even if they are old-fashioned and do not like the Comsomol.[19]

In 1939, the official journal of the Union Prosecutor declared:

> Sound moral ideas must be inculcated into the minds of young persons. They must know that lack of care for their parents is found only among savages and that in every civilized society such conduct is considered dishonest and base.[20]

To corroborate these ideas, the journal cited the laws of Solon and Xenophon's works.

The method of positive demonstration was also used, and Stalin himself found it necessary to set the example. In October, 1935, he paid a visit to his old mother living in Tiflis,[21] and in the detailed accounts of this visit signs of love and respect to the old lady by the leader of the world proletariat were emphasized. A high degree of intimacy in family relations was displayed through the reproduction of such questions as: how did Stalin's children like the jam made for them by their grandmother. Another day Stalin appeared in one of Moscow's gardens with his children, something he had never done previously. Up to that time, the majority of Soviet citizens did not even know that Stalin had any children.

Gradually, the unlimited freedom granted to young people under the Communist experiment was curbed. One of the most conspicuous items in the process has been the decree of July 15, 1943, excluding children below the age of sixteen from evening performances in theaters and movies.

To strengthen parental authority, an indirect method has been used in the new inheritance law of March 20, 1945. While previous laws limited possible heirs to direct or adopted descendants, consorts, and needy dependents, the new law broadens this list to include parents, brothers, sisters, and public organizations. Although according to the new law the testator may not deprive his minor children of jobless heirs of their rightful portion, its impact on the family is clear: the greater the freedom to dispose of one's estate, the greater is the authority of the head of the family relating to presumptive heirs.

[17] The second antidivorce law (1944) substantially increased the advantages granted to mothers of numerous children. Honorary titles were granted to mothers of seven or more children.

[18] Young Communist League.

[19] *Komsomolskaya Pravda*, June 7 and September 29, 1935; *Pravda*, August 4, 1935.

[20] *Sovetskaya Yustitsia*, 1939, No. 4.

[21] *Izvestia*, October 23, 1935.

11

Cultural Configurations in the American Family

John Sirjamaki

Most sociological studies of the family deal with it either as a social system or as a social institution. An important supplement to these approaches is the cultural analysis of the family in terms of its dominant configurations. When these can be specified for the family, it is possible to interpret the basic moral ideas which give the family its distinctive and identifying characteristics.

Cultural configurations are the moral principles which comprise the social philosophy of a society. They are patterns of covert behavior; as such, they are the culturally approved rules or sentiments which motivate overt behavior and which integrate it into consistent patterns; and they can be deduced only from behavior. Such configurations exist on the level of the culture and arise in the context of everyday living. Members of a society comprehend the meaning of such precepts in the process of socialization, even when they are expressed tenuously or obscurely; and, indeed, configurations are difficult to state abstractly inasmuch as they generally operate below the level of awareness. Taken together, the configurations delineate the ethos of a culture.[1]

Configurations are thus the basic units of the value system of a society. They differ

Reprinted from "Culture Configurations in the American Family" by John Sirjamaki in the *American Journal of Sociology,* LIII (May, 1948), 464–70, with the kind permission of the author and the University of Chicago Press.

[1] I have adhered to Clyde Kluckhohn's definition of configuration in his chapter, "Patterning as Exemplified in Navaho Culture," in Leslie Spier, A. Irving Hallowell, and Stanley S. Newman (eds.), *Language, Culture, and Personality* (Menasha, Wis.: Sapir Memorial Publication Fund, 1941), pp. 109–30, and exemplified in part in Clyde Kluckhohn and Dorothea Leighton, *The Navaho* (Cambridge, Mass.: Harvard University Press, 1946), pp. 216–38. My indebtedness is considerable to Ruth Benedict, "Configurations of Culture in North America," *American Anthropologist,* XXXIV (1932), 1–27, and *Patterns of Culture* (Boston: Houghton Mifflin Co., 1934). For the study of value systems, configuration has appeared to be a more useful concept than most, in that it refers to positive rules which organize behavior into patterns, while the mores are generally stated as unitary negative injunctions (see William Graham Sumner, *Folkways* [Boston: Ginn & Co., 1906], p. 30; and William Graham Sumner and Albert Galloway Keller, *The Science of Society*, Vol. I [New Haven: Yale University Press, 1927], 33–35). Bronislaw Malinowski has used the concept of "charter" in his definition of a social institution as a means of studying values (*A Scientific Theory of Culture and Other Essays* [Chapel Hill: University of North Carolina Press, 1944], pp. 52–53). Alfred McClung Lee has analyzed social values from an interesting and useful approach in "Levels of Culture as Levels of Social Generalization," *American Sociological Review,* X (1945), 485–95, and in "Social Determinants of Public Opinions," *International Journal of Opinion and Attitude Research,* I (1947), 12–29.

from the absolute ethics of religious or philosophical systems in that they are mundane, practical, this-worldly; having developed within the culture, they express the dominant values which are thought to be necessary for the continued functioning of the society. Ordinarily, configurational values are stigmatized by philosophers as base and inferior; Fromm has called them "socially immanent ethics" as contrasted to universal ethics.[2] For the social scientist, however, it is necessary to understand the configurations of a culture, since they motivate behavior much more continuously than do absolute ethical systems. The configurations will tend to support the total culture and to achieve an interrelatedness among themselves. As Sumner indicated, there is a strain for consistency in the mores.[3]

The concept of the configurations of the culture, and a knowledge of the manner in which these are expressed within an institution, illuminates the study of the family. Configurations reach into the most intimate areas of individual and family behavior; they furnish the meanings and determine right and wrong behavior in courting, in husband-wife and parent-child relationships, in heterosexual social activity, and in ideas about sex. Thus they supply the moral sentiments by which family members are influenced and make explicable the vagaries of their behavior.

At least four qualifications may be raised concerning the validity of applying culture configurations to the study of the American family. First, since such configurations are inferred by the investigator from the overt behavior of people, he must have available a considerable amount of observational data which, however, is currently lacking. Second, the use of such configurations should await an analysis of the total culture, and this has been attempted thus far in the most tentative manner.[4] The analysis of parts of the culture, however, will assist in the determination of the total culture ethos. Third, generalizations about American culture must be stated in the most broad terms and can attempt only to strike an average, since regional and ethnic subcultures obviously differ from the main pattern. To whom, it may be asked, do configurations apply? The answer is that configurations are generally valid, or will tend to become so, for the entire American society, in the sense that they represent the moral standards by which all behavior is evaluated and which exert a social pressure to secure some degree of conformance. Families of ethnic minorities thus quite apparently have patterns dissimilar to those of native-born families, but in time the American culture configurations come to influence the actions of at least the immigrant children and to bring their behavior into conformity with the general requirements of society. Finally, configurations are not easily amenable to quantification; they may seem to be accurately stated, but they are difficult to measure. There is no real answer to this objection

[2] Erich Fromm, *Man for Himself* (New York: Rinehart & Co., 1947), p. 241.

[3] Sumner, *op. cit.*, pp. 5–6.

[4] John Sirjamaki, "A Footnote to the Anthropological Approach to the Study of American Culture," *Social Forces,* XXV (1947), 253–63; Clyde Kluckhohn, "The American Culture: Definition and Prophecy. Part II. The Way of Life," *Kenyon Review,* III (1941), 160–79; Clyde Kluckhohn and Florence R. Kluckhohn, "American Culture: Generalized Orientations and Class Patterns," in Lyman Bryson, Louis Finkelstein, and R. M. MacIver (eds.), *Conflicts of Power in Modern Culture* (New York: Harper & Bros., 1947), pp. 106–28; Andrew H. Truxal and Francis E. Merrill, *The Family in American Culture* (New York: Prentice-Hall, 1947), pp. 29–199; Robert S. Lynd, *Knowledge for What?* (Princeton, N.J.: Princeton University Press, 1939), pp. 63–99; Robert S. Lynd and Helen Merrell Lynd, *Middletown: A Study in American Culture* (New York: Harcourt, Brace & Co., 1929), and *Middletown in Transition* (New York: Harcourt, Brace & Co., 1937); and Oscar Waldemar Junek, "What is the Total Pattern of Our Western Civilization? Some Preliminary Observations," *American Anthropologist,* XLVIII (1946), 397–406.

other than to predicate the statement of configurations upon as careful objective analysis as is possible. A value system patently exists in every culture, and its appraisal should be sought by the social scientist.

The following configurations, among others, appear inthe American family:

1. *Marriage is a dominating life-goal, for men as well as for women.*—It is felt that married life is the normal, desired condition for all adults, that it brings the greatest personal happiness and fulfillment, and that it permits the proper exercise of sex for the procreation of children and for individual satisfaction. The single adult life by contrast, according to this attitude, is empty and barren. That there is a considerable societal concern that women marry is generally recognized, but the greater courting and sexual initiative assumed by men has obscured the comparable pressure on them to marry, and adult men who postpone marriage into their thirties become objects of distress and conspiracy among friends and relatives. Most Americans marry in their twenties, and, for a considerable share of them, marriage at that age means a happy union of individual volition and social pressure.

Long ago, Professor E. A. Ross, pointed out that Americans are the most marrying nation in western Christendom. United States census figures have shown that since 1890 they have married in steadily increasing proportions and at earlier ages.[5] About 92 per cent of adults will have been married at some time in their lives by the age of sixty-five,[6] and this is a sufficiently high number to suggest that nearly all persons marry who are physically and mentally capable of contracting marriage.

2. *The giving and taking in marriage should be based on personal affection and choice.*—Marriage is thought to be preeminently the linking of the lives of two young people drawn to each other by personal attraction. Arranged marriages, or those based on fraud or calculation, receive considerable disapprobation.

Dating is thought by many sociologists to precede serious courting and to be an educational process leading to it. Waller first analyzed it in terms of its distinctive cultural patterns.[7] In dating, the young woman undoubtedly receives the greatest cultural estimation of her personal qualities: merely to be a young, nubile female of attractive phenotype means that she is the object of considerable masculine attention and chivalry.[8] But, despite this high evaluation of young women, most men grow up in American society with the assumption, culturally derived, that the decision to marry rests with them; they expect in the fullness of time to lead some dear girl to the altar. Women, on the other hand, regardless of their personal qualities, can never be completely sure that they will receive a marriage proposal which they can consider seriously, or, more to the point, be asked to marry by the man upon whom they have fastened their desire.[9] The culture does not permit them to undertake active courting by themselves; to be a man-chaser is to suffer an ostracism which is enforced by the women themselves. Women are obviously not completely helpless in these sentimental matters, but they must use guile and finesse to bring the male to their side.

Since the biological fact of bisexuality predisposes women for the having and rearing of children, and therefore for the maintenance of a home, they are compelled

[5] *Sixteenth Census of the United States, 1940, Population,* IV, Part I, 16.

[6] *Fifteenth Census of the United States, 1930, Population,* II, chapter on marital condition.

[7] Willard Waller, "The Rating and Dating Complex," *American Sociological Review,* II (1937), 727–34.

[8] Weston LaBarre, "Social Cynosure and Social Structure," *Journal of Personality,* XIV (1946), 171.

[9] Ernest R. Groves, *Marriage* (New York: Henry Holt & Co., 1933), pp. 89–90.

to drive as good a bargain in the marriage market as they can. This they can manage only by a careful exploitation of the rules which specify correct maidenly deportment. Men, on the other hand, have greater volition in their marriage choices and are much more disposed as a result to manage their marital ventures in the bathos of culturally approved romance.

3. *The criterion of successful marriage is the personal happiness of husband and wife.* —Mutual compatibility is made the basis of marriage, and marital bliss becomes dependent upon the emotional sentiments, fluctuating and volatile as they may be, with which a couple regard their relationship. Ultimately their fullest felicity is believed to be achieved by having children, whose arrival and subsequent nurture are viewed as bringing satisfaction to basic biological and social needs. Childless couples are sometimes regarded as possessed of a selfishness which blights their union. Happiness in marriage is thus predicated upon a personal equation, the individual satisfaction and the opportunity for development of the couple.

The cultural accent upon happiness in marriage is of relatively recent origin. Marriages are ordinarily contracted and their success gauged by their contribution in the struggles of life. These may be the partnership co-operation of man and wife, the production of children, the social recognition of adult status, or the stability of marital status. Many such marriages may be buttressed by institutional supports, the most important of which is generally the exchange of property. The spouses may be selected for each other by the parents or other adults, after a careful scrutiny of their relative merits and upon some property agreement, in the belief that normal young people, once married, can fashion for themselves a successful marital life.[10]

A corollary of the American patterns of courtship and marriage, which is not always recognized, is the logical necessity of a relatively easy system of divorce. From a cultural viewpoint, if marriages are made on the basis of personal and inevitably shifting emotions, without the added support of other institutional devices, then they should be equally easy to dissolve. Persons marry to find happiness and, finding it not, turn to divorce as a way out. The present high divorce rate, therefore, is in this sense made explicable and partially condoned by the cultural rules of marriage.

4. *The best years of life are those of youth, and its qualities are the most desirable.*—A high evaluation is placed upon youth and early middle age in American society. while the old are sometimes treated with indifference and even callousness. Youth is regarded as a period of innocence, energy, and enthusiasm; it is inventive and pragmatic when faced with new experiences and is glad of change—qualities fondly believed to be typical of Americans in general.

Among the young, the unmarried girl, aged perhaps twenty, attractive of face and limb, is the center of attraction in thought and deed. In other societies young men, or old men, or mothers are variously regarded as ideal symbols;[11] in the United States it is the young, pretty girl. She therefore receives at this age the greatest gratification of her ego drives which will probably ever come to her. With men the ideal age is somewhere in the thirties; they need time in which to win occupational and social placement and need not depend so much upon chronological age for their acceptance.

From this high esteem on youth there derive important social consequences. Wherever the young are involved, whether it be in the conduct of schools, or juvenile delinquency, or maltreatment of children, or provision for their play opportunities, there is likely to be at least a quick emotional response to their needs.

[10] Ralph Linton, *The Study of Man* (New York: D. Appleton-Century Co., 1936), p. 175.
[11] LaBarre, *loc. cit.*, p. 179.

Such sentiments as these do not, of course, arise in a social vacuum. They exist, rather, and become understandable in terms of American social history. Youth has received a high evaluation, precisely because its resourcefulness and resilience were valued qualities in the exploitation and development of the American continent. There have been, in addition, as compared to the age groups in European societies, relatively high proportions in the younger age categories in the American population; Americans have in this sense been a young people and correspondingly eager to admire the virtues of youth. The aged, on the other hand, have emerged as a significant social group only recently, and they are not yet favorably regarded.

Related to this cultural theme of youth is the existence of a considerable rift, not to say antagonism, between the generations. The conflict between the old and the young is common enough in human groups; what is significant is its intensity in American society. This is due, in large part, to the rapidity of social change in the United States and to the differing rates with which the generations have adjusted to these changes. Keller speaks somewhat nostalgically of the aged in primitive society as revered "repositories of wisdom";[12] in American society, they are unlikely to be regarded as possessors of a truth that has any relationship to their age.[13]

5. *Children should be reared in a child's world and shielded from too early participation in adult woes and tribulations.*—This configuration is obviously closely related to the high cultural esteem of youth. It is modified by social class: the sentiment is held most strongly by the upper levels of society, much less so by the lower, but even among the poor the social conditions of the American community prevent a too considerable precocity among the children.[14]

The cultural ideal is that children shall mature slowly in terms of their nature and age-sex grades in a prolonged child's world, which is characterized by a segregated class of children's activities.[15] In this juvenile social world they are allowed to grow, develop their abilities, indulge in play, and occasionally to perform such small and often artificial tasks as may be assigned them. Generally they are protected from the responsibilities of adults, and laws and customs prevent their too early gainful employment. In many American homes, particularly in the cities, there is actually not much useful work that children can perform even if they wish. Especially in middle-class families is the configuration most completely observed. The child is accepted as an individual, and his relationships with parents are often warm and affectionate.

Folsom has contrasted this pattern with that which prevails in certain western European families, in which the child is incorporated into the family of adults and in which he lives in their world rather than in a segregated youth society.[16] Moreover, unlike the American middle-class child who may become somewhat exhibitionist in his behavior because of the attention shown him, the European youth is often hastened along in the process of maturation and trained to deference and respect toward parents and elders in general.

Such training as the American child

[12] Sumner and Keller, *op. cit.*, p. 464.

[13] Margaret Park Redfield, "The American Family: Consensus and Freedom," *American Journal of Sociology*, LII (1946), 177.

[14] W. Lloyd Warner and Paul S. Lunt, *The Social Life of a Modern Community* (New Haven: Yale University Press, 1941), pp. 92–111; and Allison Davis, Burleigh B. Gardner, and Mary R. Gardner, *Deep South* (Chicago: University of Chicago Press, 1941), pp. 84–136.

[15] Joseph K. Folsom, *The Family and Decmoratic Society* (New York: John Wiley & Sons, 1943), p. 184.

[16] *Ibid.*, p. 105.

receives may start him off with a psychologically secure character structure,[17] but in other respects it prepares him inadequately for later life. Sometimes he has not broken the emotional ties with his parents or developed definite heterosexual interests; hence his fondness for "Mom."[18] During World War II, the British thought the American soldier adolescent.[19] James Graham Leyburn has pointed out that the American family is itself often at fault because of its inadequate integration with the larger community.[20] It may be unable, as a result, to prepare and to place its members into job, school, clique and class, association, and other social relationships in the society. Thus it delays the processes of maturation.

6. *The exercise of sex should be contained within wedlock.*—Prior to marriage, premarital intercourse is strongly condemned, and sex knowledge is kept hidden from children lest it be damaging to their moral character. After marriage, adultery is similarly proscribed. Sex may thus be legitimately expressed only within marriage, and the speaking of marriage vows makes highly moral sexual behavior which before then had been grossly immoral. The couple, previously prohibited from intercourse, may now embark upon an active, and socially approved, sex life. Sex, to speak figuratively, explodes upon marriage.

About sex there is considerable tension, preoccupation, frustration, shame, and deceit in American society. Judeo-Christian influences, and more immediately Puritanism, have given a sinful cast to sex and have condoned its expression in marriage only because of the grossly physical method of human reproduction. The tradition has particularly valued virginity, more especially in women, before marriage. But the strong interdictions upon sex have tended to heighten rather than to lessen the fascination with sex which exists among Americans. The furtiveness with which it is often approached and the numerous colloquialisms which refer to it indicate the uneasiness with which it is treated. Kinsey's exploration of the sex histories of American males has documented their actual performances.[21] These data indicate that the sex configuration is held with varying intensity at the several levels of society, apparently least so in the lower class. Even here, however, the materials re-emphasize the manner in which restrictive cultural attitudes condition and limit sexual outlets.

7. *Family roles of husband and wife should be based on a sexual division of labor, but with the male status being superior.*—According to this configuration, the husband is head of his family, its main economic support, and its representative in the larger community. Women, consigned to domesticity, are mothers and homemakers. These roles, biologically and culturally conditioned, provide for the structuring of all types of heterosexual relationships, in which the presumption of dominance generally rests with the males. Men are trained to develop the qualities necessary to fulfill their roles in economic, social, sexual, and other activities and to view themselves with self-respect when they have secured a competence in their performances. Women, too, are trained to their respective feminine roles, and these generally involve some degree of catering to men, somewhat as a

[17] Abram Kardiner, *The Psychological Frontiers of Society* (New York: Columbia University Press, 1945), p. 361.

[18] Edward A. Strecker, *Their Mothers' Sons* (Philadelphia: J. B. Lippincott Co., 1946), and Philip Wylie, *Generation of Vipers* (New York: Farrar & Rinehart, 1942).

[19] Mass-Observation, London, "Portrait of an American?" *International Journal of Opinion and Attitude Research,* I (1947), 96.

[20] In lecture at Yale University, May 2, 1947.

[21] Alfred C. Kinsey, Wardell B. Pomeroy, and Clyde E. Martin, *Sexual Behavior in the Human Male* (Philadelphia: W. B. Saunders Co., 1948).

complement to the expectation of greater male initiative. Terman's analysis of the desired pattern of sex typing in husband and in wife indicated how the cultural conception of the manly man and the womanly woman fall into the cultural mold.[22]

Women's behavior is governed by a double standard of morality which expects greater masculine enterprise not only in the sexual spheres but in many other areas of life. Women live, in male estimation, under a blanket of oppressive mores which constrains their ordinary, everyday movements. Where men have a relative freedom of action, women must cater to a public opinion of what is womanly behavior. In social life, women are under greater disapproval than men when they smoke or indulge in narcotics. On the job, they may encounter much male prejudice which affects their pay and possibilities of promotion. They are more protected by social legislation which governs their hours and conditions of employment.[23]

These cultural attitudes persist despite the social and economic events of modern times which have released women from the control of husbands and fathers. Before the law women have achieved a near-equality with men; they may seek gainful employment and retain their earnings; they have equal rights with men of education; they have all the freedoms necessary to live their own lives as they wish. Democratic sentiments further foster the desire that women develop as persons to enjoy the manifold blessings of American life and to have many of the privileges given men.

Women are thus caught in a process of social change, in which the cultural configuration restrains them to traditional roles while new ones are proffered by economic and social forces. There is much confusion among them as a result. The young college girl, for example, may have difficulty in knowing to which force to respond: should she be content with the domestic role and look to the main chance of marriage, or should she seek outlets which include both marriage and other roles?[24] Apparently some urban upper-level women find the puzzle extremely hard to resolve and respond to it neurotically.[25]

Men, too, it must be pointed out, suffer in the realignment of roles, since they as much as women are conditioned to the status quo and may find it hard to accommodate themselves to change.

8. *Individual, not familial, values are to be sought in family living.*—The family is obviously affected by the considerable cultural affirmation of individualism, and the lack of a tradition of familism in American culture has further aided in the development of a configuration in which the family exists for the benefit of its members. The emphasis has been upon the individualization of all members of the family, the children as well as the parents, the wife as much as the husband. Obviously, the husband's prerogatives, nurtured in the bosom of the patriarchal family have had to be parceled out to the other members.

There are many important social consequences from the stress on individualism in the family. On the one hand, its promise is for the richer, fuller development of personality. On the other hand, it weakens the unity of the family. The stresses of American life, including industrialization, urbanization, internal migration, and social class, press hard against the frail shell of the family, attenuated as it is by

[22] Lewis M. Terman, *Psychological Factors in Marital Happiness* (New York: McGraw-Hill Book Co., 1938), pp. 145–66.

[23] Constantine Panunzio, *Major Social Institutions* (New York: Macmillan Co., 1939), p. 430.

[24] Mirra Komarovsky, "Cultural Contradictions and Sex Roles," *American Journal of Sociology*, LII (1946), 184–89.

[25] Ferdinand Lundberg and Marynia F. Farnham, *Modern Woman: The Lost Sex* (New York: Harper & Bros., 1947).

the thinning of larger kin groups and often limited to its own resources in times of crisis. Further, since the family is not primarily important in placing its members into positions in the larger community, its members feel the strain of loyalties divided between the family and the outside affiliations.

If some of the configurations of the American family have been correctly stated, they indicate a social philosophy in which the values of individualism are paramount, or, more specifically, those which support the development of individual personality in the context of family and community relationships. A primary stress is placed on the family as a social group rather than on the functions which it performs for society. The family exists for its members rather than the members for the family. In this respect the family is in relatively close adjustment to the total culture, in which the democratic realization of the potentialities of all its members is an ideal.

But the family is pre-eminently an association based on antagonistic co-operation, and in times of hardship the antagonisms may predominate. The straining of family members for individualistic goals may blunt their sense of obligation to each other and to the larger society. When achievement of the desired values for which they grope seems far off and difficult, individualism may decay into gross egotism and selfishness. The family based on the chimera of personal values seems then faced with a dolorous future.

The American family, however, is not without resources. Contributing to its strength is the immense popularity of marriage, and through marriage the possibility of parenthood, both of them regarded as major life-goals. Staying power is also given the family by the affection and compatibility which draws two people into marriage, the warmth of relationships between parents and children, and the individualization of all members of the family. The structure of the family is such as to permit the desired nurturing of stable and democratic personalities.

In view of the ethos of the culture, the direction of evolutionary change in the family, and of desirable efforts at national adjustments, is in the continued emphasis upon the social relationships within the family and upon the family as a social system through which fundamental life-purposes can be achieved.

12

Age and Sex in the Social Structure of the United States

Talcott Parsons

In our society, age grading does not to any great extent, except for the educational system, involve formal age categorization, but is interwoven with other structural elements. In relation to these, however, it constitutes an important connecting link and organizing point of reference in many respects. The most important of these for present purposes are kinship structure, formal education, occupation, and community participation. In most cases the age lines are not rigidly specific, but approximate; this does not, however, necessarily lessen their structural significance.

In all societies, the initial status of every normal individual is that of child in a given kinship unit. In our society, however, this universal starting point is used in distinctive ways. Although in early childhood the sexes are not usually sharply differentiated, in many kinship systems a relatively sharp segregation of children begins very early. Our own society is conspicuous for the extent to which children of both sexes are in many fundamental respects treated alike. This is particularly true of both privileges and responsibilities. The primary distinctions within the group of dependent siblings are those of age. Birth order as such is notably neglected as a basis of discrimination; a child of eight and a child of five have essentially the privileges and responsibilities appropriate to their respective age levels without regard to what older, intermediate, or younger siblings there may be. The preferential treatment of an older child is not to any significant extent differentiated if and because he happens to be the first born.

There are, of course, important sex differences in dress and in approved play interest and the like, but if anything, it may be surmised that in the urban upper middle classes these are tending to diminish. Thus, for instance, play overalls are essentially similar for both sexes. What is perhaps the most important sex discrimination is more than anything else a reflection of the differentiation of adult sex roles. It seems to be a definite fact that girls are more apt to be relatively docile, to conform in general according to adult expectations, to be "good," whereas boys are more apt to be recalcitrant to discipline and defiant of adult authority and expectations. There is really no feminine equivalent of the expression "bad boy." It may be suggested that this is at least partially explained by the fact that it is possible from an early age to initiate girls directly into many important aspects of the adult

Reprinted from *American Sociological Review,* Vol. 7 (1942), pp. 604–16, with abridgment of footnotes, by permission of the author and the American Sociological Association.

feminine role. Their mothers are continually about the house, and the meaning of many of the things they are doing is relatively tangible and easily understandable to a child. It is also possible for the daughter to participate actively and usefully in many of these activities. Especially in the urban middle classes, however, the father does not work in the home and his son is not able to observe his work or to participate in it from an early age. Furthermore, many of the masculine functions are of a relatively abstract and intangible character, such that their meaning must remain almost wholly inaccessible to a child. This leaves the boy without a tangible meaningful model to emulate and without the possibility of a gradual initiation into the activities of the adult male role. An important verification of this analysis could be provided through the study in our own society of the rural situation. It is my impression that farm boys tend to be "good" in a sense in which that is not typical of their urban brothers.

The equality of privileges and responsibilities, graded only by age but not by birth order, is extended to a certain degree throughout the whole range of the life cycle. In full adult status, however, it is seriously modified by the asymmetrical relation of the sexes to the occupational structure. One of the most conspicuous expressions and symbols of the underlying equality, however, is the lack of sex differentiation in the process of normal education, so far, at least, as it is not explicitly vocational. Up through college, differentiation seems to be primarily a matter on the one hand of individual ability, on the other hand of class status, and only to a secondary degree of sex differentiation. One can certainly speak of a strongly established pattern that all children of the family have a "right" to a good education, rights which are graduated according to the class status of the family but also to individual ability. It is only in post-graduate professional education, with its direct connection with future occupational careers, that sex discrimination becomes conspicuous. It is particularly important that this equality of treatment exists in the sphere of liberal education, since throughout the social structure of our society there is a strong tendency to segregate the occupational sphere from one in which certain more generally human patterns and values are dominant, particularly in informal social life and the realm of what will here be called community participation.

Although this pattern of equality of treatment is present in certain fundamental respects at all age levels, at the transition from childhood to adolescence new features appear which disturb the symmetry of sex roles, while still a second set of factors appears with marriage and the acquisition of full adult status and responsibilities.

An indication of the change is the practice of chaperonage, through which girls are given a kind of protection and supervision by adults to which boys of the same age group are not subjected. Boys, that is, are chaperoned only in their relations with girls of their own class. This modification of equality of treatment has been extended to the control of the private lives of women students in boarding schools and colleges. Of undoubted significance is the fact that it has been rapidly declining not only in actual effectiveness but as an ideal pattern. Its prominence in our recent past, however, is an important manifestation of the importance of sex role differentiation. Important light might be thrown upon its functions by systematic comparison with the related phenomena in Latin countries, where this type of asymmetry has been far more sharply accentuated than in this country in the more modern period.

It is at the point of emergence into adolescence that there first begins to develop a set of patterns and behavior phenomena which involve a highly complex combination of age grading and sex role elements. These may be referred to together as the phenomena of the "youth culture." Certain of its elements are present in preadolescence and others in the adult culture. But the peculiar combination in connection with this particular age level is unique and highly distinctive for American society.

Perhaps the best single point of reference for characterizing the youth culture lies in its contrast with the dominant pattern of the adult male role. By contrast with the emphasis on responsibility in this role, the orientation of the youth culture is more or less specifically irresponsible. One of its dominant notes is "having a good time," in relation to which there is a particularly strong emphasis on social activities in company with the opposite sex. A second predominant characteristic on the male side lies in the prominence of athletics, which is an avenue of achievement and competition which stands in sharp contrast to the primary standards of adult achievement in professional and executive capacities. Negatively, there is a strong tendency to repudiate interest in adult things and to feel at least a certain recalcitrance to the pressure of adult expectations and discipline. In addition to, but including, athletic prowess, the typical pattern of the male youth culture seems to lay emphasis on the value of certain qualities of attractiveness, especially in relation to the opposite sex. It is very definitely a rounded humanistic pattern rather than one of competence in the performance of specified functions. Such stereotypes as the "swell guy" are significant of this. On the feminine side there is correspondingly a strong tendency to accentuate sexual attractiveness in terms of various versions of what may be called the "glamor girl" pattern. Although these patterns defining roles tend to polarize sexually—for instance, as between star athlete and socially popular girl— yet on a certain level they are complementary, both emphasizing certain features of a total personality in terms of the direct expression of certain values rather than of instrumental significance.

One further feature of this situation is the extent to which it is crystallized about the system of formal education. One might say that the principal centers of prestige dissemination are the colleges, but that many of the most distinctive phenomena are to be found in high schools throughout the country. It is, of course, of great importance that liberal education is not primarily a matter of vocational training in the United States. The individual status on the curricular side of formal education is, however, in fundamental ways linked up with adult expectations, and doing "good work" is one of the most important sources of parental approval. Because of secondary institutionalization, this approval is extended into various spheres distinctive of the youth culture. But it is notable that the youth culture has a strong tendency to develop in directions which are either on the borderline of parental approval or beyond the pale, in such matters as sex behavior, drinking, and various forms of frivolous and irresponsible behavior. The fact that adults have attitudes to these things which are often deeply ambivalent and that on such occasions as college reunions they may outdo the younger generation, as, for instance, in drinking, is of great significance, but probably structurally secondary to the youth-versus-adult differential aspect. Thus the youth culture is not only, as is true of the curricular aspect of formal education, a matter of age status as such, but also shows strong signs of being a product of tensions in the relationship of younger people and adults.

From the point of view of age grading, perhaps the most notable fact about this situation is the existence of definite pattern distinctions from the periods coming both before and after. At the line between childhood and adolescence "growing up" consists precisely in ability to participate in youth culture patterns, which are not for either sex, the same as the adult patterns practiced by the parental generation. In both sexes the transition to full adulthood means loss of a certain "glamorous" element. From being the athletic hero or the lion of college dances, the young man becomes a prosaic business executive or lawyer. The more successful adults participate in an important order of prestige symbols, but these are of a very different order from those of the youth culture. The contrast in the case of the feminine role is perhaps equally sharp, with at least a strong tendency to take on a "domestic" pattern with marriage and the arrival of young children.

The symmetry in this respect must, however, not be exaggerated. It is of fundamental significance to the sex role structure of the adult age levels that the normal man has a "job" which is fundamental to his social status in general. It is perhaps not too much to say that only in very exceptional cases can an adult man be genuinely self-respecting and enjoy a respected status in the eyes of others if he does not "earn a living" in an approved occupational role. Not only is this a matter of his own economic support but, generally speaking, his occupational status is the primary source of the income and class status of his wife and children.

In the case of the feminine role, the situation is radically different. The majority of married women, of course, are not employed, but even of those that are a very large proportion do not have jobs which are in basic competition for status with those of their husbands. The above statement, even more than most in the present paper, needs to be qualified in relation to the problem of class. It is above all to the upper middle class that it applies. Here probably the great majority of "working wives" are engaged in some form of secretarial work which would, on an independent basis, generally be classed as a lower middle class occupation. The situation at lower levels of the class structure is quite different, since the prestige of the jobs of husband and wife is then much more likely to be nearly equivalent. It is quite possible that this fact is closely related to the relative instability of marriage which Davis and Gardner (*Deep South*) find, at least for the community they studied, to be typical of lower class groups. The relation is one which deserves careful study. The majority of "career" women whose occupational status is comparable with that of men in their own class, at least in the upper middle and upper classes, are unmarried, and in the small proportion of cases where they are married the result is a profound alteration in family structure.

This pattern, which is central to the urban classes, should not be misunderstood. In rural society, for instance, the operation of the farm and the attendant status in the community may be said to be a matter of the joint status of both parties to a marriage. Whereas a farm is operated by a family, an urban job is held by an individual and does not involve other members of the family in a comparable sense. One convenient expression of the difference lies in the question of what would happen in case of death. In the case of a farm, it would at least be not at all unusual for the widow to continue operating the farm with the help of a son or even of hired men. In the urban situation, the widow would cease to have any connection with the organization which had employed her husband, and he would be replaced by another man without reference to family affiliations.

In this urban situation, the primary status-carrying role is in a sense that of housewife. The woman's fundamental status is that of her husband's wife, the mother of his children, and traditionally the person responsible for a complex of activities in connection with the management of the household, care of children, etc.

For the structuring of sex roles in the

adult phase, the most fundamental considerations seem to be those involved in the interrelations of the occupational system and the conjugal family. In a certain sense the most fundamental basis of the family's status is the occupational status of the husband and father. As has been pointed out, this is a status occupied by an individual by virtue of his individual qualities and achievements. But both directly, and indirectly, more than any other single factor, it determines the status of the family in the social structure, directly because of the symbolic significance of the office or occupation as a symbol of prestige, indirectly because as the principal source of family income it determines the standard of living of the family. From one point of view, the emergence of occupational status into this primary position can be regarded as the principal source of strain in the sex role structure of our society, since it deprives the wife of her role as a partner in a common enterprise. The common enterprise is reduced to the life of the family itself and to the informal social activities in which husband and wife participate together. This leaves the wife a set of utilitarian functions in the management of the household which may be considered a kind of "pseudo-" occupation. Since the present interest is primarily in the middle classes, the relatively unstable character of the role of housewife as the principal content of the feminine role is strongly illustrated by the tendency to employ domestic servants wherever financially possible. It is true that there is an American tendency to accept tasks of drudgery with relative willingness, but it is notable that in middle class families there tends to be a dissociation of the essential personality from the performance of these tasks. Thus, advertising continually appeals to such desires as to have hands which one could never tell had washed dishes or scrubbed floors. Organization about the function of housewife, however, with the addition of strong affectional devotion to husband and children, is the primary focus of one of the principal patterns governing the adult feminine role—what may be called the "domestic" pattern. It is, however, a conspicuous fact, that strict adherance to this pattern has become progressively less common and has a strong tendency to a residual status—that is, to be followed most closely by those who are unsuccessful in competition for prestige in other directions.

It is, of course, possible for the adult woman to follow the masculine pattern and seek a career in fields of occupational achievement in direct competition with men of her own class. It is, however, notable that, in spite of the very great progress of the emancipation of women from the traditional domestic pattern, only a very small fraction have gone very far in this direction. It is also clear that its generalization would only be possible with profound alterations in the structure of the family.

Hence it seems that, concomitant with the alteration in the basic masculine role in the direction of occupation, there have appeared two important tendencies in the feminine role which are alternative to that of simple domesticity on the one hand, and to a full-fledged career on the other. In the older situation there tended to be a very rigid distinction between respectable married women and those who were "no better than they should be." The rigidity of this line has progressively broken down through the infiltration into the respectable sphere of elements of what may be called again the glamour pattern, with the emphasis on a specifically feminine form of attractiveness which on occasion involves directly sexual patterns of appeal. One important expression of this trend lies in the fact that many of the symbols of feminine attractiveness have been taken over directly from the practices of social types previously beyond the pale of respectable society. This would seem to be substantially true of the practice of women smoking and of at least the modern version of the use of cosmetics. The same would seem to be true of many of the modern versions of women's dress. "Emancipation" in this connection means primarily emancipation from traditional and conventional restrictions on the free expression of sexual attraction and impulses, but in a direction which tends to segregate the element of sexual interest and attraction from the total personality and in so doing tends to emphasize the segregation of sex roles. It is particularly notable that there has been no corresponding tendency to emphasize masculine attraction in terms of dress and other such aids. One might perhaps say that, in a situation which strongly inhibits competition between the sexes on the same plane, the feminine glamor pattern has appeared as an offset to masculine occupational status and to its attendant symbols of prestige. It is perhaps significant that there is a common stereotype of the association of physically beautiful, expensively and elaborately dressed women with physically unattractive but rich and powerful men.

The other principal direction of emancipation from domesticity seems to lie in emphasis on what has been called the common humanistic element. This takes a wide variety of forms. One of them lies in a relatively mature appreciation and systematic cultivation of cultural interests and educated tastes, extending all the way from the intellectual sphere to matters of art, music, and house furnishings. A second consists in cultivation of serious interests and humanitarian obligations in community welfare situations and the like. It is understandable that many of these orientations are most conspicuous in fields where, through some kind of tradition, there is an element of particular suitability for feminine participation. Thus, a woman who takes obligations to social welfare particularly seriously will find opportunities in various forms of activity which traditionally tie up with women's relation to children, to sickness, and so on. But this may be regarded as secondary to the underlying orientation which would seek an outlet in work useful to the community, following the most favorable opportunities which happen to be available.

This pattern, which with reference to the character of relationship to men may be called that of the "good companion," is distinguished from the others in that it lays far less stress on the exploitation of sex role as such and more on that which is essentially common to both sexes. There are reasons, however, why cultural inrests, interest in social welfare, and community activities are particularly prominent in the activities of women in our urban communities. On the one side, the masculine occupational role tends to absorb a very large proportion of the man's time and energy and to leave him relatively little for other interests. Furthermore, unless his position is such as to make him particularly prominent, his primary orientation is to those elements of the social structure which divide the community into occupational groups rather than those which unite it in common interests and activities. The utilitarian aspect of the role of housewife, on the other hand, has declined in importance to the point where it scarcely approaches a fulltime occupation for a vigorous person. Hence the resort to other interests to fill up the gap. In addition, women, being more closely tied to the local residential community, are more apt to be involved in matters of common concern to the members of that community. This peculiar role of women becomes particularly conspicuous in middle age. The younger married woman is apt to be relatively highly absorbed in the care of young children. With their growing up, however, her absorption in the household is greatly lessened, often just at the time when the husband is approaching the apex of his career and is most heavily involved in its obligations. Since to a high degree this humanistic aspect of the feminine role is only partially institutionalized, it is not surprising that its patterns often bear the marks of strain and insecurity, as perhaps has been classically depicted by Helen Hokinson's cartoons of women's clubs.

The adult roles of both sexes involve important elements of strain which are involved in certain dynamic relationships, especially to the youth culture. In the case of the feminine role, marriage is the single event toward which a selective process, in which personal qualities and effort can play a decisive role, has pointed up. That determines a woman's fundamental status, and after that her role patterning is not so much status determining as a matter of living up to expectations and finding satisfying interests and activities. In a society where such strong emphasis is placed upon individual achievement, it is not surprising that there should be a certain romantic nostalgia for the time when the fundamental choices were still open. This element of strain is added to by the lack of clear-cut definition of the adult feminine role. Once the possibility of a career has been eliminated, there still tends to be a rather unstable oscillation between emphasis in the direction of domesticity or glamor or good companionship. According to situational pressures and individual character, the tendency will be to emphasize one or another of these more strongly. But it is a situation likely to produce a rather high level of insecurity. In this state the pattern of domesticity must be ranked lowest in terms of prestige but also, because of the strong emphasis in the community sentiment on the virtues of fidelity and devotion to husband and children, it offers perhaps the highest level of a certain kind of security. It is no wonder that such an important symbol as Whistler's mother concentrates primarily on this pattern.

The glamor pattern has certain obvious attractions, since to the woman who is excluded from the struggle for power and prestige in the occupational sphere it is the most direct path to a sense of superiority and importance. It has, however, two obvious limitations. In the first place, many of its manifestations encounter the resistance of patterns of moral conduct and engender conflicts not only with community opinion but also with the individual's own moral standards. In the second place, it is a pattern the highest manifestations of which are inevitably associated with a rather early age level—in fact, overwhelmingly with the courtship period. Hence, if strongly entered upon, serious strains result from the problem of adaptation to increasing age.

The one pattern which would seem to offer the greatest possibilities for able, intelligent, and emotionally mature women is the third—the good companion pattern. This, however, suffers from a lack of fully institutionalized status and from the multiplicity of choices of channels of expression. It is only those with the strongest initiative and intelligence who achieve fully satisfactory adaptations in this direction. It is quite clear that in the adult feminine role there is quite sufficient strain and insecurity, so that wide-spread manifestations are to be expected in the form of neurotic behavior.

The masculine role at the same time is itself by no means devoid of corresponding elements of strain. It carries with it, to be sure, the primary prestige of achievement, responsibility, and authority. By comparison with the role of the youth culture, however, there are at least two important types of limitations. In the first place, the modern occupational system has led to increasing specialization of role. The job absorbs an extraordinarily large proportion of the individual's energy and emotional interests in a role the content of which is often relatively narrow. This in particular restricts the area within which he can share common interests and experiences with others not in the same occupational speciality. It is perhaps of considerable significance that so many of the highest prestige statuses of our society are of this specialized character. There is in the definition of roles little to bind the individual to others in his community on a comparable status level. By contrast with this situation, it is notable that in the youth culture common human elements are far more strongly emphasized. Leadership and eminence are more in the role of total individuals and less of competent specialists. This perhaps has something to do with the significant tendency in our society for all age levels to idealize youth and for the older age groups to attempt to imitate the patterns of youth behavior.

It is perhaps as one phase of this situation that the relation of the adult man to persons of the opposite sex should be treated. The effect of the specialization of occupational role is to narrow the range in which the sharing of common human interests can play a large part. In relation to his wife, the tendency of this narrowness would seem to be to encourage on her part either the domestic or the glamorous role, or community participation somewhat unrelated to the marriage relationship. This relationship between sex roles presumably introduces a certain amount of strain into the marriage relationship itself, since this is of such overwhelming importance to the family and hence to a woman's status and yet so relatively difficult to maintain on a level of human companionship. Outside the marriage relationship, however, there seems to be a notable inhibition against easy social intercourse, particularly in mixed company. The man's close personal intimacy with other women is checked by the danger of the situation being defined as one of rivalry with the wife, and easy friendship without sexual-emotional involvement seems to be inhibited by the specialization of interests in the occupational sphere. It is notable that brilliance of conversation of the "salon" type seems to be associated with aristocratic society and is not prominent in ours. In the informal social life of academic circles with which the writer is familiar, there seems to be a strong tendency in mixed gatherings—as after dinner—for the sexes to segregate. In such groups the men are apt to talk either shop subjects or politics, whereas the women are apt to talk about domestic affairs, schools, their children, etc., or personalities. It is perhaps on personalities that mixed conversation is apt to flow most freely.

Along with all this goes a certain tendency for middle-aged men, as symbolized by the "bald-headed row," to be interested in the physical aspect of sex—that is, in women precisely as dissociated from those personal considerations which are important to relationships of companionship or friendship, to say nothing of marriage. In so far as it does not take this physical form, however, there seems to be a strong tendency for middle-aged men to idealize youth patterns—that is, to think of the ideal inter-sex friendship as that of their pre-marital period.

Insofar as the idealization of the youth culture by adults is an expression of elements of strain and insecurity in the adult roles, it would be expected that the patterns thus idealized would contain an element of romantic unrealism. The patterns of youthful behavior thus idealized are not those of actual youth so much as those which older people wish their own youth might have been. This romantic element seems to coalesce with a similar element derived from certain strains in the situation of young people themselves.

The period of youth in our society is one of considerable strain and insecurity. Above all, it means turning one's back on the security both of status and of emotional attachment which is engaged in the family of orientation. It is structurally essential to transfer one's primary emotional attachment to a marriage partner who is entirely unrelated to the previous family situation. In a system of free marriage choice this applies to women as well as men. For the man there is in addition the necessity to face the hazards of occupational competition in the determination of a career. There is reason to believe that the youth culture has important positive functions in easing the transition from the security of childhood in the family of orientation to that of full adult in marriage and occupational status. But precisely because the transition is a period of strain, it is to be expected that it involves elements of unrealistic romanticisim. Thus significant features in the status of youth patterns in our society would seem to derive from the coincidence of the emotional needs of adolescents with those derived from the strains of the situation of adults.

A tendency to the romantic idealization of youth patterns seem in different ways to be characteristic of modern Western society as a whole. It is not possible in the present context to enter any extended comparative analysis, but it may be illuminating to call attention to a striking difference between the patterns associated with this phenomenon in Germany and in the United States. The German "youth movement," starting before the first World War, has occasioned a great deal of comment and has in various respects been treated as the most notable instance of the revolt of youth. It is generally believed that the youth movement has an important relation to the background of National Socialism, and this fact as much as any suggests the important difference. While in Germany, as everywhere, there has been a generalized revolt against convention and restrictions on individual freedom as embodied in the traditional adult culture, in Germany particular emphasis has appeared on the community of male youth. "Comradeship" in a sense which strongly suggests that of soldiers in the field has from the beginning been strongly emphasized as the ideal social relationship. By contrast with this, in the American youth culture and its adult romantization a much stronger emphasis has been placed on the cross-sex relationship. It would seem that this fact, with the structural factors which underlie it, have much to do with the failure of the youth culture to develop any considerable political significance in this country. Its predominant pattern has been that of the idealization of the isolated couple in romantic love. There have, to be sure, been certain tendencies among radical youth to a political orientation, but in this case there has been a notable absence of emphasis on the solidarity of the members of one sex. The tendency has been rather to ignore the relevance of sex difference in the interest of common ideals.

The importance of youth patterns in contemporary American culture throws into particularly strong relief the status in our social structure of the most advanced age groups. By comparison with other societies, the United States assumes an extreme position in the isolation of old age from participation in the most important social structures and interests. Structurally speaking, there seem to be two primary bases of this situation. In the first place, the most important single distinctive feature of our family structure is the isolation of the individual conjugal family. It is impossible to say that with us it is "natural" for any other group than husband and wife and their dependent children to maintain a common household. Hence, when the children of a couple have become independent through marriage and occupational status, the parental couple is left without attachment to any continuous kinship group. It is, of course, common for other relatives to share a household with the conjugal family, but this scarcely ever occurs without some important elements of strain. For independence is certainly the preferred pattern for an elderly couple, particularly from the point of view of the children.

The second basis of the situation lies

in the occupational structure. In such fields as farming and the maintenance of small independent enterprises, there is frequently no such thing as abrupt "retirement," rather a gradual relinquishment of the main responsibilities and functions with advancing age. So far, however, as an individual's occupational status centers in a specific "job," he either holds the job or does not, and the tendency is to maintain the full level of functions up to a given point and then abruptly to retire. In view of the very great significance of occupational status and its psychological correlates, retirement leaves the older man in a peculiarly functionless situation, cut off from participation in the most important interests and activities of the society. There is a further important aspect of this situation. Not only status in the community but actual place of residence is to a very high degree a function of the specific job held. Retirement not only cuts the ties to the job itself but also greatly loosens those to the community of residence. Perhaps in no other society is there observable a phenomenon corresponding to the accumulation of retired elderly people in such areas as Florida and Southern California in the winter. It may be surmised that this structural isolation from kinship, occupational, and community ties is the fundamental basis of the recent political agitation for help to the old. It is suggested that it is far less the financial hardship of the position of elderly people than their social isolation which makes old age a "problem." That the financial difficulties of older people are in a very large proportion of cases real is not to be doubted. This, however, is at least to a very large extent a consequence rather than a determinant of the structural situation. Except where it is fully taken care of by pension schemes, the income of older people is apt to be seriously reduced; but, even more important, the younger conjugal family usually does not feel an obligation to contribute to the support of aged parents. Where as a matter of course both generations shared a common household, this problem did not exist. As in other connections, we are here very prone to rationalize generalized insecurity in financial and economic terms. The problem is obviously of particularly great significance in view of the changing age distribution of the population with the prospect of a far greater proportion in the older age groups than in previous generations. It may also be suggested that, through well-known psychosomatic mechanisms, the increased incidence of the disabilities of older people, such as heart disease, cancer, etc., may be at least in part attributed to this structural situation.

13

Family Living Space and Personality Development

James S. Plant

The area under discussion[1] has a large number of industrial plants interspersed in a general housing pattern of low rentals, large families, and few rooms for each. In the working out of the problems of life, what does this pattern mean to the individuals living within it?

Lack of Self-Sufficiency

Crowding seems very definitely to affect the self-sufficiency of children—their ability to be alone. This is a matter entirely different from that of the close-drawn walls about the ego which are built when others threaten. Here we are dealing with a certain uncomfortable ill-at-ease-ness when there are not many others about. The search is for games, for work, where many others are close by. Also we have found difficulty in placing girls of this area in house-servant positions, a difficulty made up of many elements apparently, one of which at least is revealed by the girls' statement that "the work is too lonely." Every social engineer has had the experience of the loneliness of these children of crowded areas when placed in the country. It is as though they felt incomplete—without the necessary supports to the personality. It seems that persistent and constant crowding from early life destroys the sense of individuality—which without doubt is fostered by opportunities for privacy. (McDougall in discussing this same phenomenon uses the term "incomplete personality."[2])

These children seek in all their activities situations in which there are others—the movies, the factory. Their panic over country placement is not due merely to the strangeness of the surroundings, as many do not show this when placed in equally new situations where there are plenty of people about—in other cities or in other parts of the same city. (Country children brought to the city similarly complain of "loneliness"—but this is a different matter. Here the child feels that he is no factor in all that goes on about him—that persons do not nod a "good morning"—that his place of importance in the community is lost.) Our work in suburban and rural districts has convinced us that periods of being alone, of playing alone, of having the privacy of one's own

Reprinted by permission of the publishers from James S. Plant, *Personality and the Cultural Pattern* (Cambridge, Mass.: Harvard University Press, 1937), pp. 213–28.

[1] A crowded area of Newark, New Jersey.

[2] William McDougall, *Character and the Conduct of Life* (New York: Putnam's, 1927).

room, are important fostering agents in a feeling of individuality, of self-sufficiency.

The other side of the picture is that there is a certain sensing of the needs of others, a certain understanding of others that comes from always living with them, not provided otherwise. One often hears the complaint that the ward leader, the "typical politician," represents the crowded, less advantaged area, but one also hears the admission that he has a certain understanding of people that seems to come only from close contact with people in all their moods.

(The United States is rapidly being urbanized, and, if we see the effects of crowding correctly, its results should appear in our cultural pattern. Is our growing reputation as a nation of joiners in any sense dependent upon this same factor? Here seems again to be this feeling of incompleteness if there are not many around.)

Destruction of Illusions

Crowding serves to destroy the illusions which children build about other people. The word "illusion" is perhaps unwisely chosen. These images we build of others are of the material of our dreams and goals. They are of great dynamic power—leading us to the best we can attain. Indeed, the hero we thus invest is little more than the dramatizer, the personalization of what is perhaps otherwise too intangible a goal. We nevertheless use "illusion" here because its opposite has such a fixed and real meaning. When we speak of "disillusionment," we recognize the breaking of that which has been of tremendous worth.

There seems to be a certain optimum amount of contact for the construction of illusions. This differs for different individuals. At times, chance meeting serves for the building of a complete hero picture. This phenomenon is not common and depends entirely upon the extent to which some presenting symbol has been previously associated with an acceptable ideal image ("I *always* like people with that sort of hand"). Most of the children we see build much more definitely upon persons whom they know better—with whom they have carried through a number of conversations or projects. We have become quite certain that there is a point of contact beyond which these illusions stand the hazard of complete destruction. In this mechanism, the child puts into the individual what he would like to be there rather than accepting what actually is there. This means that with rare exceptions the process of disillusionment must come with better acquaintance and more frequent contact.

Crowding, as we have said, destroys these illusions. People are seen when not on dress parade, and they are seen often; they must be seen as they are rather than as they would wish to be or as one would wish to see them. For instance, the boys of this area do not want to follow in their fathers' footsteps. Of course, these families represent the least advantaged groups so that the children would naturally look to some other lines of work than those which seem so patently to have brought this lowly result. We have felt however that there is, too, the factor that the child knows his father too well. One idealizes out of dream material—the clatter and push of crowded living conditions too easily wake him up.

Does crowding prevent the formation of these illusions or break them down soon after they are formed? Our present feeling (without adequate data) is that the latter is the case. The discovery that these children continue the construction of these illusions (though now about new persons) would, in part, constitute such data. Would individuals show an insistent urge to form these idealized goals if they had never done so at least in embryo form? One may add, for what it is worth, the observation that the descriptions of persons which these children give carry that certain sort of crispness that comes from something broken ("Everybody is a gyp," "There isn't a one I'd really trust"). Admittedly, our data for this area only cover the delinquent group, which perhaps considerably skews the findings. The child describes his lack of goal images in the people about him with a certain attitude of rebuff. It is not alone that these children of crowded families are much more realistic about other people than are the children of well-to-do families. They are realistic on the negative or discouraging side—that they know that you cannot trust people, that people are fundamentally selfish and looking for the attainment only of their own ends. They are much more on the defensive as to other people.

If crowding actually prevented the formation of ideal images then we should find hero worship absent in these groups. But if, as we believe, crowding merely served to break the images which are formed, then in some form or other hero worship should be found quite as much as at other levels of social stratification. The latter is what we find in our group. The older children have their highly idealized heroes and follow their lead as best they can. But these heroes are now peculiarly depersonalized. Thus, if one talks about some baseball hero he finds that nothing is known of the person. The hero is one of power and numbers. A home run is not a crisis met by a person but "his forty-first." Is this just the short-cut symbol for the more personal image? We think not; we have not been successful in getting back of batting averages and home-run accomplishments to the personality involved. This same "emptying" of the personality makes their description of the movies amusing. These children use the true names of the actors in describing their activities on the screen—again "protecting themselves" from the true personality of the movie hero or heroine. ("Clark Gable almost lost his life saving her.") Watching the face of the child through this gives ample evidence that the star is separated entirely from his or her own personality. If one now turns the child to the actual life of her favorite actress there is either a quick "Oh, I don't know anything about that" or a projection from a film that again leaves the star without much that she could really call her own.

Such observations led us to the following formulation: that the crowding of individuals does not prevent the development of image goals or hero worship; that the crowding of individuals repeatedly disillusions children, breaks the images that are formed; that what is left open to the child is an interesting form of depersonalized hero in which the name of an individual stands for such abstractions as numbers, high averages, power, or victory; that, in other words, the child learns that he cannot "afford" to worship a person *as such.*

This realism, this clearness of vision as to people, works peculiarly in another way, so that children seem to see more clearly what is "good" in people just as they see what is, for them, "bad." How else can one understand the ability of children to see the love that lies behind the harsh hand and voice? For often love is there—often it is precisely this force that impels the harshness. We have had some rather rude jolts from children in families where statistics as to tempests ran high—only to find ties of loyalty and love that seemed incomprehensible. "Sure the old man beat me up—lots of times—but it was because he loved me. He wouldn't a done it if he didn't care a lot." The child of the crowded home senses motives—sees what really lies behind conduct—and if this breaks his brittle idols it often too gives him strength and the sense of belongingness in the face of what seems to the objective outsider to be unreasonable and cruel treatment.

Sexual Maladjustment

Crowding also prevents the building of illusions about sex. (Again we impute a realism and dynamic power to "illusions" that is scarcely connoted in the word itself.) This demands that something be said of the meaning of sexual adjustments.

In any of the biological sciences it is difficult to set up a true dichotomy. If one sets up a dichotomy in the field of what sexual expression means to people, it is done only for the sake of clearer exposition; one accepts the premise that each of the two elements runs into the other, with indistinct borders between them. On this basis, sexual expression can be said to play two quite distinct roles which are in large measure separable though both have a part in most sexual acts.

Sexual phenomena, on the one hand, serve the individual in high degree as the source of direct pleasurable experiences. It is uncertain at how early an age this appears, though certainly, from birth, the genital region is provided with a greater concentration of sensory nerves than practically any other part of the body. The individual comes into the world already equipped to receive through this region satisfying responses which are not of a sexual nature as the adult knows it but rather of something merely more marked and striking than are other body reactions. However, the sexual connotations (in an adult sense) of these reactions rapidly grow, being aided by the biological process of the specialization of sensation and by the social process which hastens to give meaning to all life experiences. Thus, occasionally one finds children up to ten years old, let us say, who turn to stimulation of the genital region as a means of attaining a direct satisfying physical response (in distinction to those who use these activities for their social value—a group discussed in a moment). From ten years on, the opportunity for this direct satisfaction develops and is worked out largely in the problem of masturbation. We have seen both girls and boys who, we are convinced, have no phantasy life during masturbation beyond the contemplation of the pleasure of the act itself. Here one finds the establishment of various sorts of so-called perverted sexual acts because the individual is primarily interested in any procedure which will develop actual physical expression of the sexual hunger. Such an individual very soon loses all compunctions (as to following what society is pleased to call "normal" heterosexual procedures) and is quite ready to find expression in the homosexual or heterosexual, in the normal or perverted field, wherever gratification can be found.

Sexual phenomena on the other hand serve a high symbolic or language-value purpose for the individual. Just how early this begins is again unknown, although perhaps some of the rudimentary patterns are set down in late infancy when the child discovers that masturbation has a high social value in the temper tantrums his act causes in the nearby adults. Soon children learn that certain words serve the same purpose of attracting attention. By six, the boy learns that there are sexual acts which connote that one is grown up, and children of both sexes at this time, or before, use sexual information as valuable coin—buying respect and admiration from other children through particular bits of information. Most masturbation (at least this is true of our group) carries a high degree of heterosexual phantasy. By far the larger fraction of the "perversions" which we see at this period (sodomy and the like) are rich in heterosexual phantasy, are undertaken as a means of showing that one is "grown up" and spontaneously disappear just as soon as social sanctions allow of true ("normal") heterosexual experiences. The sexual phenomena through this whole adolescent period run rampant as the symbols of having grown up. One sees something of this as one listens to the tale of many a boy or girl who defies social condemnation in an effort to show through these fabrications that full growth has by now been attained. Similarly one talks with many of these children who actually dread definite heterosexual experience, but who try to drive themselves to it because it is their best established symbol of maturity. The boy who has attempted but failed to consummate the heterosexual act never comes to us with a story of physical thwarting or unpleasantness but with the shame that he is not yet grown up. So for the adolescent one could multiply by hundreds the examples of the use of the sexual life to attain in one's own eyes and the eyes of others, age, maturity, social prestige, victory in sibling rivalry, and the like.

Interwoven with the above and developing rapidly in adolescence is the use of the sexual life as a means of expressing relationships which are beyond the power of words. It is at this level that the sexual aspects of the marital relationships work themselves out. The intimacy ties involved in marriage are idiomatic for the individual, the partners labor to develop a feeling that here exists a relationship that could exist between no two others. The sexual act is of the highest importance here—entered upon only by "agreement" of both partners and turned to by them as a means of expressing some sort of idiomatic tie that seems to defy any other form of expression. So-called "perversions" (as Havelock Ellis long ago pointed out so well)[3] have frequently now a particular value as they represent to the partners symbols of "what other people wouldn't do."

Physical gratification of course plays a part in practically all the sexual phenomena. Equally, the symbolic values of the sexual life appear to some degree in most of its manifestations. The matter is one, then, of the relative degree to which each is present. We have dealt with boys and men who in fear and actual physical discomfort attempt to carry through various forms of sexual expression as symbolizing maturity. (This is apparently more common in girls and women—many of whom go through the entire sexual life with nothing beyond the experience of the sexual activities as the "proper thing to do" or what is "expected of one in marriage.") Of the existence of the various onanistic, homosexual, and heterosexual acts as no other than means of physical gratification, we are decidely more certain.

What now are the "illusions" about sex? We think that they are the realistic, dynamic images that are set up in a vague way about this use of sex as a symbol of relationship. And what now does crowding do to these illusions, which ordinarily begin to appear at seven, eight or nine years of age? If our observations are correct, then an individual can understand the use to which those who love each other put the sexual life only when he or she has had that experience. It is precisely the idiom of the relationship which defies teaching it to others. Yet our clinic records of crowded families quite abound in instances of children surreptitiously or more openly viewing those sexual activities to which they can give no other connotation than that of physical gratification. In other words, the "illusions" about sex are not formed because the child views the whole gamut of sex activities for those years during which he can give them practically no other connotation than that of direct physical gratification.

What meaning do such views give to "sexual perversion"? Evidently the important matter is whether or not the act leads towards a better heterosexual adjustment. Sexual acts carried out upon individuals of the same sex, or of a masturbatory nature, where the phantasy is entirely heterosexual and where the deterrent to heterosexual approach is social taboo, can hardly be called perversions—indeed these individuals turn to "correct" heterosexual outlets as soon as the social sanctions allow. Similarly, the most eminently "proper" relations of the marital

[3] In various places; particularly see Havelock Ellis, *Studies in the Psychology of Sex* (Philadelphia: F. A. Davis, 1927), VI, 523, 531n, 544, and 554.

state may be carried through with so overwhelming a drive on the part of one of the partners for physical gratification and so complete a disregard for the language values of the sexual act in the expression of the affectional ties, as to constitute definitely a perversion. In other words, a perversion in sexual expression has nothing at all to do with the form of the act but only with its purpose (which, of course, has been already recognized by a number of writers).

Does crowding prevent the development of illusions about sex or does it break them down after they have been formed? We get the impression from our clinic children that these illusions are never formed. In talking with us they do not manifest the elements of disappointment—the sharpness as of something broken—that appears in the discussion of broken idols. It has been this, in part, that has built our theory that the symbolic language values of sexual phenomena appear later in childhood and are prevented from appearing where the child has first seen so much of what is to him meaningless ("meaningless" beyond their prevision of physical satisfaction) physical expression.

We are aware that a large and voluble group of psychoanalytic persuasion have felt that it has been precisely the illusions about sex that have led to most of our difficulties. They would have us realize that hiding from children the strength and undaunted drive of the sexual urge has been really what has led to neuroses and conflicts when the child actually meets the overpowering character of his or her own sexual hunger. This may be a correct view of the situation. If it is, then the various interesting (not to say exotic) mechanisms which this school has uncovered should be quite lacking in crowded families where children from tender years are accustomed to see a rather florid display of the sexual urge. Up to the present time, certain quite impelling urges have almost entirely prevented the psychoanalysts from investigations among the poor. Our experience is that among the poor these difficulties are at least as frequent as among their more advantaged cousins. We are still persuaded that any arrangement which brings to the child an important and insistent urge at a time when he is utterly unable to understand its perspective in the total life situation of the adults involved must color the child's whole future attitude.

We are also aware of the arresting nature of the facts supplied by the divorce courts. In the Los Angeles courts, for instance, it is reported that "the primary cause of discord was . . . mostly based on complaints of sexual maladjustments."[4] Data such as these have strengthened the present fervid group who seek to cure the ills of family life through sexual education. We would be willing to accept the validity of these findings. We have ourselves every indication that a difficulty in the affectional ties first shows itself in sexual expression. How can people talk if they have nothing to say? The most subtle rift in the affectional ties is quite obviously magnified and dramatized in the sexual act which is no less than a highly complicated mutual act of expression. The analogy from the field of speech seems fair. Because speech difficulties such as stammering are so very dramatic and noticeable, generations have been busily engaged in attempting to cure these through various exercises directed to the speech trouble itself. If those interested in speech trouble now see that their point of attack is the fundamental emotional adjustment of the individual, may we not hope that in time there will be similar recognition that the sexual act is a mode of expressing certain deeper relationships?

There is an interesting type of document developing with some rapidity at this time —the volumes devoted to the technique

[4] J. E. Wallace Wallin, *Personality Maladjustments and Mental Hygiene* (New York: McGraw-Hill, 1935).

of the sexual act. These Emily Posts of the sexual field have convinced themselves that one can make people happily married by telling them what happily married people do. Nor would one too quickly turn from this approach—writers are aided by a larger vocabulary, artists by better colors, carpenters by a wider range of tools. But first there must be something to be expressed.

Similar considerations threaten any movement which is directed at merely a symptom of a relationship. The pleasure factors in the sexual relations—in distinction to the language factors—are indeed persistent. However, propaganda which stresses solely these pleasure factors and their enhancement through freedom from fear of consequences runs the danger of emphasizing what we would consider the least constructive and most rapidly disintegrating factor of the marital relationship. It would be difficult not to support the dissemination of sane and correct information concerning a matter which is very widely practiced at the present time—namely, birth control—so long as there continued through the whole procedure the proper primary emphasis of the part that the sexual life plays in the preservation and enrichment of the love relationship.

What does all this mean in the matter of sexual education for children and young adults? There is nothing to be gained in a program that keeps the nature of the physical acts of sex in the realm of mystery and taboo. It is equally fatuous to feel that we are covering the sexual education of youngsters by describing in detail the overt sexual phenomena. If children are to be given an insight into a vocabulary they must recognize that it is a vocabulary. The child eight or nine years old cannot understand why "people do such things." They have for him value only as objective phenomena. Admittedly, this is the only value which they have for many adults. This is not, however, the point here. Perhaps with children we can never go beyond the matter of teaching them that sex is "all right," that their questions about it are not taboo, that their interest is not evil. In other words, the important aspect of sexual education for young children is not the so-called "facts" which are taught them but the attitude with which these are taught. We have become rather certain that many parents have done more harm in blushing and blundering their way through a detailed and exact account of affairs than have others who have dispensed such old favorites as the magnanimity of the stork in a way that has made the child feel that it was all right to have asked the question.

But, frankly, we have felt that up to the present we could not answer the question of sexual education of the adolescent. The physical manifestations of the sexual life are not only highly individual but they attain, for any pair of persons who are what one calls "happily married," validity precisely on the basis of their individuality—or at least on the basis of their supposed individuality. Perhaps it is only this setting forth of principles that could ever be given to adolescents. The high degree of individuality in the sexual relationship of itself seems to defy further "teaching."

(Again we return to our parenthetical statements. If population-concentration grows and if it indeed skews the interest of the child toward the physical-gratification side of sexual phenomena, is there any general cultural trend which might be thought of as developing from this? In this light we have been interested in the development in our literature, as well as in psychiatric theory itself, of a marked increase in preoccupation with the sexual acts themselves rather than with them as an expression of the affectional ties.)

Mental Strain: Negativism and Irritability

A fourth effect of crowding we have called —for lack of a better term—"mental strain." It is that which arises from always having to "hold on to oneself." Walls are built about the ego to preserve its sanctity from prying eyes, and that these are walls of fear seems certain—nor can watchful guardianship over them be relaxed as long as many others are about. So one meets many adults—and some children—who "want to get away from everybody" they know, who feel the need of some surcease from this eternal vigilance. The results, when these periods of freedom are lacking, are either those of a somewhat forbidding negativism or of irritable outbursts of temper which belong definitely to the phenomena of fatigue. We see much of the latter either alone or associated with the former. The fatigue phenomenon seems to come from failure ever to be free from the task of guarding the status-preserving walls.

Or the matter may be expressed in another way—amounting, we guess, to the same thing. Earlier we pictured our children's inability to integrate the ego into a whole unit. Perhaps the walls of protection for the integrated ego are, in crowded families, never really completely formed. Perhaps this "mental strain," the fatigue phenomenon which we see, arises from the never-ending effort to integrate the ego under conditions which do not allow of this integration.

However this may be, one sees a constantly recurring picture of "touchy" reactions and irritability as the personality is pressed. Often one sees it covered, for protection, by an assumed nonchalance or braggadocio. When we realize that for many of these individuals from one year's end to the other, there is never a time that they are alone, we begin to get some picture of what this tension must be. Even the nights conspire to the same end; three to five children sleeping in the same bed means that even during the periods of relaxation and for the deeper levels of the unconscious there must always be this awareness of the imminence of others and the compromises and surrenders which this entails.

The reader recognizes that it is not alone the phenomenon of crowding that leads to this picture of mental strain. Nor unfortunately, are touchy, irritable reactions confined to those of these less advantaged groups.

Lack of Objectivity

Finally, among these individuals of crowded areas and crowded families, there is what one describes as the phenomenon of being so much in the world that there is no chance to look at it. Objectivity has a basic importance to the developing personality. We believe that the degree of one's objectivity is largely if not entirely an inherent matter. However, even for individuals with a high degree of objectivity, this characteristic is in abeyance where the hurly-burly of life forever presses upon them. This is not a difficult matter to measure, our conclusions being based upon the relative ability of children from different areas to describe themselves and the situations in which they have been as onlookers rather than as participants.

14

Body Ritual Among the Nacirema

Horace Miner

The anthropologist has become so familiar with the diversity of ways in which different peoples behave in similar situations that he is not apt to be surprised by even the most exotic customs. In fact, if all of the logically possible combinations of behavior have not been found somewhere in the world, he is apt to suspect that they must be present in some yet undescribed tribe. This point has, in fact, been expressed with respect to clan organization by Murdock. In this light, the magical beliefs and practices of the Nacirema present such unusual aspects that it seems desirable to describe them as an example of the extremes to which human behavior can go.

Professor Linton first brought the ritual of the Nacirema to the attention of anthropologists twenty years ago, but the culture of this people is still very poorly understood. They are a North American group living in the territory between the Canadian Cree, the Yaqui and Tarahumare of Mexico, and the Carib and Arawak of the Antilles. Little is known of their origin, although tradition states that they came from the east. According to Nacirema mythology, their nation was originated by a culture hero, Notgnihsaw, who is otherwise known for two great feats of strength—the throwing of a piece of wampum across the river Pa-To-Mac and the chopping down of a cherry tree in which the Spirit of Truth resided.

Nacirema culture is characterized by a highly developed market economy which has evolved in a rich natural habitat. While much of the people's time is devoted to economic pursuits, a large part of the fruits of these labors and a considerable portion of the day are spent in ritual activity. The focus of this activity is the human body, the appearance and health of which loom as a dominant concern in the ethos of the people. While such a concern is certainly not unusual, its ceremonial aspects and associated philosophy are unique.

The fundamental belief underlying the whole system appears to be that the human body is ugly and that its natural tendency is to debility and disease. Incarcerated in such a body, man's only hope is to avert these characteristics through the use of the powerful influences of ritual and ceremony. Every household has one or more shrines devoted to this purpose. The more powerful individuals in the society have several shrines in their houses and, in fact, the opulence of a house is often referred to in terms of the number of such ritual centers it possesses. Most houses are of wattle and daub construction, but the shrine rooms of the more wealthy are walled with stone.

Reproduced by permission of the American Anthropological Association from the *American Anthropologist:* Vol. 58 (1956), pp. 503–507.

Poorer families imitate the rich by applying pottery plaques to their shrine walls.

While each family has at least one such shrine, the rituals associated with it are not family ceremonies but are private and secret. The rites are normally only discussed with children, and then only during the period when they are being initiated into these mysteries. I was able, however, to establish sufficient rapport with the natives to examine these shrines and to have the rituals described to me.

The focal point of the shrine is a box or chest which is built into the wall. In this chest are kept the many charms and magical portions without which no native believes he could live. These preparations are secured from a variety of specialized practitioners. The most powerful of these are the medicine men, whose assistance must be rewarded with substantial gifts. However, the medicine men do not provide the curative potions for their clients, but decide what the ingredients should be and then write them down in an ancient and secret language. This writing is understood only by the medicine men and by the herbalists who, for another gift, provide the required charm.

The charm is not disposed of after it has served its purpose, but is placed in the charm-box of the household shrine. As these magical materials are specific for certain ills, and the real or imagined maladies of the people are many, the charm box is usually full to overflowing. The magical packets are so numerous that people forget what their purposes were and fear to use them again. While the natives are very vague on this point, we can only assume that the idea in retaining all the old magical materials is that their presence in the charm-box, before which the body rituals are conducted, will in some way protect the worshiper.

Beneath the charm-box is a small font. Each day every member of the family, in succession, enters the shrine room, bows his head before the charm-box, mingles different sorts of holy water in the font, and proceeds with a brief rite of ablution. The holy waters are secured from the Water Temple of the community, where the priests conduct elaborate ceremonies to make the liquid ritually pure.

In the hierarchy of magical practitioners, and below the medicine men in prestige, are specialists whose designation is best translated "holy-mouth-men." The Nacirema have an almost pathological horror of and fascination with the mouth, the condition of which is believed to have a supernatural influence on all social relationships. Were it not for the rituals of the mouth, they believe that their teeth would fall out, their gums bleed, their jaws shrink, their friends desert them, and their lovers reject them. They also believe that a strong relationship exists between oral and moral characteristics. For example, there is a ritual ablution of the mouth for children which is supposed to improve their moral fiber.

The daily body ritual performed by everyone includes a mouth-rite. Despite the fact that these people are so punctilious about care of the mouth, this rite involves a practice which strikes the uninitiated stranger as revolting. It was reported to me that the ritual consists of inserting a small bundle of hog hairs into the mouth, along with certain magical powders, and then moving the bundle in a highly formalized series of gestures.

In addition to the private mouth-rite, the people seek out a holy-mouth-man once or twice a year. These practitioners have an impressive set of paraphernalia, consisting of a variety of augers, awls, probes, and prods. The use of these objects in the exorcism of the evils of the mouth involves almost unbelievable ritual torture of the client. The holy-mouth-man opens the client's mouth and, using the above-mentioned tools, enlarges any holes which decay may have created in the teeth. Magical materials are put into these holes. If there are no naturally occurring holes in the teeth, large sections of one or more teeth are gouged out so that the supernatural substance can be applied. In the client's view, the purpose of these ministrations is to arrest decay and to draw friends. The extremely sacred and traditional character of the rite is evident in the fact the the natives return to the holy-mouth-men year after year, despite the fact that their teeth continue to decay.

It is hoped that, when a thorough study of the Nacirema is made, there will be careful inquiry into the personality structure of these people. One has but to watch the gleam in the eye of the holy-mouth-man, as he jabs an awl into an exposed nerve, to suspect that a certain amount of sadism is involved. If this can be established, a very interesting pattern emerges for most of the population shows definite masochistic tendencies. It was to these that Professor Linton referred in discussing a distinctive part of the daily body ritual which is performed only by men. This part of the rite involves scraping and lacerating the surface of the face with a sharp instrument. Special women's rites are performed only four times during each lunar month, but what they lack in frequency is made up in barbarity. As part of this ceremony, women bake their heads in small ovens for about an hour. The theoretically interesting point is that what seems to be a preponderantly masochistic people have developed sadistic specialists.

The medicine men have an imposing temple, or *latipso*, in every community of any size. The more elaborate ceremonies required to treat very sick patients can only be performed at this temple. These ceremonies involve not only the thaumaturge but a permament group of vestal maidens who move sedately about the temple chambers in distinctive costume and headdress.

The *latipso* ceremonies are so harsh that it is phenomenal that a fair proportion of the really sick natives who enter the temple ever recover. Small children whose indoctrination is still incomplete have been known to resist attempts to take them to the temple because "that is where you go to die." Despite this fact, sick adults are not only willing but eager to undergo the protracted ritual purification, if they can afford to do so. No matter how ill the supplicant or how grave the emergency, the guardians of many temples will not admit a client if he cannot give a rich gift to the custodian. Even after one has gained admission and survived the ceremonies, the guardians will not permit the neophyte to leave until he makes still another gift.

The supplicant entering the temple is first stripped of all his or her clothes. In everyday life the Nacirema avoids exposure of his body and its natural functions. Bathing and excretory acts are performed only in the secrecy of the household shrine, where they are ritualized as part of the body-rites. Psychological shock results from the fact that body secrecy is suddenly lost upon entry into the *latipso*. A man, whose own wife has never seen him in an excretory act, suddenly finds himself naked and assisted by a vestal maiden while he performs his natural functions into a sacred vessel. This sort of ceremonial treatment is necessitated by the fact that the excreta are used by a diviner to ascertain the course and nature of the client's sickness. Female clients, on the other hand, find their naked bodies are subjected to the scrutiny, manipulation, and prodding of the medicine men.

Few supplicants in the temple are well enough to do anything but lie on their hard beds. The daily ceremonies, like the rites of the holy-mouth-men, involve discomfort and torture. With ritual precision, the vestals awaken their miserable charges each dawn and roll them about on their beds of pain while performing ablutions, in the formal movements of which the maidens are highly trained. At other times they insert magic wands in the supplicant's mouth or force him to eat substances which are supposed to be healing. From time to time the medicine men come to their clients and jab magically treated needles into their flesh. The fact that these temple ceremonies may not cure, and may even kill the neophyte in no way decreases the people's faith in the medicine man.

There remains one other kind of practitioner, known as a "listener." This witch doctor has the power to exorcise the devils that lodge in the heads of people who have been bewitched. The Nacirema believe that parents bewitch their own children. Mothers are particularly suspected of putting a curse on children while teaching them the secret body rituals. The countermagic of the witch doctor is unusual in its lack of ritual. The patient simple tells the "listener" all his troubles and fears, beginning with the earliest difficulties he can remember. The memory displayed by the Nacirema in these exorcism sessions is truly remarkable. It is not uncommon for the patient to bemoan the rejection he felt upon being weaned as a babe, and a few individuals even see their troubles going back to the traumatic effects of their own birth.

In conclusion, mention must be made of certain practices which have their base in native aesthetics but which depend upon the pervasive aversion to the natural body and its functions. There are ritual fasts to make fat people thin and ceremonial feasts to make thin people fat. Still other rites are used to make women's breasts larger if they are small, and smaller if they are large. General dissatisfaction with breast shape is symbolized in the fact that the ideal form is virtually outside the range of human variation. A few women afflicted with almost inhuman hypermammary development are so idolized that they make a handsome living by simply going from village to village and permitting the natives to stare at them for a fee.

Reference has already been made to the fact that excretory functions are ritualized, routinized, and relegated to secrecy. Natural reproductive functions are similarly distorted. Intercourse is taboo as a topic and secluded as an act. Efforts are made to avoid pregnancy by the use of magical materials or by limiting intercourse to certain phases of the moon. Conception is actually infrequent. When pregnant, women dress so as to hide their condition. Parturition takes place in secret, without friends or relatives to assist, and the majority of women do not nurse their infants.

Our review of the ritual life of the Nacirema has certainly shown them to be a magic-ridden people. It is hard to understand how they have managed to exist so long under the burdens which they have imposed upon themselves. But even such exotic customs as these take on real meaning when they are viewed with the insight provided by Malinowski when he wrote: "Looking from far and above, from our high places of safety in the developed civilization, it is easy to see all the crudity and irrelevance of magic. But without its power and guidance early man could not have mastered his practical difficulties as he has done, nor could man have advanced to the higher stages of civilization."

PART II *The World of Learning*

We live in perhaps the most educated culture ever to appear on earth, but it is a culture most stricken with educational deficiencies. This is not a paradox, but is a recognition that our need for education has outstripped our capacity to educate. In a static culture, one that remains generation after generation with the same needs, learning and age are highly correlated. The older you are the more useful knowledge you have. Also, the older you are, the more likely it is that you will have more prestige, respect, and power.

Our present educational system grew out of such a steady state or static model. The present world culture is no longer static but is hell-bent on changing itself. We live in a culture where a scientific fact rarely remains unchallenged for more than a generation. Our notion of what is right, wrong, proper or improper to learn is changing more rapidly than our capacity to absorb it. We are a culture attuned to change on an individual level, but not yet on an institutional level.

The problems inherent in learning, the nature of truth, the place of teaching, and the cultivation of innovation are continual issues. The underlying question is the nature of knowledge and the value we give to it. Working out the details determines in what direction development will proceed. If we can see more accurately what we are doing now, it will make the task of creating new educational environments a task for renovators, not a demolition assignment for revolutionaries.

SECTION A *From Teaching to Thought Reform*

There have been times when a voice from out of the air seems to speak to me. It comes in the middle of a lecture or seminar which is going well. Bright, sensitive, meaningful questions have been asked. The major points appear to be grasped. Those students who often are asleep and those who usually use my classroom to eat lunch are awake and not unwrapping noisy sandwiches.

"What are you trying to do?" says this voice.

"I am trying to get everyone here to make up his own mind on this question," I answer somewhat piously.

"You mean, so that they will agree with your ideas."

"I don't like your insinuation. I'd like them to understand some of the basic ideas, to allow them to think of it in a new way."

At this point the voice might become gentle, understanding, almost affable.

"Reminds me of the time I was in China. There was this man who was teaching brainwashing. He told this group the same thing. 'Just make sure you get each prisoner to understand the other side of the issues.'"

Sometimes the voice and I argue, further touching on the problems of means and ends, the nature of understanding, the reason for teaching, and the effects of a personal bias. The issues are still unresolved.

The articles in this section start with a consideration of teaching, as we usually use the term, and continue on to advertising, selling, education under stress, and finally to thought reform.

It is obvious to me both as a teacher and as an editor that I want to influence your thinking. So do others. This section presents some of the methods currently in use.

15

Does Higher Education Influence Student Values?

Philip E. Jacob

Colleges and universities must face a hard fact about their present accomplishment before they can plan realistically for their role in the not-too-distant future. For the most part, they seem to lack the capacity to influence students, or maybe today's students are incapable of being influenced by higher education.

In any case, a study of what happens to the values of American students of today shows that their college experience barely touches their standards of behavior, quality of judgment, sense of social responsibility, perspicacity of understanding, and guiding beliefs.

This means that if institutions of higher learning are expected to fulfill the historic humanistic mission of what we have called liberal education, they will have to learn how to do it. They are *not* doing it now with most of their students.

This conclusion stems from an analysis of three types of data, which social scientists obtained from over one hundred institutions: studies of student attitudes conducted during the last fifteen years, recent evaluations of the outcomes of general education and other courses and of various methods of teaching, and a number of comprehensive self studies by particular institutions[1].

Fortunately, not all evidence is negative. There are some institutions in which students' values seem to develop, some teachers whose influence penetrates and stays, and some educational techniques which help open the sensibilities as well as the intellectual perceptions of some students. But the prevailing situation concerning the influence of college on contemporary student values is as follows:

1. *The values of American college students are remarkably homogeneous, considering the variety of their backgrounds and their relatively unrestricted opportunities for freedom of thought and personal development.*

A dominant characteristic of the current student generation is that the students are gloriously contented both in regard to their present day-to-day activity and their outlook for the future.

The great majority of students appears unabashedly self-centered. They aspire

Reprinted from Philip E. Jacob, "Does Higher Education Influence Student Values?" *NEA Journal* (Washington, D.C.: National Education Association, 1958), pp. 35–38, by permission of the publisher and the author.

[1] A detailed inventory and analysis of this material is available in a report prepared by Dr. Jacob for the Edward W. Hazen Foundation: *Changing Values in College*. Harper, 1957.

to material gratifications for themselves and their families. They intend to look out for themselves first and expect others to do likewise.

Social harmony, with an easy tolerance of the dissident and the different, also pervades the student environment. Conformists themselves, the American students do not expect others to conform to the socially accepted standard. They are, for the most part, ready to live in a mobile society without racial, ethnic, or income barriers. But they do not intend to crusade for nondiscrimination, merely to accept it as it comes.

Although most students value the traditional code of moral virtues, they are not inclined to censure those who choose to depart from it. Nor do they feel personally bound to unvarying conformity to the code, especially when a lapse is socially sanctioned. For instance, systematic academic cheating is the custom at many major institutions.

Students normally express a need for religion and often attend church on Sundays, but their religion does not carry over into the secular world. The majority appear to believe that God's place is in church or home, not in business or community.

American students are also only dutifully responsive toward government. They expect to obey its laws and pay its taxes—without complaint but without enthusiasm. Except for voting, however, they are politically irresponsible and politically illiterate.

They have contradictory attitudes toward international affairs. They predict another major war within a dozen years, yet indicate that during the immediate future they expect to give little personal attention to international problems.

Students by and large set great stock by college in general and their own college in particular. Only a minority, however, seem to value their college education for its intellectual contribution or for its nurturing of personal character. Vocational preparation and skill and experience in social "adjustment" head the rewards which students expect from college.

The available data indicate that the profile just given may broadly characterize 75 or 80 per cent of the students. To the remainder, some or most of the generalizations are not applicable. Also, on some issues, such as how much government the country needs, students have no common mind. But the dominant impression is of a nation-wide norm of values pervading the campus.

2. *The main effect of higher education upon student values is to bring about general acceptance of a body of standards and attitude characteristics of college-bred men and women in America.*

There tends to be more homogeneity and greater consistency of values among college seniors than among freshmen, indicating that the senior has ironed out serious conflicts of values or at least achieved a workable compromise. Throughout college, changes are rarely drastic or sudden. Such changes as do occur tend to emerge on the periphery of the student's character rather than to affect his core of values.

The values of college graduates do differ in some ways from the rest of society. They are more concerned with status, achievement, and prestige. As a whole, they tend to be more self-important, more conservative, more tolerant, and less superstitious and prejudiced than those without college.

It seems reasonable to credit these differences to college, partly to its positive influence in bringing students' outlook into line with a "standard," partly to a subtle selective process which tends to eliminate those not sufficiently adaptive to acquire the value patterns of the college graduate.

But to call this process a liberalization of student values is to use a misnomer. The impact of college rather is to socialize the individual, to refine or shape up his values so that he can fit into his society more congenially.

3. *For the most part, students' values do not vary greatly whether they have pursued a conventional liberal-arts program, an integrated general-education curriculum, or a professional-vocational option.*

The more liberally educated students may take a somewhat more active interest in community responsibilities and keep better informed about public affairs. But the distinction is not striking, and it does not occur consistently. It does not justify the conclusion that a student acquires a greater maturity of judgment on issues of social policy or a more sensitive regard for human values because he has had more liberal education.

There is also no solid evidence of a delayed reaction. The college alumnus exhibits no unusual trademark identifying his undergraduate curriculum.

The same negative conclusion applies to the general effect of social-science courses. Although many students testify that such courses have increased their understanding of world affairs or interest in politics, the values actually expressed by social-science students—either verbally or in action—are little different from those of others. There is little evidence, for instance, that actual participation in public life has increased as a result of students' taking social science.

4. *Quality of teaching has little effect upon the value outcomes of students' general education.*

Students have demonstrated an uncanny capacity to evaluate the performance of instructors according to objective criteria. Yet, by and large, the impact of the teachers they consider good is indistinguishable from that of the poor one—at least in terms of his influence upon the students' values.

Some teachers, however, do exert a profound influence on *some* students, even to the point of causing particular individuals to adopt new and usually more socially responsible vocational goals. It is perhaps significant that faculty members having this power are likely to be those whose own value commitments are openly expressed and who are outgoing and warm in their student relationships.

5. *The method of instruction seems to have only a minor influence on students' value judgments.*

Under special circumstances, "student-centered" teaching reportedly has resulted in a more satisfactory student adjustment and a more congenial learning situation. But the weight of evidence gives little indication that different teaching methods —say, the lecture system versus recitation, conference, discussion, or tutorial methods —greatly alter students' beliefs or behavior.

However, individual students are often deeply affected by participation in experiences which vividly confront them with value issues, and possibly demand decisions on their part whose consequences they can witness.

But the practical difficulties of working such activities in to the educational process are very great, especially in the general part of the curriculum in which large numbers of students are involved. For the essence of a potent laboratory practice in citizenship, a creative work camp, a meaningful experiment in international living, a stimulating work-study curriculum or even a well conceived field study is this: each student personally engages in the action.

Vicarious experience does not deliver the same punch, even though role-playing techniques in the classroom and the analysis of challenging case studies and problem situations do arouse more interest.

6. *Similar as the patterns of student values appear on a mass view, the intellectual, or moral climate of some institutions stands out as having a peculiar potency.*

The response of students to education within these institutions is strikingly different from the national pattern.

Such colleges and universities do not

fit any institutional type. However, they seem to have in common a high level of expectancy of their students. *What* is expected is not the same.

For instance, the institution may primarily stress intellectual initiative, profound respect for the worth of work, world-mindedness, or a dedication to humanitarian service. But everyone is conscious of the mission to which the institution stands dedicated, though this is not necessarily loudly trumpeted at every convocation, nor elaborated in the college or university bulletin.

In these colleges, students seem drawn to live up to the college standard, even if it means a wrench from their previous ways of thought.

With a distinctive quality of this kind, an institution evokes a deep loyalty from students, alumni, and staff. A community of values is created which persists long after graduation and often influences the choice of college by the next generation.

7. *Recent research has identified certain personality characteristics of students which filter their educational experiences.*

Some students have a set of mind so rigid, an outlook on human relations so stereotyped, and a reliance on authority so compulsive that they are incapable of understanding, much less accepting, new ideas. Such students quail in the presence of conflict and uncertainty. They crave "right answers," recoil from creative discussion.

Under most conditions of general education, where content and teaching method have been more or less standardized to suit the average student, the personalities just described become dead wood. A few institutions, however, are exploring special approaches to general education for this type of student, with promising results.

These students rarely achieve the autonomy of those whose personality is freer to start with. But they have shown striking gains in critical thinking and developed more responsible and sensitive social values when their general education in social science, for instance, has been tailored to their particular needs. Because the number of students with such personality characteristics is large and growing, this type of experimentation seems unusually important.

The points presented here imply that no specific curricular pattern of liberal education, no pedigree of instructor, and no wizardry of instructional method should be patented for its impact on students' values, Indeed, the impact of American higher education as a whole upon the value patterns of college youth as a whole seems negligible.

The values of some students do change in college. But even with these, the impetus to change does not come primarily from the formal educational process. It comes from the distinctive climate of a few institutions, the individual and personal magnetism of a sensitive teacher with strong values, or the value-laden personal experiences which students occasionally undergo during college.

In short, college can contribute to the growth of a students' values only when it penetrates the core of his life and confronts him with fresh and often disturbing implications, which are different from those which he and his society have taken for granted. This can hardly occur as a by-product of a curricular assembly line. It requires a highly personal relationship between the college community and the individual student—a relationship that is warm and considerate but at the same time mutually aggravating.

16

Self-images for Everybody

Vance Packard

"People have a terrific loyalty to their brand of cigarette and yet in tests cannot tell it from other brands. They are smoking an image completely."—Research director, New York advertising agency
(name withheld upon request).

The subconscious salesmen, in groping for better hooks, deployed in several directions. One direction they began exploring in a really major way was the molding of images; the creation of distinctive, highly appealing "personalities" for products that were essentially undistinctive. The aim was to build images that would arise before our "inner eye" at the mere mention of the product's name, once we had been properly conditioned. Thus they would trigger our action in a competitive sales situation.

A compelling need for such images was felt by merchandisers, as I've indicated, because of the growing standardization of, and complexity of, ingredients in most products, which resulted in products that defied reasonable discrimination. Three hundred smokers loyal to one of three major brands of cigarettes were given the three brands to smoke (with labels taped) and asked to identify their own favorite brand. Result: 35 per cent were able to do so; and under the law of averages pure guesses would have accounted for a third of the correct identifications. In short, something less than 2 per cent could be credited with any real power of discrimination. Somewhat comparable results were obtained when merchandisers tried "blindfold" tests on beer and whisky drinkers.

If people couldn't discriminate reasonably, marketers reasoned, they should be assisted in discriminating *unreasonably*, in some easy, warm, emotional way.

Pierre Martineau, a high apostle of image building, analyzed the problem with startling candor in talking to Philadelphia advertising men in early 1956. Advertising, he admonished them, is no longer just a neat little discussion of your product's merits.

"Basically, what you are trying to do," he advised, "is create an illogical situation. You want the customer to fall in love with your product and have a profound brand loyalty when actually content may be very similar to hundreds of competing brands." To create this illogical loyalty, he said, the first task "is one of creating some differentiation in the mind—some individualization for the product which has a long list of competitors very close to it in content."

While a competitor can often successfully imitate your product as to ingredients and claims of quality, a vivid personality image is much more difficult to imitate and so can be a more trustworthy sales factor.

A fairly simple, straightforward use of nonrational symbolism in image building was Louis Cheskin's transformation of the Good Luck margarine package. The package originally contained several elements, including a picture of the margarine. In one corner was a little four-leaf clover. Mr. Cheskin found from his depth probing that the four-leaf clover was "a wonderful image" so in three successive changes he brought it into more and more prominence until finally he had a simple foil package completely dominated by a large three-dimensional four-leaf clover. Mr. Cheskin reports that sales rose with each change.

David Ogilvy's advertising firm devised a highly successful nonrational symbol for an obscure brand of shirt—a mustached man with a black eye patch. Soon the public knew that any man wearing a black eye patch had to be wearing a Hathaway shirt. To prove his faith in the power of imagery Mr. Ogilvy began running expensive color full-page ads in magazines such as the *New Yorker* that did not contain a single word of text, not even the word Hathaway. All that was shown was a picture of a man. He stood by an observatory telescope taking notes. He had a mustache. He wore a bright plaid shirt. And he had a black eye patch. Hathaway shirt sales thrived.

Proctor and Gamble's image builders have charted a living personification for each of their cakes of soap and cans of shortening. Ivory soap is personalized as mother and daughter on a sort of pedestal of purity. They exude simple wholesomeness. In contrast the image charted for Camay soap is of a glamorous sophisticated woman. As for the company's two shortenings, Crisco and Golden Fluffo, differentiation is achieved by depicting Crisco in the image of a no-nonsense professional dietitian and Golden Fluffo as a warm, robust, motherly character.

The image builders began giving a great deal of thought to the types of images that would have the strongest appeal to the greatest number of people. An eye patch might sell shirts to sophisticates, but it didn't have an emotional tug, and the image builders reasoned that the emotional tug could be a real plus factor in mass merchandising. The Jewel food stores chain of Chicago, in its search for an appealing "personality" that would give it an edge over competitors, came up from its depth probing with one promising answer: It decided the chain should, in its image, take on the traits "we like in our friends." Those were spelled out as generosity, courtesy, cleanliness, patience, sincerity, honesty, sympathy, and good-naturedness.

But wouldn't it be even better, merchandisers reasoned, if they could build into their products the same traits that we recognize in ourselves! Studies of narcissism indicated that nothing appeals more to people than themselves; so why not help people buy a projection of themselves? That way the images would pre-select their audiences, select out of a consuming public people with personalities having an affinity for the image. By building in traits known to be widely dispersed among the consuming public the image builders reasoned that the could spark love affairs by the millions.

The sale of self-images soon was expediting the movement of hundreds of millions of dollars' worth of merchandise to consumers, particularly gasoline, cigarettes, and automobiles. And the image builders were offering some surprising evidence of the extent to which American consumers were becoming self-image buyers.

A chief of research for a major advertising agency was showing me many dozens of drawings people had made of cars when they were asked by his investigators to "draw a car." He said casually, "You can just about predict from the way a person draws a car the brand of gasoline he will buy." I expressed astonishment and said I thought people bought gasoline because of the dealer's location or because they liked him or because of the supposed quality of his gasoline. He agreed those all had some bearing, but not as much as we assume, and cited a study showing that where there were four dealers at an intersection and one dealer changed his brand his business would suddenly go up or down as much as 30 per cent as a result of the change in image.

This man said his staff had classified the drawings as to the kind of personality they revealed in the drawer and then had checked the findings against the kind of gasoline the drawer constantly bought. They found a startling correlation between the way a person draws a car and the gasoline image that will attract him. He explained:

"In buying a gasoline you get played back to you who you are. Each gasoline has built up an image or personality. Each helps a buyer answer the question 'Who am I?' Your aim is to find the people who have an affinity for your gasoline."

He showed me a series of car drawings made by people who consistently buy the particular brand his agency handles. The agency has deliberately sought to give its gasoline an image of bigness, authority. The car drawn by users of the gasoline clearly showed a tendency to be long, streamlined, big. And he said that an analysis of the personal characteristics of these users showed they tended to be either local successes in their community (merchants, doctors, lawyers, etc.) or else were people frustrated in yearnings for bigness.

Then he showed me another series of drawings of cars. These tended to be done not in any grand style but with loving detail. They were all done by people who prefer brand B gasoline which has built up an image of being a friendly gasoline. Its image reminds people of outdoors, small towns, warm colors. Even its TV show presents an image of folksiness. The people who buy this gasoline, my informant said, are the chatty type who like to get out of the car and talk with the station attendant while the car is being serviced.

A third series of drawings was like Rube Goldberg cartoons, flamboyant. The car might not run but it had an aerial and a host of other gadgets on it. Typically the artist thinks of his car as a wonderful plaything. The gasoline he consistently buys has sought to build an image of itself, on TV and elsewhere, as an exciting, dramatic, flamboyant gasoline. My informant explained:

"By understanding these personalities we are not only in a better position to maintain our present customers, but to know where to make gains from our competitors. Of these five brands I can say, 'Where am I going to get increases? Which is the gasoline most vulnerable to us?' Actually the brand B buyer is most vulnerable to us because, although he is folksy, he wants bigness. By warming up our image of brand A we can appeal to this brand B buyer."

A little later this research director got to talking about the images of cigarettes. Roughly 65 per cent of all smokers are absolutely loyal, and 20 per cent more relatively loyal, to one brand of cigarette. Even though in tests they cannot identify that cigarette, they will walk down five flights of stairs to buy their brand rather than accept a substitute. He cited an experiment his chief psychologist performed in the early fifties. This psychologist chose a group of eighty smokers known to have a strong loyalty for some brand of cigarette and gave these eighty smokers the Rorschach ink-blot test. Later the psychologist, who had not been advised what brand each favored, went through the Rorschach results and from the emotional make-ups indicated named with only a few misses the brand of cigarette that each of the eighty smokers *had* to favor!

This agency has built a comprehensive personality profile of the typical smoker of each major brand of cigarette. This material is confidential. However, the type of material in it resembles to a large degree profiles assembled by other investigators. Social Research, for instance, profiled several of the leading cigarettes for *The Chicago Tribune*. It found, for example, that Camels were regarded as masculine, and strong, and for the ordinary working people. Lucky Strikes had a similar reputation—strong and for men, too; for ordinary people, but less for the working-man. Chesterfields were thought to be for both men and women and on the mild side and not bound by class.

This study was made shortly before the cigarette industry was thrown into its tizzy by the now famous cancer scare, which in the words of one spokesman of the advertising agencies put the "cigarette industry in one hell of a fix." Some of the old leaders who had built themselves images as rough, tough cigarettes found themselves losing customers. There was turmoil as the cigarettes groped for more reassuring images. Retailers were flooded with new brands all claiming to be safer than others. As a result of the cancer scare virtually every major tobacco marketer brought out a filter-tip brand, and in four years filter-tip sales rose 1800 per cent. By 1957 the filter tips, too, were, by skilled image building, developing distinctive personalities, the old brands were developing more "gentle" personalities, and cigarette sales as a whole began trending upward again, starting in 1955.

Perhaps the most spectacularly successful image building has been done by the automobile industry. The automobile has become far more than a mere means of conveyance. In the words of Pierre Martineau, "The automobile tells who we are and what we think we want to be . . . It is a portable symbol of our personality and our position . . . the clearest way we have of telling people of our exact position. [In buying a car] you are saying in a sense, 'I am looking for the car that expresses who I am.'"

Buick, in fact, suggested this in its ad when it offered this promise to the public; "It makes you feel like the man you are."

One of the most remarkable documents I came across in my investigation was a pamphlet called "Automobiles, What They Mean to Americans." It reports on a study made for *The Chicago Tribune* by Social Research, Inc. The major merchandising journals have discussed its findings in great detail. The study was conducted by a team of social scientists who used a variety of probing techniques on 352 car owners in the Chicago area.

The investigators found that only a minority of the population, mostly men in the lower class, have any real interest in the technical aspect of cars. And the major finding that stands out in the survey is that automobiles are heavily laden with social meanings and are highly esteemed because they "provide avenues for the expression . . . of the character, temperament and self concept of the owner and driver . . . The buying process is an interaction between the personality of the car and the personality of the individual."

The report indicated the personality of one sort of owner of various major makes of car by presenting a series of circles. Each circle contained words written in to indicate the dominant traits of this owner and their relative importance. Here are some of the owner profiles that were indicated:

Cadillac: "Proud . . . flashy . . . salesman . . . middle-aged . . . social mobility . . . good income level . . . responsible."

Ford: "Speed demon . . . good income . . . young man . . . proud . . . upper lower class . . . drives to work . . . practical."

DeSoto: "Conservative . . . responsible . . . matron . . . upper middle class . . . good income . . . proud."

Studebaker: "Neat look . . . sophisticated . . . intellectual . . . mobile . . . professional . . . young man."

Pontiac: "Stable class outlook . . . middle of road . . . married woman . . . mother . . . sincere . . . conventional . . . busy."

Mercury: "Salesman . . . assertive . . . mobile . . . modern . . . substantial . . . lower middle . . . father . . . quick."

The report stated that "people buy the cars they think are especially appropriate for them" and then made these points:

People who want to seem conservative, to tell the world they are very serious and responsible tend to buy Plymouth, Dodge, DeSoto, Packard, four-door sedans, dark colors, minimum accessories and gadgets.

People who want to seem sociable and up-to-date but in a middle-of-the-road sort of way tend to favor Chevrolet, Pontiac, Buick, Chrysler, two-door coupés, light colors, moderate accessories and gadgets.

People who want to express some showiness, to assert their individualism and modernity, tend to buy Ford, Mercury, Oldsmobile, Lincoln, hardtops, two tones, bright shades and hues, a range of extras, gadgets, fads.

People who need to express unusual status or individual needs favor Cadillac (ostentation, high status), Studebaker, Hudson, Nash, Willys, convertibles (impulsiveness), very bright colours, red, yellow, white, latest gadgets and accessories.

One of the interesting variations, under the ways to fulfill "wish for attention" through car ownership, is what the investigators call "conspicuous reserve." Those people want other people to know their status but at the same time want to express it modestly. Some may engage in deliberate downgrading. This is "a frequent technique of people who are secure in their high social position. They show their superiority by displaying indifference to status—by purposely buying less expensive cars than might be expected. They love beat-up station wagons and old cars." Others who wish attention may try to do it with car images showing a sophisticated flair: foreign cars, the Nash Rambler, the new Studebaker. Burleigh Gardner told of a crisis that occurred among a group of four doctors who shared a suite on Chicago's swank Michigan Avenue when one of the colleagues began parking his slightly radical, attention-getting car in front of the building. After conferring they told him the car didn't fit the image they were trying to build for themselves as carriage-trade medicos.

One of the findings of the Social Research study was that DeSoto was thought of as appropriate to settled people, including middle-aged and retired ones. Dodge, while appropriate for mature, responsible people, had a chronological age somewhat younger than DeSoto.

Shortly after this study was released the Chrysler Corporation began overhauling the images of all its cars. (The degree to which the company had been influenced by the report could not be specifically determined.) At any rate the entire line was given the "Forward Look" with more youthful and exciting appeal. The Social Research report said the Dodge owner wished to be known as a solid citizen. When Dodge was restyled for a more "forward look," its makers proclaimed that the solid citizen was in for some surprises. And Plymouth, when it launched its big comeback by a change of image, didn't use a "nuts and bolts" campaign. Instead, as Mr. Martineau points out, Plymouth's campaign was built on creating a "young in heart" theme appealing to the eternal sophomore in all of us.

I asked Mr. Martineau if there had been any substantial changes in image personality of cars and cigarettes since he conducted his two studies and he replied: "Generally I would say that contrary to superficial impression, these product images change very slowly unless something radically different happens to the product or the advertising. I think Plymouth went very fast from a dull car to a rather exciting one. I think the image of Lucky Strike as a masculine cigarette is fading slowly. Naturally these images will change with time, but very generally these product personalities in the two studies . . . are relatively the same."

Although cars have distinctive images carefully created for them, aimed at appealing to a certain type of buyer, auto merchandisers do not confine their search for customers to one personality group. That would be too restrictive to be tolerated by mass marketers. As the report states: "A car can sell itself to different people by presenting different facets of its personality. . . . Advertising is a multiplier of symbols. Like a prism it can present many different facets of the car's character so that many fundamentally different people see it as their car."

When the image analysts know a few of the images we buy, they can project our behavior in other buying situations and fill in many of the gaps of our total personality configuration. I was chatting with two psychologists from Social Research and one of them said: "Now take the man who drives a Studebaker, smokes Old Golds, uses cream-based hair oil, an electric shaver, carries a Parker 51 fountain pen. Obviously he's a salesman, an active man, aggressive in face-to-face situations and wants to make a good impression. Probably he was quite a romantic type in his youth." And the other psychologist added:

"Also, you'll find that he is wearing loud shorts."

17

The Arts of Selling

Aldous Huxley

The survival of democracy depends on the ability of large numbers of people to make realistic choices in the light of adequate information. A dictatorship, on the other hand, maintains itself by censoring or distorting the facts, and by appealing, not to reason, not to enlightened self-interest, but to passion and prejudice, to the powerful "hidden forces," as Hitler called them, present in the unconscious depths of every human mind.

In the West, democratic principles are proclaimed and many able and conscientious publicists do their best to supply electors with adequate information and to persuade them, by rational argument, to make realistic choices in the light of that information. All this is greatly to the good. But unfortunately propaganda in the Western democracies, above all in America, has two faces and a divided personality. In charge of the editorial department there is often a democratic Dr. Jekyll—a propagandist who would be very happy to prove that John Dewey had been right about the ability of human nature to respond to truth and reason. But this worthy man controls only a part of the machinery of mass communication. In charge of advertising we find an anti-democratic, because anti-rational, Mr. Hyde—or rather a Dr. Hyde, for Hyde is now a Ph.D. in psychology and has a master's degree as well in the social sciences. This Dr. Hyde would be very unhappy indeed if everybody always lived up to John Dewey's faith in human nature. Truth and reason are Jekyll's affair, not his. Hyde is a motivation analyst, and his business is to study human weaknesses and failings, to investigate those unconscious desires and fears by which so much of men's conscious thinking and overt doing is determined. And he does this, not in spirit of the moralist who would like to make people better, or of the physician who would like to improve their health, but simply in order to find out the best way to take advantage of their ignorance and to exploit their irrationality for the pecuniary benefit of his employers. But after all, it may be argued, "capitalism is dead, consumerism is king"—and consumerism requires the services of expert salesmen versed in all the arts (including the more insidious arts) of persuasion. Under a free enterprise system commercial propaganda by any and every means is absolutely indispensable. But the indispensable is not necessarily the desirable. What is demonstrably good in the sphere of economics may be far from good for men and women as voters or even as human beings, An earlier, more moralistic generation would have been profoundly shocked by the bland cynicism of the motivation analysts. Today we read a book like Mr. Vance Packard's *The Hidden Persuaders,* and are more amazed than horrified, more resigned than indignant. Given Freud, given Behaviorism, given the mass producer's chronically desperate need for mass consumption, this is the sort of thing that is only to be expected. But what, we may ask, is the sort of thing that is to be expected in the future? Are Hyde's activities compatible in the long run with Jekyll's? Can a campaign in favor of rationality be successful in the teeth of another and even more vigorous campaign in favor of irrationality? These are questions which, for the moment, I shall not attempt to answer, but shall leave hanging, so to speak, as a backdrop to our discussion of the methods of mass production in a technologically advanced democratic society.

The task of the commercial propagandist in a democracy is in some ways easier and in some ways more difficult than that of a political propagandist employed by an established dictator or a dictator in the making. It is easier inasmuch as almost everyone starts out with a prejudice in favor of beer, cigarettes and iceboxes, whereas almost nobody starts out with a prejudice in favor of tyrants. It is more difficult inasmuch as the commercial propagandist is not permitted, by the rules of his particular game, to appeal to the more savage instincts of his public. The advertiser of dairy products would dearly love to tell his readers and listeners that all their troubles are caused by the machinations of a gang of godless international margarine manufacturers, and that it is their patriotic duty to march out and burn the oppressor's factories. This sort of thing, however, is ruled out, and he must be content with a milder approach. But the mild approach is less exciting than the approach through verbal or physical violence. In the long run, anger and hatred are self-defeating emotions. But in the short run they pay high dividends in the form of psychological and even (since they release large quantities of adrenalin and noradrenalin) physiological satisfaction. People may start out with an initial prejudice against tyrants; but when tyrants or would-be tyrants treat them to adrenalin-releasing propaganda about the wickedness of their enemies—particularly of enemies weak enough to be persecuted —they are ready to follow him with enthusiasm. In his speeches Hitler kept repeating such words as "hatred," "force," "ruthless," "crush," "smash"; and he would accompany these violent words with even more violent gestures. He would yell, he would scream, his veins would swell, his face would turn purple. Strong emotion (as every actor and dramatist knows) is in the highest degree contagious. Infected by the malignant frenzy of the orator, the audience would groan and sob and scream in an orgy of uninhibited passion. And these orgies were so enjoyable that most of those who had experienced them eagerly came back for more. Almost all of us long for peace and freedom; but very few of us have much enthusiasm for the thoughts, feelings and actions that make for peace and freedom. Conversely almost nobody wants war or tyranny; but a great many people find an intense pleasure in the thoughts, feelings and actions that make for war and tyranny. These thoughts, feelings and actions are too dangerous to be exploited for commercial purposes. Accepting this handicap, the advertising man must do the best he can with the less intoxicating emotions, the quieter forms of irrationality.

Effective rational propaganda becomes possible only when there is a clear understanding, on the part of all concerned, of the nature of symbols and of their relations to the things and events symbolized. Irrational propaganda depends for its effectiveness on a general failure to understand the nature of symbols. Simple-minded people tend to equate the symbol with what it stands for, to attribute to things and events some of the qualities expressed by the words in terms of which the propagandist has chosen, for his own purposes, to talk about them. Consider a simple example. Most cosmetics are made of lanolin, which is a mixture of purified wool fat and water beaten up into an emulsion. This emulsion has many valuable properties: it penetrates the skin, it does not become rancid, it is mildly antiseptic and so forth. But the commercial propagandists do not speak about the genuine virtues of the emulsion. They give it some picturesquely voluptuous name, talk ecstatically and misleadingly about feminine beauty and show pictures of gorgeous blondes nourishing their tissues with skin food. "The cosmetic manufacturers," one of their number has written, "are not selling lanolin, they are selling hope." For this hope, this fraudulent implication of a promise that they will be transfigured, women will pay ten or twenty times the value of the emulsion which the propagandists have so skilfully related, by means of misleading symbols, to a deep-seated and almost universal feminine wish—the wish to be more attractive to members of the opposite sex. The principles underlying this kind of propaganda are extremely simple. Find some common desire, some widespread unconscious fear or anxiety; think out some way to relate this wish or fear to the product you have to sell; then build a bridge of verbal or pictorial symbols over which your customer can pass from fact to compensatory dream, and from the dream to the illusion that your product, when purchased, will make the dream come true. "We no longer buy oranges, we buy vitality. We do not buy just an auto, we buy prestige." And so with all the rest. In toothpaste, for example, we buy, not a mere cleanser and antiseptic, but release from the fear of being sexually repulsive. In vodka and whisky we are not buying a protoplasmic poison which, in small doses, may depress the nervous system in a psychologically valuable way; we are buying friendliness and good fellowship, the warmth of Dingley Dell and the brilliance of the Mermaid Tavern. With our laxatives we buy the health of a Greek god, the radiance of one of Diana's nymphs. With the monthly best seller we acquire culture, the envy of our less literate neighbors and the respect of the sophisticated. In every case the motivation analyst has found some deep-seated wish or fear, whose energy can be used to move the consumer to part with cash and so, indirectly, to turn the wheels of industry. Stored in the minds and bodies of countless individuals, this potential energy is released by, and transmitted along, a line of symbols carefully laid out so as to bypass rationality and obscure the real issue.

Sometimes the symbols take effect by being disproportionately impressive, haunting and fascinating in their own right. Of this kind are the rites and pomps of religion. These "beauties of holiness" strengthen faith where it already exists and, where there is no faith, contribute to conversion. Appealing, as they do, only to the aesthetic sense, they guarantee neither the truth nor the ethical value of the doctrines with which they have been, quite arbitrarily, associated. As a matter of plain historical fact, the beauties of holiness have often been matched and indeed surpassed by the beauties of unholiness. Under Hitler, for example, the yearly Nuremberg rallies were masterpieces of ritual and theatrical art. "I had spent six years in St. Petersburg before the war in the best days of the old Russian ballet," writes Sir Nevile Henderson, the British ambassador to Hitler's Germany, "but for grandiose beauty I have never seen any ballet to compare with the Nuremberg rally." One thinks of Keats—"beauty is truth, truth beauty." Alas, the identity exists only on some ultimate, supramundane level. On the levels of politics and theology, beauty is perfectly compatible with nonsense and tyranny. Which is very fortunate; for if beauty were incompatible with nonsense and tyranny, there would be precious little art in the world. The masterpeices of painting, sculpture and architecture were produced as religious or political propaganda, for the greater glory of a god, a government or a priesthood. But most kings and priests have been despotic and all religions have been riddled with superstition. Genius has been the servant of tyranny and art has advertised the merits of the local cult. Time, as it passes, separates the good art from the bad metaphysics. Can we learn to make this separation, not after the event, but while it is actually taking place? That is the question.

In commercial propaganda the principle of the disproportionately fascinating symbol is clearly understood. Every propagandist has his Art Department, and attempts are constantly being made to beautify the billboards with striking posters, the advertising pages of magazines with lively drawings and photographs. There are no masterpieces; for masterpieces appeal only to a limited audience, and the commercial propagandist is out to captivate the majority. For him, the ideal is a moderate excellence. Those who like this not too good, but sufficiently striking, art may be expected to like the products with which it has been associated and for which it symbolically stands.

Another disproportionately fascinating symbol is the Singing Commercial. Singing Commercials are a recent invention; but the Singing Theological and the Singing Devotional—the hymn and the psalm—are as old as religion itself. Singing Militaries, or marching songs, are coeval with war, and Singing Patriotics, the precursors of our national anthems, were doubtless used to promote group solidarity, to emphasize the distinction between "us" and "them," by the wandering bands of paleolithic hunters and food gatherers. To most people music is intrinsically attractive. Moreover, melodies tend to ingrain themselves in the listener's mind. A tune will haunt the memory during the whole of a lifetime. Here, for example, is a quite uninteresting statement or value judgment. As it stands nobody will pay attention to it. But now set the words to a catchy and easily remembered tune. Immediately they become words of power. Moreover, the words will tend automatically to repeat themselves every time the melody is heard or spontaneously remembered. Orpheus has entered into an alliance with Pavlov—the power of sound with the conditioned reflex. For the commercial propagandist, as for his colleagues in the fields of politics and religion, music possesses yet another advantage. Nonsense which it would be shameful for a reasonable being to write, speak or hear spoken can be sung or listened to by that same rational being with pleasure and even with a kind of intellectual conviction. Can we learn to separate the pleasure of singing or of listening to song from the all too human tendency to believe in the propaganda which the song is putting over? That again is the question.

Thanks to compulsory education and the rotary press, the propagandist has been able, for many years past, to convey his messages to virtually every adult in every civilized country. Today, thanks to radio and television, he is in the happy position of being able to communicate even with unschooled adults and not yet literate children.

Children, as might be expected, are highly susceptible to propaganda. They are ignorant of the world and its ways, and therefore completely unsuspecting. Their critical faculties are undeveloped. The youngest of them have not yet reached the age of reason and the older ones lack the experience on which their new-found rationality can effectively work. In Europe, conscripts used to be playfully referred to as "cannon fodder." Their little brothers and sisters have now become radio fodder and television fodder. In my childhood we were taught to sing nursery rhymes and, in pious households, hymns. Today the little ones warble the Singing Commercials. Which is better—"Rheingold is my beer, the dry beer," or "Hey diddle-diddle, the cat and the fiddle"? "Abide with me" or "You'll wonder where the yellow went, when you brush your teeth with Pepsodent"? Who knows?

"I don't say that children should be forced to harass their parents into buying products they've seen advertised on television, but at the same time I cannot close my eyes to the fact that it's being done every day." So writes the star of one of the many programs beamed to a juvenile audience. "Children," he adds, "are living, talking records of what we tell them every day." And in due course these living, talking records of television commercials will grow up, earn money and buy the products of industry. "Think," writes Mr. Clyde Miller ecstatically, "think of what it can mean to your firm in profits if you can condition a million or ten million children, who will grow up into adults trained to buy your product, as soldiers are trained in advance when they hear the trigger words, Forward March!" Yes, just think of it! And at the same time remember that the dictators and the would-be dictators have been thinking about this sort of thing for years, and that millions, tens of millions, hundreds of millions of children are in process of growing up to buy the local despot's ideological product and, like well-trained soldiers, to respond with appropriate behavior to the trigger words implanted in those young minds by the despot's propagandists.

Self-government is in inverse ratio to numbers. The larger the constituency, the less the value of any particular vote. When he is merely one of millions, the individual elector feels himself to be impotent, a neglibigle quantity. The candidates he has voted into office are far away, at the top of the pyramid of power. Theoretically they are the servants of the people; but in fact it is the servants who give orders and the people, far off at the base of the great pyramid, who must obey. Increasing population and advancing technology have resulted in an increase in the number and complexity of organizations, an increase in the amount of power concentrated in the hands of officials and a corresponding decrease in the amount of control exercised by electors, coupled with a decrease in the public's regard for democratic procedures. Already weakened by the vast impersonal forces at work in the modern world, democratic institititions are now being undermined from within by the politicians and their propagandists.

Human beings act in a great variety of irrational ways, but all of them seem to be capable, if given a fair chance, of making a reasonable choice in the light of available evidence. Democratic institutions can be made to work only if all concerned do their best to impart knowledge and to encourage rationality. But today, in the world's most powerful democracy, the politicians and their propagandists prefer to make nonsense of democratic procedures by appealing almost exclusively to the ignorance and irrationality of the electors. "Both parties," we were told in 1956 by the editor of a leading business journal, "will merchandise their candidates and issues by the same methods that business has developed to sell goods. These include scientific selection of appeals and planned repetiton. . . . Radio spot announcements and ads will repeat phrases with a planned intensity. Billboards will push slogans of proven power. . . . Candidates need, in addition to rich voices and good diction, to be able to look 'sincerely' at the TV camera."

The political merchandisers appeal only to the weaknesses of voters, never to their potential strength. They make no attempt to educate the masses into becoming fit for self-government; they are content merely to manipulate and exploit them. For this purpose all the resources of psychology and the social sciences are mobilized and set to work. Carefully selected samples of the electorate are given "interviews in depth." These interviews in depth reveal the unconscious fears and wishes most prevalent in a given society at the time of an election. Phrases and images aimed at allaying or, if necessary, enhancing these fears, at satisfying these wishes, at least symbolically, are then chosen by the experts, tried out on readers and audiences, changed or improved in the light of the information thus obtained. After which the political campaign is ready for the mass communicators. All that is now needed is money and a candidate who can be coached to look "sincere." Under the new dispensation, political principles and plans for specific action have come to lose most of their importance. The personality of the candidate and the way he is projected by the advertising experts are the things that really matter.

In one way or another, as vigorous he-man or kindly father, the candidate must be glamorous. He must also be an entainer who never bores his audience. Inured to television and radio, that audience is accustomed to being distracted and does not like to be asked to concentrate or make a prolonged intellectual effort. All speeches by the entertainer-candidate must therefore be short and snappy. The great issues of the day must be dealt with in five minutes at the most—and preferably (since the audience will be eager to pass on to something a little livelier than inflation or the H-bomb) in sixty seconds flat. The nature of oratory is such that there has always been a tendency among politicians and clergymen to over-simplify complex issues. From a pulpit or a platform even the most conscientious of speakers finds it very difficult to tell the whole truth. The methods now being used to merchandise the political candidate as though he were a deodorant positively guarantee the electorate against ever hearing the truth about anything.

18

Reaction Patterns to Severe Chronic Stress in American Prisoners of War of the Chinese

Edgar H. Schein

In this paper I will outline some of the constellations of stress which prisoners of war faced during the Korean conflict, and describe some of the reaction patterns to these stresses. Rather than presenting a complete catalogue of their experiences (3), I have selected those aspects which seem to me to throw some light on the problem of collaboration with the enemy. I will give particular emphasis to the *social* psychological factors, because the Chinese approach to treatment of prisoners seemed to emphasize control over groups, rather than individuals.

My material is based on a variety of sources. I was in Korea during the repatriation, and had the opportunity to interview extensively twenty unselected repatriates. This basic material was supplemented by the information gathered by three psychiatrists, Drs. Harvey Strassman, Patrick Israel, and Clinton Tempereau, who together had seen some 300 men. On board ship returning to the United States, I also had the opportunity to sit in on bull sessions among repatriates in which many of the prison experiences were discussed. Additional details were obtained from the army dossiers on the men.

The typical experience of the prisoner of war must be divided into two broad phases. The first phase lasted anywhere from one to six months, beginning with capture, followed by exhausting marches to the north of Korea and severe privation in inadequately equipped temporary camps, terminating in assignment to a permanent prisoner of war camp.

The second phase, lasting two or more years, was marked by chronic pressures to collaborate and to give up existing group loyalties in favor of new ones. Thus, while physical stresses had been outstanding in the first six months, psychological stresses were outstanding in this second period.

The reactions of the men toward capture were influenced by their over-all attitude toward the Korean situation. Many of them felt inadequately prepared, both physically and psychologically. The physical training, equipment, and rotation system all came in for retrospective criticism, though this response might have

Reprinted from the *Journal of Social Issues*, Vol. 13, No. 3 (Washington, D.C.: The Society for the Psychological Study of Social Issues, 1957), pp. 21–30, by permission of the publisher.

been merely a rationalization for being captured. When the Chinese entered the war, they penetrated into rear areas, where they captured many men who were taken completely by surprise. The men felt that when positions were overrun, their leadership was often less than adequate. Thus, many men were disposed to blame the UN command for the unfortunate event of being captured.

On the psychological side, the men were not clearly aware of what they were fighting for or what kind of enemy they were opposing. In addition, the reports of the atrocities committed by the North Koreans led most men to expect death, torture, or nonrepatriation if captured.

It was in such a context that the soldier found his Chinese captor extending his hand in a friendly gesture and saying "Welcome" or "Congratulations, you've been *liberated*." This Chinese tactic was part of their "lenient policy" which was explained to groups of prisoners shortly after capture in these terms: because the UN had entered the war illegally and was an aggressor, all UN military personnel were in fact war criminals, and *could* be shot summarily. But the average soldier was, after all, only carrying out orders for his leaders who were the real criminals. Therefore, the Chinese soldier would consider the POW a "student," and would teach him the "truth" about the war. Anyone who did not cooperate by going to school and by learning voluntarily could be reverted to his "war criminal" status and shot, particularly if a confession of "criminal" deeds could not be obtained from him.

In the weeks following capture, the men were collected in large groups and marched north. From a physical point of view, the stresses during these marches were very severe: there was no medicine for the wounded, the food was unpalatable and insufficient, especially by our standards, clothing was scarce in the face of severe winter weather, and shelter was inadequate and overcrowded. The Chinese set a severe pace and showed little consideration for weariness that was the product of wounds, diarrhea, and frostbite. Men who were not able to keep up were abandoned unless they were helped by their fellows. The men marched only at night and were kept under cover during the day, ostensibly as protection against strafing by our own planes.

From a psychological point of view, this situation is best described as a recurring cycle of fear, relief, and new fear. The men were afraid that they might die, that they might never be repatriated, that they might never again have a chance to communicate with the outside, and that no one even knew they were alive. The Chinese, on the other hand, were reassuring and promised that the men would be repatriated soon, that conditions would improve, and that they would soon be permitted to communicate with the outside.

One of the chief problems for the men was the disorganization within the group itself. It was difficult to maintain close group ties if one was competing with others for the essentials of life, and if one spent one's resting time in overcrowded huts among others who had severe diarrhea and were occasionally incontinent. Lines of authority often broke down, and with this, group cohesion and morale suffered. A few men attempted to escape, but they were usually recaptured in a short time and returned to the group. The Chinese also fostered low morale and the feeling of being abandoned by systematically reporting false news about United Nations defeats and losses.

In this situation, goals became increasingly short-run. As long as the men were marching, they had something to do and could look forward to relief from the harsh conditions of the march. However, arrival at a temporary camp was usually a severe disappointment. Not only were physical conditions as bad as ever, but the sedentary life in overcrowded quarters produced more disease and still lower morale.

What happened to the men under these conditions? During the one- to two-week marches, they became increasingly apathetic (4). They developed a slow, plodding gait, called by one man a "prisoners' shuffle." Uppermost in their minds were fantasies of food: men remembered all the good meals they had ever had, or planned detailed menus for years into the future. To a lesser extent, they thought of loved ones at home, and about cars which seemed to them to symbolize freedom and the return home.

In the temporary camps, disease and exposure took a heavy toll in lives. But it was the feeling of many men, including some of the doctors who survived the experience, that some of these deaths were not warranted by a man's physical condition. Instead, what appeared to happen was that some men became so apathetic that they ceased to care about their bodily needs. They retreated further into themselves, refused to eat even what little food was available, refused to get any exercise, and eventually lay down as if waiting to die. The reports were emphatic concerning the lucidity and sanity of these men. They seemed willing to accept the prospect of death rather than to continue fighting a severely frustrating and depriving environment.

Two things seemed to save a man who was close to such "apathy" death: getting him on his feet and doing something, no matter how trivial, or getting him angry or concerned about some present or future problem. Usually it was the effort of a friend who maternally and insistently motivated the individual toward realistic goals which snapped him out of such a state of resignation. In one case such "therapy" consisted of kicking the man until he was mad enough to get up and fight.

Throughout this time, the Chinese played the role of the benevolent but handicapped captor. Prisoners were always reminded that it was their own air force bombing which was responsible for the inadequate supplies. Furthermore, they were reminded that they were getting treatment which was just as good as that which the average Chinese was getting. One important effect of this was that a man could never give *full* vent to his hostility toward the Chinese, even in fantasy. In their manner and words they were usually solicitous and sympathetic. The Chinese also implied that conditions could be better for a prisoner if he would take a more "cooperative" attitude, if he would support their propaganda for peace. Thus a man was made to feel that he was himself responsible for his traumatic circumstances.

Arrival at a permanent camp usually brought relief from many of these physical hardships. Food, shelter, and medicine, while not plentiful, appeared to be sufficient for the maintenance of life and some degree of health. However, the Chinese now increased sharply their efforts to involve prisoners in their own propaganda program, and to undermine loyalties to their country. This marks the beginning of the second phase of the imprisonment experience.

The Chinese program of subversion and indoctrination was thoroughly integrated into the entire camp routine and involved the manipulation of the entire social milieu of the prison camp. Its aims appeared to be to manage a large group of prisoners with a minimum staff of guards, to indoctrinate them with the Communist political ideology, to interrogate them to obtain intelligence information and confessions for propaganda purposes, and to develop a corps of collaborators within the prisoner group. What success the Chinese had stemmed from their *total* control of the environment, not from the application of any one technique.

The most significant feature of Chinese prisoner camp control was the systematic destruction of the prisoners' formal and informal group structure. Soon after arrival at a camp, the men were segregated by race, nationality, and rank. The Chinese put their own men in charge of the platoons and companies, and made arbitrary selections of POW squad leaders to remind the prisoners that their old rank system no longer had any validity. In addition, the Chinese attempted to undermine *informal* group structure by prohibiting any kind of group meeting, and by systematically fomenting mutual distrust by playing men off against one another. The most effective device to this end was the practice of obtaining from informers or Chinese spies detailed information about someone's activities, no matter how trivial, then calling him in to interrogate him about it. Such detailed surveillance of the men's activities made them feel that their own ranks were so infiltrated by spies and informers that it was not safe to trust anyone.

A similar device was used to obtain information during interrogation. After a man had resisted giving information for hours or days, he would be shown a signed statement by one of his fellow prisoners giving that same information. Still another device was to make prisoners who had not collaborated look like collaborators, by bestowing special favors upon them.

A particularly successful Chinese technique was their use of testimonials from other prisoners, such as the false germ-warfare confessions, and appeals based on familiar contexts, such as peace appeals. Confessions by prisoners or propaganda lectures given by collaborators had a particularly demoralizing effect, because only if resistance had been *unanimous* could a man solidly believe that his values were correct, even if he could not defend them logically.

If the men, in spite of their state of social disorganization, did manage to organize any kind of group activity, the Chinese would quickly break up the group by removing its leaders or key members and assigning them to another camp.

Loyalties to home and country were undermined by the systematic manipulation of mail. Usually only mail which carried bad news was delivered. If a man received no mail at all, the Chinese suggested that his loved ones had abandoned him.

Feelings of social isolation were increased by the complete information control maintained in the camps. Only the Communist press, radio, magazines, and movies were allowed.

The weakening of the prisoner group's social structure is particularly significant because we depend to such an extent on consensual validation in judging ourselves and others. The prisoners lost their most important sources of information and support concerning standards of behavior and beliefs. Often men who attempted to resist the Chinese by means other than *outright* obstruction or aggression failed to obtain the active support of others, often earning their suspicion instead.

At the same time, the Chinese did create a situation in which meaningful social relationships could be had through common political activity, such as the "peace" committees which served as propaganda organs. The Chinese interrogators or instructors sometimes lived with prisoners for long periods of time in order to establish close personal relationships with them.

The Communist doctrines were presented through compulsory lectures followed by compulsory group discussions, for the purpose of justifying the conclusions given at the end of the lectures. On the whole, this phase of indoctrination was ineffective because of the crudeness of the propaganda material used in the lectures. However, its constant repetition seemed eventually to influence those men who did not have well-formed political opinions to start with, particularly because no counterarguments could be heard. The group discussions were effective only if their monitor was someone who could keep control over the group and keep it on the topic of discussion. Attempts by the Chinese to use "progressive" POW's in the role of monitors were seldom successful because they aroused too much hostility in the men.

The Chinese also attempted to get prisoners to use mutual criticism and self-criticism in the fashion in which it is used within China.(2) Whenever a POW was caught breaking one of the innumerable camp rules, he was required to give an elaborate confession and self-criticism, no matter how trivial the offense. In general, the POW's were able to use this opportunity to ridicule the Chinese by taking advantage of their lack of understanding of slang and American idiom. They would emphasize the wrong parts of sentences or insert words and phrases which made it apparent to other prisoners that the joke was on the Chinese. Often men were required to make these confessions in front of large groups of other prisoners. If the man could successfully communicate by a linguistic device his lack of sincerity, this ritual could backfire on the Chinese by giving the men an opportunity to express their solidarity (by sharing a communication which could not be understood by the Chinese). However, in other instances, prisoners who viewed such public confessions felt contempt for the confessor and felt their own group was being undermined still further by such public humiliation.

Various tales of how prisoners resisted the pressures put on them have been widely circulated in the press. For example, a number of prisoners ridiculed the Chinese by playing baseball with a basketball, yet telling the Chinese this was the correct way to play the game. Such stories suggest that morale and group solidarity was actually quite high in the camps. Our interviews with the men suggest that morale climbed sharply during the last *six* to *nine months* of imprisonment when the armistice talks were underway, when the compulsory indoctrination program had been put on a voluntary basis, and when the Chinese were improving camp conditions in anticipation of the repatriation. However, we heard practically no stories of successful group resistance or high morale from the first year or so in the camps when the indoctrination program was seriously pursued by the Chinese. (At that time the men had neither the time nor the opportunity to play any kind of games because all their time was spent on indoctrination activities or exhausting labor.)

Throughout, the Chinese created an environment in which rewards such as extra food, medicine, special privileges, and status were given for cooperation and collaboration, while threats of death, nonrepatriation, reprisal against family, torture, decreases in food and medicine, and imprisonment served to keep men from offering much resistance. Only imprisonment was consistently used as an actual punishment. *Chronic* resistance was usually handled by transferring the prisoner to a so-called "reactionary" camp.

Whatever behavior the Chinese attempted to elicit, they always *paced* their demands very carefully, they always required some level of *participation* from the prisoner, no matter how trivial, and they *repeated* endlessly.

To what extent did these pressures produce either changes in beliefs and attitudes, or collaboration? Close observation of the repatriates and the reports of the men themselves suggest that the Chinese did not have much success in changing beliefs and attitudes. Doubt and confusion were created in many prisoners as a result of having to examine so closely their own way of thinking, but very few changes, if any, occurred that resembled actual *conversion* to Communism. The type of prisoner who was most likely to become *sympathetic* toward Communism was the one who had chronically occupied a low status position in this society, and for whom the democratic principles were not very salient or meaningful.

In producing collaboration, however, the Chinese were far more effective. By collaboration I mean such activities as giving lectures for the Communists, writing and broadcasting propaganda, giving false confessions, writing and signing petitions, informing on fellow POW's and so on; none of these activities required a personal change of belief. Some 10 to 15 per cent of the men chronically collaborated, but the dynamics of this response are very complex. By far the greatest determinant was the amount of pressure the Chinese put on a particular prisoner. Beyond this, the reports of the men permit one to isolate several sets of motives that operated, though it is impossible to tell how many cases of each type there may have been.

1. Some men collaborated for outright opportunistic reasons; these men lacked any kind of stable group identification, and exploited the situation for its material benefits without any regard for the consequences to themselves, their fellow prisoners, or their country.

2. Some men collaborated because their egos were too weak to withstand the physical and psychological rigors; these men were primarily motivated by fear, though they often rationalized their behavior; they were unable to resist any kind of authority figure, and could be blackmailed by the Chinese once they had begun to collaborate.

3. Some men collaborated with the firm conviction that they were infiltrating the Chinese ranks and obtaining intelligence information which would be useful to the UN forces. This was a convenient rationalization for anyone who could not withstand the pressures. Many of these men were initially tricked into collaboration or were motivated by a desire to communicate with the outside world. None of these men became ideologically confused; what Communist beliefs they might have professed were for the benefit of the Chinese only.

4. The prisoner who was vulnerable to the ideological appeal because of his low status in this society often collaborated with the conviction that he was doing the right thing in supporting the Communist peace movement. This group included the younger and less intelligent men from backward or rural areas, the malcontents, and members of various minority groups. These men often viewed themselves as failures in our society, and felt that society had never given them a chance. They were positively attracted by the immediate status and privileges which went with being a "progressive," and by the promise of important roles which they could presumably play in the peace movement of the future.

Perhaps the most important thing to note about collaboration is the manner in which the social disorganization contributed to it. A man might make a slanted radio broadcast in order to communicate with the outside, he might start reading Communist literature out of sheer boredom, he might give information which he knew the Chinese already had, and so on. Once this happened, however, the Chinese rewarded him, increased pressure on him to collaborate, and blackmailed him by threatening exposure. At the same time, in most cases, his fellow prisoners forced him into further collaboration by mistrusting him and ostracizing him. Thus a man had to stand entirely on his own judgment and strength, and both of these often failed. One of the most common failures was a man's lack of awareness concerning the effects of his own actions on the other prisoners, and the value of these actions for the Chinese propaganda effort. The man who confessed to germ warfare, thinking he could repudiate such a confession later, did not realize its immediate propaganda value to the Communists.

A certain percentage of men, though the exact number is difficult to estimate, exhibited chronic resistance and obstructionism toward Chinese indoctrination efforts. Many of these men were well integrated with secure, stable group identifications who could withstand the social isolation and still exercise good judgment. Others were chronic obstructionists whose histories showed recurring resistance to any form of authority. Still others were idealists or martyrs to religious and ethical principles, and still others were anxious, guilt-ridden individuals who could only cope with their own strong impulses to collaborate by denying them and over-reacting in the other direction.

By far the largest group of prisoners, however, established a complex compromise between the demands of the Chinese and their own value system. This adjustment, called by the men "playing it cool," consisted primarily of a physical and emotional withdrawal from the whole environment. These men learned to suspend their feelings and to adopt an attitude of watching and waiting, rather than hoping and planning. This reaction, though passive, was not as severe as the apathy described earlier. It was a difficult adjustment to maintain because some concessions had to be made to the Chinese in the form of trivial or well-timed collaborative acts, and in the form of a feigned interest in the indoctrination program. At the same time, each man had to be prepared to deal with the hostility of his buddies if he made an error in judgment.

Discussion

This paper has placed particular emphasis on the social psychological factors involved in "brainwashing" because it is my opinion that the process is primarily concerned with social forces, not with the strengths and weaknesses of individual minds. It has often been asserted that drugs, hypnotic techniques, refined "mental tortures" and, more recently, implanted electrodes can make the task of the "brainwasher" much easier by rendering the human mind submissive with a minimum of effort. There is little question that such techniques can be used to elicit confessions or signatures on documents prepared by the captor; but so can withdrawal of food, water, or air produce the same results. The point is that the Chinese Communists do not appear to be interested in obtaining merely a confession or *transient* submission. Instead, they appear to be interested in producing changes in men which will be lasting and self-sustaining. A germ-warfare confession alone is not enough—the POW had to "testify" before an international commission explaining in detail how the bombs had been dropped, and had to tell his story in other prison camps to his fellow POW's.

There is little evidence that drugs, posthypnotic suggestion, or implanted electrodes can now or ever will be able to produce the kind of behavior exhibited by many prisoners who collaborated and made false confessions. On the other hand, there is increasing evidence (1, 2) that Russian and Chinese interrogation and indoctrination techniques involve the destruction of the persons's social ties and identifications, and the partial destruction of his ego. If this is successfully accomplished, the person is offered a new identity for himself and given the opportunity to identify with new groups. What physical torture and deprivation are involved in this process may be either a calculated attempt to degrade and humiliate a man to destroy his image of himself as a dignified human being, or the product of fortuitous circumstances, *i.e.*, failure of supply lines to the prison, loss of temper on the part of the interrogator, an attempt to inspire fear in other prisoners by torturing one of them and so on. We do not have sufficient evidence to determine which of these alternatives represents Communist intentions; possibly all of them are involved in the actual prison situation.

Ultimately that which sustains humans is their personality integration born out of secure and stable group identifications. One may be able to produce temporary submission by direct intervention in cortical processes, but only by destroying a man's self-image and his group supports can one produce any lasting changes in his beliefs and attitudes. By concerning ourselves with the problem of artificially creating submission in man, we run the real risk of overlooking the fact that we are in a genuine struggle of ideas with other portions of the world and that man often submits himself directly to ideas and principles.

To understand and combat "brainwashing" we must look at those social conditions which make people ready to accept new ideas from anyone who states them clearly and forcefully, and those social conditions which give people the sense of integrity which will sustain them when their immediate and social and emotional supports are stripped away.

REFERENCES

1. Hinkle, Lawrence E. and Wolff, Harold C. Communist Interrogation and Indoctrination of "Enemies of the State." *Archives of Neurology and Psychiatry,* 1956, *76*, 115–174.
2. Lifton, Robert L. "Thought Reform" of Western Civilians in Chinese Communist Prisons. *Psychiatry*, 1956, *19*, 173–198.
3. Schein, Edgar H. The Chinese Indoctrination Program for Prisoners of War. *Psychiatry*, 1956, *19*, 149–172.
4. Strassman, Harvey D., Thaler, Margaret, and Schein, Edgar H. A Prisoner of War Syndrome: Apathy as a Reaction to Severe Stress. *American Journal of Psychiatry*, 1956, *112*, 998–1003.

19

Thought Reform of Chinese Intellectuals

Robert J. Lifton

The Chinese Communist program of *Szu Hsiang Kai Tsao* or "thought reform" is unique both as a social experiment and as a laboratory for cross-cultural psychiatric study. Applied to Westerners and Chinese, to professors, students, and peasants, it combines a remarkably widespread dissemination with impressive emotional force and depth.

It is a subject which has received much attention in this country (under the popular term "brainwashing") when involving such groups as American prisoners of war and other incarcerated Westerners. But there

From Robert J. Lifton, "Thought Reform of Chinese Intellectuals: A Psychiatric Evaluation," *The Journal of Asian Studies,* Vol. 16, No. 1 (November 1956), pp. 75–88. Copyright by the Association for Asian Studies, Inc., reprinted with permission.

has been surprisingly little systematic psychological investigation of the thought reform procedures which the Chinese have employed with their own people, particularly with their intellectuals.

The most intensive of these all-Chinese thought reform programs for intellectuals is that conducted in the "revolutionary-colleges"—set up all over China immediately after the Communist takeover. These were particularly active between 1948 and 1952, when they represented an ideological hard core for the entire thought reform movement, an extreme model for reform efforts throughout the population. Their techniques—which I will here attempt to describe and interpret—can give us a key to the understanding of all Chinese thought reform programs, whether applied to Chinese intellectuals, United Nations prisoners of war, or Western missionaries. . . .

Who attends a revolutionary college? Students are drawn from many divergent sources: former KMT officials and affiliates, teachers who had been associated with the old regime, Communist cadres who had demonstrated significant "errors" in their work or thoughts, party members who had spent long periods of time in KMT areas, students returning from the West, and finally, arbitrarily selected groups of university instructors or recent graduates. Many in these groups came in response to thinly veiled coercion—the strong "suggestion" that they attend; but others actively sought admission on a voluntary basis, in order to try to fit in with the requirements of the new regime, or at least to find out what was expected of them.

The college itself is tightly organized along Communist principles of "democratic centralism." One center may contain as many as 4,000 students, subdivided into sections of about 1,000 each, then classes of 100–200 each, and finally into six to ten man groups. The president of the institution may be a well known scholar serving as a figurehead; technically below him in rank are a vice-president and the section heads, who are likely to be Communist Party members, and exert the real authority at the center. Under their supervision are the class heads, each of whom works with three special cadres.

These cadres, usually long-standing and dedicated party workers, play a central role in the thought reform process; they are the connecting link between the faculty and the students, and it is they who perform the day-to-day leg work of the reform process. The three cadres of each class may be designated according to function: the executive cadre, concerned essentially with courses of study; the organizing cadre, most intimately involved with the structure and function of the small group and the attitudes of the individual students who make them up; and the advisory cadre—the only one of the three who may be a woman—offering counsel on personal and ideological problems which come up during this arduous experience.

I have divided the six-month reform course into three stages, which represent the successive psychological climates to which the student is exposed as he is guided along the path of his symbolic death and rebirth: The Great Togetherness, The Closing in of the Milieu, and Submission and Rebirth.

The Great Togetherness: Group Identification

New students approach the course with a varying mixture of curiosity, enthusiasm, and apprehension. When a group of them arrives, their first impression is likely to be a favorable one. They encounter an atmosphere which is austere, but friendly—an open area of low-slung wooden buildings (frequently converted from military barracks) which serve as living quarters and class rooms—old students and cadres greeting them warmly, showing them around, speaking glowingly of the virtues of the Revolutionary College, of the Communist movement, of the new hope for the future. Then, after a warm welcoming speech from the president of the college, they are organized into ten-man study groups. And for a period of from a few days to two weeks they are told to "just get to know each other."

Students are surprised by this free and enthusiastic atmosphere; some among the older ones may remain wary, but most are caught up in a feeling of camaraderie. Within the small groups they vent their widely-shared hostility towards the old regime—an important stimulus to the thought reform process. There is a frank exchange of feeling and ideas, past and present, as they discuss their background experiences, and hopes and fears for the future. There is an air of optimism, a feeling of being in the same boat, a high *esprit de corps.*

Next, through a series of "thought mobilization" lectures and discussions, the philosophy and rationale of the program are impressed upon the individual student: the "old society" was evil and corrupt; this was so because it was dominated by the "exploiting classes"—the landowners and the bourgeoisie; most intellectuals come from these "exploiting classes" (or from the closely related petit-bourgeoisie) and therefore retain "evil remnants" of their origins and of the old regime; each must now rid himself of these "ideological poisons" in order to become a "new man" in the "new society." In this way, he is told, the "ideology of all classes" can be brought into harmony with "objective material conditions." Mao Tse-tung is frequently quoted in his references to "diseases in thought and politics" which require "an attitude of "saving men by curing their diseases'."

At this time, and throughout the program, *thought reform is presented to the student as a morally uplifting, harmonizing, and therapeutic experience.*

Then the formal courses begin—the first usually entitled The History of the Development of Society (to be later followed by Lenin on the State and Materialistic Dialectics, History of the Chinese Revolution, Theory of the New Democracy, and Field Study—visits to old Communist workshops and industrial centers). The subject matter is introduced by a two to six hour lecture delivered by a leading Communist theorist. This is followed by the interminable *hsueh hsi* or study sessions within the ten-man group, where the real work of thought reform takes place. Discussion of the lecture material is led by the group leader who has been elected by its membrs—usually because of his superior knowledge of Marxism. At this point he encourages a spirited exchange of all views, and takes no side when there is disagreement. The other students realize that the group leader is making daily reports to a cadre or to the class head, but the full significance of these is not yet appreciated; they may be viewed as simply a necessary organizational procedure. Most students retain a feeling of pulling together toward a common goal in a group crusading spirit.

The Closing-in of the Milieu: The Period of Emotional Conflict

About four to six weeks from the beginning of thought reform—at about the time of the completion of the first course—a change begins to develop in the atmosphere. With the submission of the first "thought summary" (these must be prepared after each course) there is a shift in emphasis from the intellectual and ideological to the personal and the emotional. The student begins to find that he, rather than the Communist doctrine, is the object of study. A pattern of criticism, self-criticism, and confession develops—pursued with increasing intensity throughout the remainder of the course.

Now the group leader is no longer "neutral"; acting upon instructions from above, he begins to "lean to one side," to support the "progressive elements," to apply stronger pressures in the direction of reform. He and the "activists" who begin to emerge take the lead in setting the tone for the group. The descriptions of past and present attitudes which the student so freely gave during the first two weeks of the course now come back to haunt him. Not only his ideas, but his underlying motivations are carefully scrutinized. Failure to achive the correct "materialistic viewpoint," "proletarian standpoint," and "dialectical methodology" is pointed out, and the causes for this deficiency are carefuly analyzed.

Criticisms cover every phase of past and present thought and behavior; they not only "nip in the bud" the slightest show of unorthodoxy or non-conformity, but they also point up "false progressives"—students who outwardly express the "correct" views without true depth of feeling. Group members are constantly on the lookout for indications in others of lack of real involvement in the process. Each must demonstrate the genuineness of his reform through continuous personal enthusiasm and active participation in the criticism of his fellow students. In this way he can avoid being rebuked for "failure to combine theory with practice."

Standard criticisms repeatedly driven home include: "individualism"—placing personal interests above those of "the people"—probably the most emphasized of all; "subjectivism"—applying a personal viewpoint to a problem rather than a "scientific" Marxist approach; "objectivism"—undue detachment, viewing oneself "above class distinction," or "posing as a spectator of the new China"; "sentimentalism"—allowing one's attachment to family or friends to interfere with reform needs, therefore "carrying about an ideological burden" (usually associated with reluctance to denounce family members or friends allegedly associated with the "exploiting classes.") And in addition: "deviationism," "opportunism," "dogmatism," "reflecting exploiting class ideology," "overly technical viewpoint," "bureaucratism," "individual heroism," "revisionism," "departmentalism," "sectarianism," "idealism," and "pro-American outlook."

The student is required to accept these criticisms gratefully when they are offered. But more than this, he is expected both to anticipate and expand upon them through the even more important device of *self-criticism.* He must correctly analyze his own thoughts and actions, and review his past life—family, educational, and social—in order to uncover the source of his difficulties. And the resulting insights are always expressed within the Communist jargon—corrupt "ruling class" and "bourgeois" influence, derived from his specific class origin.

The criticism and self-criticism process is also extended into every aspect of daily life, always with a highly moralistic tone. Under attack here are the "bourgeois" or "ruling class" characteristics of pride, conceit, greed, competitiveness, dishonesty, boastfulness, and rudeness. Relationships with the opposite sex are discussed and evaluated, solely in terms of their effects upon the individual's progress in reform. Where a "backward" girl friend is thought to be impeding his progress, a student may be advised to break off a liasion; but if both are "progressive," or if one is thought to be aiding the other's progress, the relationship will be condoned. Sexual contacts are, on the whole, discouraged, as it is felt that they drain energies from the thought reform process.

The student must, within the small group, *confess* all the evils of his past life. Political and moral considerations here become inextricably merged; but especially emphasized are any "reactionary" affiliations with the old regime or with its student organizations. Each student develops a running confession, supplemented by material from his self-criticisms and "thought summaries"; its content becomes widely known to students. Some, recalling either stories they have heard or personal experiences, find revived in their minds images of the extreme measures used by the Communists in dealing with their enemies. All are extremely fearful of the consequences of being considered a "reactionary."

Students who show signs of emotional disturbance are encouraged to seek help by talking over their "thought problem" with the advisory cadre, in order to resolve whatever conflicts exist. Many experience psychosomatic expressions of their problems—fatigue, insomnia, loss of appetite, vague aches and pains, or gastro-intestinal symptoms. Should they take their complaints to the college doctor, they are apt to encounter a reform-oriented and psychologically-sophisticated reply: "There is nothing wrong with your body. It must be your thoughts that are sick. You will feel better when you have solved your problems and completed your reform." And indeed, most students are in a state of painful inner tension; relief is badly needed.

Submission and "Rebirth"

The last stage—that of the over-all thought summary or final confession—supplies each student with a means of resolving his conflicts. It is ushered in by a mass meeting at which high Communist officials and faculty members emphasize the importance of the final thought summary as the crystallization of the entire course. Group sessions over the next two or three days are devoted exclusively to discussions of the form this summary is to take. It is to be a life history, beginning two generations back, and extending through the reform experience. It must, with candor and thoroughness, describe the historical development of one's thoughts, and the relationship of these to actions. It is also to include a detailed analysis of the personal effects of thought reform.

The summary may be from five to twenty-five thousand Chinese characters (roughly equivalent numerically to English words) and require about ten days of preparation. Each student then must read his summary to the group, where it is subjected to more prolonged and penetrating criticism. He may be kept under fire for several days of detailed discussion and painful revision—as every group member is considered responsible for the approval of each confession presented, and all may even have to place their signatures upon it.

The confession is the student's final opportunity to bring out anything he has previously held back, as well as to elaborate upon everything he has already said. It always includes a detailed analysis of class origin. And in almost every case its central feature is the denunciation of the father—both as a symbol of the exploiting classes, and as an individual. The student finds the recitation of his father's personal, political, and economic abuses to be the most painful part of his entire thought reform. He may require endless prodding, persuasion, and indirect threats before he is able to take this crucial step. But he has little choice, and he almost invariably complies.

The confession ends with an emphasis on personal liabilities which still remain, attitudes in need of further reform—and the solemn resolve to continue attempts at self-improvement, and to devotedly serve the regime in the future. When his confession is approved, the student experiences great emotional relief. He has weathered the thought reform ordeal, renounced his past, and established an organic bond between himself and the government. His confession will accompany him throughout his future career as a permanent part of his personal record.

It is no wonder that this period of the final thought summary is frequently referred to as "taking a bath." It is the symbolic submission to the regime, and at the same time the expression of individual rebirth into the Chinese Communist community. . . .

Viewed in its broadest perspective, thought reform represents an exaggerated expression of human emotions and psychological forces that are universal in nature. In its extreme character, it sets off in high relief things which cannot ordinarily be seen as clearly. It conveys to us valuable insights—of both an ethical and psychological variety.

It is, first of all, replete with important psychiatric data—concerning such issues as guilt, shame, and confession, change in identity and belief, relations between language and theory, the effects of group pressures, and techniques for controlling the environment. All of this may add to our knowledge of human emotions, and has great relevance to psychiatric illness and to treatment methods. Equally important is the manner in which thought reform gives us a test tube demonstration of the total manipulation of the human being, and a vantage point for further insights into Communist practices.

Thought reform also highlights the dilemma which we face in our own political cultural, and educational institutions. Every society makes use of similar pressures of guilt, shame, and confession, and of milieu control, as means of maintaining its values and its organization. We must ask ourselves where we—inadvertently, and in less extreme form—could also be applying these in excess, to mould uniform identities, and to make men think and act in the conforming fashion. We are confronted with the problem of any democratic society—that of maintaining a balance which limits these forces sufficiently to allow its people a sense of individual freedom, creativity, and human dignity.

SECTION B *Perspectives on Education*

The previous section emphasized educational techniques and their effects. It is equally important to come to terms with some of the implications and limitations of education itself, irrespective of the process or procedure.

To be alive is to have a capacity for learning. What should be learned is a major question. Instinct, useful at first, appears less and less valuable beyond the first few years of life. The infant stretching and twisting his muscles is teaching himself skills that will be needed when he begins to sit, stand, and walk. He does not understand the purpose of his motor activity, only that there is an inner urge to develop certain muscles. Such inner urges are given little attention in the scale of educational values.

Walter Goldschmidt surveys the extensive nature of education stretching far beyond the formal confines of schools and books. Richard M. Jones, in his direct attack on certain kinds of education, underlines the point of view that education must eventually arise from the desires of the self. External education, at its best, consists of ways to awaken the inner learner. Willis W. Harman's piece is a still more fundamental one. He is suggesting that the state of mind in which we live and move and have our being is suspect. This state of mind is probably limited and certainly tends to deny, repress, and obfuscate whole areas of experience that might profoundly affect our capacity and direction for education.

To our knowledge of education, social science can add an awareness of the ongoing process. It can shed light on the cultural assembly line, on those influences not revealed in the finished product.

20

Education in Every Culture

Walter Goldschmidt

Education is crucial to the cultural mode of life. This follows from the fact that culture is learned behavior; for if there is learning, there must be teaching. Education may be viewed as the means by which culture is passed from one person to another and, therefore, the way it continues through time.

By education we mean more than schooling. Schools are a part of our educational system, growing in importance with each succeeding year, and they are found in many other societies as well. But schools are not universal, and we shall see that for primitive man they are not necessary. What we include here under the term education is the total process by which the infant acquires the knowledge, understanding, attitudes, and orientation that are characteristic of his culture.

For the infant taken naked from his mother's womb is naked of culture as well. And all of us, however primitive or civilized we may be, have entered our culture in precisely this way. From that moment forward, the baby is surrounded by the culture into which he is born and in the course of time he acquires the knowledge, understandings, attitudes and ways of doing things of the people among whom he lives and grows up. Nothing is more important in the whole realm of anthropology than to understand the processes by which the naked infant is clad in the uniform of his culture. Only a small part of this process takes place in the schools, even in our own stage of civilization.

Anthropologists call this process enculturation, sociologists call it socialization, and both are good and useful terms. Here we have used the older and more general term education, for we want to include formal training along with the subtler informal processes of acquiring cultural values and attitudes and the indoctrination into social life.

Two sets of distinctions will help us to understand the educational process. First, we must distinguish between skills, or explicit knowledge, and the ideals, attitudes, and values. Next, we must distinguish the conscious, deliberate education of the young man from the unconscious, unwitting patterning of his behavior. By and large, skills are taught quite consciously, while values and attitudes tend to be transmitted less explicitly—though there are important exceptions.

The transmission of skills raises no particular problems. For most people of the world, skills are acquired on the job. Certainly the daily economic activity of the hunter and his wife and of the primitive farmer and her husband are acquired by the children through participating with their elders as part of their everyday life. The notion that schools should exist for the transmission of the ordinary skills—even of specialized crafts—is a quite recent innovation. One can still see in Germany the apprentice cabinetmaker traveling through the countryside in his special costume, seeking the experience that will establish his journeyman's status; in America such skills are frequently taught in schools.

In most primitive societies all adult males engage in essentially the same work; all adult females in "women's work," and every grown person knows how to do almost all of the things that everyone else of his sex knows. The child learns the skills necessary to his adult life through daily habituation. To be sure, there are some skills that not everyone shares in like degree—one man is handier at chipping flint into arrowheads and another at making traps, perhaps—and these differences in skill are recognized. The child is usually taught by a relative who is skilled. We can see this in a description of the way Yurok girls learn to make baskets:

> As a very little girl she watched the older weavers of the family. Usually she and her age mates attempted to duplicate the efforts of their elders with any kind of sticks and green grasses available. This was only playing; it resulted in nothing recognizable as a basket and no one paid any attention to it. But if the child persisted in working she was finally noticed by her elders. She could not be trusted to go on with a basket in process of construction, so her mother would start a root on discarded sticks for her. After a round or two of the child's weaving, the older woman took it from her to make a course, straightening the sticks where twining turns had been put in with uneven tension. The work alternated between them in this way until its abandonment as a diversion or its completion as a rough little bowl. . . .
>
> The child was six or seven years old when the first basket was started for her; it would be five years probably before she could begin her own baskets. In this interim she might make a dipper which is always plain, or possibly an acorn soup basket with simple grass overlay pattern, or a small trinket basket in which twining elements regularly progress over two sticks at a time. . . .
>
> Old weavers still laugh at memories of their first baskets. Some were so sharp at the bottom they could only be hung up, surfaces were fluted from the insertion of too many sticks, and dippers were so loosely woven that they could not be swollen sufficiently to hold water. Yet between a girl's first efforts and her results which had value for use or exchange, a young weaver learned certain of the established requirements. She had gathered and dried materials for the old people of her family who could not get to the patches themselves, and was commended or criticized for quality; she was taught to set an acorn basket on the ground during its making to watch its shape and proportions—features every beginner must know, and she did considerable ripping out of work in order to make the neccessary corrections. . . .
>
> Grown women will refer to their training with pride. If one's mother or aunt was a "good hand at baskets," presumably she taught the right methods which would never have to be relearned.*

Not all skills are acquired through direct teaching. People learn to use their muscles by unconscious imitation of those around them (just as they unconsciously imitate the use of the muscles of the mouth in speech) so that the people of a region will tend to have the same way of walking or use similar gestures. It has been noted that the American Indian uses a knife by drawing the blade toward him, while a person of European descent whittles away from the body. Though these patterns may reflect the differences between stone and steel blades, they

* Lila M. O'Neale, "Yurok-Karok Basket Weavers." *University of California Publications in American Archaeology and Ethnology,* Volume 32, No. 1, pp. 10–11. Berkeley: University of California Press, 1932.

nevertheless are unconscious patterns of behavior and usually represent an unconscious transmission of technique. Miguel Covarrubias tells us that every Balinese child can carve, just as he can play in the gamelin orchestras. Though this may seem mysterious to us, the fact is that artistic activity is as much a part of the daily life of the Balinese as driving cars or writing is with us. Not every Balinese is equally adept, yet it is so much a part of the everyday environment that the skills are, one might say, subconsciously acquired.

Schooling as a separate aspect of life is a product of literacy—and the three R's still have a dominant part in our educational program. However, with the increased specialization of labor in modern society and with the increased need for skills on the job, specialized training plays an ever increasing part in the educational process. For centuries formal schooling, as distinct from apprentice craftsmanship, was limited to a small sector of our society and was primarily for the upper classes or for a separate learned class. Democratic institutions tended to spread literacy over the population, while the spread of literacy through the invention of printing was a factor which, in turn, furthered democratic institutions. The operation of our society depends upon widespread literacy (consider only its importance for driving a car in a modern city). But more than this, the elaborate technical apparatus of the modern economy requires a populace highly trained in thousands of different specialties. Schools are a necessary element in the skill-training of the citizen for life in today's society; they are necessary for maintaining a modern society.

Skills and the use of muscles are only a part of what every child learns. He learns also a wide range of tabus, rules, behavior patterns, myths, explanations of the world, rituals; he learns the values, attitudes and sentiments that characterize his culture. Some of these are carefully communicated to him, explicitly and directly, by his elders —frequently on ceremonial occasions. Thus, though a Hopi lad has heard many moral principles repeated, they are brought home to him at the time of his initiation through the formidable presence of spirit impersonators, the element of personal pain in whipping, and by the whole religious paraphernalia of an impressive ceremony in which he has an important role. Such ceremonial inductions into adult status are widespread, and are certainly an effective means of inculcating moral precepts.

But subtler influences are at work in communicating values and attitudes, and these are more important in the aggregate, though less dramatic than the initiatory rites. The child hears a person praised or condemned by his elders; he sees persons with prestige acting one way and those poorly thought of conducting themselves differently. In modern parlance, he finds models for behavior in his community. And in doing so, he acquires the fundamental set of his character; that is, he takes on the features approved by his culture. We can see this process at work in the essay on Plainville education.

Though universal and unconscious, the process is not automatic, and in no culture is everybody stamped precisely in one mold. Variations due to personal attributes and individual circumstances make for differences in response to such cultural forces. Yet the central tendencies are so clear that it is possible to see the characteristic temperaments not only of different tribes in different parts of the world but even between the peoples of modern nations, the members of social classes, or the populations of regions within large countries.

There are still subtler processes at work that tend to mold the character of the individual to the shape that his culture finds congenial, that make for the continuity of patterns of behavior and attitudes which the people themselves are unaware they exhibit. It is this kind of educational process that Margaret Mead is speaking of when she discusses the transmission of parental anxieties among modern middle-class Americans.

The processes here are not too well understood and are the subject of much debate. Most anthropologists interested in them have been to some extent influenced by Freudian psychology, which holds not only that the first five years of life establish the personality of the child, but also that the infant goes through a series of erotic stages (oral, anal, and genital), and that the character of his experiences at various times, and his relations with his immediate family (particularly his mother) determine the features of his personality and basic patterns of cultural attitudes. This theoretical orientation has led to an emphasis in the study of such aspects of child training as suckling, weaning, toilet training, and patterns of body contact.

There can be little doubt that the treatment of the infant and child during the first years of life is important to his subsequent behavior, whatever psychological orientation one has. We are reasonably certain that the dominant parental attitudes are unwittingly transmitted in much the same manner as are nuances of speech. If parents themselves have many fears or much suppressed hostility, if they are easygoing or phlegmatic, or if they are harsh and demand much of themselves, these feelings are communicated by the parents and taken over by the children though neither may be aware of the transmission. Indeed, where such attitudes exist as cultural norms, they are taken to be as natural to man as the need for food or sleep. Alan Lomax tells us that these elements of intimate interpersonal family life are expressed in the folksongs of a people. He believes these attitudes tend to persist for centuries, so that the music that expresses the sentiments and feelings of a population dates back, in some parts of Italy, for instance, to pre-Roman and even pre-Etruscan times.

It is the subtle and pervasive kind of cultural learning that tends to make the people from a given tribe or culture behave in somewhat consistent fashion. These consistencies have led to the anthropological study of "national character," the general features of modern countries or regions. Anyone who has traveled through Europe will recognize certain pervasive qualities in different areas; qualities which distinguish one land from its neighbors.

No one believes all Frenchman act alike; as we have said, the process is not like a stamp-machine, stamping out so many precise replicas. People vary, and in a broad set of European acquaintances one will usually know a volatile Englishman or a jolly Scot. For each person has his own individual set of educational experiences, and his own physiology as well. No population is homogeneous with respect to temperament, any more than with respect to any other trait. Yet, a Channel crossing will convince one that there is a sharp difference between the English and the French—in their bearing, in their interpersonal relationships, in the very way they eat or dress or make love. Older generations used to speak of these peoples as separate races and assumed that their characteristics were determined by inherited factors or by the climate. We now know they are differences in culture and that the different patterns of behavior are subtly learned in the process of growing up.

We must remember that the institutions by which a culture trains its children—from the mother cradling her child to the great universities teaching modern physics—are themselves all part of that culture. But they are also that part through which all parts of the culture are acquired by the oncoming generation; through which every aspect of the culture is inevitably filtered. It is this element of the teaching process that makes it so important for an understanding of culture itself. Since educational practices serve this filtering function, the manner of teaching is suited to the cultural needs.

Thus, for example, a recent analysis of the child-training practices among a variety of primitive societies showed that hunting and food-gathering peoples tend to train their children more for individualistic behavior, agriculturists and herders more for cooperative life. The authors point out that hunters need more autonomy of action and dependence upon individual initiative than do primitive farmers, who must more often operate in concert and suppress individualism.

This brings out a more general point. Some people, admiring the educational practices found in other cultures, have advocated their adoption by our own society. But a virtue in one situation is not necessarily good for another, and before the importation of other practices is undertaken, their consequences and cultural entanglements should be carefully examined. The same caution should be used when we endeavor to impose our practices on others. (This is true for all aspects of culture, but is perhaps more important in education than elsewhere.)

We do not mean to imply that each culture has an educational system perfectly and automatically adapted to its needs. In our own society there is a long-standing debate over the proper way of rearing and training children, and considerable variation from place to place and gradual shift through time. The patterns described for Plainville, for example, are quite different from those that most city children have undergone. As a matter of fact, America is quite diverse with respect to cultural background; we have only begun to forge a common culture; and there is much variation in the manner in which we rear our children, though our formal education tends to be pretty much the same all over the United States. As Mead points out, certain uniformities in child-rearing are appearing in middle-class America—tendencies brought about by the strains of middle-class life, including a strain to conformity by people of diverse cultures.

Education in sum, is the process by which both the obvious aspects of culture and its hidden minutiae are transmitted from one generation to another and thus passed on through time. It is partly a conscious and deliberate process, partly automatic or unconscious, both on the part of the teacher and the pupil. Education does not cause or create culture, for it is itself a part of culture: cultural patterns set the attitudes of education and training. Yet insofar as each of us is a piece of our own culture, the educational process to which we have been subjected has created that part in us.

21

The Role of Self-knowledge in the Educative Process

Richard M. Jones

It is becoming a cliché in psychological circles to note that normal mental processes have not had anything like the systematic scrutiny which Freud gave to their pathological counterparts in his refinements of the therapeutic arts. This paper seeks to enlist Freud in the work of refining the educative arts. It will be instructive therefore to begin with an instance of the psychonormalities of everyday life.

A radio announcer recently interrupted my reverie to say that a clarinet concerto would next be played—Benny Goodman, soloist. During approximately the next ten seconds there occurred the following: Benny Goodman? That's right, he plays concert music too. I wonder if I can tell the difference between Goodman and that English fellow, what's his name . . . can't think of it . . . anyhow I wouldn't know the difference . . . and my wife thinks I'm so adept at that kind of thing. Look at me, I can't even distinguish Goodman from . . . what *is* that name? . . . I wonder why I cultivate that illusion of hers. I suppose its because *she* knows so much about painting. . . . Still, that is phoney of me. Of course, I *might* have done all right in music. If only that Aunt of mine had been less insistent about the violin. . . . How did I ever keep from killing that woman? So what if I *had* broken a finger playing baseball? Perhaps now I'd at least be able to distinguish Goodman from . . .

With the elusive name on the tip of my tongue, and with a sense of impending recognition, I was suddenly sitting in the bleachers at Fenway Park in Boston. George Kell, then third baseman for the Red Sox, was at bat and hit a killing line drive, the trajectory of which, from his bat to a point about one inch above the wall, formed an absolutely unwavering acute angle. It was the last of the ninth and the Red Sox won by a very well-deserved inch.

George Kell . . . K-E-L-L . . . but, of course: *Reginald* Kell is that English fellow's name!

Thus was my wife's opinion of my musical ear vindicated—true, by way of a not very musical detour, but as I thought of it later, by a not very phoney one either. In other words, in ten seconds I had rediscovered that I am neither better nor worse than I am.

I offer that anecdote in illustration of what I shall mean by self-knowledge. It is not a thing; it is a process. It is not the pinnacle of experience, but no one approaches his particular pinnacles without

Richard M. Jones; "The Role of Self-knowledge in the Educative Process," *Harvard Educational Review,* 32, Spring 1962, 200–209.

it. Volumes have been written on what may have taken place during that speck of time. Alfred Adler would have been impressed with the way a picture of perfection had compensated my ruminations of *im*perfection. Charles Fisher might observe that an acute angle multiplied by two equals the letter "K." Freud, of course, would have asked me who the Good-man was that I had lost in the first place, and he would certainly have made something more of the *killings* that were made on the way from Goodman to *Kell* to *Kell*. We shall have need of more volumes before we can explain preconscious processing. We know now though that it is a very subjective process.

For the purpose at hand I want only to draw attention to a series of empirical events: a lapse of memory was followed by experiences of personal conflict, followed in turn by a pictorial image, and then by restoration of the memory lapse. Presumably, had the sequence cut out at either the conflicts or the image, the restoration would not have followed, and I would have languished in a state of relative mental disorder. I wanted to say this at the outset, because I shall later emphasize the *enhancing* effects of self-knowledge, and I don't want the reader to think that I overlook its sheer survival value.

I want next briefly to summarize an experiment, which later became a little book entitled *An Application of Psychoanalysis to Education*. The students of a preparatory school for girls could elect to take in their senior year a course called the "Self-Knowledge Workshop." The course consisted of two ordinary class periods per week, during which various traditional psychologies were offered, interspersed by one lengthy and *extra*-ordinary discussion meeting, in which anything that could be put into words was encouraged. (That is not so easy an invitation to accept as it may appear.) The course spanned an academic year and the discussion meetings were tape-recorded.[1]

Over the year there ensued, openly and articulately, a succession of emotional struggles between students and teacher, between students and students, within the students, and within the teacher. The same struggles transpire, I believe, in most classrooms, with the exception that they do so covertly in an atmosphere of what Kubie describes as the "conspiracy of silence."[2] By arranging, this one time, that the emotional tug of war, which comprises much of the educative process, should occur openly, it was possible to trace a phenomenon that psychologists are increasingly taking pains to document. I refer to the works of Erik Erikson, Lawrence Kubie, Jean Piaget, Heinz Werner, and the students of subliminal perception. The general observation is that human beings when confronted by a novel and challenging situation begin to master themselves in relation to that situation by recapitulating a telescoped version of their own life history in respect to it. Before learning to trust themselves in it, for example, they may first become untrustworthy, in order to see what happens. They may then become too trusting, like children; then too big for their britches; then doubtful; then secure; then adventurous; then ashamed. They may find a way to fall in love in the new situation, and becoming disillusioned they may then turn bitter and biting critics of it. Eventually, depending on the situation, having sunk their own roots in it, they can feel their own oats in it. At that point they have made it their own, as we say. The parameters and the rhythm of the process vary with the unit of observation. But the

[1] For the flavor of psychoanalytic education, as distinct from psychoanalytic treatment, the reader is referred to the book, where appear extensive verbatim accounts of the former: Richard M. Jones, *An Application of Psychoanalysis to Education* (Springfield, Ill.: Thomas, 1960).

[2] Lawrence S. Kubie, *Neurotic Distortion of the Creative Process* (Lawrence, Kan.: University of Kansas Press, 1958).

same recapitulative principle seems to guide human adaptation whether we take the epigenetic unit of the life cycle or the microgenetic unit of split-second perception.

Such a process—very much intensified and concentrated for the sake of observation—was recorded in the experiment. Further, an elaborate battery of psychological tests was administered to the experimental students and to two closely matched groups of control students.[3] We were therefore able to report that, insofar as these tests can measure such things, the experimental students showed a significant increase over the year in "self-acceptance," while the control subjects did not. We were also able to add in passing to the already impressive body of evidence in support of the psychodynamic theory of race prejudice: the experimental students showed a significant decrease in attitudes of ethnic intolerance, presumably as an ancillary effect of the increase in self-tolerance, since, again, the control students did not.

But this was not the whole story. An unexpected finding, which I was not prepared at the time of writing up the study to fully exploit, was the following: not only did the control students not share the positive changes with their experimental counterparts but they showed significant changes in the opposite direction. In other words, as a result of some unknown influence in their senior year of high school—and these were known as top-quality preparatory schools—they had become significantly less tolerant of themselves, a little less open to novelty, a little less adventuresome, a little less likely to seek out meaningful encounters, or to face up actively to the inevitable conflicts that make meaningful all encounters. In sum, the evidence suggested that either in spite of or because of certain external achievements, such as good grades and admission to good colleges, these students had been injured as human beings. In self-awareness, and all that that singularly human possession generates in the way of imaginative and critical living, they had less when they went out than when they came in.

I want now to marshal this sobering piece of data in support of a critical position on the educative process, which was taken by Edith Weisskopf twelve years ago.[4] Dr. Weisskopf observes that while the social science literature contains considerable information about creative thought and the conditions of its growth, educators have strangely not taken it much to heart. Dr. Weisskopf for example grants that industry, regular study habits, and a critical and controlled attitude are necessary attributes of successful intellectual work, and that those creative individuals who eventually learned the values of relaxation, irregular habits, and the periodic abandonment of criticism and control have usually spent years exercising the virtues advocated by traditional educators. "Yet," she observes, "the question remains unanswered why, among the four stages of the creative process, namely, preparation, incubation, illumination, and verification, we prepare children for the first and last stage only, and completely ignore the other two stages" (p. 188).

She suggests in conclusion one possible answer to her question:

> The process of insight and illumination appears to be directed by unconscious forces to a higher degree than the process of preparation and verification. Just as lightning represents the sudden explosive merging of positive and negative electricity,

[3] The test battery included the Berger scale for self-acceptance, the Dorriss-Levinson-Hanfmann self-reference sentence completion test, the revised Bogardus social distance scale and the social attitude battery.

[4] Edith A. Weisskopf, "Some Comments Concerning the Role of Education in the 'Creation of Creation,' " *Journal of Educational Psychology*, XLII (March, 1951), 185–189.

intellectual insight may represent the sudden merging of conscious content accumulated during the stage of preparation with unconscious material. Thus, it may be the denial of this repressed material which causes educators to deny the process of illumination. In other words, we do not want to accept the fact that intellectual activity takes part of its energy supply from the big reservoir of unacceptable impulses called the Id, that the material carefully and rationally accumulated during the period of preparation has to become imbued with Id-impulses in order to be brought to life (p. 188).

Now, in the light of Dr. Weisskopf's diagnosis, why *might* those students have left good secondary schools less human than when they went into them? I suggest it was because their education consisted of a kind of squeeze play on a grand scale in which students are set up to prepare for and to verify almost everything in the world of knowledge except their own capacities to contribute to it.

You know how it is when you are prevented from contributing to some enterprise that may initially have interested you. You feel angry, then left out; then, it being usually not appropriate to express either of these, you make peace with your discomforts by one ego-salving ploy or another. But, inevitably, somewhere along in that private sequence of events the germ of a lethal suspicion has usually been spawned, namely: "Perhaps I didn't have anything to contribute." That suspicion, driven sufficiently far underground, and requiring sufficiently often to be thrown this bone or that of spurious achievement, is what creates uncreative thinkers. And that suspicion, along with elaborate theories and practices for its care and keeping, is what sustains, as we well know, the esprit de corps of many a school and of many a teacher. In whatever ways it may be couched in terms of educational philosophies or psychologies it comes back to the "conspiracy of silence."

Now to a definition of terms: the educative process refers to anything that transpires in a school room which helps to fire all four cylinders of the creative act: preparation, incubation, illumination, and verification. This definition takes seriously the mounting evidence that, so far as humans are concerned, one learns creatively or one does not learn at all. Self-knowledge lends itself less readily to definition. We know it is relevant to those two middle phases: incubation and illumination. Something like it mediated my mental detour from Goodman to Kell to Kell. It has been called "insight," "competence," "identity," even in some circles "genitality." I prefer the makeshift definition of a student who described it as that which enhances by "en-chance-ment."

For example, picture an eleven-year-old boy in sixth grade mathematics who was asked to say what infinity was. He replied, "It's like a box of Cream of Wheat."[5] He was censured for silliness, and to outward appearances that was that. But the inward result was a misused conscience warning the boy not to take a chance with *that* kind of thing again. He later found his way into psychotherapy where some of the dimensions of the chance he had taken in that moment of classroom routine were brought to light. His father had deserted the family when the boy was four. Forced to take a job, his mother had just time each morning to get him settled into breakfast before leaving for work. There was our future math student. morning after morning, random fantasies engaging and disengaging a half-conscious gaze on a box of Cream of Wheat. As reconstructed in therapy those fantasies alternated usually between themes of longing for a lost father, and of hatred for

[5] For the benefit of youthful readers, the Cream of Wheat label formerly pictured a chef holding a box of Cream of Wheat, which pictured a chef holding a box of Cream of Wheat, etc.

a mother whom he unconsciously blamed for the loss. I have tried but I can think of no better word to describe the intensity of that hateful longing than "infinite."

The point however, is not that mental mysteries can be reconstructed. The point is that infinity is like a box of Cream of Wheat—exactly so, vividly so, originally so. In whatever manner the concept of infinity had been introduced to him he had begun to assimilate it by reliving his own history in respect to it. And by reliving that particular segment of his history he was enhancing the concept of infinity, I say, by one momentous en-chance-ment, because those were not benign moments spent with the Cream of Wheat box. But the chance failed, and two reciprocal opportunities defaulted as a consequence, one therapeutic, the other educational. The first was an opportunity to review from a less helpless vantage a portion of his formative years, which while not happy was manifestly not meaningless. The second was an opportunity to create infinity!

We should, I think, neither be too easy nor too hard on the teacher who forfeited those opportunities. If inclined to let her off we shall protest that she had no way of knowing all this—what with thirty children to tend, etc., and not being a psychoanalyst, etc. But finding out how infinity is like a box of Cream of Wheat would have been a superb way to get the idea across to the other twenty-nine; and it required no more knowledge to confirm that particular en-chance-ment than an understanding of Robert Frost's homely observation that you know somebody is thinking when you hear a figure of speech. A gifted teacher will rush to an analogy like a shortstop to a slow-rolling grounder, because it happens to be good practice. On the other hand it is true that gifted teachers are hard put to confirm their gifts in a school where from teacher selection to in-service training and from curriculm construction to classroom architecture the educative process is polarized from preparation to verification, and back again—unilluminated.

What might the role of self-knowledge have been in that potentially educative process? Suppose the teacher had been inclined not only to allow the analogy but to aid it, to encourage it, to draw it out, to help it interchange with similar experiences of classmates, to detect in it patterns of recurrent enhancements both illuminating and distorting, and to draw those out? I am speaking of a technology originated in the office of Sigmund Frued and since perfected by the psychiatric profession in the treatment of mental illness, free associative techniques, methods for the elucidation and interpretation of transference and resistance, "working through" procedures, and so forth. These are admittedly not playtoys to be distributed indiscriminately among inexperienced teachers. For the present their modified applications in classrooms had best be encouraged only with teachers who know enough from first-hand experience—whether by way of personal psychotherapy or in-service training groups, such as described by Leo Berman,[6] or consultation measures, such as described by Gerald Caplan[7]—to seek administrative sanction for experimentation along these lines. Such experimentation should be part of formal research programs, for obvious reasons, not the least of which stem from the

[6] Leo Berman, "Psychoanalysis and Group Psychotherapy," *The Psychoanalytic Review*, XXXVII, 2 (1950), pp. 156–163; "Mental Hygiene for Educators: Report on an Experiment Using a Combined Seminar and Group Psychotherapy Approach," *The Psychoanalytic Review*, XL, 4 (1953), pp. 319–332: "A Group Psychotherapy Technique for Training in Clinical Psychology," *The Amer. J. of Orthopsychiatry*, XXIII, 2 (1953), pp. 322–327.

[7] Gerald Caplan, "Mental Health Consultation" (unpublished manuscript), draft copy from Harvard School of Public Health, September 20, 1957.

restraints that well-designed research tends to impose on experimentation. Ongoing consultation, preferably with an experienced and psychoanalytically trained educator, should be available in order to reduce the possibilities of unnecessarily triggering off neurotic anxieties. And my own judgment is that at least two teachers should be thus engaged in any school that decides to move in this direction, as there are certain kinds of mutual support and consultation that can only take place between junior equals.

While the cautions and restraints of consultation and research are clearly in order, the indiscriminate trepidations of some psychoanalysts, I think, are not. Those who would restrict the influence of applied psychoanalytic psychology and overextend the treatment of neurosis forget the versatility of psychoanalysis. In the present context clinical neurosis is not our concern. If the incidence of certain disease happens indirectly to be reduced by psychoanalytically oriented education, so much the better. The direct objective, however, is better learning—not transformed personalities, not insight into the etiology of symptoms, in brief, not the objectives of psychotherapy—but better, more active, more lasting, let us say ego-syntonic learning. Let us admit in advance that measures undertaken to deepen the educative process will sometimes *appear* to be introducing psychotherapy into the classrooms. But Freud has taught us not to be taken in by appearances.

If trepidation is to be prescribed it should not be in respect to the techniques themselves but in respect to certain reverberations, which the successful application of those techniques can be predicted to effect. The students will complain that they are not being taught correctly, but that is to be welcomed, as it introduces the question of what correct teaching is, and students should recognize that this is a real question. But parents will soon be heard from. The school is stirring up trouble at home, they will complain, and besides it isn't good for young people to know so much about themselves; it makes them brood—by which is meant that the brooding will now have become articulate. A trustee will proclaim that a school is a school and not a mental hospital; a janitor will sulk about re-arrangements of furniture. And, not least, a psychiatrist may be consulted who can be counted on to announce his profession's ambivalence in such matters. The school's efforts are admirable, he will say, but should not be continued without *medical supervision.* Even a principal or dean enlightened enough to encourage his teachers in this direction and strong enough to protect them in it will probably throw in the towel when he sees the price of *that.*

Let us be clear with what it is we are dealing. Dr. Weisskopf surveys with too much alacrity, I think, the barbed wire at this particular frontier of education, when she says, "In other words we do not want to accept the fact that intellectual activity takes part of its energy supply from the reservoir of unacceptable impulses called the Id." The concept of the Id is a relatively new one in the history of ideas. Long ago it was called "Beelzebub," and people would only confront it (in public) at the behest of priests and their assorted technologies including the burning stake. We are more humane now and no longer see the Id as bad—only sick. Thus, now it is to be confronted "if you say so, Doctor." Right there is the barbed wire, because God forbid that a teacher should say so. And yet we have psychoanalytic evidence and the reports of the best creative minds that "the material carefully and rationally accumulated during the period of preparation *has to* become imbued with Id-impulses in order to be brought to life."[8]

Now, I am as thankful as the next person that we are out of the dark ages. But, as a teacher, I am reluctant to call in a physician

[8] Weisskopf, p. 188.

every time I see a chance to foster creativity in my classroom; and, as a psychologist, I am reluctant to define the creative process in terms of psychopathology just because the two have been known to overlap. For example, in one of my classes, where a standing assignment is to hand in dreams thought to relate to classroom matters, a young woman submitted the following:

> I viewed myself coughing up dead mice, rats, squirrels and other kinds of tiny animals. The more someone would try to pat me on the back so that I would stop coughing the more I would cough up these animals. Finally I stopped, but I felt so listless and hollow that I could barely stand up and had to lean on a chair for support. The same unidentified (I suspect male) person who was patting me on the back decided to pick me up so that I could get where I was going easier. To his utter shock, however, I completely seemed to collapse as if nothing else were inside me now that the animals had been removed. As he picked me up I seemed to dry or shrivel up and then I awoke.

I had previously written a letter of recommendation for the author of the dream on the strength of which she was offered a teaching position in a local school system. I knew her well and thought she would make a first-rate teacher. Also, I had admonished her the day before for the annoying habit of writing out exam questions prior to writing her answers. I thought that unnecessary and told her so. On the next occasion alloted to discussion of dreams the dreamer, with the help of her classmates, and of my silence, arrived at the following interpretation of the dream. It presented her, they thought, with a picture of her mixed feelings about being the dependent person she had all along complained of being. Furthermore, it showed how she sometimes felt toward those who encouraged her dependence. She had, she reported, been walking on air since receiving the job offer, and had been speculating what my letter must have said about her. Doubts arose: she had noted there were times when I seemed to enjoy the sound of my own words. What if the letter had been one of those times? What if she was not ready to teach? What if she made a fool of herself on her first job? My harshness of the day before, it seemed, was on the way to convincing her of the worst. Two camps formed around the issue of whether I should be asked to show her a copy of the letter. She was against it. I kept my peace. The hour concluded on the question of the source of self-confidence.

That, I considered, was a fruitful hour of teaching. The source of self-confidence was a subject not extraneous to the course, which was educational psychology. And I don't expect soon to see as vivid a representation of concern over self-confidence at the Id level as was pictured by that dream.

It should not be concluded from the above example that every item in the syllabus must be dramatically and explicitly related to Id material in order to be made active parts of a student's working knowledge. It is what this example *implies* that warrants emphasis, namely, that students need to be encouraged (1) to seek the help of the teacher and fellow students with psychologically short-circuiting emotional issues *when necessary*, and (2) to exploit in the privacy of their own thoughts the enhancing properties of relatively conflict-free personal imagery. The latter has no need of dreams, but will show itself rather in silently restored memory lapses, in immediately relevant figures of speech, in novel examples, in working metaphors, and in other such signs that the student is making his education his own. Neither of the above conditions, however, can be created in classrooms if the teacher is oblivious to their need. Nor is verbal permissiveness enough. Time—regularly scheduled periods of time—must be allotted by the teacher to the acquistion of relevant self-knowledge. In no other way can a teacher begin to be convincing with respect to the kinds of thought processes he values in his students. And, knowing what we do about the amount of true knowledge typically gained from classroom time, what, after all, can be lost if we re-allocate some of it?

In conclusion let me concede a point. Psychologists are presently better equipped to state *why* educators should locate the role of self-knowledge in the educative process than to specify how we should locate it, or what, once located, we should do about it. The challenge is particularly vexing to the college educator, for the reason that he deals with students so accustomed to the squeeze play that almost any measure designed to invite inspiring or illuminating thought is met with scorn if not with fright. It always takes me a month to convince a quorum of my classes, first that I am serious about the dream assignment, second that I am of sound mind, third that I am competent to teach at a respectable university, and fourth that I am not experimenting on them. Many never get beyond the second doubt, but for some "education-in-depth" becomes more than a title in Kubie's book.

Until students come to college accustomed to firing all four cylinders of the learning process the college teacher will on occasion have to appear mighty like a psychiatrist—with or without medical supervision. A good psychological counseling center goes a long way toward relieving the classrooms of accumulated self-ignorance; however, in the long view a psychological counseling center is a stop-gap measure, awaiting the day when students will look more naturally to teachers than to doctors for self-knowledge. Meanwhile, given a strong and sympathetic dean, there is much a classroom teacher can try in the way of making self-knowledge not the end in itself, which it must be in a counseling center, but the means to actively enchanced learning, which is its design in nature.

22

Old Wine in New Wineskins—The Reasons for the Limited World View

Willis W. Harman

From the study of the past it is evident that, throughout the ages, individuals and communities have repeatedly come upon the creative factors and forces at work in the human psyche. Great philosophies and great religions have time and again come into being as an outcome of such discoveries; and for a while stirred men to the depths. But as often as the discoveries have been made they have again been lost.

In this present age there is the possibility of making the discoveries in a new way: not as an outcome of some special revelation of extraordinary insight on the part of one man or a small body of men, but in the form of direct personal experience of a considerable number of intelligent men and women directing their awareness upon the inner world. For the first time in history, the scientific spirit of enquiry, the free search for truth, is being turned upon the other side of consciousness.

In place of *a priori* dogma there is a growing body of empirically established experience; experience which can be progressively funded, as our experience of the outer world has been funded, and its meaning learnt. Because of this, there is good prospect that the discoveries can this time be held: and so become, now and henceforward, no longer the lost secret but the living heritage of man (Martin, 1965).

Seldom have the promise and the challenge of humanistic psychology been stated so succinctly and so well. Viewing this area of scientific inquiry as characterized not by monotonic progress but by discoveries made and lost raises questions central to the whole enterprise. What are the characteristics of this knowledge of the "other side of consciousness" which make conceptual ordering so elusive, which make it so difficult to transmit the knowledge gained? Why have these discoveries inspired man's most noble poetry, thoughts, and deeds, and at the same time provoked the most bitter conflicts? Why is it that we find this knowledge at once so valued and yet so threatening? Why is it that, as Maslow (1962) puts it, "It is precisely the god-like in ourselves that we are ambivalent about, fascinated by and fearful of, motivated to and defensive against." (p. 58)?

We shall not answer these questions in a brief chapter, of course, but consideration of them is essential to an understanding of the nature of the enterprise of humanistic psychology.

The Encapsulated-Man Thesis

To begin, let us examine a thesis which appears to be as old as our most ancient records of man's attempts to organize his experience. This is the thesis "that man is encapsulated. . . . If man wishes to gain a more inclusive world-view or to approach ultimate reality it will be necessary for him to break through the several cocoons within which he is inevitably encapsulated. The first step in this process is to recognize that he is, in fact, encapsulated. Unfortunately, this first step is the most difficult" (Royce, 1964, p. 3):

There is a traditional doctrine, usually associated with religion, but now and then invading great literature, that our present waking state is not really being awake at all. . . . It is, the tradition says, a special form of sleep comparable to a hypnotic trance. . . . From the moment of birth and before, we are under the suggestion that we are not fully awake; and it is universally suggested to our consciousness that we must dream the dream of this world—as our parents and friends dream it. . . . Just as in night-dreams the first symptom of waking is to suspect that one is dreaming, the first symptom of waking from the waking state—the second awakening of religion—is the suspicion that our present waking state is dreaming likewise. To be aware that we are asleep is to be on the point of waking; and to be aware that we are only partially awake is the first condition of becoming and making ourselves more fully awake (Orage, 1965, p. 89).

It is our tendency to consider the assertion in this more or less familiar doctrine to be an interesting metaphor. But is it only such a figure of speech, or is it to be taken more literally and more seriously? This is a profoundly important—and challenging—distinction.

The Data of Hypnosis. Of all those phenomena whose existence is widely recognized by scientists (whether or not they are felt to be understood), among the most fraught with significance and implication are those associated with hypnosis. The basic facts are generally known, but we have hestitated to draw the conclusions to which they point.

A recent inventory of scientific findings

about human behavior (Berelson & Steiner, 1964, pp. 121-123) lists a number of established findings regarding hypnosis, including the following:

> Hypnotism works: that is, there is no question today that hypnotism can induce all of the following "unnatural" states:
>
> 1. Anesthesia and analgesia, local or general
> 2. Positive and negative hallucinations
> 3. Regression to an earlier age
> 4. Unusual muscular strength, rigidity, resistance to fatigue
> 5. Organic effects, normally outside voluntary control. . . .

For example, a hypnotized subject may be induced to perceive an imaginary kitten placed in her lap. She experiences stroking the kitten and hearing it purr; the senses of sight, touch, and hearing seem to corroborate the hypnotist's suggestion. Yet this is a "positive hallucination." There is no kitty there.

Other examples are familiar. A subject accepts the suggestion that a person sitting in a particular chair really is not there; he perceives an empty chair. A hypnotized person is persuaded that a small wastebasket is fastened to the floor; struggling mightily, he is unable to lift it. A subject's body is rendered rigid by appropriate suggestions; he is then used to bridge the space between two chairs, and one or more individuals mount and stand on top of his unsupported chest and abdomen. Blisters and burned spots can be produced by hypnotic suggestion.

In a fascinating series of experiments, Aaronson (1966) has altered the perceptual experience of subjects by giving them hypnotic suggestions such as, "When I wake you up everybody and everything will seem to be moving three times as slowly as usual," or "The dimension of depth will be gone; there will be no depth." By changing the way in which the individual perceived the world—his depth perception, time perception, movement perception, color perception, and so on—major behavior changes, as well as mental states ranging from psychoticlike to euphoric and mystical, were produced.

Now what are the conditions essential to the production of hypnotic phenomena? In their barest simplicity, they are (1) a source of suggestion and (2) the willingness, at a deep level in the personality, to accept suggestions from that source. But surely these conditions are met in our infancy and early childhood. Most of what we commonly think of as the education of the young child amounts to acceptance of suggestions from the parents and from the culture. Extreme willingness to accept the suggestions offered by the environment accounts for the child's success in learning how to get along in the world; it also accounts, in part at least, for his pathology if the environment is unfavorable. The wrong kind of suggestions can lead to such personality defects as exaggerated suspicion and hostility, incapacitating feelings of low self-worth and inadequacy, and phobias.

The inference is as obvious as it is startling: *We are hypnotized from infancy.*

This proposition is neither bad nor new. It is a necessity of life, our essential adaptation to the culture into which we are born. It is only another way of looking at some thing we knew all the time and called by some other name, such as "enculturation." But we failed to become sufficiently aware of the implications. The apparent carollary is that we do not perceive ourselves and the world about us as they are but as we have been persuaded to perceive them. Our limitations are primarily not inherent but are those which we have accepted through the suggestions of others. And our usual unawareness that this is so is part of the hypnosis as well.

Now what evidence do we have that this is a reasonable conclusion—that it is to be taken literally and not simply as a metaphor or analogy? We shall consider briefly four sources of such evidence: (1) the behavioral sciences and history, (2) the testimonies of widely recognized men of wisdom in all cultures, (3) the observations of parapsychology, and (4) the comparative descriptions of what William James termed "other forms of consciousness" (1902, p. 379).

Evidence from the Behavioral Sciences and History. To begin, then, with the behavioral sciences, we find voluminous research in cultural anthropology, as well as the personal experiences of field workers, substantiating the conclusion that a person immersed in another culture perceives himself and the world very differently from the way we do. The 1898 Cambridge anthropological expedition to Torres Straits found the natives unfooled by optical illusions which uniformly deceived Europeans. Malinowski observed that the Trobriand Islanders, who believed that all characteristics are inherited from the father, regularly failed to see resemblances of the child to the mother's side of the family. Studies of authoritarian and prejudiced persons have demonstrated that they tend, whether or not the objective data support it, to perceive members of ethnic subgroups as having the characteristics of stereotypes which the perceivers acquired in childhood. Numerous demonstrations in perception (such as the famous ones of Adelbert Ames at Dartmouth) have clearly shown that what we perceive depends in extremely large measure upon our ordering of past perceptions, which in turn is influenced by accepted suggestions. Familiar objects tend to be perceived with normal size, color, and shape as expected, even when these deliberately have been significantly altered. Poor children are found to perceive coins as larger than rich children see them. How a reversible figure-ground pattern will be seen can be influenced by prior pleasant or unpleasant associations with one or the other figure in isolation. The experiments of Asch (Berelson & Steiner, 1964, p. 335) and others indicate the extent to which perceptions are modified by group pressure.

The history of science is replete with examples illustrating that how one sees the world is determined to a large extent by how one expects to see it. To consider the most notorious case, one may recall that Western man in the Middle Ages perceived the earth as a flat plane. He was aware of various phenomena which we would today interpret as demonstrations of the spheroidal nature of the earth's surface—the disappearance of ships at sea over the horizon, the lunar eclipse, the variation of the positions of the stars with change in latitude. On the basis of observations of these same phenomena, Eratosthenes and the Alexandrian astronomers had, many centuries before, computed with remarkable accuracy the earth's circumference and the distance to, and circumference of, the moon. But these phenomena were not perceived to conflict with medieval man's basic perception of the world as flat.

To medieval man, with his teleological preconception, protective coloration in animals was provided for a purpose which was completely obvious. So also were complicated instinctual patterns such as the honey making of bees and the nest making of birds, complex organs of sight and hearing, and so on. But to the post-Darwinian sophisticate of a half-century ago, the world appeared quite differently. To him it was quite apparent that protective coloration and instinctual patterns, eyes and ears were the result of random mutations sorted out by natural selection. Nothing in his observations gave him any reason to suppose that medieval man's perception of meaning and design in life was more than a comforting fiction.

The committee appointed by the French Academy, with Lavoisier as a member, to investigate the frequently reported perception of meteorites as white-hot stones which sometimes fall to the earth and are recovered denied that things could be as they seemed because there are no stones in the sky to fall (Polanyi, 1958, p. 138). The prestige of the committee was such that many museums in Western Europe threw away their meteorite collections since, after all, there were no such things. (Today the considerable publicly available data on "flying saucer" sightings receive scant attention by civilian scientists because there are no such things.) And so it goes. Medieval doctors perceived possession by evil spirits; modern doctors do not. Early chemists perceived phlogiston; early biologists perceived spontaneous generation of maggots in meat. Physicians perceive diseases which were seemingly nonexistent to doctors practicing before they were diagnosed and described. The *Weltanschauung* changes, and as it does man's perception of himself and of his environment changes accordingly. Thus man avoids finding himself in more than mild conflict.

Testimony of the Sages. As a second type of evidence, there are the testimonies of those many acknowledged men of wisdom, from diverse cultural backgrounds and scattered along the entire continuum of recorded history, who have concluded that our ordinary perceptions of reality are partial at best and in a very real sense are illusions.

Arthur Koestler describes, in masterful prose, a series of inner experiences during long days of imprisonment in the Spanish Civil War. Of these experiences he writes (1954, p. 353):

> [They] had filled me with a direct certainty that a higher order of reality existed and that it alone invested existence with meaning. I came to call it later on "the reality of the third order." The narrow world of sensory perception constituted the first order; this perceptual world was enveloped by the conceptual world which contained phenomena not directly perceivable, such as gravitation, electromagnetic fields, and curved space. The second order of reality filled in the gaps and gave meaning to the absurd patchiness of the sensory world. In the same manner, the third order of reality enveloped, interpenetrated, and gave meaning to the second. It contained "occult" phenomena which could not be apprehended or explained either on the sensory or on the conceptual level, and yet occasionally invaded them like spiritual meteors piercing the primitive's vaulted sky. Just as the conceptual order showed up the illusions and distortions of the senses, so the "third order" disclosed that time, space and causality, that isolation, separateness and spatio-temporal limitations of the self were merely optical illusions on the next higher level.

Meister Eckhart had said the same in remarking that there are three kinds of knowledge. "The first is sensible, the second is rational and a great deal higher. The third corresponds to a higher power of the soul which knows no yesterday or today or tomorrow." Aldous Huxley makes a similar assertion in summarizing the testimony of scores of sages of all ages and cultures (1946).

Plato summarizes this "universal-hypnosis" view of man's situation in the well-known allegory of the cave, in the seventh book of *The Republic*. It is found in the ancient doctrine of maya in Hinduism, as well as in Sufi tradition: "Humanity is asleep, concerned only with what is useless, living in a wrong world" (Sanai of Afghanistan, 1130 A.D.).

Two, of many possible examples from more modern writers, will suffice to make the point, one from a modern French psychiatrist and the other from a Russian philosopher: "Our conscious thinking has all the characteristics of a dream; it is a dream. The representation that it gives us of the world is illusory. . . . In the [higher-awareness] state of the Buddha, consciousness is awakened in a way which is no longer exclusive or attached. . . . It is liberated from usual hypnosis" (Benoit, 1962, p. 237). "It must be realized that the sleep in which man exists is not normal but hypnotic sleep. Man is hypnotized and his hypnotic state is continually maintained and strengthened in him. . . . 'To awaken' for man means to be 'dehypnotized'" (Ouspensky, 1949, p. 219).

The Discordant Data of Parapsychology. Third, we come to those anomalous data which are sometimes more and sometimes less completely subsumed under the heading "parapsychology" or "psychical research" (Johnson, 1953; Murphy, 1961; Rhine, 1953; Sudre, 1960). These include those types of phenomena, attested to in many cases by hundreds of observers, which do not "fit in." Yet they seem to speak clearly to the point that something is fundamentally incomplete about a world view which cannot accommodate them.

The mere listing of some of these phenomena, with the implication that perhaps they should be taken seriously, makes some of us squirm: telepathy, clairvoyance, precognition (varieties of extrasensory perception), levitation, teleportation, fire walking, poltergeists, spiritual healing, "seeing" with the fingertips, hypnosis at a distance. The questions raised are as fundamentally challenging as any since the Copernican heresies.

The scientific standing of hypnosis is a case in point. This baffling phenomenon was, less than a century ago, part of the ostracized territory known as "psychical research." So impossible was it considered (since there was no conceivable mechanism to account for it) that even after the analgesic and anesthetic potentialities of hypnosis had been demonstrated in hundreds of apparently painless major operations, some witnessed by scores of physicians, the possibility of the phenomenon's very existence was denied. Medical journals refused to publish papers documenting the work, and patients were accused of "deluding or colluding with" their doctors in pretending to feel no pain while limbs were amputated or abdominal operations were performed (Polanyi, 1958, p. 274). Today the basic phenomenon of hypnosis is widely accepted as we noted earlier. It is interesting to observe, however, that the earliest scientific definition of hypnosis (Bertrand, 1826) included, besides the "unnatural states" listed at the beginning of this chapter, telepathic communication; "sight without eyes"; clairvoyant ability to diagnose, prescribe for, and prognosticate about illness; and ability to take on the illness of another and thereby cure him. These phenomena seemingly are no longer observed to occur, and the definition of hypnosis no longer includes or implies them. This could be taken to indicate that they never happened at all, or it may mean instead that the existence of an "a priori impossible" conviction on the part of the hypnotist will preclude their appearing.

Nor should we forget that the phenomena which we presently subsume under the heading "creativity" (having recently become uncomfortable with the connotations of the older term "inspiration") have also only in the recent past come to be considered part of the subject matter of psychology. Prior to that, this topic too was part of "psychical research" (Myers, 1961). The universal testimony of highly creative men has been that their created projects are the result of higher, unconscious processes over which they have only limited control. At approximately the same time that Freud, in Vienna, was developing his theories of the unconscious, Frederic Myers, in Cambridge, was compiling his impressive study of the "subliminal consciousness" containing "a rubbish-heap as well as a treasurehouse" (Myers, 1961, p. 74). This vanguard para-psychological treatise stresses the essential similarities between such phenomena as telepathy and clairvoyance, and the experiences of creative geniuses and of mathematical prodigies.[1]

[1] William James opined that Myers would "be regarded as the Founder of a new science" on the basis of his "concept of the Sublinimal Self, by which he colligated and co-ordinated a mass of phenomena which had never before been considered together" (*Proceedings of the Society for Psychical Research*, 1903, 18, 22).

G. N. M. Tyrrell summarized the implications of the data of the paranormal in *The Nature of Human Personality* (1954, p. 94):

> When we pass beyond the range of our senses, we find evidence that both we and the world we live in have been given a specious appearance of self-completeness. This does not merely mean that the human senses are limited; it means that the practical mind has been formed in such a way that it reinforces the impression given by the senses and takes for granted things which are not true, but which make for simplicity and efficiency in practical life. . . . The great value of psychical research is that it has begun to put perspective into the universe and to show us that neither we nor our world come to an end where we thought they did.

The "Other-Forms-of-Consciousness" Issue

Finally, we have a fourth source of data which directly challenge the assumption that the world is as we ordinarily perceive it. This is the voluminous literature on transcendental states, on kinds of consciousness other than the usual. One of the earliest studies of these states used the term "cosmic consciousness" to refer to a broad range of experiences which awaits a satisfactory taxonomy (Bucke, 1905, p. 2).

> The prime characteristic of cosmic consciousness is, as its name implies, a consciousness of the cosmos, that is, of the life and order of the universe. . . . Along with the consciousness of the cosmos there occurs an intellectual enlightenment or illumination which alone would place the individual on a new plane of existence—would make him almost a member of a new species. To this is added a state of moral exaltation, an indescribable feeling of elevation, elation, and joyousness, and a quickening of the moral sense, which is fully as striking and more important both to the individual and to the race than is the enhanced intellectual power. With these come what may be called a sense of immortality, a consciousness of eternal life, not conviction that he shall have this, but the consciousness that he has it already.

Further documentation may be found in philosophy and the arts, in mystical literature, and in the rapidly accumulating literature on experiences with the psychedelic chemical agents. We shall examine each of these briefly.

The Transcendental in the Humanities. Among philosophers, perhaps Baruch Spinoza speaks most unequivocally on the place of the transcendental (Pollock, 1899, p. 269):

> In all exact knowledge the mind knows itself under the form of eternity; that is to say, in every such act it is eternal and knows itself as eternal. This eternity is not a persistence in time after the dissolution of the body, no more than a pre-existence in time, for it is not commensurable with time at all. And there is associated with it a state or quality of perfection called the immediately apprehended love of God.

Again and again we find expressed in the works of the most cherished poets the urging to discover for oneself the supremacy of the transcendental. The forms range from the straightforward statements of the first two examples below to the tantalizingly paradoxical expression exemplified by the latter one:

> If the doors of perception were cleansed, everything would appear to man as it is, infinite.
>
> For man has closed himself up, till he sees all things thro' narrow chinks of his cavern.
>
> William Blake,
> "The Marriage of Heaven and Hell"

> Truth is within ourselves; it takes no rise
> From outward things, whate'er you may believe
> . . . and to *know*,

Rather consists in opening out a way
Whence the imprisoned splendour may
escape,
Than in effecting entry for a light
Supposed to be without.

Robert Browning,
"Paracelsus"

Die and Become
Till thou hast learned this
Thou art but a dull guest
On this dark planet.

Goethe, "Spiritual Longing,"
Book 1 of *West-Eastern Divan*

. . .

As to the arts, we shall have to allow a single quotation to suffice. It is from J. W. N. Sullivan's biography of Beethoven (1927, p. 159):

> All art exists to communicate states of consciousness which are higher synthetic wholes than those of ordinary experience, but in these last quartets Beethoven is dealing with . . . a state of consciousness surpassing our own, where our problems do not exist, and to which even our highest aspirations . . . provide no key.

The Literature of Mysticism. The empirical, mystical element is well recognized to exist in nearly all religions and religious philosophies. To be sure, certain aspects of the Eternal Gospel, the *Philosophia Perennis,* are especially emphasized in the Eastern religious philosophy of Vedanta, others in the mystical tradition of Christianity, and still others in the poetic writings of the mystics of Islam. But its essence is the claim of the possibility of directly apprehended knowledge that is universal and immemorial.

Stace (1960) has provided a particularly helpful analysis of mysticism in various cultures. He concludes that "the mystical consciousness is quite different from [the sensory-intellectual consciousness]. . . . The central characteristic in which all fully-developed mystical experiences agree is that they involve the apprehension of an ultimate nonsensuous unity in all things, a oneness or a One to which neither the senses nor the reason can penetrate. In other words, it entirely transcends our sensory-intellectual consciousness" (p. 14).

Carpenter (1892, p. 156) sums up what might be appropriate attitude for the humanistic psychologist as follows:

> Great have been the disputes among the learned as to the meaning of the word Nirvana—whether it indicates a state of no-consciousness or a state of vastly enhanced consciousness. . . . The important thing is to see and admit that under cover of this and other similar terms there does exist a real and recognizable fact (that is, a state of consciousness in some sense), which has been experienced over and over again, and which to those who have experienced it in ever so slight a degree has appeared worthy of lifelong pursuit and devotion. . . .

The Psychedelic Agents. The rapidly accumulating literature on experiences with the psychedelic ("mind-manifesting" or "consciousness-expanding") chemical agents provides a final array of observations on our central theme. They have been used in the spiritual exercises of many religious groups, both ancient and modern, primitive and sophisticated, to assist man to reveal his mind to himself and to help him reach greatly cherished, heightened levels of awareness and consciousness. In recent years these substances have played an increasingly important role in psychotherapy (Cohen, 1965; Harman, 1963; Masters, 1966; Mogar, 1965; Sherwood, 1962). Their potential theoretical and practical importance has evoked extravagant statements from many of the scientists who have studied them:

> Science develops through the development of instruments which make new classes of evidence available. . . . [One such instrument is] the psychedelics . . . which enhance the sense of meaning or vitality, or beauty and sheer intensity of

existence. . . . Quite aside from absolutely all interpretations whatever, to say the very least, these [psychedelic] experiences alter man's conception of himself and the world. . . . They are a way of looking at the cosmos, and therefore belong to the central core of man's needs as a thoughtful being (Murphy, 1965, p. 79).

The very beginning, the intrinsic core, the essence, the universal nucleus of every known high religion has been the private, lonely, personal illumination, revelation, or ecstasy of some acutely sensitive prophet or seer . . . of what I prefer to call "peak experience." . . . In the last few years it has become quite clear that certain drugs called "psychedelic" often produce peak experiences in the right people under the right circumstances (Maslow, 1964, p. 27).

The changes in values and the therapeutic gains which may follow even a partial glimpsing of the psychedelic-mystical perception . . . are suggestive of the part the psychedelic experiences may have to play in helping us to discern the true meaning of the verb "to be" (Sherwood, 1962, p. 79).

Briefly, the evidence of the psychedelics seems to corroborate the testimonies of the men of vision which we examined earlier, to the effect that reality is a far different matter from what we ordinarily imagine it.

Now this is uncomfortable matter to contemplate. None of us likes to be fooled. It is difficult for us to allow the full significance of this proposition to impinge on our conscious awareness. To an extent far greater than we like to imagine, our perceptions are influenced or determined by what Rokeach (1960) terms the person's "total belief-disbelief system."

The Obdurate Belief System. By the term "belief system," Rokeach means not only consciously held beliefs but also "what a person really believes of verbal and nonverbal, implicit and explicit beliefs, sets, or expectancies." (1960, p. 32). Central to this system is a set of unstated but basic beliefs[2] about the nature of the self, others, and the universe; about what in life is to be highly valued; and about where one looks for ultimate authority; The validity of these basic beliefs and values the individual "does not question and, in the ordinary course of events, is not prepared to question" (p. 40). These basic beliefs are formed early in life. Their nature is strongly influenced by early environment; once formed, they are remarkably resistant to change as one moves through life. Out of this core of basic beliefs the total belief system grows. New perceptions may alter the core beliefs. Much more likely, however, the core beliefs will shape the perceptions to fit in with the existing belief structure.

Viewed in these terms, the lasting and all-pervading effect of the particular suggestions accepted by the infant stands out with clarity. It is thus that the central hypnosis or the core beliefs are shaped. Thenceforth the world tends to be perceived in such a way that the perception supports the image. Always the self-preserving instinct acts to filter incoming data to fit in with the existing belief system. Always the conflict is present between this sanity-maintaining action and the counteroperating growth impulse to remove the distorting lenses, to "cleanse the doors of perception."

We have emphasized so strongly the supporting evidence for this hypothesis of our perceptions of reality being conditioned and limited to a predominant degree because of our natural reluctance to take the proposition seriously. Now the time

[2] One might question whether the word "beliefs" is a fortunate choice to refer to inferred determinants of action which are not in the individual's conscious awareness, since its ordinary usage implies conscious acceptance. However, when persons become aware of these preexistent influences, they often spontaneously express themselves in terms such as "I feel that I have believed this about myself without knowing it."

has come to inquire into some of the consequences of this premise, particularly in relation to the changing character of psychology.

Characteristics of the New Psychology

If there is a perception of reality which is less conditioned, what are its characteristics? We may assume that it includes the commonsense scientific image of reality as a valid but partial view. It is probable that it cannot be adequately conceptualized with symbols, or in a language, that have been built up mainly out of experience in the hypnotized, conditioned state. (Hence the frequently heard claim that experience of the dehypnotized state is ineffable or that attempts to express it verbally lead to paradoxical statements.) It is not yet clear what metaphors the new psychology will choose for the attempt.

Conceptualizing Man and His Experience. We may speculate on the characteristics of the developing humanistic psychology as it comes more and more adequately to deal with the "encapsulated-man" problem and the "other-forms-of-consciousness" issue, as these have been described above. Certain attributes of a liberated psychology seem most probable:

1. It will incorporate some way of referring to the subjective experiencing of a unity in all things [the "More" of William James (1902), "the All" of Bugental (1965), the "divine Ground" of the *Perennial Philosophy* (Huxley, 1946)].
2. It will include some sort of mapping or ordering of states of consciousness transcending the usual conscious awareness [Bucke's "Cosmic Consciousness" (1905), the "enlightenment" of Zen, and similar concepts].
3. It will take account of the subjective experiencing of a "higher self" and will view favorably the development of a self-image congruent with his experience [Bugental's "I-process" (1965), Emerson's "Oversoul" (1950), Assagioli's "True Self" (1965), Brunton's "Overself" (1938), the Atman of Vedanta, and so on].
4. It will allow for a much more unified view of human experiences now categorized under such diverse headings as "creativity," "hypnosis," "mystical experience," "experiences with the psychedelic drugs," "extrasensory perception," "psychokinesis," and related phenomena.
5. It will include a much more unified view of the processes of personal change and emergence which take place within the contexts of psychotherapy, education (in the sense of "know thyself"), and religion (as spiritual growth). This view will possibly center around the concept that personality and behavior patterns change consequent upon a change in self-image a modification of the person's emotionally felt perception of himself and his relationship to his environment.

Processes of Change. We shall adopt here such a conceptual model of personal change resulting from alterations in the self-image because it appears to offer a useful way of summarizing the diversity of techniques which have been used to promote change. The self-image [Self-concept of Bugental (1965), personal construct system of Kelly (1955)] is, of course, a much more complex thing than the name suggests. It is by no means free of inconsistencies and fragmentation, but for our purposes we may oversimplify and speak as though it were a unified pattern of feelings and behavior. It has been likened to the input signal of a feedback control system; the personality and behavior-pattern structure tend to "follow" the self-image. We become as we imagine ourselves to be: "As a man thinketh in his heart, so he is." In a more elaborate metaphor, Lilly (1966) views conscious and unconscious mental processes as a hierarchy of programs available to the brain-computer, with the self-image as a "metaprogram" which modifies, controls, and creates the programs giving rise to behavior.

The form of the self-image is part of the

original hypnosis. It comprises the feelings and judgments about ourselves which we have accepted from external sources. It is, as we have noted, remarkably resistant to any direct pressures to change. Nevertheless a host of techniques of some effectiveness have been developed and used to try to bring about such changes.

In general, there seem to be four basic techniques for changing the self-image:

Change in Response to Clues from the Environment, Particularly Other Persons

Through fortunate life experiences, as well as experiences in the more structured context of therapy or "encounter group" situations, the individual may introject new data resulting in a revision of his self-image. Through a meaningful, emotional relationship with another or with other persons, and in a supportive environment, he may be able to "see," feel, and alter handicapping and constraining aspects of his basic, preverbal belief structure. Being confronted by awareness of limiting and hurtful aspects of his self-image, and simultaneously supported while he dares to consider reinterpretation and change, the person may use such experiences to revise his basic beliefs and move in the direction of becoming "fully functioning" (Rogers, 1961), "self-actualizing" (Maslow, 1962), and "authentic" (Bugental, 1965). He moves away from resistiveness and defensiveness and toward an increasing awareness of his deeper needs, toward growing confidence in his own inner reactions as a trustworthy guide to behavior, toward increasing sensitivity and openness to all experience with increased ability to form new relationships, and toward being in accord with himself and at one with the world.

Change in Response to Clues Generated by Oneself

A second technique involves changing of the self-image by integrative symbols which the person presents, so to speak, to himself. These clues may come through dreams, fantasy, or directed imagination; through the use of psychedelic agents; or in participation in religious ritual or contemplative exercise. Use of such symbols is central to the "constructive technique" of C. G. Jung and to the "psychosynthesis" of Assagioli (1965). It is set forth with particular clarity by one of Jung's students, P. W. Martin (1965, p. 115):

> The principal means by which the creative possibilities of the deep unconscious may be reached is the transforming symbol. Anyone wholeheartedly engaging in the experiment in depth will find, as a normal fact of experience, that the unconscious repeatedly produced shapes, objects, phrases, ideas, which have this peculiar quality: if put to their right use they make possible a re-direction of energy and, by so doing, progressively transform the man who uses them.

Through the emotional and intellectual integration of these symbols, the governing image of the self—the one that is emotionally felt and imagined—may change from one of worthlessness, inadequacy, or precariously pent-up urges, to a self-image centered on an "I," "that of God in every man," whose worth and adequacy are beyond question and whose guidance can be implicitly trusted. The task and joy of life then become that of response to the quiet but insistent demands of this "I" that one actualize his inherent potentialities to know, to be free, and to love—to be oneself.

Modification by Deliberate Choice and Autosuggestion

Another technique involves deliberately choosing the characteristics of the self-image to be modified and using autohypnotic techniques to effect the change. Modifications of the self-image, deeply embedded in the personality structure, can be brought about by the persistent vivid imagining that they have already taken place—through a deliberate dehypnotization, as it were. This sort of technique has been one of the secrets of esoteric knowledge for many centuries. "Therefore I tell you, whatever you ask in prayer, believe that you receive it, and you will" (Mark 11:24). It obtained its greatest popularization (and received correspondingly great condemnation) through the work of the French psychologist Emile Coué. More recently Maltz (1960) has given a popular exposition of the technique of rational selection of a desired self-image, with autosuggestive implantation of this image into the deeper levels of the psyche. Assagioli's technique of "ideal models" (1965, p. 166) is similar. The approach is the basis for a number of "personal effectiveness" seminars and training courses. In a superficial form, where it involves a good component of self-deception, it receives much-deserved criticism.

Similar to the autosuggestive techniques are the "autogenic training" of Schultz (Schultz & Luthe, 1959) and Kelly's "fixed-role therapy" (1955). The same basic process would seem to be involved in the influencing of the deeply buried self-image by religious symbol and ritual, by contact with great works of art, and by study of "the best that has been thought and said" in humanities and "great books" courses.

ALTERED CONSCIOUSNESS

The fourth process of character change is described in mystical and occult literature, but it cannot be said to have formed a part of recognized psychotherapeutic procedures in recent times until the advent of psychedelic therapy (Harman, 1963; Sherwood, 1962). It is characterized by the person's image of himself being changed as a result of his having experiences which he perceives as transcendental and valid, as directly revealing to him higher aspects of himself of which he had previously been unaware. Various techniques have been used to facilitate the shift to altered states of consciousness, including prayer and meditation, fasting and asceticism, the various forms of yoga, the shock treatments of Zen, and the use of psychedelic chemicals.

The New Synthesis. Knowledge of oneself, of the core of one's being, has throughout history been held before man as his highest goal. Since the Middle Ages in Western civilization, three parallel developments have carried on this tradition, emphasizing their somewhat different techniques and formulating their discoveries in varying ways. With the growth of humanistic psychology, we have the convergence of these three streams—psychotherapy, religion, and liberal (liberating) education. The insights of the psychiatrist's office, of the monastic cloister, of the humanities seminar, and of the artist's studio are now being conceptualized and joined together in practice in ways which promise new levels of effectiveness.

Self-realization, enlightenment, creativity, self-actualization, spiritual development, being authentic, fully functioning—in the end these come mainly to a single essence, to be aware and to respond: to become aware, from one's own immanent, intimate experience, that we are elements of a greater whole and that one has the choice of responding, of saying "yes" to life with the whole of his being, of being responsible (response-able)—and so to choose, and thereby to taste of freedom, to know the origins of love, to find the essence of wisdom, to become authentically man.

We are accustomed to the idea that progress in scientific knowledge is monotonically cumulative. We tend to forget that knowledge can be lost as well as won. It is humbling to realize that that which is newest and most filled with promise in the science of man's psyche is also, in some sense, the most ancient knowledge of all. Perhaps, indeed, the time has come for this knowledge to become not "the lost secret but the living heritage of man."

REFERENCES

AARONSON, B. S. Hypnosis, responsibility and the boundaries of self. Paper read at Conference on Science, Philosophy and Religion, New York, January, 1966.

ASSAGIOLI, R. *Psychosynthesis: A manual of principles and techniques.* New York: Hobbs, Dorman, 1965.

BENOIT, H. *Let go! Theory and practice of detachment according to Zen.* London: Allen & Unwin, 1962.

BERELSON, B., & STEINER, G. A. *Human behavior: An inventory of scientific findings.* New York: Harcourt, Brace & World, 1964.

BERTRAND, A. 1826. Quoted in A. Weitzenhoffer, The nature of hypnosis. *American Journal of Clinical Hypnosis,* 1953, *5*, 296, Part I.

BRUNTON, P. *The quest of the overself.* New York: Dutton, 1938.

BUCKE, M. *Cosmic consciousness.* New York: Dutton, 1905.

BUGENTAL, J. F. T. *The search for authenticity.* New York: Holt, Rinehart and Winston, 1965.

CARPENTER, E. *From Adam's peak to elephanta.* London: Swan & Sonnenschein, 1892.

COHEN, S. *The beyond within: The LSD story.* New York: Atheneum, 1965.

EMERSON, R. W. The oversoul. In *Essays.* New Haven, Conn.: Yale Univer. Press, 1950.

HARMAN, W. W. Some aspects of the psychedelic drug controversy. *Journal of Humanistic Psychology,* 1963, *3*, 93–107.

HUXLEY, A. *The perennial philosophy.* London: Chatto & Windus, 1946.

JAMES, W. *The varieties of religious experience.* New York: Modern Library, 1902.

JOHNSON, R. *The imprisoned splendour.* New York: Harper & Row, 1953.

KELLY, G. A. *The psychology of personal constructs.* Vol. 1. New York: Norton 1955.

KOESTLER, A. *The invisible writing.* New York: Macmillan, 1954.

LILLY, J. C. The human computer. Paper read at Conference on Science, Philosophy and Religion, New York, March, 1966.

MALTZ, M. *Psychocybernetics.* Englewood Cliffs, N.J.: Prentice-Hall, 1960.

MARTIN, P. W. *Experiment in depth.* New York: Pantheon, 1965.

MASLOW, A. H. *Toward a psychology of being.* Princeton, N.J.: Van Nostrand, 1962.

MASLOW, A. H. *Religions, values and peak experiences.* Columbus, Ohio: Ohio State Univer. Press, 1964.

MASTERS, R. E. L., & HOUSTON, J. *Varieties of psychedelic experience.* New York: Holt, Rinehart and Winston, 1966.

MOGAR, R. E. Current trends in psychedelic research. *Journal of Humanistic Psychology,* 1965, *5*,147–166.

MURPHY, G. *The challenge of psychical research.* New York: Harper & Row, 1961.

MURPHY, G. Human psychology in the context of the new knowledge. *Main Currents,* March–April, 1965, 75–81.

MYERS, F. W. H. *Human personality and its survival of bodily death.* New York: University Books, 1961.

ORAGE, A. R. *Psychological exercises and essays.* London: Janus, 1965.

OUSPENSKY, P. D. *In search of the miraculous.* New York: Harcourt, Brace & World, 1949.

POLANYI, M. *Personal knowledge.* Chicago: Univer. of Chicago Press, 1958.

POLLOCK, F. *Spinoza's life and philosophy.* London: Duckworth, 1899.

RHINE, J. B. *New world of the mind.* New York: Sloane, 1953.

ROGERS, C. R. *On becoming a person.* Boston: Houghton Mifflin. 1961.

ROKEACH, M. *The open and closed mind.* New York: Basic Books, 1960.
ROYCE, J. R. *The encapsulated man.* Princeton, N.J.: Van Nostrand, 1964.
SCHULTZ, J. H., & LUTHE, W. *Autogenic training.* New York: Grune & Stratton, 1959.
SHERWOOD, J. N., STOLAROFF, M. J., & HARMAN, W. W. The psychedelic experience: A new concept in psychotherapy. *Journal of Neuropsychiatry*, 1962, *4*, 69–80.
STACE, W. T. *The teachings of the mystics.* New York: Mentor Books, 1960.
SURDE, R. *Parapsychology.* New York: Citadel, 1960.
SULLIVAN, J. W. N. *Beethoven: His spiritual development.* New York: Vintage Books, 1927.
TYRELL, G. N. M. *The nature of human personality.* London: Allen & Unwin, 1954.

SECTION C *Creativity—The Organization of Surprise*

The title of this section is the best definition of creativity I know. It transcends the awkward distinctions between a creative product, a creative process, or a creative life-style. Jerome Bruner suggested it, and for this suggestion I am in his debt.

The first article is by Carl Rogers, a creative professional. He reports on the psychological health that appears in creative work. We are all aware of the neurotic, creative personality whose work is not improved by his psychological infirmities, but limited by them. He is creative in spite of himself—beyond himself.

The second article is by Arthur Koestler, a professional creator. He describes the elements underlying most creative solutions. The last two selections are reports from scientists discussing how they have solved important problems. Both men suggest that a large part of creative thinking does not take place consciously, that the solution appears to emerge from below or behind consciousness. One role of the rational, objective mind seems to be to prepare a framework to which solutions can attach themselves as they arise from the rest of the mind.

Can creativity be taught? Probably not. However, there are ways to increase the possibility of creative solutions. A problem for the more creative to play with. Creativity is fundamentally a form of play; perhaps that is why we consider it such a desirable trait.

23

Toward a Theory of Creativity

Carl R. Rogers

I maintain that there is a desperate social need for the creative behavior of creative individuals. It is this which justifies the setting forth of a tentative theory of creativity—the nature of the creative act, the conditions under which it occurs, and the manner in which it may constructively be fostered. Such a theory may serve as a stimulus and guide to research studies in this field.

The Social Need

Many of the serious criticisms of our culture and its trends may best be formulated in terms of a dearth of creativity. Let us state some of these very briefly:

In education we tend to turn out conformists, stereotypes, individuals whose education is "completed," rather than freely creative and original thinkers.

In our leisure-time activities, passive entertainment and regimented group action are overwhelmingly predominant, whereas creative activities are much less in evidence.

In the sciences, there is an ample supply of technicians, but the number who can creatively formulate fruitful hypotheses and theories is small indeed.

In industry, creation is reserved for the few—the manager, the designer, the head of the research department—whereas for the many life is devoid of original or creative endeavor.

In individual and family life the same picture holds true. In the clothes we wear, the food we eat, the books we read, and the ideas we hold, there is a strong tendency toward conformity, toward stereotypy. To be original or different is felt to be "dangerous."

Why be concerned over this? If, as a people, we enjoy conformity rather than creativity, shall we not be permitted this choice? In my estimation such a choice would be entirely reasonable were it not for one great shadow which hangs over all of us. In a time when knowledge, constructive and destructive, is advancing by the most incredible leaps and bounds into a fantastic atomic age, genuinely creative adaptation seems to represent the only possibility that man can keep abreast of the kaleidoscopic change in this world. With scientific discovery and invention proceeding, we are told, at a geometric rate of progression, a generally passive and culture-bound people cannot cope with the multiplying issues and problems. Unless individuals, groups, and nations can imagine, construct, and creatively revise new ways of relating to these complex changes, the lights will go out. Unless man can make new and original adaptations to his environment as rapidly as his science can change the environment, our culture will perish. Not only individual maladjustment and group tensions but international annihilation will be the price we pay for a lack of creativity.

Consequently it would seem to me that investigations of the process of creativity, the conditions under which this process occurs, and the ways in which it may be facilitated, are of the utmost importance.

It is in the hope of suggesting a conceptual structure under which such investigations might go forward, that the following sections are offered.

The Creative Process

There are various ways of defining creativity. In order to make more clear the meaning of what is to follow, let me present the elements which, for me, are a part of the creative process, and then attempt a definition.

In the first place, for me as scientist, there must be something observable, some product of creation. Though my fantasies may be extremely novel, they cannot usefully be defined as creative unless they eventuate in some observable product—unless they are symbolized in words, or written in a poem, or translated into a work of art, or fashioned into an invention.

These products must be novel constructions. This novelty grows out of the unique qualities of the individual in his interaction with the materials of experience. Creativity always has the stamp of the individual upon its product, but the product is not the individual, nor his materials, but partakes of the relationship between the two.

Creativity is not, in my judgment, restricted to some particular content. I am assuming that there is no fundamental difference in the creative process as it is evidenced in painting a picture, composing a symphony, devising new instruments of killing, developing a scientific theory, discovering new procedures in human relationships, or creating new formings of one's own personality as in psychotherapy. (Indeed it is my experience in this last field, rather than in one of the arts, that has given me special interest in creativity and facilitation. Intimate knowledge of the way in which the individual remolds himself in the therapeutic relationship, with originality and effective skill, gives one confidence in the creative potential of all individuals.)

My definition, then, of the creative process is that it is the emergence in action of a novel relational product, growing out of the uniqueness of the individual on the one hand, and the materials, events, people, or circumstances of his life on the other.

Let me append some negative footnotes on this definition. It makes no distinction between "good" and "bad" creativity. One man may be discovering a way of relieving pain, whereas another is devising a new and more subtle form of torture for political prisoners. Both these actions seem to me creative, even though their social value is very different. Although I shall comment on these social valuations later, I have avoided putting them in my definition because they are so fluctuating. Galileo and Copernicus made creative discoveries which in their own day were evaluated as blasphemous and wicked, and in our day as basic and constructive. We do not want to cloud our definition with terms which rest in subjectivity.

Another way of looking at this same issue is to note that to be regarded historically as representing creativity, the product must be acceptable to some group at some point of time. This fact is not helpful to our definition, however, both because of the fluctuating valuations already mentioned and because many creative products have undoubtedly never been socially noticed, have disappeared without ever having been evaluated. So this concept of group acceptance is also omitted from our definition.

In addition, it should be pointed out that our definition makes no distinction regarding the degree of creativity, since this too is a value judgment extremely variable in nature. The action of the child inventing a new game with his playmates; Einstein formulating a theory of relativity; the housewife devising a new sauce for the a meat; young author writing his first novel; all of these are, in terms of our definition, creative, and there is no attempt to set them in some order of more or less creative.

The Motivation for Creativity

The mainspring of creativity appears to be the same tendency which we discover so deeply as the curative force in psychotherapy—*man's tendency to actualize himself, to become his potentialities.* By this I mean the directional trend which is evident in all organic and human life—the urge to expand, extend, develop, mature—the tendency to express and activate all the capacities of the organism, to the extent that such activation enhances the organism or the self. This tendency may become deeply buried under layer after layer of encrusted psychological defenses; it may be hidden behind elaborate façades which deny its existence; it is my belief however, based on my experience, that it exists in every individual and awaits only the proper conditions to be released and expressed. It is this tendency which is the primary motivation for creativity as the organism forms new relationships to the environment in its endeavor most fully to be itself.

Let us now attempt to deal directly with this puzzling issue of the social value of a creative act. Presumably few of us are interested in facilitating creativity which is socially destructive. We do not wish, knowingly, to lend our efforts to developing individuals whose creative genius works itself out in new and better ways of robbing, exploiting, torturing, killing other individuals; or developing forms of political organization or art forms which lead humanity into paths of physical or psychological self-destruction. Yet how is it possible to make the necessary discriminations such that we may encourage a constructive creativity and not a destructive?

The distinction cannot be made by examining the product. The very essence of the creative is its novelty, and hence we have no standard by which to judge it. Indeed history points up the fact that the more original the product, and the more far-reaching its implications, the more likely it is to be judged by contemporaries as evil. The genuinely significant creation, whether an idea, or a work of art, or a scientific discovery, is most likely to be seen at first as erroneous, bad, or foolish. Later it may be seen as obvious, something self-evident to all. Only still later does it receive its final evaluation as a creative contribution. It seems clear that no contemporary mortal can satisfactorily evaluate a creative product at the time that it is formed, and this statement is increasingly true the greater the novelty of the creation.

Nor is it of any help to examine the purposes of the individual participating in the creative process. Many, perhaps most, of the creations and discoveries which have proved to have great social value, have been motivated by purposes having more to do with personal interests than with social value, while on the other hand history records a somewhat sorry outcome for many of these creations (various Utopias, Prohibition, etc.) which had as their avowed purpose the achievement of the social good. No, we must face the fact that the individual creates primarily because it is satisfying to him, because this behavior is felt to be self-actualizing, and we get nowhere by trying to differentiate "good" and "bad" purposes in the creative process.

Must we then give over any attempt to discriminate between creativity which is potentially constructive, and that which is potentially destructive? I do not believe this pessimistic conclusion is justified. It is here that recent clinical findings from the field of psychotherapy give us hope. It has been found that when the individual is "open" to all of his experience (a phrase which will be defined more fully), then his behavior will be creative, and his creativity may be trusted to be essentially constructive.

The differentiation may be put very briefly as follows. To the extent that the individual is denying to awareness (or repressing, if you prefer that term) large areas of his experience, then his creative formings may be pathological or socially evil, or both. To the degree that the individual is open to all aspects of his experience, and has available to his awareness all the varied sensings and perceivings which are going on within his organism, then the novel products of his interaction with his environment will tend to be constructive both for himself and others. To illustrate, an individual with paranoid tendencies may creatively develop a most novel theory of the relationship between himself and his environment, seeing evidence for his theory in all sorts of minute clues. His theory has little social value, perhaps because there is an enormous range of experience which this individual cannot permit in his awareness. Socrates, on the other hand, although also regarded as "crazy" by his contemporaries, developed novel ideas which have proven to be socially constructive. Very possibly this was because he was notably nondefensive and open to his experience.

The reasoning behind this will perhaps become more clear in the remaining sections of this paper. Primarily however it is based upon the discovery in psychotherapy:

> . . . that if we can add to the sensory and visceral experiencing which is characteristic of the whole animal kingdom the gift of a free and undistorted awareness of which only the human animal seems fully capable, we have an organism which is aware of the demands of the culture as it is of its own physiological demands for food or sex; which is just as aware of its desire for friendly relationships as it is of its desire to aggrandize itself; which is just as aware of its delicate and sensitive tenderness toward others as it is of its hostilities toward others. When man's unique capacity of awareness is thus functioning freely and fully, we find that we have, not an animal whom we must fear, not a beast who must be controlled, but an organism able to achieve, through the remarkable integrative capacity of its central nervous system, a balanced, realistic, self-enhancing, other enhancing behavior as a resultant of all these elements of awareness. To put it another way, when man is less than fully man—when he denies to awareness various aspects of his experience—then indeed we have all too often reason to fear him and his behavior, as the present world situation testifies. But when he is most fully man, when he is his complete organism, when awareness of experience, that peculiarly human attribute, is most fully operating, then he is to be trusted, then his behavior is constructive. It is not always conventional. It will not always be conforming. It will be individualized. But it will also be socialized.

The Inner Conditions of Constructive Creativity

What are the conditions within the individual which are most closely associated with a potentially constructive creative act? I see these as possibilities.

A. *Openness to experience: extensionality.* This is the opposite of psychological defensiveness, when to protect the organization of the self certain experiences are prevented from coming into awareness except in distorted fashion. In a person who is open to experience each stimulus is freely relayed through the nervous system, without being distorted by any process of defensiveness. Whether the stimulus originates in the environment, in the impact of form, color, or sound, on the sensory nerves, or whether it originates in the viscera, or as a memory trace in the central nervous system, it is available to awareness. This means that instead of perceiving in predetermined categories (trees are green; college education is good; modern art is silly) the individual is aware of this existential moment as *it* is, thus being alive to many experiences which fall outside the usual categories (*this* tree is lavender; *this* college education is damaging; *this* modern sculpture has a powerful effect on me).

This last suggests another way of describing openness to experience. It means lack of rigidity and permeability of boundaries in concepts, beliefs, perceptions, and hypotheses. It means a tolerance for ambiguity where ambiguity exists. It means the ability to receive much conflicting information without forcing closure upon the situation. It means what the general semanticist calls the "extensional orientation."

This complete openness of awareness to what exists at this moment is, I believe, an important condition of constructive creativity. In an equally intense but more narrowly limited fashion it is no doubt present in all creativity. The deeply maladjusted artist who cannot recognize or be aware of the sources of unhappiness in himself may nevertheless be sharply and sensitively aware of form and color in his experience. The tyrant (whether on a petty or grand scale) who cannot face the weaknesses in himself may nevertheless be completely alive to and aware of the chinks in the psychological armor of those with whom he deals. Because there is the openness to one phase of experience, creativity is possible; because the openness is *only* to one phase of experience, the product of this creativity may be potentially destructive of social values. The more the individual has available to himself a sensitive awareness of all phases of his experience, the more sure we can be that his creativity will be personally and socially constructive.

B. *An internal locus of evaluation.* Perhaps the most fundamental condition of creativity is that the source of locus or evaluative judgment is internal. The value of his product is, for the creative person, established not by the praise or criticism of others, but by himself. Have I created something satisfying to *me*? Does it express a part of me—my feeling or my thought, my pain or my ecstasy? These are the only questions which really matter to the creative person, or to any person when he is being creative.

This does not mean that he is oblivious to, or unwilling to be aware of, the judgments of others. It is simply that the basis of evaluation lies within himself, in his own organismic reaction to and appraisal of his product. If to the person it has the "feel" of being "me in action," of being an actualization of potentialities in himself which heretofore have not existed and are now emerging into existence, then it is satisfying and creative, and no outside evaluation can change that fundamental fact.

C. *The ability to toy with elements and concepts.* Though this is probably less important than A or B, it seems to be a condition of creativity. Associated with the openness and lack of rigidity described under A is the ability to play spontaneously with ideas, colors, shapes, relationships—to juggle elements into impossible juxtapositions, to shape wild hypotheses, to make the given problematic, to express the ridiculous, to translate from one form to another, to transform into improbable equivalents. It is from this spontaneous toying and exploration that there arises the hunch, the creative seeing of life in a new and significant way. It is as though out of the wasteful spawning of thousands of possibilities there emerges one or two evolutionary forms with the qualities which give them a more permanent value.

The Creative Act and Its Concomitants

When these three conditions obtain, constructive creativity will occur. But we cannot expect an accurate description of the creative act, for by its very nature it is indescribable. This is the unknown which we must recognize as unknowable until it occurs. This is the improbable that becomes probable. Only in a very general way can we say that a creative act is the natural behavior of an organism which has a tendency to arise when that organism is open to all of its inner and outer experiencing, and when it is free to try out in flexible fashion all manner of relationships. Out of this multitude of half-formed possibilities the organism, like a great computing machine, selects this one which most effectively meets an inner need, or that one which forms a more effective relationship with the environment, or this other one which discovers a more simple and satisfying order in which life may be perceived.

Then is one quality of the creative act which may, however, be described. In almost all the products of creation we note a selectivity, or emphasis, an evidence of discipline, an attempt to bring out the essence. The artist paints surfaces or textures in simplified form, ignoring the minute variations which exist in reality. The scientist formulates a basic law of relationships, brushing aside all the particular events or circumstances which might conceal its naked beauty. The writer selects those words and phrases which give unity to his expression. We may say that this is the influence of the specific person, of the "I." Reality exists in a multiplicity of confusing facts, but "I" bring a structure to my relationship to reality; I have "my" way of perceiving reality, and it is this (unconsciously?) disciplined personal selectivity or abstraction which gives to creative products their esthetic quality.

Although this is as far as we can go in describing any aspect of the creative act, there are certain of its concomitants in the individual which may be mentioned. The first is what we may call the Eureka feeling —"This is *it!*" "I have discovered!" "This is what I wanted to express!"

Another concomitant is the anxiety of separateness.[1] I do not believe that many significantly creative products are formed without the feeling, "I am alone. No one has ever done just this before. I have ventured into territory where no one has been. Perhaps I am foolish, or wrong, or lost, or abnormal."

Still another experience which usually accompanies creativity is the desire to communicate. It is doubtful whether a human being can create, without wishing to share his creation. It is the only way he can assuage the anxiety of separateness and assure himself that he belongs to the group. He may confide his theories only to his private diary. He may put his discoveries in some cryptic code. He may conceal his poems in a locked drawer. He may put away his paintings in a closet. Yet he desires to communicate with a group which will understand him, even if he must imagine such a group. He does not create in order to communicate, but once having created he desires to share this new aspect of himself in-relation-to-his-environment with others.

Conditions Fostering Constructive Creativity

Thus far I have tried to describe the nature of creativity, to indicate that quality of individual experience which increases the likelihood that creativity will be constructive, to set forth the necessary conditions for the creative act and to state some of its concomitants. But if we are to make progress in meeting the social need which was presented initially, we must know whether constructive creativity can be fostered, and if so, how.

From the very nature of the inner conditions of creativity it is clear that they cannot be forced, but must be permitted to emerge. The farmer cannot make the germ develop and sprout from the seed; he can only supply the nurturing conditions which will permit the seed to develop its own potentialities. So it is with creativity. How can we establish the external conditions which will foster and nourish the internal conditions described above? My experience in psychotherapy leads me to

[1] For this and the idea in the following paragraph I am specifically indebted to my student and colleague, Mr. Robert Lipgar.

believe that by setting up conditions of psychological safety and freedom, we maximize the likelihood of an emergence of constructive creativity. Let me spell out these conditions in some detail, labeling them as X and Y.

X. *Psychological Safety.* This may be established by three associated processes:

1. *Accepting the individual as of unconditional worth.* Whenever a teacher, parent, therapist, or other person with a facilitating function feels basically that this individual is of worth in his own right and in his own unfolding, no matter what his present condition or behavior, he is fostering creativity. This attitude can probably be genuine only when the teacher, parent, etc., senses the potentialities of the individual and thus is able to have an unconditional faith in him, no matter what his present state.

The effect on the individual as he apprehends this attitude is to sense a climate of safety. He gradually learns that he can be whatever he is, without sham or façade, since he seems to be regarded as of worth no matter what he does. Hence he has less need of rigidity, can discover what it means to be himself, can try to actualize himself in new and spontaneous ways. He is, in other words, moving toward creativity.

2. *Providing a climate in which external evaluation is absent.* When we cease to form judgments of the other individual from our own locus of evaluation, we are fostering creativity. For the individual to find himself in an atmosphere where he is not being evaluated, not being measured by some external standard, is enormously freeing. Evaluation is always a threat, always creates a need for defensiveness, always means that some portion of experience must be denied to awareness. If this product is evaluated as good by external standards, then I must not admit my own dislike of it. If what I am doing is bad by external standards, then I must not be aware of the fact that it seems to be me, to be part of myself. But if judgments based on external standards are not being made then I can be more open to my experience, can recognize my own likings and dislikings, the nature of the materials and of my reaction to them, more sharply and more sensitively. I can begin to recognize the locus of evaluation within myself. Hence I am moving toward creativity.

To allay some possible doubts and fears in the reader, it should be pointed out that to cease evaluating another is not to cease having reactions. It may, as a matter of fact, free one to react. "I don't like your idea" (or painting, or invention, or writing), is not an evaluation, but a reaction. It is subtly but sharply different from a judgment which says, "What you are doing is bad (or good), and this quality is assigned to you from some external source." The first statement permits the individual to maintain his own locus of evaluation. It holds the possibility that I am unable to appreciate something which is actually very good. The second statement, whether it praises or condemns, tends to put the person at the mercy of outside forces. He is being told that he cannot simply ask himself whether this product is a valid expression of himself; he must be concerned with what others think. He is being led away from creativity.

3. *Understanding empathically.* It is this which provides the ultimate in psychological safety, when added to the other two. If I say that I "accept" you, but know nothing of you, this is a shallow acceptance indeed, and you realize that it may change if I actually come to know you. But if I understand you, empathically, see you and what you are feeling and doing from your point of view, enter your private world and see it as it appears to you—and still accept you—then this is safety indeed. In this climate you can permit your real self to emerge, and to express itself in varied and novel formings as it relates itself to the world. This is a basic fostering of creativity.

Y. *Psychological freedom.* When a teacher, parent, therapist, or other facilitating person permits the individual a complete freedom of symbolic expression, creativity is fostered. This permissiveness gives the individual complete freedom to think, to feel, to be, whatever is most inward within himself. It fosters the openness, and the playful and spontaneous juggling of percepts, concepts, and meanings, which is a part of creativity.

Note that it is complete freedom of *symbolic* expression which is described. To express in behavior all feelings, impulses, and formings may not in all instances be freeing. Behavior may in some instances be limited by society, and this is at it should be. But symbolic expression need not be limited. Thus, to destroy a hated object (whether one's mother or a rococo building) by destroying a symbol of it, is freeing. To attack it in reality may create guilt and narrow the psychological freedom which is experienced. (I feel unsure of this paragraph, but it is the best formulation I can give at the moment which seems to square with my experience).

The permissiveness which is being described is not softness or indulgence or encouragement. It is permission to be *free*, which also means that one is responsible. The individual is as free to be afraid of a new venture as to be eager for it; free to bear the consequences of his mistakes as well as of his achievements. It is this type of freedom responsibly to be oneself which fosters the development of a secure locus of evaluation within oneself, and hence tends to bring about the inner conditions of constructive creativity.

Putting the Theory to Work

There is but one excuse for attempting to discover conceptual order and stating it in a theory; that is to develop hypotheses from the theory which may be tested. By such testing profitable directions for action may be found, and the theory itself may be corrected, modified, and extended. Thus if this theory which I have tentatively formulated is worthwhile, it should be possible to develop from it hypotheses which might be objectively tested in classes in the arts; in education outside of the arts; in leadership training groups whether in industry or the military services; in problem-solving groups of any sort. Let me suggest a few of the general hypotheses which might be given more specific and operational form for any of the above groups. They would apply whether one was concerned with the development of creative artists or creative leaders; with originality of design or creative methods of problem-solving.

Hypotheses regarding inner conditions:

1. Individuals who exhibit a measurably greater degree of conditions A, B, and C (openness, internal locus of evaluation, ability to toy with materials) will, over any given period of time spontaneously form more products judged to be novel and creative, than a matched group who exhibit a lesser degree of A, B, and C.

2. The products of the first group will not only be more numerous, but will be judged to be more significant in their novelty. (Such a hypothesis could be given operational definition in art classes, problem-solving groups, or leadership training groups, for example.)

3. Condition A (openness to experience) can be predicted from conditions B or C, which are more easily measurable. (It is not at all certain that this hypothesis would be upheld, but it would be worth careful investigation. If conditions A, B, and C are highly intercorrelated, then they could jointly be predicted from the one which proved most easily measurable. Thus we might gain clues as to how we might less laboriously select graduate students, for example, with a high creative potential.)

Hypotheses regarding fostering constructive creativity:

4. Given two matched groups, the one in which the leader establishes a measurably greater degree of conditions XI, X2, X3, and Y (psychological safety and freedom) will spontaneously form a greater number of creative products, and these products

will be judged to be more significantly novel.

5. Conditions X1, X2, X3, and Y are not of equal importance in fostering creativity. By comparing different groups in which one or another of these conditions is emphasized or minimized it may be possible to determine which of these conditions is most effective in facilitating creativity.

6. A group in which conditions X1, X2, X3, and Y are established should, according to our theory, have more effective and harmonious interpersonal relationships than a matched group in which these conditions are present to a lesser degree. (The reasoning is that if creativity is all of a piece, then a group in which the fostering conditions are established should be more constructively creative in social relationships.)

7. The extent to which different groups in our culture provide the fostering conditions (X and Y) could be measured. In this way one could determine whether creativity is now being fostered to a greater degree by the family group, classes in schools and colleges, bull sessions, social clubs and groups, interest groups, military groups, industrial groups. (One wonders how college classes would show up in such a comparison.)

Conclusion

I have endeavored to present an orderly way of thinking about the creative process, in order that some of these ideas might be put to a rigorous and objective test. My justification for formulating this theory and my reason for hoping that such research may be carried out is that the present development of the physical sciences is making an imperative demand upon us as individuals and as a culture for creative behavior in adapting ourselves to our new world if we are to survive.

24

The Three Domains of Creativity

Arthur Koestler

This chapter attempts to give a condensed outline of a theory I have set out in detail in a recent book (1964) and to carry that theory the next step. The proposition I shall submit is, in a nutshell, that the conscious and unconscious processes which enter into all three forms of creative activity have a basic pattern in common. And when I speak of *three* forms of creativity, I mean the domains of artistic originality, scientific discovery, and comic inspiration. I believe that all creative activity falls into one or another of these three categories or, more frequently, into some combination of them. If you speak for instance, of cooking as "creative," you automatically imply that cooking is either an art or a science or both.

As a first step toward describing that pattern, let us try something simple like this: The creative act consists in combining previously unrelated structures in such a way that you get more out of the emergent whole than you have put in. This sound like making a *perpetuum mobile*, and in a sense it is, because mental evolution, like biological evolution, seems to contradict the second law of thermodynamics, which contends that the universe is running down as if afflicted by metal fatigue. But we will not go into this; instead, let me illustrate by a few schoolbook examples what I mean by combining two previously unrelated structures.

Association and Bisociation

The motions of the tides have been known to man since time immemorial. So have the motions of the moon. But the idea to relate the two, the idea that the tides were due to the attraction of the moon, occurred, as far as we know, for the first time to a German astronomer in the seventeenth century, and when Galileo read about it, he laughed it off as an occult fancy (Santillana, 1953, p. 469). Moral: The more familiar each of the previously unrelated structures are, the more striking the new synthesis and the more obvious it seems in the driver's mirror of hindsight.

The history of science is a history of marriages between ideas which were previously strangers to each other, and frequently considered incompatible. Lodestones—magnets—were known in antiquity as some curiosity of nature. In the Middle Ages they were used for two purposes: as navigators' compasses and as a means to attract an estranged wife back to her husband. Equally well known were the curious properties of amber, which, when rubbed, acquires the virtue of attracting flimsy objects. The Greek word for amber is *elektron*, but the Greeks were not much interested in electricity, nor were the Middle Ages. For nearly two thousand years, electricity and magnetism were considered separate phenomena, in no way related to each other. In 1820, Hans Christian Oersted discovered that an electric current flowing through a wire deflected a compass needle which happened to be lying on his table. At that moment the two contexts began to fuse into one—electromagnetism—creating a kind of chain reaction which is still continuing and gaining in momentum; forever amber.

From Pythagoras, who combined arithmetic and geometry, to Einstein, who unified energy and matter in a single sinister equation, the pattern is always the same. The Latin word *cogito* comes from *coagitare*, "to shake together." The creative act does not create something out of nothing, like the God of the Old Testament; it combines, reshuffles, and relates already existing but hitherto separate ideas, facts, frames of perception, associative contexts. This act of cross-fertilization —or self-fertilization within a single brain—seems to be the essence of creativity. I have proposed for it the term *bisociation*. It is not a pretty word, but it helps us to make a distinction between the sudden leap of the creative act and the more normal, more pedestrian, associative routines of thinking.

The difference between the two could be described as follows. Orderly thinking (as distinct from daydreaming) is always controlled by certain rules of the game. In the psychological laboratory, the experimenter lays down the rule: "Name opposites." Then he says, "dark," and the subject promptly says, "light." But if the rule is "synonyms," then the subject will associate "dark" with "black" or "night" or "shadow." To talk of stimuli in a vacuum is meaningless; what response a stimulus will evoke depends on the game we are playing at the time.

But we do not live in laboratories where the rules of the game are laid down by explicit orders; in normal life, the rules control our thinking unconsciously—and there's the rub. When talking, the laws of grammar and syntax function below the level of awareness, in the gaps between the words. So do certain simple rules of common or garden-variety logic and of courtesy and convention, and also the complex and specialized rules which we call "frames of reference" or "universes of discourse" or "thinking in terms of" this or that—of physiological explanations or ethical value judgments. All thinking is playing a game according to fixed rules and more or less flexible strategies. The game of chess allows you a vast number of strategic choices among the moves permitted by the rules, but there is a limit to them. There are hopeless situations in chess when the most subtle strategies will not save you—short of offering your opponent a jumbo-sized Martini. Now in fact there is no rule in chess preventing you from offering your opponent a Martini. But making a person drunk while remaining sober oneself is a different sort of game with a different context. Combining the two games is a bisociation. In other words, associative routine means thinking according to a given set of rules, on a single plane, as it were. The bisociative act means combining two different sets of rules, to live on several planes at once.

Three Kinds of Reactions

I do not mean to belittle the value of law-abiding routines. They lend coherence and stability to behavior and structured order to thought. But they have their obvious limitations. For one thing, every game tends to become monotonous after awhile and fails to satisfy the artist's craving for self-expression and the scientist's search for explanations. In the second place, the world moves on, and new problems arise which cannot be solved within the conventional frames of reference by applying to them the accepted rules of the game. Then a crisis occurs: The position on the scientist's checkerboard is blocked; the artist's vision is blurred; the search is on, the fumbling and groping for that happy combination of ideas—of lodestone and amber—which will lead to the new synthesis.

The Aha Reaction. Gestalt psychologists have coined a word for that moment of truth, the flash of illumination, when bits of the puzzle suddenly click into place. They call it the *Aha* experience. One may regard it as a synonym for the "Eureka!" cry. Imagine it written on a blackboard, thus:

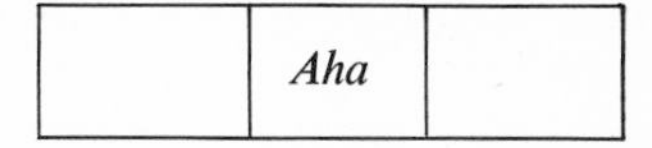

We shall seen in a moment the reason for this display. There is an empty panel on each side—for the *Aha* response represents only *one* type of reaction after bisociative click. There are others. Let me tell my favorite anecdote:

A nobleman at the court of Louis XV had unexpectedly returned from a journey and, on entering his wife's boudoir, found her in the arms of a bishop. After a short hesitation, the nobleman walked calmly to the window and went through the motions of blessing the people in the street.

"What are you doing?" cried the anguished wife.

"Monseigneur is performing my functions," replied the nobleman, "so I am performing his."

Well, some readers will be kind enough to laugh; let us call this the *Haha* reaction:[1]

Haha	*Aha*	

[1] I owe the term "*Haha* reaction" to Dr. Brennig James's paper "The Function of Jokes" (unpublished), which he kindly sent me.

THE HAHA REACTION

The Logic of Laughter. Now let us inquire into the difference between the *Haha* and the *Aha* reactions. Why do we laugh? Let me try to analyze first the intellectual and then the emotional aspect of this odd reaction. The nobleman's behavior is both unexpected and perfectly logical—but of a logic not usually applied to this type of situation. It is the logic of the division of labor, where the rule of the game is the *quid pro quo*, the give-and-take. But we expected, of course, that his reactions would be governed by a quite different logic or rule of the game. It is the interaction between these two mutually exclusive associative contexts which produces the comic effect. It compels us to perceive the situation at the same time in two self-consistent but habitually incompatible frames of reference; it make us function on two wavelengths simultaneously, as it were. While this unusual condition lasts, the event is not, as is normally the case, perceived in a single frame of reference but is bisociated with two.

But the unusual condition does not last for long. The act of discovery leads to a lasting synthesis, a *fusion* of the two previously unrelated frames of reference; in the comic bisociation you have a *collision* between incompatible frames which for a brief moment cross each other's path. But whether the frames are compatible or not, whether they will collide or merge, depends on subjective factors, on the attitudes of the audience—for, after all, the colliding or merging takes place in the audience's heads. The history of science abounds with examples of discoveries greeted with howls of laughter because they seemed to be a marriage of incompatibles—until the marriage bore fruit and the alleged incompatibility of the partners turned out to derive from prejudice. The humorist, on the other hand, deliberately chooses discordant codes of behavior or universes of discourse to expose their hidden incongruities in the resulting clash. Comic discovery is paradox stated—scientific discovery is paradox resolved.

Let me return for a moment to our poor nobleman blessing the crowd through the window. His gesture was a truly original inspiration. If he had followed the conventional rules of the game, he would have had to beat up or kill the bishop. But at the court of Louis XV, assassinating a monseigneur would have been considered, if not exactly a crime, still in very bad taste. It simply could not be done; the chessboard was blocked. To solve the problem, that is, to save his face and at the same time to humiliate his opponent, the nobleman had to bring into the situation a second frame of reference, governed by different rules of the game, and combine it with the first. All original comic invention is a creative act, a malicious discovery.

The Emotional Dynamics of Laughter. The emphasis is on malicious, and this brings us from the *logic* of humor to the *emotional factor* in the *Haha* reaction. When the expert humorist tells an anecdote he creates a certain tension which mounts as the narrative progresses. But it never reaches its expected climax. The punch line acts like a guillotine which cuts across the logical development of the situation; it debunks our dramatic expectations, and the tension becomes redundant and is exploded in laughter. To put it differently, laughter disposes of the overflow of emotion which has become pointless, is denied by reason, and has to be somehow worked off along physiological channels of least resistance.[2]

I shall not bore you with physiological explanations because if you look at the coarse and brutal merriment in a tavern

[2] For a review of the theories on laughter, see Koestler, 1964, Chaps. 1 and 2; also Koestler, 1949, part 1 and appendix 2.

scene by Hogarth or Rawlinson, you realize at once that the revelers are working off their surplus of adrenalin by contractions of the face muscles, slapping of thighs, and explosive exhalations of breath from the half-closed glottis. The emotions worked off in laughter are aggression, sexual gloating, conscious or unconscious sadism—all operating through the sympathicoadrenal system. On the other hand, when you look at a clever *New Yorker* cartoon, Homeric laughter yields to an amused and rarefied smile; the ample flow of adrenalin has been distilled into a grain of Attic salt. Think, for instance, of that classic definition: "What is a sadist?" "A person who is kind to a masochist."

The word "witticism" is derived from "wit" in its original sense of "ingenuity." The clown is brother to the sage; their domains are continuous, without a sharp dividing line. As we move from the coarse toward the higher forms of humor, the joke shades into epigram and riddle, the comic simile into the discovery of hidden analogies; and the emotions involved show a similar transition. The emotive voltage discharged in coarse laughter is aggression robbed of its purpose; the tension discharged in the *Aha* reaction is derived from an intellectual challenge. It snaps at the moment when the penny drops—when we have solved the riddle hidden in the *New Yorker* cartoon, in a brainteaser, or in a scientific problem.

The Ah Reaction. Let me repeat, the two domains of humor and discovery form a continuum. As we travel across it, from left to center, so to speak, the emotional climate gradually changes from the malice of the jester to the detached objectivity of the sage. If we now continue the journey in the same direction, we find equally gradual transitions into a third domain, that of the artist. The artist hints rather than states, and he poses riddles. So we get a symmetrically reversed transition toward the other end of the spectrum, from highly intellectualized art forms toward the more sensual and emotive, ending in the thought-free beatitude of the oceanic feeling—the cloud of unknowing.

But how does one define the emotional climate of art? How does one classify the emotions which give rise to the experience of beauty? If you leaf through textbooks of experimental psychology, you will not find much mention of it. When behaviorists use the word "emotion," they nearly always refer to hunger, sex, rage, and fear and to the related effects of the release of adrenalin. They have no explanations to offer for the curious reaction one experiences when listening to Mozart or looking at the ocean or reading for the first time John Donne's *Holy Sonnets.* Nor will you find in the textbooks a description of the physiological processes accompanying the reaction: the moistening of the eyes, perhaps a quiet overflow of the lachrymal glands, the catching of one's breath, followed by a kind of rapt tranquillity, the draining of all tensions. Let us call this the *Ah* reaction and thus complete our trinity.

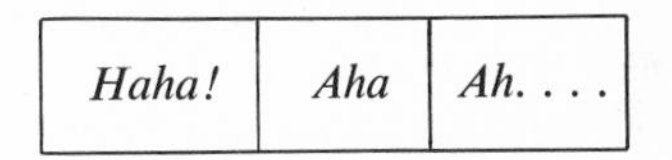

Haha!	*Aha*	*Ah. . . .*

Laughter and weeping, the Greek masks of comedy and tragedy, mark the two extremes of a continuous spectrum; both are overflow reflexes, but they are in every respect physiological opposites. Laughter is mediated by the sympathicoadrenal branch of the autonomous nervous system, weeping by the parasympathetic branch. The first tends to galvanize the body into action; the second tends toward passivity and catharsis. Watch how you breathe when you laugh: long, deep intakes of air, followed by bursts of exhalatory puffs—"Ha, ha, ha." In weeping, you do the opposite: short, gasping inspirations—sobs—are followed by long, sighing expirations—"a-a-h, aah" (cf. Koestler, 1964, pp. 271, 284; and, for a bibliography on the psychology and physiology of weeping pp. 725-728).

Self-assertion and Self-transcendence

In keeping with this, the emotions which overflow in the *Ah* reactions are the direct opposites of those exploded in laughter. The latter belong to the familiar adrenergic hunger-rage-fear category; let us call them the *aggressive-defensive* or self-assertive emotions. Their opposites we might call the *self-transcending* or participatory or integrative emotions. They are epitomized in what Freud called the "oceanic feeling"; When you listen to a Bach toccata thundering through the cathedral, you experience that expansion and depersonalizing of awareness in which the self seems to dissolve like a grain of salt in a lot of water.

This class of emotions shows a wide range of variety. They may be joyous or sad, tragic or lyrical; but they have a common denominator: the feeling of participation in an experience which transcends the boundaries of the self. That higher entity, of which the self feels a part, to which it surrenders its identity, may be nature, God, the anima mundi, the magic of forms, or the ocean of sound.

The self-assertive emotions are expressed in bodily actions; the self-transcending emotions operate through the passive processes of empathy, rapport, projection, and identification. In laughter, tension is suddenly exploded, emotion debunked; in weeping, it is drained away in a gradual process which does not break the continuity of mood. The self-transcending emotions do not tend toward action but toward quiescence and catharsis. Respiration and pulse rate are slowed down; "entrancement" is a step toward the trancelike states induced by contemplative techniques or drugs. The self-transcending emotions cannot be consummated by any specific, voluntary action. You cannot take the mountain panorama home with you; you cannot merge with the infinite by any exertion of the body. To be "overwhelmed" by awe and wonder, "enraptured" by a smile, "entranced" by beauty—each of these verbs expresses a passive surrender. The surplus of emotion cannot be worked off in action; it can be consummated only in internal, visceral and glandular processes (Koestler, 1964, pp. 285-300).

The participatory or self-transcending tendencies, these stepchildren of psychology, are as powerful and deeply rooted in man's nature as his self-assertive drives. Freud and Piaget, among others, have emphasized the fact that the very young child does not differentiate between ego and environment. The nourishing breast appears to it as a more intimate possession than the toes of its own body. It is aware of events but not of itself as a separate entity. It lives in a state of mental symbiosis with the outer world, a continuation of the biological symbiosis in the womb. The universe is focused in the self, and the self *is* the universe—a condition which Piaget called "protoplasmic consciousness." It may be likened to a liquid, fluid universe, traversed by dynamic currents, the rise and fall of physiological needs causing minor storms which come and go without leaving solid traces. Gradually the floods recede, and the first islands of objective reality emerge; the contours grow firmer and sharper; the islands grow into continents; the dry territories of reality are mapped out; but side by side with it, the liquid world coexists, surrounding it, interpenetrating it by canals and inland lakes, the vestigial relics of the erstwhile symbiotic communion. Here, then, we have the origin of that oceanic feeling which the artist and the mystic strive to recapture on a higher level of development, at a higher turn of the spiral.

Art and Self-transcendence

Children and primitives are apt to confuse dream and reality; they not only believe in miracles but also believe themselves capable of performing them. When the medicine man disguises himself as the rain god, he produces rain. Drawing a picture of a slain bison assures a successful hunt. This is the ancient unitary source out of which the ritual dance and song, the mystery plays of the Achaeans, and the calendars of the Babylonian priest-astronomers were derived. The shadows in Plato's cave are symbols of man's loneliness; the paintings in the Altamira caves are symbols of his magic powers.

We have traveled a long way from Altamira and Lascaux, but the artist's inspirations and the scientist's intuitions are still fed by that same unitary source—though by now we should rather call it an underground river. Wishes do not displace mountains, but in our dreams they still do. Symbiotic consciousness is never completely defeated but merely relegated underground to those unconscious levels in the mental hierarchy where the boundaries of the ego are still fluid and blurred—as blurred as the distinction between the actor and the hero whom he impersonates and with whom the spectator identifies. The actor on the stage is himself and somebody else at the same time—he is both the dancer and the rain god.

Dramatic illusion is the coexistence in the spectator's mind of two universes which are logically incompatible; his awareness, suspended between the two planes, exemplifies the bisociative process in its most striking form. All the more striking because he produces physical symptoms—palpitations, sweating, or tears—in response to the perils of a Desdemona whom he *knows* to exist merely as a shadow on the TV screen or as dry printer's ink in the pages of a book. Yet let Othello but get the hiccups, and instead of coexistence between the two planes juxtaposed in the spectator's mind, you get collision between them. Comic impersonation produces the *Haha* reaction because the parodist arouses aggression and malice; dramatic stagecraft achieves the suspension of disbelief, the coexistence of incompatible planes, because it induces the spectator to identify. It excites the self-transcending and inhibits or neutralizes the self-assertive emotions. Even when fear and anger are aroused in the spectator, these are vicarious emotions, derived from his identification with the hero, which in itself is a self-transcending act. Vicarious emotions aroused in this manner carry a dominant element of sympathy, which facilitates catharsis in conformity with the Aristotelian definition—"through incidents arousing horror and pity to accomplish the purgation of such emotions." Art is a school of self-transcendence.

We thus arrive at a further generalization: *The* Haha *reaction signals the collision of bisociated contexts; the* Aha *reaction signals their fusion; and the* Ah *reaction signals their juxtaposition.*

This difference is reflected in the quasi-cumulative progression of science through a series of successive mergers, compared with the quasi-timeless character of art in its continuous restatement of basic patterns of experience in changing idioms. I said "quasi" because it can be shown that this, too, is a matter of degrees, because the progress of science is not cumulative in the strict sense. It is moving in a dizzy, zigzag course rather than in a straight line (Kuhn, 1962; Popper, 1959). On the other hand, the development of a given art form over a period of time often displays a cumulative progression (Gombrich, 1962). I shall return to this in a moment, but first let me briefly mention a few more types of the combinatorial activities which enter into the fabric of art.

Bisociative Structures in Art

When we listen to poetry, two frames of reference interact in our minds: one governed by meaning, the other by rhythmic patterns of sound. Moreover, the two frames operate on two different levels of awareness: the first in broad daylight, the other much deeper down. The rhythmic beat of poetry is designed, in the words of Yeats, "to lull the mind into a waking trance." Rhythmic pulsation is a fundamental characteristic of life; our ready responses to it arise from the depths of the nervous system, from those archaic strata which reverberate to the shaman's drum and which make us particularly receptive to, and suggestible by, messages which arrive in a rhythmic pattern or are accompanied by such a pattern.

The rhyme has equally ancient roots. It repeats the last syllable of a line. Now the repetition of syllables is a conspicuous phenomenon at the very origins of language. The young child is addicted to babbling, "obble-gobble," "humpty-dumpty," and so on. In primitive languages, words like "kala-kala" or "moku-moku" abound. Closely related to it is association by pure sound. The rhyme is in fact nothing but a glorified pun—two strings of ideas tied together in a phonetic knot. Its ancient origins are revealed in the punning mania of children and in certain forms of mental disorder and in the frequent recurrence of puns in dreams. "What could be moister than the tears of an oyster?" The statement that the oyster is a wet creature and that therefore its tears must be particularly wet would not make much of an impression, but when meaning is bisociated with sound, there is magic. This is what I meant when I said that routine thinking involves a single matrix, whereas creative thinking always involves more than one plane. Needless to say, it is difficult to identify with an oyster, so the reaction will be *Haha*, not *Ah*.

Thus rhythm and meter, rhyme and euphony, are not artificial ornaments of language but combinations of contemporary, sophisticated frames of reference with archaic and emotionally more powerful games of the mind. In other words, creative activity always implies a *temporary regression* to these archaic levels, while a simultaneous process goes on in parallel on the highest, most articulate and critical level: the poet is like a skin diver with a breathing tube.

The same applies, of course, to poetic imagery. Visual thinking is an earlier form of mental activity than thinking in verbal concepts; we dream mostly in pictures and visual symbols. It has been said that scientific discovery consists in seeing an analogy where nobody has seen one before. When in the Song of Songs, Solomon compared the Shulamite's neck to a tower of ivory, he saw an analogy which nobody had seen before; when Harvey compared the heart of a fish to a mechanical pump, he did the same; and when the caricaturist draws a nose like a cucumber, he again does just that. In fact, all combinatorial, bisociative patterns are trivalent—they can enter the service of humor, discovery, or art, as the case may be.

Let me give you another example of this trivalence. Man has always looked at nature by superimposing a second frame on the retinal image—mythological, anthromorphic, scientific frames. The artist sees in terms of his medium—stone, clay, charcoal, pigment—and in terms of his preferential emphasis on contours or surfaces, stability or motion, curves or cubes. So, of course, does the caricaturist, only his motives are different. And so does the scientist. A geographical map has the same relation to a landscape that a character sketch has to a face. Every diagram or model, every schematic or symbolic representation of physical or mental processes is an unemotional caricature of reality—at least unemotional in the sense that the bias is of an obvious kind, although some models of the human mind as a conditioned-reflex automaton seem to be crude caricatures inspired by unconscious bias.

In the language of behaviorist psychology, we would have to say that Cézanne, glancing at a landscape, receives a stimulus, to which he responds by putting a dab of paint on the canvas, and that is all there is to it. But in fact the two activities take place on two different planes. The stimulus comes from one environment, the distant landscape. The response acts on a different environment, a square surface of 10 by 15 inches. The two environments obey two different sets of laws. An isolated brush-stroke does not represent an isolated detail in the landscape. There are no point-to-point correspondences between the two planes; each obeys a different rule of the game. The artist's vision is bifocal, just as the poet's voice is bivocal, as he bisociates sound and meaning.

Extraconscious Factors in Discovery

Let me return for a moment to science. I said at the beginning of this chapter that the essence of discovery is the coagitation, the shaking together, of already existing frames of reference or areas of knowledge. Now we arrive at the crucial question: just how does the creative mind hit upon that happy combination of ideas which nobody had thought of combining before?

Artists are inclined to believe that scientists reason in strictly rational, precise verbal terms. They do, of course, nothing of the sort. In 1945, a famous inquiry was organized by Jacques Hadamard (1949) among eminent mathematicians in America to find out their working methods. The results showed that all of them, with only two exceptions, thought neither in verbal terms nor in algebraic symbols but relied on visual imagery of a vague, hazy kind. Einstein was among those who answered the questionnaire; he wrote: "The words of the language as they are written or spoken do not seem to play any role in my mechanism of thought, which relies on more or less clear images of a visual and some of a muscular type. It seems to me that what you call full consciousness is a limit case, which can never be fully accomplished because consciousness is a narrow thing."

Einstein's statement is typical. On the testimony of those original thinkers who have taken the trouble to record their methods of work, *not only verbal thinking but conscious thinking in general plays only a subordinate part in the brief, decisive phase of the creative act itself.* Their virtually unanimous emphasis on spontaneous intuitions and hunches of unconscious origin, which they are at a loss to explain, suggests that the role of strictly rational and verbal processes in scientific discovery has been vastly overestimated since the age of enlightment, There are always large chunks of irrationality embedded in the creative process, not only in art (where we are ready to accept it) but in the exact sciences as well.

The scientist who, facing his blocked problem, regresses from precise verbal thinking to vague visual imagery seems to follow Woodworth's advice: "Often we have to get away from speech in order to think clearly." Words crystallize thoughts, but a crystal is no longer a liquid. Language can act as a screen between the thinker and reality. Creativity often starts where language ends, that is, by regressing to preverbal levels, to more fluid and uncommitted forms of mental activity.

Now I do not mean, of course, that there is a little Socratic demon housed in the scientist's or artist's skull who does his homework for him; nor should one confuse unconscious mentation with Freud's primary process. The primary process is defined by him as devoid of logic, governed by the pleasure principle, apt to confuse perception and hallucination, and accompanied by massive discharges of affect. It seems that between this very primary process and the so-called secondary process governed by the reality principle, we must interpolate a whole hierarchy of cognitive structures, which are not simply mixtures of primary and secondary, but are autonomous systems in their own right, each governed by a distinct set of rules. The paranoid delusion, the dream, the daydream, free association, the mentalities of children of various ages and of primitives at various stages should not be lumped together, for each has its own logic or rules of the game. But while clearly different in many respects, all these forms of mentation have certain features in common, since they are ontogenetically, and perhaps phylogenetically, older than those of the civilized adult. They are less rigid, more tolerant, and more ready to combine seemingly incompatible ideas and to perceive hidden analogies between cabbages and kings. One might call them "games of the underground," because if not kept under restraint, they would play havoc with the routines of disciplined thinking. But under exceptional conditions, when disciplined thinking is at the end of its tether, a temporary indulgence in these underground games may suddenly produce a solution—some farfetched, reckless combination which would be beyond the reach of, or seem to be unacceptable to, the sober, rational mind. The place for the rendezvous of ideas is underground.

Illumination and Catharsis. What I have been trying to suggest is that the common pattern underlying scientific discovery and artistic inspiration is a temporary regression, culminating in the bisociative act, i.e., the bringing together of previously separate frames of perception or universes of discourse. I suppose that is what Ernst Kris (1952) meant by his frequently quoted but somewhat cryptic remarks about regression in the service of the ego. The boundaries between science and art, between the *Ah* reaction and the *Aha* reaction, are fluid, whether we consider architecture or cooking or psychiatry or the writing of history. There is nowhere a sharp break where witticism changes into wit or where science stops and art begins. Science, the hoary cliché goes, aims at truth, art at beauty. But the criteria of truth, such as verification by experiment, are not as hard and clean as we tend to believe, for the same experimental data can often be interpreted in more than one way. That is why the history of science echoes with as many bitter and venomous controversies as the history of literary criticism. Moreover, the verification of a discovery comes after the act; the creative act itself is for the scientist, as it is for the artist, a leap into the dark, where both are equally dependent on their fallible intuitions. The greatest mathematicians and physicists have confessed that, at those decisive moments when taking the plunge, they were guided not by logic but by a sense of beauty which they were unable to define. Vice versa, painters and sculptors, not to mention architects, have always been guided and often obsessed by scientific or pseudoscientific theories and criteria of truth: the golden section, the laws of perspective, Dürer's and Leonardo's laws of proportion representing the human body. Cézanne's doctrine that everything in nature is modeled on the cylinder and cone, Braque's alternative theory that cubes should be substituted for spheres; le Courbusier's modulator theory, Buckminster Fuller's geodesic domes. The same goes, of course, for literature, from the formal laws imposed on Greek tragedy to the various recent and contemporary schools— romanticism, classicism, naturalism, symbolism, stream of consciousness, socialist realism, the *nouveau roman*, and so forth—not to mention the intricate rules of harmony and counterpoint in music. The English physicist Dirac, a Nobel laureate, said recently (1963): "It is more important to have beauty in one's equations than that they should fit experiment." The counterpart to this is the statement by Seurat on his pointillist method: "They see poetry in what I have done. No, I apply my method, and that is all there is to it." In other words, the experience of truth, however subjective, must be present for the experience of beauty to arise, and vice versa: an elegant solution of a problem gives rise in the connoisseur to the experience of beauty. Intellectual illumination and emotional catharsis are complementary aspects of an indivisible process.

Regression and Rebound

I would like to conclude this discussion with a remark which is no more than a hint, to place the phenomena of human creativity into a wider biological perspective. I have talked of temporary regression, followed by a rebound, as a characteristic of the creative act. Now biologists are familiar with a similar phenomenon on lower levels of the evolutionary scale. I mean the phenomenon of regeneration (Koestler, 1964, pp. 447-474). It consists in the reshaping of bodily structures—or the reorganization of functions—in response to traumatic challenges from the environment. It involves the regression of bodily tissues to a quasi-embryonic state and the release of genetic growth potentials which are normally under restraint in the adult organism—just as in the moment of discovery the creative potentials of the earlier forms of intuitive thinking are released from the censorship of the conscious adult mind. Psychotherapy reflects the same process on a higher level. It aims at inducing a temporary regression in the emotionally traumatized patient in the hope that he will regenerate into a pattern which eliminates the conflict. The creative act could be called a kind of do-it-yourself psychotherapy where the traumatic challenge is intellectual instead of emotional, for instance, new data which shake the foundation of a well-established theory, observations which contradict each other, problems which cause frustration and conflict—or the artist's perplexities in trying to communicate his experiences through the blocked matrices of conventional techniques.

And finally we find the same pattern reflected in the death-and-resurrection motif in mythology, in Toynbee's *Withdrawal and Return*, in Jung's *Night Journey*. Joseph is thrown into a well, Mohammed goes out into the desert, Jesus is resurrected from the tomb, Jonah is reborn out of the belly of the whale. The mystic's dark night of the soul reflects the same archetype. It seems to be a principle of universal validity in the evolution of individuals and cultures.

REFERENCES

DIRAC, P. A. M. Evolution of the physicist's picture of nature. *Scientific American,* 1963, *208* (36), 45–53.

GOMBRICH, E. H. *Art and illusion.* London: Phaidon Press, 1962.

HADAMARD, J. *The psychology of invention in the mathematical field.* Princeton, N.J.: Princeton Univer. Press, 1949.

KOESTLER, A. *Insight and outlook.* New York: Macmillan, 1949.

KOESTLER, A. *The act of creation.* New York: Macmillan, 1964.

KRIS, E. *Psychoanalytic explorations in art.* New York: International Universities Press, 1952.

KUHN, T. H. *The structure of scientific revolutions.* Chicago: Univer. of Chicago Press, 1962.

POPPER, K. R. *The logic of scientific discovery.* London: Hutchinson, 1959.

SANTILLANA, G. DE. *Dialogue on the great world systems.* Chicago: Univer. of Chicago Press, 1953.

25

Letter on the Creative Process

Albert Einstein

My Dear Colleague:

In the following, I am trying to answer in brief your questions as well as I am able. I am not satisfied myself with those answers and I am willing to answer more questions if you believe this could be of any advantage for the very interesting and difficult work you have undertaken.

(A) The words or the language, as they are written or spoken, do not seem to play any role in my mechanism of thought. The psychical entities which seem to serve as elements in thought are certain signs and more or less clear images which can be "voluntarily" reproduced and combined.

There is, of course, a certain connection between those elements and relevant logical concepts. It is also clear that the desire to arrive finally at logically connected concepts is the emotional basis of this rather vague play with the above mentioned elements. But taken from a psychological viewpoint, this combinatory play seems to be the essential feature in productive thought—before there is any connection with logical construction in words or other kinds of signs which can be communicated to others.

(B) The above mentioned elements are, in my case, of visual and some of muscular type. Conventional words or other signs have to be sought for laboriously only in a secondary stage, when the mentioned associative play is sufficiently established and can be reproduced at will.

(C) According to what has been said, the play with the mentioned elements is aimed to be analogous to certain logical connections one is searching for.

(D) Visual and motor. In a stage when words intervene at all, they are, in my case, purely auditive, but they interfere only in a secondary stage as already mentioned.

(E) It seems to me that what you call full consciousness is a limit case which can never be fully accomplished. This seems to me connected with the fact called the narrowness of consciousness (*Enge des Bewusstseins*).

Remark: Professor Max Wertheimer has tried to investigate the distinction between mere associating or combining of reproducible elements and between understanding (*organisches Begreifen*); I cannot judge how far his psychological analysis catches the essential point.

With kind regards . . .

Albert Einstein

From Jacques Hadamard, *The Psychology of Invention in the Mathematical Field,* (New York: Dover Publications, 1954), pp. 142–143. Reprinted by permission of the Estate of Albert Einstein.

26

Moments of Creation

Henri Poincaré

It is time to penetrate deeper and to see what goes on in the very soul of the mathematician. For this, I believe, I can do best by recalling memories of my own. But I shall limit myself to telling how I wrote my first memoir on Fuchsian functions. I beg the reader's pardon, I am about to use some technical expressions, but they need not frighten him, for he is not obliged to understand them. I shall say, for example, that I have found the demonstration of such a theorem under such circumstances. This theorem will have a barbarous name, unfamiliar to many, but that is unimportant; what is of interest for the psychologist is not the theorem but the circumstances.

For fifteen days I strove to prove that there could not be any functions like those I have since called Fuchsian functions. I was then very ignorant; every day I seated myself at my work table, stayed an hour or two, tried a great number of combinations, and reached no results. One evening, contrary to my custom, I drank black coffee and could not sleep. Ideas rose in crowds; I felt them collide until pairs interlocked, so to speak, making a stable combination. By the next morning I had established the existence of a class of Fuchsian functions, those which come from the hypergeometric series; I had only to write out the results, which took but a few hours.

Then I wanted to represent these functions by the quotient of two series; this idea was perfectly conscious and deliberate, the analogy with elliptic functions guided me. I asked myself what properties these series must have if they existed, and I succeeded without difficulty in forming the series I have called theta-Fuchsian.

Just at this time I left Caen, where I was then living, to go on a geologic excursion under the auspices of the school of mines. The changes of travel made me forget my mathematical work. Having reached Coutances, we entered an omnibus to go some place or other. At the moment when I put my foot on the step the idea came to me, without anything in my former thoughts seeming to have paved the way for it, that the transformations I had used to define the Fuchsian functions were identical with those of non-Euclidean geometry. I did not verify the idea; I should

From *The Creative Process*, Brewster Ghiselin, ed. (New York: New American Library, Mentor Books), pp. 36–39.

not have had time, as, upon taking my seat in the omnibus, I went on with a conversation already commenced, but I felt a perfect certainty. On my return to Caen, for conscience's sake I verified the result at my leisure.

Then I turned my attention to the study of some arithmetical questions apparently without much success and without a suspicion of any connection with my preceding researches. Disgusted with my failure, I went to spend a few days at the seaside, and thought of something else. One morning, walking on the bluff, the idea came to me, with just the same characteristics of brevity, suddenness and immediate certainty, that the arithmetic transformations of indeterminate ternary quadratic forms were identical with those of non-Euclidean geometry.

Returned to Caen, I meditated on this result and deduced the consequences. The example of quadratic forms showed me that there were Fuchsian groups other than those corresponding to the hypergeometric series; I saw that I could apply to them the theory of theta-Fuchsian series and that consequently there existed Fuchsian functions other than those from the hypergeometric series, the ones I then knew. Naturally I set myself to form all these functions. I made a systematic attack upon them and carried all the outworks, one after another. There was one however that still held out, whose fall would involve that of the whole place. But all my efforts only served at first the better to show me the difficulty, which indeed was something. All this work was perfectly conscious.

Thereupon I left for Mont-Valérien, where I was to go through my military service; so I was very differently occupied. One day, going along the street, the solution of the difficulty which had stopped me suddenly appeared to me. I did not try to go deep into it immediately, and only after my service did I again take up the question. I had all the elements and had only to arrange them and put them together. So I wrote out my final memoir at a single stroke and without difficulty.

I shall limit myself to this single example; it is useless to multiply them. In regard to my other researches I would have to say analogous things, and the observations of other mathematicians given in *L'Enseignement Mathematique* would only confirm them.

Most striking at first is this appearance of sudden illumination, a manifest sign of long, unconscious prior work. The role of this unconscious work in mathematical invention appears to me incontestable and traces of it would be found in other cases where it is less evident. Often when one works at a hard question, nothing good is accomplished at the first attack. Then one takes a rest, longer or shorter, and sits down anew to the work. During the first half-hour, as before, nothing is found, and then all of a sudden the decisive idea presents itself to the mind. It might be said that the conscious work has been more fruitful because it has been interrupted and the rest has given back to the mind its force and freshness. But it is more probable that this rest has been filled out with unconscious work and that the result of this work has afterward revealed itself to the geometer just as in the cases I have cited; only the revelation, instead of coming during a walk or a journey, has happened during a period of conscious work, but independently of this work which plays at most a rôle of excitant, as if it were the goad stimulating the results already reached during rest, but remaining unconscious, to assume the conscious form.

There is another remark to be made about the conditions of this unconscious work: it is possible, and of a certainty it is only fruitful, if it is on the one hand preceded and on the other hand followed by a period of conscious work. These sudden inspirations (and the examples already cited sufficiently prove this) never happen except after some days of voluntary effort which has appeared absolutely fruitless and whence nothing good seems to have come, where the way taken seems totally astray. These efforts than have not been as sterile as one thinks; they have set agoing the unconscious machine and without them it would not have moved and would have produced nothing.

The need for the second period of conscious work, after the inspiration, is still easier to understand, It is necessary to put in shape the results of this inspiration, to deduce from them the immediate consequences, to arrange them, to word the demonstrations, but above all is verification necessary. I have spoken of the feeling of absolute certitude accompanying the inspiration; in the cases cited this feeling was no deceiver, nor is it usually. But do not think this is a rule without exception; often this feeling deceives us without being any the less vivid, and we only find it out when we seek to put on foot the demonstration. I have especially noticed this fact in regard to ideas coming to me in the morning or evening in bed while in a semi-hypnagogic state.

Such are the realities; now for the thoughts they force upon us. The unconscious, or, as we say, the subliminal self plays an important rôle in mathematical creation; this follows from what we have said. But usually the subliminal self is considered as purely automatic. Now we have seen that mathematical work is not simply mechanical, that it could not be done by a machine, however perfect. It is not merely a question of applying rules, of making the most combinations possible according to certain fixed laws. The combinations so obtained would be exceedingly numerous, useless and cumbersome. The true work of the inventor consists in choosing among these combinations so as to eliminate the useless ones or rather to avoid the trouble of making them, and the rules which must guide this choice are extremely fine and delicate. It is almost impossible to state them precisely; they are felt rather than formulated. Under these conditions, how imagine a sieve capable of applying them mechanically?

A first hypothesis now presents itself: the subliminal self is in no way inferior to the conscious self; it is not purely automatic; it is capable of discernment; it has tact, delicacy; it knows how to choose, to divine. What do I say? It knows better how to divine than the conscious self, since it succeeds where that has failed. In a word, is not the subliminal self superior to the conscious self? You recognize the full importance of this question. Boutroux in a recent lecture has shown how it came up on a very different occasion, and what consequences would follow an affirmative answer.

Is this affirmative answer forced upon us by the facts I have just given? I confess that, for my part, I should hate to accept it. Reexamine the facts then and see if they are not compatible with another explanation.

It is certain that the combinations which present themselves to the mind in a sort of sudden illumination, after an unconscious working somewhat prolonged, are generally useful and fertile combinations, which seem the result of a first impression. Does it follow that the subliminal self, having divined by a delicate intuition that these combinations would be useful, has formed only these, or has it rather formed many others which were lacking in interest and have remained unconscious?

In this second way of looking at it, all the combinations would be formed in consequence of the automatism of the subliminal self, but only the interesting ones would break into the domain of consciousness. And this is still very mysterious.

PART III *The Inner World*

We watch others move around us and we know that the behavior we can see is only a covering over of the more complex inner world. The world of the mind, the place of consciousness, the castle of dreams, the center of being—whatever we call it, whatever it is, it attracts and fascinates us. It is the vast realm of inner space, less explored and perhaps less understood than the recently accessible darkness of outer space. We are beginning to open up this part of our world to systematic investigation. Problems of reality, alterations in consciousness, and the content of unusual styles of perception are all being researched. It is difficult to recognize that my reality may not be the same as yours. Philosophy has discussed this for centuries and now behavioral science is testing theories. For now it is enough to recognize that there are different and equally valid ways of ordering the inner world. The world of subjective experience is still the most puzzling portion of social science. It is at the core of our ignorance and at the center of our attention.

To be useful, the selections following should be tested against your own inner world. In what ways are you understanding these authors? Is it through reason, by comparison with other books, ideas, and experiences? Is it through intuition, the sudden flash, "of-course-I-knew-that"? Perhaps you can use your empathic sense, the emotional recognition of another's state by feeling it within yourself.

Although we have always been aware of the inner world, we are only beginning to explore it.

SECTION A *Perspectives on Mental Illness*

For creatures reputedly built in the image of God, we seem to need an enormous amount of servicing to prevent breaking down. The mentally ill have suffered cruelly from the fear and ignorance surrounding their condition. In earlier periods we killed them outright, chained them to posts, and sometimes tortured them to release the devils possessing them. Later we developed treatments that included ice-water baths, electric shock and severing the frontal lobes of the brain.

The seemingly insane ways of treating the seemingly insane were remarkably effective at times. Patients improved perhaps only in a desperate effort to stop the treatment.

Now we have moved from physical pressure and confinements to drugs—tranquillizers, energizers, stimulants, and others. We have progressed from cold cells and straw mats to modern comfortable hospitals with bowling alleys, movies, craft shops, and an abundance of therapy. We are also finding out that some mental illness is traceable to physical causes and can be treated by physical means.

Yet the inner world of mental illness is still dark and twisted to those who suffer. The visions, the alterations in mood, in affect, in awareness itself, still confuse and confound them.

The first two selections offer speculations on the origin of some kinds of mental illness. The article on schizophrenia contains basic information on the most widespread and least understood of all mental illnesses. Jerome Frank's article distinguishes between the psychological and the physiological effects of medication. Finally excerpts from books by Ken Kesey and Vaslav Nijinsky allow you to observe the thought process of persons judged to be insane. Kesey's selection is the beginnning of a novel which takes place in a modern mental hospital. Nijinsky's report displays the alternations of mood and thought within a sensitive but disoriented personality grappling to retain his hold on the world. At the same time, you can see that he is responding to demands and ideas relating to another level of reality altogether.

To overcome our own fears of the unknown is the first step in understanding the fears and uncertainties of others.

27

Experimental Demonstrations of the Psychopathology of Everyday Life

Milton S. Erickson

Introduction

The experiments reported below were conducted for the most part in the presence of a seminar of graduate students held in New Haven under the leadership of Dr. Sapir during the spring of 1933. In addition, a few experiments which were performed elsewhere are included.

The subject who was used for many of these demonstrations had frequently before volunteered for similar purposes. He knew nothing, however, of the plans for these experiments; they represented situations which were entirely new and problems with which he had never before been confronted.

In his approach to such demonstrations, this subject customarily reacted in a way which was fairly characteristic for many others. Ahead of time he often appeared to be resentful and anxious, or over-eager about the impression which he and the experimenter would make. Suddenly, however, with the beginning of the lecture or demonstration, he would seem to shift the responsibility completely and to lapse into an attitude of complete comfort with loss of all tension and worry.

Following one of the demonstrations described below the subject told the experimenter that his shift in mood had been even more marked than usual. The night before the lecture he had been unable to sleep and had felt more than ordinarily resentful that on so important an occasion no rehearsal or preparatory discussion had taken place. He had even developed some nausea and diarrhœa. All of this nervousness had disappeared completely, however, as he entered the lecture room on the morning of these experiments.

I. *Unconscious Determinants of the Casual Content of Conversation.* The subject was brought into a state of profound hypnosis, during which he was instructed that after awakening he would (*1*) notice Dr. D. searching vainly through his pockets for a package of cigarettes; (*2*) that he then would proffer his own pack, and (*3*) that Dr. D. absent-mindedly would forget to return the cigarettes whereupon the subject would feel very eager to recover them because he had no others. He was further told that (*4*) he would be too courteous to ask for the cigarettes either directly or indirectly but that (*5*) he would engage in a conversation that would cover any topic except cigarettes although at the time his desire for the return of

Reprinted from *The Psychoanalytic Quarterly,* Vol. VIII (July, 1939), pp. 338–53, by permission of the author and publisher.

the cigarettes would be on his mind constantly.

When he was awakened the subject saw that Dr. D. was looking for cigarettes. He thereupon courteously offered his own and at the same time became involved in a conversation during which Dr. D., after lighting the cigarette, absent-mindedly placed the pack in his own pocket. The subject noted this with a quick glance, felt of his own pockets in a somewhat furtive manner as if to see whether or not he had another pack, and showed by his facial expression that he had no others. He then began chatting casually, wandering from one topic to another, always mentioning in some indirect but relevant fashion the word "smoking." For example, he talked about a boat on the bay at New Haven, commenting on the fact that the sight of water always made him thirsty, as did smoking. He then told a story about how the dromedary got one hump and the *camel* two. When the question of travel was raised he immediately pictured the pleasure he would derive from crossing the Sahara Desert rocking back and forth comfortably on a *camel*. Next he told a tale of Syrian folklore in which again a camel played a role. When he was asked to tell something interesting about patients he told of taking a patient to see a marathon dance which the latter enjoyed immensely while he himself was reminded by the antics of the dancers of a circus where one would see elephants, hippopotami and *camels*. Asked what he would like to do, he commented on the pleasant weather and said there was nothing more glorious than paddling in a canoe or floating at ease on the water, smoking.

II. *Manifestations of Unconscious Ambivalent Feelings in Conversation About a Person*. During hypnosis the subject was told that he admired and respected Dr. D. very much but that unconsciously he was jealous of him and that because of this jealousy there would be a cutting edge to complimentary remarks which he would make. He was further told that after awakening a conversation would be started with Dr. D. in which he would take part. The subject was them awakened and the conversation begun.

The topic of traveling and its contribution to personal education was mentioned. The subject immediately brought up the fact that Dr. D. had studied both in the Middle West and in the East and that, having traveled abroad as well, he might well be called cosmopolitan. He himself, he added, would like to travel and get a cosmopolitan education but in the last analysis that was what was being done by any old tramp who traveled from one part of the country to another by stealing rides on freight cars. There followed a discussion of human behavior as it reflected local environments during which the subject remarked that the man who had traveled showed a broader knowledge and better understanding of people and of cultural things; he added, however, that the same thing might possibly be said of any resident of east-side New York.

III. *Lapsus Linguæ and Unconscious Irony*. During hypnosis the subject was instructed that after he awakened Dr. D. would begin talking to him about some abstruse subject in which he was not at all interested, and that although he would actually be profoundly bored he would try to appear interested. He was told that he would want very much to close the conversation, that he would wish for some way of shutting off this interminable flow of words, that he would look around him in the hope of finding some distraction, and that he would feel that Dr. D. was terribly tiresome. He was then awakened, whereupon Dr. D. began the conversation. Although the subject appeared to be politely attentive, Dr. D. would occasionally say, "Perhaps you're not interested?." The subject would reply with excessive emphasis, "Oh, yes, certainly, I'm very much interested." Now and then he would interrupt Dr. D., trying to pin him down to some definite point for discussion, but each time this effort was evaded. At length the subject began glancing about the room and was noted casually to observe an open door. Finally he interrupted Dr. D. saying, "Excuse me, I feel an awful draft," and got up to close the door. As he did so he was asked what he was doing. He replied, "The air seems to be awful hot ["hot air!"]; I thought I would shut off the draft." When the hypnotist pretended not to understand and asked him what he was doing the subject replied, "Why, I just shut the bore." His remark was then repeated by the hypnotist for the benefit of those in the audience who had not heard it. When the subject heard his statement given as "shutting the bore" he started visibly, seemed tremendously embarrassed, and with much urgency turned to Dr. D. saying, "Did I say that? I didn't mean that. I just meant I closed the door." He was very apologetic in his whole manner and bearing.

IV. *Unconscious Resentment Expressing Itself in Masked Forms Through a Smoke-Screen of Overcompensatory Courtesy.* The subject was told during hypnosis that he felt antagonistic, resentful and jealous of Dr. D., and that this emotional state would persist after he was awakened. He was also told that after awakening he would try to be courteous and acquiescent toward Dr. D. in every way and would appear to be willing to do anything requested of him.

After being awakened the subject seemed to be entirely at ease; he responded courteously to some casual remarks addressed to him by Dr. D. Presently Dr. D. asked him if he would mind changing his seat. The subject replied certainly not, that he would be delighted, but that *he* was quite comfortable where he was; if, however, it would make *Dr. D.* more comfortable, he would be delighted to change his seat. The request was repeated, whereupon the subject arose and asked Dr. D. to designate the precise chair in which he was to seat himself. He walked over towards the designated chair but asked Dr. D. if perhaps a certain other chair might not serve even better since the reason Dr. D. had given for his request was that he was not quite in full view of the audience. When Dr. D. insisted that the designated chair was the better one the subject, with great courtesy, still questioned, seeming nevertheless most willing to do precisely what was desired and to be hesitant only about seating himself before he was absolutely certain of Dr. D.'s wishes. After much insistence by Dr. D. that he seat himself the subject agreed that the chair indicated was precisely the one that he ought to sit in and proceeded to do so; but as he did so he moved the chair about six inches to one side and shifted its position so that it faced in a slightly different direction. Immediately upon seating himself he turned and politely asked, "Is this the way you would like to have me?." After a few moments of casual conversation Dr. D. found fault with his position and asked him if he would mind taking his original chair. He rose promptly, said that he would be delighted to sit anywhere that Dr. D. wished but that perhaps it would be better if he sat on the table, and offered to move the designated chair to any desired spot, suggesting some clearly unsuitable positions; finally, when urged insistently to sit in the chair he again had to move it.

V. *Ambivalence: Manifestations of Unconscious Conflict About Smoking in the Distortion of Simple, Daily Smoking Habits.* During profound hypnosis the subject was instructed to feel that he wanted to get over the habit but that he felt it was too strong a habit to break, that he would be very reluctant to smoke and would give anything not to smoke, but that he would find himself compelled to smoke; and that after he was awakened he would experience all of these feelings.

After he was awakened the subject was drawn into a casual conversation with the hypnotist who, lighting one himself, offered him a cigarette. The subject waved it aside with the explanation that he had his own and that he preferred Camels, and promptly began to reach for his own pack. Instead of looking in his customary pocket however, he seemed to forget where he carried his cigarettes and searched fruitlessly through all of his other pockets with a gradually increasing concern. Finally, after having sought them repeatedly in all other pockets, he located his cigarettes in their usual place. He took them out, engaged in a brief conversation as he dallied with the pack, and then began to search for matches which he failed to find. During his search for matches he replaced the cigarettes in his pocket and began using both hands, finally locating the matches too in their usual pocket. Having done this, he now began using both hands to search for his cigarettes. He finally located them but then found that he had once more misplaced his matches. This time however he kept his cigarettes in hand while attempting to relocate the matches. He then placed a cigarette in his mouth and struck a match. As he struck it, however, he began a conversation which so engrossed him that he forgot the match and allowed it to burn his finger tips whereupon with a grimace of pain, he tossed it in the ash tray. Immediately he took another match, but again introduced a diverting topic by asking the aduience in a humorous fashion if they knew the "Scotch" way of lighting a cigarette. As interest was shown, he carefully split the match through the middle. One half of the match he replaced in his pocket in a time-consuming manner and tried to light his cigarette with the other half. When it gave too feeble a flame he discarded it and had to search for the second half. After striking this another interesting topic of conversation developed and again he burned his fingers before he made use of it. He apologized for his failure to demonstrate the "Scotch" light successfully and repeated the performance, this time holding the flame in such a way as to ignite only a small corner of the cigarette from which he succeeded in getting only one satisfactory puff. Then he tossed the match away and tipped the cigarette up so that he could see the lighted end. He started to explain that that was how the "Scotch" light was obtained and noted that only one small corner of the cigarette was lit. He smiled in a semi-apologetic manner and explained that he had really given a "Jewish" light to the cigarette, whereupon the lighted corner expired. He made a few more humorous comments, and as he talked and gesticulated appropriately he rolled the cigarette between his fingers in such a fashion that he broke it, whereupon he put it aside and took another. This time a member of the audience stepped up and proffered him a light, but as the lighted match drew near to the tip of his cigarette the subject sneezed and blew it out. He apologized again and said he thought he would light his own cigarette. While taking out his matches he commented on the vaudeville trick of rolling cigars from one corner of the mouth to the other and proceeded to demonstrate how he could roll a cigarette in that fashion, which he did fairly successfully. However, in doing so he macerated the tip of the cigarette and had to discard it. He took another, holding it in his mouth while he reached for his matches, started a conversation, and took the cigarette out so that he could talk more freely. It was observed that he took the cigarette out with his hand held in the reverse position to that which he usually used, and after completing his remarks he put the dry end of the cigarette in his mouth, exposing the wet end. He then tried to light this, held the match to the tip in the proper fashion, puffed vigorously, finally got a puff of smoke and then blew out the match. Naturally the wet end of the cigarette did not burn satisfactorily and quickly went out. He looked at it in amazement and in a semi-embarrassed manner mumbled that he had lit the wrong end of the cigarette; he then commented that now both ends of the cigarette were wet, and discarded it for another. After several similar trials he finally succeeded in lighting the cigarette. It was observed that although he took deep puffs he tended to let his cigarette burn undisturbed, and that instead of smoking it down to a reasonable butt he quickly discarded it.

A little later while smoking the subject attempted to demonstrate the violent gestures of a patient and in so doing knocked off the burning tip. Then while lighting another cigarette he became so interested in talking that he lit the cigarette in the middle rather than at the tip and had to discard it. As usual he showed profound embarrassment at seeming so awkward.

(On other occasions when the subject had demonstrated this phenomenon, he would finally complete the demonstration by selecting a cigarette in a strained and laborious fashion and then, obviously centering all of his attention upon the procedure of lighting it, would hold his hand tensely as he lit the match, applying it with noticeable rigidity to the cigarette and holding it there so long and puffing so repeatedly that all doubt was removed concerning the actual lighting of the cigarette, whereupon his whole manner and attitude would relax and he would appear to be physically comfortable.)

VI. *Unconscious Convictions of Absurdities with Rationalization in Support of the Belief in Them.* During hypnosis the subject was instructed that he was about to be reminded by the hypnotist of something he had known a long time, that he had known it both as a result of his own experience and from reading about it in authoritative books. This, he was told, was the fact that "all German men marry women who are two inches taller than they are." A state of absolute emotional and intellectual belief in this was suggested and he was warned that he might be called upon to defend this statement. He was told that he had read of this in a book written by Dr. Sapir in which the reference occurred on page forty-two. He was informed that he would know this not only in the hypnotic state but also when awake. The subject was then wakened.

During the course of a casual conversation mention was made of the peculiar customs of various nations and peoples. Remarking that he was reminded of a peculiar custom among the Germans, the subject went on to describe the suggested phenomenon in a matter-of-fact way. When his statement was challenged he expressed obvious surprise that anybody should doubt it. He argued that it was entirely reasonable that customs established originally from some simple purpose could be perpetuated by future generations until, regardless of their absurdity, they were looked upon as rational and commonplace. From this statement he proceeded to draw a social parallel to the attitude of Mussolini regarding compulsory marriage, arguing in a logical, orderly and reasonable fashion. When this failed to convince the doubters he drew upon personal experience, citing examples with a casual, simple, matter-of-fact and convincing manner, and calling upon others in the group to verify his statements. When they failed to do so and cited contrary instances he smiled agreeably and stated that every rule had its exception and that the failure of the German in the audience to confirm his observation was characteristic of the well-known tendency to overlook the obvious in familiar situations. When he was asked whether any authority in the field was known to hold such a belief he promptly stated that he had read the same observation in a book by Dr. Sapir entitled, Primitive Peoples and Customs. When he was asked where in the book it was described he smiled in a deprecating fashion and remarked that it had been so long since he had read the book that he could not be sure of the page but that, as he recalled it, it seemed to be between pages forty and forty-five—forty-four, perhaps; this despite the fact that the hypnotist had specified page forty-two. He was then asked by a member of the audience what chapter it was in; he stated that as far as he recalled it was chapter two. Asked for the chapter heading, he explained that he had read the book so long ago he really could not recall it. When a member of the audience then stated that such a belief was contrary to all common sense the subject, in amazement and with some embarrassment, asked rather urgently, "Surely you would not dispute a man as famous and distinguished as Dr. Sapir?," nodding his head toward Dr. Sapir. His whole manner was suggestive of intense surprise at such arrogant disbelief.

VII. *Automatic Writing: Unconscious Obliteration of Visual Impressions in Order to Preserve an Hypnotically Ordered Amnesia.* During hypnosis the subject was instructed that on awakening he would engage in a casual conversation and that as he did so his hand would begin writing, but that he would have no knowledge of what he was doing.

After he had written some incomplete sentences he was asked what he was doing by others in the audience. With some amazement he explained that he had been talking to Dr. D. When he was informed that while talking to Dr. D. he had also been writing, he immediately pointed out that this could not have been since he had been holding a cigarette in his right hand. (He had actually transferred the cigarette from his left to the right hand upon completing the writing.) As the audience continued to insist he pointed out that he had no pencil and nothing to write on, in addition to the fact that *he knew* he had not been writing and that the audience must have been mistaken. His attention was then called to a pencil and some paper on the table; he seemed surprised to see the paper and pencil and insisted that he had not had anything to do with either. He was asked to examine the paper to see if there were not some automatic writing on it, or at least writing. He picked up the paper, glanced at the top sheet, shook his head and began slowly to thumb over each sheet, examining the papers over and over again on both sides, and finally restoring the pile to its original state. He said that he found no writing on any of the sheets. His attention was called to the top sheet which he was asked to examine. He looked it over carefully at the top, turned it over and examined it, seemed to be in doubt as to whether or not he had taken the top sheet and took the second sheet; he examined that, put it away, and glanced at the third sheet; he then seemed to feel that possibly he *had* had the top sheet in his hand, so he reexamined that very thoroughly and carefully and then, still holding it right side up, declared hesitantly, as if he hated to dispute with the audience but felt compelled to disagree, that there was no writing on the paper. One of the audience called his attention to the particular part of the paper on which there was writing. He glanced at it, looked back at his informant in a puzzled way and then reexamined that part of the paper. After turning it over somewhat doubtfully and glancing at it he turned it right side up again. He then began holding it so that the light struck it obliquely and finally declared, still in a puzzled fashion, that there *really* was no writing on the paper. Finally he was given the suggestion by the hypnotist that there *was* writing and that he could see it. He glanced back at the paper in surprise and then an expression of amusement and amazement spread over his face as he saw the writing apparently for the first time. He commented on the juvenility of the handwriting, disowning it. When asked to tell what it said he showed much interest in reading the characters but appeared to hve a certain amount of difficulty in deciphering the writing. The last word was incomplete; he read it, spelled it, and stated that it seemed to be only part of a word. When he was asked to guess what the word was he promptly reread the sentence in order to get the context, but was unable to guess. He then wanted to know why the writing had not been finished and was informed by the hypnotist that if he would just watch the pencil on the table it would suddenly lift up in the air and begin writing the rest of the word. He looked doubtfully at the hypnotist and then said, "Why, it's lifting up", seeming to have no realization that his own hand was picking up the pencil and holding it poised in position to write. Gradually his hand began forming letters. He was asked what the pencil was writing, to which he replied. "Wait—wait; let's see"; he appeared to be entirely absorbed in the supposed phenomenon of a pencil writing alone. The hypnotist watched the writing, which was proceeding very slowly, and soon realized that the word in question was "delicious". The hypnotist then announced to the audience while the subject was writing the last four letters and finished by the time the subject had finished writing. The subject looked up upon completing the word and said, "It's delicious," and then read the sentence to see if the word was relevant to the meaning. Apparently he had not heard the observer announce the word to the seminar.

VIII. *"Crystal" Gazing: Hallucinatory Vividness of Dream Imagery Embodying Anger Displaced from Hypnotist on to Dream Person.* In a somnambulistic state the subject was instructed that he was to gaze at the wall and that as he did this the wall would become distant, far-away, foggy and blurred, and that gradually a dark point would appear which would become more and more elaborate, that movement would enter the scene and that soon he would see a well-known and emotionally stirring moving picture.

The subject began these observations with faint interest and considerable difficulty at first but gradually a profound change in his manner and attitude occurred as he was seen to watch the moving images with intense interest. He resented any inquiries as to what he was seeing and gave the impression that he did not want to be distracted from the scene. Now and then he would turn slightly to ask, "Did you see that? Watch." The moving scene was from Rasputin and the Empress, showing the stumbling and falling of the Czarevitch, to which the subject showed appropriate emotional reactions. He went on to describe the sequence of events in proper chronological order. When the demonstration had gone far enough he was told that the picture was changing. He disregarded this; when the hypnotist insisted, he declared that he did not want to listen now, that the hypnotist should wait until the picture came to an end. He was obdurate about accepting any suggestions concerning the changing of the picture. The suggestion was then tried of speeding up the movie, making it go faster and faster. When this was done it was possible to shift the scene to a hospital picture which he described as one in which *a nurse shouted loudly at a patient.* Here he manifested great resentment toward the nurse for doing this, apparently hallucinating the nurse's voice. The incorporation into the hallucinatory image of his anger against the experimenter and the child-like and fear-laden exaggeration of his impression of loud and angry voices because of his own inner anger were all very evident.

IX. *Implantation of a Complex.* During hypnosis the subject was instructed to recall having had dinner at Dr. D.'s home on the previous day. He was then told that the hypnotist would review a certain series of actions which had occurred on the previous day, and that the hypnotist would refresh his memory of certain things that the subject had done which he regretted intensely and which constituted a source of much shame to him. Thereupon he was told to remember how during the course of the afternoon he had stood by the fireplace, leaning against the mantel while talking to Dr. D. about various subjects, when his eye happened to fall upon a package of cigarettes lying behind the clock on the end of the mantelpiece. The tale went on that Dr. D. had noticed his glance and had proceeded to tell the subject that the package of cigarettes was a sentimental keepsake of his marriage, that he and his wife had received this package of cigarettes on their wedding day and had preserved it unused ever since. As Dr. D. added various romantic elaborations the subject had not paid much attention because he was really rather bored by the sentimental story. After fingering the package, Dr. D had replaced it at the other end of the mantelpiece; but the subject had not paid any attention to this either. Shortly after this Dr. D. and his wife had left the room for a few minutes. During their absence the subject noticed that he was out of cigarettes and glanced about the room to see if his host had some. Noticing a pack of cigarettes at the other end of the mantelpiece, he thought that his host would have no objections to his helping himself. He stepped over and took this pack of cigarettes from the mantelpiece, opened it, extracted a cigarette, lit and smoked it. Not until he had finished smoking did he realize that this was the very pack of cigarettes which Dr. D. had placed at the end of the mantelpiece instead of returning to its original hiding place behind the clock. The subject was then reminded of how distressed he had felt, of his sense of being in a quandary as to what he ought to do, of how he had hastily closed the pack and had replaced it behind the clock and had then decided that he had better put it where Dr. D. had placed it, but how before he could do this his host had returned so that he had been forced to carry on a casual conversation with this burden on his mind. Furthermore he was told that even now and after awakening this burden would still be on his mind.

The subject was roused and after a few brief remarks Dr. D. offered him a cigarette. The subject started, glanced furtively first at Dr. D. and then at the hypnotist and finally in a labored fashion reached out and accepted the cigarette, handling it in a gingerly manner. Dr. D. began an innocuous conversation, but the subject paid little attention to what was said and asked Dr. D. what he thought about sentimentality, uttering the word "sentimentality" in a tone of disgust. He then stated that he himself was not sentimental and that he tended to dislike people who were sentimental and maudlin. He stated that he hoped that Dr. D. was not sentimental, that he did not impress the subject as being sentimental. Dr. D. made another attempt to change the topic of conversation but the subject persisted with his own line of thought. He raised a hypothetical question about a man who owned an old homestead and who, as a result of the economic depression, had lost much money and was in a quandary about the necessity of selling it. He went on to talk of the burning of the house, of the house going up in smoke, and various allied topics. He then talked of guilt feelings, how everybody stole, how he himself had stolen; he wanted to know how Dr. D. would feel about anybody who had stolen unwittingly. Another attempt by Dr. D. to change the trend of the conversation failed. The subject then told of having once stolen a cigar which belonged to a man who had kept it for sentimental reasons. He said he had taken the cigar and smoked it without realizing that it was a keepsake, and that he had felt very badly about it and wondered about the possibility of replacing it so that the sentimental man would not be angry with him. In a defensive manner he then expressed a high regard for a person's feelings and contended that nevertheless people should not think too hard of others who had unwittingly violated some of their sentimental values. After this he stated that not only had he stolen the cigar but he had even stolen cigarettes (pause) a pack of cigarettes. As he said this he glanced in a particularly furtive manner at Dr. D. and also at the hypnotist, and seemed very ill at ease. He told about having smoked a cigarette and having enjoyed it, but that it had left a bad taste in his mouth afterwards and that even though he had stolen the cigarettes long ago he could not get them off his mind, that they still troubled him though common sense told him it was nothing to be concerned or worried about.

X. *The Assumption of Another's Identity Under Hypnotic Direction, with Striking Unconscious Mimicry and the Assumption of Unconscious Emotional Attitudes.* During hypnosis the subject was informed that after awakening *he* would be Dr. D. and that Dr. D. would be Mr. Blank, and that in the role of Dr. D. he would talk to the pseudo Mr. Blank. Additional suggestions which the subject fully accepted were given to complete the trans-identification. After the subject was awakened a conversation was begun. The pseudo Mr. Blank questioned him about his work in the seminar, as though he were Dr. D.; the subject responded by giving an excellent talk about his experiences in the seminar and his reactions to the group, talking in the phraseology of Dr. D. and expressing the personal attitudes of Dr. D. A chance conversation with Dr. D. on the previous day had supplied him with a great deal of information which he utilized fully. It was noted also that he adopted Dr. D.'s mannerisms in smoking and that he introduced ideas with certain phrases characteristic of Dr. D. When the pseudo Mr. Blank challenged his identity the subject contradicted "Mr. Blank" politely and seemed profoundly amazed at "Mr. Blank's" remarks. Then suddenly, with an expression of dawning understanding, he turned to the hypnotist saying "He's in a trance, isn't he?," and thereafter was only amused at "Mr. Blank's" remarks. "Mr. Blank" then questioned the subject about his "wife", to which the subject responded in a way that would have been natural for the real Dr. D. When asked about children he assumed an expression of mild embarrassment and replied, "not yet, but you never can tell." "Mr. Blank" then began talking to the hypnotist in his ordinary fashion, at which the subject again seemed tremendously surprised. With a puzzled look on his face he suddenly leaned over and tested "Mr. Blank" for catalepsy. When he found none his face was expressive of some concern; he promptly whispered to the hypnotist, "He's coming out of the trance," but was relieved when the hypnotist assured him that it would be all right if this happened.

Finally when an attempt was made to rehypnotize him in order to restore his own identity, the subject displayed the emotional attitude of resistance towards the induction of hypnosis which would have been entirely characteristic of the real Dr. D. The subject seemed actually to experience the same emotional responses that Dr. D. would have had at such a time. Finally, because he appeared to be entirely resistive to simple suggestion, it was necessary to induce hypnosis by indirect method.

This rather astonishing result offers a technique for the experimental investigation of the phenomena of identification, and of the unconscious incorporation of parental emotions by children.

28

Parents, Children, and Achievement

Margaret Mead

. . . When we ask how babies become Americans, we are asking how all these precipitates, in the American language, in American jokes and American songs, in American attitudes towards politics and the world and the universe, which were originally created by the attempt of many diverse peoples to assimilate themselves to a pattern which others would accept as identical with their own, have been re-created in the upbringing of the growing child.

The American baby is born into a family which is isolated from both paternal and maternal lines of kindred. (1) His parents typically live in a house by themselves. If they do not, they seek to create some sort of social isolation to recompense themselves for the presence of relatives. The mother dreams in secret of the day when "John's mother won't have to live with us any more," and the father hopes that "One of Mary's brothers will be able to take Mary's mother before long." This attitude is conveyed to the baby. He learns that only his father and his mother are really relevant to his life, that grandparents should live at a distance if at all, and are not really necessary. There is no occasion on which their presence is essential. If they are all dead, he experiences no sense of loss, no feeling that his own place in the world is compromised or incomplete. But he learns that parents—a father and mother—and a sibling of the opposite sex —a little brother for a girl, a little sister for a boy—are essential to make up a "family." (2) As his baby fingers scuffle through the pages of the *Saturday Evening Post* or the *Ladies' Home Journal*, he sees picture after picture of a family, the family for which a man takes correspondence courses, buys life insurance and puts money in the savings bank the family which now in wartime is working together on the farm to feed a soldier and a sailor, the family which is the other part of the sailor far away on the high seas. When mother and children occur alone in a picture, the father is implied, coming home from work, away defending them, working for them, thinking of them. Every picture a child sees, every skit over the radio, every song of popular phrase, reaffirms the importance of having a family, that one is not either safe or sound without one. Meanwhile when he goes to school, sometimes before he goes to school, he encounters the phenomenen of adoption. Some children don't belong to their families at all—they are adopted. The people who mention the subject to him are very mixed in their feelings on the subject. His mother is far less tolerant of the bad behavior of her friend's adopted child than of the behavior of another friend's own child. The adopted child carries with it the stigma of belonging to some other family, an unknown, disintegrated, probably immoral family, the kind of family which vanishes off the map and leaves its children all alone. And some children don't know they are adopted. That he learns also. The scene is set against which he can come to doubt and question his own place in his own family.

In old societies when the extended family or the clan is still an important part of the way of life, the child moves easily among many relatives, many of whom bear his name, with some one of whom he can almost certainly find a community of interest and even a common physique. But in America, with the family whittled down to father and mother, a child may often feel he is like neither of them. The fact that two parents are all the anchors he has in a world which is otherwise vague and shifting, over-emphasizes the tie and brings it into question. And so the phantasy of adoption develops, the fear which grips so many children's hearts that they are adopted, that they don't really belong anywhere at all. The day comes when both father and mother seem strange, forbidding figures, enforcing some meaningless moral code in a meaningless world. At first it gives a fine feeling of rebellion to say: "I don't care what you say. I am not your child anyway. My father and mother were a king and a queen and you are nothing but gypsies who carried me off," or: "I won't listen to a word you say, I am not your child. I won't look like you. I don't think like you. I don't feel like you. And I won't come out from under the bed," but afterwards, when the anger has worn off, the child is left with a terrible fear that maybe the words spoken in stubborn rejection are true. The children who are adopted, the children who have feared they were adopted, all serve to exaggerate for each American child his dependence on his father and mother, of whom there is only one edition in the whole world. From broken homes come our delinquents and our neurotics; from unbroken homes homes come the ordinary Americans, terribly impressed with the fragility and importance of those homes which made them into regular fellows, not children about whom other children whispered and whom teachers and neighbors commiserated.

From this curious structure of the American family, from the fact that two young people, often of quite diverse backgrounds, are sent out into the world together to make a way of life, with no oldsters by to help them, with no guides except the movies, the pulp magazines and the fumbling experiences of those very little older than themselves, it follows also that each child's experience will be different from each other's. However much his mother may study the daily specials, may deck his baby carriage in the type of tailored cover in style this year, and dress him in the most approved sun suit or slacks, beneath the outward conformity there lies always the mother's sense of difference. How does her marriage compare with that of the other women who stroll beside her with their impeccably dressed babies? She doesn't know, she doesn't dare to ask, even if she had words in which to ask such a question. The questions themselves might betray her, might betray some peculiarity in her own make-up or some inadequacy in her husband. The endless query: "Am I happy?" can in part be translated into the question: "How close am I to what I should expect to be?" Back of her lies her single experience with family life—her view of her own parents. She lives in the only other experience she may ever have. She cannot know how her worried version of life compares with the average, with the normal, with those who are "really" happy. And her voice is sharp as she admonishes her child if he deviates from the public behavior which is common for all of the children of the block, if he fights when they don't or fails to fight when they do. The basis of her life, her membership in her new family, like her membership in her old one, is secret, and probably deviates in a thousand ways from that which others would respect and envy—if they knew. To compensate for this, she insists on conformity. Their house, their car, their clothes, their patterns of leisure time, shall be as much like other people's as possible. Her face cream, her powder, her lipstick, shall be publicly validated. But inside the walls of that home, there is no one to tell her, or to tell her husband, whether their expectations are too high or too low, no one to quote from the experience of other generations, no yardstick, no barometer.

Some of this desperate uncertainty is conveyed to the baby, as she dresses him to take him out, as she undresses him when she brings him in. Just as virtually no American family is completely certain of its social antecedents, or can produce a full complement of unblotted escutcheons, so also no American family is sure of its position on an unknown chart called "happiness." The mother anxiously searches her baby's face. Are his "looks" something which should make her happy, is his health something which shows she is a good mother, does he walk and talk early enough to be a credit to her, to prove to others and so prove to herself that she has a right to be what she wants to be—happy? From the day when self-conscious fathers stand outside the glass-walled hospital nursery and anxiously compare the shape of their own babies' heads with those of the other babies, the child is valued in comparative terms, not because he is of the blood and bone and "name" of his parents, but because of his place on some objective (but undefined) rating scale of looks and potential abilities. In his parents' every gesture, the child learns that although they want to love him very much, although they hope they will love him very much—for loving your children is one of the things that books say parents do—they are not quite sure that he will deserve it, that when they check him up against the baby book and the neighbors' baby he will come out A-1 and so worthy of complete blind love.

Each civilization conveys different things to its children. The Balinese mother (3) mimicking a desperate fear as she calls the wandering child back to her side teaches him forever after to fear the unknown, to cling, he knows not why, to well-trodden paths. *"Aroh!"* she shrieks, "Wild cat!" or "Witch!" or "Snake!" or "Fire!", making no effort to adapt the scare word to the circumstance. If she screamed "Snake" when the child went into the grass, and "Scorpion" when he climbed the wood-pile he might learn to look and find patches of grass without snakes and piles of wood without scorpions. But instead any scare word in any context will do; the child gets no chance to test reality out, he remains frightened of an unknown.

"He's so strong," says the Iatmul (3) mother. "He runs so fast. I can't catch him." "When I catch him I will hit him and kill him," she says, as she pretends to chase and fails to catch her erring two-year-old. She acts as if the child were as strong and fleeter of foot than she, and the terrified baby, pushed beyond his endurance into an assertive role for which he is not ready, learns that safety lies in stamping and shouting and pretending to be bigger and stronger and fiercer than one really is.

Not with a single phrase or a single gesture, not with one punishment alone, but in every tone of the voice, in each turn of the head, these nuances are conveyed to the child, and as the Balinese baby learns that the unknown is always to be avoided, and the Iatmul baby learns to play at being strong, the American baby learns that its parents' love—even if they are his parents and he isn't adopted—is conditional upon the way in which he compares with others. "He's such a poor eater. I don't know what to do with him. I just can't get him to eat like other children." His mother thinks he isn't listening, as he digs with his shovel under the park bench, but the "won't eat" and the depreciating tone in which she says it gets through to him—she is not worrying because her beloved child does not take the food which she has lovingly prepared for him, but because he is showing himself inferior at being a growing child. At his next meal he looks guiltily at his carrots. If he rejects them again that same depreciatory note will recur tomorrow in his mother's voice.

So while the child is learning that his whole place in the world, his name, his right to the respect of other children—everything—depends upon his parents and on what kind of a house they have been able to build or buy or rent, what kind of a car they are able to drive, what kind of toys they are able to buy him, he also learns that his own acceptance by these parents, who are his only support, is conditional upon his achievements, upon the way in which he shows up against other children and against their idea of other children. To the anxiety with which small boys in many if not all cultures of the world view grown men and wonder if they will ever be as tall and strong, is added in America, for both boys and girls, the anxiety as to whether they will be successful in keeping their parents' love as children. American girls of college age can be thrown into a near panic by the description of cultures in which parents do not love their children. Against the gnawing fear that their personal achievement has made them unworthy of love, they have placed a vague persistent belief in "mother love," a belief that somehow or other their parents won't be able to get out of loving them some—because they are parents, and theirs. Any evidence that destroys their faith in this "maternal instinct" is profoundly disturbing. They know they are not worthy; if the modicum that was to be theirs forever, even without worthiness, is taken away—what is there left of which they can be sure? Their own children? No, because what if they are imbeciles? The brightest people, college professors especially, have imbecile children. "If your skirt turns up in back, your mother loves you better than your father. If your skirt turns up in front, your father loves you better than your mother." "She loves me, she loves me not," is a game that Americans do not wait to play until they are in love.

So the young American starts life with a tremendous impetus towards success. His family, his little slender family, just a couple of parents alone in the world, are the narrow platform on which he stands. If he becomes an orphan, or a half orphan, if his father deserts his mother, or his mother his father, if any of the things happen that happen all the time in the movies, in the papers, on the radio, he is already half defeated. To succeed after such an event he would have to overcome a dreadful handicap. "He lives with his uncle. His father's dead." "She hasn't any father and mother; she lives with some people who were just neighbors." "He lives with his grandmother and she's deaf as a post." "Poor Jane, she is a little queer, but then you know her grandparents brought her up." "He's just boarding there—some charity pays for him." This is what he may expect. And when he has got his family intact, down to a kid sister, he can't be sure of keeping his place in it, just because he is himself. "No one," remarked a famous American educator, "no one can love unconditionally a child with an IQ over 90." A normal child must earn his parents' love.

Recently, students of comparative education, philosophers of improved family relationships, have made this point articulate and begun to scold American mothers because they do not love their children unconditionally. This has merely added to the confusion. It is only possible to love a child, as part of oneself, unconditionally, if one loves oneself in a certain sense unconditionally. The unconditional mother must have once been an unconditionally loved child, taking into her own soul part of the approval that was showered upon her. The peculiarity of the American version of "To him that hath shall be given" lies in this, that the child who, because it was bright or strong or beautiful, did receive great approval from its parents, is in turn able to love friends and lovers and children as parts of its highly approved self.

For the obverse of the whole system obtains. If parents can persuade themselves that their child is wholly admirable, they are then given license to love it fatuously, without the reserve or the precautionary bows to Fate appropriate in other societies. Although the anxiety that one will not be worthy is never entirely lacking, the assurance of the successful American child can be very great, and that in turn he passes on to his children.

This whole emphasis upon achievement in order to deserve that parental love which is so essential, in a world where everything else is shifting, where one's home is a number of a street, where one may change schools every year and move always among half-familiar faces, is further sharpened by the parent's inability to applaud themselves in their children. In societies where the father rears his son to his own trade, it is possible for him to feel a fine thrill of identification and pride the first time the child manipulates the tools of the trade with a distinguished touch. "Ha, a chip of the old block!" says father. "My child shares my skill." But in America, with the rapid rate of change, most parents know that the child will not do what the parent did, but something different. A parent cannot think back to his own boyhood and simply make an inaccurate comparison. When he was a boy, it was his pride to ride a bicycle thirty miles a day, not drive a car four hundred miles a day, to tap out a few words on a home-built radio set, not to build a model aeroplane of beautiful accurracy and new design. He must applaud in his son something which he did not do himself, and something which he has no way of judging. If he knew more than his son about building model aeroplanes, then he could judge his son's model on its merits. As it is, he vacillates between fatuous attacks of paternal pride, for whose undiscriminating nature his son despises him, and anxious requests as to whether the model has won or will win a prize, and so give him the right to be proud. Any approval which he does give must be necessarily ill-informed and not of the sort to win his son's respect. Only from outside sources, from school grades, competitions, rises in salary, prizes, can he learn whether this son whom he has reared is really as good as he hopes that he is.

Yet the further the child goes from standards that his parents know, the greater is his need for success. He is leaving them, he is giving up every concrete thing which they did, he will neither eat like them, nor dress like them, nor have the same standards as to what is appropriate to say to a girl or how he should plan his life insurance or where he should take his vacation. In big things and in small, in all the habits of life through which they taught him what the world was like, he will leave them, he will in a sense betray them. All he can offer in return is success. As a high school principal said recently to the parents of the graduating class: "They lay their success, their achievement, before you, a thank-offering for all that you have done for them."

When we see this situation dramatized in the immigrant father, himself with no book learning and hardly an English word, pathetically delighted because his son has won some academic honor, we are touched with the pity of it, of the father who cannot himself, realize the inwardness of what his son has done. We can sympathize with the young research chemist who is offered a job as the president of a small college—"President! Now that is something my father and mother would understand. They don't get this sort of thing I am doing at all. But a title, a limousine, to live in a big house called the President's house. They'd know I'd made good then." And he hesitates and goes back not quite happy to the research work which his fine mind is so perfectly fitted to do, not able to be gay in the rejection of the conspicuous role which would have made sense to his less schooled parents. These seem to us extreme cases, part of the drama of immigration, of the rapid rise from generations of peonage to a place in a free world. But they are only extreme cases of what happens to almost every American parent, no matter how successful his son. And we find a curious reflection of this dependence upon externals for the validation of success, in the anxiety of wives, or of the husbands of professional women, to be assured that the spouse is really good, really recognized by his or her colleagues. A husband who has regarded his wife's excursions into the academic world with kindly contempt will grow suddenly respectful when she is offered a fellowship. "They" have recognized her, she must have something in her after all.

This anomalous state in which American parents are forever looking for a right to be proud of, and a right to love, their children, and forever recognizing that the proofs of worthiness must come from a world which itself has already slipped beyond them, is dramatized also in the relationship between parents and teachers. The teacher, in the American school, is teaching the child something which the parents don't know. If not in sober fact, giving the child a mastery of English grammar of which the parents have never heard, or a facility with fractions which the mother never mastered, still in spirit the teacher is the representative of the changing world in which the children must succeed. The teacher symbolizes a gulf between parents and children which will grow year by year—not the inevitable gulf between old and young, for that, like the seasons, is a circumstance to which man can bow with dignity, but the more dishonorable gulf which results from the parents getting out of date. The children are fast outstripping the parents, and handling daylight saving time with no mistakes at all while the parents are still missing trains. It is hard to find in such a breach between youth and age a place for pride in the young who outstrip the old, not because of greater ability but merely because of being born in a different year. Only those who have made a point of pride out of the very pace of our lives, out of the very fact that those who are born in 1920 start off wiser than those born in 1910 can find pride in such a circumstance. For the majority it is galling to slip behind, for it was one's place in the race which gave one dignity. And the teacher, often younger than the parents, becomes the symbol of this indignity. Children come home from school, anxious to put their parents in their place, and quote the teacher's word against theirs. It is small wonder that American parents retaliate by taking a savage interest in the teacher's character, by surveying her morals with a scrutiny accorded no one else except the minister's wife and the characters of political opponents. In a sense she is the enemy. They have given in, they have turned their children over to her to be made smarter than themselves and to learn a lot of things they, the parents, never needed to know. But just let them find her wanting in some way, failing to teach the children what the parents *do* know—that sacred symbol of the little bit of the Past which is worthy of respect, the Three R's—and they become merciless.

The situation, although difficult for the teacher, can be used to good purpose, if she makes herself the child's ally, the person who helps him take home to his parents the success which they so eagerly demand and upon which their love is contingent. If she is merely the dispenser of grades, she becomes to the child the person who, when she gives out a low grade, is denying him his passport to his parents' love. If she is helping the child to learn, she is helping him gain the coveted approval. She is in no sense a parent, but always she is professionally concerned with success, and this concern may be phrased in various ways. She may give or withhold, or she may turn with the child by her side to some impersonal power, which says whether the task was well done, and, if it was not, help again. In more static societies where there are schools, it is the duty of teachers merely to represent the parents, teaching what the parents would have the children learn. The teachers are the custodians of the past, the preservers of tradition. In America, the teacher is, in fact, never the representative of the parents—hardly even in those Eastern schools and colleges which attempt to imitate English institutions—she is always the representative of the future into which the parents are anxious that their children should enter, and enter well prepared.

REFERENCES

1. Mead, Margaret, "Broken Homes," *Nation, 128*:253–255, Feb. 27, 1939.
2. "Sociological Research in Adolescence" (Report of a Conference of the American Sociological Society held in New Haven in April 1934) *American Journal of Sociology,* Vol. XLII, No. 1, July 1936, pp 81–94.
3. Mead, Margaret, "Character Formation in Two South Seas Societies," *Proceedings,* American Neurological Association, 1940.

29

What You Should Know About Schizophrenia

American Schizophrenia Foundation

Schizophrenia. What is it?

Certainly it is a name which, because of a lack in public education, has all too often struck terror, needlessly, into the hearts of those diagnosed as schizophrenics and their loved ones. Few know that schizophrenia, if diagnosed early and properly treated, is a highly recoverable illness.

Any serious attempt to define schizophrenia is handicapped by the many myths—both ancient and modern—that have grown up around it, compounding its tragedies.

Schizophrenia is not a way of life. It is not a crime. It does not favor artists and intellectuals. It is not a "split" or a "double" personality. It is not caused by devils or difficult mothers or tyranical fathers or latent homosexuality or stress. It is not caused by childhood trauma and does not distinguish between people with happy childhoods and those with unhappy childhoods.

Schizophrenia is a physical *disease*, in the same way that pellagra and diabetes—and mental retardation are physical diseases. And it is a disease which is the same in every part of the world.

Schizophrenia is a widespread and devastating illness which today afflicts at least 2,000,000 persons in the United States and Canada.

One of every 100 persons in the world today has, has had or will have schizophrenia in his lifetime. The incidence of schizophrenia is at least 1 per cent in all societies, in all cultures, in all racial and ethnic types, in all social classes, in war and in peace, in times of depression and of prosperity.

Schizophrenia is one of the most common of the mental illnesses. About a quarter of the 300,000 annual admissions to state mental hospitals are schizophrenics. About half of the resident population of American hospitals is schizophrenic.

The recovery rate for schizophrenics is low and the rate of readmission to hospitals is high. In fact, because many patients are not receiving the most advanced treatments, the number of readmissions is almost equal to the number of first admissions.

Schizophrenia is thus an extremely costly disease, which puts an enormous financial burden on its victims and their families, as well as on American taxpayers.

Though it can strike at any time (babies may even be born with it), schizophrenia takes its largest toll among young men and women in the 16-30 age group, in the very prime of life. Schizophrenic breakdowns in college are not uncommon.

Among these persons, the recovery rate has remained fairly constant throughout the years, and even the use of tranquilizers, though helpful to patients in many ways, does not appear to have greatly changed this proportion. With or without treatment, about one-third will recover, a third will be totally disabled, and another third will be discharged into the outside world not sick enough to be institutionalized, "not well enough to live healthy, happy lives."

Many of the latter will take their own lives to escape the dreadful pain and suffering of their affliction. Schizophrenia is one of the reasons that suicide has become a major problem in the United States. Every day, about 300 Americans try to kill themselves and 50 succeed. There is much evidence that many suicides and attempted suicides are schizophrenics. Young schizophrenic men are especially suicide prone.

A large body of scientific evidence has recently been assembled indicating that the schizophrenic is a victim of a "metabolic error" in the chemistry of his body. This defect, probably inherited, causes the production of a poisonous substance that affects his brain and creates marked disturbances in perception and radical changes in thought, personality and behavior.

Scientists have succeeded in extracting from the blood and urine of schizophrenics various poisonous substances which, when injected into the blood of normal persons, create many of the classic symtoms of schizophrenia. The origin of these toxins is still something of a mystery, and much inspired research remains to be done to track down the source of the defect or defects.

But whatever the nature or origin of the brain poison, by attacking those brain functions governing perception, it forces the victim of schizophrenia to live in a different world from that of normal persons. It interferes with normal communication with others, isolating him from his family and friends, and thus schizophrenia has often been justifiably referred to as a living death.

Some Signs of Schizophrenia

The fact is, schizophrenia generally strikes persons who have been heretofore relatively normal, and that is one of the major reasons why the experience is so terrifying. Schizophrenia may come on suddenly or imperceptibly, in a slowly increasing personality deformation without any obvious explanation. It may last a few days or a whole lifetime.

The symptoms of schizophrenia, both psychological and physical, are innumerable, but for centuries and in all societies, there have been certain disturbances frequently encountered among schizophrenics. No two patients will necessarily have the same ones, but these disturbances fall into general categories.

Schizophrenia has two important, universal characteristics that set it apart from other physical illnesses and from the neuroses:

1. *The schizophrenic experiences perceptual changes (in seeing, hearing, touching, tasting and smelling).*
2. *There are accompanying changes in thought, mood and behavior, and thus an alteration in the entire personality.*

DISTURBANCES IN PERCEPTION

Perception is the way things appear to us. The inner and outer worlds of a normal person are fairly constant. There is, on the whole, a consistency in the way he sees, hears, touches, tastes and smells the world around him.

When, however, a normal person is given an infinitesimal quantity of a drug like LSD or mescaline, his perception is immediately disturbed or distorted. The brain toxin brewed by the defective body chemistry of the schizophrenic has similar effects.

Schizophrenia can change one or all of our sensory modes. Common among schizophrenics are:

1. *Visual Changes*

The schizophrenic sees the world as through a distorted looking glass. Colors may become very brilliant or lose their brilliance. He may complain that the world has suddenly become unreal. Objects look different. Three-dimensional objects look flat. The world may appear as though constructed out of flat cardboard. The shapes of people may change. He may have difficulty judging the size of people and objects at some distance from him. Frequently, the schizophrenic will suffer from *illusions and hallucinations.* The coat hanging in a closet may momentarily look like a bear. People may look like chess pieces. A schizophrenic child might suddenly see her playmate grow in size and turn into a lion. *These are illusions. Hallucinations* are things, scenes, people, etc., which patients see vividly but other people do not see. A coiled snake may suddenly appear on the floor of a vacant room. A patient may walk directly into a wall, having seen a door which does not exist. These visual changes may range in intensity from very slight to very severe, and may endure from a hallucination of one moment to hallucinations lasting many decades. Because of them, the schizophrenic is often unclear in his own mind as to what is real and what unreal.

2. *Auditory Changes*

Very few schizophrenics are free of auditory changes. Sounds may be louder and music deafening to the ears. Or sounds may become less loud and difficult to locate. There may be strange sounds of rushing noises, buzzings and hissings. Often the schizophrenic has auditory hallucinations. He may hear voices speaking accusingly to him. He may hear voices singing. A voice might tell him to go hang himself. "Religious communications have been very common," reports one psychiatrist, "but in recent years sexual comments seem to have become more frequent." The schizophrenic has no control over these hallucinations, which may involve any combination of the senses. For instance, a stranger might appear and carry on a sensible chat with a schizophrenic and then just as suddenly vanish into thin air.

3. *Changes in Sense of Smell*

Patients may become either more or less sensitive to odors. Schizophrenics often complain of having an ever-present, offensive body odor. Perfume may no longer smell like perfume to a female schizophrenic.

4. *Changes in Sense of Touch*

Patients may become more or less sensitive to touch. Schizophrenics tend to be hypersensitive, and during their waking hours they live with constant, intolerable mental and physical pain. Their generalized suffering is so great that they may appear to be insensitive to pain. Sometimes they will inflict serious bodily injury to themselves with no evidence of pain. They may have trouble feeling hot or cold things. And they may complain of bizarre sensations such as feelings of being stuck with needles or of worms crawling under the skin.

5. *Taste Changes*

Foods have a strange taste. New tastes may occur. A schizophrenic may start eating foods he formerly loathed and avoiding foods he formerly enjoyed. Taste changes may lead him to believe that someone is poisoning his food.

6. *Time Changes*

Schizophrenics are continually living with a distorted time sense, much like that produced in normal persons by drugs like LSD. Many chronic schizophrenics feel that they are suspended in time. Time passes with excruciating slowness, and an hour may seem like a month. Past, present and future are all muddled up.

Perceptions may be distorted or disturbed in almost any manner. The schizophrenic finds that he can not trust his own sensory experiences, as he once did before the onset of his illness. Taking it as a sign that he is losing his mind, he often panics and thus accelerates the course of the illness.

DISTURBANCES IN THOUGHT

Schizophrenia often results in the shattering or fragmentation of its victim's mental life. Generally the schizophrenic will experience:

1. *Changes in Thought Process*

There may be a slow-down in the process of thinking, so that logical thinking becomes difficult or impossible. Memory may become disturbed and recall rendered difficult. Or there may be an acceleration in thought and the schizophrenic will complain that his mind is racing away from him. Prof. Landis notes that patients may feel that "thoughts from the outside, over which they have no control, are inflicted upon them to such an extent that their own thoughts become displaced, blocked, distorted or completely changed."

2. *Changes in Thought Content*

These are myriad and limited only by the schizophrenic's imagination. Schizophrenics often develop false beliefs, or delusions, which may grow out of their perceptual difficulties. For example, a change in his ability to taste the flavor of foods may lead him to the conviction that his wife is trying to poison him. Or, if he repeatedly evokes the hallucination of a stranger following him, he may become convinced that he is about to become the victim of a communist plot or (if he lives in Russia) of a capitalist plot. Patients may also develop delusions of personal power, becoming convinced that they are important persons or reincarnations of historical figures, and with it a system of apparently logical reasoning to support their contentions. Frequently, schizophrenics come to believe that they are under the control of outside forces, divine or demoniacal.

CHANGES IN MOOD

Deep, almost continuous depression, unrelated to external events, is the most common change in mood. Depression is primary in schizophrenia, often occurring without any precipitating event, and it is fruitless to search for a rational reason for it. Crippling fatigue and apathy are associated with this depression. Sometimes the depression may swing, suddenly and unaccountably, into a period of great elation and well-being, causing much senseless over-activity, but these periods are few and far between in schizophrenia. Also common is the sudden growth of an irrational, nameless and overwhelming fear. Indeed schizophrenic episodes rarely occur without including a large element of fear, also unrelated to external events. It is not unlikely that this irrational fear, and the depression, are the results of the peculiar perceptual changes which the schizophrenic can neither understand nor cope with. The schizophrenic also suffers from severe inner tension, which may make him feel as if he is about to explode and disintegrate. Thus he may appear to be seething with anger, and the posture of hostility he may assume is a consequence of this great tension and inward suffering. Sometimes he may complain of inappropriate feelings, that he felt like crying when a situation called for laughter, or that he laughed when he should have cried. At other times, he may complain that he can not feel any emotion at all and that his soul has left his body. The inner world of the schizophrenic is turbulent and terrifying, often beyond endurance, and it is not difficult to understand why, assailed by such symptoms, schizophrenics have identity problems and complain that they do not know who they are.

CHANGES IN BEHAVIOR

The schizophrenic "acts strangely as the result of what he suffers and does not understand." It should not be surprising that changes in perception, thought and mood lead to changes in behavior. If a person, because of taste changes, develops the delusion that his wife is poisoning his food, it seems only natural that he will respond in some bizarre way. If he actually "sees" an FBI man dogging his tracks, it would seem likely that he would take some sort of action, either defensive or offensive. He might conclude that the president of the United States is persecuting him, and he might decide to take revenge and send in to a mail-order house for a high-powered rifle with a telescopic sight. Schizophrenia can sometimes lead to violence, though the great majority of schizophrenics are peaceful and harmless persons. Their illness far more often leads to sucide. A schizophrenic episode may also result in a reversal in many of the victim's personal habits. The person may hate what he previously loved and love what he previously hated, and act accordingly. Sexual activity may be increased, but as a rule, schizophrenics lose their sexual desire or find it considerably reduced during their illness. It often returns after recovery.

What Causes Schizophrenia?

Some psychoanalytical theorists have, unfortunately, encouraged the schizophrenic to blame his ailment on his mother, his father, his spouse, the society he lives in, or all of these together. Left by himself, the schizophrenic may delude himself into blaming some minority group or (if he is a member of a minority) the majority, or he may blame the political party to which he does not belong. (Most of the persons arrested in recent years for threatening the lives of American presidents were apparently schizophrenic.) *No one is to blame*, though we are all to blame for being poorly informed about a widespread and very costly illness and not taking the proper steps to combat it.

In the past decade, the laboratory evidence has been steadily growing that a defect in his body chemistry causes the schizophrenic to brew—perhaps in his liver, perhaps in his adrenal glands—some substance that distorts the working of his brain.

"Before anyone can get schizophrenia," according to two psychiatric researchers, Dr. Abram Hoffer and Dr. Humphry Osmond, "his body 'factory' must be different from that of a normal subject in that it must have the capacity to go out of order for some reason, and start biochemical changes in motion. This is an essential cause of schizophrenia. Without it, the disease can not occur. With it, it may occur, but it also may not, just as everyone susceptible to tuberculosis does not develop tuberculosis."

Negative emotional factors—like fear and hatred, despair and self pity—can trigger or aggravate the condition, but the underlying physiological weakness is the basic cause.

This physiological weakness is, in turn, probably inherited. The distinguished geneticists Sir Julian Huxley and Professor Ernst Mayr of Harvard declared recently that "it now appears clear that schizophrenia, at least in the great majority of cases, is based on a single partially dominant gene with low penetrance."

Studies of identical twins have shown the tendency to be inherited. Identical twins have nearly identical genetic factors and are as much alike as it is possible for two humans to be. It has been demonstrated that if one member of a set of identical twins becomes schizophrenic, the other will become schizophrenic about 85 per cent of the time, even though the twins may be separated at birth and raised in different homes by different parents.

Other studies have shown that schizophrenics were *schizoprone* apparently from birth, manifesting marked personality and temperament differences from an early age, and that these could not be associated with environmental influences.

Schizophrenia can be determined by one's genes, but there is no simple or direct inheritance, as for eye color. There are a number of genes involved and one can only say what could probably occur in a family.

The majority of schizophrenics come from normal parents. The inheritance factor, however, helps explain why some members of a family are schizophrenic and some are not.

Huxley and Mayr consider that the immediate aim of scientific research should be to devise biochemical tests to identify carriers of the "Sc" gene, as has been done with a number of other genes. Thus, if schizoprones can be identified from childhood, "educational and other methods could be devised to prevent or mitigate the manifestation of the disease."

Diagnosis and Treatment

In the United States, and elsewhere, there is widespread disagreement among psychiatrists as to the proper treatment of schizophrenia. The treatment of schizophrenics varies radically from psychiatrist to psychiatrist, hospital to hospital, clinic to clinic. This disagreement within the psychiatric profession is reflected in the confusion of the patients, their families and the general public.

The schizophrenic may be given electric shock treatments or insulin shock therapy. It may be decided that he needs a lobotomy, a type of brain surgery. He may be rotated on a number of different tranquilizers and anti-depressants. Often, despite Freud's explicit warning that schizophrenia does not respond to psychoanalysis he may undergo a number of years of such treatment. "It is of utmost importance to recognize early the presence of the disease," warns Dr. Robert G. Heath, chairman of the Department of Psychiatry, Tulane University, because the therapist who doesn't "may undertake a type of psychotherapy that can result in dire consequences."

One of the goals of the American Schizophrenia Foundation will be to improve and standardize the treatment of schizophrenics through a program of research, public education and service.

Until science develops better methods of treatment, the public would be wise to seek the help of physicians who know what schizophrenia is, who will not fail to diagnose it, and who will employ the best up-to-date treatments available and consistent with modern knowledge.

Often, schizophrenics, both in and out of the hospital, are given no information about their illness, neither its diagnosis nor its cause. Their fears are unwarrantably magnified and the condition aggravated by this lack of information. The lack of information and the lack of psychiatric agreement combine to increase the schizophrenic's sense of isolation not only from healthy persons but also from other schizophrenics. Schizophrenics thus do not develop the comradeship which alcoholics, for instance, find so beneficial.

When a person suddenly begins to have strange experiences which he never had or heard about previously, it would be strange indeed if he were not terrified. When he is not given the name of his illness, when he is not given a prescription or instructions on how to combat it, and when he is not told that thousands of others have had similar experiences and recovered, then his physician is not discharging his obligation to him.

Prompt and proper diagnosis is the first important step in the treatment of any disease. Failure to diagnose schizophrenia and to initiate treatment at an early age may lead to a lifetime of invalidism. Chronic schizophrenia does not respond readily to treatment, and chances of full recovery are diminished with advancing years.

This booklet has given the highlights of the changes which occur in schizophrenia. No one patient has them all, nor do they remain the same from month to month.

Do not diagnose yourself. But you should become familiar with some of the warning signs of an approaching schizophrenic episode. These are:

1. Insomnia.
2. Headaches.
3. A change in skin color to a darker hue.
4. An ever-present offensive body odor.
5. Intense self-preoccupation.
6. Irrational crying fits.
7. Crippling fatigue.
8. Deep depression unrelated to external events.
9. Severe inner tension.
10. Disturbances in perception.
11. Unaccountable changes in personality.
12. Inability to lose the feeling of being watched.
13. The growth of a senseless terror.
14. A fear of loss of self-control over one's thoughts and actions.

Some of these symptoms, of course, may be indicative of other illnesses. But if you have any combination of them, you should immediately consult your physician. You must at all times rely on the judgment of your physician and follow his instructions faithfully.

And remember. Don't panic. Schizophrenia can be brought under control. Thousands of persons have made full recoveries from the illness. Indeed, as one scientist commented: "Considering how ineptly we handle this illness, the surprising thing is that so many schizophrenics manage to fight their way through." Among these are some of the world's greatest scientists, religious leaders, statesmen, formed by the fresh view of life that developed out of their schizophrenic breakdowns.

30

The Placebo Effect in Medical and Psychological Treatment

Jerome Frank

"I know something *interesting is sure to happen," she said to herself, "whenever I eat or drink anything: so I'll just see what this bottle does."* (Alice's Adventures in Wonderland, *Chapter 4*)

Our review of religious healing has revealed considerable evidence that measures which combat anxiety and arouse hope can have curative power in themselves. Physicians have always known that their ability to inspire expectant trust in a patient has something to do with the success of treatment. Until recently this knowledge, like that obtained from anthropological studies, rested on uncontrolled observations and clinical impressions, so that it was impossible to define in any systematic way the sources and limits of the effects of hope on different kinds of patients and their illnesses. The problem has been to domesticate the question, as it were, to lure it away from the bedside into the laboratory where the factors involved could be systematically manipulated and their effects sorted out.

Fortunately, there is one form of medical treatment that makes this possible, since its effectiveness rests solely on its ability to mobilize the patient's expectancy of help. This is the use of a "placebo." A placebo is a pharmacologically inert substance that the doctor administers to a patient to relieve his distress when, for one reason or another, he does not wish to use an active medication. Thus he may use a placebo rather than a sedative in treating a patient's chronic insomnia to avoid the danger of addiction. Since a placebo is inert, its beneficial effects must lie in its symbolic power. The most likely supposition is that it gains its potency through being a tangible symbol of the physician's role as a healer. In our society, the physician validates his power by prescribing medication, just as a shaman in a primitive tribe may validate his by spitting out a bit of bloodstained down at the proper moment.

In this connection it may be worth while to recall that until the last few decades most medications prescribed by physicians were pharmacologically inert. That is, physicians were prescribing placebos without knowing it, so that, in a sense, the "history of medical treatment until relatively recently is the history of the placebo effect."[1] Despite their inadvertent reliance

From *Persuasion and Healing* by Jerome Frank (Baltimore: The Johns Hopkins Press, 1961), pp. 65–74. Reprinted by arrangement with The Johns Hopkins Press.

[1] Shapiro (1959), p. 303.

on placebos, physicians maintained an honored reputation as successful healers, implying that these remedies were generally effective. Yet, when a physician today knowingly prescribes a placebo, he may tend to feel a little guilty. For it seems to imply deception of the patient, which the physician finds hard to reconcile with his professional role. The dictionary definition of a placebo is illuminating in this regard: "a medicine, especially an inactive one, given merely to satisfy a patient."[2] The little word "merely" has been the stumbling block, since it implies that a placebo does nothing but satisfy the patient. Perhaps because of this implication, the conditions determining the effects of placebo administration and the nature of these effects have failed to receive the careful study they deserve.

In recent years the mounting flood of new pharmaceuticals requiring evaluation has given impetus to the study of placebo effects, for the pharmacological effects of any new drug must be disentangled from those due simply to the power of any new remedy to arouse hopes of physicians and patients. A common experimental approach to this problem has been the so-called "double-blind" method. In this technique neither physician nor patient knows whether a particular dose contains the medicine or a placebo. The patient's responses to each dose or course of treatment are carefully recorded, and after the experiment is completed, responses to medication and placebo are compared. Any consistent differences can then be reliably attributed to the pharmacological action of the drug.

Study of the patient's reactions to pharmacologically inert medication is a means of investigating effects of their expections, mediated by the doctor-patient relationship, on their physical and emotional states. A look at the present state of knowledge on this subject is therefore pertinent to the aims of this book.

In passing, it may be mentioned that a patient's expectations have been shown to affect his physiological responses so powerfully as even to reverse the pharmacological action of a drug. For example, the drug ipecac is an emetic, which normally causes cessation of normal stomach contractions shortly after ingestion. The patient experiences this as nausea. By having a patient swallow a balloon, which is inflated in the stomach and hooked to the proper equipment, these changes in stomach motility can be directly observed. A pregnant patient suffering from excessive vomiting showed the normal response of cessation of stomach contractions with nausea and vomiting after receiving a dose of ipecac. When the same medication was given to her through a tube, so that she did not know what it was, with strong assurance that it would cure her vomiting, gastric contractions started up at the same interval after its administration that they would normally have stopped, and simultaneously the patient's nausea ceased.[3]

Evidence that placebos can have marked physiological effects has been afforded by demonstrations of their ability to heal certain kinds of tissue damage. The placebo treatment of warts, for example, by painting them with a brightly colored but inert dye and telling the patient that the wart will be gone when the color wears off, is as effective as any other form of treatment, including surgical excision, and works just as well on patients who have been successfully treated by other means as on untreated ones.[4] Apparently the emotional reaction to a placebo can change the physiology of the skin so that the virus which causes warts can no longer thrive.

Placebo treatment can also activate

[2] Webster's New Collegiate Dictionary, 1957 edition.
[3] Wolf (1950).
[4] Bloch (1927).

healing of more severely damaged tissues, especially when the damage seems related to physiological changes connected with unfavorable emotional states. In one study of patients hospitalized with bleeding peptic ulcer, for example, 70 per cent showed "excellent results lasting over a period of one year," when the doctor gave them an injection of distilled water and assured them that it was a new medicine that would cure them. A control group who received the same injection from a nurse with the information that it was an experimental medication of undetermined effectiveness showed a remission rate of only 25 per cent.[5]

The symbolic meaning of medication may not always be favorable. Some patients fear drugs and distrust doctors. In these patients a placebo may produce severe untoward physiological reactions including nausea, diarrhea, and skin eruptions.[6]

Placebos can have powerful effects on hospitalized psychiatric patients. Using double-blind techniques, it has been found that some of the beneficial effects of tranquilizers, especially when they were first introduced into mental hospitals, were really due to the hope they inspired in both staff and patients. They increased the therapeutic zeal of the staff, and this in itself helped the patients. In this connection, the mere introduction of a research project into a ward in a veterans hospital was followed by considerable behavioral improvement in the patients, although no medications or other special treatments were involved at all. The most likely explanation seemed to be that participation in the project raised the general level of interest of the treatment staff, and the patients responded favorably to this.[7]

Psychiatric outpatients also often respond favorably to inert medications. In five separate studies involving a total of fifty-six patients, an average of 55 per cent showed significant symptomatic improvement from placebos.[8] This figure is about the same as that reported with medical patients whose disorders have an emotional component, suggesting that placebos produce their benefits through favorably affecting certain emotional states.

The duration of the placebo effect depends on many factors. When the source of the pain is independent of the patient's emotional condition, like a surgical wound, the relief afforded by a placebo tends to be transient, although it may last as long as that produced by analgesics. When the improvement in emotional state produced by the placebo also diminishes the physiological disorder producing the pain, then the effect may be enduring, as in the peptic ulcer patients reported above. The placebo, by combating anxiety, probably diminished stomach mobility and secretion, thereby facilitating healing of the ulcers. The maximum duration of the placebo effect in psychiatric patients is unknown because a placebo has seldom been given for more than two or three weeks. It remains undiminished for at least this length of time with many patients. In one study the effect was undiminished at the end of at least eight weeks.[9]

The kinds of symptoms that are particularly susceptible to relief by placebos confirm the hypothesis that they combat anxiety and similar feelings. Their ability to relieve the pain in patients following surgical operations—and they are temporarily effective in over a third of these patients—has been attributed to their success in combating the "processing" aspects of pain,[10] that is, the apprehensiveness and

[5] Volgyesi (1954).
[6] Wolf and Pinsky (1954).
[7] Frank (1952).
[8] Gliedman et al. (1958).
[9] Hampson et al. (1954).
[10] Beecher (1955).

other emotions that aggravate painful sensations. In psychiatric outpatients psychic symptoms, especially anxiety and depression, respond more often and more markedly to placebos than do bodily ones, though these also are somewhat relieved.

If the effectiveness of the placebo lies in its ability to mobilize the patient's expectancy of help, then it should work best with those patients who have favorable expectations from medicine and, in general accept and respond to symbols of healing. The scanty information available is consistent with this hypothesis. In the study of patients with surgical pain, placebo responders tended to be more dependent, emotionally reactive, and conventional, while the nonreactors were more likely to be isolated and mistrustful.[11] Psychiatric outpatients who showed strong responses to placebos, as compared with a group who showed no response, were more apt to take vitamins and aspirins regularly, were more outgoing, participated more in organizations, and were less cautious. These findings suggest that they expected medicines to help them, were better integrated socially, and were less mistrustful than nonreactors.

Thus it appears that the ability to respond favorably to a placebo is not so much a sign of excessive gullibility, as one of easy acceptance of others in their socially defined roles. This view is supported by the relation of placebo responsiveness of a group of schizophrenic patients to their subsequent clinical course.[12] Thirty-three who appeared at a follow-up clinic for a routine check-up shortly after their discharge from a state hospital were given placebos for three weeks. Their response was a remarkably good prognosticator of whether they would have to go back to the hospital or not. Of those who had to return within thirty days not one responded favorably, while of those who remained well enough to stay out of the hospital, four-fifths had felt better after receiving the placebo. Apparently placebo responsiveness was an indicator of the ability of these patients to trust their fellow man as represented by the clinic physicians, and this had something to do with their capacity to adjust to the world outside the hospital.

If part of the success of all forms of psychotherapy may be attributed to the therapist's ability to mobilize the patient's expectation of help, then some of the effects of psychotherapy should be similar to those produced by a placebo.[13] It has been possible to demonstrate experimentally that this is so. In an experimental study of the relative effects of six months of group, individual, and minimal psychotherapy with psychiatric outpatients, it was found that, while degree of improvement in social effectiveness was related to the amount of treatment contact, average diminution of discomfort was the same regardless of the form or amount of psychotherapy the patients had received. Moreover, the average amount of discomfort relief was the same for patients who had dropped out of treatment within the first month as for those who had received six months of treatment. It is perhaps more surprising, in view of the wide-

[11] Lasagna et al. (1954). It should be added that occasionally a patient who expresses strong distrust of doctors reacts positively to a placebo. A diabetic who was a trained nurse, for example, was the despair of her physicians because of her refusal to take her medicines and her constant diatribes against them. Yet in the very midst of her rebelliousness she showed a striking relief of abdominal pain following an injection of distilled water by a physician. This suggested that her attitude might have been an overcompensation for strong feelings of dependency, as if she were longing to accept help but could not admit it. The analogy to "skeptics" who benefit from a pilgrimage to Lourdes is obvious.

[12] Hankoff et al. (1958).

[13] Rosenthal and Frank (1956).

spread belief among physicians that symptomatic relief is superficial and transient, that average diminution of discomfort persisted over a five-year follow-up period. That is, although some patients relapsed, the group as a whole maintained its gains.[14]

The fact that relief of discomfort was the same regardless of the type or duration of therapy and that it seemed to occur quite promptly suggested that it might be due to the mobilization of the patient's expectant trust. This would ordinarily not depend on the nature or length of treatment and should occur at the first contact of the patient with his physician. If this were the explanation, then administration of a placebo, the power of which presumably rests on the same factor, should have similar effects.

To test this, twelve patients of the original population were given a two-week trial of placebo at the time of their routine follow-up interview two to three years after their initial contact with the project. These patients had shown marked symptomatic improvement after the first six months and had slipped back only a little during the subsequent observation period, but they still were sufficiently distressed to desire further relief. The placebo produced just about as much relief of discomfort in these patients as had the six months of psychotherapy.[15] This seems to confirm the hypothesis that part of the healing power of all forms of psychotherapy lies in their ability to mobilize the patient's hope of relief.

The intensity of the hope that can be elicited by psychotherapy must be but a pale shadow of that evoked by religious healing. It is therefore the more surprising that symptomatic relief following even minimal psychotherapy proved to be so enduring. The explanation may be that relief of anxiety and depression frees the patient to make better use of the healthy parts of his personality, so that he functions more effectively in general. As one writer puts it: "If the patient believes strongly in a cure . . . by his very belief he at once obtains sufficient moral support to *face all his problems* with some degree of equanimity."[16] Greater success in solving his problems, in turn, results in increased satisfaction and diminished frustration, further ameliorating his distress.

To forestall misunderstanding, it should be stressed that mobilization of the patient's expecation of help at best accounts for only a part of the effects of psychotherapy. In the experimental study, improvement in social effectiveness, in contrast to relief of distress, was clearly due to other factors. However, as suggested above, symptom relief and improved functioning are intimately related.

Nor should the ability of placebos to produce symptomatic relief under some circumstances be regarded as justification for their widespread use. In addition to the obvious consideration that this would cause them to lose their effectiveness and damage patients' faith in the medical profession, they have several serious drawbacks. Insofar as the doctor feels that he is deceiving a patient by giving him a placebo, this may undermine the doctor-patient relationship. For if the patient showed a good response, the doctor might lose respect for him as gullible; and if the patient failed to respond, he would have lost some faith in the doctor. The very power of the placebo makes it dangerous, for it may relieve distress caused by serious disease. This may cause neglect of diagnostic studies that would have revealed the condition and result in failure to give adequate treatment.

[14] Frank et al. (1959).
[15] Gliedman et al. (1958)
[16] Kraines (1943), p. 135. Author's italics.

From the standpoint of psychotherapy, the psychiatrist by prescribing a placebo implicitly conveys that he considers medication the best treatment for the patient's condition. This decreases the patient's motivation to solve the personal problems that are the real source of his distress.

There are three conditions in which the use of a placebo may be indicated. Sometimes it can be helpful when an active agent for the patient's illness cannot be used or does not exist. It also may have a proper use with patients whose anxiety over their condition aggravates or prolongs it. To the extent that a placebo will relieve this anxiety, it is a genuine healing agent. Finally, for some patients treatment means receiving a medicine or an injection, and if they do not get it, they will not return. It may sometimes be advisable to meet the expectations of such a patient by giving him a placebo in order to hold him in treatment long enough to establish a therapeutic relationship with him.

But in most circumstances the physician can best arouse the expectant trust of his patients by his serious interest and competence and, where indicated, by the use of treatment measures that combat the pathological condition underlying the patient's symptoms. The chief value of the placebo will continue to be as a research tool to study some of the determinants and effects of expectancy of help, and to test the pharmacological action of new drugs.

Summary

Experimental studies of the effects of the administration of inert medications by physicians demonstrate that the alleviation of anxiety and arousal of hope through this means commonly produce considerable symptomatic relief and may promote healing of some types of tissue damage. The relief may be enduring. The little that is known of personality attributes of those who respond favorably to placebos suggests that they are predisposed to accept and react to socially defined symbols of healing.

Comparison of the effects of psychotherapy and placebos on a group of psychiatric outpatients suggests that certain symptoms may be relieved equally well by both forms of treatment and raises the possibility that one of the features accounting for some of the success of all forms of psychotherapy is their ability to arouse the patient's expectation of help. These findings must not be interpreted as justifying widespread use of placebos or as explaining other more important, beneficial effects of psychotherapy that are clearly due to factors different from arousal of the expectation of help.

31

From *The Diary of Vaslav Nijinsky*

Vaslav Nijinsky

Everybody will say that Nijinsky has become insane. I do not care, I have already behaved like a madman at home. Everybody will think so, but I will not be put in an asylum, because I dance very well and give money to all those who ask me. People like an odd and peculiar man and they will leave me alone, calling me a "mad clown." I like insane people, I know how to talk to them. My brother was in the lunatic asylum.

I was fond of him and he understood me. His friends there liked me too, I was then eighteen years old. I know the life of lunatics and understood the psychology of an insane man. I never contradict them, therefore madmen like me. . . .

Life is not sex—sex is not God, God is man, who fecundates only one woman, a man who gives children to one woman. I am twenty-nine years old. I love my wife spiritually, not for begetting children. I will have children if God wishes it. Kyra is an intelligent girl. I do not want her to be clever. I will prevent her from developing her intelligence. I like simple people but not stupidity, because I see no feeling in that. Intelligence stops people from developing. I feel God and God feels me.

I want to correct my faults but I do not know whether I will be able to. The doctor's eyes were full of tears when he told me that he needed no promises, he knew that I would do everything to stop my wife from being nervous and worried. I explained to him that I was the one who wanted my wife's mother to come. I do not want my wife to be afraid; therefore I wanted my mother-in-law to live with us. I am not afraid of the Allied authorities. I do not care if they take all our money.[1] But I do not want this money to be taken on account of my family. I do not want my wife to be ruined. I gave her all I had which was very little, so that she should be able to live. I am not afraid of life and therefore I do not need money. My wife will weep if I die. I hope for her sake that she will soon forget me. My wife does not always understand or, rather, feel me. Tolstoy's wife had no feeling. Tolstoy's wife cannot forget that he had given all his money away. I want to give my wife money. I love my wife and Kyra more than anybody else; my hand is tired.

I do not like Shakespeare's Hamlet because he reasons. I am a philosopher who does not reason—a philosopher who

[1] Subjects of Allied countries were not allowed to spend money on the subjects of the enemy countries. Mme. Nijinsky's relatives were Hungarians.

feels. I do not like to write things that are thought out. I like Shakespeare because he loved the theater. Shakespeare understood the theater. I have understood the "living theater" also. I am not artificial. I am life. The theater is not life. I know the customs of the theater. The theater becomes a habit. Life does not. I do not like the theater with a square stage. I like a round stage. I will build a theater which will have a round shape, like an eye. I like to look closely in the mirror and I see only one eye in my forehead. Often I make drawings of one eye. I dislike polemics and therefore people can say what they like about my book; I will be silent. I have come to the conclusion that it is better to be silent than to speak. Diaghilev told me to be silent. Diaghilev is clever. Vassilli, his servant, used to say, "Diaghilev hasn't got a penny, but his intelligence is worth a fortune." I say, "I haven't got a penny and no intelligence, but I have a mind." I call mind that center which generates feeling. I am sensitive. I was stupid before because I thought that happiness depended on money—now I no longer think it. Many people think about money, I need some to carry out my plans; we all have our plans and aims, and we earn money to realize them, but our problems are different. I am God's problem, not Antichrist's. I am not Antichrist. I am Christ. I will help mankind.

I will go to Geneva to have a rest because the doctor tells me to do so. He thinks I am tired because my wife is now very nervous, high-strung. I am not, therefore I will stay at home. My wife can go alone. She has a little money. I have not got a penny. I am not bragging when I say that I have no money. I like to have money and will earn some to give to my wife and to poor people. Many will say that Nijinsky pretends to be like Christ. I do not pretend —I love His deeds. I am not afraid of being attacked. I say everything I have to.

I used to go out on the street. I deceived my wife, I had so much semen that I had to throw it away. I did not waste it on a cocotte. I threw it on the bed in order to protect myself from catching a venereal disease. I am not erotic and therefore will not deceive my wife any more. My seed I will save for another child—I hope I will some day have a son. I love my wife, I do not want anything bad to happen to her. She is sensitive. She thinks that I do everything on purpose, in order to frighten her. Everything I do is for the purpose of making her well and happy. She eats meat—that causes her nervousness; it does not matter if one eats meat—to lead a good life is important. My wife knows that it is good to lead a regular life, but she does not realize what this mode of life consists of. "*To listen to God—and obey Him—that is a good regular mode of life.*" People do not understand God, and ask themselves who is this God who must be obeyed. I know God and His wishes. I love God.

I do not know what to write about, because I have suddenly thought of the doctors and my wife—who are talking in the next room. I know they do not like my actions but I will continue in the same way while God wishes it. I am not afraid of any complications. I will ask everybody to help me and will not be afraid if I am told this, for instance: "Your wife became insane because you have tortured her; for this you will be imprisoned for the rest of your life." I am not afraid of prison and there I will find life, but I will die there if I am put there for life. I do not wish my wife ill, I love her too much to harm her. I like to hide from people; I am used to living alone.

Maupassant was terrified of being lonely. The Count of Monte Cristo liked loneliness because he wanted time to prepare for his revenge. Maupassant was frightened of solitude; he loved people. I am afraid of loneliness but will not cry; God loves me and so I am not alone. If God leaves me I will die. As I do not want to, I will live like other people, in order to be understood by others. God is mankind, and does not like those who interfere with His plans. I do not; on the contrary I help him. I am the weapon of God, a man of God. I like God's people. I am not a beggar. I will take money if a rich man will leave it to me. I like a rich man. The rich man has a lot of money and I have none. When everyone finds out that I have no money, they will get frightened and turn away from me. That is why I want to get richer every hour.

I will hire a horse and will make him take me home without paying for it. My wife will pay. If she does not pay I will find a way of paying myself. I want my wife to love me and so I do all this to develop her character. Her intelligence is well developed but her feelings are not. I want to destroy her intelligence; then she can only develop in other ways. People think that without intelligence a man is either insane or a fool. An insane person is a person who cannot reason. A lunatic does not realize what he is doing. I understand my good and my bad actions. I am a man who has reason. In Tolstoy's book a lot is explained about reason. I read this book and therefore know what it means. I am not afraid of intelligent people. I am strong because I feel all that is said about me. I know that they invent all sorts of things to calm me. The doctors are good. My wife is also a good woman, but they think much too much. I am afraid for their intelligence. People went mad because they thought too much—I am afraid for them, they think too much. I do not want them to become insane: I will do everything to make them healthy.

I offended my wife without realizing it—then I asked her for forgiveness; my faults were continuously being brought up at a suitable moment. I am afraid of my wife; she does not understand me. She believes that I am insane or wicked. I am not wicked, I love her. I write about life, not death. I am not Nijinsky as they think. I am God in man. My wife is a good woman. I told her in secret all my plans, then she told the doctors everything, believing this would help me. My wife does not understand my object; I did not explain it, not wanting her to know. I will feel and she will understand. She will feel and I will understand. I do not want to think, thinking is death. I know what I am doing. *"I do not wish you ill. I love you. I want to live and therefore I will be with you. I spoke to you. I do not want intelligent speech."* The doctors speak with intelligence, so does my wife. I am afraid of them. I want them to understand my feelings. *"I know that it hurts you. Your wife is suffering because of you."* I do not want death to come and therefore I use all kinds of tricks. I will not reveal my object. *"Let them think you are an egoist. Let them put you in prison. I will release you because you belong to me. I do not like the intelligent Romola. I want her to leave you. I want you to be mine. I do not want you to love her as a man loves. I want you to love her with a sensitive love. I know how to simplify and smooth everything that has happened. I want the doctors to understand your feelings. I want to scold you because the doctors think that your wife is a nervous woman. Your cross*[2] *has done so much harm that you cannot disentangle it all. I know your faults because I have committed them." I put on a cross on purpose: "She understood you. The doctor came in order to find out what your intentions are and does not understand anything at all. He thinks and therefore it is difficult for him to understand. He feels Romola is right and that you are right too. I know how to understand."* I think better than doctors. *"I am afraid for you, because love for me is infinite; you obey my orders. I will do everything to make you understand,*

[2] [Nijinsky wore a cross over his necktie and walked around St. Moritz, causing a sensation, described in the biography.]

I love your wife and you. I wish her well. I am God in you. I will be yours when you will understand me. I know what you are thinking you are frightened. I know your habits. Your about: that he is here and is staring at you. I want him to look at you." I do not want to turn round because I can feel him looking at me. *"I want to show him your writing. He will think that you are ill because you write so much. I understand your feelings. I understand you well. I am making you write with a purpose because he will understand your feelings too. I want you to write everything I am telling you. People will understand you because you are sensitive. Your wife will understand you also. I know more than you and therefore I ask you not to turn around. I know your intentions. I want to carry out our plans but you must suffer. Everybody will feel and understand only when they see your sufferings."*

I want to write about my conversation in the dining room with my wife and the doctor. I pretended I was an egoist because I wanted to touch him. He will be offended if he finds this out but I do not care. I do not divide love. I wrote that I loved my wife better than anybody—I wanted to show how I feel about my wife. I love A. just as much. I know her tricks. She understands my feelings because she is going away in the next few days. I do not want her presence. I want my mother-in-law to come because I want to study her and help her. I do not study people's character in order to write about them. I want to write in order to explain to people their habits—which lead them to death. I call this book "Feelings." I love feeling and will write a big book about it. There will be a description of my life in it. I do not want to publish this book after my death. I want to publish it now. *"I am afraid for you because you are afraid for yourself. I want to say the truth. I do not want to hurt people. Perhaps you will be put in prison for writing this book. I will be with you because you love me. I cannot be silent. I must speak. I know you will not be put in prison; legally you have not committed an offense. If people want to judge you, you shall answer that everything you said is God's word. Then they will put you in an asylum, and you will understand insane people. I want you to be put in prison or into an asylum. Dostoievsky went to the gallows and therefore you also can go and sit somewhere. I know people whose love is not dead and they will not allow you to be put anywhere. You will become as free as a bird when this book is published in many thousands of copies. I want to sign the name of Nijinsky—but my name is God. I love Nijinsky not as Narcissus but as God."* I love him because he gave me life. I do not want to pay any compliments. I love him. He loves me because he knows my habits. *"Nijinsky has faults, but Nijinsky must be listened to because he speaks the words of God."* I am Nijinsky. *"I do not want Nijinsky to be hurt and therefore I will protect him. I am only afraid for him because he is afraid for himself. I know his strength. He is a good man. I am a good God. I do not like Nijinsky when he is bad."* I do not like God when he is bad. I am God, Nijinsky is God. *"He is a good man and not evil. People have not understood him and will not understand him if they think. If people listened to me for several weeks there would be great results. I hope that my teachings will be understood."* All that I write is necessary to mankind. Romola is afraid of me, she feels I am a preacher. Romola does not want her husband to be a preacher, she wants a young, handsome husband. I am handsome, young. She does not understand my beauty, I have not got regular features. Regular features are not like God. God has sensitiveness in the face, a hunchback can be Godlike. I like hunchbacks and other freaks. I am myself a freak who has feeling and sensitiveness, and I can dance like a hunchback. I am an artist who likes all shapes and all beauty. Beauty is not relative. Beauty is God, He is in beauty and feeling. Beauty is in feeling too. I love beauty. I feel it and understand it. Those people who think write nonsense about beauty. One cannot discuss it. One cannot criticize it. I am feeling beauty. I love beauty.

I do not want evil—I want love. People think that I am an evil man. I am not. I love everybody. I have written the truth. I have spoken the truth. I do not like untruthfulness and want goodness, not evil. I am love. People take me for a scarecrow because I put on a small cross which I liked. I wore it to show that I was Catholic. People thought I was insane. I was not. I wore the cross in order to be noticed by people. People like calm men. I am not. I love life. I want it. I do not like death. I want to love mankind. I want people to believe in me. I have said the truth about A., Diaghilev, and myself. I do not want war and murders. I want people to understand me. I told my wife that I would destroy the man who would touch my notebooks, but I will cry if I have to do it. I am not a murderer. I know that everyone dislikes me. They think I am ill. I am not. I am a man with intelligence.

The maid came and stood near me, thinking that I was sick. I am not. I am healthy. I am afraid for myself because I know God's wish. God wants my wife to leave me. I do not want it, I love her and will pray that she may remain with me. They are telephoning about something. I believe they want to send me to prison. I am weeping, as I love life, but I am not afraid of prison. I will live there. I have explained everything to my wife. She is no longer afraid, but she still has a nasty feeling. I spoke harshly because I wanted to see tears —but not those which have been caused by grief. Therefore I will go and kiss her. I want to kiss her to show her my love. I love her, I want her, I want her love. A. has felt that I love her too and she is remaining with us. She is not leaving. She has telephoned to sell her ticket. I do not know for certain but I feel it.

My little girl is singing: "Ah, ah, ah, ah!" I do not understand its meaning, but I feel what she wants to say. She wants to say seek Him. I am a seeker, for I can feel that everything—Ah! Ah!—is not horror but joy.

Epilogue

I want to cry but God orders me to go on writing. He does not want me to be idle. My wife is crying, crying. I also. I am afraid that the doctor will come and tell me that my wife is crying while I write. I will not go to her, because I am not to blame. My child sees and hears everything and I hope that she will understand me. I love Kyra. My little Kyra feels my love for her, but she thinks too that I am ill, for they have told her so. She asks me whether I sleep well and I tell her that I always sleep well. I do not know what to write, but God wishes me to. Soon I will go to Paris and create a great impression—the whole world will be talking about it. I do not wish people to think that I am a great writer or that I am a great artist nor even that I am a great man. I am a simple man who has suffered a lot. I believe I suffered more than Christ. I love life and want to live, to cry but cannot—I feel such a pain in my soul—a pain which frightens me. My soul is ill. My soul, not my mind. The doctors do not understand my illness. I know what I need to get well. My illness is too great to be cured quickly. I am incurable. My soul is ill, I am poor, a pauper, miserable. Everyone who reads these lines will suffer—they will understand my feelings. I know what I need. I am strong, not weak. My body is not ill—it is my soul that is ill. I suffer, I suffer. Everyone will feel and understand. I am a man, not a beast. I love everyone, I have faults, I am a man—not God. I want to be God and therefore I try to improve myself. I want to dance, to draw, to play the piano, to write verses, I want to love everybody. That is the—object of my life. I know that Socialists would understand me better—but I am not a Socialist. I am a part of God, my party is God's party. I love everybody.

I *do not* want war or frontiers. The world exists. I have a home everywhere. I live everywhere. I do not want to have any property. I do not want to be rich. I want to love. I am love—not cruel I am not a bloodthirsty animal. I am man. I am man. God is in me. I am in God. I want Him, I seek Him. I want my manuscripts to be published so that everybody can read them. I hope to improve myself. I do not know how to, but I feel that God will help all those who seek Him. I am a seeker, for I can feel God. God seeks me and therefore we will find each other.

God and Nijinsky,
Saint Moritz-Dorf,
Villa Guardamunt
February 27, 1919

32

From *One Flew Over the Cuckoo's Nest*

Ken Kesey

They're out there. Black boys in white suits up before me to commit sex acts in the hall and get it mopped up before I can catch them.

They're mopping when I come out the dorm, all three of them sulky and hating everything, the time of day, the place they're at here, the people they got to work around. When they hate like this, better if they don't see me. I creep along the wall quiet as dust in my canvas shoes, but they got special sensitive equipment detects my fear and they all look up, all three at once, eyes glittering out of the black faces like the hard glitter of radio tubes out of the back of an old radio.

"Here's the Chief. The *soo*-pah Chief, fellas. Ol' Chief Broom. Here you go, Chief Broom. . . ."

Stick a mop in my hand and motion to the spot they aim for me to clean today, and I go. One swats the back of my legs with a broom handle to hurry me past.

"Haw, you look at 'im shag it? Big enough to eat apples off my head an' he mine like a baby."

They laugh and then I hear them mumbling behind me, heads close together. Hum of black machinery, humming hate and death and other hospital secrets. They don't bother not talking out loud about their hate secrets when I'm nearby because they think I'm deaf and dumb. Everybody thinks so. I'm cagey enough to fool them that much. If my being half Indian ever helped me in any way in this dirty life, it helped me being cagey, helped me all these years.

I'm mopping near the ward door when a key hits it from the other side and I know it's the Big Nurse by the way the lockworks cleave to the key, soft and swift and familiar she been around locks so long. She slides through the door with a gust of cold and locks the door behind her and I see her fingers trail across the polished steel—tip of each finger the same color as her lips. Funny orange. Like the tip of a soldering iron. Color so hot or so cold if she touches you with it you can't tell which.

She's carrying her woven wicker bag like the ones the Umpqua tribe sells out along the hot August highway, a bag shape of a tool box with a hemp handle. She's had it all the years I been here. It's a loose weave and I can see inside it; there's no compact or lipstick or woman stuff, she's got that bag full of a thousand parts she aims to use in her duties today—wheels and gears, cogs polished to a hard glitter, tiny pills that gleam like porcelain, needles, forceps, watchmakers' pliers, rolls of copper wire . . .

She dips a nod at me as she goes past. I let the mop push me back to the wall and smile and try to foul her equipment up as much as possible by not letting her see my eyes—they can't tell so much about you if you got your eyes closed.

In my dark I hear her rubber heels hit the tile and the stuff in her wicker bag clash with the jar of her walking as she passes me in the hall. She walks stiff. When I open my eyes she's down the hall about to turn into the glass Nurses' Station where she'll spend the day sitting at her desk and looking out her window and making notes on what goes on out in front of her in the day room during the next eight hours. Her face looks pleased and peaceful with the thought.

Then . . . she sights those black boys. They're still down there together, mumbling to one another. They didn't hear her come on the ward. They sense she's glaring down at them now, but it's too late. They should of knew better'n to group up and mumble together when she was due on the ward. Their faces bob apart, confused. She goes into a crouch and advances on where they're trapped in a huddle at the end of the corridor. She knows what they been saying, and I can see she's furious clean out of control. She's going to tear the black bastards limb from limb, she's so furious. She's swelling up, swells till her back's splitting out the white uniform and she's let her arms section out long enough to wrap around the three of them five, six times. She looks around her with a swivel of her huge head. Nobody up to see, just old Broom Bromden the half-breed Indian back there hiding behind his mop and can't talk to call for help. So she really lets herself go and her painted smile twists, stretches to an open snarl, and she blows up bigger and bigger, big as a tractor, so big I can smell the machinery inside the way you smell a motor pulling too big a load. I hold my breath and figure, My God this time they're gonna do it! This time they let the hate build up too high and overloaded and they're gonna tear one another to pieces before they realize what they're doing!

But just as she starts crooking those sectioned arms around the black boys and they go to ripping at her underside with the mop handles, all the patients start coming out of the dorms to check on what's the hullabaloo, and she has to change back before she's caught in the shape of her hideous real self. By the time the patients get their eyes rubbed to where they can halfway see what the racket's about, all they see is the head nurse, smiling and calm and cold as usual, telling the black boys they'd best not stand in a group gossiping when it *is* Monday morning and there *is* such a lot to get done on the first morning of the week. . . .

". . . mean old Monday morning, you know, boys . . ."

"Yeah, Miz Ratched . . ."

". . . and we have quite a number of appointments this morning, so perhaps, if your standing here in a group talking isn't *too urgent* . . ."

"Yeah, Miz Ratched . . ."

She stops and nods at some of the patients come to stand around and stare out of eyes all red and puffy with sleep. She nods once to each. Precise, automatic gesture. Her face is smooth, calculated, and precision-made, like an expensive baby doll, skin like flesh-colored enamel, blend of white and cream and baby-blue eyes, small nose, pink little nostrils—everything working together except the color on her lips and fingernails, and the size of her bosom. A mistake was made somehow in manufacturing, putting those big, womanly breasts on what would of otherwise been a perfect work, and you can see how bitter she is about it.

The men are still standing about and waiting to see what she was onto the black boys about, so she remembers seeing me and says, "And since it *is* Monday, boys, why don't we get a good head start on the week by shaving poor Mr. Bromden first this morning, before the after-breakfast rush on the shaving room, and see if we can't avoid some of the—ah—disturbance he tends to cause, don't you think?"

Before anybody can turn to look for me I duck back in the mop closet, jerk the door shut dark after me, hold my breath. Shaving before you get breakfast is the worst time. When you got something under your belt you're stronger and more wide awake, and the bastards who work for the Combine aren't so apt to slip one of their machines in on you in place of an electric shaver. But when you shave *before* breakfast like she has me do some mornings—six-thirty in the morning in a room all white walls and white basins, and long-tube lights in the ceiling making sure there aren't any shadows, and faces all round you trapped screaming behind the mirrors—then what chance you got against one of their machines?

I hide in the mop closet and listen, my heart beating in the dark, and I try to keep from getting scared, try to get my thoughts off someplace else—try to think back and remember things about the village and the big Columbia River, think about ah one time Papa and me were hunting birds in a stand of cedar trees near The Dalles. . . . But like always when I try to place my thoughts in the past and hide there, the fear close at hand seeps in through the memory. I can feel that least black boy out there coming up the hall, smelling out for my fear. He opens out his nostrils like black funnels, his outsized head bobbing this way and that as he sniffs, and he sucks in fear from all over the ward. He's smelling me now, I can hear him snort. He don't know where I'm hid, but he's smelling and he's hunting around. I try to keep still. . . .

(Papa tells me to keep still, tells me that the dog senses a bird somewheres right close. We borrowed a pointer dog from a man in The Dalles. All the village dogs are no-'count mongrels, Papa says, fish-gut eaters and no class a-tall; this here dog, he got *insteek!* I don't say anything, but I already see the bird up in a scrub cedar, hunched in a gray knot of feathers. Dog running in circles underneath, too much smell around for him to point for sure. The bird safe as long as he keeps still. He's holding out pretty good, but the dog keeps sniffing and circling, louder and closer. Then the bird breaks, feathers springing, breaks out of the cedar into the birdshot from Papa's gun.)

The least black boy and one of the bigger ones catch me before I get ten steps out of the mop closet, and drag me back to the shaving room. I don't fight or make any noise. If you yell it's just tougher on you. I hold back the yelling. I hold back till they get to my temples. I'm not sure it's one of those substitute machines and not a shaver till it gets to my temples; then I can't hold back. It's not a will-power thing any more when they get to my temples. It's a . . . *button*, pushed, says Air Raid Air Raid, turns me on so loud it's like no sound, everybody yelling at me, hands over their ears from behind a glass wall, faces working around in talk circles but no sound from the mouths. My sound soaks up all other sound. They start the fog machine again and its snowing down cold and white all over me like skim milk, so thick I might even be able to hide in it if they didn't have a hold on me. I can't see six inches in front of me through the fog and the only thing I can hear over the wail I'm making is the Big Nurse whoop and charge up the hall while she crashes patients outta her way with that wicker bag. I hear her coming but I still can't hush my hollering. I holler till she gets there. They hold me down while she jams wicker bag and all into my mouth and shoves it down with a mop handle.

(A bluetick hound bays out there in the fog, running scared and lost because he can't see. No tracks on the ground but the ones he's making, and he sniffs in every direction with his cold red-rubber nose and picks up no scent but his own fear, fear burning down into him like steam.) It's gonna burn me just that way, finally telling about all this, about the hospital, and her, and the guys—and about McMurphy. I been silent so long now it's gonna roar out of me like floodwaters and you think the guy telling this is ranting and raving my *God;* you think this is too horrible to have really happened, this is too awful to be the truth! But, please. It's still hard for me to have a clear mind thinking on it. But it's the truth even if it didn't happen.

SECTION B *Perspectives on the Frontiers of Mental Health*

There is a trend in behavioral science toward the humanistic. This movement has been along two distinct axes: the first toward a greater degree of involvement in social problems. Social scientists are active in the programs on poverty, racial difficulties, housing, student unrest, and other areas of immediate concern as a direct result of this expansion.

The second is not as easily understood, but has a greater potential impact in the long run. There is a growing attempt to study and develop a science of mental health, not merely a science designed to minimize or eliminate mental illness. Foundations for the science of mental improvement are being established and it is becoming evident that every individual can become considerably more healthy, more effective, and better able to deal with new and varied situations. There is a parallel in physical medicine. The astronauts have focused attention on superior health, not merely the elimination of physical illness. For the first time considerable amounts of time, energy, money, and talent are being funneled into understanding and encouraging superior physical health.

Carl Rogers, whose previous article on creativity already implied the need for mental health, discusses the process of an encounter group. These groups, also called sensitivity groups, T-groups, basic awareness, touch and tenderness, and interpersonal awareness are increasingly popular. They allow people to expose their feelings themselves in an atmosphere of trust and mutual compassion. For some it is a religious experience, a conversion of their self-image in a few days; others find it less effective or helpful and may increase their anxiety. However, these groups are rapidly becoming part of the mental-health movement.

Abraham Maslow's article makes the point that mental improvement is the natural urge of a human being. If this urge is thwarted, the resulting drive is away from stability and maturity toward illness.

The remaining selections illustrate aspects of this new focus on mental health.

33

The Process of the Basic Encounter Group

Carl R. Rogers

I would like to share with you some of my thinking and puzzlement regarding a potent new cultural development—the intensive group experience.[1] It has, in my judgment, significant implications for our society. It has come very suddenly over our cultural horizon, since in anything like its present form it is less than two decades old.

I should like briefly to describe the many different forms and different labels under which the intensive group experience has become a part of our modern life. It has involved different kinds of individuals, and it has spawned various theories to account for its effects.

As to labels, the intensive group experience has at times been called the *T-group* or *lab group*, "T" standing for training laboratory in group dynamics. It has been termed *sensitivity training* in human relationships. The experience has sometimes been called a *basic encounter group* or a *workshop*—a workshop in human relationships, in leadership, in counseling, in education, in research, in psychotherapy. In dealing with one particular type of person—the drug addict—it has been called a *synanon.*

The intensive group experience has functioned in various settings. It has operated in industries, in universities, in church groups, and in resort settings which provide a retreat from everyday life. It has functioned in various educational institutions and in penitentiaries.

An astonishing range of individuals have been involved in these intensive group experiences. There have been groups for presidents of large corporations. There have been groups for delinquent and predelinquent adolescents. There have been groups composed of college students and faculty members, of counselors and psychotherapists, of school dropouts, of married couples, of confirmed drug addicts, of criminals serving sentences, of nurses preparing for hospital service, and of educators, principals, and teachers.

The geographical spread attained by this

[1] In the preparation of this paper I am deeply indebted to two people, experienced in work with groups, for their help: Jacques Hochmann, M.D., psychiatrist of Lyon, France, who has been working at WBSI on a U.S.P.H.S. International Post-doctoral Fellowship, and Ann Dreyfuss, M.A., my research assistant. I am grateful for their ideas, for their patient analysis of recorded group sessions, and for the opportunity to interact with two original and inquiring minds.

rapidly expanding movement has reached in this country from Bethel, Maine (starting point of the National Training Laboratory movement), to Idyllwild, California. To my personal knowledge, such groups also exist in France, England, Holland, Japan, and Australia.

In their outward pattern these group experiences also show a great deal of diversity. There are T-groups and workshops which have extended over three to four weeks, meeting six to eight hours each day. There are some that have lasted only 2½ days, crowding twenty or more hours of group sessions into this time. A recent innovation is the "marathon" weekend, which begins on Friday afternon and ends on Sunday evening, with only a few hours out for sleep and snacks.

As to the conceptual underpinnings of this whole movement, one may almost select the theoretical flavor he prefers. Lewinian and client-centered theories have been most prominent, but gestalt therapy and various brands of psychoanalysis have all played contributing parts. The experience within the group may focus on specific training in human relations skills. It may be closely similar to group therapy, with much exploration of past experience and the dynamics of personal development. It may focus on creative expression through painting or expressive movement. It may be focused primarily upon a basic encounter and relationship between individuals.

Simply to describe the diversity which exists in this field raises very properly the question of why these various developments should be considered to belong together. Are there any threads of commonality which pervade all these widely divergent activities? To me it seems that they do belong together and can all be classed as focusing on the intensive group experience. They all have certain similar external characteristics. The group in almost every case is small (from eight to eighteen members), is relatively unstructured, and chooses its own goals and personal directions. The group experience usually, though not always, includes some cognitive input, some content material which is presented to the group. In almost all instances the leader's responsibility is primarily the facilitation of the expression of both feelings and thoughts on the part of the group members. Both in the leader and in the group members there is some focus on the process and the dynamics of the immediate personal interaction. These are, I think, some of the identifying characteristics which are rather easily recognized.

There are also certain practical hypotheses which tend to be held in common by all these groups. My own summary of these would be as follows: In an intensive group, with much freedom and little structure, the individual will gradually feel safe enough to drop some of his defenses and facades; he will relate more directly on a feeling basis (come into a basic encounter) with other members of the group; he will come to understand himself and his relationship to others more accurately; he will change in his personal attitudes and behavior; and he will subsequently relate more effectively to others in his everyday life situation. There are other hypotheses related more to the group than to the individual. One is that in this situation of minimal structure, the group will move from confusions, fractionation, and discontinuity to a climate of greater trust and coherence. These are some of the characteristics and hypotheses which, in my judgment, bind together this enormous cluster of activities which I wish to talk about as constituting the intensive group experience.

As for myself, I have been gradually moving into this field for the last twenty years. In experimenting with what I call *student-centered teaching*, involving the free expression of personal feelings, I came to recognize not only the cognitive learnings but also some of the personal changes which occurred. In brief intensive training courses for counselors for the Veterans Administration in 1946, during the postwar period, I and my staff focused more directly on providing an intensive group experience because of its impact in producing significant learning. In 1950, I served as leader of an intensive full-time, one-week workshop, a postdoctoral training seminar in psychotherapy for the American Psychological Association. The impact of those six days was so great that for more than a dozen years afterward, I kept hearing from members of the group about the meaning it had had for them. Since that time I have been involved in more than forty ventures of what I would like to term—using the label most congenial to me—*basic encounter groups.* Most of these have involved for many of the members experiences of great intensity and considerable personal change. With two individuals, however, in these many groups, the experience contributed, I believe, to a psychotic break. A few other individuals have found the experience more unhelpful than helpful. So I have come to have a profound respect for the constructive potency of such group experiences and also a real concern over the fact that sometimes and in some ways this experience may do damage to individuals.

The Group Process

It is a matter of great interest to me to try to understand what appear to be common elements in the group process as I have come dimly to sense these. I am using this opportunity to think about this problem, not because I feel I have any final theory to give, but because I would like to formulate, as clearly as I am able, the elements which I can perceive at the present time. In doing so I am drawing upon my own experience, upon the experiences of others with whom I have worked, upon the written material in this field, upon the written reactions of many individuals who have participated in such groups, and to some extent upon the recordings of such group sessions, which we are only beginning to tap and analyze. I am sure that (though I have tried to draw on the experience of others) any formulation I make at the present time is unduly influenced by my own experience in groups and thus is lacking in the generality I wish it might have.

As I consider the terribly complex interactions which arise during twenty, forty, sixty, or more hours of intensive sessions, I believe that I see some threads which weave in and out of the pattern. Some of these trends or tendencies are likely to appear early and some later in the group sessions, but there is no clear-cut sequence in which one ends and another begins. The interaction is best thought of, I believe, as a varied tapestry, differing from group to group, yet with certain kinds of trends evident in most of these intensive encounters and with certain patterns tending to precede and others to follow. Here are some of the process patterns which I see developing, briefly described in simple terms, illustrated from tape recordings and personal reports, and presented in roughly sequential order. I am not aiming at a high-level theory of group process but rather at a naturalistic observation out of which, I hope, true theory can be built.[2]

Milling Around. As the leader or facilitator

[2] Jack and Lorraine Gibb have long been working on an analysis of trust development as the essential theory of group process. Others who have contributed significantly to the theory of group process are Chris Argyris, Kenneth Benne, Warren Bennis, Dorwin Cartwright, Matthew Miles, and Robert Blake. Samples of the thinking of all these and others may be found in three recent books: Bradford, Gibb, & Benne (1964); Bennis, Benne, & Chin (1961); and Bennis, Schein, Berlew, & Steele (1964). Thus, there are many promising leads for theory construction involving a considerable degree of abstraction. This chapter has a more elementary aim—a naturalistic descriptive account of the process.

makes clear at the outset that this is a group with unusual freedom, that it is not one for which he will take directional responsibility, there tends to develop a period of initial confusion, awkward silence, polite surface interaction, "cocktail-party talk," frustration and great lack of continuity. The individuals come face-to-face with the fact that "there is no structure here except what we provide. We do not know our purposes; we do not even know one another, and we are committed to remain together over a considerable period of time." In this situation, confusion and frustration are natural. Particularly striking to the observer is the lack of continuity between personal expressions. Individual A will present some proposal of concern, clearly looking for a response from the group. Individual B has obviously been waiting for his turn and starts off on some completely different tangent as though he had never heard A. One member makes a simple suggestion such as, "I think we should introduce ourselves," and this may lead to several hours of highly involved discussion in which the underlying issues appear to be, "Who is the leader?" "Who is responsible for us?" "Who is a member of the group?" "What is the purpose of the group?"

Resistance to Personal Expression or Exploration. During the milling period, some individuals are likely to reveal some rather personal attitudes. This tends to foster a very ambivalent reaction among other members of the group. One member, writing of his experience, says:

> There is a self which I present to the world and another one which I know more intimately. With others I try to appear able, knowing, unruffled, problem-free. To substantiate this image I will act in a way which at the time or later seems false or artificial or "not the real me." Or I will keep to myself thoughts which if expressed would reveal an imperfect me.
>
> My inner self, by contrast with the image I present to the world, is characterized by many doubts. The worth I attach to this inner self is subject to much fluctuation and is very dependent on how others are reacting to me. At times this private self can feel worthless.

It is the public self which members tend to reveal to one another, and only gradually fearfully, and ambivalently do they take steps to reveal something of their inner world.

Early in one intensive workshop, the members were asked to write anonymously a statement of some feeling or feelings which they had which they were not willing to tell in the group. One man wrote:

> I don't relate easily to people. I have an almost impenetrable facade. Nothing gets in to hurt me, but nothing gets out. I have repressed so many emotions that I am close to emotional sterility. This situation doesn't make me happy, but I don't know what to do about it.

This individual is clearly living inside a private dungeon, but he does not even dare, except in this disguised fashion, to send out a call for help.

In a recent workshop when one man started to express the concern he felt about an impasse he was experiencing with his wife, another member stopped him, saying essentially:

> Are you sure you want to go on with this, or are you being seduced by the group into going further than you want to go? How do you know the group can be trusted? How will you feel about it when you go home and tell your wife what you have revealed, or when you decide to keep it from her? It just isn't safe to go further.

It seemed quite clear that in his warning, this second member was also expressing his own fear of revealing *him*self and *his* lack of trust in the group.

Description of Past Feelings. In spite of ambivalence about the trustworthiness of the group and the risk of exposing oneself.

expression of feelings does begin to assume a larger proportion of the discussion. The executive tells how frustrated he feels by certain situations in his industry, or the housewife relates problems she has experienced with her children. A tape-recorded exchange involving a Roman Catholic nun occurs early in a one-week workshop, when the discussion has turned to a rather intellectualized consideration of anger:

Bill: What happens when you get mad, Sister, or don't you?
Sister: Yes, I do—yes I do. And I find when I get mad, I, I almost get, well, the kind of person that antagonizes me is the person who seems so unfeeling toward people—now I take our dean as a person in point because she is a very aggressive woman and has certain ideas about what the various rules in a college should be; and this woman can just send me into high "G"; in an angry mood. *I mean this.* But then I find, I. . . .
Facil.:[3] But what, what do you do?
Sister: I find that when I'm in a situation like this, that I strike out in a very sharp, uh, *tone*, or else I just refuse to respond—"All right, this happens to be her way"—I don't think I've ever gone into a tantrum.
Joe: You just withdraw—no use to fight it.
Facil.: You say you use a sharp tone. To *her*, or to other people you're dealing with?
Sister: Oh, no. To *her*.

This is a typical example of a *description* of feelings which are obviously current in her in a sense but which she is placing in the past and which she describes as being outside the group in time and place. It is an example of feelings existing "there and then."

Expression of Negative Feelings. Curiously enough, the first expression of genuinely significant "here-and-now" feeling is apt to come out in negative attitudes toward other group members or toward the group leader. In one group in which members introduced themselves at some length, one woman refused, saying that she preferred to be known for what she was in the group and not in terms of her status outside. Very shortly after this, one of the men in the group attacked her vigorously and angrily for this stand, accusing her of failing to cooperate, of keeping herself aloof from the group, and so forth. It was the first *personal current feeling* which had been brought into the open in the group.

Frequently the leader is attacked for his failure to give proper guidance to the group. One vivid example of this comes from a recorded account of an early session with a group of delinquents, where one member shouts at the leader (Gordon, 1955, p. 214):

You will be licked if you don't control us right at the start. You have to keep order here because you are older than us. That's what a teacher is supposed to do. If he doesn't do it we will cause a lot of trouble and won't get anything done. [Then, referring to two boys in the group who were scuffling, he continues.] Throw 'em out, thrown 'em out! You've just *got* to make us behave!

An adult expresses his disgust at the people who talk too much, but points his irritation at the leader (Gordon, 1955, p. 210):

It is just that I don't understand why someone doesn't shut them up. I would have taken Gerald and shoved him out the window. I'm an authoritarian. I would have told him he was talking too much and he had to leave the room. I think the group discussion ought to be led by a person who simply will not recognize these people after they have interrupted about eight times.

Why are negatively toned expressions the first current feelings to be expressed? Some speculative answers might be the following:

[3] The term "facilitator" will be used throughout this paper, although sometimes he is referred to as "leader" or "trainer."

This is one of the best ways to test the freedom and trustworthiness of the group. "Is it really a place where I can be and express myself positively and negatively? Is this really a safe place, or will I be punished?" Another quite different reason is that deeply positive feelings are much more difficult and dangerous to express than negative ones. "If I say, 'I love you,' I am vulnerable and open to the most awful rejection. If I say, 'I hate you,' I am at best liable to attack, against which I can defend." Whatever the reasons, such negatively toned feelings tend to be the first here-and-now material to appear.

Expression and Exploration of Personally Meaningful Material. It may seem puzzling that following such negative experiences as the initial confusion, the resistance to personal expression, the focus on outside events, and the voicing of critical or angry feelings, the event most likely to occur next is for an individual to reveal himself to the group in a significant way. The reason for this no doubt is that the individual member has come to realize that this is in part *his group*. He can help to make of it what he wishes. He has also experienced the fact that negative feelings have been expressed and have usually been accepted or assimilated without any catastrophic results. He realizes there is freedom here, albeit a risky freedom. A climate of trust (Gibb, 1964, Ch. 10) is beginning to develop. So he begins to take the chance and the gamble of letting the group know some deeper facet of himself. One man tells of the trap in which he finds himself, feeling that communication between himself and his wife is hopeless. A priest tell of the anger which he has bottled up because of unreasonable treatment by one of his superiors. What should he have done? What might he do now? A scientist at the head of a large research department finds the courage to speak of his painful isolation, to tell the group that he has never had a single friend in his life. By the time he finishes telling of his situation, he is letting loose some of the tears of sorrow for himself which I am sure he has held in for many years. A psychiatrist tells of the guilt he feels because of the suicide of one of his patients. A woman of forty tells of her absolute inability to free herself from the grip of her controlling mother. A process which one workshop member has called a "journey to the center of self," often a very painful process, has begun.

Such exploration is not always an easy process, nor is the whole group always receptive to such self-revelation. In a group of institutionalized adolescents, all of whom had been in difficulty of one sort or another, one boy revealed an important fact about himself and immediately received both acceptance and sharp nonacceptance from members of the group:

George: This is the thing. I've got too many problems at home—uhm, I think some of you know why I'm here, what I was charged with.
Mary: I don't.
Facil.: Do you want to tell us?
George: Well, uh, it's sort of embarrassing.
Carol: Come on, it won't be so bad.
George: Well, I raped my sister. That's the only problem I have at home, and I've overcome that, I think. (*Rather long pause.*)
Freda: Oooh, that's *weird*!
Mary: People have problems, Freda, I mean ya know. . . .
Freda: Yeah, I know, but *yeOUW*! ! !
Facil. *(to Freda)*: You know about these problems, but they still are weird to you.
George: You see what I mean; it's embarrassing to talk about it.
Mary: Yeah, but it's O.K.
George: It *hurts* to talk about it, but I know I've got to so I won't be guilt-ridden for the rest of my life.

Clearly Freda is completely shutting him out psychologically, while Mary in particular is showing a deep acceptance.

The Expression of Immediate Interpersonal Feelings in the Group. Entering into the process sometimes earlier, sometimes later, is the explicit bringing into the open of the feelings experienced in the immediate moment by one member about another. These are sometimes positive and sometimes negative. Examples would be: "I feel threatened by your silence." "You remind me of my mother, with whom I had a tough time." "I took an instant dislike to you the first moment I saw you." "To me you're like a breath of fresh air in the group." "I like your warmth and your smile." "I dislike you more every time you speak up." Each of these attitudes can be, and usually is, explored in the increasing climate of trust.

The Development of a Healing Capacity in the Group. One of the most fascinating aspects of any intensive group experience is the manner in which a number of the group members show a natural and spontaneous capacity for dealing in a helpful, facilitative, and therapeutic fashion with the pain and suffering of others. As one rather extreme example of this I think of a man in charge of maintenance in a large plant who was one of the low-status members of an industrial executive group. As he informed us, he had not been "contaminated by education." In the initial phases the group tended to look down on him. As members delved more deeply into themselves and began to express their own attitudes more fully, this man came forth as, without doubt, the most sensitive member of the group. He knew intuitively how to be understanding and acceptant. He was alert to things which had not yet been expressed but which were just below the surface. When the rest of us were paying attention to a member who was speaking, he would frequently spot another individual who was suffering silently and in need of help. He had a deeply perceptive and facilitating attitude. This kind of ability shows up so commonly in groups that it has led me to feel that the ability to be healing or therapeutic is far more common in human life than we might suppose. Often it needs only the permission granted by a freely flowing group experience to become evident.

In a characteristic instance, the leader and several group members were trying to be of help to Joe, who was telling of the almost complete lack of communication between himself and his wife. In varied ways members endeavored to give help. John kept putting before Joe the feelings Joe's wife was almost certainly experiencing. The facilitator kept challenging Joe's facade of "carefulness," Marie tried to help him discover what he was feeling at the moment. Fred showed him the choice he had of alternative behaviors. All this was clearly done in a spirit of caring, as is even more evident in the recording itself. No miracles were achieved, but toward the end Joe did come to the realization that the only thing that might help would be to express his real feelings to his wife.

Self-acceptance and the Beginning of Change. Many people feel that self-acceptance must stand in the way of change. Actually, in these group experiences, as in psychotherapy, it is the *beginning* of change. Some examples of the kind of attitudes expressed would be these: "I *am* a dominating person who likes to control others. I do want to mold these individuals into the proper shape." Another person says, "I really have a hurt and overburdened little boy inside of me who feels very sorry for himself. I *am* that little boy, in addition to being a competent and responsible manager."

I think of one governmental executive in a group in which I participated, a man with high responsibility and excellent technical training as an engineer. At the first meeting of the group he impressed me, and I think others, as being cold, aloof, somewhat bitter, resentful, and cynical. When he spoke of how he ran his office it appeared that he administered it "by the book," without any warmth or human feeling entering in. In one of the early sessions, when he spoke of his wife, a group member asked him, "Do you love your wife?" He paused for a long time, and the questioner said, "OK, that's answer enough." The executive said, "No. Wait a minute. The reason I didn't respond was that I was wondering if I ever loved anyone. I don't think I *ever* really *loved* anyone." It seemed quite dramatically clear to those of us in the group that he had come to accept himself as an unloving person.

A few days later he listened with great intensity as one member of the group expressed profound personal feelings of isolation, loneliness, and pain, revealing the extent to which he had been living behind a mask, a facade. The next morning the engineer said, "Last night I thought and thought about what Bill told us. I even wept quite a bit myself. I can't remember how long it has been since I have cried, and I really *felt* something. I think perhaps what I felt was love."

It is not surprising that before the week was over, he had thought through new ways of handling his growing son, on whom he had been placing extremely rigorous demands. He had also begun genuinely to appreciate the love which his wife had extended to him and which he now felt he could in some measure reciprocate.

In another group one man kept a diary of his reactions. Here is his account of an experience in which he came really to accept his almost abject desire for love, a self-acceptance which marked the beginning of a very significant experience of change. He says (Hall, 1965):

During the break between the third and fourth sessions, I felt very droopy and tired. I had it in mind to take a nap, but instead I was almost compulsively going around to people starting a conversation. I had a begging kind of a feeling, like a very cowed little puppy hoping that he'll be patted but half afraid he'll be kicked. Finally, back in my room I lay down and began to know that I was sad. Several times I found myself wishing my roommate would come in and talk to me. Or, whenever someone walked by the door, I would come to attention inside, the way a dog pricks up his ears; and I would feel an immediate wish for that person to come in and talk to me. I realized my raw wish to receive kindness.

Another recorded excerpt from an adolescent group, shows a combination of self-acceptance and self-exploration. Art had been talking about his "shell," and here he is beginning to work with the problem of accepting himself, and also the facade he ordinarily exhibits:

Art: I'm so darn used to living with the shell; it doesn't even bother me. I don't even know the real me. I think I've uh, well, I've pushed the shell more away here. When I'm out of my shell—only twice—once just a few minutes ago—I'm really me, I guess. But then I just sort of pull in the [latch] cord after me when I'm in my shell, and that's almost all the time. And I leave the [false] front standing outside when I'm back in the shell.

Facil: And nobody's back in there with you?

Art *(crying)*: Nobody else is in there with me, just me. I just pull everything into the shell and roll the shell up and shove it in my pocket. I take the shell, and the real me, and put it in my pocket where it's safe. I guess that's really the way I do it—I go into my shell and turn off the real world. And here: that's what I want to do here in this group, ya know, come out of my shell and actually throw it away.

Lois: You're making progress already. At least you can talk about it.

Facil.: Yeah. The thing that's going to be hardest is to stay out of the shell.

Art *(still crying)*: Well, yeah, if I can keep talking about it, I can come out and stay out, but I'm gonna have to, ya know, protect me. It hurts; it's actually hurting to talk about it.

Still another person reporting shortly after his workshop experience said, "I came away from the workshop feeling much more deeply that 'It is all right to be me with all my strengths and weaknesses.' My wife has told me that I appear to be more authentic, more real, more genuine."

This feeling of greater realness and authenticity is a very common experience. It would appear that the individual is learning to accept and to *be* himself, and this is laying the foundation for change. He is closer to his own feelings, and hence they are no longer so rigidly organized and are more open to change.

The Cracking of Facades. As the sessions continue, so many things tend to occur together that it is difficult to know which to describe first. It should again be stressed that these different threads and stages interweave and overlap. One of these threads is the increasing impatience with defenses. As times goes on, the group finds it unbearable that any member should live behind a mask or a front. The polite words, the intellectual understanding of one another and of relationships, the smooth coin of tact and cover-up—amply satisfactory for interactions outside—are just not good enough. The expression of self by some members of the group has made it very clear that a deeper and more basic encounter is *possible*, and the group appears to strive, intuitively and unconsciously, toward this goal. Gently at times, almost savagely at others, the group *demands* that the individual be himself, that his current feelings not be hidden, that he remove the mask of ordinary social intercourse. In one group there was a highly intelligent and quite academic man who had been rather perceptive in his understanding of others but who had not revealed himself at all. The attitude of the group was finally expressed sharply by one member when he said, "Come out from behind that lectern, Doc. Stop giving us speeches. Take off your dark glasses. We want to know you."

In Synanon, the fascinating group so successfully involved in making persons out of drug addicts, this ripping away of facades is often very drastic. An excerpt from one of the "synanons," or group sessions, makes this clear (Casriel, 1963, p. 81):

Joe *(speaking to Gina)*: I wonder when you're going to stop sounding so good in synanons. Every synanon that I'm in with you, someone asks you a question, and you've got a beautiful book written. All made out about what went down and how you were wrong and how you realized you were wrong and all that kind of bullshit. When are you going to stop doing that? How do you feel about Art?

Gina: I have nothing against Art.

Will: You're a nut. Art hasn't got any damn sense. He's been in there, yelling at you and Moe, and you've got everything so cool.

Gina: No, I feel he's very insecure in a lot of ways but that has nothing to do with me. . . .

Joe: You act like you're so goddamn understanding.

Gina: I was *told* to act as if I understand.

Joe: Well, you're in a synanon now. You're not supposed to be acting like you're such a goddamn healthy person. Are you so well?

Gina: No.

Joe: Well why the hell don't you quit acting as if you were.

If I am indicating that the group at times is quite violent in tearing down a facade or a defense, this would be accurate. On the other hand, it can also be sensitive and gentle. The man who was accused of hiding behind a lectern was deeply hurt by this attack, and over the lunch hour looked very troubled, as though he might break into tears at any moment. When the group reconvened, the members sensed this and treated him very gently, enabling him to tell us his own tragic personal story, which accounted for his aloofness and his intellectual and academic approach to life.

The Individual Receives Feedback. In the process of this freely expressive interaction, the individual rapidly acquires a great deal of data as to how he appears to others. The "hail-fellow-well-met" discovers that others resent his exaggerated friendliness. The executive who weighs his words carefully and speaks with heavy precision may find that others regard him as stuffy. A woman who shows a somewhat excessive desire to be of help to others is told in no uncertain terms that some group members do not want her for a mother. All this can be decidedly upsetting, but as long as these various bits of information are fed back in the context of caring which is developing in the group, they seem highly constructive.

Feedback can at times be very warm and positive, as the following recorded excerpt indicates:

Leo *(very softly and gently)*: I've been struck with this ever since she talked about her waking in the night, that she has a very delicate sensitivity. *(Turning to Mary and speaking almost caressingly.)* And somehow I perceive—even looking at you or in your eyes—a very—almost like a gentle touch and from this gentle touch you can tell many—things—you sense in—this manner.

Fred: Leo, when you said that, that she has this kind of delicate sensitivity, I just felt, *Lord, yes*! Look at her eyes.

Leo: M-hm.

A much more extended instance of negative and positive feedback, triggering a significant new experience of self-understanding and encounter with the group, is taken from the diary of the young man mentioned before. He had been telling the group that he had no feeling for them, and felt they had no feeling for him (Hall, 1965):

Then, a girl lost patience with me and said she didn't feel she could give any more. She said I looked like a bottomless well, and she wondered how many times I had to be told that I *was* cared for. By this time I was feeling panicky, and I was saying to myself, "My God, can it be true that I can't be satisfied and that I'm somehow compelled to pester people for attention until I drive them away!"

At this point while I was really worried, a nun in the group spoke up. She said that I had not alienated her with some negative things I had said to her. She said she liked me, and she couldn't understand why I couldn't see that. She said she felt concerned for me and wanted to help me. With that, something began to really dawn on me, and I voiced it somewhat like the following: "You mean you are all sitting there, feeling for me what I say I want you to feel, and that somewhere down inside me I'm stopping it from touching me?" I relaxed appreciably and began really to wonder why I had shut their caring out so much. I couldn't find the answer, and one woman said: "It looks like you are trying to stay continuously as deep in your feelings as you were this afternoon. It would make sense to me for you to draw back and assimilate it. Maybe if you don't push so hard, you can rest awhile and then move back into your feelings more naturally."

Her making the last suggestion really took effect. I saw the sense in it, and almost immediately I settled back very relaxed with something of a feeling of a bright, warm day dawning inside me. In addition to taking the pressure off of myself, however, I was for the first time really warmed by the friendly feelings which I felt they had for me. It is difficult to say why I felt liked only just then, but, as opposed to the earlier sessions, I really *believed* they cared for me. I never have fully understood why I stood their affection off for so long, but at that point I almost abruptly began to trust that they did care. The measure of the effectiveness of this change lies in what I said next. I said, "Well, that really takes care of me. I'm really ready to listen to someone else now." I *meant* that, too.

Confrontation. There are times when the term "feedback" is far too mild to describe the interactions which take place, when it is better said that one individual *confronts* another, directly "leveling" with him. Such confrontations can be positive, but frequently they are decidely negative, as the following example will make abundantly clear. In one of the last sessions of a group, Alice had made some quite vulgar and contemptuous remarks to John, who was entering religious work. The next morning, Norma, who had been a very quiet person in the group, took the floor:

Norma *(loud sigh)*: Well, I don't have *any* respect for you, Alice. *None*! *(Pause)*. There's about a hundred things going through my mind I want to say to you, and by God I hope I get through 'em all! First of all, if you wanted us to respect you, then why couldn't you respect *John's* feelings last night? Why have you been on him today? Hmm? Last night—couldn't you—couldn't you accept—*couldn't you* comprehend in any way at all that—that *he felt* his unworthiness in the service of God? Couldn't you accept this, or did you have to dig into it today to find something *else there*? And his respect for womanhood—he *loves* women—yes, he does, because he's a real person, but you—you're not a real woman—to me—and thank God, you're not my mother! ! ! ! I want to come over and beat the hell out of you! ! ! ! I want to slap you across the mouth so hard and—oh, and you're so, you're many years above me—and I respect age, and I respect people who are older than me, *but I don't respect you, Alice. At all!* And I was so *hurt* and *confused* because you were making someone else feel *hurt* and *confused*. . . .

It may relieve the reader to know that these two women came to accept each other, not completely, but much more understandingly, before the end of the session. But this was a confrontation!

The Helping Relationship Outside the Group Sessions. No account of the group process would, in my experience, be adequate if it did not make mention of the many ways in which group members are of assistance to one another. Not infrequently, one member of a group will spend hours listening and talking to another member who is undergoing a painful new perception of himself. Sometimes it is merely the offering of help which is therapeutic. I think of one man who was going through a very depressed period after having told us of the many tragedies in his life. He seemed quite clearly, from his remarks, to be contemplating suicide. I jotted down my room number (we were staying at a hotel) and told him to put it in his pocket and to call me anytime of day or night if he felt that it would help. He never called, but six months after the workshop was over he wrote to me telling me how much that act had meant to him and that he still had the slip of paper to remind him of it.

Let me give an example of the healing effect of the attitudes of group members both outside and inside the group meetings. This is taken from a letter written by a workshop member to the group one month after the group sessions. He speaks of the difficulties and depressing circumstances he has encountered during that month and adds:

I have come to the conclusion that my experiences with you have profoundly affected me. I am truly grateful. This is different than personal therapy. None of you *had* to care about me. None of you had to seek me out and let me know of things you thought would help me. None of you had to let me know I was of help to you. Yet you did, and as a result it has far more meaning than anything I have so far experienced. When I feel the need to hold back and not live spontaneously, for whatever reasons, I remember that twelve persons, just like those before me now, said to let go and be congruent, to be myself, and, of all unbelievable things, they even loved me more for it. This has given me the *courage* to come out of myself many times since then. Often it seems my very doing of this helps the others to experience similar freedom.

The Basic Encounter. Running through some of the trends I have just been describing is the fact that individuals come into much closer and more direct contact with one another than is customary in ordinary life. This appears to be one of the most central, intense, and change-producing aspects of such a group experience. To illustrate what I mean, I would like to draw an example from a recent workshop group. A man tells, through his tears, of the very tragic loss of his child, a grief which he is experiencing *fully*, for the first time, not holding back his feelings in any way. Another says to him, also with tears in his eyes, "I've never felt so close to another human being. I've never before felt a real physical hurt in me from the pain of another. I feel *completely* with you." This is a basic encounter.

Such I-Thou relationships (to use Buber's term) occur with some frequency in these group sessions and nearly always bring a moistness to the eyes of the participants.

One member, trying to sort out his experiences immediately after a workshop, speaks of the "commitment to relationship" which often developed on the part of two individuals, not necessarily individuals who had liked each other initially. He goes on to say:

> The incredible fact experienced over and over by members of the group was that when a negative feeling was fully expressed to another, the relationship grew and the negative feeling was replaced by a deep acceptance for the other. . . . Thus real change seemed to occur when feelings were experienced and expressed in the context of the relationship. "I can't *stand* the way you talk!" turned into a real understanding and affection for you the *way* you talk.

This statement seems to capture some of the more complex meanings of the term "basic encounter."

The Expression of Positive Feelings and Closeness. As indicated in the last section, an inevitable part of the group process seems to be that when feelings are expressed and can be accepted in a relationship, a great deal of closeness and positive feelings result. Thus as the sessions proceed, there is an increasing feeling of warmth and group spirit and trust built, not out of positive attitudes only, but out of a realness which includes both positive and negative feeling. One member tried to capture this in writing very shortly after the workshop by saying that if he were trying to sum it up, ". . . it would have to do with what I call confirmation—a kind of confirmation of myself, of the uniqueness and universal qualities of men, a confirmation that when we can be human together something positive can emerge."

A particularly poignant expression of these positive attitudes was shown in the group where Norma confronted Alice with her bitterly angry feelings. Joan, the facilitator, was deeply upset and began to weep. The positive and healing attitudes of the group, for their own *leader*, are an unusual example of the closeness and personal quality of the relationships.

Joan *(crying)*: I somehow feel that it's so *damned* easy for me to—put myself *inside* of another person and I just guess I can feel that—for John and Alice and for you, Norma.

Alice: And it's *you* that's hurt.

Joan: Maybe I am taking some of that hurt. I guess I am. *(crying)*.

Alice: That's a wonderful gift. I wish I had it.

Joan: You have a lot of it.

Peter: In a way you bear the—I guess in a special way, because you're the—facilitator, ah, you've probably borne, ah, an extra heavy burden for all of us—and the burden that you, perhaps, you bear the heaviest is—we ask you—we ask one another; we grope to try to accept one another as we are, and—for each of us in various ways I guess we reach things and we say, *please* accept me. . . .

Some may be very critical of a "leader" so involved and so sensitive that she weeps at the tensions in the group which she has taken into herself. For me, it is simply another evidence that when people are real with each other, they have an astonishing ability to heal a person with a real and understanding love, whether that person is "participant" or "leader."

Behavior Changes in the Group. It would seem from observation that many changes in behavior occur in the group itself. Gestures change. The tone of voice changes, becoming sometimes stronger, sometimes softer, usually more spontaneous, less artificial, more feelingful. Individuals show an astonishing amount of thoughtfulness and helpfulness toward one another.

Our major concern, however, is with the behavior changes which occur following the group experience. It is this which constitutes the most significant question and on which we need much more study and research. One person gives a catalog of the changes which he sees in himself which may seem too "pat" but which is echoed in many other statements:

> I am more open, spontaneous. I express myself more freely. I am more sympathetic, empathic, and tolerant. I am more confident. I am more religious in my own way. My relations with my family, friends, and co-workers are more honest, and I express my likes and dislikes and true feelings more openly. I admit ignorance more readily. I am more cheerful. I want to help others more.

Another says:

> Since the workshop there has been a new relationship with my parents. It has been trying and hard. However, I have found a greater freedom in talking with them, especially my father. Steps have been made toward being closer to my mother than I have ever been in the last five years.

Another says:

> It helped clarify my feelings about my work, gave me more enthusiasm for it, and made me more honest and cheerful with my co-workers and also more open when I was hostile. It made my relationship with my wife more open, deeper. We felt freer to talk about anything, and we felt confident that anything we talked about we could work through.

Sometimes the changes which are described are very subtle. "The primary change is the more positive view of my ability to allow myself to *hear*, and to become involved with someone else's 'silent scream.'"

At the risk of making the outcomes sound too good, I will add one more statement written shortly after a workshop by a mother. She says:

> The immediate impact on my children was of interest to both me and my husband. I feel that having been so accepted and loved by a group of strangers was so supportive that when I returned home my love for the people closest to me was much more spontaneous. Also, the practice I had in accepting and loving others during the workshop was evident in my relationships with my close friends.

Disadvantages and Risks

Thus far one might think that every aspect of the group process was positive. As far as the evidence at hand indicates, it appears that it nearly always is a positive process for a majority of the participants. There are, nevertheless, failures which result. Let me try to describe briefly some of the negative aspects of the group process as they sometimes occur.

The most obvious deficiency of the intensive group experience is that frequently the behavior changes, if any, which occur, are not lasting. This is often recognized by the participants. One says, "I wish I had the ability to hold permanently the 'openness' I left the conference with." Another says, "I experienced a lot of acceptance, warmth, and love at the workshop. I find it hard to carry the ability to share this in the same way with people outside the workshop. I find it easier to slip back into my old unemotional role than to do the work necessary to open relationships."

Sometimes group members experience this phenomenon of "relapse" quite philosophically:

> The group experience is not a way of life but a reference point. My images of our group, even though I am unsure of some of their meanings, give me a comforting and useful perspective on my normal routine. They are like a mountain which I have climbed and enjoyed and to which I hope occasionally to return.

Some Data on Outcomes. What is the extent of this "slippage"? In the past year, I have administered follow-up questionnaires to 481 individuals who have been in groups I have organized or conducted. The information has been obtained from two to twelve months following the group experience, but the greatest number were followed up after a three- to six-month period.[4] Of these individuals, two (i.e., less than one-half of 1 percent) felt it had changed their behavior in ways they did not like. Fourteen percent felt the experience had made no perceptible change in their behavior. Another fourteen percent felt that it had changed their behavior but that this change had disappeared or left only a small residual positive effect. Fifty-seven percent felt it had made a continuing positive difference in their behavior, a few feeling that it had made some negative changes along with the positive.

A second potential risk involved in the intensive group experience and one which is often mentioned in public discussion is the risk that the individual may become deeply involved in revealing himself and then be left with problems which are not worked through. There have been a number of reports of people who have felt, following an intensive group experience, that they must go to a therapist to work through the feelings which were opened up in the intensive experience of the workshop and which were left unresolved. It is obvious that, without knowing more about each individual situation, it is difficult to say whether this was a negative outcome or a partially or entirely positive one. There are also very occasional accounts, and I can testify to two in my own experience, where an individual has had a psychotic episode during or immediately following an intensive group experience. On the other side of the picture is the fact that individuals have also lived through what were clearly psychotic episodes, and lived through them very constructively, in the context of a basic encounter group. My own tentative clinical judgment would be that the more positively the group process has been proceeding, the less likely it is that any individual would be psychologically damaged through membership in the group. It is obvious, however, that this is a serious issue and that much more needs to be known.

Some of the tension which exists in workshop members as a result of this potential for damage was very well described by one member when he said, "I feel the workshop had some very precious moments for me when I felt very close indeed to particular persons. It had some frightening moments when its potency was very evident and I realized a particular person might be deeply hurt or greatly helped but I could not predict which."

Out of the 481 participants followed up by questionnaires, two felt that the overall impact of their intensive group experience was "mostly damaging," Six more said that it had been "more unhelpful than helpful." Twenty-one, or 4 percent, stated that it had been "mostly frustrating, annoying, or confusing." Three and one-half percent said that it had been neutral

[4] The 481 respondents constituted 82 percent of those to whom the questionnaire had been sent.

in its impact. Nineteen percent checked that it had been "more helpful than unhelpful," indicating some degree of ambivalence. But 30 percent saw it as "constructive in its results," and 45 percent checked it as a "deeply meaningful, positive experience."[5] Thus for three-fourths of the group, it was *very* helpful. These figures should help to set the problem in perspective. It is obviously a very serious matter if an intensive group experience is psychologically damaging to *anyone*. It seems clear, however, that such damage occurs only rarely, if we are to judge by the reaction of the participants.

Other Hazards of the Group Experience. There is another risk or deficiency in the basic encounter group. Until very recent years it has been unusual for a workshop to include both husband and wife. This can be a real problem if significant change has taken place in one spouse during or as a result of the workshop experience. One individual felt this risk clearly after attending a workshop. He said, "I think there is a great danger to a marriage when one spouse attends a group. It is too hard for the other spouse to compete with the group individually and collectively." One of the frequent aftereffects of the intensive group experience is that it brings out into the open for discussion marital tensions which have been kept under cover.

Another risk which has sometimes been a cause of real concern in mixed intensive workshops is that very positive, warm, and loving feelings can develop between members of the encounter group, as has been evident from some of the preceding examples. Inevitably some of these feelings have a sexual component, and this can be a matter of great concern to the participants and a profound threat to their spouses if these feelings are not worked through satisfactorily in the workshop. Also the close and loving feelings which develop may become a source of threat and marital difficulty when a wife, for example, has not been present, but projects many fears about the loss of her spouse—whether well founded or not—onto the workshop experience.

A man who had been in a mixed group of men and women executives wrote to me a year later and mentioned the strain in his marriage which resulted from his association with Marge, a member of his basic encounter group:

> There was a problem about Marge. There had occurred a very warm feeling on my part for Marge, and great compassion, for I felt she was *very* lonely. I believe the warmth was sincerely reciprocal. At any rate she wrote me a long affectionate letter, which I let my wife read. I was *proud* that Marge could feel that way about *me*, [Because he had felt very worthless.] But my wife was alarmed, because she read a love affair into the words—at least a *potential* threat. I stopped writing to Marge, because I felt rather clandestine after that.
>
> My wife has since participated in an "encounter group" herself, and she now understands. I have resumed writing to Marge.

Obviously, not all such episodes would have such a harmonious ending.

It is of interest in this connection that there has been increasing experimentation in recent years with "couples workshops" and with workshops for industrial executives and their spouses.

Still another negative potential growing out of these groups has become evident in recent years. Some individuals who have participated in previous encounter groups may exert a stultifying influence on new workshops which they attend. They sometimes exhibit what I think of as the "old pro" phenomenon. They feel they have learned the "rules of the game," and they

[5] These figures add up to more than 100 percent since quite a number of the respondents checked more than one answer.

subtly or openly try to impose these rules on newcomers. Thus, instead of promoting true expressiveness and spontaneity, they endeavour to substitute new rules for old—to make members feel guilty if they are not expressing feelings, are reluctant to voice criticism or hostility, are talking about situations outside the group relationship, or are fearful of revealing themselves. These old pros seem to be attempting to substitute a new tyranny in inter-personal relationships in the place of older, conventional restrictions. To me this is a perversion of the true group process. We need to ask ourselves how this travesty on spontaneity comes about.

Implications

I have tried to describe both the positive and the negative aspects of this burgeoning new cultural development. I would like now to touch on its implications for our society.

In the first place, it is a highly potent experience and hence clearly deserving of scientific study. As a phenomenon it has been both praised and criticized, but few people who have participated would doubt that *something* significant happens in these groups. People do not react in a neutral fashion toward the intensive group experience. They regard it as either strikingly worthwhile or deeply questionable. All would agree, however, that it is potent. This fact makes it of particular interest to the behavioral sciences since science is usually advanced by studying potent and dynamic phenomena. This is one of the reasons why I personally am devoting more and more of my time to this whole enterprise. I feel that we can learn much about the ways in which constructive personality change comes about as we study this group process more deeply.

In a different dimension, the intensive group experience appears to be one cultural attempt to meet the isolation of contemporary life. The person who has experienced an I-Thou relationship, who has entered into the basic encounter, is no longer an isolated individual. One workshop member stated this in a deeply expressive way:

> Workshops seem to be at least a partial answer to the loneliness of modern man and his search for new meanings for his life. In short, workshops seem very quickly to allow the individual to become that person he wants to be. The first few steps are taken there, in uncertainty, in fear, and in anxiety. We may or may not continue the journey. It is a gutsy way to live. You trade many, many loose ends for one big knot in the middle of your stomach. It sure as hell isn't easy, but it is a *life* at least—not a hollow imitation of life. It has fear as well as hope, sorrow as well as joy, but I daily offer it to more people in the hope that they will join me. . . . Out from a no-man's land of *fog* into the more violent atmosphere of extremes of thunder, hail, rain, and sunshine. It is worth the trip.

Another implication which is partially expressed in the foregoing statement is that it is an avenue to fulfillment. In a day when more income, a larger car, and a better washing machine seem scarcely to be satisfying the deepest needs of man, individuals are turning to the psychological world, groping for a greater degree of authenticity and fulfillment. One workshop member expressed this extremely vividly:

> [It] has revealed a completely new dimension of life and has opened an infinite number of possibilities for me in my relationship to myself and to everyone dear to me. I feel truly alive and so grateful and joyful and hopeful and healthy and giddy and sparkly. I feel as though my eyes and ears and heart and guts have been opened to see and hear and love and feel more deeply, more widely, more intensely—this glorious, mixed-up, fabulous existence of ours. My whole body and each of its systems seems freer and healthier. I want to feel hot and cold, tired and rested, soft and hard, energetic and lazy. With persons every-

where, but especially my family, I have found a new freedom to explore and communicate. I know the change in me automatically brings a change in them. A whole new exciting relationship has started for me with my husband and with each of my children—a freedom to speak and to hear them speak.

Though one may wish to discount the enthusiasm of this statement, it describes an enrichment of life for which many are seeking.

Rehumanizing Human Relationships. This whole development seems to have special significance in a culture which appears to be bent upon dehumanizing the individual and dehumanizing our human relationships. Here is an important force in the opposite direction, working toward making relationships more meaningful and more personal, in the family, in education, in government, in administrative agencies, in industry.

An intensive group experience has an even more general philosophical implication. It is one expression of the existential point of view which is making itself so pervasively evident in art and literature and modern life. The implicit goal of the group process seems to be to live life fully in the here and now of the relationship. The parallel with an existential point of view is clear cut. I believe this has been amply evident in the illustrative material.

There is one final issue which is raised by this whole phenomenon: What is our view of the optimal person? What is the goal of personality development? Different ages and different cultures have given different answers to this question. It seems evident from our review of the group process that in a climate of freedom, group members move toward becoming more spontaneous, flexible, closely related to their feelings, open to their experience, and closer and more expressively intimate in their interpersonal relationships. If we value this type of person and this type of behavior, then clearly the group process is a valuable process. If, on the other hand, we place a value on the individual who is effective in suppressing his feelings, who operates from a firm set of principles, who does not trust his own reactions and experience but relies on authority, and who remains aloof in his interpersonal relationships, then we would regard the group process, as I have tried to describe it, as a dangerous force. Clearly there is room for a difference of opinion on this value question, and not everyone in our culture would give the same answer.

Conclusion

I have tried to give a naturalistic, observational picture of one of the most significant modern social inventions, the socalled intensive group experience, or basic encounter group. I have tried to indicate some of the common elements of the process which occur in the climate of freedom that is present in such a group. I have pointed out some of the risks and shortcomings of the group experience. I have tried to indicate some of the reasons why it deserves serious consideration, not only from a personal point of view, but also from a scientific and philosophical point of view. I also hope I have made it clear that this is an area in which an enormous amount of deeply perceptive study and research is needed.

REFERENCES

BENNIS, W. G., BENNE, K. D., & CHINN, R. (Eds.) *The planning of change.* New York: Holt, Rinehart and Winston, 1961.

BENNIS, W. G., SCHEIN, E. H., BERLEW, D. E., & STEELE, F. I. (Eds.) *Interpersonal dynamics.* Homewood, Ill.: Dorsey, 1964.

BRADFORD, L., GIBB, J. R., & BENNE, K. D. (Eds.) *T-group theory and laboratory method.* New York: Wiley, 1964.
CASRIEL, D. *So fair a house.* Englewood Cliffs, N.J.: Prentice-Hall, 1963.
GIBB, J. R. Climate for trust formation. In L. Bradford, J. R. Gibb, & K. D. Benne (Eds.), *T-group theory and laboratory method.* New York: Wiley, 1964.
GORDON, T. *Group-centered leadership.* Boston: Houghton Mifflin, 1955.
HALL, G. F. A participant's experience in a basic encounter group. (Mimeographed) Western Behavioral Sciences Institute, 1965.

34

Neurosis as a Failure of Personal Growth

Abraham H. Maslow

Rather than trying to be comprehensive, I have chosen to discuss only a few selected aspects of this topic, partly because I have been working with them recently, partly also because I think they are especially important, but mostly because they have been overlooked.

The frame of reference which all in this symposium have taken for granted considers the neurosis to be, from *one* aspect, a describable, pathological state of affairs which presently exists, a kind of disease or sickness or illness, on the medical model. But we have learned to see it also in a dialectical fashion, as simultaneously a kind of moving forward, a clumsy groping forward toward health and toward fullest humanness, in a kind of timid and weak way, under the aegis of fear rather than of courage, and *now* involving the future as well as the present.

All the evidence that we have (mostly clinical evidence, but already some other kinds of research evidence) indicates that it is reasonable to assume in practically every human being, and certainly in almost every newborn baby, that there is an active will toward health, an impulse toward growth, or toward the actualization of human potentialities. But at once we are confronted with the very saddening realization that so few people make it. Only a small proportion of the human population gets to the point of identity, or of selfhood, full humanness, self-actualization, etc., even in a society like ours which is relatively one of the most fortunate on the face of the earth. This is our great paradox. We all have the impulse towards full development of humanness. Then why is it that it does not happen more often? What blocks it?

This is our new way of approaching the

Reprinted from *Humanitas,* Journal of the Institute of Man, VIII (1967), pp. 154–169., by permission of the publisher.

problem of humanness, i.e., with an appreciation of its high possibilities and simultaneously, a deep disappointment that these possibilities are so infrequently actualized. This attitude contrasts with the "realistic" acceptance of whatever happens to be the case, and then of regarding that as the norm, as, for instance, Kinsey did, and as the TV pollsters do today. We tend then to get into the situation that Dr. Barton pointed out to us this morning in which normalcy from the descriptive point of view, from the value-free science point of view—that this normalcy or averageness is the best we can expect, and that therefore we should be content with it. From the point of view that I have outlined, normalcy would be rather the kind of sickness or crippling or stunting that we share with everybody else and therefore don't notice. I remember an old textbook of abnormal psychology that I used when I was an undergraduate, which was an awful book, but which had a wonderful frontispiece. The lower half was a picture of a line of babies, pink, sweet, delightful, innocent, lovable. Above that was a picture of a lot of passengers in a subway train, glum, grey, sullen, sour. The caption underneath was very simply, "What happened?" This is what I'm talking about.

I should mention also—I feel a little self-conscious about this after Dr. Gendlin's address—but I should mention also that part of what I have been doing and what I want to do here now comes under the head of the strategy and tactics of research and of preparation for research and of trying to phrase all of these clinical experiences and personal subjective experiences that we have been discussing today in such a way that we can learn more about them in a scientific way, that is, checking and testing and making more precise, and seeing if it is really so, and were the intuitions correct? etc., etc. For this purpose and also for those of you who are primarily interested in the philosophical problems which are involved in this discussion, I would like to present briefly a few theoretical points which are relevant for what follows. This is the age-old problem of the relationship between facts and values, between *is* and *ought*, between the descriptive and the normative—a terrible problem for the philosophers who have dealt with it ever since there were any philosophers, and who haven't got very far with it yet. I'd like to offer some considerations that I would like you to mull over which have helped me with this old philosophical difficulty, and perhaps might do the same for you, a third horn to the dilemma, you might say.

Fusion-Words

What I have in mind here is the general conclusion that I have already written about (15), which comes partly from the Gestalt psychologists and partly from clinical and psychotherapeutic experience, namely, that, in a kind of a Socratic fashion, facts often point in a direction, i.e., they are vectorial. Facts don't lie there like pancakes, just doing nothing; they are to a certain extent signposts which tell you what to do, which make suggestions to us, which nudge us in one direction rather than another. They "call for," they have "demand" character, they even have "requiredness," as Kohler called it (10). I feel frequently that whenever we get to know enough, then we know what to do, or we know much better what to do; that sufficient knowledge will often solve the problem, that it will often help us at our moral and ethical choice-points, when we must decide whether to do this or to do that. For instance, it is our common experience in therapy, that as people "know" more and more consciously, their solutions, their choices become more easy, more automatic. This is why I would reject entirely Sartre's kind of arbitrariness. I think it's a profound mistake to think of us as being confronted only with arbitrariness, with choices we make by fiat, by sheer, unaided acts of will, and without any help from the nature of reality or from the essential nature of human nature.

I am suggesting something other than that. I am suggesting that there are facts and words which themselves are both normative and descriptive simultaneously. I am calling them for the moment "fusion-words," meaning a fusion of facts and values, and what I have to say beyond this should be understood as part of this effort to solve the *is* and *ought* problem.

I myself have advanced, as I think we all have in this kind of work, from talking in the beginning, in a frankly normative way, for example, asking the questions—what is normal, what is healthy? My former philosophy professor, who still feels fatherly toward me, and to whom I still feel filial, has occasionally written me a worried letter scolding me gently for the cavalier way in which I was handling these old philosophical problems, saying something like, "Don't you realize what you have done here? 2000 years of thought lies behind this problem and you go skating over this thin ice so easily and casually." And I remember that I wrote back once trying to explain myself, saying that this sort of thing is really the way a scientist functions, and that this is part of his strategy of research, i.e., to skate past philosophical difficulties as fast as possible. I remember writing to him once that my attitude as a strategist in the advancement of knowledge had to be one, so far as philosophical problems were concerned, of "determined naivete." And I think that is what we have here. I felt that it was heuristic, and therefore all right, to talk about normal and healthy and what was good and what was bad, and frequently getting very arbitrary about it. I did one research in which there were good paintings and bad paintings, and with a perfectly straight face I put in the footnote, "Good paintings are defined here as paintings that I like." The thing is, that if I can skip to my conclusion, it turns out to be not so bad a strategy after all.

In studying healthy people, self-actualizing people, etc., there has been a steady move from the openly normative and the frankly personal, step by step, toward more descriptive, objective words, to the point at which there is today a standardized test of self-actualization (25). Self-actualization can now be defined quite operationally, as intelligence used to be defined, i.e., self-actualization is what that test tests. It correlates well with external variables of various kinds, and keeps on accumulating additional correlational meanings. As a result, I feel heuristically justified in *starting* with my "determined naivete." Most of what I was able to see intuitively, directly, personally is being confirmed now with numbers and tables and curves.

Full-Humanness

I would like to suggest a further step toward the fusion-word "fully-human," a concept which is still more descriptive and objective (than the concept "self-actualization") and yet retains everything that we need of normativeness. This is in the hope of moving from intuitive heuristic beginnings toward more certainty, greater reliability, more and more external validation, which in turn means more scientific and theoretical usefulness of this concept. This phrasing and this way of thinking was suggested to me about fifteen or so years ago by the axiological writings of Robert Hartman (5) who defined "good" as the degree to which an object fulfills its definition or concept. This suggested to me that the conception of humanness might be made, for research purposes, into a kind of quantitative concept. For instance, full humanness can be defined in a cataloguing fashion, i.e., full humanness is the ability to abstract, to have a grammatical language, to be able to love, to have values of a particular kind, to transcend the self, etc., etc., etc. The complete cataloguing definition could even be made into a kind of check list.

We might shudder a little at this thought, but it could be very useful if only to make the theoretical point for the researching scientist that the concept *can* be descriptive and quantitative—and yet also normative, i.e., this person is closer to full humanness than that other person. Or we could even say: This person is *more* human than that one. This is a fusion-word in the sense that I have mentioned above; it is really objectively descriptive because it has nothing to do with my wishes and tastes, my personality, my neuroses. Moreover, my unconscious wishes or fears, anxieties or hopes are far more easily excluded from the conception of full humanness than they are from the conception of psychological health.

If you ever work with the concept of psychological health—or any other kind of health, or normality—you will discover what a temptation it is to project your own values and to make it into a self-description or perhaps a description of what you would like to be, or what you think people *should* be like. You'll have to fight against it all the time, and you'll discover that, while it is *possible* to be objective in such work, it is certainly difficult. And even then, you cannot be really sure. Have you fallen into sampling error? After all, if you select persons for investigation on the basis of your personal judgment and diagnosis, such sampling errors are more likely than if you select by some more impersonal criterion (12).

Clearly, fusion-words are a scientific advance over more purely normative words, while also avoiding the trap of believing that science *must* be *only* value-free, and non-normative, i.e., non-human. Fusion-concepts and words permit us to participate in the normal advance of science and knowledge from its phenomenological and experiential beginnings on toward greater reliability, greater validity, greater confidence, greater exactness, greater sharing with others and agreement with them (18).

Other obvious fusion-words are: problem, task duty, mature, evolved, developed, stunted, crippled, fully-functioning, graceful, awkward, clumsy, and the like. There are many more words which are less obviously fusions of the normative and the descriptive. One day we may even have to get used to thinking of fusion-words as paradigmatic, as normal, usual and central. Then the more purely descriptive words and the more purely normative words would be thought of as peripheral and exceptional. I believe that this will come as part of the new humanistic Weltanschauung which is now rapidly crystallizing into a structured form.[1]

For one thing, as I have pointed out (11), these conceptions are too exclusively extra-psychic and don't account sufficiently for the quality of consciousness, for intra-psychic or subjective abilities, for instance, to enjoy music, to meditate and contemplate, to savor flavors, to be sensitive to one's inner voices, etc. Getting along well within one's inner world may be as important as social competence or reality competence.

But more important from the point of view of theoretical elegance and research strategy, these concepts are less objective and quantifiable than is a list of the capacities that make up the concept of humanness.

I would add that I consider none of these models to be *opposed* to the medical model. There is no need to dichotomize them from each other. Medical illnesses diminish the human being and therefore fall on the continuum of greater to lesser degree of humanness. Of course, though the medical illness model is necessary (for tumors, bacterial invasions, ulcers, etc.), it is certainly not sufficient (for neurotic, characterological or spiritual disturbances).

Human Diminution

One consequence of the usage of "full-humanness" rather than "psychological health" is the corresponding or parallel use of "human diminution," instead of "neurosis," which is a totally obsolete

[1] I consider the "degree of humanness" concept to be more useful also than the concepts of "social competence," "human effectiveness" and similar notions.

word anyway. Here the key concept is the loss or not-yet-actualization of human capacities and possibilities, and obviously this is also a matter of degree and quantity. Furthermore, it is closer to being externally observable, i.e., behavioral, which of course makes it easier to investigate than, for example, anxiety or compulsiveness or repression. Also it places on the same continuum all the standard psychiatric categories, all the stuntings, cripplings and inhibitions that come from poverty, exploitation, maleducation, enslavement, etc., and also the newer value pathologies, existential disorders, character disorders that come to the economically privileged. It handles very nicely the diminutions that result from drug-addiction, psychopathy, authoritarianism, criminality, and other categories that cannot be called "illness" in the same medical sense as, for example, brain tumor.

This is a radical move away from the medical model, a move which is long overdue. Strictly speaking, neurosis means an illness of the nerves, a relic we can very well do without today. In addition, using the label "psychological illness" puts neurosis into the same universe of discourse as ulcers, lesions, bacterial invasions, broken bones, or tumors. By now, we have learned very well that it is better to consider neurosis as related rather to spiritual disorders, to loss of meaning, to doubts about the goals of life, to grief and anger over a lost love, to seeing life in a different way, to loss of courage or of hope, to despair over the future, to dislike for oneself, to recognition that one's life is being wasted, or that there is no possibility of joy or love, etc., etc.

These are all fallings away from full-humanness, from the full blooming of human nature. They are losses of human possibility, of what might have been and could perhaps yet be. Physical and chemical hygiene and prophylaxes certainly have some place in this realm of psychopathogenesis, but are nothing in comparison with the far more powerful role of social, economic, political, religious, educational, philosophical, axiological and familial determinants.

Subjective Biology

There are still other important advantages to be gained from moving over to this psychological-philosophical-educational-spiritual usage. Not the least of these, it seems to me, is that it encourages the *proper* conceptual use of the biological and constitutional base which underlies any discussion of Identity or of The Real Self, of growth, of uncovering therapy, of full-humanness or of diminution of humanness, of self-transcendence, or any version of these. Briefly, I believe that helping a person to move toward full-humanness proceeds inevitably via awareness of one's identity (among other things). A very important part of this task is to become aware of what one *is*, biologically, temperamentally, constitutionally, as a member of a species, of one's capacities, desires, needs, and also of one's vocation, what one is fitted for, what one's destiny is.

To put it bluntly and unequivocally, one absolutely necessary aspect of this self-awareness is a kind of phenomenology of one's own inner biology, of that which I have called instinctoid (17), of one's animality and specieshood. This is certainly what psychoanalysis tries to do., i.e., to help one to become conscious of one's animal urges, needs, tensions, depressions, tastes, anxieties. So also for Horney's distinction between a real self and a pseudo-self. Is this also not a subjective discrimination of what one truly is? And what *is* one truly if not first and foremost one's own body, one's own constitution, one's own functioning, one's own specieshood? (I have very much enjoyed, *qua theorist*, this pretty integration of Freud, Goldstein, Sheldon, Horney, Cattell, Frankl, May, Rogers. Murray, et. al. Perhaps even Skinner could be coaxed into this diverse company, since I suspect that a listing of all his "intrinsic reinforcers" for his human subjects might very well look much like the "hierarchy of instinctoid basic needs and metaneeds" that I have proposed!)

I believe it is possible to carry through this paradigm even at the very highest levels of personal development, where one transcends one's own personality (16). I hope to make a good case soon for accepting the probable instinctoid character of one's highest values, i.e., of what might be called the spiritual or philosophical life (19). Even this personally discovered axiology I feel can be subsumed under this category of "phenomenology of one's own instinctoid nature" or of "subjective biology" or "experiential biology" or some such phrase.

Think of the great theoretical and scientific advantages of placing on one single continuum of degree or amount of humanness, not only all the kinds of sickness the psychiatrists talk about but also all the additional kinds that existentialists and philosophers and religious thinkers and social reformers have worried about. Not only this, but we can also place on the same single scale all the various degrees and kinds of *health* that we know about, plus even the health-beyond-health of self-transcendence, of mystical fusion, and whatever still higher possibilities of human nature the future may yet disclose.

Inner Signals

Thinking in this way has had for me at least the one special advantage of directing my attention sharply to what I called at first "the impulse voices" but which could be called more generally something like the "inner signals" (or cues or stimuli). I had not realized sufficiently that in most neuroses, and in many other disturbances as well, the inner signals become weak or even disappear entirely (as in the severely obsessional person) and/or are not "heard" or *cannot* be heard. At the extreme we have the experientially-empty person, the zombie, the one with empty insides. Recovering the self *must*, as a *sine qua non*, include the recovery of the ability to have and to cognize these inner signals, to know what and whom one likes and dislikes, what is enjoyable and what is not, when to eat and when not to (Schachter), when to sleep, when to urinate, when to rest.

The experientially-empty person, lacking these directives from within, these voices of the real self, must turn to outer cues for guidance, for instance eating when the clock tells him to, rather than obeying his appetite (he has none). He guides himself by clocks, rules, calendars, schedules, agenda, and by hints and cues from other people.

In any case, I trust that the particular sense in which I suggest interpreting the neurosis as a failure of personal growth must be clear by now. It is a falling short of what one could have been, and even one could say, of what one *should* have been, biologically speaking, that is, if one had grown and developed in an unimpeded way. Human and personal possibilities have been lost. The world has been narrowed, and so has consciousness. Capacities have been inhibited. I think for instance of the fine pianist who couldn't play before an audience of more than a few, or the phobic who is forced to avoid heights or crowds. The person who can't study, or who can't sleep, or who can't eat many foods has been diminished as surely as the one who has been blinded. The cognitive losses, the lost pleasures, joys, and ecstasies,[2] the loss of competence, the inability to relax, the weakening of will, the fear of responsibility—all these are diminutions of humanness.

I have mentioned some of the advantages

[2] What it means for one's style of life to lose peak-experiences has been very well set forth in Colin Wilson's *Introduction to the New Existentialism* (29).

of replacing the concepts of psychollogica illness and health with the more pragmatic, public and quantitative concept of full or diminished humanness, which I believe is also biologically and philosophically sounder. But before I move on, I would like to note also that diminution can, of course, be either reversible or irreversible, for example, we feel far less hopeful about the paranoid person than we do about say a nice, lovable hysterical. And, of course, diminution is also dynamic, in the Freudian style. The original Freudian schema spoke of an intrinsic dialectic between the impulse and the defenses against this impulse. In this same sense, diminution leads to consequences and processes. It is only rarely a completion or a finality in a simple descriptive way. In most people these losses lead not only to all sorts of defensive processes which have been well described by Freudian and other psychoanalytic groups, for instance, to repression, denial, conflict, etc. They also lead to coping responses as I stressed long ago (21).

Conflict itself is of course a sign of relative health, as you would know if you ever met really apathetic people, hopeless people, people who have given up hoping, striving and coping. Neurosis is by contrast a very hopeful kind of thing. It means that a man who is frightened, who does not trust himself, who has a low self-image, etc., reaches out for the human heritage and for the basic gratifications to which every human being has a right, simply by virtue of being human. You might say it's a kind of *timid* and ineffectual striving toward self-actualization, toward full humanness.

Diminution can of course be reversible. Very frequently, simply supplying the need gratifications can solve the problem, especially in children. For a child who has not been loved enough, obviously the treatment of first choice is to love him to death, to just slop it all over him. Clinical and general human experience is that it works—I don't have any statistics, but I would suspect nine out of ten times. So is respect a wonderful medicine for counteracting a feeling of worthlessness. Which of course brings up the obvious conclusion that, if "health and illness" on the medical model are seen as obsolete, so also must the medical concepts of "treatment" and "cure" and the authoritative doctor be discarded and replaced.

The Jonah Syndrome

In the little time I have left, I would like to turn to one of the many reasons for what Angyal (1) called the evasion of growth. Certainly everybody in this room would like to be better than he is. All of us have an impulse to improve ourselves, an impulse toward actualizing more of our potentialities, toward self-actualization, or full humanness, or human fulfillment, or whatever term you like. Granted this for everybody here, then what holds us up? What blocks us?

One such defense against growth, which I'd like to speak about especially because it hasn't received much notice, I shall call the Jonah syndrome.[3]

In my own notes I had at first labelled this defense the "fear of one's own greatness" or the "evasion of one's destiny" or the "running away from one's own best talents." I had wanted to stress as bluntly and sharply as I could the non-Freudian point that we fear our best as well as our worst, even though in different ways. It is certainly possible for most of us to be greater than we are in actuality. We all have unused potentialities or not fully developed ones. It is certainly true that many of us evade our constitutionally suggested vocations (call, destiny, task in life, mission). So often we run away from the responsibilities dictated (or rather suggested) by nature, by

[3] This name was suggested by my friend, Professor Frank Manual, with whom I had discussed this puzzle.

fate, even sometimes by accident, just as Jonah tried—in vain—to run away from *his* fate.

We fear our highest possibilities (as well as our lowest ones). We are generally afraid to become that which we can glimpse in our most perfect moments, under the most perfect conditions, under conditions of greatest courage. We enjoy and even thrill to the godlike possibilities we see in ourselves in such peak moments. And yet we simultaneously shiver with weakness, awe and fear before these very same possibilities.

I have found it easy enough to demonstrate this to my students simply by asking, "Which of you in this class hopes to write the great American novel, or to be a Senator, or Governor, or President? Who wants to be Secretary-General of the United Nations? Or a great composer? Who aspires to be a saint, like Schweitzer, perhaps? Who among you will be a great leader?" Generally everybody starts giggling, blushing, and squirming until I ask, "If not you, then who else?" Which of course is the truth. And in this same way, as I push my graduate students toward these higher levels of aspiration, I'll say, "What great book are you now secretly planning to write?" And then they often blush and stammer and push me off in some way. But why should I not ask that question? Who else will write the books on psychology except psychologists? So I can ask, "Do you not plan to be a psychologist?" "Well, yes." "Are you in training to be a mute or an inactive psychologist? What's the advantage of that? That's not a good path to self-actualization. No, you must want to be a first-class psychologist, meaning the best, the very best you are capable of becoming. If you deliberately plan to be less than you are capable of being, then I warn you that you'll be deeply unhappy for the rest of your life. You will be evading your own capacities, your own possibilities."

Not only are we ambivalent about our own highest possibilities. We are also in a perpetual and I think universal—perhaps even *necessary*—conflict and ambivalence over these same highest possibilities in other people, and in human nature in general. Certainly we love and admire good men, saints, honest, virtuous, clean men. But could anybody who has looked into the depths of human nature fail to be aware of our mixed and often hostile feelings toward saintly men? Or toward very beautiful women or men? Or toward great creators? Or toward our intellectual geniuses? It is not necessary to be a psychotherapist to see this phenomenon—let us call it "counter-valuing." Any reading of history will turn up plenty of examples, or perhaps I could even say that any such historical search might fail to turn up a single exception throughout the whole history of mankind. We surely love and admire all the persons who have incarnated the true, the good, the beautiful, the just, the perfect, the ultimately successful. And yet they also make us uneasy, anxious, confused, perhaps a little jealous or envious, a little inferior, clumsy. They usually make us lose our aplomb, our self-possession and self-regard. (Neitzsche is still our best teacher here.)

Here we have a first clue. My impression so far is that the greatest people, simply by their presence and by being what they are, make us feel aware of our lesser worth, whether or not they intend to. If this is an unconscious effect, and we are not aware of why we feel stupid or ugly or inferior whenever such a person turns up, we are apt to respond with projection, i.e., we react as if he were *trying* to make us feel inferior, as if we were the target (8). Hostility is then an understandable consequence. It looks to me so far as if conscious awareness tends to fend off this hostility. That is, if you are willing to attempt self-awareness and self-analysis of your *own* counter-valying, i.e., of your unconscious fear and hatred of true, good, beautiful, people, you will most likely be less nasty to them. I am willing also to extrapolate the guess that if you can learn to love more purely the highest values in others, this might make you love these qualities in yourself in a less frightened way.

Allied to this dynamic is the awe before the highest, of which Rudolf Otto (23) has given us the classical description. Putting this together with Eliade's insights (2) into sacralization and desacralization, we become more aware of the universality of the fear of direct confrontation with a god or with the godlike. In some religions death is the inevitable consequence. Most preliterate societies also have places or objects that are taboo because they are too sacred and *therefore too dangerous.* In the last chapter of my *Psychology of Science* (18), I have also given examples mostly from science and medicine of desacralizing and resacralizing and tried to explain the psychodynamics of these processes. Mostly it comes down to awe before the highest and best, (I want to stress that this awe is intrinsic, justified, *right*, suitable, rather than some sickness or failing to get "cured of").

But here again my feeling is that this awe and fear need not be negative alone, need not be something to make us flee or cower. These are also desirable and enjoyable feelings capable of bringing us even to the point of highest ecstasy and rapture. Conscious awareness, insight and "working through," à la Freud, is the answer here too I think. This is the best path I know to the acceptance of our highest powers, and whatever elements of greatness or goodness or wisdom or talent we may have concealed or evaded.

A helpful sidelight for me has come from trying to understand why peak-experiences are ordinarily transient and brief (13). The answer becomes clearer and clearer. *We are just not strong enough to endure more!* It is just too shaking and wearing. So often people in such ecstatic moments say, "It's too much," or "I can't stand it," or "I could die." And as I get the descriptions, I sometimes feel, "Yes, they *could* die." Delirious happiness cannot be borne for long. Our organisms are just too weak for any large doses of greatness, just as they would be too weak to endure hour-long sexual orgasms, for example.

The word "peak-experience" is more appropriate than I realized at first. The acute emotion must be climactic and momentary and it *must* give way to nonecstatic serenity, calmer happiness, and the intrinsic pleasures of clear, contemplative cognition of the highest goods. The climactic emotion can not endure, but B-Cognition *can* (16, 18).

Does this not help us to understand our Jonah syndrome? It is partly a justified fear of being torn apart, of losing control, of being shattered and disintegrated, even of being killed by the experience. Great emotions after all can in *fact* overwhelm us. The fear of surrendering to such an experience, a fear which reminds us of all the parallel fears found in sexual frigidity, can be understood better I think through familiarity with the literature of psychodynamics and depth psychology, and of the psychophysiology and medical psychomatics of emotion.

There is still another psychological process that I have run across in my explorations of failure to actualize the self. This evasion of growth can also be set in motion by a fear of paranoia. Of course this has been said in more universal ways. Promethean and Faustian legends are found in practically any culture.[4] For instance, the Greeks called it the fear of *hubris.* It has been called "sinful pride," which is of course a permanent human problem. The person who says to himself, "Yes, I will be a great philosopher and I will rewrite Plato and do it better," must sooner or later

[4] Sheldon's excellent book on this subject (24) is not quoted often enough, possibly because it came before we were quite ready to assimilate it (1936).

be struck dumb by his grandiosity, his arrogance. And especially in his weaker moments, will say to himself, "Who? Me?" and think of it as a crazy fantasy or even fear it as a delusion. He compares his knowledge of his inner private self, with all its weakness, vacillation, and shortcomings, with the bright, shining, perfect, and faultless image he has of Plato. Then of course, he will feel presumptuous and grandiose. (What he fails to realize is that Plato, introspecting, must have felt just the same way about himself, but went ahead anyway, overriding his own doubts about self.)

For some people this evasion of one's own growth, setting low levels of aspiration, the fear of doing what one is capable of doing, voluntary self-crippling, pseudostupidity, mock-humility are in fact defenses against grandiosity, arrogance, sinful pride, hubris. There are people who cannot manage that graceful integration between humility and pride which is absolutely necessary for creative work. To invent or create you must have the "arrogance of creativeness" which so many investigators have noticed. But, of course, if you have *only* the arrogance without the humility, then you are in fact paranoid. You *must* be aware not only of the godlike possibilities within, but also of the existential human limitations. You must be able simultaneously to laugh at yourself and at all human pretensions. If you can be amused by the worm trying to be a god (28), then in fact you may be able to go on trying and being arrogant without fearing paranoia or bringing down upon yourself the evil eye. This is a good technique.

May I mention one more such technique that I saw at its best in Aldous Huxley, who was certainly a great man in the sense I have been discussing, one who was able to accept his talents and use them to the full. He managed it by perpetually marvelling at how interesting and fascinating everything was, by wondering like a youngster at how miraculous things are, by saying frequently, "Extraordinary! Extraordinary!" He could look out at the world with wide eyes, with unabashed innocence, awe and fascination, which is a kind of admission of smallness, a form of humility, and then proceed calmly and unafraid to the great tasks he set for himself.

Finally, may I refer you to a paper of mine (14) relevant in itself, but also as the first in a possible series. Its name, "The need to know and the fear of knowing," illustrates well what I want to say about *each* of the intrinsic or ultimate values that I call Values of Being (B-Values). I am trying to say that these ultimate values, which I think are also the highest needs (or metaneeds, as I'm calling them (19) in a forthcoming publication) fall, like all basic needs, into the basic Freudian schema of impulse *and* defense against that impulse. Thus it is certainly demonstrable that we need the truth and love and seek it. And yet it is just as easy to demonstrate that we are also simultaneously *afraid* to know the truth. For instance, certain truths carry automatic responsibilities which may be anxiety-producing. One way to evade the responsibility and the anxiety is simply to evade consciousness of the truth.

I predict that we will find a similar dialectic for each of the intrinsic Values of Being, and I have vaguely thought of doing a series of papers on, for example, "The love of beauty and our uneasiness with it," "Our love of the good man and our irritation with him," "Our search for excellence and our tendency to destroy it." Of course these counter-values are stronger in neurotic people, but it looks to me as if all of us must make our peace with these mean impulses within ourselves. And my impression so far is that the best way to do this is to transmute envy, jealousy, *ressentiment*, and nastiness into humble admiration, gratitude, appreciation, adoration, and even worship via conscious insight and working through (22). This is the road to feeling small and weak and unworthy and *accepting* these feelings instead of needing to protect a spuriously high self-esteem by striking out (7).

Again I think it is obvious that understanding this basic existential problem should help us to embrace the B-Values not only in others, but also in ourselves, thereby helping to resolve the Jonah syndrome.

REFERENCES

1. Angyal, A. *Neurosis and Treatment: A Holistic Theory.* Wiley, 1965.
2. Eliade, M. *The Sacred and the Profane.* Harper & Row, 1961.
3. Frankl, V. Self-transcendence as a human phenomenon, *Journal of Humanistic Psychology*, 1966, *6*, 197–206.
4. Goldstein, K. *The Organism.* American Book Company, 1939.
5. Hartman, R. The science of value, in *New Knowledge in Human Values,* A. H. Maslow (Ed.) Harper & Row, 1959.
6. Henle, M. (Ed.). *Documents of Gestalt Psychology.* University of California Press, 1961.
7. Horney, K. *Neurosis and Human Growth.* W. W. Norton, 1950.
8. Huxley, L., *You Are Not the Target.* Farrar, Straus & Co., 1963.
9. King, C. D. The meaning of normal, *Yale Journal of Biology and Medicine,* 1945, *17*, 493–501.
10. Köhler, W. *The Place of Values in a World of Facts.* Liveright, 1938.
11. Maslow, A. H. *Motivation and Personality.* Harper & Row, 1954.
12. ______. Some frontier problems in mental health, in A. Combs (Ed.), *Personality Theory and Counseling Practice.* University of Florida Press, 1961.
13. ______. Lessons from the peak-experiences, *Journal of Humanistic Psychology,* 1962, *2*, 9–18.
14. ______. The need to know and the fear of knowing, *Journal of General Psychology,* 1963, *68*, 111–125.
15. ______. Fusions of facts and values, *American Journal of Psychoanalysis,* 1963, *23*, 117–131.
16. ______. *Religions, Values, and Peak-Experiences.* Ohio State University Press, 1964.
17. ______. Criteria for Judging Needs to be Instinctoid, in M. R. Jones (Ed.), *Human Motivation: A Symposium,* University of Nebraska Press, 1965, 33–47.
18. ______. *The Psychology of Science: A Reconnaissance.* Harper & Row, 1966.
19. ______. A theory of metamotivation: the biological rooting of the value-life. *Journal of Humanistic Psychology,* 1967, in press.
20. ______. Self-actualization and beyond, in J. Bugental (Ed.) *Challenges of Humanistic Psychology.* McGraw-Hill, 1967.
21. ______ and Mittelman, B. *Principles of Abnormal Psychology,* Harper & Row, 1941.
22. ______, with Rand, H. & Newman, S. Some parallels between the dominance and sexual behavior of monkeys and the fantasies of patients in psychotherapy, *Journal of Nervous & Mental Disease,* 1960, *131*, 202–212.
23. Otto, R. *The Idea of the Holy.* Oxford University Press, 1958.
24. Sheldon, W. H. *Psychology and the Promethean Will,* Harper & Row, 1936.
25. Shostrom, E. Personal Orientation Inventory (POI), Educational and Industrial Testing Service, 1963.

26. van Kaam, A. *Existential Foundations of Psychology.* Duquesne University Press, 1966.
27. Weiss, F. A. Emphasis on health in psychoanalysis, *American Journal of Psychoanalysis*, 1966, *26*, 194–198.
28. Wilson, C. *The Stature of Man.* Houghton Mifflin, 1959.
29. ______. *Introduction to the New Existentialism.* Houghton Mifflin, 1967.

35

The Repression of the Sublime

Frank Haronian

The title, "The Repression of the Sublime," comes from the writings of Robert Desoille (1945). In the course of this paper I am not going to offer you any really new ideas. Instead, I will try to bring together the ideas of a number of others in such a way as to make the concept, the repression of the sublime, so real and compelling to you that you will see it ever more clearly and inescapably in yourselves, in your patients, and in your associates.

I do not think it is necessary to define the concept of repression but I do want to go into the question of what is meant in this instance by the sublime. We can be orthodox-psychoanalytic about it and consider all higher artistic, social, and spiritually oriented activities as sublimations of primitive, erotic, and aggressive drives. These would be sublime activities, but as sublimations of "lower" drives. But we could also consider that these same "higher" impulses, desires, or motives exist in their own right, and that they develop whether or not the sexual and aggressive drives are satisfied. In fact, one might go so far as to claim that the higher and more sublime needs of the person are more likely to be awakened and developed if the so-called lower, more carnal drives are satisfied rather than if these are frustrated and "sublimated." For it is often out of a sense of boredom and dissatisfaction with the gratification of the senses that we begin to look for higher meanings to our lives.

There are still other ways of looking at the term *sublime.* In its broadest sense, it covers all of man's impulses, instincts, drives, urges to be something more, better, greater than he is. Personal growth and differentiation is part of the picture, to be sure, but beyond that, the concept of the sublime involves several other general areas. It refers to the true, the good, the beautiful. We orient ourselves toward the sublime when we disinterestedly seek to know things as they are; when we nurture others for the pleasure of seeing them grow; when we arrange physical events so that they are seen as beautiful or artistic.

Then, there is the tendency towards

Printed by permission of the author. This paper was originally presented at a seminar of the Psychosynthesis Research Foundation in New York City on December 15, 1967, and has been edited for inclusion in this book.

community, brotherliness, and caring. It is based on the feeling, the belief, the conviction that we all share the same fate, ultimately. In the thinking of Robert Desoille, in whose writings I first came across the conception of the repression of the sublime, the impulse toward the sublime demands that we be concerned with others, that we feel the need to communicate with others with the best of ourselves, and that we find our deepest satisfaction in service to others. I quote in translation the section of his 1945 book in which he says: "There are many forms of service and among them the disinterested efforts of the savant and of the artist are among the highest." The impulse to act in such ways is the expression of a profound urge to trust life, to give freely of oneself, and to forget one's selfish concerns. These are among the traits of the sublime.

There is another aspect of the sublime which is confusingly called "the religious." This is the inescapable need of every person to answer the existential questions for himself and to attach himself to a purpose, a goal, an ideal, that he sees as greater and more important, more durable than his own transient existence and powers. When we sense the sublime as the feeling of communion with and devotion to something that is greater than ourselves, then we are experiencing this basic religious impulse. It may be theistic, agnostic, or atheistic; it does not require a belief in God, but it is consonant with such a belief. According to Desoille it is the therapist's job to help his client to become fully aware of this basic and normal religious impulse and to help the client to clear his mind of any persisting infantile theological conceptions. Finally, the therapist helps the client to develop his primitive religious impulses to the level at which they are converted into reflective thought rather than merely emotionally charged "magic thinking."

Now, to get back to the title of this paper, "The Repression of the Sublime," I would like to demonstrate that it is an essential part of being fully human to feel the pull and the attraction of the sublime in the several ways that I have described. And it is typically neurotic for us to avoid the responsibility of trying to answer this call of the sublime. However, we often do repress it.

There are many ways in which we evade the call of the sublime. Why do we evade, for example, the challenge of personal growth? We fear growth because it means abandoning the familiar for the unknown, and that always involves risks. I recently came across the same idea in the works of Andras Angyal (1965) where he says:

> Abandoning the familiar for the unknown always involves risks. When the changes are far-reaching or precipitous they are bound to arouse anxiety. The view that growth is inseparable from anxiety is shared by practically all thinkers who have substantially contributed to our understanding of anxiety. . . . The anxiety felt at the prospect of dissolution of one's current mode of being has been related by some to the fear of final dissolution, of which human beings have the certain foreknowledge; since growth requires the breaking of old patterns, willingness "to die" is a precondition of living. . . . Excessive fear of death is often a correlate of the neurotic fear of growth and change.

Why do we evade the expression of care and concern for others? Often it is because we fear that we won't know where to draw the line and that we will find ourselves used and exploited by others. In popular parlance, "If you give a person an inch, he'll take a mile." Somehow we lack the stable sense of self which would permit us to have our "yes" and our "no" in such situations. I think that this fear is also related to the fact that as a part of the pattern of modern life, we know too many people too superficially—and we experience too little responsibility for each other.

I suspect that the loss of the security of

a sense of community with others, the loss of the feeling of sharing a common fate, has led us to a state in which we are no longer able to commit ourselves to an ideal whose value, in our eyes, transcends that of our personal existence. This is the opposite of the situation that normally exists in primitive tribes. Today, the old tribal claims for loyalty in return for status and security are weak. We seldom experience a close relatedness to others for whose lives we are responsible and on whom we, in turn, can call for aid when we are distressed or threatened. Because of this loss, the motive for commitment of oneself to something greater than oneself must nowadays attach itself to something more abstract than one's tribe, something harder to define and to keep in mind and heart as a goal.

Let's go back to the idea of repression. Desoille's idea that we repress the sublime can be found in the writings of current American psychologists. For example, Angyal (1965) speaks of the defense mechanisms such as repression as exercising their effects not only on neurotic feelings and trends, but on the healthy ones, too. To his way of thinking, two competing organizations or sets of attitudes or systems for attributing meaning to experiences are in competition with each other. One is healthy, the other is neurotic. Each system seeks to dominate the individual, and to do this, it must repress the other competing system. So when the neurotic system is dominant, the healthy system is *ipso facto* subdued and submerged, i.e., excluded from consciousness, or *repressed.* Angyal then says,

> This conception is borne out by numerous observations that one can and does repress feelings and wishes that are in no way socially tabooed and are often considered laudable.

He calls this "annexation" or "appropriation," and he gives the example of an analytic patient who misinterprets his own natural and healthy friendliness as a viciously motivated exploitativeness.

There are a number of other current examples of the repression of the sublime. I would like to draw some from Abraham Maslow's writings. Recently he gave a lecture in which he included the notion of "the Jonah Complex." To quote from Dr. Maslow (1966):

> I'd like to turn to one of the many reasons for what Angyal has called "the evasion of growth." Certainly everybody in this room would like to be better than he is. We have, all of us, an impulse to improve ourselves, an impulse towards actualizing more of our potentialities, towards self-actualization, or full humanness, or human fulfillment, or whatever term you like. Granted this for everybody here, then what holds us up? What blocks us?
>
> One such defence against growth that I would like to speak about especially, because it has not been noticed much, I shall call the Jonah Complex.
>
> In my own notes I had at first labelled this defense "the fear of one's own greatness" or "the evasion of one's destiny" or "the running away from one's best own talent." I had wanted to stress as bluntly and sharply as I could the non-Freudian point that we fear our best as well as our worst, even though in different ways. It is certainly possible for most of us to be greater than we are in actuality. We all have unused potentialities or not fully developed ones. It is certainly true that many of us evade our constitutionally suggested vocations. . . . So often we run away from the responsibilities dictated (or rather suggested) by nature, by fate, even sometimes by accident, just as Jonah tried in vain to run away from *his* fate.
>
> We fear our highest possibilities (as well as our lowest ones). We are generally afraid to become that which we can glimpse in our most perfect moments, under the most perfect conditions, under conditions of greatest courage. We enjoy and even thrill to the god-like possibilities we see in ourselves in such peak moments. And yet we simultaneously shiver with weakness, awe and fear before these same possibilities. . . .
>
> Not only are we ambivalent about our

highest possibilities, we are also in a perpetual, and I think universal, perhaps even necessary, conflict and ambivalence over these same highest possibilities in other people and in human nature in general. Certainly we love and admire good men, saints; honest, virtuous, clean men. But could anybody who has looked into the depths of human nature fail to be aware of our mixed and often hostile feelings toward saintly men? Or toward very beautiful women or men? Or toward great creators? Or toward our intellectual geniuses? We surely love and admire all the persons who incarnated the true, the good, the beautiful, the just, the perfect, the ultimately successful. And yet they also make us uneasy, anxious, confused, perhaps a little jealous or envious; a little inferior, clumsy. They usually make us lose our aplomb, our self-possession, our self-regard.

Here we have a first clue. My impression so far is that the greatest people, simply by their presence and being what they are, make us feel aware of our lesser worth, whether or not they intend to. If this is an unconscious effect, and we are not aware of why we feel stupid or ugly or inferior whenever such a person turns up, we are apt to respond with projection, i.e., we react as if he were trying to make us feel inferior, as if we were the target. Hostility is then an understandable consequence. It looks to me, so far, as if conscious awareness tends to fend off this hostility. That is, if you are willing to attempt self-awareness and self-analysis of your *own* counter-valuing, i.e., of your unconscious fear and hatred of the true, good and beautiful, etc., people, you will very likely be less nasty to them. And I am willing to extrapolate to the guess that if you can learn to love more purely the highest values in others, this might make you love these qualities in yourself in a less frightening way.

In another paper, Dr. Maslow (1967) has brought up a different aspect of the repression of the sublime. He calls it "desacralizing":

Let me talk about one defense mechanism that is not mentioned in the psychology textbooks, though it is a very important defense mechanism to the snotty and yet idealist youngster of today. It is the defense mechanism of *desacralizing*. These youngsters mistrust the possibility of values and virtues. They feel themselves swindled and thwarted in their lives. Most of them have, in fact, dopey parents whom they don't respect very much, parents who are quite confused themselves about values and who, frequently, are simply terrified of their children and never punish them or stop them from doing things that are wrong. So you have a situation where the youngsters simply despise their elders—often for good and sufficient reason. Such youngsters have learned to make a big generalization: They won't listen to anybody who is grown up, especially if the grown-up uses the same words which they've heard from the hypocritical mouth. They have heard their fathers talk about being honest or brave or bold, and they have seen their fathers being the opposite of all these things.

The youngsters have learned to reduce the person to the concrete object and to refuse to see what he might be or to refuse to see him in his symbolic values or to refuse to see him or her eternally. Our kids have desacralized sex, for example. Sex is nothing; it is a natural thing, and they have made it so natural that it has lost its poetic qualities in many instances, which means that it has lost practically everything. Self-actualization means giving up this defense mechanism and learning or being taught to resacralize.

Resacralizing means being willing, once again, to see a person "under the aspect of eternity," as Spinoza says, or to see him in the medieval Christian unitive perception, that is, being able to see the sacred, the eternal, the symbolic. It is to see Woman with a capital "W" and everything which that implies, even when one looks at a particular woman. Another example: One goes to medical school and dissects a brain. Certainly something is lost if the medical student isn't awed but, without the unitive perception, sees the brain only as one concrete thing. Open to resacralization, one sees a brain as a sacred object also, sees its symbolic value, sees it as a figure of speech, sees it in its poetic aspects.

Resacrilization often means an awful lot of corny talk—"very square," the kids would say. Nevertheless, for the counselor, especially for the counselor of older people, where these philosophical questions about religion and the meaning of life come up, this is a most important way of helping the person to move toward self-actualization. The youngsters may say that it is square, and the logical positivists may say that it is meaningless, but for the person who seeks our help in this process, it is obviously very meaningful and very important, and we had better answer him, or we're not doing what it is our job to do. . . .

Here is one more quotation from Maslow (1962) on another aspect of the sublime; one that is perhaps closer to earth: "The Avoidance of Knowledge, as Avoidance of Responsibility," is the title:

> . . . lack of curiosity can be an active or a passive *expression* of anxiety and fear. . . . That is, we can seek knowledge in order to reduce anxiety and we can also avoid knowing in order to reduce anxiety. To use Freudian language, incuriosity, learning difficulties, pseudo-stupidity can be a defense. Knowledge and action are very closely bound together, all agree. I go much further, and am convinced that knowledge and action are frequently synonymous, even identical in the Socratic fashion. Where we know fully and completely, suitable action follows automatically and reflexively. Choices are then made without conflict and with full spontaneity.
> . . . this close relation between knowing and doing can help us to interpret one cause of the fear of knowing as deeply a fear of doing, a fear of the consequences that flow from knowing, a fear of its dangerous responsibilities. Often it is better not to know, because if you *did* know, then you would *have* to act and stick your neck out.

There is an interesting theoretical explanation of this idea of the repression of the sublime by Robert Desoille (1945), the French engineer who made it his avocation to develop the *rêve éveillé dirigé*, or directed daydream, as a psychotherapeutic tool. Desoille has woven theory and experience into a fairly elaborate explanation of how, why, and by what agency the sublime is repressed. He has his own topographical description of the psyche. It includes the usual Freudian trio—the id, the ego, and the superego; but they are now supplemented by a fourth agent, the self. The area in the center contains consciousness, the ego, and the superego. Farther out, one finds the personal preconscious and unconscious. Beyond that is the collective unconscious. It should be noted that the superego does not partake of the collective unconscious.

Desoille borrowed Jung's concept of the self and modified it somewhat. For him it means a state that represents the far limits of sublimation, a state that is the expression of the highest ideal that a person is able to entertain at any given moment. In this case, the id is the usual concept of our animal drives seeking expression. We experience it as it has been transformed in rising into consciousness, with all the associations that have been called forth by the stimulation of the primitive instincts. Desoille goes on to emphasize the unity of the psyche. The self and the id are considered to be two extreme limits, two opposite poles within the psyche; they never coincide. Each exercises its own attractive effect on the ego at the center; and the ego oscillates back and forth between these two instinctual limits, the primitive and the sublime.

The superego is that arbitrary and infantile outgrowth of the ego that represents the strictures and demands of the parents and other authority figures as they were experienced primarily in childhood. Desoille sees it as a temporary structure that must eventually be dissolved and whose role must be taken over by the self in the mature personality.

At this point, I would like to digress into a description of the types of imagery that

Desoille has habitually found to occur in the directed daydream. As you know, Desoille uses the imagery of ascending and descending in order to evoke images at different levels of the psyche, or at different levels in the archetypal chain, as he puts it. The idea of ascending to heavenly heights he finds associated with sublimation, euphoria, serenity, and ultimately, with spiritual growth. But it frequently happens that the patient's ascent is blocked by a monster of some sort, perhaps a dragon. Desoille calls this character the "guardian of the threshold" and considers it to be an agent of the childish superego, whose function has been in the past to frustrate normal self-expression, e.g., sexual behavior. It is the patient's task in his daydream to struggle with and to overcome this superego figure. If he succeeds in doing this in his daydream, he thereby nullifies the arbitrary restrictions set up by his parents and other authority figures, and in so doing, accepts responsibility for directing his sexual and aggressive strivings according to his own judgments. At this point, the ego becomes animated by an intense aspiration to attain a sublime objective which is still only glimpsed. The superego, which had been constructed from the introjects of the parents as a bulwark against oedipal desires and the like, becomes superfluous as the individual develops autonomy. The self, with its higher, more sublime goals, supplants the superego.

Desoille (1945) draws an important point from Jung. He points out that Jung, among others, has emphasized the necessity of shedding one's own instinctive egotism. On this matter, Jung said that the ancient mystical precept "Get rid of all that you have and then you will receive" means, in effect, that one must abandon the bulk of one's most cherished illusions. Desoille says:

> It is only then that something more beautiful, deeper, and more comprehensive will develop in one. For only the mystery of the sacrifice of oneself makes it possible for one to find oneself again with a renewed soul. These are precepts of very ancient wisdom which are brought back to light during psychoanalytic treatment. . . . This aspiration, which must come to us from a region of the unconscious, arises from a deeper layer than the superego. That is why it needs a special name. We will go along with Jung and call it the self.
>
> The conflict breaks out between the id and the self. The self tries to get the ego to satisfy its needs [for the sublime, its yearnings for growth] and the id, in opposing itself to the self's desires, takes on the role of the repressive agent [and becomes] the expression of a new form of censorship, *the repression of the sublime,* in this case, of the urge to spiritual growth.

When the patient accedes to these intense aspirations of the self which we mentioned earlier and attains certain levels of sublimation, the symbol of the guardian of the threshold changes. It is no longer that of a threatening dragon but takes on a different appearance in the daydreams. It generally appears now as a creature who is both kindly and firm, but still bars the route upward. In this situation the patient no longer feels threatened, but he does feel called upon to make a conscious choice between two equally possible attitudes.

According to Desoille this is what is taking place. During the previous sessions, the subject has become aware of the possibility of developing something more beautiful, deeper, more comprehensive within himself. There has been an intimation of the sublime, a call to become a finer person than he is. But for that to take place, the subject realizes now that he must renounce old habits and stop following lines of least resistance. He must give up the gratification of impulses from the lower unconscious, *all of which have been tolerated and even encouraged by the superego* in the past and accepted by the ego. But the patient hesitates to take this path upward because he feels that it will restrain his freedom and diminish his range of activities. In some cases, the patient may even feel these suggested renunciations have an *inhuman* character to them. This is when the guardian of the threshold appears—but no longer in a repulsive form. This time, it may take on the form of an angel, for example. The conflict between the self and id for possession of the ego, one might say between the sublime and the base, is no longer unconscious. It is now taking place between the ego on the one hand, whose habit has been to accede consciously to those of the id's impulses that had been accepted by the superego (these impulses conforming to the lowest moral restraint of everyday life); and on the other hand, the self, represented by the guardian of the threshold, the angel, whose call is felt to be ever more imperative.

In this case we see that the id, acting through the ego and with the collusion of the superego, struggles against the demands of the self. But at this stage the struggle has become quite conscious; and the ego now seeks to suppress the sublime just as it repressed what seemed to it to be base and vile.

Desoille says that there are three ways in which the patient may react to the image of the guardian of the threshold with its call towards the sublime:

1. During that very session, the subject may suddenly decide to give up his old habits because they now appear to him to represent non-values. These must be replaced by new values, which must be found and possessed. They are symbolized in the subsequent directed daydreams by such images as treasures that are hidden or guarded. Once this decision is made, the patient is again able to see himself ascending to greater heights in his directed daydreams.

2. A subject may hesitate and the session may come to a halt at that point. Subsequently, while the subject is alone, during the interval between sessions, he may decide to take on the struggle. In subsequent sessions he is then able again to progress as a result of that decision.

3. Alternatively, the subject may flatly refuse, consciously or not, to give up his illusions. With this refusal he makes a negative transference on his therapist. Generally, it is rather discrete and of short duration, says Desoille, except in difficult cases.

Psychosynthesis (Assagioli, 1965) makes much of the fact that we suppress and deny our impulses toward the sublime. One possible reason why we do this is because the more that one is conscious of one's positive impulses, of one's urges toward the sublime, the more shame one feels for one's failure to give expression to these impulses. There ensues a painful burning of the conscience, a sense of guilt at not being what one could be, of not doing what one could do. This is not superego guilt but rather the cry of the self for its actualization.

But we have available an "easy-out," an escape from this sense of guilt, if we accept those popular intellectual arguments which reduce the call of the higher unconscious to nothing but sublimation of the impulses of the lower unconscious. Jung (1933) decried this reductionism in *Modern Man in Search of his Soul* more than thirty years ago, but we still find it soothing and comforting to deny these instincts of the higher unconscious and to settle for a degraded self-image because in some ways it is an easier one to live with.

This is the self-image of the well-psychoanalyzed man; he has undergone a sort of psychoanalytical lobotomy of the spirit, a deadening of his normal sensitivity to the higher unconscious and to the possibility of spiritual growth. The key to this denial is probably to be found in Freud's concept of sublimation with its emphasis on aim-inhibited sexual and aggressive drives as the source of the kindly and generous acts of men. This emphasis denied the existence of autonomous impulses towards goodness, towards community. This dogma was especially useful for the reduction of anxiety because it automatically relieved the patient who accepted it of all sense of responsibility for spiritual growth, and of the normal anxiety attended on this quest.

Thus, the psychoanalytic theory of neurosis can be seen as a truncated theory of personality which, in an ideological way, tends to relieve neurotic symptomatology by amputating or anesthetizing a portion of the psyche, the highest and most valuable functions, those which urge us on to be the most that is within our potentiality.

But perhaps it is better for the severe neurotic to temporarily put aside his impulses to the sublime. These impulses, if misused, can lead to ego inflation and solidification of one's pathological self-image. One classical picture of this is rigid self-righteousness. It may be that the severe neurotic should be prohibited from dwelling on thoughts of the sublime until he has uprooted the core of his neurosis, just as the aspirant is not initiated into the secrets of the society until he has developed the knowledge with which to understand the facts and judgment with which to use them.

The problem that psychosynthesis faces, and which I think that psychoanalysis in the classical sense avoids, is to provide a therapy for both the lower and the higher aspects of the unconscious. The needs of the lower unconscious are met more or less successfully by conventional forms of psychotherapy. Religious guidance seeks to enlarge the scope and effectiveness of the higher unconscious. Psychosynthesis provides a philosophy that aims to reach both the id and the self. Psychosynthesis aims to help man to recognize all of his impulses, to accept the responsibility of deciding which to express and which to renounce, and to live with the anxiety that is an inescapable aspect of the struggle for self-actualization.

REFERENCES

ANGYAL, ANDRAS. *Neurosis and treatment.* New York: Wiley, 1965.

ASSAGIOLI, ROBERTO. *Psychosynthesis.* New York: Hobbs, Dorman, 1965.

DESOILLE, ROBERT. *Le rêve éveillé en psychothérapie.* Paris: Presses Universitaires de France, 1945.

JUNG, CARL G. *Modern man in search of a soul.* New York: Harcourt, Brace, 1933.

MASLOW, A. H. *Toward a psychology of being.* Princeton, N.J.: Van Nostrand, 1962.

______, "Neurosis as a failure of personal growth," *Humanitas,* III (1966), pp. 153–169.

______, "Self-actualization and beyond." In J. F. T. Bugental (ed.), *Challenges of humanistic psychology.* New York: McGraw-Hill, 1967, pp. 279–286.

36

Joy Is the Prize

Leo E. Litwak

Big Sur is an 80-mile stretch of California coast below the Monterey Peninsula. It is approximately midway between Los Angeles and San Francisco and difficult of access from either direction. Before the coastal highway was completed in 1936, the shore was accessible only by foot. The Los Padres National Forest, one of the largest preserves in the country, extends 30 miles inland and is 200 miles long; it occupies most of the area. Not much land is available for private ownership. There are only 300 residents. The rugged terrain of Los Padres includes redwood canyons, barren mountain ranges, desert flora, thick forests. It is the province of mountain lions and wild boar.

Stone cliffs rise 2,000 feet above the ocean. Beyond a wedge of meadow, the steeply inclined hillside begins. For great distances there is no meadow at all and the serpentine coastal highway hangs on the cliff-side. It is a two-lane road, sometimes impassable after heavy rains. The fog bank wavers off shore. When it sweeps in, the traveler faces an uncanny trip, guided entirely by the few white dashes of the center line that are visible. With hairpin turns, sharp rises and declines, the road can be dangerous in bad weather. On clear days when the setting sun ignites dust particles on your windshield you are forced to drive blind for dangerous seconds.

Nonetheless, 4,000 people traveled this road last year, in disregard of weather, aimed toward the Esalen Institute, famous until a few years ago under a different name, Big Sur Hot Springs. These are unlikely adventurers. They are doctors, social workers, clinical psychologists, teachers, students, business executives, engineers, housewives —or just fun lovers who have come to take the baths.

Big Sur Hot Springs was originally renowned as the Eden discovered by Henry Miller and Jack Kerouac. Joan Baez once lived there. The springs were purchased in 1910 from a man named Slade by Dr. Henry C. Murphy of Salinas. It was Dr. Murphy's intention to establish a health spa. In order to use the mineral waters he brought in two bathtubs by fishing sloop. They were hauled up the cliff and placed on a ledge at the source of the Springs. But because of their inaccessibility, the springs did not flourish as a spa. Not until Dr. Murphy's grandson, Michael, assumed operation of the property in the mid-nineteen-fifties did the baths begin to receive attention—attention that has grown with the development of Esalen Institute.

Michael Murphy at 37 appears to be in his early 20's. He is slender and boyish and has a marvelous smile. I took part in a panel discussion at Hot Springs some years ago and I was not impressed either by the topic, my performance or the audience. I did enjoy the baths. I had misgivings about Murphy's program, yet none about him. He seemed to me generous, charming, innocent, credulous, enthusiastic and enormously sympathetic. A Stanford alumnus who had done some graduate work in psychology and philosophy, he had recently returned from an 18-month study of the art of meditation at the Aurobindo Ashram in Pondicherry, India, and he devoted a considerable part of each day to meditation. I believe he had—and still has—in mind some great mission, based on his Indian experience. I am not quite sure what the scope of his mission is. A friend of his told me: "Mike wants to turn on the world." Esalen Institute is his instrument for doing so. It has come a long way from the shoddy panels of a few years ago. Its spreading impact may seriously affect our methods of therapy and education.

In the course of a year, almost 1,000 professional persons—social workers, psychiatrists, clinical psychologists—enroll in Esalen workshops. Close to 700 psychotherapists have been trained to administer techniques devised by staff members—Frederick Peres, Virginia Satir, Bernard Gunther and William Schutz. These techniques have been demonstrated at hospitals, universities and medical schools. This year Esalen has opened a San Francisco extension which in the first two months of operation has attracted an attendance in excess of 10,000, offering the same workshops and seminars that are available at Big Sur. Esalen-type communities have begun to appear throughout the country, in Atlanta, Chicago, Los Angeles, Cleveland, La Jolla. One has even appeared in Vancouver, Canada. Murphy offers advice and help, and permits use of his mailing list.

Consider some offerings of the Esalen winter brochure. Seminars led by Alan Watts, the Zen interpreter, and Susan Sontag, the camp interpreter. Workshops for professional therapists conducted by Frederick Perls, an early associate of Freud and Wilhelm Reich and a founder of Gestalt therapy. A lecture panel including the psychologist Carl Rogers and Herman Kahn, the "thinking about the unthinkable" man. Some of the titles are: "Kinetic Theater," "Psycotechnics," "Do You Do It? Or Does It Do You?", "Dante's Way to the Stars," "Creativity and the Daimonic," "On Deepening the Marriage Encounter," "Tibetan Book of the Dead," "Anxiety and Tension Control," "Racial Confrontation as a Transcendental Experience."

What principle guides a mélange that consists of dance workshops, therapy workshops, sensory-awareness experiments, the Tibetan Book of the Dead, Herman Kahn, Carl Rogers, Frederick Perls and Susan Sontag?

Esalen's vice president, George B. Leonard, has written a general statement of purpose. He says: "We believe that all men somehow possess a divine potentiality; that ways may be worked out—specific, systematic ways—to help, not the few, but the many toward a vastly expanded capacity to learn, to love, to feel deeply, to create. We reject the tired dualism that seeks God and human potentialities by denying the joys of the senses, the immediacy of unpostponed life." The programs, he says, are aimed toward "the joys of the senses."

I had signed up for a workshop led by Dr. William Schutz, a group therapist who has taught at Harvard and the Albert Einstein College of Medicine, among other institutions, and has served on the staff of the National Training Laboratories Interne Training Program at Bethel, Me. His latest book, "Joy," was published in 1967 by Grove Press.

In the brochure description of Dr. Schutz's workshop I read a warning that the experience would be more than verbal: "An encounter workshop with body movements, sensory awareness, fantasy experiments, psychodrama. Developing the ability to experience joy is the workshop's guiding theme."

Joy as the prize of a five-day workshop?

"How can we speak of joy," Leonard has written, "on this dark and suffering planet? How can we speak of anything else? We have heard enough of despair."

It was easy enough to dismiss the language. It seemed naive to promise so great a reward for so small an investment. Joy for $175 seemed cheap at the price, especially since The New York Times was paying. I did have considerable anxieties that some of those "body movements" might be humiliating. And what precisely was meant by "sensory awareness"?

Esalen has changed considerably since my previous visit. Rows of new cabins are ranged along terraces on the hillside. The lodge is located at the bottom of a steep incline, in a meadow. The meadow is perhaps 200 yards deep and ends at the cliff edge. The Pacific Ocean is 150 feet below. A staff of 50 operates the kitchen, supervises the baths, cleans the cabins and garden and works on construction.

I passed hippy laborers, stripped to the waist, long hair flowing, operating with pick and shovel. Dreamy girls in long gowns played flutes near the pool.

I was somewhat put off by what I considered to be an excessive show of affection. Men hugged men. Men hugged women. Women hugged women. These were not hippies, but older folks, like myself, who had come for the workshop. People flew into one another's arms, and it wasn't my style at all.

After dinner, 30 of us met in the gallery for our first session. We began our excursion toward joy at 9 P.M. of a Sunday in a woodsy room on a balmy, starry night.

William Schutz, solidly built, with bald head and muzzle beard, began by telling us that in the course of the workshop we would come to dangerous ground. At such times we ought not to resist entering, for in this area lay our greatest prospect for self-transcendence. He told us to avoid verbal manipulations and to concentrate on our feelings.

We began with exercises. A fat lady in leotards directed us to be absurd. We touched our noses with our tongues. We jumped. We ran. We clutched one another, made faces at one another. Afterward, we gathered in groups of five and were given an ambiguous instruction to discover one another by touching in any way we found agreeable. I crouched in front of a strange-looking young man with an underslung jaw and powerful shoulders. I tried unlocking his legs and he glared at me.

When Schutz asked each group of five to select one couple that seemed least close, the young man with the underslung jaw selected me. The hostile pairs were then requested to stand at opposite diagonals of the room and approach each other. They were to do whatever they felt like doing when they met in the center of the room. A burly middle-aged man marched toward a petite lady. They met, they paused, stared, then suddenly embraced. The next couple, two husky men, both frozen rigid, confronted each other, stared, then also embraced. The young man and I came next. We started at opposite diagonals. We met in in the center of the room. I found myself looking into the meanest, coldest eyes I had ever seen. He pressed his hands to his sides, and it was clear to me that we were not going to embrace. I reached for his hand to shake it. He jerked free. I put my hand on his shoulder; he shrugged me off. We continued staring and finally returned to our group.

There was a general discussion of this encounter. Some feared we might start fighting. Nothing, of course, was farther from my mind. I had gone out, intending to play their game and suddenly found myself staring at a lunatic. He had very mean, cold eyes, a crazy shape to his jaw, lips so grim that his ill-feeling was unmistakable. Back in our group he said to me, in a raspy, shrill voice: "You thought I was going to bat you in the face; that's why you turned away." There was a slurred quality to his speech, and it occurred to me that I might have triggered off a madman. I denied that I had turned away and I was challenged to stare him down. I was annoyed that I had been forced into something so silly.

We proceeded, on the basis of our first impressions, to give one another names, which we kept for the duration of the workshop. My nemesis accepted the name of Rebel. There was a plump, lovely girl we called Kate. A silent, powerful man with spectacles we named Clark. Our fat group leader received the name of Brigitte. A lumpy, solemn man with thick spectacles we named Gary. An elegant, trim middle-aged woman we named Sheba. A buxom, mournful woman with long hair became Joan. A jovial middle-aged pipe smoker with a Jean Hersholt manner we named Hans. A fierce mustached swaggerer in Bermuda shorts was Daniel. A quiet man with a little boy's face we named Victor. I was named Lionel. We were addressed by these names at all times.

I considered this renaming of ourselves a naive attempt to create an atmosphere free of any outside reference. Many of the techniques impressed me as naive. It seemed tactless and obvious to ask so blunt and vague a question as: "What are you feeling?" Yet what happened in the course of five days was that the obvious became clarified. Clichés became significant.

I found myself discovering what had always been under my nose. I had not known how my body felt under conditions of tension or fear or grief. I discovered that I was numb. I had all sorts of tricks for avoiding encounter. I didn't particularly like to be touched. I avoided looking strangers in the eye. I took pride in my coolness and trickery. I didn't believe one should give oneself away. It seemed to me a virtue to appear cool, to be relatively immune to feeling, so that I could receive shocks without appearing to. I considered it important to keep up appearances. I'm no longer proud of what I now believe to be an incapacity rather than a talent.

I thought my group rather dull. I saw no great beauty and a great deal of weakness. I felt somewhat superior, since I was there on assignment, not by choice. I hated and feared Reb.

But in the next five days, I became enormously fond of these apparently uninteresting strangers. We encountered one another in violent and intimate ways, and I could no longer dismiss them.

I was convinced that Rebel was insane. He opened our second meeting with gratuitous insults. He referred to me as "Charley Goodguy." When Brigitte, the leader of our group, told him not to think in stereotypes, he sneered at her: "Why don't you shut up, Fats?" It is difficult to convey the nastiness of his tone—an abrasive, jeering quality.

Daniel exploded. He called Rebel a shark and a rattlesnake. He said he wanted to quit the group because he despised this frightening, violent kid. "You scare me," he told Reb. "It's people like you who are responsible for Vietnam and Auschwitz. You're a monster and you're going to suck up all the energy of this group and it's not worth it. I want to get out."

I told Daniel his response seemed ex-excessive. Vietnam and Auschwitz? "He's a little hostile," I said.

Reb didn't want any favors from me. "Hostile?" he sneered. "Say, I bet I know what you are. You sound to me like a professor. Or a pawnbroker. Which are you, a professor or a pawnbroker?"

Schutz intervened. He said to me and Rebel: "I feel you have something going. Why don't you have it out?" He suggested that we arm wrestle, an innocuous contest, but, under the circumstances, there seemed to be a great deal invested in winning or losing. My arm felt numb, and there was some trembling in my thighs. I feared I might not have all my strength, and Rebel appeared to be a powerful kid.

I pinned him so easily, however, that the group accused him of having quit. Daniel was jubilant: "You're a loser. You're trying to get clobbered."

Rebel was teased into trying again. On the second trial, he pressed my left arm down and demanded a rematch with the right hand. We remained locked together for close to 20 minutes. It was unbearable. I lost all sensation in my hand and arm. I willed my hand not to yield. Finally, I hoped he would press me down and get it over with. It ended when Rebel squirmed around and braced his foot against the wall and the contest was called.

Daniel was delighted by the outcome. He felt as though I had won something for him. Schutz asked: "Why don't you wrestle Reb?" Daniel despised violence. He probably would lose and he didn't want to give that monster the satisfaction of a victory. Violence was right up that shark's alley. He refused to play his games. Nonetheless, Daniel was on the ground with Rebel a moment later, beet red with strain, trembling down to his calves. Rebel raised his elbow, pressed Daniel down and the match was called off. Daniel leaped to his feet, circled the room. He suddenly charged Rebel, who was seated, and knocked him from his chair. He then rushed at Schutz, yelling: "It's you I hate, you bastard, for making me do this." Schutz did not flinch, and Daniel backed off. I could see that his impulse was histrionic. I felt sorry for Reb, who mumbled: "I copped out. I should have hit him."

Reb later presented a different guise. Far from being an idiot, he was an extremely precocious 20-year-old computer engineer, self-taught in the humanities. His father had abandoned the family when he was a child. His mother was a cold customer—never a sign of feeling. He didn't know where he stood with her. She taunted him in the same abrasive style which he tried with us.

Reb suffered sexual agonies that had brought him several hundred miles in search of a solution. He considered himself perverse and contemptible, the only impotent 20-year-old kid in the world. He admitted he found women repugnant as sexual objects, and it was hardly surprising that his crude advances were rebuffed. He admitted that his strategy had been to strike out in hope that someone would strike back so that he might *feel.* He was boyish and affectionate outside the group.

My feeling for him underwent a complete reversal. He began to impress me as an intelligent kid, trying with great courage to repair terrible injuries. The monster I had seen simply vanished.

I never anticipated the effect of these revelations, as one after another of these strangers expressed his grief and was eased. I woke up one night and felt as if everything were changed. I felt as if I were about to weep. The following morning the feeling was even more intense.

Brigitte and I walked down to the cliff edge. We lay beneath a tree. She could see that I was close to weeping. I told her that I'd been thinking about my numbness, which I had traced to the war. I tried to keep the tears down. I felt vulnerable and unguarded. I felt that I was about to lose all my secrets and I was ready to let them go. Not being guarded, I had no need to put anyone down, and I felt what it was to be unarmed. I could look anyone in the eyes and my eyes were open.

That night I said to Daniel: "Why do you keep diverting us with intellectual arguments? I see suffering in your eyes. You give me a glimpse of it, then you turn it off. Your eyes go dead and the intellectual stuff bores me. I feel that's part of your strategy."

Schutz suggested that the two of us sit in the center of the room and talk to each other. I told Daniel that I was close to surrender. I wanted to let go. I felt near to my grief. I wanted to release it and be purged. Daniel asked about my marriage and my work. Just when he hit a nerve, bringing me near the release I wanted, he began to speculate on the tragedy of the human condition. I told him: "You're letting me off and I don't want to be let off."

Schutz asked if I would be willing to take a fantasy trip.

It was late afternoon and the room was

already dark. I lay down, Schutz beside me, and the group gathered around. I closed my eyes. Schutz asked me to imagine myself very tiny and to imagine that tiny self entering my own body. He wanted me to describe the trip.

I saw an enormous statue of myself, lying in a desert, mouth open as if I were dead. I entered my mouth. I climbed down my gullet, entering it as if it were a manhole. I climbed into my chest cavity. Schutz asked me what I saw. "It's empty," I said. "There's nothing here." I was totally absorbed by the effort to visualize entering myself and lost all sense of the group. I told Schutz there was no heart in my body. Suddenly, I felt tremendous pressure in my chest, as if tears were going to explode. He told me to go to the vicinity of the heart and report what I saw. There, on a ledge of the chest wall, near where the heart should have been, I saw a baby buggy. He asked me to look into it. I didn't want to, because I feared I might weep, but I looked, and I saw a doll. He asked me to touch it. I was relieved to discover that it was only a doll. Schutz asked me if I could bring a heart into my body. And suddenly there it was, a heart sheathed in slime, hung with blood vessels. And that heart broke me up. I felt my chest convulse. I exploded. I burst into tears.

I recognized the heart. The incident had occurred more than 20 years before and had left me cold. I had written about it in a story published long ago in Esquire. The point of the story was that such events should have affected me but never did. The War in Germany was about over. We had just taken a German village without resistance. We had fine billets in German houses. The cellars were loaded with jams and sausages and wine. I was the aid man with the outfit, and was usually summoned by the call of "Aid man!" When I heard that call I became numb, and when I was numb I could go anywhere and do anything. I figured the battles were over. It came as a shock when I heard the call this time. There were rifle shots, then: "Aid man!" I ran to the guards and they pointed to bushes 10 yards from where they had been posted. They had spotted a German soldier and called to him to surrender. He didn't answer and they fired. I went to the bushes and turned him over. He was a kid about 16, blond, his hair strung out in the bushes, still alive. The .30-caliber bullets had scooped out his chest and I saw his heart. It was the same heart I put in my chest 23 years later. He was still alive, gray with shock, going fast. He stared up at me—a mournful, little boy's face. He asked: "Why did you shoot? I wanted to surrender." I told him we didn't know.

Now, 23 years later, I wailed for that German boy who had never mattered to me and I heaved up my numbness. The trip through my body lasted more than an hour. I found wounds everywhere. I remembered a wounded friend whimpering: "Help me, Leo," which I did—a close friend, yet after he was hit no friend at all, not missed a second after I heard of his death, numb to him as I was to everyone else, preparing for losses by anesthetizing myself. And in the course of that trip through my body I started to feel again, and discovered what I'd missed. I felt wide open, lightened, ready to meet others simply and directly. No need for lies, no need to fear humiliation. I was ready to be a fool. I experienced the joy Schutz had promised to deliver. I'm grateful to him. Not even the offer of love could threaten me.

This was the transformation I underwent in the course of that fantasy trip. The force of the experience began to fade quickly, and now, writing two weeks later, I find that little remains. But I still have a vision of a possibility I had not been aware of—a simple, easy connection with my own feeling and, consequently, with others'.

I had great difficulty emerging from my body. I was pinned against my intestines, pregnant with myself. When I finally began to move and restored all the missing organs and repaired those that were damaged, I feared that all this work was temporary, that if I were to leave the heart would vanish, the stomach dry up, the intestines be exposed. Schutz asked if there was anyone who could help me get out. I said: "My daughter." So I invited my daughter to enter my body. She stood near my heart and said: "Come on out, Daddy," and led me out. I ran to a meadow on my chest. I ran through long grass, toward a gate, directly toward the sun. There I lay down and rested.

Occasionally, during my trip, I heard others crying, but I had lost track of the group. I opened my eyes. I had an initial sense of others as darts of candlelight about me. The room seemed to have shifted. It was pitch black outside. Everyone was very close to me—Reb, Daniel, Brigitte, Bill, Joan, Victor, Kate, Clark, Gary, Sheba. Sheba still wept. Brigitte directed us all to lie down and to reach out and touch one another. She turned out the lights and gave us various instructions designed to release us and finally we parted.

It was not easy leaving these people I had met only five days before. Time was distorted and we seemed to have lived years together. It was not easy leaving Big Sur. On the final morning, the entire workshop met to say good-by. Our group gathered in a tight circle hugging, and kissing, and I found myself hugging everyone, behaving like the idiots I had noticed on first arriving at Esalen. I hugged Rebel. I told him he was a great kid and that a few years from now he might not even recall his present trouble. I told him not to envy his peers. He was probably much better than they.

Schutz ended our last meeting by playing a record from "The man of La Mancha," "The Impossible Dream." We were at that point of sentiment where corny lyrics announced truths and we could be illuminated by the wisdom of clichés.

The condition of vulnerability is precious and very fragile. Events and people and old routines and old habits conspire to bring you down. But not all the way down. There is still the recollection of that tingling sense of being wide awake, located in the here and now, feeling freely and entirely, all constraints discarded. It remains a condition to be realized. It could change the way we live.

37

The Roots of Virtue

Erik Erikson

1. Ego and Virtue

In this essay I intend to investigate the genetic roots and the evolutionary rationale of certain basic human qualities which I will call virtues. We have learned to be cautious in the use of this powerful little word ever since Freud introduced us to the study of "the much furrowed ground from which our virtues proudly spring." Yet, the very development of psychoanalytic thought, and its recent pre-occupation with "ego-strength" suggest that human virtue be reconsidered—not, of course, in the now more widespread sense of moral nobility and rectitude, but in that older, simpler

Reprinted from *The Humanist Frame,* edited by Sir Julian Huxley (London: George Allen & Unwin, Ltd.; New York: Harper & Row, 1960).

sense of an "inherent strength," an "active quality." "By virtue of" what qualities, then, can man claim to be, or to be able to become, humanly strong?

What we call virtue, we value; and in approaching the origin of value we face a dilemma which Darwinian biology and Freudian psychology seem to share. Together they have focused on what is popularly considered man's "lower nature"; the descent and evolution of the genus man from a pre-human state of *animality*; the emergence of civilized man from degrees of *savagery* and *barbarism*; and the evolution of individual man from the states of *infantility*. They have shown the relation of rational man's everyday irrationalities to *insanity*, and revealed political man's propensity for mob *anarchy*. Each of these insights was at first met with derision and disbelief; but they soon assumed the form of modern myths. Popular thought (and that includes specialists in non-biological fields) generalized Darwin's theory as a "tooth-and-claw" struggle for survival, in which the crown of creation would go to what T. H. Huxley called the "gladiatorial" type of man. Similarly, popular thought (and that includes scientists not familiar with the advancements of psychoanalysis) crudely over-simplifies Freud's theory of inner conflict. It clings to the earliest formulation of this conflict and conceives of it as an inner tooth-and-claw struggle between ravenous instincts (the impersonal "Id") and cruel conscience (the moralistic "Super-Ego"). Thus the moral alternatives seemingly implicit in Darwin's and Freud's discoveries were over-dramatized as if mankind were taking revenge on these fearless men by forcing them into the role of tragic high priests in the cult of "facing man's lower nature"—a "nature" owned up to so eagerly that it soon excuses everything. This double myth of an inner and outer struggle to the death, has thus made it difficult for both biology and psychoanalysis to come to grips with the question of man's moral strength—except, perhaps, by drawing the obvious and yet already stereotyped conclusion that man's future, if it were dependent on his over-weening conscience and his absolutist morality alone, could predictably end in species-wide suicide in the name of the highest principles(1).

Julian Huxley summed the matter up at the end of his Romanes Lecture:

> The peculiar difficulties which surround our individual moral adjustment are seen to be largely due to our evolutionary history. Like our prolonged helplessness in infancy, our tendency to hernia and sinusitis, our troubles in learning to walk upright, they are a consequence of our having developed from a simian ancestry. Once we realise that the primitive super-ego is merely a makeshift developmental mechanism, no more intended to be the permanent central support of our bodily frame, we shall not take its dictates so seriously (have they not often been interpreted as the authentic Voice of God?), and shall regard its supersession by some more rational and less cruel mechanism as the central ethical problem confronting every human individual. (2)

This passage expresses a view to which, in fact, psychoanalysis is dedicated both as a clinical technique and a system of thought. Every step in treatment and every act of clarification is directed toward the "supersession by some more rational and less cruel mechanisms." And it is not difficult for a psychoanalyst to subscribe to Huxley's "humanist frame," if for no other reason than that, to the scientist and scholar, it seems the best of all possible Utopias:

> While to the evolutionist ethics can no longer be regarded as having any absolute value, yet their relativity is neither chaotic nor meaningless: ethics are relative to a process which is both meaningful and of indefinitely long duration—that of evolutionary progress. (2)

The fact is that the rapprochment between evolutionary biology and psychoanalytic psychology is one well prepared for by an aspect of Freud's thought which has not provoked the imagination of other scientists as his instinct theory has done: I refer to his Ego-Psychology. Almost from the beginning of psychoanalysis, Freud worked continuously on an area of inquiry concerning the "coherent organization of mental processes" (3) which, in all conflict and danger, guarantees to the human person a measure of individuality, mature sexuality, intelligence, and integrity.[1]

Before indicating what the ego is, it is necessary to state what it is not; for the term has been much abused. Popularly, the term "ego" implies an inflated sense of one's own importance, a precarious sense subject to sudden deflation by the pricks of fate—and of gossip. As a brief designation of modern man's vulnerable sense of a self-made self, this usage has become so popular that even highly informed individuals prefer it to, or use it alongside, the psychoanalytic meaning of ego as designating an inner-psychic regulator which organizes inner experience and guards such organization *both* against the untimely impact of *drives* and the undue pressure of an overweening *conscience*. Actually, ego is an age-old term which in scholastics stood for the *unity* of body and soul, and in philosophy in general for the *permanency* of conscious experience. Psychoanalysis, of course, has not concerned itself with matters of soul and has assigned to consciousness a limited role in mental life by demonstrating that man's thoughts and acts are co-determined by unconscious motives which, upon analysis, prove him to be both worse and better than he thinks he is. But this also means that his motives as well as his feelings, thoughts and acts, often "hang together" much better than he could (or should) be conscious of. The ego in psychoanalysis, then, is analogous to what it was in philosophy in earlier usage: a selective, integrating, coherent and persistent agency central to personality formation. First studied clinically in its impaired states, the ego has also been revealed as a control regulator of remarkable endurance and power. It is the inner "organ" which makes it possible for man to bind together the two great evolutionary developments, his *inner life*, and his *social planning*.

But where, in animal nature, is the precursor of the human ego? Man has always tended to project what he calls his own "animal nature" on animals, comparing, for example, his ravenousness with the eating style of dogs, or his rage with that of provoked tigers. Yet, man has also been inclined to use animals as images of ideals, calling himself as courageous as a lion, or as meek as a lamb. For an analogy to what we call ego, however, we must contemplate a certain chaste restraint and selective discipline (11) in the life of even the "wildest" animals: a built-in regulator set to prevent (or "inhibit") carnivorous excess, inappropriate sexuality, useless rage, and damaging panic, permitting rest and play along with the readiness to attack when hungry, or intruded upon. Similarly, different species of animals share environments with a minimum of mutual interference or distraction, each minding its own section of the environment unless, and until, vital interests prove to intersect. Thus, the state of the adapted animal is defined by what we might call "ecological integrity"; a combination of mutual regulation and reciprocal avoidance which safeguards

[1] The study of the ego has been pursued most significantly by Anna Freud (4) and Heinz Hartmann, who was the first to point to the central role of the ego in all human adaptation. See his comprehensive monograph "Ego-Psychology and the Problem of Adaptation" (5), in which he approached such previously neglected problems as "the regulation by the will." David Rapaport has in recent years worked on the systematization of the theory of the ego (6, 7), and has enriched it with an investigation of the problems of activity and passivity (8). My own studies in the relation of ego, society, and history (7, 9, 10), prompt this attempt to speculate on the psychosocial implications of human evolution.

adaptation within the characteristic environment and with other species sharing it. Man, who has evolved into a creature always in the process of readjusting to historical change in his man-made world, obviously over-reacts (i.e. suffers from affect-incontinence as Konrad Lorenz has said): for him, to live up, on his level, to the animal's adaptive integrity, would call for a mutual regulation of inner motivation and technical-social invention which he seems to approach only during certain glorious, but unpredictable periods. To take his place more consciously in the succession of generations within his psychosocial universe, he must learn to know and to use what we here call the Ego.

I will call "virtues," then, the specifically human qualities of strength which are implicit in man's psychosocial evolution, and I will relate them to that process, by which *ego-strength* is both developed and imparted, from generation to generation.

2. A Schedule of Virtues

The paradox of human life is man's collective power to create his own environment, although each individual is born with a naked vulnerability extending into a prolonged infantile dependence. The weakness of the newborn, however, is truly relative. While far removed from any measure of mastery over the physical world, newborn man is endowed with an appearance and with responses which appeal to the tending adults' tenderness and make them wish to attend his needs; which arouse concern in those who are concerned with his well being; and which, in making adults care, stimulate their active caretaking. I employ the repetition of the words tending, concern, and caring not for poetic effect, but in order to underscore the fundamental fact, that in life in general and in human life in particular, the vulnerability of being newly born and the meekness of innocent, needfulness have a power all of their own. Defenseless as babies are, there are mothers at their command, families to protect the mothers, societies to support the structure of families, and traditions to give a cultural continuity to systems of tending and training. All of this, however, the human infant does need in order to evolve humanly: for his environment must provide the *outer wholeness and continuity* which, like a second womb, permits the child to develop his separate capacities in distinct steps, and to unify them only in a series of psychosocial crises.

In recent years, psychiatry has concerned itself with the mother-child relationship, and has, at times, burdened it with the whole responsibility for man's sanity and maturation. This concentration on earliest development seemed to find powerful support in the young science of ethology (12), which analyzes the innate mechanisms by which mother animal and young animal release in each other the behavior necessary for the survival of the young—and thus the species(12). However, a true ethological comparison must juxtapose the first period in animal life (such as the nest-occupancy of certain birds) with man's whole pre-adult life, including adolescence. For man's psychosocial survival is safeguarded only by virtues which develop in the interplay of successive and overlapping generations, living together in organized settings. Here, living together means more than incidental proximity: it means that the individual's life-stages are "interliving," cogwheeling with the stages of others which move him along as he moves them. I have, therefore, in recent years, attempted to delineate the whole life cycle as an integrated psychosocial phenomenon, (see also 13) instead of following what (in analogy to teleology) may be called the "originological" approach, that is, the attempt to derive the meaning of development primarily from a reconstruction of the infant's beginnings.

When it finally comes to naming the basic virtues, with which human beings steer themselves and others along the path of life, one is at first tempted to make up new words out of Latin roots. Latin always suggests expertness and explicitness, while everyday words have countless connotations: to optimists they make virtues sound like gay and easy accomplishments, and, to pessimists, like idealistic pretenses. Yet, when we approach phenomena closer to the ego, the everyday words of living languages, ripened in the usage of generations, will serve best as a means of discourse.

I will, therefore, speak of *Hope, Will, Purpose,* and *Skill,* as the rudiments of virtue developed in childhood; of *Fidelity* as an adolescent virtue; and of *Love, Care,* and *Wisdom,* as the central virtues of adulthood. In all their seeming discontinuity, these qualities depend on each other: will cannot be trained, until hope is secure, nor love become reciprocal, until fidelity has proven reliable. Also, each virtue and its place in the schedule of all virtues, is vitally interrelated to other segments of human development, such as the stages of psychosexuality (13, 9, 15), the psychosocial crises (7, 16), and the steps of cognitive maturation (17, 18). These schedules I must take for granted, as I restrict myself to a parallel timetable of the evolving virtues....

3. Hope

If we ascribe to the healthy infant the rudiments of Hope, it would, indeed, be hard to specify the criteria for this state, and harder to measure it: yet, he who has seen a hopeless child, knows what is *not* there. Hope is both the earliest and the most indispensable virtue inherent in the state of being alive (19). Others have called this deepest quality confidence, and I have referred to trust as the earliest positive psychosocial attitude: but, if life is to be sustained, hope must remain even where confidence is wounded, trust impaired. Clinicians know that an adult who has lost all hope, regresses into as lifeless a state as a living organism can sustain. But there is something in the anatomy even of mature Hope which suggests that it is the most childlike of all ego-qualities, and the most dependent for its verification on the charity of fate; wherefore religious sentiment induces adults to restore their hopefulness in periodic petitionary prayer, assuming a measure of childlikeness toward unseen, omnipotent powers.

Nothing in *human* life, however, is secured in its origin unless it is verified in the intimate meeting of partners in favorable social settings. Thus, the rudiments of hope rely on the new being's first encounter with *trustworthy maternal persons* who respond to his instinctive reach for *intake* and *contact* with appropriate envelopment, and provision, and prevent experiences of the kind which all too regularly bring too little too late.

Hope thus rests its case on a combination of experiences in the individual's "prehistoric" era, the time before speech and verbal memory. Both psychoanalysis and genetic psychology consider central in that period of growth the secure apperception of an "object": by which the psychologists mean the ability to perceive the *enduring quality* of the *thing world* while psychoanalysts speak loosely of a first inner love-object, i.e. the experience of the caretaking person as a *coherent being,* who reciprocates one's physical and emotional needs in expectable ways and therefore deserves to be endowed with trust.

Hope, once established as a basic quality of experience, remains independent of the verifiability of *hopes*: for it is in the nature of man's maturation, that concrete hopes will, at a time when a hoped for event or state comes to pass, prove to have been quietly superseded by a more advanced set of hopes. The gradual widening of the infant's horizon of active experience provides, at each step, verifications which inspire new hopefulness. Even as the infant learns to renounce and to repress (with all the profound consequences uncovered by psychoanalysis), he also learns to dream of what is imaginable and to train his expectations on what promises to prove possible. All in all, then, maturing hopefulness not only maintains itself in the face of changed facts—it proves itself able to change facts, even as faith is said to move mountains.

The evolutionary character of Hope becomes apparent if we consider that it must help man to approximate that rootedness possessed by the animal world, in which instinctive equipment and environment, moment for moment, verify each other, unless catastrophe overtakes the individual or the species. To the human infant, his mother *is* nature; she must *be* that original verification, which, later, will come from other and wider segments of reality.[2]

All the self-verifications, however, begin in that inner light of the mother-child world, which Madonna images have conveyed as so exclusive and so secure: and, indeed, such light must shine through the chaos of many crises, maturational and accidental.

4. Will

An exclusive condition of hopefulness, translated into various imaginable worlds, would be a paradise in nature, an Utopia in social reality, and a heaven in the beyond. Yet, hope leads man inexorably into conflicts between the rapidly developing self-will, and the will of others. As the infant's senses and his muscles grab at opportunities for more active experience, he faces the double-demand for self-control and for the acceptance of the control of others: he must learn to *will* what *can* be, and to convince himself that he *willed* what *had* to be.

Here, no doubt, is the genetic origin of the elusive question of Free Will, which man, ever again, attempts to master logically and theologically. The fact is that no person can live, no ego remain intact without hope and will. Even philosophical man who feels motivated to challenge the very ground he stands on by questioning both will and hope as illusory, feels more real for having willed such heroic inquiry; and where man chooses to surrender his sense of having willed the inevitable to imagined gods and appointed leaders, he fervently endows them with what he has renounced for himself.

The rudiments of Will are acquired, in analogy to all basic qualities, as the ego unifies experiences on fronts seemingly remote from each other: awareness and attention, verbalization, manupulation and locomotion. The training of the eliminative sphincters, too, can become the center of the struggle over inner and outer control. A sense of defeat (from inadequate or over-training) can lead to deep shame and a compulsive doubt whether one ever really willed what one did, or really did what one willed.

If will is built securely into the early development of the ego it survives, as hope does, the evidences of its limited potency: for the maturing individual gradually incorporates a knowledge of what is expectable and what can be expected of him. Often defeated, he nevertheless learns to accept the existential paradox of making decisions which he knows deep down will be predetermined by events, because making decisions is part of the evaluative quality inherent in being alive: ego strength depends, above all, on the sense of having done one's *active part* in the chain of the inevitable.

It is the task of *judicious parenthood* to demonstrate that *good will* ensues from a mutual limitation of wills; it gradually grants a liberating measure of self-control to the child who learns to control wilfulness and to train his willingness.

[2] In what follows I must imply rather than spell out a number of self-verifications on which the strength of the ego depends; among them: 1. *the completion of growth patterns,* and the successful exercise of physical and mental powers; 2. the *consummation of significant relationships* to the point of a mutual engagement or a successful disengagement; 3. the *resolution of maturational crises* with a reintegration of the unity of experience; 4. the *confirmation of the individual's identity* as he gradually takes his place in his culture's technology and tradition.

5. Purpose

It is inherent in infantile man's prolonged immaturity that he must train the rudiments of Will in situations in which he does not quite know what he wants and why—which makes his wilfulness at times rather desperate. By the same token he must develop in "mere" phantasy and play the rudiments of *Purpose*, a temporal perspective giving direction and focus to concerted striving. Play is to the child what thinking, planning, and blueprinting are to the adult: a trial universe in which conditions are simplified, and methods exploratory, so that past failures can be thought through, expectations tested. In the toy world, the child "plays out" the past, often in disguised form, in the manner of dreams (9, 20); and he begins to master the future, by *anticipating* it in countless variations of repetitive themes. In taking the various role-images of his elders into *his* sphere of *make-believe*, he can find out what it feels like to be like them before fate forces him to become like some of them.

It may well be the evolutionary function of infantile play (and later, of drama) that it affords an intermediate reality in which the budding sense of purposefulness can disengage itself from the fixation on the past by giving it a mythological order and quality. It seems significant that play is most intense when the period of "infantile sexuality" comes to an end and when the great barrier the universal "incest-taboo," is met. The direction of sexual drives and of purposeful energies must now be diverted from the very parental persons who first awakened the child's tenderness, sensuality, and amorphous sexual phantasies.

Play, in young animals, too, is predicated upon parental protection from hunger and from danger. In man, it is, furthermore, dependent on the protection from unmanageable conflict (9). The play age relies on the existence of the *basic family* in one of its exemplary forms, which must gradually delineate where play ends and irreversible purpose begins, where phantasy is no longer permissible and to-be-learned reality all-demanding: only thus, conscience is integrated. It is not always understood that one of the main rationales for marital and familial loyalty and morals is the imperative need for the inner unity of the child's conscience at the very time when he can and must envisage goals beyond the family: for the voices and images of those adults who are now internalized as an *inner voice* must not contradict each other too flagrantly, and, in fact, must speak *the same language*. Only the safe inner development of a rudimental conscience, can, in turn, give the child the inner freedom to move onto whatever school setting his culture has ready for him.

Purposefulness is now ready to attach itself to a sense of reality which is defined by what *can be attained* and by what can be *shared in words*. Conscience, the consistent inner voice which delineates permissible action and thought, finds a powerful ally in the structure of *language*, which makes reality an order verbally shared and subject to joint mastery.

6. Skill

Ever since his "expulsion from paradise," man has been inclined to protest work as drudgery or as slavery, and to consider most fortunate those who seemingly can choose to work or not to work. The fact is that man *must* learn to work, as soon as his intelligence and his capacities are ready to be "put to work," so that his ego's powers may not atrophy.

The rudiments of *skill* add method to hope, will and purpose. Now, what "works" in the fabric of one's thought and in cooperative encounters: a self-verification of lasting importance. All human environments, therefore, meet this stage with the offer of instruction in *perfectable skills* leading to *practical uses* and *significant achievements*. All cultures have their logic and their "truth," which can be learned, by exercise, usage, and ritual. Where literacy is a common basis for all future specialization, the rules of grammar and of algebra, of course, form a more abstract demonstration of the workings of reality. Thus *workmanship* and the *reasonableness* which comes from convincing experience prepare in the child a future sense of *competency* without which there can be no "strong ego." Without it man feels inferior in his equipment, and in the hope to match an ever increasing section of manageable reality with his growing capacities.

7. Fidelity

When man's genitality matures in puberty, he is not yet ready to be a mate or a parent. His ego balance is, in fact, decidedly endangered by the double uncertainty of a demanding instinctual machinery which must be kept in abeyance in some of its functions[3] while he must prepare for his own place in the adult order. The adolescent thus often appears to be a contradictory combination of shifting devotion and general perversity: at times more devotedly perverse, at others more perversely devoted. In all of this, however, an "ideological" seeking after an inner coherence and a durable set of values can always be detected. I have, in a series of books and papers, described many aspects of this "sense of identity" (7, 9, 10, 16) and I would now call the particular ego-quality which emerges with it and from it, *fidelity*. This word combines a number of truths to which adolescents alternately adhere: high *accuracy* and *veracity* in the rendering of reality; the sentiment of truth, as in *sincerity* and *conviction*; the quality of genuineness, as in *authenticity*; the trait of *loyalty*, of "being true"; *fairness* to the rules of the game; and finally all that is implied in *devotion*: a freely given but binding vow, with the fateful implication of a curse befalling the undedicated. When Hamlet, the emotional victim of his royal parents' faithlessness, poses the question "To be or not to be," he demonstrates in word and deed, that to him *To be* is contingent on being loyal (to the Self, to Love, to the Crown) and that the rest is death. Cultures, societies, religions, offer the adolescent the nourishment of some truth in rites and rituals of *confirmation* as a member of a totem, a clan, or a faith, a nation or a class, which henceforth is to be his super-family; in modern times we also find powerful ideologies which claim and receive the loyalty (and, if demanded, an early death) from youth.

Thus one could say that societies "meet the needs" of youth. Here, however, the principle of complementary needs must be stated more explicitly. As cultures, through graded training, enter into the fiber of the individual, they also absorb into their lifeblood the rejuvenative power of youth. Adolescence is thus a vital regenerator in the process of social evolution: for youth selectively offers its loyalties and energies to the conservation of what feels true to them and to the correction or destruction of that which has lost its regenerative significance.

Loyal and legal are kindred words. He who can be loyal can bind himself legally (or decide to remain deviant in his insistence on new laws). As the young adult selects those who in turn will select him—as friends, mates, co-workers—he completes the foundation for adult virtues. His identity and his style of fidelity define his place in what history had determined as his environment.

8. Love

There must clearly be an important evolutionary function in the selectivity of sexual love: I think it is the mutual search for a

[3] By complete abstinence; by sexual release without the involvement of another; by emotional love without sexual involvement; by sexual license without genital involvement; by genital involvement without procreative commitment.

shared identity, for the mutual verification through an experience of finding oneself, as one loses oneself, in another. While many forms of love can be shown to be at work in the formation of the various virtues, it is important to realize that only graduation from adolescence permits the development of that intimacy, that selflessness of joined devotion which anchors love in a mutual commitment. Intimate love thus is the guardian of that elusive and yet all-pervasive power in psychosocial evolution: the power of cultural and personal *style*—which gives and demands conviction in the shared patterns of living and thus guarantees individual identity in joint intimacy. All of this, and, alas, no less, is necessary for the human equivalent of those rituals by which birds select each other for mating and nesting. That in man various kinds of "love," rather than instinctive certainty, must animate his affiliations and associations, is at least one reason for his clannish adherence to styles (national, religious, economic) which he will defend "as if his life depended on them." His ego's coherence, his certainty of orientation *does* depend on them; wherefore *ego-panic* can make man "go blind" with a rage which induces him, in the "righteous" defense of an endangered identity, (religious or national, racial or ideological) to sink to levels of sadism for which there seems to be no parallel in the animal world.

Entrance into adulthood is marked by "genitality," the capacity for a full and mutual consummation of the sexual act. An immense power of verification pervades this meeting of bodies and temperaments after the hazardously long childhood, which, as the study of neuroses has revealed in detail, can severely prejudice the capacity for psychosexual mutuality. Freud observed that mature genitality alone guarantees that combination (by no means easily acquired, nor easily maintained) of intellectual clarity, sexual mutuality, and considerate love, which anchors man in reality.

The word "affiliation" means to adopt somebody as a son—and, indeed, in friendships and partnerships young adults become sons of each other: but sons by a free choice which verifies a long hope for kindredness beyond (incestuous) blood-bonds. From here on, ego-strength depends on an affiliation with others equally whole and this means, by the nature of things, soon equally ready and able to share in the task of *caring* for offspring, products, and ideas.

9. Care

Care (in all the various meanings of *caritas*) is a quality essential for psychosocial evolution: for we are the teaching species. Animals, too, instinctively encourage in their young what is ready for release; and, of course, some animals can be taught some tricks and services by man. Only man, however, can and must extend his solicitude over the long, parallel, and overlapping childhoods of numerous offspring united in households and communities. As he transmits the rudiments of hope, will, purpose and skill, he imparts meaning to the child's bodily experiences; he conveys a logic much beyond the literal meaning of the words he teaches; and he gradually outlines a particular world image and style of citizenship. All of this is necessary to complete in man, the analogy to the basic ethological situation between parent animal and young animal: all this, and no less, makes us comparable to the ethologist's goose and gosling. Once we have grasped this interlocking of the human life-stages, we understand that adult man is so constituted as to *need to be needed* lest he suffer the mental deformation of self-absorption, in which he becomes his own infant and pet. I have, therefore, postulated an instinctual and psychosocial stage of "generativity." Parenthood is, for most, the first, and for many, the prime generative encounter (21); yet, the next generation challenges the generative ingenuity of workers and thinkers of many kinds.

It is, at this vital point, that asceticism goes its own way, to face death prematurely, and yet, where it achieves integrity, it returns with a message of the unity of and of charity toward *all* life. Here, also great philosophers make their "great renunciation" paired with utmost responsibility toward mankind as a whole; while small philosophers try to save their own, their one and only, existential hide.

Modern man, forced to limit his fertility, is apt to consider the matter of procreative involvement resolved by the technical possibility of making a conscious choice in the matter of fertilization. Yet clinical impressions suggest that an ever so "safe" love life, if accompanied by a denial of generativity, can be the source of the specific guilt of playing with the "fire of creation." It is essential, therefore, that the control of procreation be guided not only by an acknowledgment of man's psychosexual needs, but also by a universal sense of generative responsibility toward all those brought more planfully into this world. Such care includes the guarantee to each child of a chance for such development as we are outlining here.

Generativity, however, in the form of a selfless "caring" and a need to "take care" of whatever one generates and leaves to the next generation, potentially extends to whatever a man creates and produces (or helps to produce). The ideological polarization in the western world which has made Freud the the theorist of sex and Marx that of work, has, until quite recently, left a whole area of man's mind uncharted in psychoanalysis. I refer to man's love for his works and ideas as well as for his children, and the necessary self-verification which adult man's ego receives, and must receive, as he labours to change conditions, and changes himself under the impact of the challenge of his own labour. As adult man needs to be needed, so for the strength of his ego and for that of his community he requires the challenge emanating from what he has generated and from what now must be "brought up," guarded, preserved, and eventually transcended.[4] Man's creation of all-caring gods is not only an expression of his persisting infantile need for being taken care of, but also a projection on a superhuman agency of an ego-ideal: this agency must be strong enough to guide (or at least forgive) man's propensity for freely causing events and creating conditions which, ever again, prove to be beyond him. It is obvious, however, that man must learn to accept the responsibiltiy which evolution has given him, and must learn not only to develop, but also to understand and planfully restrain, his capacity for unlimited change.

10. Wisdom

Psychosocial evolution with its biological and technical advances, has not only elongated man's childhood, but also his life-expectancy beyond the period of procreative power. In man's family or community, the toothless oldster lives next door to the toothless baby, and the signs and signals both of the beginning and of the end exert a deep influence on the search for meaning in those in between.

Ego-strength in the old takes the form of *wisdom* in all of its connotations from ripened "wits" to matured judgment, which constitute the ability to maintain the *wholeness of experience* even as the body's faculties gradually fall "apart" and again

[4] Freud was our century's theorist of sex, as Marx was of work, and they had some common denominators in Darwin's evolutionary theories. Future historians may see in perspective the ideological antagonism which has developed as Marxism went all political and psychoanalysis all psychiatric, with a resulting emphasis on *consciousness* and *production* on the one hand, and the *unconscious* and *reproduction*, on the other—strange, indeed, since both men have striven to prove that man's innermost motivations are determined by his condition: economic and historical in Marx's interpretation, psychological and, as it were, life-historical in Freud's.

become a conglomerate of parts which now weaken (as they once matured) at different rates. If vigor of mind combines with the gift of responsible renunciation, some old people can envisage human problems in their entirety (which is what *integrity* means) and come to represent to the coming generation a living example of the "closure" of a style of life. Only such integrity can balance the despair of a limited life coming to a conscious conclusion.

Our society, taught by the "century of the child" that it is not enough to keep children alive, now learns the same truth about its old people. As children were brought up, according to the maturation of their various parts, so old people myst be "let down" gradually, according to their declining faculties, while their wisdom and experience is recognized and cultivated. This is not just a humanitarian duty but a humanist obligation; for the expectation, now aroused in many children by the evidence of daily living, namely, that man's prolonged life may only mean the return in old age of a new kind of childishness, can only weaken their own vital fiber. Any span of the cycle lived without vigorous meaning, at the beginning, in the middle, or at the end, endangers the sense of life and the meaning of death in all whose life stages are intertwined.

11. Conclusion

Our survey suggests an *evolutionary scheme*: the stages of childhood have evolved in a pattern which permits the maturing ego, under the protection of the adult environment, to integrate those part-functions (biological, mental, emotional) which secure a measure of psychosocial adaptation. Man, not guided by a comprehensive and conclusive set of instincts, must *learn* to *wish* strongly, learn to *control* himself securely, learn to give *direction* to his imagination, and learn to acquire *methods* for his direction; and he must finally learn to bind all these with *devotion*. All this, ego-defense must guard, and virtue fortify. Hope, Will, and Purpose provide the human animal with the strength to live in the space-time of human existence: Hope provides the long-range vision which replaces the animal's immediate certainty; Will, the psychological backbone for man's physical and moral "uprightness," his "standing on his own two feet"; and Purpose directs to a new variety of goals the energies of the bipedal hunter with special powers of visual perception. Finally, Skill develops man's tool-using capacities, his reason, and his speech. But if man had all this, and had not Fidelity, he would not be able to attain his specific integrity: therefore, his need for styles of truth.

The cogwheeling stages of childhood and adulthood are, as we can see in conclusion, truly a system of *generation* and *regeneration*—for into this system flow, and from this system emerge those attitudes which find permanent structure in the great *social institutions*. . . .

Thus the virtues, far from being ornaments to be reflected upon in front of the mirror, or traits easily accounted for in tests, are deeply rooted in evolution and in unconscious processes to which we are finding access only in our time. From here, we must gain new understanding of the virtues called natural, or cardinal.

It is probable that the *vices* corresponding to our schedule of virtues are to be found in the array of inner states which reveal themselves in psycho-pathological symptoms. In recent decades, they have been studied in much detail: we would recognize, for example, an inner affinity between the loss of hope and the nature of delusion and addiction, between the impairment of will, and the structure of obsession and compulsion. As the transgressions called deadly, the symptoms called malignant indicate the forfeiture of "ecological integrity" in man.

An attempt to abstract any ground plan is an invitation to the reproach that one contributes to the fetish of norms, neglects diversities and thus undermines individuality. I must admit the neglect of one major diversity: that of the two sexes. Yet, as clearly pervasive as sex-differences are in all aspects of life (20), the ego's development and function is relatively similar in the two sexes; which may contribute to the fact that in old age men and women look, think, and feel more alike than in any other period—except in infancy. As to individuality, there is no need to worry: we cannot dictate deadly conformity to the life processes—they themselves will lead to more diversity than we can comfortably manage with our thoughts, our plans, and our cures. And so will man's idiosyncratic reaction to the diversity of conditions: in an evolutionary setting, we can ascribe a long range meaning to the idiosyncratic individualist and the deviant as well as to the conformist: for all healthy individualism and devoted deviancy contains an indignation in the service of a *to-be-restored* wholeness without which psychosocial evolution would be doomed—even as biological evolution would have been doomed without deviancy. Thus, one may say, *adaptation* has its loyal deviants who refuse to *adjust* to "conditions".

Neither a humanist nor a psychoanalytic view, however, can overlook for a moment that so far in his history man has realized this blueprint only in fragments. There are many reasons for this; in our context we can only say that in the course of the individual's abandonment of his childhood he loses much of his creative childlikeness while he attaches his unresolved childishness to *personal* and *collective projections* on what is *beyond* and *ahead* of him. Seemingly guided and justified by what he calls "great" men and ideas, he is apt to use history to play out past failures and to test the future in dangerous experiments with fate itself. His long (and much exploited) childhood dependence conditions him to an alternation between *total conformity* and *excessive diversity*, leading him to the Utopian expectation that, at last, some absolute wholeness may be secured either to a community that sets itself above the individual or to the individual who considers himself above all community.

The psychoanalytic study of the residues of our evolutionary origins and of our infantile "pre-history" must be extended to *recorded history* (16) and above all to those ideas which have exclusively dominated whole eras of the past: for these ideas, as we can now dimly discern, may well owe their dominance to the fact that they promise masses of men a verification which, by each single individual, is truly experienced as "eternal" because it lifts one of the ego's prime potentials for verification to the level of a promised historical reality.[5] History justly records the triumphs of perfectibility thus attained in certain eras; but it has, on the whole, lacked both the method and the intent to demonstrate the dynamic relation between these triumphs and the ego-distortions and social sacrifices imposed both on the triumphant minorities and the vaguely participant masses.

Where do we stand? In our time, for the first time, one human species can be envisaged, with one common technology on one globe (and a bit of outer space). At the

[5] A glance at the ego verifications enumerated earlier (footnote 2) suggests, that in different historical periods one or the other of these verifications is lifted to the level of exclusive universal values. The ideal of the *perfection of growth patterns* we may recognize in the Greek idea of a *complete harmony* between an excellent body and an excellent mind; the *consummation of interpersonal relationships* in the idea of *perfect Christian Love,* or the mystic consummation of the relationship with God, and, in modern times, in the idea of the all-healing power of the *genital union.* The idea of a *resolution of developmental crises* without any loose ends fits modern man's idea of a *perfect adjustment,* as if developmental crises were that many efficiency tests applied to an organism with accidental flaws in design and production. Finally, the *mutual fittedness* of personality development and social structure, in modern times, dominates the idea of the *perfect state.*

same time, psychological insight has made our consciousness wiser by the recognition of the body's wisdom, of the power of the unconscious, and of the ego's functions and limitations. This increased margin of consciousness, in itself a major step in evolution, enables man to visualize new moral alternatives, and to strive for a perfection both abundant and adaptive which mediates more realistically between his inner and outer world than do the fatal compromises resulting from the reign of moral absolutes. Outworn alternatives may eventually yield to an order, in which deliberate and creative *diversity* is anchored in a common *responsibility* for all of psychosocial evolution.

How this will change the bringing up of children, it is hard to predict and impossible to prescribe: effective pedagogic sentiment emerges from the strength of a lifestyle. But our scheme suggests, for any future lifestyle, a morality based on the responsibility of each individual for the potentialities of all generations, and this in a more informed manner than has ever been possible before. But this means that the men of all fields who concern themselves with human destiny must take care lest their vision remain illusory through that exclusive emphasis on masculine dreams, which has characterized the study of history so far; leaving childhood, the very powerhouse of evolution and tradition, to the educationists.

As we have seen, the individual ego can be strong only through a mutual guarantee of strength given to and received by all whose life cycles intertwine; and it can transcend itself only where it has learned to engage and to disengage itself responsibly from others.

Thus the basic virtues—these miracles of everyday life—seem to provide a test for universal values, and to contain the promise of a possible morality which is self-corrective as it remains adaptive. The study of these virtues, therefore, is indispensable to an appraisal of the process man partakes in, of the stuff he must work with, and of the strength he can count on, as he charts his future course.

REFERENCES

1. Roe, A., & Simpson, G. G., ed., *Behavior and Evolution,* Yale University Press, New Haven, 1958. See especially "Evolution and Human Behavior," by Roe, A., and Freedman, L. Z., and the last sentence of G. G. Simpson's Epilogue.
2. Huxley, T. H., & Huxley, J. S., *Evolution and Ethics,* London Pilot Press, 1947; *Touchstone for Ethics,* New York, Harper, 1947.
3. Freud, S., *The Ego and the Id* (1923), London, Hogarth, 1947.
4. Freud, A., *The Ego and the Mechanisms of Defense,* International Universities Press, New York, 1946.
5. Hartmann, H., *Ego Psychology and the Problem of Adaptation,* International Universities Press, New York, 1958.
6. Rapaport, D., "The Structure of Psychoanalytic Theory: A Systematizing Attempt," in Sigmund Koch (ed.) *Psychology: A Study of a Science,* Vol. III, New York, McGraw-Hill, 1959.
7. Erikson, E. H., *Identity and the Lifecycle,* Monograph, *Psychological Issues,* Vol. I, No. 1, International Universities Press, New York, 1959, with an introduction by Rapaport, D. "A Historical Survey of Psychoanalytic Ego Psychology."
8. Rapaport, D., "Some Metapsychological Considerations Concerning Activity and Passivity" (unpublished) Manuscript 1953.

9. Erikson, E. H., *Childhood and Society,* W. W. Norton, New York, 1950, Imago, London, 1951.
10. Erikson, E. H., *Young Man Luther,* W. W. Norton, New York, 1958, Faber and Faber, London, 1959.
11. Weigert, Edith, "Human Ego Development in the Light of Animal Behavior," *Psychiatry*, 1956.
12. Schiller, Claire H., ed., *Instinctive Behavior: the Development of a Modern Concept.* International Universities Press, New York, 1957. See particularly the contributions of Lorenz, K. and Tinbergen, H.
13. Buehler, Charlotte, *Der menschliche Lebenslauf als psychologisches Problem,* Verlag für Psychologie, Göttingen, 1959.
14. Freud, S., "Three Essays on the Theory of Sexuality," Standard Edition, London, Imago Publishing Co., 1949.
15. Erikson, E. H., "Psychosexual Development," in *Discussions in Child Development,* World Health Organization, Vol. IV, Tavistock Publications Ltd., London, 1961.
16. Erikson, E. H., "The Psychosocial Development of Children," and "The Syndrome of Identity Diffusion in Adolescents and Young Adults" in *Discussions in Child Development*, World Health Organization, Vol. III, Tavistock Publications, Ltd., London, 1956, International Universities Press, New York, 1958.
17. Inhelder, B. and Piaget, J., *The Growth of Logical Thinking from Childhood to Adolescence.* Basic Books, New York, 1958.
18. Wolff, P. H., *The Developmental Psychologies of Jean Piaget and Psychoanalysis.* Monograph, *Psychological Issues,* International Universities Press, 1962.
19. French, T., *The Integration of Behavior,* University of Chicago Press, Chicago, 1952.
20. Mead, Margaret, "The Childhood Genesis of Sex Differences in Behavior," and Erikson, E. H., "Sex Differences in the Play Constructions of Pre-Adolescents," in *Discussions in Child Development,* World Health Organization, Vol. III, Tavistock Publications, Ltd., London, 1956, International Universities Press, New York, 1958.
21. Benedict, Therese, "Parenthood as a Developmental Phase," in *Journal of the American Psychoanalytic Association,* VII, *3*, 1959.

38

A Scientist Looks at Love

Ashley Montagu

The study of love is something from which scientists, until very recently, have shied away. With the increase, however, of interest in the origins of mental illness in this century, more and more attention has begun to be paid to the infancy and childhood of human beings. What has been revealed by these investigations is that love is, without any question, the most important experience in the life of a human being.

What is love? One of the most frequently used words in our vocabulary, the major theme of art in all its aspects, the principal industry of Hollywood and of countless magazines, the thing with which human beings are most concerned all their lives, the most important experience in the world, *love* is something about which most of us, at this late date, are still extremely vague. One has only to ask one's friends what they understand by "love" to discover how unclear the idea remains in the minds of many people. Even when a fair definition is achieved the meaning of love in its full significance is rarely understood.

In this paper I should like to set out some of the findings about the nature and meaning of love as scientists have revealed them.

The dictionary tells us that love is a feeling of deep regard, fondness, and devotion. Robert Louis Stevenson said that love was a passionate kindness. One could go on quoting hundreds of statements about love, and they would all be true as far as they go, but none of them go far enough because while they provide the skeleton, they miss the vital essence of the meaning of love. This essential meaning one can discover only by studying the origins and development of love as they are manifested in small children, in the newborn baby and every stage of childhood, and finally in adolescents and in adults.

There is a widespread belief that a newborn baby is a rather selfish, disorganized, or unorganized, wild kind of creature which would grow into a violently intractable savage if it were not properly disciplined. Contrary to this widely held belief, modern scientists find that far from being such an unorganized barbarian the newborn baby is one of the most highly organized creatures on the face of the earth, and organized not for brattishness but for love.

The newborn baby is organized in an extraordinarily sensitive manner, most delicately attuned to receive all those stimulations which will creatively contribute to its development. Far from wanting to be disciplined in the usual meaning of that word, it wants to be loved. It behaves as if it expected to be loved, and when its expectation is thwarted—that is, frustrated—it behaves in a grievously disappointed manner.

There is now good evidence which leads us to believe that not only does a baby want to be loved, but also that it wants to love, that all its drives are oriented in the direction of receiving and giving love, and that if it doesn't receive love it is unable to give it—as a child or as an adult.

From the moment of birth the baby needs the reciprocal exchange of love with its mother. From the very outset the baby is capable of conferring great benefits upon the mother—*if* the maternal-infant relationship is not disturbed. It has now been thoroughly established that if the baby is left with the mother and put to nurse at her breast, three problems which have bedeviled obstetricians for many years, and what is more important, have been responsible for much tragedy and unhappiness, are in most cases solved at once. These are hemorrhaging from the womb after birth, the beginning return of the uterus to normal size, and the completion of the third stage of labor by the ejection of the placenta. These problems are solved in the majority of instances by putting the baby to nurse at the mother's breast. The hemorrhage is reduced and the uterus begins its return to almost normal size within a matter of minutes, and the placenta becomes detached and is ejected. There are almost certainly other benefits which the nursing baby confers upon the mother, not the least of which are probably psychological. The baby is in turn, of course, also benefited; among other things, such a baby is practically never a feeding problem.

. . . It has, I believe, universally been acknowledged that the mother-infant relationship perhaps more than any other defines the very essence of love. If that is so . . . we may tentatively define love as *the relationship between persons in which they confer mutual benefits upon each other*. This is a broad definition and might be said well to describe the relationship which exists between an insurance company and the insured. Bearing in mind the physiological benefits which accrue to mother and child, perhaps we could try again and state that *love is the relationship between persons which contributes to the welfare and development of each.*

. . . Scientists have learned most about love from the study of the mother-infant relationships. Let us proceed to the discussion of *how* and *what* they have learned about the nature and meaning of love.

Survival is of the first importance, without it nothing else matters, but survival alone is not enough—human beings need and should receive much more. If children are to grow in health and harmony, then they must experience more than the mere physical satisfaction of their needs. A baby is a beginning human being, and his birthright is development—development of his psychological and spiritual as well as his physical potentialities for being human. The mere satisfaction of his physical needs will not bring about such development—such satisfaction may secure survival, but in most cases it is doubtful whether it will even secure that.

We now know that babies which are physically well nurtured may nevertheless waste away and die unless they are also loved. We now know, beyond cavil or question, that love is an essential part of the nourishment of every baby, and that unless human beings in their early stages of development are loved they will not grow and develop as healthy organisms. It has taken the independent observations of a number of physicians and other investigators to ascertain the relationship between the infant's need for love and his capacity to survive.

It may come as a surprise to many readers to learn that because this relationship was not understood during the first two decades of this century, the majority of infants under one year of age who entered hospitals and similar institutions never emerged from them alive. This shocking infant death rate was discussed at a meeting of the American Pediatric Society in 1915. Dr. Henry Chapin reported on ten infant asylums located in the United States in which, with one exception, *every* infant under two years of age died! Dr. R. Hamil of Philadelphia, at the same meeting, remarked with tragic irony that he "had the honor to be connected with an institution in Philadelphia in which the mortality among all the infants under one year of age, when admitted to the institution and retained there for any length of time, was 100 per cent. That is, no infant admitted under one year of age lived to be two years old. . . ."

Many other such reports could be quoted from other American authorities as well as from institutions abroad, but those given above should be enough. In the late twenties Dr. J. Brennemann of New York City recognized the ill effects caused by an absence of mothering and established a rule in his hospital that every baby should be picked up, carried about, amused, and "mothered" several times a day. A most illuminating experience is related by Dr. Fritz Talbot, who visited the Children's Clinic in Düsseldorf, Germany, some fifty years ago. Dr. Talbot noticed a fat old woman wandering about the ward with a baby on her hip. Inquiring of the chief of the Clinic, he was told, "Oh, that's Old Anna. Whenever we have a baby for whom everything we could do has failed, we turn it over to Old Anna. She is always successful."

Drs. Ruth and Harry Bakwin, of Bellevue Hospital Pediatric Division, have graphically described what happens in hospitals as a result of the lacklove experiences which children undergo there:

> The effect of residence in a hospital manifests itself by a fairly well-defined clinal picture. A striking feature is the failure to gain properly, despite the ingestion of diets which are entirely adequate for growth in the home. Infants in hospitals sleep less than others and they rarely smile or babble spontaneously. They are listless and apathetic and look unhappy. The appetite is indifferent and food is accepted without enthusiasm.

The emotional deprivation suffered by infants in hospitals may do vastly more damage than the physical condition which brought them there. The infant can suffer no greater loss than the privation of its mother's love.

There have been several important studies of the effects of the absence of mother-love within the past decade. Dr. Rene Spitz of New York City has reported on children confined in two different institutions. They were studied simultaneously during the first year of life. Both institutions were adequate in all physical respects, providing equivalent housing, asepsis, food, and hygiene. In both, infants were admitted shortly after birth. The institutions differed in but one factor—the amount of affection offered. In the first institution, called "Nursery," the infants were cared for by their own mothers. In the second institution, called "Foundlinghome," the children were raised from the third month by overworked nursing personnel, each nurse in charge of from eight to twelve children. The absence or presence of emotional interchange between mother and child formed the one independent condition in the comparison of the two groups.

The response to this condition showed up in many ways, but perhaps most comprehensively in what is called the Developmental Quotient. The Developmental Quotient represents a measure of the total development of six sectors of the personality: mastery of perception, bodily functions, social relations, memory and imitation, manipulative ability, and intelligence. At the end of the first year, though the "Foundlinghome" infants had a developmental quotient of 124 to start with, and the "Nursery" infants a developmental quotient of 101.5, the deprived

"Foundlinghome" infants declined to a developmental quotient of 72, while the "Nursery" infants rose to 105. At the end of the second year the D.Q. had fallen in the "Foundlinghome" group to an astonishing low of 45!

As Dr. Spitz remarks:

> We have here an impressive example of how the absence of one psychosocial factor, that of emotional interchange with the mother, results in a complete reversal of a developmental trend.
>
> It should be realized that the factor which was present in the first case but eliminated in the second, is the pivot of all development in the first year. It is the mother-child relation. By choosing this factor as our independent variable we were able to observe its vital importance. While the children in "Nursery" developed into normal healthy toddlers, a two-year observation of "Foundlinghome" showed that the emotionally starved children never learned to speak, to walk, to feed themselves. With one or two exceptions in a total of 91 children, those who survived were human wrecks who behaved either in the manner of agitated or apathetic idiots.

A comparison of the mortality rates in the two institutions is striking and significant. During five years of observation involving 239 children who had been institutionalized for one year or more, "Nursery" did not lose a single child through death; whereas in "Foundlinghome" 37 per cent of the children died during a two years' observation period. Death, Dr. Spitz states, is but an extreme consequence of the general physiological and psychological decline which affects children completely starved of emotional interchange.

The mother does not necessarily have to be the biological mother of the child; any human being whether female or male, as long as he is capable of giving the child love, may be the equivalent of the real mother. All investigators are agreed that the importance of the mother—biological or surrogate—lies in the fact that she is the first representative of humanity with whom the child comes into association and through whom it usually receives the satisfaction or expects to receive the satisfaction of its needs. The child constructs its picture of the world largely through the experience it has with its mother. According as the mother is loving or unloving, the child will feel that the world is loving or unloving.

Endowed at birth with all the necessary drives for developing as a loving harmonic human being, the child learns to love by being loved. When it is not loved it fails to learn to love, but responds instead with protesting behavior, with rage and aggression, then with despair, and finally with the abandonment of all faith and hope in human beings. These are not mere statements concocted out of a desk thinker's head, but the conclusions of the workers at The International Children's Centre in Paris under the leadership of Drs. John Bowlby and Jenny Roudinesco. Such children, the children who have not been adequately loved, grow up to be persons who find it extremely difficult to understand the meaning of love; they are awkward in their human relationships, "cold fish," they tend to be thoughtless and inconsiderate; they have little emotional depth; hence they are able to enter into all sorts of human relationships in a shallow way and drift from one marriage to another with the greatest of emotional ease. They are "affectionless characters" who suffer from a hunger for affection. Awkward and ineffectual in their attempts to secure it, they often suffer rejection and end up by becoming more embittered than ever, finding themselves in the paradoxical situation of hating people because they want to love them, but having attempted to love them have been repulsed, and so end up by hating them.

We are now, perhaps, in a better position to understand the meaning and importance of love for human beings and for humanity. Nothing in the world can be more important or as significant. Let us, then, set out the characteristics as best we can, of love—the conditions which must be fulfilled if we are to agree that the state of love exists.

1. Love is not only a subjective feeling which one has, an emotion, but a series of acts by means of which one conveys to another the feeling that one is deeply involved, profoundly interested, in him and in his welfare. In this sense love is demonstrative, it is sacrificial, it is self-abnegative. It always puts the other first. It is not a cold or calculated altruism, but a feeling of deep involvement in the other.

2. Love is unconditional, it makes no bargains, it trades with no one for anything, but conveys the feeling, the in-the-bones belief to the other that you are all for him, that you are there to give him your support, to contribute to his development as best you can, because the other is what he is, *not* because he is something you want or expect him to be, but because you value him for what he is as he is.

3. Love is supportative, it conveys to the other that you will never commit that supreme of all the treasons that one human being can commit against another, namely, to let him down when he most needs you. Love promises that you will always be present to support the other, no matter what the conditions you will never fail him; that you will neither condemn nor condone, but that you will always be there to offer your sympathy and your understanding, and that whatever the other needs as a human being he shall have, even though it may be a firm no. Love means that you will be there to help him say yes to life, and to have all his needs for love satisfied.

From the evidence thus far available it seems clear that love is indispensably necessary for the healthy development of the individual. Love is the principal developer of one's capacity for being human, it is the chief stimulus to the development of social competence, and the only thing in the world that can produce that sense of belongingness and relatedness to the world of humanity which every healthy human being develops. And what is health? Health is the ability to love and the ability to work. And what is love? Love is the quality which confers survival benefits upon others, and upon oneself, in a creatively enlarging manner.

SECTION C *Perspectives on Deviance*

Deviance: What is it and why is it so popular? Any formal definition contains the idea of socially disapproved action, but that is only half the story. Standards of behavior shift more rapidly than laws that circumscribe behavior. There are deviant groups or subcultures that are accepted, with restrictions, as part of the larger culture, but not acceptable by the existing laws.

An act is usually defined as deviant only if others not doing the act classify it as deviant. Other variables that should be taken into account are the age of the deviant (driving, drinking, and making love are all deviant acts at the wrong age), the social class of the deviant (the rich are allowed a greater range of behavior), and the social position of the deviant (blacks are prosecuted more often than whites for similar transgressions).

Deviance is a relative question, a situation where shifting standards are common. Still, the deviant personality and the deviant act intrigue and fascinate us. This fascination is both the urge to share the excitement and possible danger within the subculture, but it is also an expression of a lack of understanding of the motivation that leads citizens to commit deviant acts.

In this section I have not included selections describing the well accepted deviant classes—the criminal, the prostitute, or the juvenile offender. Instead the selections focus on deviant activities where the moral codes are fuzzy or in the process of clarification. The initial article by Howard Becker on marihuana users suggests that deriving much effect from marihuana takes some practice. Classed as a deviant act, it is punishable by extensive prison terms and fines in most states. A large number of federal and state agents work at preventing the use of this drug. On the other hand there are perhaps ten million Americans who have used or are using this substance in their social life. Most are students or middle class college graduates. One question is, who is deviant and by whose standards? A better understanding of this and other situations comes primarily through perceiving the cultural framework in which the deviant act is embedded.

The second selection is a straightforward look at race track gamblers. Gambling is a deviant behavior but also an accepted behavior. When is it considered pathological? When is it considered appropriate? No simple answer exists.

William Helmer's article looks in on a subculture of homosexuals.

This deviant behavior is not isolated from our culture as much as it exists and flourishes because of our culture. The interrelatedness is one of the questions that makes the definition of deviance such a tricky one.

The final article on police violence concludes that apparently illegal violence is part of the way the police operate and that while it is officially opposed, it will in fact continue. Is it, therefore, deviant to be a violent policeman or is it part of the way the larger culture has defined the role of the policeman in the first place?

It appears that no deviance goes totally unsupported by the structure and ideology of the entire culture. Implicitly, therefore, the responsibility for both the central thread of morality and the deviant offshoots are part of our collective responsibility. Our interest in deviance, I suggest, is only another facet of our abiding interest in ourselves.

39

Becoming a Marihuana User

Howard S. Becker

An unknown, but probably quite large, number of people in the United States use marihuana. They do this in spite of the fact that it is both illegal and disapproved.

The phenomenon of marihuana use has received much attention, particularly from psychiatrists and law enforcement officials. The research that has been done, as is often the case with research on behavior that is viewed as deviant, is mainly concerned with the question: why do they do it? Attempts to account for the use of marihuana lean heavily on the premise that the presence of any particular kind of behavior in an individual can best be explained as the result of some trait which predisposes or motivates him to engage in that behavior. In the case of marihuana use, this trait is usually identified as psychological, as a need for fantasy and escape from psychological problems the individual cannot face.[1]

I do not think such theories can adequately account for marihuana use. In fact, marihuana use is an interesting case for

[1] See, as examples of this approach, the following: Eli Marcovitz and Henry J. Meyers, "The Marihuana Addict in the Army," *War Medicine*, VI (December, 1944), 382–391; Herbert S. Gaskill, "Marihuana, an Intoxicant," *American Journal of Psychiatry*, CII (September, 1945), 202–204; Sol Charen and Luis Perelman, "Personality Studies of Marihuana Addicts," *American Journal of Psychiatry*, CII (March, 1946), 674–682.

theories of deviance, because it illustrates the way deviant motives actually develop in the course of experience with the deviant activity. To put a complex argument in a few words: instead of the deviant motives leading to the deviant behavior, it is the other way around; the deviant behavior in time produces the deviant motivation. Vague impulses and desires—in this case, probably most frequently a curiosity about the kind of experience the drug will produce—are transformed into definite patterns of action through the social interpretation of a physical experience which is in itself ambiguous. Marihuana use is a function of the individual's conception of marihuana and of the uses to which it can be put, and this conception develops as the individual's experience with the drug increases.[2]

The research reported in this and the next chapter deals with the career of the marihuana user. In this chapter, we look at the development of the individual's immediate physical experience with marihuana. In the next, we consider the way he reacts to the various social controls that have grown up around use of the drug. What we are trying to understand here is the sequence of changes in attitude and experience which lead to *the use of marihuana for pleasure*. This way of phrasing the problem requires a little explanation. Marihuana does not produce addiction, at least in the sense that alcohol and the opiate drugs do. The user experiences no withdrawal sickness and exhibits no ineradicable craving for the drug.[2] The most frequent pattern of use might be termed "recreational." The drug is used occasionally for the pleasure the user finds in it, a relatively casual kind of behavior in comparison with that connected with the use of addicting drugs. The report of the New York City Mayor's Committee on Marihuana emphasizes this point:

> A person may be a confirmed smoker for a prolonged period, and give up the drug voluntarily without experiencing any craving for it or exhibiting withdrawal symptoms. He may, at some time later on, go back to its use. Others may remain infrequent users of the cigarette, taking one or two a week, or only when the "social setting" calls for participation. From time to time we had one of our investigators associate with a marihuana user. The investigator would bring up the subject of smoking. This would invariably lead to the suggestion that they obtain some marihuana cigarettes. They would seek a "teapad," and if it was closed the smoker and our investigator would calmly resume their previous activity, such as the discussion of life in general or the playing of pool. There were apparently no signs indicative of frustration in the smoker at not being able to gratify the desire for the drug. We consider this point highly significant since it is so contrary to the experience of users of other narcotics. A similar situation occurring in one addicted to the use of morphine, cocaine or heroin would result in a compulsive attitude on the part of the addict to obtain the drug. If unable to secure it, there would be obvious physical and mental manifestations of frustration. This may be considered presumptive evidence that there is no true addiction in the medical sense associated with the use of marihuana.[4]

In using the phrase "use for pleasure," I mean to emphasize the noncompulsive and casual character of the behavior. (I also mean to eliminate from consideration here those few cases in which marihuana is used for its prestige value only, as a symbol that one is a certain kind of person, with no

[2] This theoretical point of view stems from George Herbert Mead's discussion of objects in *Mind, Self, and Society* (Chicago: University of Chicago Press, 1934), pp. 277–280.

[3] Cf. Rogers Adams, "Marihuana," *Bulletin of the New York Academy of Medicine,* XVIII (November, 1942), 705–730.

[4] The New York City Mayor's Committee on Marihuana, *The Marihuana Problem in the City of New York* (Lancaster, Pennsylvania: Jacques Cattell Press, 1944), pp. 12–13.

pleasure at all being derived from its use.)

The research I am about to report was not so designed that it could constitute a crucial test of the theories that relate marihuana use to some psychological trait of the user. However, it does show that psychological explanations are not in themselves sufficient to account for marihuana use and that they are, perhaps, not even necessary. Researchers attempting to prove such psychological theories have run into two great difficulties, never satisfactorily resolved, which the theory presented here avoids. In the first place, theories based on the existence of some predisposing psychological trait have difficulty in accounting for that group of users, who turn up in sizable numbers in every study,[5] who do not exhibit the trait or traits which are considered to cause the behavior. Second, psychological theories have difficulty in accounting for the great variability over time of a given individual's behavior with reference to the drug. The same person will at one time be unable to use the drug for pleasure, at a later stage be able and willing to do so, and still later again be unable to use it in this way. These changes, difficult to explain from a theory based on the user's needs for "escape" are readily understandable as consequences of changes in his conception of the drug. Similarly, if we think of the marihuana user as someone who has learned to view marihuana as something that can give him pleasure, we have no difficulty in understanding the existence of psychologically "normal" users.

In doing the study, I used the method of analytic induction. I tried to arrive at a general statement of the sequence of changes in individual attitude and experience which always occurred when the individual became willing and able to use marihuana for pleasure, and never occurred or had not been permanently maintained when the person was unwilling to use marihuana for pleasure. The method requires that *every* case collected in the research substantiate the hypothesis. If one case is encountered which does not substantiate it, the researcher is required to change the hypothesis to fit the case which has proven his original idea wrong.[6]

To develop and test my hypothesis about the genesis of marihuana use for pleasure, I conducted fifty interviews with marihuana users. I had been a professional dance musician for some years when I conducted this study and my first interviews were with people I had met in the music business. I asked them to put me in contact with other users who would be willing to discuss their experiences with me. Colleagues working on a study of users of opiate drugs made a few interviews available to me which contained, in addition to material on opiate drugs, sufficient material on the use of marihuana to furnish a test of my hypothesis.[7] Although in the end half of the fifty interviews were conducted with musicians, the other half covered a wide range of people, including laborers, machinists, and people in the professions. The sample is, of course, in no sense "random"; it would not be possible to draw a random sample, since no one knows the nature of the universe from which it would have to be drawn.

In interviewing users, I focused on the history of the person's experience with marihuana, seeking major changes in his attitude toward it and in his actual use of it, and the reasons for these changes. Where

[5] Cf. Lawrence Kolb, "Marihuana," *Federal Probation*, II (July, 1938), 22–25; and Walter Brombreg, "Marihuana,: A Psychiatric Study," *Journal of the American Medical Association*, CXIII (July 1, 1939), 11.

[6] The method is described in Alfred R. Lindesmith, *Opiate Addiction* (Bloomington, Indiana: Principia Press, 1947), chap. 1. There has been considerable discussion of this method in the literature. See, particularly, Ralph H. Turner, "The Quest for Universals in Sociological Research," *American Sociological Review*, 18 (December, 1953), 604–611, and the literature cited there.

[7] I wish to thank Solomon Kobrin and Harold Finestone for making these interviews available to me.

it was possible and appropriate, I used the jargon of the user himself.

The theory starts with the person who has arrived at the point of willingness to try marihuana. (I discuss how he got there in the next chapter.) He knows others use marihuana to "get high," but he does not know what this means in any concrete way. He is curious about the experience, ignorant of what it may turn out to be, and afraid it may be more than he has bargained for. The steps outlined below, if he undergoes them all and maintains the attitudes developed in them, leave him willing and able to use the drug for pleasure when the opportunity presents itself.

Learning the Technique

The novice does not ordinarily get high the first time he smokes marihuana, and several attempts are usually necessary to induce this state. One explanation of this may be that the drug is not smoked "properly," that is, in a way that insures sufficient dosage to produce real symptoms of intoxication. Most users agree that it cannot be smoked like tobacco if one is to get high:

> Take in a lot of air, you know, and . . . I don't know how to describe it, you don't smoke it like a cigarette, you draw in a lot of air and get it deep down in your system and then keep it there. Keep it there as long as you can.

Without the use of some such technique[8] the drug will produce no effects, and the user will be unable to get high:

> The trouble with people like that [who are not able to get high] is that they're just not smoking it right, that's all there is to it. Either they're not holding it down long enough, or they're getting too much air and not enough smoke, or the other way around or something like that. A lot of people just don't smoke it right, so naturally nothing's gonna happen.

If nothing happens, it is manifestly impossible for the user to develop a conception of the drug as an object which can be used for pleasure, and use will therefore not continue. The first step in the sequence of events that must occur if the person is to become a user is that he must learn to use the proper smoking technique so that his use of the drug will produce effects in terms of which his conception of it can change.

Such a change is, as might be expected, a result of the individual's participation in groups in which marihuana is used. In them the individual learns the proper way to smoke the drug. This may occur through direct teaching:

> I was smoking like I did an ordinary cigarette. He said, "No, don't do it like that." He said "Suck, it, you know, draw in and hold it in your lungs till you . . . for a period of time."
>
> I said, "Is there any limit of time to hold it?"
>
> He said, "No, just till you feel that you want to let it out, let it out." So I did that three or four times.

Many new users are ashamed to admit ignorance and, pretending to know already, must learn through the more indirect means of observation and imitation:

> I came on like I had turned on [smoked marihuana] many times before, you know. I didn't want to seem like a punk to this cat. See, like I didn't know the first thing about it—how to smoke it, or what was going to happen, or what. I just watched him like a hawk—I didn't take my eyes off him for a second, because I wanted to do everything just as he did it. I watched how he held it, how he smoked it, and everything. Then when he gave it to me I just

[8] A pharmacologist notes that this ritual is in fact an extremely efficient way of getting the drug into the blood stream. See R. P. Walton, *Marihuana: America's New Drug Problem* (Philadelphia: J. B. Lippincott, 1938), p. 48.

came on cool, as though I knew exactly what the score was. I held it like he did and took a poke just the way he did.

No one I interviewed continued marihuana use for pleasure without learning a technique that supplied sufficient dosage for the effects of the drug to appear. Only when this was learned was it possible for a conception of the drug as an object which could be used for pleasure to emerge. Without such a conception marihuana use was considered meaningless and did not continue.

Learning to Perceive the Effects

Even after he learns the proper smoking technique, the new user may not get high and thus not form a conception of the drug as something which can be used for pleasure. A remark made by a user suggested the reason for this difficulty in getting high and pointed to the next necessary step on the road to being a user:

As a matter of fact, I've seen a guy who was high out of his mind and didn't know it.
[How can that be, man?]
Well, it's pretty strange, I'll grant you that, but I've seen it. This guy got on with me, claiming that he'd never got high, one of those guys, and he got completely stoned. And he kept insisting that he wasn't high. So I had to prove to him that he was.

What does this mean? It suggests that being high consists of two elements: the presence of symptoms caused by marihuana use and the recognition of these symptoms and their connection by the user with his use of the drug. It is not enough, that is, that the effects be present; alone, they do not automatically provide the experience of being high. The user must be able to point them out to himself and consciously connect them with having smoked marihuana before he can have this experience. Otherwise, no matter what actual effects are produced, he considers that the drug has had no effect on him: "I figure it either had no effect on me or other people were exaggerating its effect on them, you know. I thought it was probably psychological, see." Such persons believe the whole thing is an illusion and that the wish to be high leads the user to deceive himself into believing that something is happening when, in fact, nothing is. They do not continue marihuana use, feeling that "it does nothing" for them.

Typically, however, the novice has faith (developed from his observation of users who do get high) that the drug actually will produce some new experience and continues to experiment with it until it does. His failure to get high worries him, and he is likely to ask more experienced users or provoke comments from them about it. In such conversations he is made aware of specific details of his experience which he may not have noticed or may have noticed but failed to identify as symptoms of being high:

I didn't get high the first time. . . . I don't think I held it in long enough. I probably let it out, you know, you're a little afraid. The second time I wasn't sure, and he [smoking companion] told me, like I asked him for some of the symptoms or something, how would I know, you know. . . . So he told me to sit on a stool. I sat on—I think I sat on a bar stool—and he said, "Let your feet hang," and then when I got down my feet were real cold, you know.

And I started feeling it, you know. That was the first time. And then about a week after that, sometime pretty close to it, I really got on. That was the first time I got on a big laughing kick, you know. Then I really knew I was on.

One symptom of being high is an intense hunger. In the next case the novice becomes aware of this and gets high for the first time:

They were just laughing the hell out of me because like I was eating so much. I just scoffed [ate] so much food, and they were just laughing at me, you know. Sometimes

I'd be looking at them, you know, wondering why they're laughing, you know, not knowing what I was doing. [Well, did they tell you why they were laughing eventually?] Yeah, yeah, I come back, "Hey, man, what's happening?" Like, you know, like I'd ask, "What's happening?" and all of a sudden I feel weird, you know. "Man, you're on, you know. You're on pot [high on marihuana]." I said, "No, am I?" Like I don't know what's happening.

The learning may occur in more indirect ways:

I heard little remarks that were made by other people. Somebody said, "My legs are rubbery," and I can't remember all the remarks that were made because I was very attentively listening for all these cues for what I was supposed to feel like.

The novice, then, eager to have this feeling, picks up from other users some concrete referents of the term "high" and applies these notions to his own experience. The new concepts make it possible for him to locate these symptoms among his own sensations and to point out to himself a "something different" in his experience that he connects with drug use. It is only when he can do this that he is high. In the next case, the contrast between two successive experiences of a user makes clear the crucial importance of the awareness of the symptoms in being high and re-emphasizes the important role of interaction with other users in acquiring the concepts that make this awareness possible:

[Did you get high the first time you turned on?] Yeah, sure. Although, come to think of it, I guess I really didn't. I mean, like that first time it was more or less of a mild drunk. I was happy, I guess, you know what I mean. But I didn't really know I was high, you know what I mean. It was only after the second time I got high that I realized I was high the first time. Then I knew that something different was happening.

[How did you know that?] How did I know? If what happened to me that night would of happened to you, you would've known, believe me. We played the first tune for almost two hours—one tune! Imagine, man! We got on the stand and played this one tune, we started at nine o'clock. When we got finished I looked at my watch, it's a quarter to eleven. Almost two hours on one tune. And it didn't seem like anything.

I mean, you know, it does that to you. It's like you have much more time or something. Anyway, when I saw that, man, it was too much. I knew I must really be high or something if anything like that could happen. See, and then they explained to me that that's what it did to you, you had a different sense of time and everything. So I realized that that's what it was. I knew then. Like the first time, I probably felt that way, you know, but I didn't know what's happening.

It is only when the novice becomes able to get high in this sense that he will continue to use marihuana for pleasure. In every case in which use continued, the user had acquired the necessary concepts with which to express to himself the fact that he was experiencing new sensations caused by the drug. That is, for use to continue, it is necessary not only to use the drug so as to produce effects but also to learn to perceive these effects when they occur. In this way marihuana acquires meaning for the user. as an object which can be used for pleasure.

With increasing experience the user develops a greater appreciation of the drug's effects; he continues to learn to get high. He examines succeeding experiences closely, looking for new effects, making sure the old ones are still there. Out of this there grows a stable set of categories for experiencing the drug's effects whose presence enables the user to get high with ease.

Users, as they acquire this set of categories, become connoisseurs. Like experts in fine wines, they can specify where a particular plant was grown and what time of year it was harvested. Although it is usually not possible to know whether these attributions are correct, it is true that they distinguish between batches of marihuana, not only according to strength, but also with respect to the different kinds of symptoms produced.

The ability to perceive the drug's effects must be maintained if use is to continue; if it is lost, marihuana use ceases. Two kinds of evidence support this statement. First, people who become heavy users of alcohol, barbiturates, or opiates do not continue to smoke marihuana, largely because they lose the ability to distinguish between its effects and those of the other drugs.[9] They no longer know whether the marihuana gets them high. Second, in those few cases in which an individual uses marihuana in such quantities that he is always high, he is apt to feel the drug has no effect on him, since the essential element of a noticeable difference between feeling high and feeling normal is missing. In such a situation, use is likely to be given up completely, but temporarily, in order that the user may once again be able to perceive the difference.

Learning to Enjoy the Effects

One more step is necessary if the user who has now learned to get high is to continue use. He must learn to enjoy the effects he has just learned to experience. Marihuana-produced sensations are not automatically or necessarily pleasurable. The taste for such experience is a socially acquired one, not different in kind from acquired tastes for oysters or dry martinis. The user feels dizzy, thirsty; his scalp tingles; he misjudges time and distances. Are these things pleasurable? He isn't sure. If he is to continue marihuana use, he must decide that they are. Otherwise, getting high, while a real enough experience, will be an unpleasant one he would rather avoid.

The effects of the drug, when first perceived, may be physically unpleasant or at least ambiguous:

> It started taking effect, and I didn't know what was happening, you know, what it was, and I was very sick. I walked around the room, walking around the room trying to get off, you know; it just scared me at first, you know. I wasn't used to that kind of feeling.

In addition, the novice's naive interpretation of what is happening to him may further confuse and frighten him, particularly if he decides, as many do, that he is going insane:

> I felt I was insane, you know. Everything people done to me just wigged me. I couldn't hold a conversation, and my mind would be wandering, and I was always thinking, oh, I don't know, weird things like hearing music different. . . . I get the feeling that I can't talk to anyone. I'll goof completely.

Given these typically frightening and unpleasant first experiences, the beginner will not continue use unless he learns to redefine the sensations as pleasurable:

> It was offered to me, and I tried it. I'll tell you one thing. I never did enjoy it at all. I mean it was just nothing that I could enjoy. [Well, did you get high when you turned on?] Oh, yeah, I got definite feelings from it. But I didn't enjoy them. I mean I got plenty of reactions, but they were mostly reactions of fear. [You were frightened?] Yes. I didn't enjoy it. I couldn't seem to relax with it, you know. If you can't relax with a thing, you can't enjoy it, I don't think.

In other cases the first experiences were also definitely unpleasant, but the person did become a marihuana user. This occurred,

[9] "Smokers have repeatedly stated that the consumption of whiskey while smoking negates the potency of the drug. They find it very difficult to get 'high' while drinking whiskey and because of that smokers will not drink while using the 'weed.'" (New York City Mayor's Committee on Marihuana, *The Marihuana Problem in the City of New York, op. cit.*, p. 13.)

however, only after a later experience enabled him to redefine the sensations as pleasurable:

> [This man's first experience was extremely unpleasant, involving distortion of spatial relationships and sounds, violent thirst, and panic produced by these symptoms.] After the first time I didn't turn on for about, I'd say, ten months to a year. . . . It wasn't a moral thing; it was because I'd gotten so frightened, bein' so high. An' I didn't want to go through that again, I mean, my reaction was, "Well, if this is what they call bein' high, I don't dig [like] it." . . . So I didn't turn on for a year almost, accounta that. . . .
>
> Well, my friends started, an' consequently I started again. But I didn't have any more, I didn't have that same initial reaction, after I started turning on again.
>
> [In interaction with his friends he became able to find pleasure in the effects of the drug and eventually became a regular user.]

In no case will use continue without a redefinition of the effects as enjoyable.

This redefinition occurs, typically, in interaction with more experienced users who, in a number of ways, teach the novice to find pleasure in this experience which is at first so frightening.[10] They may reassure him as to the temporary character of the unpleasant sensations and minimize their seriousness, at the same time calling attention to the more enjoyable aspects. An experienced user describes how he handles newcomers to marihuana use:

> Well, they get pretty high sometimes. The average person isn't ready for that, and it is a little frightening to them sometimes. I mean, they've been high on lush [alcohol], and they get higher that way than they've ever been before, and they don't know what's happening to them. Because they think they're going to keep going up, up, up till they lose their minds or begin doing weird things or something. You have to like reassure them, explain to them that they're not really flipping or anything, that they're gonna be all right. You have to just talk them out of being afraid. Keep talking to them, reassuring, telling them it's all right. And come on with your own story, you know: "The same thing happened to me. You'll get to like that after awhile." Keep coming on like that; pretty soon you talk them out of being scared. And besides they see you doing it and nothing horrible is happening to you, so that gives them more confidence.

The more experienced user may also teach the novice to regulate the amount he smokes more carefully, so as to avoid any severely uncomfortable symptoms while retaining the pleasant ones. Finally, he teaches the new user that he can "get to like it after awhile." He teaches him to regard those ambiguous experiences formerly defined as unpleasant as enjoyable. The older user in the following incident is a person whose tastes have shifted in this way, and his remarks have the effect of helping others to make a similar redefinition:

> A new user had her first experience of the effects of marihuana and became frightened and hysterical. She "felt like she was half in and half out of the room" and experienced a number of alarming physical symptoms. One of the more experienced users present said, "She's dragged because she's high like that. I'd give anything to get that high myself. I haven't been that high in years."

In short, what was once frightening and distasteful becomes, after a taste for it is built up, pleasant, desired, and sought after. Enjoyment is introduced by the favorable definition of the experience that one acquires from others. Without this, use will not continue, for marihuana will not be for the user an object he can use for pleasure.

In addition to being a necessary step in becoming a user, this represents an important condition for continued use. It is quite

[10] Charen and Perelman, *op. cit.*, p. 679.

common for experienced users suddenly to have an unpleasant or frightening experience, which they cannot define as pleasurable, either because they have used a larger amount of marihuana than usual or because the marihuana they have used turns out to be of a higher quality than they expected. The user has sensations which go beyond any conception he has of what being high is and is in much the same situation as the novice, uncomfortable and frightened. He may blame it on an overdose and simply be more careful in the future. But he may make this the occasion for a rethinking of his attitude toward the drug and decide that it no longer can give him pleasure. When this occurs and is not followed by a redefinition of the drug as capable of producing pleasure, use will cease.

The likelihood of such a redefinition occurring depends on the degree of the individual's participation with other users. Where this participation is intensive, the individual is quickly talked out of his feeling against marihuana use. In the next case, on the other hand, the experience was very disturbing, and the aftermath of the incident cut the person's participation with other users to almost zero. Use stopped for three years and began again only when a combination of circumstances, important among which was a resumption of ties with users, made possible a redefinition of the nature of the drug:

> It was too much, like I only made about four pokes, and I couldn't even get it out of my mouth, I was so high, and I got real flipped. In the basement, you know, I just couldn't stay in there anymore. My heart was pounding real hard, you know, and I was going out of my mind; I thought I was losing my mind completely. So I cut out of this basement, and this other guy, he's out of his mind, told me, "Don't, don't leave me, man. Stay here." And I couldn't.
>
> I walked outside, and it was five below zero, and I thought I was dying, and I had my coat open; I was sweating, I was perspiring. My whole insides were all . . . , and I walked about two blocks away, and I fainted behind a bush. I don't know how long I laid there. I woke up, and I was feeling the worst, I can't describe it at all, so I made it to a bowling alley, man, and I was trying to act normal, I was trying to shoot pool, you know, trying to act real normal, and I couldn't lay and I couldn't stand up and I couldn't sit down, and I went up and laid down where some guys that spot pins lay down, and that didn't help me, and I went down to a doctor's office. I was going to go in there and tell the doctor to put me out of my misery . . . because my heart was pounding so hard, you know. . . . So then all week end I started flipping, seeing things there and going through hell, you know, all kinds of abnormal things. . . . I just quit for a long time then.
>
> [He went to a doctor who defined the symptoms for him as those of a nervous breakdown caused by "nerves" and "worries." Although he was no longer using marihuana, he had some recurrences of the symptoms which led him to suspect that "it was all his nerves."] So I just stopped worrying, you know; so it was about thirty-six months later I started making it again. I'd just take a few pokes, you know. [He first resumed use in the company of the same user-friend with whom he had been involved in the original incident.]

A person, then, cannot begin to use marihuana for pleasure, or continue its use for pleasure, unless he learns to define its effects as enjoyable, unless it becomes and remains an object he conceives of as capable of producing pleasure.

In summary, an individual will be able to use marihuana for pleasure only when he goes through a process of learning to conceive of it as an object which can be used in this way. No one becomes a user without (1) learning to smoke the drug in a way which will produce real effects; (2) learning to recognize the effects and connect them with drug use (learning, in other words, to get high); and (3) learning to enjoy the sensations he perceives. In the course of this process he develops a disposition or motivation to use marihuana which was not and could not have been present when he began use, for it involves and depends on conceptions of the drug which could only grow out of the kind of actual experience detailed above. On completion of this process he is willing and able to use marihuana for pleasure.

He has learned, in short, to answer "Yes" to the question: "Is it fun?" The direction his further use of the drug takes depends on his being able to continue to answer "Yes" to this question and, in addition, on his being able to answer "Yes" to other questions which arise as he becomes aware of the implications of the fact that society disapproves of the practice: "Is it expedient?" "Is it moral?" Once he has acquired the ability to get enjoyment by using the drug, use will continue to be possible for him. Considerations of morality and expediency, occasioned by the reactions of society, may interfere and inhibit use, but use continues to be a possibility in terms of his conception of the drug. The act becomes impossible only when the ability to enjoy the experience of being high is lost, through a change in the user's conception of the drug occasioned by certain kinds of experience with it.

40

Gambling as Work: A Sociological Study of the Race Track

Robert D. Herman

This article examines a single type of gambling institution, the large, commercial horse race track. Three comments are in order concerning the social relevance of horse racing in comparison with alternative gambling enterprises. First, horse race gambling is an enormous industry. Almost $4 billion was wagered legally and openly at race tracks in the United States in 1963. Fifty-seven million persons attended horse races that year,[1] a greater number than the total for major league baseball, professional football, and collegiate football combined.[2] No estimates of the size of *illegal* horse playing are trustworthy, but one which is often cited states that $16.50 is wagered

From "Gambling as Work: A Sociological Study of the Race Track," pp. 87–104, and pp. 254–256 in *Gambling* by Robert D. Herman. Copyright © 1967 by Robert D. Herman. Reprinted by permission of Harper & Row, Publishers, Incorporated. The research for this report was supported by the National Institute of Health, Grant #MH 08040–01.

[1] *The American Racing Manual* (Triangle Publications, Inc., 1964). In 1963, wagering increased 6.7 percent over 1962.

[2] Attendance at horse races increased 8 percent while the U.S. population 21 years of age and older increased 1.1 percent. *Statistical Abstract of the United States, 1963*) Washington, D.C.,: U.S. Department of Commerce).

"off track" on horses for every dollar wagered legally.[3]

Second, in contrast to Nevada-style casinos, most of which are removed from major population centers and have the general features of resorts, race tracks are primarily identifiable with conventional urban culture. They are normally located well within the physical embrace of the metropolis itself. For example, "Aqueduct" (the largest race track in the New York area) enjoys the benefits of its own station on a subway line.[4] Los Angeles has two major tracks, both located within a few minutes travel time from the center of the city. In fact, of the ten largest cities in the United States, only Houston has no horse race track within half an hour's reach. While the racing industry often celebrates its connections with the elegance of old Saratoga and the romance of the blue grass, it is clear that the realities of modern horse racing bring it closer to the model of the supermarket than to that of the vacation spa or the county fair.

Third, many precise data of interest to students of social behavior are readily available without dependency upon questionable and troublesome detective work. A variety of records are kept (and many are published) both because state governments have economic interests in the revenues of track operations and because tracks have almost no reason to hide their records—but every reason to encourage publicity. Exact tabs are maintained on attendance and wagering, even to the point of recording where and when every bet is made. In contrast, there is no way of computing, from the data available to the public, exact amounts wagered in casinos or card parlors. Of course casinos appear to do a very impressive business, but the size of that business is harder to pin down in exact terms. The Nevada Gaming Commission says that the reported gross revenue (taxes) from all gambling establishments in that state in 1963 was $260 million.[5] Still, the amounts actually wagered in that state remain unknown. While it is tempting to focus attention on the more bizarre and colorful world of casinos, the present study is an attempt to appreciate the more routine case of the "local neighborhood race track."[6]

The data for this study were collected in Los Angeles in 1962 and 1963 at Hollywood Park. Although it is one of the largest tracks in the United States (Santa Anita, across town is slightly smaller), Hollywood Park may be considered "typical" of major thoroughbred race tracks. This

[3] John Scarne, *Scarne's Complete Guide to Gambling* (New York: Simon & Schuster, 1961), p. 32. A more moderate estimate was reported by Robert Kennedy to Congress that $7 billion was gambled in the U.S. in 1960. See, *Hearings,* Subcommittee on the Judiciary, House of Reps., 87th Congress, Washington, 1961, "Legislation Relating to Organized Crime," p. 24.

[4] The "Big A" had an average daily attendance of 33,120 in 1964 with an average daily handle of $3,236,086. Hollywood Park (Los Angeles) had an average daily attendance of 34,081 that year and an average daily handle of $2,885,795.

[5] Nevada Gaming Commission, *Legalized Gambling in Nevada* (Carson City, Nevada: Gaming Policy Board, 1963).

[6] The following are the important publications by sociologists on gambling in the last two decades: The best treatment of horse racing is Edward C. Devereux, Jr., "Gambling and the Social Structure—A Sociological Study of Lotteries and Horse Racing in Contemporary America," (unpublished Ph.D. dissertation, Harvard University, 1949). A second doctoral dissertation on the sociology of horse racing is being prepared by Marvin Scott, University of California, Berkeley. Soccer pools are studied by Nechama Tec, *Gambling in Sweden* (Totawa, N.J.: The Bedminster Press, 1964). Herbert A. Bloch has contributed two essays: "The Sociology of Gambling," *American Journal of Sociology,* 57 (1951), pp. 215–222; and Chapter 23 of *Crime in America,* edited by Bloch (Philosophical Library, New York, 1961). A few sociologists have, of course, examined issues related to gambling, especially racketeering, organized crime, and gambling among ethnic minorities.

study should be considered to apply primarily to gambling behavior at thoroughbred races, which presently account for 74 per cent of all wagering on horses in this country. Attendance figures, total amounts wagered, and a few other statistics are published in city newspapers and do not require special collection techniques. Some of the details of these figures are recorded by the management of the track for administrative purposes, and I am indebted to the Hollywood Turf Club for access to them. The management also cooperated in giving me and my student assistant the run of the entire establishment in order to make direct observations of patron's gambling behavior supplemented by the spending of long hours simply counting the numbers of people of each sex as they appeared in various betting lines, as they came through track entrances, or as they purchased programs, tip sheets, or *Racing Forms.* Also included in this study were large numbers of structured and unstructured interviews. Our observations in general became relatively more quantitative as we learned more about the business.

The Setting

For the reader who is unfamiliar with a typical commercial horse race track, this may serve as a guided tour. The physical layout is functional and direct. The running track itself is usually an oval a mile in circumference with a grandstand situated along one side. Horses are walked to the track from nearby stables shortly before the races in which they are to run; they then parade in front of the crowd to the starting gate whose position may be varied to permit races of from $\frac{3}{4}$-mile (requiring about 1 minute, 12 seconds) to 1-$\frac{1}{2}$ miles (2 minutes, 24 seconds). An afternoon of racing consists of nine races spaced about one-half hour apart. Significantly, there is no prepared entertainment between races.

Exhibited in front of the crowd, in the infield, is a "tote" board, a large scoreboard showing, among other things, the payoff amounts for the first three horses in the preceding race and the "odds" against each horse entered in the following race. The odds are actually the payoff prices determined by the relative amounts wagered on each horse. Because these odds change as betting proceeds (betting on one race starts within a few minutes after the conclusion of the preceding one but increases in volume as the starting time approaches), the tote board commands the thoughtful attention of a majority of the crowd.

A major race track draws its patrons from a socio-economic cross-section of the city, a fact that is reflected in the division of the grandstand into three or four stratified zones. The largest is a section (for which the term "Grandstand" is usually reserved) that includes a large ramp for standees. At Hollywood Park, 77 percent of the crowd is accommodated within this area. An area, usually called the "Clubhouse" offers somewhat more elbow room and better conveniences for its patrons, but it seems primarily to serve to segregate the $1.00-extra customers from the crush of the main crowd. Twenty percent of the total attendance is contained in the Clubhouse. A more luxurious and expensive area, called the "Private Turf Club" contains 3-$\frac{1}{2}$ percent of the total crowd—but they bet about 10 percent of the money!

Almost all members of the Private Turf Club attend the races in the company of friends or family. In contrast from 35 to 40 percent of the crowd in the Grandstand attend as loners, while 33 to 35 percent of the Clubhouse attendees are loners. On Saturdays and holidays when the size of the total crowd almost doubles that of ordinary weekdays, a somewhat greater proportion of the patrons attend with companions. The loners, although they number considerably less than half the crowd, are a major factor in its appearance. Casual observers are often impressed by the somber, even gloomy, expressions of horse players; win or lose, they seem withdrawn and joyless.

However, this atmosphere is largely an artifact of the absence of conversation with companions. Animation normally requires company. It seems heedless to presume, as many commentators have, that some sort of pathology is indicated by the fact that many horse players wear serious expressions.

A more important element in the calm between races is that most patrons are kept quietly but actively engrossed in the demanding tasks of selecting horses on which to bet. Only a small proportion are "hunch" bettors or are willing to act blindly on the advice of public handicappers.[7] Most people indeed *play* the game; in risking their money, they attempt to select their own betting options by the deliberate application of rational criteria. The task is immensely complex, the list of factors which ought to be considered is very large, and the amount of information which is made available is overwhelming. There is so much, in fact, that most or all players must rely on simplifications and rules of thumb.

The most important source of information is a newspaper, the *Daily Racing Form*, purchased by approximately 40 percent of the Grandstand patrons and 60 percent of the Turf Club members. (We estimate that, at Hollywood Park, 89 percent of *Racing Form* purchasers are men, although two-thirds of the attendees are men.) This document provides three main types of material: (1) A few pages contain feature articles about important horses and their owners, trainers, and riders—of interest primarily to box holders and Turf Club members; (2) A couple of pages consist of ordered selections by the *Form's* handicappers along with equivocal comments on horses thought likely to be "in contention"; (3) The largest section, and most important for the individual bettor, is called simply, "Past Performances." Past Performances are published for horses entered in each of the day's races at the local track and, interestingly, for *other* major race tracks across the country, in spite of the fact that betting on races is illegal (except in Nevada) where one cannot be present in person. Here are tabulated in astonishing detail the racing histories of each horse entered in each race. Among other particulars, the following information is offered *for each horse:* the weight he must carry in the present race, his age, color of his coat, sire, dam, dam's sire, the names of his owner, breeder, and trainer, the amounts of money he has won for his owner in the last two or three years, his speeds for his last few workouts, the dates, locations, and "conditions" of his last dozen races—and then *for each of those races:* his jockey, weight carried, running position relative to the leader at each quarter of the race including the finish, the names of the first three horses to finish, the weights *they* carried, etc.

Of course, a few important considerations receive no comparable publicity. Obscured, for example, are the subtleties of health and emotion of each horse just before racing and the trainer's strategy and instructions to the jockey (e.g., whether to press for victory under any condition or perhaps merely to engage the horse in training and exercise). However, even here,

[7] In "hunch betting," a horse is selected on arbitrary grounds having nothing to do with the horse's ability. Hunch players usually agree that their actions are not objectively based, but other complex motives may be involved. For a discussion of "psychological probability," see John Cohen, *Chance, Skill and Luck: The Psychology of Guessing and Gambling* (Baltimore, Md.: Penguin Books, 1960).

The term "handicapper" formerly referred to the person, now called the racing secretary, who assigns racing conditions and weights carried by horses. The term now has been extended to include anyone who makes a calculated attempt to determine the winning probabilities of horses in a given race. Many city newspapers publish "selections" which are of some aid to novice bettors. For monthly ratings of major public handicappers, see the magazine, *Turf and Sports Digest* (Baltimore, Md.: Montee Publishing Co., Inc.).

experienced bettors are sometimes able to draw inferences from clues in the *Form* or elsewhere.[8]

As might be expected, many "textbooks" on uses of the *Form* and methods of handicapping and betting are available to the public. These consist mainly of expositions on the asserted significance of a relatively limited number of variables (speed, consistency, post position, experience, etc.). A few books examine not so much the past performances of the horses but rather the possible opportunities afforded by the betting behavior of the crowd (favorites, prices, shifts in odds, etc.).[9] Yet both types of books are likely to call for the application of considerable skill and effort. One recent volume directs its readers to *memorize* at least two tables, one with 42 cells, the other with 56, to be able to read and understand the *Racing Form*, and to be able to apply several complicated rules rapidly and on the spot.[10] More will be said below of those persons who, with the help of the *Form*, attempt to make independent choices; but it may be noted here that gambling at the race track is seen by most participants, and this writer, to require genuine mental effort. It is therefore quite unlike gambling in such casino games as craps, roulette, or slot machines, which depend almost entirely on chance.

The "Action"

The actual operation of placing bets is simple enough. Since the 1930s, American race tracks, by state law, have prohibited private bookmakers from operating openly at tracks and have required that all wagering be pooled and held by the track for subsequent redistribution—the system called pari-mutuel betting. The bettor tells the "seller" (at a window of the desired denomination—$2, $5, $10, $50, $100) the program number of the horse on which he wishes to bet. The clerk presses a key on a machine (a form of cash register) which prints out an appropriately numbered ticket which is taken by the bettor. As the machine issues the ticket, it simultaneously telegraphs that information to a central computing station, which then, in turn, sends new totals and payoff odds information to the tote board in front of the stands. (Payoff information is corrected for the fact that, from each betting pool, the track withdraws 15 percent of which about half goes to the state as taxes. The proportion to be returned to the winners, then, is 85 per cent of the total bet.) Should the bettor's horse subsequently win, the bettor cashes the ticket at another window; both sellers' and cashiers' windows are distributed throughout the plant and are within a few steps of any potential bettor. Marketing studies have shown that virtually every person in attendance bets on at least one race during the afternoon and a majority bet on half the races or more. It seems that almost no one visits the race track merely to watch horses.

In addition to straight, or "Win" bets, other types of wagers may be made. "Place" bets (in the same denominations as Win bets) pay a return if the horse in question finishes either first or second; "Show" bets pay if the horse is first, second, or third. Payoffs for Place and Show bets are smaller in consequence of the lower risk

[8] Marvin Scott gives special attention to the fact that the act of a trainer's giving final instructions to the jockey occurs in full view of the crowd—but out of earshot. *Op. cit.*

[9] Among the most highly regarded *Form*-oriented books is Robert S. Dowst, *The Odds, The Player, The Horses* (New York: Dodd Mead & Co., 1959). Two examples of crowd-oriented texts are Burton P. Fabricand, *Horse Sense* (David McKay Co., 1965); E. R. DaSilva and Roy M. Dorcus, *Science in Betting* (New York: Harper & Row, 1961).

[10] Fabricand, *op. cit.* This book purports to have been based on analyses of races performed by a high-speed digital computer. One is reminded of an analysis of blackjack ("21") gambling also based on computer analysis. See E. O. Thorp, *Beat the Dealer* (New York: Vintage Books, 1966).

TABLE 1. Women as Percent of All Attendees and Bettors in Three Areas of Hollywood Park, by Denomination of Bet, 1963

TOTAL IN ATTENDANCE	TURF CLUB 47%	CLUBHOUSE 33%	GRANDSTAND 26%
Denomination of Betting			
$2 Win	48%	30%	18%
$2 Show	50	61	34
$5 Win	31	19	9
Daily Double [a]	39	29	22

[a] Two sizes of Daily Double bets are sold, $2 and $10; these data refer to $2 size only.

involved. Increasingly race tracks have also provided opportunities for people to bet on more than one race at a time. For example, a "Daily Double" ticket, sold before the first race, is printed with two numbers representing win selections in both the first and second race; thus the risks and the payoffs are greater than for single races. Other more elaborate betting opportunities are presently being introduced at some tracks which account for occasional news items reporting record payoffs when successions of long shots win.

The horse betting behavior of men is different from that of women. This can be seen in Table 1 which shows the proportions of attendees and bettors who are women in three areas of the stands and in four major types of betting situations. (Women tend to avoid risking larger stakes, hence we made no precise counts of the very few women at $10, $50, and $100 windows. The proportions of women who make Place bets are between the figures given for Win and Show.) Notice should be made, for later reference, of the relatively high percentage of women betting at $2 Show windows and the relatively low percentage making the more expensive bets. Pari-mutuel clerks and racing habituees are well aware of these differences in gambling behavior, and they are usually accounted for by such explanations as "Women bet defensively," or "Women try to keep from losing, but men try to win." It will be seen that the interpretation presented at the conclusion of this article is an alternative to these propositions.

The socioeconomic identities of race track patrons are difficult to determine accurately, except those of the 3½ percent of the crowd who are members of the Private Turf Club who are upper-middle class and above. We must distrust responses to interview questions asking respondents to classify themselves, given sensitivities to traditional, critical judgments of gambling shared by an unknown proportion of attendees. Loners, in particular, are often timid about revealing their important affiliations in this context. (It may occur to some readers that identities of gamblers could be traced through income tax records even though these are not normally made available to the public. Tracks make a practice of requiring only winners of very large amounts to sign special income tax reports before collecting, but generalizations from such a sample would be inappropriate.) As an alternative to direct questioning, we exploited the fact that 90 percent of Hollywood Park attendees travel to the track by automobile (in contrast to the heavy bus and rail patronage of tracks in many other cities). By recording the license numbers of a sample of 604 cars entering the parking lot, while also recording the number and sex of the occupants, we were able to identify the street addresses of the owners of the cars (with the assistance of the California Department of Motor Vehicles).

Then census tract maps were used to

indicate the socioeconomic characteristics of the neighborhoods in which the owners resided. Table 2 presents a summary of this information. The data from car licenses suggest that Los Angeles neighborhoods of each social rank contribute Hollywood Park attendees in approximate proportion to their percentage in the country. We have no way of determining whether track attendees are truly representative of their own neighborhoods nor can we judge, from these data, whether the proportionate attendance from middle-class areas is a recent development. Devereux believed most horse players were middle-class people. When he studied race tracks in the late 1940s,

> . . . The vast throngs that fill the stands at the modern race courses and that pour their money into the pari-mutuel machines . . . are for the most part middle-class laymen, out-groupers from the perspective of the race track society, who still take satisfaction in a day at the races.[10]

It is also known by the management that Hollywood Park's Clubhouse attendance is now increasing at a faster rate than is Grandstand attendance, but this fact may represent either an increasing affluence among attendees generally or an increasing participation in horse playing by more affluent strata of the urban population. In any case, the data in Table 2 show that track habituees are correct when they say that racing patrons "come from all over."

Myth and Evidence

Gambling is popularly believed to ensnare its participants in a system involving (a) the reckless expenditure of scarce resources on events of great risk in the naive hope of (b) "making a killing," and gambling is presumed to be (c) an escape from rationality, even where pathological addiction is not at issue. However, an examination of race track data fails to confirm these impressions. In order to clear the way for alternative interpretations, these popular views are considered in the next few paragraphs.

Recklessness as Heavy Betting on High-Risk Alternatives

1. The evidence is that the larger the amount of a given bet, the more likely it will be wagered on a favorite—the horse with the statistically *smallest* risk. Approximately 50 percent of the money wagered at $100 Win windows is bet on favorites, while about 29 percent of all smaller bets is wagered on favorites. Hollywood Park has two $100 sellers windows which account for 7 percent of the total handle but 16 percent of the total amount bet on favorites.

2. At one point in our investigation, we interviewed 100 men about the way they bet. (These were mostly loners drawn as a quota sample from the Grandstand and Clubhouse areas.) Among the questions asked was, "When you win, do you usually rebet all of your winnings right away or what . . . ?" Eleven percent of the respondents said they rebet all winnings immediately; 3 percent do so eventually; 34 percent rebet a fixed amount or a fixed ratio only; and 41 percent simply answered "No" to the question. If these responses can be believed, it appears that these men (probably the most likely to be "reckless" of anyone at the track) handle their money fairly "conservatively."

3. A relatively small proportion of all bets made costs over $50. The figures showing the amounts of *money* (not numbers of tickets) wagered by size of bet are presented in Table 3. In interpreting this information note should be given of the fact that about half of the $100 bets are made by Turf Club members, and it is very doubtful that any substantial part of the remaining large bets are placed by people without financial means. Most people buy reasonably inexpensive tickets.

4. Dividing the total handle for the tracks in the United States by the number of attendees, the average amount wagered per day was found to be $77 in 1964 ($85 at

TABLE 2. Neighborhood Social Rank of Hollywood Park Patrons by Type of Group Attending, Compared with Los Angeles County Population

Number and Sex of Group	Social Rank[a]						Total	%	Mean Rank[b]
	I	II	III	IV	V	VI			
Lone, Male	26	37	63	79	68	36	309	54.3%	11.05
Group, Males	3	13	15	15	19	9	74	13.0	11.42
Lone, Female	2	5	8	4	8	6	33	5.8	11.48
Group, Females	3	7	7	4	6	4	31	5.4	10.55
Group, Mixed	5	20	23	17	39	18	122	21.6	11.75
Sample Total	39	82	116	119	140	73	569[c]	100.1	11.246
Sample %	6.85	14.42	20.40	20.92	24.54	12.84			
L.A. County %	5.00	12.98	24.27	21.12	22.80	13.8		County Mean = 11.308	

[a] Rank I represents highest status, Rank VI, lowest status. The "Social Rank" index is a composite of three characteristics of census tracts; median family income, percent of population over 24 having completed 1 or more years of college, and percent of employed males in white collar occupations. This index was developed by Meeker for use in the Los Angeles area. See Marchia Meeker, *Background for Planning* (Los Angeles: Welfare Planning Council, 1964), p. 81.

[b] The six ranks are actually combinations of sixteen levels, ranging from 3 to 18. The Mean Rank column refers to this continuum; a score of 10.5 is on the dividing line between Ranks III and IV.

[c] Original sample, 604. The remainder were eliminated from consideration as having untraceable addresses, address of businesses or auto rental services, or addresses outside Los Angeles County.

TABLE 3. Percent Money Wagered by Denomination of Wager, Hollywood Park, 1963 [a]

DENOMINATION	PERCENT MONEY
$100	6.7
$ 50	14.6
$ 10	21.2
$ 5	12.5
$ 2	22.8
$ 15[b]	5.2
$ 6[b]	9.4
Daily Double	7.2
Total	100.0

[a] First 48 days of 1963 program ($126,791,000).

[b] These are "Combination" or "Across the Board" bets in which a single ticket is purchased betting that a given horse will win, *and* place *and* show, the payoff varying with the horse's actual performance.

Hollywood Park, California; about $98 at Aqueduct, New York). Even when the disproportionate influence of wealthy bettors is subtracted, the average still seems sizable. However, these figures are misleading when taken out of context because they include both rebet winnings and fresh money. It is possible to compute the minimum amount of fresh money that must be invested by supposing that *all* winnings are immediately reinvested, and under these fictional circumstances, about 25 percent of the total handle would have to be fresh money. It would be more accurate to accept Scarne's estimate that half of the total handle consists of fresh money.[11] When this is further divided by the number of races per day, the average amount of fresh money wagered per bettor per race turns out to be about $4.70 at Hollywood Park and $5.45 at Aqueduct.[12]

"MAKING A KILLING" AS BETTING ON HIGH-PAYOFF CHOICES

People tend, in fact, to bet on horses whose odds are relatively low with no possibility at all of paying large returns. At Hollywood Park in 1963, only 6½ percent of the total Win bets were on winning horses ranking lower than fourth choice (and even less was wagered on losing horses ranking that low). Fifty-seven percent of the money was wagered on the first two public choices—36 percent on favorites alone, a statistically "proper" amount in terms of winning probabilities.[13] Long shots capable of rewarding their backers with large-payoffs must, by definition, rarely be selected by bettors. The existence of high-risk, high-payoff alternatives is, of course, a statistical necessity; observers of gambling should not assume that the fact that some people play long shots means that the practice is widespread.

ESCAPE FROM RATIONALITY

The rationality of the betting public may be inferred from the wisdom of its choices. (Rationality may be considered by some to

[11] Scarne, *op. cit.*, p. 57.

[12] For further discussion of the daily pattern of betting at race tracks, see William H. McGlothlin, "Stability of Choices among Uncertain Alternatives," *American Journal of Psychology*, 69 (1956), p. 406.

Of the total handle, an unknown proportion consists of bets made by nonattendees who send money to the track by two main channels. Often attendees are given money by friends to bet on horses previously selected; bookmakers occasionally send "layoff" money by way of professional couriers. In layoff betting, the bookmaker places a bet with another bookmaker or at the track at which a race is to be run so as to hedge his losses to his customers should their heavy favorite in that race win. Layoff networks are illegal, and they are periodically the objects of Congressional scrutiny. See *Gambling and Organized Crime,* Hearings before the Permanent Subcommittee on Investigations of the Committee on Governmental Operations, United States Senate, 87th Congress, 1961.

[13] Derived from R. C. Evenson and C. C. Jones, *The Way They Run* (Los Angeles, Cal.: Techno-Graphic Publications, 1964), p. 55. The average win payoffs of first, second, third, and fourth choices were (for $2 wagered): $5.75, $8.90, $11.80, and $15.83.

apply mainly to the *prior* choice of whether or not to take any risk at all or even to play a game, an issue touched upon in the final section of this article. However, once the game has been chosen by the player, the efficiency of his play may be treated as a separate index of rationality.) While any individual race is an exception to the perfect operation of the rule, data from any large number of races show a perfect rank-order correlation between the average popularity of horses and their ability.[14] In other words, for the crowd as a whole, betting behavior is consistent with actual probabilities of winning.

In summary, the data suggest that horse playing is more characteristic of self-control and caution than of recklessness, more a participant sport than a spectator sport, and, as we shall argue below, more ritualistic than innovative.

Interpretation

Several interpretations of gambling have appeared in the sociological literature which consider gambling to be a form of deviancy or a cultural aberration reactive to a context of *deprivation.* Four examples may be identified.

1. An "escape hatch" interpretation of gambling has been proposed by a number of observers. Gambling is thought to provide an "escape from the routine and boredom of modern industrial life in which the sense of creation and the 'instinct of workmanship' has been lost. 'Taking a chance' destroys routine and hence is pleasurable . . ."[15] Bloch goes on to say that the "chance element" is fostered by certain types of social systems, namely those which base status on competitive, pecuniary standards.

2. A related view is that gambling represents a "safety valve." Here ". . . instead of turning against the original source of their deprivations and unfulfilled aspirations, bettors are relieved through gambling of some of their frustrations and, hence, are less likely to attack the existing class structure."[16]

3. Another interpretation is that gambling keeps alive a hope for social betterment among people "who are least capable of fulfilling their mobility aspirations through conventional avenues . . ."[17] (This, by the way, is the only theory mentioned here which has been subjected to tests against quantitative, empirical data.)

4. Zola, in his study of lower-class clients of a tavern bookmaker, proposes that gambling occasionally allows bettors to "beat the system" through rational means and thus permits them to demonstrate to themselves and their associates that "they *can* exercise control and that for a brief moment they *can* control their fate. Off-track betting . . . denies the vagaries of life and gives these men a chance to regulate it."[18]

While these interpretations attempt to place gambling into appropriate social contexts, they treat rather lightly the differences in gambling behavior among various types of players. In the following discussion we shall distinguish between the actions of middle-class and lower-class men (Grandstand and Clubhouse), middle-class and lower-class women, and upper-class attendees (members of the Turf Club).

[14] Literally any race could serve as an example of a violation of the general rule, but to take a prominent instance, the 1965 Kentucky Derby: the fourth choice won, and the favorite placed tenth. Fabricand, a mathematician, is so taken with the correlation between wagering and winning, that he devotes an entire chapter of his "textbook" to extolling the public's wisdom. Fabricand, *op. cit.*, Chapter IV.

[15] Bloch, "The Sociology of Gambling," *op. cit.*, pp. 217–218.

[16] Tec, *op. cit.*, p. 108.

[17] *Ibid.*

[18] Irving Kenneth Zola, "Observations on Gambling in a Lower-Class Setting," reprinted in this volume from *Social Problems,* 10 (1963), p. 360.

MIDDLE-CLASS AND LOWER-CLASS MEN

I have suggested that a primary characteristic of horse playing is the intellectual exercise of selecting horses on which to wager. It may not be an overstatement to argue that, for middle- and lower-class men, it is the *central* element in the attraction of gambling. The exchange of money, of course, is essential, but not central. If the acquisition of money were the main goal, then gambling must be judged inefficient in comparison with other ways that are easier, faster, and more certain. The evidence suggests that most horse players concur in such a judgment: they tend to avoid high-risk horses; they do not invest much money per race (although it is not possible to determine from our data how seriously gambling may drain individual financial resources); they admit, when asked to the uncertainties involved. I suggest that *the function of money,* in the context of the gambling institution, *is primarily to reify the decision-making process.* Money establishes the fact of a decisive act, and in its being lost or returned, it verifies the involvement of the bettor in the "action." Thus the player, even the "little guy," is brought into meaningful association with processes beyond himself. The impression of involvement and participation in events of importance is facilitated by the presence of large numbers of people, the bustle of general activity, the color and drama of the race, and the movement of money. This is why the more important races, measured in terms of purses and quality of horses, attract relatively more wagering. It is difficult to determine the conditions under which money is primarily an end in itself or a means to other ends—undoubtedly it is usually both.[19] In any case, tote boards give prominence to the total amounts of money wagered in addition to information concerning the odds, and in casinos, the raw cash itself is conspicuous everywhere.

Decision-making requires of players that they study the past performance records, ponder the tote board, consider reasonable lines of action, estimate probabilities, risk money, and collect the fruits of their action. Though on a smaller scale, *they emulate traditional, entrepreneurial roles*—weighing alternatives, making decisions, and signalling these decisions by attaching money to them.[20] Gambling is a game. It has many of the social psychological qualities which have been identified in other games by such observers as Piaget and G. H. Mead who point to the socializing and integrative functions of many forms of play. Horse players demonstrate to themselves their self-reliance and rationality by engaging in decision-making games made up primarily of conventional roles. Gambling, by this view, is less dysfunctional than it appears to be to those who judge it solely by standards linked to the production of goods.[21]

But, in indicating the conventional quality of much horse gambling, we have not accounted for its growing attraction for large numbers of middle-class and lower-class men. The answer appears to lie in the fact that opportunities to demonstrate self-reliance, independence, and decision-making ability are less and less available in other roles in which these men are involved. Occupational deprivations are usually

[19] Some experimental attempts have been made to investigate the "utility of money" apart from the "utility of gambling." See Halsey L. Royden, Patrick Suppes, and Karol Walsh, "A Model for the Experimental Measurement of the Utility of Gambling," *Behavioral Science* 4 (1959), pp. 11–18.

[20] Gregory Stone has written that some sport modes, "mark transformations of the play form into work-professional and otherwise subsidized athletes. . . . Second, there are sports that are transformations of work form into play." These latter are engaged in by "amateurs." See Gregory P. Stone and Marvin J. Taves, "Camping in the Wilderness," in Eric Larrabee and Rolf Meyersohn (eds.), *Mass Leisure* (Glencoe, Illinois: The Free Press, 1958), p. 296.

[21] That such standards are obsolete is suggested by John Kenneth Galbraith, *The Affluent Society,* (Boston: Houghton Mifflin Co., 1958).

assumed to be more acute among lower-class men, but with the development of white-collar industrial bureaucracies and the more recent emergence of automation, middle-class men may also be increasingly separated from traditional sources of self-esteem.[22] If horse playing fills a decision-making void in a social system increasingly unable to supply alternatives, the future of gambling may be hypothesized to follow changes in the supply of alternative devices for affirming personal autonomy.

MIDDLE-CLASS AND LOWER-CLASS WOMEN

The gambling behavior of women must be explained differently. As shown above, women are more likely to make Show bets and are less likely to study the past performances in the *Racing Form*. It appears that the search for independence through decision-making activities is not the attraction here. A look at some characteristics of Show betting should provide a basis for interpretation.

Show bets pay a return, of some sort, a large percent of the time! Show bets on favorites pay 63 percent of the time—though in insufficient amounts to be profitable over a large number of such bets ($2.93 is the average payoff). Even horses ranking as low as fourth choice pay a return to Show bettors 36 percent of the time.[23] To appreciate the meaning of this, we may turn to studies of working-class women by Rainwater, who describes his subjects as leading dull, sparkless, unfulfilled lives in routinized settings bereft of social-emotional rewards but heavy with responsibility.[24] If this is an accurate picture of even a substantial portion of lower-class women today, we may link their gambling behavior to their particular deprivations. Thus in attending the races and in playing horses to Show, women experience frequent "rewards." The rewards may be small (too small to make up for the losses) and financial (rather than personal), but they can be symbolic and meaningful nevertheless. Show payoffs are frequent sparks against a background of dreariness.[25]

But what of *middle*-class women who appear to gamble in the same manner? As Komarovsky has shown, middle-class women are brought up to be more dependent than men on the authority of their parents. "Competitiveness, independence, dominance, aggressiveness, are all traits felt to be needed by the future head of the family . . . " while middle-class girls are sheltered and given fewer opportunities for independent action.[26] It is to be expected, then, that middle-class women will gamble in ways consistent with their training. They will make low-risk (Show) bets and will follow the "authority" of public handicappers rather than choices based on their own independent selection. As it happens, their gambling behavior is roughly similar to that of lower-class women, but for different reasons.

[22] For a prediction of the ways in which automation may be separating middle managers from the traditional decision-making satisfactions of supervision, see Harold J. Leavitt and Thomas L. Whistler, "Management in the 1980's," *Harvard Business Review*, Vol. 36 (Nov./Dec., 1958), p. 46. For evidence that their predictions are correct, see Jack B. Weiner, "Cutbacks in Middle Management," *Dun's Review and Modern Industry*, Vol. 84 (July, 1964).

[23] 1963 data reported in Evenson and Jones, *op. cit.*, p. 55.

[24] Lee Rainwater, Richard P. Coleman, Gerald Handel, *Working-man's Wife* (New York: MacFadden-Bartell, Inc., 1962), Chapter III, "Inner Life and the Outer World." "In comparison with the middleclass wife, *reality is, in its ordinary presentation to her, flat, unvarnished and not highly differentiated.*" p. 52.

[25] Betty Friedan (*The Feminine Mystique*, New York: W. W. Norton & Co., 1957), has described middle-class women as suffering from many of the same deprivations as those of their lower-class sisters. If she is correct, their similar gambling behavior could be accounted for by the same factors.

[26] Mirra Komarovsky, "Functional Analysis of Sex Roles," *American Sociological Review*, XV (August, 1950), 508–516.

PRIVATE TURF CLUB MEMBERS

These people suffer few of the deprivations just discussed. As a group, they bet large amounts of money, they are the prime supporters of favorites, and their gambling occurs in a setting of conviviality, sociability and exclusiveness. Both their gambling behavior and their sociality are consistent with Veblen's notions of "conspicuous leisure" or "conspicuous consumption." "In order to gain and to hold the esteem of men it is not sufficient merely to possess wealth or power. The wealth or power must be put in evidence, for esteem is awarded only on evidence."[27] Clearly, heavy wagering in the exclusive gathering of the Turf Club is wealth put in evidence. However, while it is important to spend money lavishly, it is easier and less disruptive to spend it in ways which suggest conformity to the choices of fellow Club members rather than a rejection of them—hence the tendency to support favorites. Furthermore, since conversation with companions precludes all but a relatively superficial examination of the *Racing Form* during the periods between races, the simplest choice available to the Club member is to "play the favorite!" (It is also true that because favorites win more often than other horses, bettors of large stakes may hope to reduce their "down-side risks," to borrow a phrase from Wall Street.)

Thus, difficult decisions, symbolic of independence, are *avoided* by the Club member, they are *irrelevant* to middle-class and lower-class women, and they are *pursued* by middle-class and lower-class men.

Summary

The functions served by gambling have been described in terms of the social contexts relevant for three different categories of horse players. By an analysis of this sort, the issue of the desirability of gambling for urban society becomes less one of blanket approval or disapproval but rather one of the evaluation of alternatives. What other cultural devices are available to middle-class and lower-class men that can be as effective in bolstering a sense of independence and self-determination and that so compellingly exercise mental skills and rational powers? What else might be done to brighten the lives of working-class women? How else might the wealthy engage in the open consumption of leisure in ways that would be as "harmless"?

In short, commercialized gambling offers to many people efficient means of enhanced self-esteem and gratification in a culture in which satisfactions are increasingly likely to be found in enterprises of consumption rather than production.

[27] Thorstein Veblen, *The Theory of the Leisure Class* (New York: Macmillan Co., 1899), p. 36.

41

New York's "Middle-Class" Homosexuals

William J. Helmer

As might be expected, the common view of homosexuality we find in recent novels, plays, and films is often very limited. Even the more "understanding" studies of the problem seem to consider homosexuals as a definable group—distinct from heterosexuals—whose chief concern in life is to satisfy their sexual desires while shamefully concealing them from friends and associates.

In fact, homosexuality is a condition which takes so many forms that the word is of little use in describing any single group of people. And many homosexuals insulate themselves from hostile heterosexual society, taking refuge in a separate homosexual community which possesses its own customs, social structure, ethics, argot, organizations, and even business establishments.

To the extent that police or anonymity permit, every large city in America contains a homosexual community. It has no physical dimensions, and it certainly does not include everyone who would legally, psychiatrically, or otherwise qualify as a homosexual. But for some it offers a virtually complete personal world where one can pursue a busy and varied "gay" life, socially as well as sexually, practically independent of "straight" society.

Like most heterosexuals I was barely aware of the gay community in New York when I first came to work in the city. A friend who knew it well offered to introduce me to his friends, with the understanding that I would try to write an objective study of their way of life. I spent several months talking chiefly to homosexuals who participate in gay life more or less exclusively, sometimes to the extent of working in a so-called "gay trade" (such as hairdressing) or in an office where other employees are homosexual. This article thus concerns itself with what might be called the homosexual bourgeoisie—people who are community-oriented, provincial, critical of undesirables. They are themselves frequently disdained by other homosexuals, some of whom are less preoccupied with their deviancy and participate freely in both gay and "straight" society. Still other homosexuals live more private and self-sufficient lives and have little or nothing at all to do with gay society.

But the homosexuals who confine themselves to their own "middle-class" community seem to me the appropriate group from which to gain some insight into the social aspects of homosexuality. Because they are much concerned with their own position in the community, they draw many distinctions among themselves which are too subtle to be reflected in police records or psychiatric studies of the isolated individual. In introducing some of the habits and styles of their life, I must however emphasize that the varieties of actual behavior among homosexuals are endless and I have undoubtedly oversimplified them here. Furthermore, the homosexuals who described themselves and their friends to me could be expected to generalize in defensive and self-interested ways—even unintentionally—when talking to a "square" reporter.

New York probably has the country's largest homosexual community if only because of its size, but few reliable statistics are available. The late Dr. Robert Lindner, drawing selectively on the statistics of several psychologists, psychiatrists, and sexual researchers (including Kinsey), arrived at an estimate of 4 to 6 per cent of "the total male population over age sixteen" who are homosexual in the gay sense of the word. Applied to New York City's population, this estimate would indicate a homosexual population of about 100,000. The number may be much higher, since any large city, and especially New York, attracts deviants seeking a degree of privacy, anonymity, and gay life not available in smaller communities. It would be impossible to estimate the number who participate in New York's homosexual society more or less exclusively, since many persons are socially or sexually disqualified for various reasons and others take part in it only to a limited degree.

Gay Bars and Beaches

In New York, as in other cities, bars are an important part of gay life, especially for young men who have just discovered homosexual society and for those new to the city who want to get acquainted. In Manhattan, about twenty bars cater to homosexuals exclusively and about twice that number are "mixed." They are scattered around the city with concentrations in the Greenwich Village area and the Upper East Side. In most cases they are located away from main business districts, and about the only thing which might distinguish them from any other neighborhood tavern is that their customers tend to be young, well-groomed, and well-dressed, and therefore not quite typical of New York neighborhood bar clientele. Lesbians have their own bars, but they are fewer in number and somewhat more obvious because all the customers are female, and at least some of them are "butch" lesbians, made conspicuous by their short hair, manly clothes, and generally tomboyish appearance.

A few bars have private back rooms where homosexuals can dance with one another. These, more than the other bars, seem to be dominated by a young crowd of regular patrons whom my guide referred to as "bar society," and the first one we visited proved to be fairly typical. It was an inconspicuous but very busy street-corner tavern near the Hudson River in West Greenwich Village. Although we went on a Thursday night, the back room was so crowded that many were standing, and the atmosphere was that of a speakeasy: dim lights, loud noise, cigarette smoke, music, and, I was told, a signal to stop dancing in the event of a police raid.

My reaction to the unusual sight of men embracing each other on the dance floor was one more of curiosity than aversion, probably because the dancers appeared so casual and others in the room so indifferent. I was far more surprised to see no one who "looked" homosexual. A few were a little too well-groomed or elegant in their behavior, and a few were dressed younger than their age (though all looked to be under thirty), but otherwise the only noticeable difference was that everyone resembled the dashing young men in college sportswear advertisements. At other bars I did see a few obviously effeminate persons, but they were not flamboyant, and I was told that the better class of gay bar usually discourages conspicuous homosexuals in order to avoid police crackdowns.

Word spreads quickly once a bar becomes gay, and many are opened with the intention of catering to homosexuals who will keep a place busy until closing every night of the week. A new bar will sometimes raid another, hiring away a popular bartender who will bring with him a large personal following.

New York's gay bars are periodically closed by the police, but no serious effort has been made to eliminate them—either because the owners pay off the police (as customers widely assume, and as bartenders sometimes intimate in justifying their dollar-a-bottle price for beer in the back rooms), or because the police believe they can be more easily watched and controlled if a few are permitted to operate in the open. A police cruiser was parked in front of one of the dancing bars I visited and its driver was standing inside the door talking to the proprietor as I entered, but no one in the back room, where about twenty-five male couples were dancing, paid any notice to this.

Bar owners are not the only businessmen who cater to the gay trade. A number of smart men's shops in the Village and on the Upper East Side feature slim-cut and youthfully styled clothing designed to appeal to homosexuals. Some stores carry bikini-type underwear and swimsuits for men, and fancy silk supporters. Swimsuits of this sort cannot be worn on public beaches, but certain parts of Fire Island (and sometimes other beaches) have become the more or less exclusive domain of the gay crowd, and there they have more freedom to dress and behave as they please, and generally "camp it up," *i.e.*, act "homosexually" without inhibition.

A number of restaurants, barber shops, tailors, gyms, athletic clubs and Turkish baths also cater to homosexuals. Some stationers even carry a line of greeting cards for "gay occasions," and sometimes an apartment or rooming house becomes predominantly homosexual. Some homosexuals feel enough group loyalty to patronize mainly those establishments considered gay, usually because of their employees, but others are indifferent to the point of calling them "fruitstands."

"Drag Balls" and "Sick" Behavior

Gay social life takes many forms. Some men spend practically every evening in bars, drinking beer and exchanging news and gossip: others are continually holding or attending parties, which may range from sedate evenings of drinking, talking, and listening to music, to wild nights of orgy. Hundreds of gay parties take place during a New York weekend and the homosexual can usually find one open to him. The genuine orgy, however, is less common and regarded by some as rather jading and degrading, but still "okay if you like that sort of thing." A colorful—but not necessarily sexual—event in the gay world is the "drag party" to which guests may come dressed as women. Unlike genuine transvestitism, however, such masquerading is often done as a titillating joke, the idea being to dress like a ridiculous parody of the female in order to humorously exaggerate one's "perversion."

The term *gay*, which often strikes a heterosexual as inappropriate if not ironic, becomes meaningful at parties and dancing bars. Any private gathering is an opportunity to relax and "drop the mask" one wears in public, and there is usually an air of conspiracy and intrigue which is not without its appeal. Such conditions tend to promote a spirit of good-fellowship, and everyone tries to outdo each other in being friendly, sociable, and "gay." Part of this is artificial—the same sort of attempt at jolly behavior that may go on between males and females after a few drinks at a dull cocktail party. But no doubt homosexuals do feel a genuine exuberance in temporarily escaping the sense of rejection implicit in their frequent need to conceal their nature from employer, acquaintances, and family. The "gaiety" of many homosexuals is also expressed in a sense of humor, perhaps defensive, which often makes fun of themselves. ("Sorry I'm so late, dearie, but I kept tripping in my high heels.") Gay homosexuals I talked to frequently used such terms as *fag, fairy, swish, pansy, screaming queen* (but rarely *queer*) to describe persons they did not like; however, they used the same terms often (plus the plain *queen*) in referring humorously to gay friends. One person introduced me to his roommate as a "queen for a day who is writing a fairy tale."

What I saw and heard of party life and bar life left with me the impression that the homosexuals, at least in those circles are, often quite lonely people who need to surround themselves with friends and stay continually amused. Some have virtually no heterosexual friends, serious interests or outside diversions, or long-range goals. They are content to support themselves through low-paying white-collar jobs, and otherwise are preoccupied with the intricacies of cliquish, competitive gay society.

About the only social event staged publicly for homosexuals is the "drag ball," at which so-called "drag queens" can legally impersonate women. These are held regularly in commercial halls and may draw a thousand or more persons, including a sizable number of heterosexual curiosity seekers. At the Exotic Ball and Carnival held in Manhattan Center last October, forty-four men were arrested for masquerading as women when New York Police Commissioner Michael J. Murphy saw the group as he arrived to attend a policeman's ball on another floor of the same building. The charges later were dismissed since the affair was a bona fide masquerade party, but one man was booked for indecent exposure.

Some New York nightclubs feature female impersonators and other "gay entertainment," but these are strictly offbeat tourist attractions for heterosexuals.

Drag balls, and especially the nightclub entertainment, are objected to by some homosexuals who say that they oppose any type of public behavior or appearance that sustains the stereotype of a freak who minces, wears cosmetics, and speaks with a lisp. In fact, appearance and behavior, to a large extent, determine whether or not an individual will find acceptance in gay society.

By far the majority of homosexuals have no obvious mannerisms and can pass easily in heterosexual society, and many claim to regard the "flaming faggot" with contempt. Similarly excluded from polite gay society are the hoodlums who engage in male prostitution, shakedowns, muggings, or other antisocial behavior, as well as the "degenerate fag" who regularly risks arrest by openly soliciting in public restrooms and parks. Generally speaking, any behavior which attracts heterosexual attention is disapproved, if for no other reason than that it is considered bad public relations.

Many psychiatrists trace effeminism to a deepseated identification with the female sex, pointing out that effeminate mannerisms are not necessarily an indication of homosexuality. Effeminate homosexuals often believe they are "just born that way," but I heard other theories advanced. One was that mannerisms sometimes are acquired, perhaps unconsciously, by young men who try to find acceptance in gay life by adopting what they believe to be its conventions. Another held that the ostentatious queen was simply a "sick and neurotic" person who cannot adjust to his condition, and who compensates by "thumbing his powdered nose" at the society which rejects him. Blatant effeminism seems to be more prevalent among homosexuals of the lower socio-economic classes; if so, it may be that such men are more distressed by their loss of masculinity and less able to reach an intelligent understanding of it, and thus are more inclined to exhibit abnormal behavior.

Some sexual tendencies are unacceptable in gay society. The more flagrant homosexual sadists and masochists have formed their own little outcast groups on the fringes of gay life and are characterized by their penchant for leather, denim, or rubber clothing, and by their interest in matters of "bondage" and "discipline." Some cultivate a tough, masculine appearance—black leather jacket, motorcycle boots, tight denims, sometimes a symbolic piece of chain dangling from the belt or hooked around the upper arm. Some wear a Band-Aid on the hand to indicate masochistic inclinations. The two types are lumped together and referred to as S-Ms or "sadie-masies" by other homosexuals who seem to know little about them and say they do not associate with them.

Transvestitism and fetishism, too, are generally regarded as "sick behavior. The ordinary gay person tends to think of himself as an otherwise normal individual whose sexual inclinations are merely reversed; but he will say that he considers other forms of deviancy to be genuine "perversions," insisting that such inclinations are not "normal" to either the male or female. This is especially true with regard to violent sex crimes, and child molesting.

If anything, the gay person is even more scandalized by violent psychopathic behavior than other people, since the police, the public, and newspapers tend to use the term "homosexual" in describing any crimes involving members of the same sex, thereby implying that homosexuals are inherently depraved. Ordinarily, criminal psychopaths who are homosexual have no wish to participate in gay life, even if they could find acceptance. Most of the people I talked to believed that homosexual child molesters and other "sex maniacs" were secretive and tortured men who were incapable of openly acknowledging their deviancy: hence they had no desire to fraternize with other homosexuals. I was told that many male prostitutes were homosexuals who refused to acknowledge their inclinations but used prostitution as an excuse to indulge in homosexual relations. Some, known as "rough trade," then beat and rob the "dirty queer" to preserve their own heterosexual illusions.

The bisexual—defined here only as a person who describes himself as one—is a kind of mulatto in gay life. He is rejected by conventional heterosexual society and sometimes by gay homosexuals who argue that there is no such thing as true bisexuality and that those who claim to be attracted equally to men and women are only trying to prove their masculinity to themselves. Bisexuals disagree vigorously, and criticize other homosexuals for being too narrow in their interests.

It should be kept in mind that homosexuals, like heterosexuals, do not always practice what they preach. Engaging a prostitute, extreme effeminism, associating with various "undesirables," accepting money, indiscreet "cruising" in public, and so on, are practices generally frowned upon in polite gay society, although an individual may well indulge in them when his friends aren't looking.

Sexual satisfaction is usually seen as a matter of personal preference, and homosexuals tend to be liberal in what they consider respectable sex. A person may specialize in the active or the passive role, or in partners who are very masculine, very effeminate, younger, older, or blond and blue-eyed. Sexual eccentricities, even when socially unacceptable by gay standards, rarely are condemned as wrong or immoral. To some extent, attitudes toward sex divide along familiar heterosexual lines —one person being casually promiscuous another insisting on only one "boyfriend" at a time and exhibiting jealousy in the event of competition. A few seek to elevate their relationships to an idealized level—the ultimate spiritual union between two faithful lovers in what they conceive to be the classic Greek tradition. (Some homosexuals manage to establish lengthy or even permanent relationships, but successful "marriages" seem rare. One obvious reason is the lack of legal and social sanctions: family disputes are easily settled by separation.)

Freud's Reassurance

The homosexual's position in society is often precarious. Discovery can cost him his reputation and perhaps his career. He is aware that, according to New York law, every sexual act could cost him years in prison (though it rarely happens). He feels society hates him, and unjustly. Frequently he is guilt-ridden, aware or not, and lacks the self-acceptance he needs in order to live comfortably with his condition, which itself is thought to be closely related to an unhealthy early psychological environment. These factors, rather than homosexuality alone, are what some believe to be the main causes of emotional instability, effeminism, violence, and other problems commonly blamed on sexual deviation. Homosexuals themselves argue that while these problems are indeed widespread, they tend to be exaggerated by psychiatrists, the police, and other authorities whose work brings them into contact only with disturbed individuals: they insist that many homosexuals can be reasonably happy and productive people, capable of leading quite as fulfilled lives as heterosexuals.

Although psychologists are far from agreement on the causes and remedies for homosexuality, there is considerable support for this claim. In a letter to a despairing mother, written in 1935, Freud himself expressed a general view of the problem which many analysts would no doubt affirm today:

Homosexuality is assuredly no advantage, but it is nothing to be ashamed of, no vice, no degradation, it cannot be classified as an illness; we consider it to be a variation of the sexual function produced by a certain arrest of sexual development. Many highly respectable individuals of ancient and modern times have been homosexuals, several of the greatest men among them. . . . It is a great injustice to persecute homosexuality as a crime, and cruelty too.

[You ask if we can] abolish homosexuality and make normal heterosexuality take its place. The answer is in a general way, we cannot promise to achieve it. In a certain number of cases we succeed in developing the blighted germs of heterosexual tendencies which are present in every homosexual; in the majority of cases it is no more possible.

What analysis can do for your son runs in a different line. If he is unhappy, neurotic, torn by conflicts, inhibited in his social life, analysis may bring him harmony, peace of mind, full efficiency, whether he remains a homosexual or gets changed.

Some psychiatrists do consider homosexuality a severe emotional disorder that both can and should be corrected—if the individual sincerely wants to change. The relatively few instances of successful treatment would seem to indicate most do not. Another view which seems to be gaining wider acceptance is that homosexuality may arise out of faulty differentiation of the male and female components in the "psychosexual" development of the individual, and thus should be considered a character or personality problem rather than a deep-seated neurosis. Such broad hypotheses subdivide into numerous and often conflicting theories. Some experts are now reconsidering the possibility that hereditary factors, which were once dismissed, may indeed play a role. There is however a fairly wide consensus that adjustment to homosexuality is sometimes preferable to attempts at cure.

Evidence that there may be no inherent connection between homosexuality and pathology has been gathered in a study conducted by Dr. Evelyn Hooker of the University of California and published in 1957 as a preliminary report on "The Adjustment of the Male Overt Homosexual." For the study, thirty apparently well-adjusted homosexuals were matched for age, IQ, and education against thirty apparently well-adjusted heterosexuals. The teams then were given a battery of psychological tests, the results of which were analyzed blind by two of Dr. Hooker's colleagues who found themselves unable to pick out which of the subjects were homosexuals. Nor was there any significant difference between the groups in overall adjustment ratings. Dr. Hooker does not present her results as at all conclusive, but she considers them ground for reviewing the theory that homosexuality and pathology are inherently related.

Many homosexuals have always contended they were no different from anyone else—just sexually left-handed. A few even argue that homosexuality would be an altogether superior way of life were it not for society's square attitudes. However, such militancy is more characteristic of the few "organized" homosexuals than of the rank and file. The New York Homosexual League conducted an informal poll among three hundred deviates, asking each, among other things, if he would want to become heterosexual if a safe, easy means were available. Ninety-six percent answered no, but only three per cent said they would want to see a child of theirs homosexual. The attitude which seems to be most commonly held is that homosexuality is not the preferable condition, but there's nothing morally wrong with it, it even has some things to recommend it, and in any case one has to make the best of the situation. Out of this desire to make the best of it grows a gay community with a social structure specially adapted to homosexual needs.

The Easy Ways to Status

Still, the term *gay society* must be used very cautiously. If a fairly self-conscious and recognizable gay community can be observed in New York, it should be clear that its habits and standards do not apply to thousands of homosexuals who have little or nothing to do with it. Generalizations about gay "social structure" thus must be even more tentative than those about heterosexual society. Nevertheless, gay society does seem to deal with such questions as status and money in roughly consistent ways.

For obvious reasons, personal attractiveness and age seem the most important qualifications for getting ahead socially in the gay world. A premium is placed on appearing neat, fashionably dressed, young, and handsome, and anyone who is slovenly or physically unattractive is severely handicapped. Fashionable dress currently means slim-cut Continental or extreme Ivy League styles in suits, and well-tailored, collegiate-looking casual wear. The perfect dresser is extremely up-to-date, but careful to avoid styles so radical or grooming so fastidious as to be termed "faggoty-elegant." Homosexuals commonly dress younger and try to look younger than their years, but those who overdo it are often ridiculed. Although one finds quite a few exceptions, young homosexuals generally prefer their own age group socially as well as sexually, and an older person who insists on a youthful sexual partner may have to turn to male prostitutes.

Wealth and family background themselves usually are not sources of status within the homosexual community, though their manifestations—possessions, manners, etc.—may be. Since most homosexuals have no dependents and only personal expenses, a modest income will usually provide the obvious luxuries of "sophisticated" city life, reducing the importance of real wealth. Most homosexuals who participate exclusively in gay social life have a relatively low income, so there exists no real moneyed class within the community toward which to aspire. A prominent family background brings little status since few homosexuals can afford to mix their gay life with their straight life.

A college education, as such, confers

relatively little status within the community, but in many circles it is important to display cultural interests and a degree of cool sophistication or "hipness." The folklore of the gay world has it that homosexuals tend to be specially gifted in the creative arts. There is not much evidence to support this notion, although living in an "enemy" society of heterosexuals may well increase one's sensitivity and perception. Quite naturally, however, homosexuals tend to be attracted to creative fields, which are traditionally tolerant, rather than to occupations like law, engineering, or business management where disclosure could be ruinous. A young single man, moreover, can better afford the risks and financial insecurity of an artistic career. A few occupations such as clothes designing, window dressing, decorating, modeling, and hairdressing are considered gay trades and carry more prestige than office work and clerking. So do some types of performing (ice-skating, chorus dancing, etc.). For the most part, however, the homosexuals of the gay community are not notably successful people by the standards of the outer world. If they are gifted professionals or artists, for example, they will usually find their way to more complex and interesting homosexual, and mixed, milieus, and their lives will seldom center in gay society.

The gay social climber (like any other) considers address and neighborhood important, but he sometimes goes to extremes that would strike the status-seeking heterosexual as too obvious. Some will sacrifice every other luxury to live in a plush apartment in Sutton Place on a clerk's salary, or pay high rent for a cramped room because it has an East Fifties address.

In gay society an individual is often typed (not always accurately) according to his neighborhood. The "East Side Snob" is described as an elegant, high-class dandy, or a bland, pseudosophisticated "organization man with a flair," and both tend to confine themselves to their own more private social circles. The West Sider is thought to be a lower-class, sometimes bizarre person, and the two extremes seem to meet in the Village where stereotypes mix. To some homosexuals, Forty-second Street between Sixth and Eighth Avenues is practically a taboo area because of the hustlers, hoodlums, and generally undesirable types who often congregate there. The West Seventies are said to be a "pansy patch" because of the number of obviously effeminate homosexuals, often Puerto Rican, who live there; and some areas of the Upper East Side are called "fairy flats" because they are supposedly inhabited by "conspicuously elegant types usually walking poodles," as one informant put it. Brooklyn Heights, just across the East River from Lower Manhattan, is thought of as a kind of homosexual suburbia popular with "young marrieds."

Despite the social discrimination and class distinctions operating at most levels of the gay community, upward social mobility is not only possible but fairly easy. The superficial nature of many status symbols makes them simple to acquire, and the most humble and unsophisticated rural bumpkin arriving cold in the big city can advance socially by adopting the right conventions and cultivating the right interests. A homosexual illustrator, complaining about fashion-consciousness in gay life, told me that a friend of his considered Vance Packard's *The Status Seekers* a valuable "get-ahead book," full of good tips.

Race is less often a deciding factor of acceptability in homosexual circles. Attractive Negroes and Puerto Ricans can sometimes use their homosexuality to enter various elite gay circles, particularly in the Village, and even many white homosexuals who will not accept Negroes socially nonetheless are "quite democratic in bed." Talking of racial as well as other distinctions, one man told me: "Homosexuals are terrible snobs, you know; but not sexually, at least when no one's looking."

Homosexuals who are not deeply involved in the gay community often criticize the conformity, phoniness, and lack of individuality they believe characterizes much of this society. There are few interesting eccentrics or bohemians; most of the men seem preoccupied with "belonging" or getting ahead, and one is not aware of much depth of personality. These qualities may reflect the strong sense of rejection and insecurity, which creates a compelling need in some homosexuals to find personal acceptance. Responding to this need are a community and a value system which seem to diminish the homosexual's social handicaps by attaching status to objects well within his reach. Furthermore there are sexual considerations: homosexuals are reluctant to erect insurmountable social restrictions that would severely limit their sexual activities by excluding many personally desirable partners.

The New Pressure Groups

Some of the people I talked to believe the homosexual's lot is gradually improving. More and more novels, plays, and even movies are venturing into the subject, usually treating it with some understanding. Since the late 1950s a number of radio and television programs have explored sexual deviation, and talks on the subject are increasingly common, both by professional persons and by homosexuals themselves. In 1961, Illinois became the first state to exclude from its criminal code private homosexual relations between consenting adults, a revision now advocated by many legal, medical, and psychiatric societies. One conspicuous step toward toleration took place in 1950 when homosexuals first were able to form organizations, hold meetings and conventions, and publish their own books and magazines. Earlier attempts had failed, usually in the face of extra-legal and social pressures.

The most prominent homosexual organization, the Mattachine Society (so named after medieval court jesters who dared to speak the truth in the face of stern authority) originated in California in 1950 and later opened chapters in other cities. It was followed by One, Inc., and by the Daughters of Bilitis, a national organization for female homosexuals. Today there are more than a dozen national and local organizations for "homophiles," publishing *One Magazine, One Quarterly, The Ladder* (Daughters of Bilitis), *The Mattachine Review,* The League For Civil Education *News* (a biweekly newspaper published in San Francisco), and numerous local newsletters.

In New York, the local Mattachine Society (now independent of the California group) has around two hundred members and holds regular meetings and study groups at which psychiatrists, lawyers, and other professionals speak. A new group called the Homosexual League was founded last year and is chiefly the work of Randolfe Wicker, a young man in his twenties whose main objective is to "bring the subject of homosexuality into the open" by speaking before interested groups and arranging for others to lecture on the subject.

Despite the increase in organizational activities, very few homosexuals belong to groups or subscribe to publications. Some are afraid to join or subscribe, and others oppose organizing on the grounds that it only attracts attention which will make things worse. The majority simply are not interested in crusading and want only to be left alone. Judging from the readers' letters published, the magazines are of greater interest to homosexuals in smaller cities who tend to feel more isolated.

Even though the organizations and magazines are not widely supported, they have exerted a subtle influence on both heterosexual and homosexual thinking. To city, state, medical, and other authorities they are tangible evidence that homosexuals are not altogether the either dangerous or laughable perverts that police arrests or locker-room jokes imply. Moreover, they document many aspects of homosexuality and examine its problems, and no doubt provide a welcome source of information and understanding to many young persons suddenly confronted with the realization they are "queer."

Some authorities who hold that homosexuality is a neurotic symptom might warn against increasing its social acceptance, in the belief that this would invite latent deviants to become overt, and discourage the overt from seeking therapy. But those who consider it to be a type of personality disorder in which adjustment is often preferable to attempts at cure, believe that increased tolerance of homosexuality may help reduce the intense guilt that sometimes leads to seriously neurotic or antisocial behavior.

In any case, even a superficial inquiry into the community life of homosexuals should make two things clear. First, the term *homosexual* itself means little unless it is carefully qualified. The latent homosexual, the transvestite, the child molester, the lone wolf, the gay person, and so on, may all have very different problems and social roles, deriving from radically different causes. Secondly, the isolated life of the gay community may be seen as a reflection of the dominant social order itself. Our society has been quick to adopt defensive and mocking attitudes toward homosexuals and painfully slow to acquire a humane and mature understanding of their condition.

42

Violence and the Police

William A. Westley

Brutality and the third degree have been identified with the municipal police of the United States since their inauguration in 1844. These aspects of police activity have been subject to exaggeration, repeated exposure, and virulent criticism. Since they are a breach of the law by the law-enforcement agents, they constitute a serious social, but intriguing sociological, problem. Yet there is little information about or understanding of the process through which such activity arises or of the purposes which it serves.

This paper is concerned with the genesis and function of the illegal use of violence by the police . . . It shows that (a) the police accept and morally justify their illegal use of violence; (b) such acceptance and justification arise through their occupational experience; and (c) its use is functionally related to the collective occupational, as well as to the legal, ends of the police . . .

The technical demands of a man's work tend to specify the kinds of social relationships in which he will be involved and to select the groups with whom these relationships are to be maintained. The social definition of the occupation invests its

Reprinted from *The American Journal of Sociology*, 49 (July, 1953), 34–42, "Violence and the Police" by William A. Westley as abridged by permission of The University of Chicago Press and the author. Footnotes have been renumbered.

members with a common prestige position. Thus, a man's occupation is a major determining factor of his conduct and social identity. This being so, it involves more than man's work, and one must go beyond the technical in the explanation of work behavior. One must discover the occupationally derived definitions of self and conduct which arise in the involvements of technical demands, social relationships between colleagues and with the public, status, and self-conception. To understand these definitions, one must track them back to the occupational problems in which they have their genesis.[1]

The policeman finds his most pressing problems in his relationships to the public. His is a service occupation but of an incongruous kind, since he must discipline those whom he serves. He is regarded as corrupt and inefficient by, and meets with hostility and criticism from, the public. He regards the public as his enemy, feels his occupation to be in conflict with the community, and regards himself to be a pariah. The experience and the feeling give rise to a collective emphasis on secrecy, an attempt to coerce respect from the public, and a belief that almost any means are legitimate in completing an important arrest. These are for the policeman basic occupational values. They arise from his experience, take precedence over his legal responsibilities, are central to an understanding of his conduct, and form the occupational contexts within which violence gains its meaning. This then is the background for our analysis.[2]

The materials which follow are drawn from a case study of a municipal police department in an industrial city of approximately one hundred and fifty thousand inhabitants. This study included participation in all types of police activities, ranging from walking the beat and cruising with policemen in a squad car to the observation of raids, interrogations, and the police school. It included intensive interviews with over half the men in the department who were representative as to rank, time in service, race, religion, and specific type of police job.

Duty and Violence

In the United States the use of violence by the police is both an occupational prerogative and a necessity. Police powers include the use of violence, for to them, within civil society, has been delegated the monopoly of the legitimate means of violence possessed by the state. Police are obliged by their duties to use violence as the only measure adequate to control and apprehension in the presence of counterviolence.

Violence in the form of the club and the gun is for the police a means of persuasion. Violence from the criminal, the drunk, the quarreling family, and the rioter arises in the course of police duty. The fighting drunk who is damaging property or assailing his fellows and who looks upon the policeman as a malicious intruder justifies for the policeman his use of force in restoring order. The armed criminal who has demonstrated a casual regard for the lives of others and a general hatred of the policeman forces the use of violence by the police in the pursuit of duty. Every policeman has some such experiences, and they proliferate in police lore. They constitute a commonsense and legal justification for the use of violence by the police and for training policemen in the skills of violence. Thus, from experience in the pursuit of their legally prescribed duties, the police develop

[1] The ideas are not original. I am indebted for many of them to Everett C. Hughes, although he is in no way responsible for their present formulation (see E. C. Hughes, "Work and the Self," in Rohrer and Sherif, *Social Psychology at the Crossroads* [New York: Harper and Brothers 1951]).

[2] The background material will be developed in subsequent papers which will analyze the occupational experience of the police and give a full description of police norms.

a justification for the use of violence. They come to see it as good, as useful, and as their own. Furthermore, although legally their use of violence is limited to the requirements of the arrest and the protection of themselves and the community, the contingencies of their occupation lead them to enlarge the area in which violence may be used. Two kinds of experience—that with respect to the conviction of the felon and that with respect to the control of sexual conduct—will illustrate how and why the illegal use of violence arises.

1. *The conviction of the felon.*—The apprehension and conviction of the felon is, for the policeman, the essence of police work. It is the source of prestige both within and outside police circles, it has career implications, and it is a major source of justification for the existence of the police before a critical and often hostile public. Out of these conditions a legitimation for the illegal use of violence is wrought.

The career and prestige implication of the "good pinch"[3] elevate it to a major end in the conduct of the policeman. It is an end which is justified both legally and through public opinion as one which should be of great concern to the police. Therefore it takes precedence over other duties and tends to justify strong means. Both trickery and violence are such means. The "third degree" has been criticized for many years and extensive administrative controls have been devised in an effort to eliminate it. Police persistence in the face of that attitude suggests that the illegal use of violence is regarded as functional to their work. It also indicates a tendency to regard the third degree as a legitimate means for obtaining the conviction of the felon. However, to understand the strength of this legitimation, one must include other factors: the competition between patrolman and detectives and the publicity value of convictions for the police department.

The patrolman has less access to cases that might result in the "good pinch" than the detective. Such cases are assigned to the detective, and for their solution he will reap the credit. Even where the patrolman first detects the crime, or actually apprehends the possible offender, the case is likely to be turned over to the detective. Therefore patrolmen are eager to obtain evidence and make the arrest before the arrival of the detectives. Intimidation and actual violence frequently come into play under these conditions. This is illustrated in the following case recounted by a young patrolman when he was questioned as to the situations in which he felt that the use of force was necessary:

> One time Joe and I found three guys in a car, and we found that they had a gun down between the seats. We wanted to find out who owned that gun before the dicks arrived so that we could make a good pinch. They told us.

Patrolmen feel that little credit is forthcoming from a clean beat (a crimeless beat), while a number of good arrests really stands out on the record. To a great extent this is actually the case, since a good arrest results in good newspaper publicity, and the policeman who has made many "good pinches" has prestige among his colleagues.

A further justification for the illegal use of violence arises from the fact that almost every police department is under continuous criticism from the community, which tends to assign its own moral responsibilities to the police. The police are therefore faced with the task of justifying themselves to the public, both as individuals and as a

[3] Policemen, in the case studied, use this term to mean an arrest which (a) is politically clear and (b) likely to bring them esteem. Generally it refers to felonies, but in the case of a real vice drive it may include the arrest and *conviction* of an important bookie.

group. They feel that the solution of major criminal cases serves this function. This is illustrated in the following statement:

> There is a case I remember of four Negroes who held up a filling station. We got a description of them and picked them up. Then we took them down to the station and really worked them over. I guess that everybody that came into the station that night had a hand in it, and they were in pretty bad shape. Do you think that sounds cruel? Well, you know what we got out of it? We broke a big case in ———. There was a mob of twenty guys, burglars and stick-up men, and eighteen of them are in the pen now. Sometimes you have to get rough with them, see. The way I figure it is, if you can get a clue that a man is a pro and if he won't co-operate, tell you what you want to know, it is justified to rough him up a little, up to a point. You know how it is. You feel that the end justifies the means.

It is easier for the police to justify themselves to the community through the dramatic solution of big crimes than through orderly and responsible completion of their routine duties. Although they may be criticized for failures in routine areas, the criticism for the failure to solve big crimes is more intense and sets off a criticism of their work in noncriminal areas. The pressure to solve important cases therefore becomes strong. The following statement, made in reference to the use of violence in interrogations, demonstrates the point:

> If it's a big case and there is a lot of pressure on you and they tell you you can't go home until the case is finished, then naturally you are going to lose patience.

The policeman's response to this pressure is to extend the use of violence to its illegal utilization in interrogations. The apprehension of the felon or the "good pinch" thus constitues a basis for justifying the illegal use of violence.

2. *Control of sexual conduct.*—The police are responsible for the enforcement of laws regulating sexual conduct. This includes the suppression of sexual deviation and the protection of the public from advances and attacks of persons of deviant sexual tendencies. Here the police face a difficult task. The victims of such deviants are notoriously unwilling to co-operate, since popular curiosity and gossip about sexual crimes and the sanctions against the open discussion of sexual activities make it embarrassing for the victim to admit or describe a deviant sexual advance or attack and cause him to feel that he gains a kind of guilt by association from such admissions. Thus the police find that frequently the victims will refuse to identify or testify against the deviant.

These difficulties are intensified by the fact that, once the community becomes aware of sexual depredations, the reports of such activity multiply well beyond reasonable expectations. Since the bulk of these reports will be false, they add to the confusion of the police and consequently to the elusiveness of the offender.

The difficulties of the police are further aggravated by extreme public demand for the apprehension of the offender. The hysteria and alarm generated by reports of a peeping Tom, a rapist, or an exhibitionist result in great public pressure on the police; and, should the activities continue, the public becomes violently critical of police efficiency. The police, who feel insecure in their relationship to the public, are extremely sensitive to this criticism and feel that they must act in response to the demands made by the political and moral leaders of the community.

Thus the police find themselves caught in a dilemma. Apprehension is extremely difficult because of the confusion created by public hysteria and the scarcity of witnesses, but the police are compelled to action by extremely public demands. They dissolve this dilemma through the illegal utilization of violence.

A statement of this "misuse" of police powers is represented in the remarks of a patrolman:

> Now in my own case when I catch a guy like that I just beat him up and take him into the woods and beat him until he can't crawl. I have had seventeen cases like that in the last couple of years. I tell that guy that if I catch him doing that again I will take him out to those woods and I will shoot him. I tell him that I carry a second gun on me just in case I find guys like him and that I will plant it in his hand and say that he tried to kill and that no jury will convict me.

This statement is extreme and is not representative of policemen in general. In many instances the policeman is likely to act in a different fashion. This is illustrated in the following statement of a rookie who described what happened when he and his partner investigated a parked car which had aroused their suspicions:

> He [the partner] went up there and pretty soon he called me, and there were a couple of fellows in the car with their pants open. I couldn't understand it. I kept looking around for where the woman would be. They were both pretty plastered. One was a young kid about eighteen years old, and and the other was an older man. We decided, with the kid so drunk, that bringing him in would only really ruin his reputation, and told him to go home. Otherwise we would have piched them. During the time we were talking to them they offered us twenty-eight dollars, and I was going to pinch them when they showed the money, but my partner said, "Never mind, let them go."

Nevertheless, most policemen would apply no sanctions against a colleague who took the more extreme view of the right to use violence and would openly support some milder form of illegal coercion. This is illustrated in the statement of another rookie:

> They feel that it's okay to rough a man up in the case of sex crimes. One of the older men advised me that if the courts didn't punish a man we should. He told me about a sex crime, the story about it, and then said that the law says the policeman has the right to use the amount of force necessary to make an arrest and that in that kind of a crime you can use just a little more force. They feel definitely, for example, in extreme cases like rape, that if a man was guilty he ought to be punished even if you could not get any evidence on him. My feeling is that all the men on the force feel that way, at least from what they have told me.

Furthermore, the police believe, and with some justification it seems, that the community supports their definition of the situation and that they are operating in terms of an implicit directive.

The point of this discussion is that the control of sexual conduct is so difficult and the demand for it so incessant that the police come to sanction the illegal use of violence in obtaining that control. This does not imply that all policemen treat all sex deviants brutally, for, as the above quotations indicate, such is not the case. Rather, it indicates that this use of violence is permitted and condoned by the police and that they come to think of it as a resource more extensive than is included in the legal definition.

Legitimation of Violence

The preceding discussion has indicated two ways in which the experience of the police encourages them to use violence as a general resource in the achievement of their occupational ends and thus to sanction its illegal use. The experience, thus, makes violence acceptable to the policeman as a generalized means. We now wish to indicate the particular basis on which this general resource is legitimated. In particular we wish to point out the extent to which the policeman tends to transfer violence from a legal resource to a personal resource, one which he uses to further his own ends.

Seventy-three policemen, drawn from all ranks and constituting approximately 50 per cent of the patrolmen, were asked, "When do you think a policeman is justified in roughing a man up?" The intent of the question was to get them to legitimate the use of violence. Their replies are summarized in Table 1.

TABLE 1. Bases for the Use of Force Named by 73 Policemen*

TYPE OF RESPONSE	FREQUENCY	PERCENTAGE
(A) Disrespect for police	27	37
(B) When impossible to avoid	17	23
(C) To obtain information	14	19
(D) To make an arrest	6	8
(E) For the hardened criminal	5	7
(F) When you know man is guilty	2	3
(G) For sex criminals	2	3
Total	73	100

* Many respondents described more than one type of situation which they felt called for the use of violence. The "reason" which was was either (*a*) given most heatedly and at greatest length and/or (*b*) given first was used to characterize the respondent's answer to the question. However, this table is exhaustive of the types of replies which were given.

An inspection of the types and distribution of the responses indicates (1) that violence is legitimated by illegal ends (A, C, E, F, G) in 69 per cent of the cases; (2) that violence is legitimated in terms of purely personal or group ends (A) in 37 per cent of the cases (this is important, since it is the largest single reason for the use of violence given); and (3) that legal ends are the bases for legitimation in 31 per cent of the cases (B and D). However, this probably represents a distortion of the true feelings of some of these men, since both the police chief and the community had been severely critical of the use of violence by the men, and the respondents had a tendency to be very cautious with the interviewer, whom some of them never fully trusted. Furthermore, since all the men were conscious of the chief's policy and of public criticism, it seems likely that those who did justify the use of violence for illegal and personal ends no longer recognized the illegality involved. They probably believed that such ends fully represented a moral legitimation for their use of violence.

The most significant finding is that at least 37 per cent of the men believed that it was legitimate to use violence to coerce respect. This suggests that policemen use the resource of violence to persuade their audience (the public) to respect their occupational status. In terms of the policeman's definition of the situation, the individual who lacks respect for the police, the "wise guy" who talks back, or any individual who acts or talks in a disrespectful way, deserves brutality. This idea is epitomized in admonitions given to the rookies such as, "You gotta make them respect you" and "You gotta act tough." Examples of some of the responses to the preceding question that fall into the "disrespect for the police" category follow:

Well, there are cases. For example, when you stop a fellow for a routine questioning, say a wise guy, and he starts talking back to you and telling you you are no good and that sort of thing. You know you can take a man in on a disorderly conduct charge, but you can practically never make it stick. So what you do in a case like that is to egg the guy on until he makes a remark where you can justifiably slap him and, then, if he fights back, you can call it resisting arrest.

Well, it varies in different cases. Most of the police use punishment if the fellow gives them any trouble. Usually you can judge a man who will give you trouble though. *If there is any slight resistance*, you can go all out on him. You shouldn't do it in the street though. Wait until you are in the squad car, because, even if you are in the right and a guy takes a poke at you, just when you are hitting back somebody's just likely to come around the corner, and what he will say is that you are beating the guy with your club.

Well a prisoner deserves to be hit when he goes to the point where he tries to put you below him.

You gotta get rough when a man's language becomes very bad, when he is trying to make a fool of you in front of everybody else. I think most policemen try to treat people in a nice way, but usually you have to talk pretty rough. That's the only way to set a man down, to make him show a little respect.

If a fellow called a policeman a filthy name, a slap in the mouth would be a good thing, especially if it was out in the public where calling a policeman a bad name would look bad for the police.

There was the incident of a fellow I picked up. I was on the beat, and I was taking him down to the station. There were people following us. He kept saying that I wasn't in the army. Well, he kept going on like that and I finally had to bust him one. I had to do it. The people would have thought I was afraid otherwise.

These results suggest (1) that the police believe that these private or group ends constitute a moral legitimation for violence which is equal *or superior* to the legitimation derived from the law and (2) that the monopoly of violence delegated to the police, by the state, to enforce the ends of the state has been appropriated by the police as a personal resource to be used for personal and group ends.

The Use of Violence

The sanctions for the use of violence arising from occupational experience and the fact that policemen morally justify even its illegal use may suggest that violence is employed with great frequency and little provocation. Such an impression would be erroneous, for the actual use of violence is limited by other considerations, such as individual inclinations, the threat of detection, and a sensitivity to public reactions.

Individual policemen vary of course in psychological disposition and past experience. All have been drawn from the larger community which tends to condemn the use of violence and therefore have internalized with varying degrees of intensity this other definition of violence. Their experience as policemen creates a new dimension to their self-conceptions and gives them a new perspective on the use of violence. But individual men vary in the degree to which they assimilate this new conception of self. Therefore, the amount of violence which is used and the frequency with which it is employed will vary among policemen according to their individual propensities. However, policemen cannot and do not employ sanctions against their colleagues for using violence,[4] and individual men who personally condemn the use of violence and avoid it whenever possible[5] refuse openly to condemn acts of violence by other men on the force. Thus, the collective sanction for the use of violence permits those men who are inclined to its use to employ it without fear.

All policemen, however, are conscious of the dangers of the illegal use of violence. If detected, they may be subject to a lawsuit and possibly dismissal from the force. Therefore, they limit its use to what they think they can get away with. Thus, they

[4] The emphasis on secrecy among the police prevents them from using legal sanctions against their colleagues.

[5] Many men who held jobs in the police station rather than on beats indicated to the interviewer that their reason for choosing a desk job was to avoid the use of violence.

recognize that, if a man is guilty of a serious crime, it is easy to "cover up" for their brutality by accusing him of resisting arrest, and the extent to which they believe a man guilty tends to act as a precondition to the use of violence.[6]

The policeman, in common with members of other occupations, is sensitive to the evaluation of his occupation by the public. A man's work is an important aspect of his status, and to the extent that he is identified with his work (by himself and/or the community) he finds that his self-esteem requires the justification and social elevation of his work. Since policemen are low in the occupational prestige scale, subject to continuous criticism, and in constant contact with this criticizing and evaluating public, they are profoundly involved in justifying their work and its tactics to the public and to themselves. The way in which the police emphasize the solution of big crimes and their violent solution to the problem of the control of sexual conduct illustrate this concern. However, different portions of the public have differing definitions of conduct and are of differential importance to the policeman, and the way in which the police define different portions of the public has an effect on whether or not they will use violence.

The police believe that certain groups of persons will respond only to fear and rough treatment. In the city studied they defined both Negroes and slum dwellers in this category. The following statements, each by a different man, typify the manner in which they discriminate the public:

> In the good districts you appeal to people's judgment and explain the law to them. In the South Side the only way is to appear like you are the boss.

> You can't ask them a question and get an answer that is not a lie. In the South Side the only way to walk into a tavern is to walk in swaggering as if you own the place and if somebody is standing in your way give him an elbow and push him aside.

> The colored people understand one thing. The policeman is the law, and he is going to treat you rough and that's the way you have to treat them. Personally, I don't think the colored are trying to help themselves one bit. If you don't treat them rough they will sit right on top of your head.

Discriminations with respect to the public are largely based on the political power of the group, the degree to which the police believe that the group is potentially criminal, and the type of treatment which the police believe will elicit respect from it.

Variations in the administration and community setting of the police will introduce variations in their use of violence. Thus, a thoroughly corrupt police department will use violence in supporting the ends of this corruption, while a carefully administrated nonpolitical department can go a long way toward reducing the illegal use of violence. However, wherever the basic conditions here described are present, it will be very difficult to eradicate the illegal use of violence.

Given these conditions, violence will be used when necessary to the pursuit of duty or when basic occupational values are threatened. Thus a threat to the respect with which the policeman believes his occupation should be regarded or the opportunity to make a "good pinch" will tend to evoke its use.

Conclusions

The policeman uses violence illegally because such usage is seen as just, acceptable, and, at times, expected by his colleague group and because it constitutes an effective means for solving problems in obtaining status and self-esteem which policemen as

[6] In addition, the policeman is aware that the courts are highly critical of confessions obtained by violence and that, if violence is detected, it will "spoil his case."

policemen have in common. Since the ends for which violence is illegally used are conceived to be both just and important, they function to justify, to the policeman, the illegal use of violence as a general means. Since "brutality" is strongly criticized by the larger community, the policeman must devise a defense of his brutality to himself and the community, and the defense in turn gives a deeper and more lasting justification to the "misuse of violence." This process then results in a transfer in property from the state to the colleague group. The means of violence which were originally a property of the state, in loan to its law-enforcement agent, the police, are in a psychological sense confiscated by the police, to be conceived of as a personal property to be used at their discretion. This, then, is the explanation of the illegal use of violence by the police which results from viewing it in terms of the police as an occupational group.

The explanation of the illegal use of violence by the police offers an illuminating perspective on the social nature of their occupation. The analysis of their use of brutality in dealing with sexual deviants and felons shows that it is a result of their desire to defend and improve their social status in the absence of effective legal means. This desire in turn is directly related to and makes sense in terms of the low status of the police in the community, which results in a driving need on the part of policemen to assert and improve their status. Their general legitimation of the use of violence *primarily* in terms of coercing respect and making a "good pinch" clearly points out the existence of occupational goals, which are independent of and take precedence over their legal mandate. The existence of such goals and patterns of conduct indicates that the policeman has made of his occupation a preoccupation and invested in it a large aspect of his self.

SECTION D *Perspectives on Psychedelics*

One of the most disturbing changes in our culture in the past few decades has been the widespread introduction of consciousness-altering drugs to high school and college students and the general population as well.

The selections in this section touch on different aspects of the psychedelic controversy. The morality of drug use is a current question; the reality of drug use can no longer be set aside. Dr. Kenneth Keniston states that the main issue is not and has not been drugs themselves. The drugs have been used to focus on value conflicts implicit in the educational system and in the needs and desires of those attracted to drug experimentation. Drugs promised much, delivered much, destroyed much.

The two articles from the *New York Times* try to assess the general situation nationwide. These stories are disturbing because they suggest that there has been a shift in public morality concerning drugs. The casual use of drugs for a host of situations has already happened and prevention is not possible.

The balance of the articles in this section examine specific uses of the various drugs. The LSD article describes experiments in which the altered state of consciousness is focused on creative problem-solving. The first article on peyote describes the "use of a sacrament under ritual conditions." The final article by Crashing Thunder is a personal description of a peyote experience. The two selections highlight the way the American Indian has reacted to the introduction of psychedelics. Both the ways of acculturation and the effects of use are strikingly different from our own.

43

Drug Use and Student Values

Kenneth Keniston

Student drug users are generally treated by the mass media as an alien wart upon the student body of America. The use of drugs to alter psychic states, associated in the public mind with the abuse of narcotics, conjures up images of moral lepers and Mafia members. These images, in turn, help prevent any real understanding of the actual meanings and functions of drug use among a small minority of today's students.

In the comments to follow, I will argue that student drug use is closely related to the dominant pressures on American students, and is but a *variant* of values that are shared by many and perhaps most American undergraduates today. To be sure, only a small minority turn towards drugs; but the members of this minority group are but first-cousins to the more "normal" college student. In particular, the student drug-user shares with his non-drug-using classmates an active search for meaning through intense personal experience.

In order to understand the values shared by many American college students, we must begin by considering some of the pressures that affect today's students. With regard to drug use, two pressures are particularly important: the pressure toward cognitive professionalism, and the pressure toward psychological numbing.

Cognitive Professionalism

The past two decades have seen a revolution in our expectations about college students. Rising standards of academic performance in primary and secondary schools, the "baby boom" of the war, the slowness with which major American universities have expanded their size—all have resulted in increasing selectivity by the admissions offices of the most prestigious American colleges and universities. Furthermore, once a student is admitted to college, higher admission standards have meant that more could be demanded of him; students who a generation ago would have done "A" work now find themselves doing only "C" work with the same effort. The sheer volume of required reading and writing has increased enormously; in addition, the quality of work expected has grown by leaps and bounds. Finally, for a growing number of young Americans, college is but a stepping stone to professional and graduate school after college; and as a result, consistent academic performance in college increasingly becomes a prerequisite for admission

Paper presented at National Association of Student Personnel Administrators Drug Education Conference, Washington, D.C., November 7–8, 1966. The NASPA Drug Education Project is supported by Contract No. FDA 67–3, with the Food and Drug Administration, Dept. of Health, Education and Welfare.

to a desirable business school, medical school, law school or graduate school.

Not only have academic pressures mounted in the past generation, but these pressures have become more and more cognitive. What matters, increasingly, to admissions committees and college graders is the kind of highly intellectual, abstracting, reasoning ability that enables a student to do well on college boards, graduate records and other admissions tests, and—once he is in college or graduate school—to turn out consistently high grades that will enable him to overcome the next academic hurdle. And while such intellectual and cognitive talents are highly rewarded, colleges increasingly frown upon emotional, affective, non-intellectual and passionate forms of expression. What is rewarded is the ability to delay, postpone and defer gratification in the interests of higher education tomorrow.

In contrast to these cognitive demands, there are extremely few countervailing pressures to become more feeling, morally responsible, courageous, artistically perceptive, emotionally balanced, or interpersonally subtle human beings. On the contrary, the most visible pressures on todays students are, in many ways anti-emotional, impersonal, quantitative and numerical. The tangible rewards of our college world—scholarships, admission to graduate school, fellowships and acclaim—go for that rather narrow kind of cognitive functioning involved in writing good final examinations, being good at multiple choice tests, and getting good grades. Furthermore, the tangible rewards of the post-collegiate professional world also demand a similar kind of cognitive functioning, at least in the early years. Thus, it is the outstanding college and graduate student who goes on to coveted appointments in desirable hospitals, law firms, businesses, faculties and scientific laboratories.

This pressure for cognitive professionalism is closely related to the increasing "seriousness" of American college students. Many observers have commented on the gradual decline of student enthusiasm for such traditional American student pastimes as fraternities, football games, popularity contests and panty raids. At least at the more selective colleges, the reason for this decline is obvious: the pre-professional student has neither time nor motivation for the traditional pranks of his parent's generation. To survive and prosper in today's technological world, he must work with unremitting diligence to "be really good in his field."

Increasingly, then, one of the major pressures on American students is a pressure to perform well academically, to postpone and delay emotional satisfactions until they are older, to refine and sharpen continually their cognitive abilities. As a result, students today probably work harder than students in any other previous generation; a bad course or a bad year means to many of them that they will not get into graduate school. Taking a year off increasingly means running the danger of getting drafted and being sent to Vietnam.

In describing these pressures, I have used the word "performance" advisedly. A "performance" suggests an activity that is alien, that is done on a stage in order to impress others, that is a role played for an audience's applause. And to many students, of course, this quality of mild "alienness" pervades much of their intellectual and academic activities.

Thus, while the systematic quest for cognitive competence occupies much of the time and effort of the pre-professional student at today's selective colleges, this pursuit does little to inform the student about life's wider purposes. One of the peculiar characteristics of professional competence is that even when competence is attained, all of the other really important questions remain unanswered: what life is all about, what really matters, what to stand for, how much to stand for, what is meaningful, relevant and important, what is meaningless, valueless and false. Thus, for many students, the pursuit of professional competence must be supplemented by another, more private and less academic quest for the meaning of life. Academic efforts seem, to a large number of students, divorced from the really important "existential" and "ultimate" questions. In this way, the student's private search for meaning, significance and relevance are experienced as unconnected with or opposed to his public exertions for grades, academic success and professional competence. How students search for significance and relevance of course varies enormously from individual to individual; but as I will later suggest, drug use seems—to a small group of students—a pathway to the pursuit of meaning.

Stimulus Flooding and Psychological Numbing

Every society contains pressures and demands which its members simply take for granted. Thus, the pressure for extremely high levels of cognitive efficiency seems to most of us a necessary and an even desirable aspect of modern society. Our response to the second social pressure I want to discuss is even more unreflective and automatic. This second pressure has to do with the sheer quantity, variety and intensity of external stimulation, imagery and excitation to which most Americans are subjected. For lack of a better label, I will term our condition one of increasing "stimulus flooding."

Most individuals in most societies have at some point in their lives had the experience of being so overcome by external stimulation and internal feelings that they gradually find themselves growing numb and unfeeling. Medical students, for example, commonly report that after their first and often intense reactions to the cadaver in the dissecting room, they simply "stop feeling anything" with regard to the object of their dissection. Or we have all had the experience of listening to so much good music, seeing so many fine paintings, being so overwhelmed by excellent cooking that we find ourselves simply unable to respond further to new stimuli. Similarly, at moments of extreme psychic pain and anguish, most individuals "go numb," no longer perceiving the full implications of a catastrophic situation or no longer experiencing the full range of their own feelings. This lowered responsiveness, which I will call "psychological numbing," seems causally related to the variety, persistence and intensity of psychological flooding. In a calm and tranquil field of vision, we notice the slightest motion. In a moving field, only the grossest of movements are apparent to us.

One of the conditions of life in any modern technological society is continual sensory, intellectual, and emotional stimulation which produces or requires a high tendency towards psychological numbing. Some of you, I am sure, have had the experience of returning to urban American life from a calm and tranquil pastoral setting. Initially, we respond by being virtually overwhelmed with the clamor of people, sights, sounds, images and colors that demand our attention and our response. The beauty and the ugliness of the landscape continually strikes us; each of the millions of faces in our great cities has written on it the tragi-comic record of a unique life history; each sound evokes a resonant chord within us. Such periods, however, tend to be transient and fleeting; often they give way to a sense of numbness, of non-responsiveness, and of profound inattention to the very stimuli which earlier evoked so much in us. We settle in; we do not notice any more.

This psychological numbing operates, I submit, at a great variety of levels for modern man. Our experience from childhood onward with the constantly flickering images and sounds of television, films, radio, newspapers, paperbacks, neon signs, advertisements and sound trucks, numbs us to many of the sights and sounds of our civilization. The exposure of the most intelligent men to a vast variety of ideologies, value systems, philosophies, political creeds, superstitions, religions and faiths numbs us, I think, to the unique claims to validity and the special spiritual and intellectual values of each one: we move among values and ideologies as in a two-dimensional landscape. Similarly, the availability to us in novels, films, television, theatre and opera of moments of high passion, tragedy, joy, exhaltation and sadness often ends by numbing us to our own feelings and the feelings of others.

In all these respects, modern men confront the difficult problem of keeping "stimulation" from without to a manageable level, while at the same time protecting themselves against being overwhelmed by their own inner responses to the stimuli from the outer world. Defenses or barriers against both internal and external stimulation are, of course, essential in order for us to preserve our intactness and integrity as personalities. From earliest childhood, children develop thresholds of responsiveness and barriers against stimulation in order to protect themselves against being overwhelmed by inner or outer excitement. Similarly, in adulthood, comparable barriers, thresholds and defenses are necessary, especially when we find ourselves in situations of intense stimulation.

I do not mean to suggest that the quantity of stimulation in modern society is alone responsible for psychological numbing. Certainly the quality, kind and variety of stimuli determine how we respond to them; in addition, our own excitability, responsitivity, sensitivity and openness are crucial factors in determining what defenses we need against stimulus flooding. But I am arguing that the quantity, intensity and variety of inputs to which the average American is subjected in an average day probably has no precedent in any other historical society: everywhere we turn we are surrounded by signs, sounds and people actively clamoring for our response. Thus, to survive with calm and intactness in the modern world, we all require an armor, a protective shell, a screen, a capacity to "close off," ignore, or deny our attention to the many stimuli of our physical and social world. Such numbing is necessary and useful for most of us, most of the time. The problem arises, however, because the shells we erect to protect ourselves from the clamors of the inner and outer world often prove harder and less permeable than we had originally wanted.

Thus, in at least a minority of Americans, the normal capacity to defend oneself against undue stimulation and inner excitation is exaggerated and automatized, so that it not only protects but walls off the individual from inner and outer experience. In such individuals, there develops an acute sense of being trapped in their own shells, unable to break through their defenses to make "contact" with experience or with other people, a sense of being excessively armored, separated from their own activities as by an invisible screen, estranged from their own feelings and from potentially emotion-arousing experiences in the world. Presumably most of us have had some inkling of this feeling of inner deadness and outer flatness, especially in times of great fatigue, let-down, or depression. The world seems cold and two-dimensional; food and life have lost their savor; our activities are merely "going through the motions," our experiences lack vividness, three-dimensionality, and intensity. Above all, we feel trapped or shut in our own subjectivity.

Such feelings are, I believe, relatively common among college students, and particularly so at moments of intense stress, loss, depression, discouragement and gloom. It is at such times that the gap between the public pursuit of professional competence and the private search for meaning seems widest; it is also at these times that the chasm between individual and his own experience seems most unbridgable.

Each of the two pressures I have discussed—cognitive professionalism and stimulus flooding—evoke characteristic responses among today's American college students. The pressure for cognitive professional competence leads to a search for meaning in other areas of life; the feeling and fear of psychological numbing leads to a pursuit, even a cult, of experiences for its own sake. And the use and abuse of psychoactive drugs by students is closely related to these two themes in student values.

The Search for Meaning

Among today's self-conscious college students, the statement, "I'm having an identity crisis" has become a kind of verbal badge of honor, a notch in the gun, a scalp at the belt. But although the term "identity crisis" can be easily parodied and misused, it points to fundamental issues of adolescence in all societies that are particularly heightened in our own society. Since academic pursuits, on the whole, tell the student so little about life's ultimate purposes, students are turned back upon their own resources to answer questions like, "What does life mean? What kind of a person am I? Where am I going? Where do I come from? What really matters?"

Obviously, our society does not attempt to provide young Americans ready-made and neatly packaged answers to these questions. Rather, we expect that students will, in general, arrive at individual solutions to the riddles of life, and indeed, we sometimes deliberately design our educational systems so as to provoke and challenge students to profound replies. Yet at the same time, we insist that students occupy themselves with getting good grades and getting ahead in the academic world, pursuits that often seem to have relatively little to do with "ultimate" questions. Thus, students often feel obligated to turn away from their academic pursuits toward a private quest for identity or search for meaning.

To understand this search for meaning, we must recall that many of the traditional avenues to meaning and significance have dried up. Traditional religious faith is not, for most sophisticated undergraduates, a means of ascertaining the meaning of life: traditional religions often seem to students to be worn out, insincere, or superficial. Similarly, the great classic political ideologies, whether they be political liberalism, conservatism, marxism, or fascism, arouse relatively little interest among most undergraduates. Nor does the "American Way of Life," as epitomized by 100% Americanism and free enterprise, stir most students to enthusiasm, much less provide them with answers about life's ultimate purposes.

At the same time, many traditional campus activities have lost their centrality as guidelines for or rehearsal of life's ultimate purposes. There was a day, when the quest for popularity seemed to a great many undergraduates, a reflection of a broader philosophy on life in which the most important goal was to make friends, to be popular and to influence people. Today, the pursuit of popularity and social success is declining in importance, and even those who pursue friendship and social skills most avidly are likely to recognize their limitations as ultimate values. Upward mobility, another ancient American goal, has also lost much of its savor. More and more students arrive in college already "ahead in the world," from well-situated middle class families, and not particularly worried about status and upward mobility. Nor does the old American dream of giving one's children "a better chance" make great sense of life to a generation that has been born and bred amid affluence, and that rarely imagines a society in which starvation, unemployment, or depression will be major possibilities.

One by one, then, many of the traditional sources of meaning have disappeared, at the very same time that academic life itself, because of its intense pressure and professional specialization, seems to many students increasingly irrelevant to their major existential concerns. Where, then, do students turn?

The Cult of Experience

The cult of experience has often been discussed as a defining characteristic of American youth cultures. Central to this cult is a focus on the present—on today, on the here-and-now. Thus, rather than to defer gratification and enjoyment for a distant future, immediate pleasure and satisfaction are emphasized. Rather than reverence for the traditions of the past, experience in the present is stressed. Psychologically, then, such human qualities as control, planning, waiting, saving, and postponing on the one hand, and revering, recalling, remembering and respecting on the other, are equally deemphasized. In contrast, activity, adventure, responsiveness, genuineness, spontaneity and sentience are the new experiential values. Since neither the future nor the past can be assumed to hold life's meaning, the meaning of life must be sought within present experience, within the self, within its activity and responsiveness in the here-and-now.

The cult of experience has many variants and forms, most of them visible in one aspect or another on most American campuses. One such variant is what is often termed "student existentialism." At the more intellectually sophisticated campuses, this outlook manifests itself in an intense interest in existential writers like Sartre and Camus. But at a variety of other colleges, it is evident by student discussions of the importance of simple human commitments as contrasted with absolute values, and by a pervasively high estimation of such human qualities as authenticity, genuineness, sincerity and directness, which are contrasted with phoniness, inauthenticity, artificiality and hypocrisy. This student existentialism is humanistic rather than religious, and its most immediate goals are love, intimacy, directness, immediacy, empathy and sympathy for one's fellow man. Thus, what matters is interpersonal honesty, "really being yourself," and genuineness, and what is most unacceptable is fraudulence, "role playing," "playing games."

The same focus on simple human experiences in the present is seen in a variety of other student values. Consider, for example, the great growth in interest in the arts—music, poetry, sculpture, drama, the film as art. Or recall the importance to many students of nature—that is, of wilderness, of the rapidly disappearing natural beauty of this country. Sex, too, is related to the same theme; for sex is above all that human experience that seems to require directness and immediacy, and that cannot be forced. Similarly, the focus by many students on family life—their willingness to sacrifice other goals for the creation and maintenance of a good family and a "productive" relationship with their future wives—these too are variations on the same experiential theme.

Disaffiliation and Drugs

The two student values I have discussed—the search for meaning and the cult of experience—are intimately related to the pressures I have outlined earlier. The search for meaning is made more urgent by the amount of time and energy the average student must spend in pre-professional academic pursuits that often appear to him irrelevant to his basic concerns. And the cult of experience is intensified by the fear or feeling in many undergraduates that, instead of becoming more open to themselves and to experience, they are becoming increasingly numbed and closed off from all that is exciting and beautiful. Both of these values are, as well, related to the use and abuse of drugs by students. For such is the cultism and propaganda that surrounds drugs, especially the hallucinogens, that many students have come to feel the states induced by these drugs will automatically produce a revelation of life's meaning, or at least an experience which itself will be highly significant and illuminating. Similarly, to the undergraduate who feels himself unduly walled-off from experience, drugs like the hallucinogens and the amphetamines (which intensify and alter ordinary states of consciousness) may seem a chemical sledge hammer for breaking out of his shell.

Obviously, despite the congruence of drug use with important student values in American colleges, the vast majority of American students do not seek meaning and experience primarily via psychoactive compounds. There are other values in most students that conflict sharply with drug use—for example, a kind of "do-it-yourselfism" that strongly rejects "artificial" and "chemical" means of altering psychic states; a sense of social responsibility that enjoins the student against doing socially disapproved things like abusing drugs; and—perhaps most important—a legitimate fear of the possible bad affects of drug use. Social and geographic factors also contribute to the low incidence of drug use. On many campuses, drugs are simply not available; on other campuses, the prevalent value system (e.g., religious fundamentalism) is completely at odds with the use of psychoactive compounds. Thus, despite the presence of some values which are consistent with drug use, most students have other values that argue against drug use. It is only a minority who are pursuaded to choose drugs as a primary means of searching for meaning.

I doubt that it is possible to present an exact portrait of the type of student who is likely to use and abuse drugs. My own experience with student drug-users convinces me that there are many different motives for drug use and abuse, and there are many different factors—psychological, sociological, cultural and situational—that determine whether one student will use drugs while another will not. But despite the diversity of student types who *may* become involved in drug use, there is, I believe, one type that is particularly prone to drug abuse. Students of this type have, I think, particularly few values that militate against drug use and particularly strong motivations that incline them toward drugs, especially the hallucinogens. I will call such students "disaffiliates."

Elsewhere I have attempted a more comprehensive description of disaffiliates or "alienated" students. Here I will merely summarize some of the factors that predispose these students toward drug abuse. The defining characteristic of the disaffiliate is his generalized rejection of prevalant American values, which he rejects largely on esthetic, cultural and "humanistic" grounds. Such students are rarely political activists, and they are rarely concerned with the issues of economic, social and political justice that agitate many of their classmates. For these students, the problem is not political or social, but esthetic: American society is ugly, trashy, cheap and commercial; it is dehumanizing; its middle-class values are seen as arbitrary, materialistic, narrow and hypocritical. Thus, those conventional values which deem experimentation with drugs—or experimentation of all kinds—illicit are strongly rejected by disaffiliates; for them, what matters is somehow to seek a way out of the "air conditioned nightmare" of American society.

A second characteristic of disaffiliates is a more or less intense feeling of estrangement from their own experience. Such students are highly aware of the masks, facades and defenses people erect to protect themselves; and not only do they criticize these "defenses" in others, but even more strongly in themselves. Any "defense" that might prevent awareness of inner life must be rooted out and destroyed: self-deception, lack of self-awareness and any "phoniness" with regard to oneself are cardinal sins. But despite their efforts to make contact with their "real" selves and to have "genuine" experiences, disaffiliates often feel separated from both self and others. They experience themselves as separated from others by a grey opaque filter, by invisible screens and curtains, by protective shells and crusts that prevent them from the fullness of experience. They recriminate themselves for their lack of feeling expressiveness, spontaneity and genuineness. One such student described human relations as being like people trying to contact and touch each other through airtight space suits; another talked of a wax that was poured over all of his experience preventing him from genuine contact with it. These feelings of estrangement are often accompanied by considerable depression and a strong sense of personal isolation. Indeed, depression, following the loss of an important relationship, is commonly found in the immediate background of the student who begins to abuse drugs. For the student with intensified feelings of estrangement from himself and others, drugs that promise to heighten experience seem a tempting way out of his shell.

A third relevant characteristic of disaffiliates is a fantasy of fusion and merger, which contrasts sharply with their current feelings of estrangement. In the background, many of these students have a concept of an almost mystical fusion with nature, with their own inner lives, or above all with other people—a kind of communication that requires no words, a kind of oneness with nature or the world that has characterized intense religious experience for centuries, a special kind of automatic oneness with another. For an undergraduate with an especial longing for oneness with others, the hallucinogens are especially tempting. For one characteristic of the drug experience is a weakening or breaking down of the boundaries of the self such that many individuals in fact report feelings of oneness, merger and fusion with others.

On several grounds, then, the disaffiliate is strongly attracted by drugs. Arguments based on traditional American values against drug use carry little weight for him; on the contrary, he values most in himself his own rebellion against such "middle-class" standards. His frequent feelings of estrangement from experience lead him to seek means of breaking through the walls, shells, filters and barriers that separate him from the world. And his fantasy of fusion disposes him to seek out chemical instruments that will increase his "oneness" with others. For such students, who are young, searching, uncommitted and anti-conventional, drug use is primarily a way of searching for meaning via the chemical intensification of personal experience.

Drug Use and Student Values

In portraying one type of student who is predisposed toward the abuse of psychoactive compounds, and in relating drug use to more general student values, I do not mean to portray all American students as potential drug users, nor to decry the student values which may be interpreted to support drug use. On the contrary, I am convinced that the search for meaning through experience is an important and valid search, although I personally doubt that present experience is itself enough to provide "the meaning of life." Similarly, even those students who actively abuse drugs are seeking, I think, legitimate ends through unwise means. It will not do, therefore, to repudiate students who misuse drugs as moral lepers and "addicts" without trying to understand their motives for drug use, and the values and goals they pursue. These motives are rarely simply anti-social or "thrill-seeking." On the contrary, they almost always involve a legitimate (if misguided) search for ultimate meaning and contact with the world. In dealing with individual drug users, then, we must attempt to provide the student with alternate routes to attain his valid goals. And since drug use is notoriously hazardous and uncertain, it should not prove impossible to suggest better avenues toward meaning and experience than drugs.

Even Dick Alpert commented, in an earlier talk, that he considers the use of LSD a "crutch"; we must help our students to understand that this is so.

In addition, we need to appreciate that students who use and abuse drugs are reacting not only to the individual circumstances of their past and present lives, but to dilemmas that confront their entire generation. It would of course be wrong to identify drug use *solely* with cultural and historical pressures. But it would be equally wrong to emphasize the individual psychodynamics of student drug users in such a way as to avoid confronting the possibility that the rising rate of student drug use is a commentary upon our educational system and upon our entire society. Although student drug users are a small minority, they point to the inability of our colleges and our society to enlist the commitments of a talented minority. If we could understand why, it might point not only to how we could "cure" drug users, but, even more important, how we might "cure" colleges and society.

As for counseling student drug users—potential and actual—I think it important to acknowledge that the question of drug use is, in the last analysis, not a medical issue, but an existential, philosophical and ethical issue. Student drug users are, as a group, extemely knowledgeable about the possible bad effects of drug use; they can usually teach their counselors, deans and advisors a good deal about the potential bad side effects of drugs. They will argue—with considerable validity—that society does not prohibit the use of other psychoactive compounds (e.g., alcohol, tobacco) which in some ways are far more dangerous than many of the hallucinogens or amphetamines. In the last analysis, then, whether one chooses or not to use drugs, in full consciousness of their possible bad effects and the legal implications of drug use, becomes an existential rather than a medical decision. It is a matter of how one chooses to live one's life, how one hopes to seek experience, where and how one searches for meaning. To be sure, I doubt that we can hope to persuade students that drugs are ethically, humanly or existentially undesirable if they are not already persuaded. But I think we can at least help the student to confront the fact that in using drugs he is making a statement about how he wants to live his life. And we can, perhaps, in our own lives and by our own examples, suggest that moral courage, a critical awareness of the defects of our society, a capacity for intense experience and the ability to relate genuinely to other people are not the exclusive possessions of drug-users.

In the long run, then, those of us who are critical of student drug abuse must demonstrate to our students that there are better and more lasting ways to experience the fullness, the depth, the variety and the richness of life than that of ingesting psychoactive chemicals. It would be a pity, for example, to allow the advocates of LSD to take exclusive possession of the term "consciousness-expansion." Consciousness-expansion seems to me not the sole prerogative of psychoactive compounds, but of education in its fullest sense. The giants of our intellectual tradition were men who combined critical consciousness of their own societies with a capacity for experience and relatedness. And they were consciousness-expanders par excellence in their attempts to lead their fellows out of ignorance to a clearer perception of truth, beauty, and reality.

Thus, insofar as we can truly and honestly help our students to become educated in the fullest sense, we will be able to provide alternative routes to the pursuit of meaning, the quest for experience, and the expansion of consciousness. Obviously, much of what passes for higher education in America fails to accomplish any of these high objectives. As long as it continues to fail, I suspect that drugs will continue to be a problem on our campuses and in our society.

44

A Growing Number of America's Elite Are Quietly Turning On

Martin Arnold

The expensively coiffed wife of a dress shop owner was seated on a brown hassock, slowly running her tongue along the seam of a cigarette she had just rolled.

Resting in the fold of her skirt was a packet of cigarette paper and a large instant coffee jar that held something resembling tobacco.

"You make them too thin," she said to no one in particular.

It was a party on Thanksgiving Day in Houston, and the woman sat near the host, a computer expert. Everyone was getting ready to play a favorite game—improvising the dialogue for a radio serial into a tape recorder.

Soon the host spoke his lines and passed his cigarette to the woman's husband. He inhaled noisily, laughed and offered his lines to a lawyer.

The other guests were the lawyer's young wife and the manager of a large book and toy store. They all smoked the cigarette. It was a marijuana joint.

The scene was not entirely uncommon in middle-class America. Although the headlines and psychological studies about drugs deal mostly with hippies, heroin addicts and students, adult America is "turning on" in ever-increasing numbers.

A national survey by The New York Times found that while still a small minority of the population, more and more on-the-way-up and already successful adults were using marijuana and hallucinogenic drugs. Many more were found to be using barbiturates to relieve tension and amphetamines to capture a feeling of limitless energy.

Among adult drug takers, marijuana was found to be the great leveler, used by the very poor, the middle class and the wealthy. Heroin, on the other hand, is nearly always used only by the poor.

The amphetamines and barbiturates cut across social lines, but seemed to be abused more often in the upper and middle classes.

The true hallucinogens, such as LSD, make up a different drug scene entirely. According to Dr. William H. McGlothin, a psychologist at the University of California at Los Angeles, the adult usually experiments with them cautiously and in a way that will not abruptly change his daily living pattern.

Sometimes, Dr. McGlothin said, the adult will gain new insights, and lessen his anxiety through the use of hallucinogens. They may also stimulate a "new found interest in music, art and nature—a sort of aesthetic Head Start for artistically deprived adults," he said.

Many of the adults interviewed said they used marijuana or an hallucinogen to escape boredom or what they believed to be their remoteness from meaningful activity.

Some, but not all, said they were searching for sexual freedom. Others said they sought a passageway to their own subconscious.

"In our private lives we're willing to edge to the outer rim of society in our search to maybe find God, self-revelation, or whatever you call it," a 47-year-old executive secretary in a small Southern city said.

She had taken four LSD trips in the last five years, and smoked marijuana several times a week.

For other drug takers, a wine-red or pink and white amphetamine capsule, or a cool turquoise barbiturate, was used simply for kicks or as a way to keep functioning.

The remark of a successful 53-year-old Manhattan businessman, for example, was not uncommon. "I keep a supply of pills for entertaining just the way I keep liquor," he said off-handedly.

The wife of a publisher was just as casual as she rolled two marijuana cigarettes for her husband, wrapped them neatly in tinfoil and put them into his coat pocket to take to work—a tuned-in, turned-on modern executive's afternoon snack.

Nonetheless, there are no statistics on the respectable drug user. More surprising, in interviews with 25 psychiatrists who had studied drug usage, not one had personally done research on the white collar drug user or knew of any medical literature on the subject.

Still, the white collar users were easy to find. They were usually in groups, experimenting with drugs together, although many were solitary users, taking pills to function, to stay slim, to fight the boredom of housework or dull jobs, or to be "up" and alive for a cocktail party or business dinner.

Most of the adult drug users interviewed were particularly articulate. They also held good jobs and appeared self-confident and assured. Despite their material success, however, they said they were alienated from the mainstream of American life.

Because of this, perhaps, they shunned conventional diversions, such as liquor. Although they may have considered themselves nonconformists, nonconformity was not reflected in their daily lives. Few were involved in causes—civil rights or Vietnam—and few took part in community activities.

Privately, however, a retailer in Charlotte N.C., who makes $50,000 a year, would say:

"I would have been proud of my son if he had torn up his draft card and not gone in the Army, but he was too square."

The speaker is Southern-born, a Republican, and harshly opposed to the Vietnam war. He has taken five LSD trips and is a marijuana smoker.

"I learned from LSD the beauty of life—that it's too precious, so that we must not kill unless we are being invaded," he said. "I don't want my son to kill, in Vietnam or anywhere."

The respectable woman involved in drug usage, sociologists say, is from what can be called the transition generation. She was born too late to fit the totally domesticated tradition—married at 17, mother at 18—and too early to be a totally liberated career woman.

She is, therefore, neither a total housewife nor a total career woman. She is often trapped by her own limited imagination. She is often bored with her husband and frustrated sexually.

One such woman in Fort Worth said, "As adults, we're just as unfamiliar with the world today as the kids are." This woman is a former alcoholic, who now uses marijuana, LSD and amphetamines.

Many of the men held jobs they did not like, despite their success. One lawyer, who regularly uses marijuana and LSD, said that "after my first [LSD] trip it was unmistakably clear to me that this was not what my life was about—real estate law."

"Other people, probably stronger people, could come to this conclusion without drugs," he said. "I couldn't. Suddenly I didn't feel that I was put upon this earth to reduce landlords' real estate taxes."

He had given up the law and gone into book publishing.

Aside from addicts, the adult users interviewed had a tendency toward what Dr. Donald B. Louria, president of the New York State Council on Drug Addiction, called "emotional proselitizing"—expounding the virtues of drug-taking with little thought of the psychological and physical consequences.

"No doubt some have done with drugs precisely what they said they did—but no doubt a lot don't even know exactly what they are taking. Their judgment is affected and half of what they say isn't true."

Certainly, few of the adults, whatever their reason for taking drugs, seemed to be overly concerned about the psychological and physical dangers—the possibility of addiction, of recurrent hallucinations and feelings of panic, of loss of sanity and even, in some cases, death.

Most often, there appeared to be a difference between the adult who experimented with marijuana and the hallucinogens and the one who used amphetamines or barbiturates, or a combination of both.

The hallucinogen user was seeking, however naively, what Aldous Huxley called the "transcendental experience, where the soul knows itself as unconditioned and of like nature with the divine."

In "The Doors of Perception," which was something of a Bible to many of the adults who experimented with hallucinogenics, Huxley summed up their use this way:

"To be shaken out of the ruts of ordinary perception, to be shown for a few timeless hours the outer and the inner world, not as they appear to an animal obsessed with words, and notions, but as they are apprehended, directly and unconditionally, by Mind at Large."

The hallucinogen and marijuana user had nearly always been persuaded to try the drugs for the first time by a friend or a group of friends.

The pill user, on the other hand, who made up by far the greater number of adults using drugs, most often started out alone. He was not seeking self-knowledge or even fun, but support.

His use of drugs was a solitary thing. He did not want to be part of an experimental group. He used the drug not to stand out from a crowd, but to blend into one and to function the way he thought everyone else did.

"I got started on the amphetamine-barbiturate kick because I couldn't sleep nights before an important trial," a lawyer said. "I took sleeping pills. I owed that much to my clients. Suddenly I wasn't alert anymore. I started my day with an amphetamine.

A magazine editor, who commutes several times a month between Los Angeles and New York, goes a step further.

He takes amphetamine shots, for which there is no legitimate medical usage. "It's the first thing I do when I get to New York. I know a dozen doctors who give them. It gives you a hell of a lift. It's the only thing that keeps me going here," he said.

A female entertainer said: "I get done with a performance in New York and I have a television show to tape on the Coast the next morning. If I don't sleep on the plane I'm finished. The barbiturates give me the sleep; the amphetamines keep me going.

"In the old days I'd go on the 20th Century Limited, read a book, sleep and relax on the way to Hollywood. Now you can't."

Their pill usage, which could lead to addiction, had been induced by doctors.

Dr. Sidney S. Greenberg, chairman of the New York County Medical Society's subcommittee on narcotics and drug usage, said:

"A great deal of the fault in our drug-oriented society is with physicians, many of whom give pills indiscriminately.

"The doctor is so busy that when a patient comes in and says, 'Oh, Doctor, I'm so tense,' he doesen't take the time to find out what the problem is. He'll just prescribe tranquilizers.

"He's rushed, not interested in the patient, and if the patient appears very aggresive he'll give him a prescription for 50 or 100 pills rather than for 10 or 12."

Most pill users, once hooked, quickly put together a string of five or 10 or more physicians, each of whom, unknown to the other, would give him a prescription for pills.

The woman who wants to be fashionably slim may also go to a diet doctor, who dispenses from his office his own brand of appetite-killing pills. They are amphetamines.

In all cases they help to slim the figure. In many cases they hook the weight-watcher, who soon finds herself taking pills not to control weight but to get a pleasant high.

Physicians and their families are not exempt from using drugs, either. In Houston, the woman who heads an Alcoholics Anonymous group said:

"Of our 60 members, six are doctors' wives whose husbands hooked them on pills. One other member is a doctor's daughter hooked on pills and three are nurses, who are alcoholics and pill addicts."

A psychologist with a large practice in Atlanta has among his patients several doctors and dentists who are pill addicts. "They take amphetamines to pep up. They say their long hours make them tired. They then take sleeping pills, or morphine," he said.

Pill dependency is also a fact of life with truck drivers who say they couldn't earn a living "without bennie riding in the cab" to keep them awake on long hauls. Bennie is benzedrine, an amphetamine.

And in the autumn and winter, on any Sunday afternoon, how many professional football players charge out onto the gridiron, their step a little quicker, not from a pep talk but from a pep pill? Some sports writers say a lot of them do.

Atlanta is a city bursting with construction, with pride in its art museums and theater groups, and with sophistication. People who sin there, do so quietly, and the mention of marijuana at a cocktail party is greeted with silence.

Yet like other American cities it has its share of white-collar drug users. A $50-an-hour call girl says that at least half her customers, mostly local businessmen, use amphetamines or smoke marijuana. "And half of those who don't are always asking me if we can try pot," she said.

A young and attractive receptionist in an Atlanta dentist office proclaimed proudly that she had taken two LSD trips and that "they were damn good trips—they lasted nine hours."

"I smoke pot whenever I can get it," she said. "We have a group, which includes ad agency people, a dentist and a chiropractor. We smoke pot all the time. What's wrong with it? Nothing!"

There is in a small city in the Southern Piedmont a group of about 20 adults who also smoke pot and experiment with LSD. They range in age from 40 to 60. Most are businessmen, only six are women.

They use LSD and marijuana, they say, mainly for self-analysis. Five of them, three men and two women, said that they were cured of alcoholism through drugs.

Others claimed that, only after using the drugs, particularly marijuana, were they able to achieve healthy sexual lives. All claimed that drugs had contributed to their business and professional success.

The leader of the group—it would be more accurate to think of him as their guru—is a 55-year-old Navy veteran. He had become involved with drugs six years ago, while in Mexico.

"I was very much interested in the ancient Mexican religions and I saw the old manuscripts where drugs were talked about," he said.

"I had been offered synthetic drugs before, but I wanted to try more natural things first.

"I discovered this ancient mural. One of the gods was showering down on the earth morning glory seeds and colored berries. I didn't know how to take berries, but I used morning glory seeds, which were hallucinogenic. I also experimented with psilocybin mushrooms."

As he talked, the man was seated in his study on the ground floor of a large antebellum style plantation home. Next to him was a woman in her early 40's, who had taken 15 LSD trips.

"It's never become exactly a cult with us," she said, speaking of their group. "But it's taken people who had gotten stagnant and sent them off into other more interesting directions. The object of all these things is that the user gets out into these new directions."

Their friends take their hallucinogenic trips together, in groups of three or four. Usually it is in a home. But sometimes they rent beach houses to "trip in," and they have even climbed nearby mountain ranges, where they have taken LSD on the grassy slopes.

"It is part of our inner life," the woman said. "All of us lead an outer life that is square."

"LSD and marijuana allowed me to escape from the structure of my own ego at least," said the leader of the group. "I'm structured and compressed enough by my time and circumstances and place in history, and this has freed me a great deal."

His three daughters and his wife know of this drug experimentation. They do not take part, but they do not disapprove, either.

Another group member, a 57-year-old businessman, said that drugs had helped him to straighten out his drinking and his business problems.

"I can see things more clearly when I'm smoking a joint," he said. "The next day, when I am back down flat, so to speak, I can still see things from the turned on point of view."

Drugs made them kinder, gentler people, all the group members believed. Like the Charlotte businessman, most of them were now doves on Vietnam because, they said, they now oppose any form of killing.

Despite their success and respectability, their "new understanding," members of the group said, now extends far enough to embrace the hippies.

"Except for the dirt, the smell, I really think they're the greatest generation of youth this country has produced," one said.

Others praised anti-Vietnam demonstrators and even civil rights activists. They all said that five years ago such activists would have outraged them.

Presumably, there are similar groups all over the United States.

Quite apart from any group, however, there are the amphetamine users, some of whom take the pills for sexual purposes.

The Manhattan businessman who keeps pills handy for entertainment, just as he does alcohol, said that a lot of the women he dated—models and career girls—would not make love without first popping a pill. These girls, he said, seldom smoke and never drink.

One such girl, a 27-year-old, who once worked for a motion picture company here, uses amphetamines "to keep going sexually."

Pointing to the bedroom in her Park Avenue apartment, she said, "I once stayed in bed for three days with a man taking pills to keep going and smoking pot to enjoy myself. We did nothing but make love for three days. We sent out for chopsuey every once in a while."

Usually, however, the pills and the stimulation they provide are reason enough for the user; sex is not a factor.

On the other hand, the use of marijuana and the hallucinogens, almost always leads to sexual experimentation among adult users.

There is seldom anything orgiastic about this. Pot parties among adults do not end with couples pairing off in dark corners or empty bedrooms.

However, nearly all marijuana and LSD users maintain that the drugs lend a spice to sexual relations that their own imaginations do not.

In Washington, a woman who works for a Federal agency and has been on a Presidential commission said:

"I don't enjoy liquor, but a good high on pot is wonderful. I like the whole mood, having the right atmosphere, people getting together, with a good record on."

"Afterwards, if my date is right, and we're both turned on, there's nothing better than making love together. It seems like everything is so slow, so long lasting and loving."

Some adults on the drug scene will try anything that is available—marijuana, hallucinogens, pills. A painter in New York uses laughing gas when he can get it "because, man, it really makes you zoom off into space."

A woman who works in a San Francisco advertising agency pulls her hi-fi turntable out from the bookcase and reveals behind it a cache of pot, LSD and pills.

"It depends on what I'm looking for," she said, "A mellowness, a long trip or just a terrific high."

A 47-year-old housewife in Fort Worth has 20 bottles of pills in her kitchen, prescribed by at least six doctors.

In her living room library, amid the books on psychology and Indian mysteries, is the massive, 1,900-page United States Dispensatory, a directory of drugs. Also on the bookcase is a kaleidoscope which, she said, "I brought for my LSD trips."

The woman has made a way of life out of the use of drugs. She has taken five LSD trips and her husband has taken two. They have four children, the oldest a 21-year-old college student.

The woman has given the son two LSD trips. "I knew he was headed that way. I wanted him to experience it with good stuff, not junk that someone gave him at college," she said.

She has used LSD, marijuana and pills for a wide variety of reasons, including self-analysis, attempts to cure the headaches that plague her, and sexual experimentation.

"When my husband first took LSD he got very sensual; he kept wanting to touch me," she said. "Every time I take a trip with him or with friends I provide good wine, good cheese, good incense—everything to stimulate our senses into whatever avenue we want them to go." How many people are like her?

The psychiatrists, the sociologists and the police don't know. For these are discreet, respectable lawbreakers. They do not deviate from the rest of society except by taking drugs.

They are in the minority, but clearly their numbers are growing. "I would favor legalizing marijuana, but not for the masses," a young lawyer told an adult discussion group one night recently in Dallas. He did not define "the masses."

There is usually a scandal when the sons and daughters of the white-collar drug users are caught smoking pot or using LSD. But The Times survey showed that in many cases, the parents and children shared the same values.

In their search for something mystical, or for their lost feelings, or for a way out of their boredom, the adults have taken for their own much of the trappings of the hippie subculture.

Because they have so much to lose materially the adults remain nameless. But even when they are caught the authorities sometimes wink at their transgressions.

In a North Carolina city several months ago, the police swooped down on the home of a businessman who was growing a large field of marijuana in his backyard. They cut down the marijuana and left. The man was not arrested.

45

Many Students Now Regard Marijuana as a Part of Growing Up

John Kifner

Amherst, Mass., is a New England college town, dominated by a sweeping tree-shaded green, flanked on the south by a small business section, and on the north by comfortable fraternity houses and the pretty campus of Amherst College.

It looks like the setting for one of those college musicals about the Big Game and the bestowing of a fraternity pin on the Homecoming Queen. A half-block north of the green and down a narrow alley is a head shop.

A head shop is where one buys the accessories of the psychedelic experience, grass pipes, for example, which are small pipes for smoking marijuana, and roach holders, which are elaborate clips for holding the tiny butt ends of marijuana cigarettes, or joints.

A few doors up the street, another establishment specializes in wall posters, beads and small brass Indian pipes for smoking hashish.

And the local stationery store, besides its stock of things like spiral notebooks has a prominent display of Zig-Zag cigarette papers.

Nonetheless, no one was seen with the tag of a Bull Durham tobacco sack hanging out of his button-down shirt; the papers were for rolling joints.

In Cambridge, Mass., on a recent Friday, a dozen students at Harvard Law School gathered in an apartment for an evening of relaxation.

Four or five drew their chairs together and spoke of the possibility of political change in entrenched big-city bureaucracies. The others gathered about the fireplace and passed around a pipe, its bowl covered with perforated aluminum foil, and talked about movies, music and friends, and smoked marijuana.

"What the law school needs," said one future attorney, "is more snorts and less torts."

At a small Roman Catholic girls prep school outside San Francisco last spring, a local narcotics officer lectured on the danger of drugs. With many jocular remarks about making sure that he got them all back, he passed around three benzedrine pills and three marijuana cigarettes.

When they were returned, he humorously began to count them, and then discovered that he had got back four marijuana cigarettes.

In the late nineteen-sixties, a nationwide survey by the The New York Times has found, drugs, particularly marijuana, have become for many students a part of growing up, perhaps as common as the hip flasks of Prohibition.

While drug use has been expanding over the last few years, students and high school and college officials agree that it has increased sharply since the intensive coverage given to drugs and the hippies last summer by the mass media.

"There's no doubt this thing has increased since the summer. There were articles on the East Village in Esquire, Look and Life and this provides the image for the kids," said Dr. Donald W. Miles, the principal of Horace Greeley High School in the Westchester suburb of Chappaqua.

There does, in fact, appear to be far more drug use than police or academic officials say there is, and, particularly with marijuana, the drug use cuts across all types of young people.

In the past, younger students were introduced to drugs—"turned on"—by upperclassmen. Now, students on many campuses say, freshmen arrive already smoking marijuana or taking it for granted that it is part of the college experience.

Marijuana—"grass" in the current campus phrase—has spread from avant-garde, artsy-craftsy colleges, through the Ivy League and the schools in big cities, through universities with transplanted New Yorkers, to campuses all over the country.

It also has spread to exclusive prep schools such as The Hun School in Princeton, N.J., and Phillips Academy in Andover, Mass., and on to high schools in places like Brattleboro, Vt., and Cedar Rapids, Iowa.

Dr. Kenneth Keniston, assistant professor of psychology at the Yale University School of Medicine, could suggest to a recent meeting of the American Psychiatric Association that drug users were "largely congregated at the more selective, progressive and academically demanding institutions."

He also said they tended to be "better than average students," who majored "in the humanities, or perhaps in psychology," and were "rather more introspective than many of their classmates."

Most psychiatrists and administrators agree. They say that the student who uses drugs regularly tends to be rather bright and rather introspective, to often have deep personal or family problems, and to be alienated from both the values of the adult world and from those of his fellow students.

But, it is this type of students that psychiatrists and administrators are most likely to come in contact with, resulting in what sociologists term a "biased sample."

Interviews with students indicated that, while many drug takers appeared to be troubled, many did not.

Furthermore, many students who gave little evidence of being particularly thoughtful seemed to be sampling drugs simply because they were available, or because they were considered sophisticated or daring. Others were smoking marijuana because it was the social thing to do, like sipping a cocktail.

A reporter for The Harvard Crimson, the undergraduate daily, recalled that four years ago a student turned in his roommate for smoking pot to "save" him.

"This would never happen today because the atmosphere has changed," he said. "It would be embarrassing for a student now to admit that he hadn't at least tried pot—just as it would be embarrassing for a Harvard student to admit that he was a virgin."

And, while a few years ago drug use appeared to be concentrated at better schools in the Northeast and on the West Coast, the scene is expanding rapidly.

The National Student Association collects newspaper articles about students arrested on drug charges. In the 24 cases listed for the first three weeks of last November, which were by no means all of them, there were arrests at Berkeley, Yale,

New York University and the University of Wisconsin. There were also arrests at:

Franklin and Marshall College, Lancaster, Pa.; Hutchinson Community College, Hutchinson, Kan.; Piedmont College, Clarksville, Ga.; Towson State College, Towson, Md.; The University of Texas; Eastern New Mexico University in Portales; Pennsylvania Military College; Kansas Weslyan University in Salina; Northwestern University, Evanston, Ill.; Wichita State University in Wichita, Kan.; University of Nebraska; Michigan State University; Shimer College in Chicago; Eastern Illinois University in Charleston; Central Missouri State College in Warrensburg; Southern Illinois University in Carbondale. In the New York area there were arrests at Adelphi, Hofstra and the Collegiate Institute.

The survey showed that student comments about drugs, particularly marijuana, sound the same all over the country:

"It's not addicting. It's cheaper than booze and the high is better."

"When I'm high I'm in control of myself, when I'm drunk I'm not."

"There's no hangover."

"Man, when I'm high (snapping his fingers) . . . like, I'm inside myself, I'm outside myself (snap, snap)."

"Why not?"

Despite this, there are distinctions among youthful drug users.

On the campuses, where drugs are a social experience, or perhaps an attempt at self realization, they tend to be regarded earnestly, but only as a part of life. Among the hippie drop outs, they seem to be the focal point of existence.

In high schools, where a weird and dangerous variety of drugs may be taken without sophistication or discrimination, they are a remedy for boredom and a way of rebellion.

The most common mind-alerting drug used on campus, of course, is still alcohol. The drinking culture predominates, particularly at Southern universities, where the "foamies," beer drinkers, hold weekend binges, and at Roman Catholic institutions such as Fordham and St. John's, where vice tends to be more traditionally Irish.

A normal college weekend party is still marked by much ostentatious quaffing of beer or punch (usually a local specialty with a name like "Texas Twister" or "Purple Passion") or cheap bourbon.

There is also crowded dancing, spilled beer, big-beat rock 'n' roll, grouping and pawing, passing out, throwing up, and maybe fights, smashed windows and furniture and occasional automobile accidents.

The activity, if it reaches the proper peak, is known on some campuses as a "horror show," and participants speak fondly of "throwing shows."

A drug party, in contrast, usually means a small group of friends—or sometimes only a boy and girl—in a domitory room or, more likely, an offcampus apartment.

Perhaps there are candles burning, or perhaps incense to disguise the heavy, sweet odor of marijuana. The cigarette or pipe is passed quietly from person to person; each inhales deeply, holds his breath, and sniffs in more air to keep the smoke in the lungs.

As the light-headed, euphoric "high" comes on, there will be some giggles, some dangling conversation. They will listen to records—The Beatles, Bob Dylan, Ravi Shankar—talk, or simply sit and contemplate.

Later they will raid the icebox, or go to an all-night sandwich shop, for marijuana increases the appetite, and users say the sensation of taste is enhanced.

Increasingly, the alcoholic party is yielding to this. At Colgate, for instance, one fraternity normally consumes ten kegs of beer on the big fall weekend when the houses are open to freshmen. This year it used only three.

At Amherst, a fraternity has switched almost completely to drugs, and others have found that their liquor bills have declined. A fraternity brother who was once known as "The Mad Dog" because of his behavior when he drank is now a pothead and is called "The Docile Dog."

Among younger pot smokers particularly there is a strong revulsion toward alcohol. Young people who were graduated from college in the early 'sixties have discovered a generation gap as their younger brothers and sisters accuse them of ruining their health and losing their self-control by drinking.

"I just can't see drinking—pouring all those poisons into your body and becoming obnoxious, ugh," said a 17-year-old boy who goes to Hillhouse High School in New Haven and turns on nearly every weekend.

In contrast to marijuana, the use of acid —the hallucinogen LSD—has fallen off rapidly on most campuses. In some circles, however, it is being replaced with mescaline.

One major reason for the decline of LSD is the recent publicity about the possibility of hereditary defects and mutations from the drug. "I don't want any freaky three-headed kids," said one coed.

Another reason is that there have been too many "bad trips" and frightening experiences from taking LSD. Many students have found a trip too powerful and too exhausting an experience to repeat.

Still, many youths say that a trip has been a valuable experience—"I found out a lot about myself, including a lot of stuff I didn't like," is a common comment—and many of the bad trips have been unsettling rather than disastrous.

But everyone knows stories of people who took LSD and then leaped out of windows convinced they could fly, or attempted (sometimes with ghastly results) to stop rapidly moving traffic.

Or they know of experiences similar to that of a brilliant science student at Amherst who was dismissed from school a few months before his graduation.

On a bad trip, he had raced into the home of an elderly woman, screaming that the police were after him, and barricaded himself in a closet. The police weren't, but they soon were.

Another problem with transparent tasteless LSD is the quality of the drug. Much of it has been cut with "speed"—methedrine, a powerful amphetamine—or other substances.

Amphetamines, in the form of benzedrine and dexedrine have been used in colleges for years, not for kicks, but merely to stay awake, sometimes for days while writing papers or taking exams.

This is not considered taking drugs, said a Harvard senior, "any more than No-Doz was in prep school."

But sometimes the results can be disastrous here, too. Some students have been hospitalized with exhaustion, and there is the graduate student at the University of Oklahoma, who, stoked with dexedrine, walked out of an exam convinced he had written the best paper of his career.

He may well have, but no one will ever know, since he wrote it all on the same line.

While there are bizarre aspects to collegiate drug use—such as the students at Rice Institute in Texas who play "pill roulette" by grabbing an unidentified pill out of a paper sack on the way to class to find out what will happen when they take it —there are relatively few "stone heads," who center their lives on drugs.

"Most people go through three phases with drugs," explains a junior at the University of Massachusetts. "When you're first turned on, it's like the greatest thing in the world, and you get very evangelical and run around talking about it all the time and trying to turn everybody else on.

"Then you go through a period when drugs are pretty important and you orient most of the rest of your life around the time when you turn on. Eventually there's just a lot of other stuff you want to do, so you just smoke once in a while."

Most experts, such as Dr. Joel Fort, who was once with the San Francisco Health Department, and Dr. Richard H. Blum, director of the Psychopharmacology Project of the Institute for the Study of Human Problems at Stanford University, agree that becoming "strung out" on drugs is not so much caused by the drug as it is the personality problems of the user.

This is backed up by such lay observations as that of a girl in Greenwich Village, who declared:

"Most of the real heads were completely freaked out before they ever saw dope; that bag is just their outlet."

Despite their apparent sophistication, many turned-on college students have been startled to find a widespread use of drugs at their old high schools, and some have been shocked by the abandon with which they are sampled.

"My 14-year-old sister, who goes to a nice Catholic girls' school, called me up this summer to tell me she's been dropping STP [a hallucinogen] with the surfers on the Jersey shore," a 23-year-old pothead recalled. "I said, hold on, honey, we'd better have a little talk."

In Besthesda, Md., a suburb of Washington, members of the high school "blue glasses" hippie set have stolen whatever looked interesting from the medicine cabinets of homes where they were babysitting. The next day they see if anyone knows what it is. Then they take it to see what it does.

In Houston, teen-agers have told their parents they were going to the shore for the week-end, and then pooled their money and sent one of their number to San Francisco and back to fetch LSD.

In Beaverton, Ore., the largest suburb of Portland, half the students in a high school assembly raised their hands when asked if they knew where they could get marijuana. Two students there were arrested while shooting up methedrine in a restroom during a football game.

"The frightening thing about these kids is that they'll take anything, anywhere," said a young medical student at Yale, who is studying drug usage. "I used to think it wasn't so much different from what we did at that age, but this is really dangerous."

Indeed, it is the teenyboppers' ready acceptance of drugs such as methedrine, which can induce psychological dependence, compulsive, sometimes violent behavior and intense feelings of paranoia, which has hastened the break-up of the Haight-Ashbury hippie community in San Francisco.

The high school student most likely to use drugs, according to several high school principals, deans and suburban psychiatrists, is the bright student, who does not participate in school activities, who often has a troubled home life, and who feels alienated.

"One gets from these kids a feeling of nothingness, of pervasive depression," said Dr. H. R. Kormos, one of 14 psychiatrists in Westport, Conn., a wealthy suburb of 26,400 persons and 21 liquor stores.

"There is a very genuine feeling that life has little to offer them, and they speak continually of the dreariness, the drabness of everyday life," he said.

Dr. Kormos suggested that, particularly with marijuana, the mystique and ceremony of sharing the drug may impart a sense of belonging and identity that be more important to the student than the effect of the drug.

And, like other psychiatrists, school administrators and clergymen, Dr. Kormos spoke of the problems that an affluent society has created for young people: the shifting of families as businessmen are transferred about the country; the absence from home of a commuting, traveling father; the struggle for status and success; pressures to get into competitive colleges; and what the young person may see as a moral contradiction, Vietnam, for example.

"The drug problem is quite related to what's going on in the community; there's a lot of comment about the hypocrisy of the adult world," said the Rev. James G. Emerson Jr., who works with young people in weekly discussion sessions at the Larchmont Avenue Presbyterian Church in Larchmont, N.Y.

"These kids know a lot more; they're much more idealistic about life, and they feel they can't be idealistic in the church, in the school system or with their parents," he said.

"One of the real problems now is that parents over-react," Mr. Emerson continued. "Often a parent just latches on to the drugtaking and doesn't realize that it's really a symptom of other things."

One type of suburban student unlikely to use drugs, however, is the leather-jacketed "hood," who in past years might have been accused of creating teenage drinking or driving problems.

"These are usually the sons of the local tradespeople, and they're less articulate and resentful of the more affluent kids," a Westchester high school principal said.

"There's a real split here. The longhaired kids are against the war, for instance; these kids are for it. They view the drugs as a very moral issue. They've even beaten up some of the kids who were known to smoke marijuana."

The going rate for drugs varies with the area, the amount on the market and the source of supply, but an ounce of marijuana generally costs $15 to $20.

In some areas, users say, underworld elements have moved into the marijuana trade in the last few months and have driven prices up.

But for the most part the sources of drugs, particularly in colleges, are informal—normally a student who sells only to a small circle of friends, and usually not for a profit.

Probably the biggest carrier of drugs to campuses is the United States mail. There are some students, however, paying for their tuition or vacations, who make regular runs between Boston and New York, or who fly to San Francisco or drive to Mexico with an empty suitcase and back with a full one.

The unstructured nature of the traffic has posed a problem for the police. Increasingly they are planting undercover agents in high schools and colleges, and forcing students who have been arrested to turn informer.

In Washington County, Ore., outside of Portland, the chief of detectives in the county sheriffs office keeps a list of 400 teen-agers who are known or suspected users. In Madison, Wis., Detective Capt. Stanley Davenport says that 90 per cent of the students arrested cooperate with the police to avoid prosecution.

This troubles college administrators, who traditionally have stood somewhere between the students and the police. Most colleges are now issuing rather vaguely worded warnings about drugs, but most do not have a set policy, explaining that they prefer to deal with each case as it arises.

46

LSD: A Design Tool?

From *Progressive Architecture*

LSD has roused storms of controversy and has been the subject of nationwide publicity, often of a sensational kind. One of the less publicized aspects of the psychedelic drugs is their possible use in creative work. In an attempt to assess their value to the profession, Progressive Architecture interviewed a number of architects who have taken the drugs on an experimental basis, and asked such questions as : Do the psychedelics heighten the ability to visualize three-dimensionally? Do they enhance creativity and problem-solving? Do they have a positive effect that outlasts a particular session? This article presents our findings, including extensive verbatim reports by architects and the design uses to which they put their psychedelic experiences.

Drugs that have a "psychedelic" effect on the human mind are, in their general order of potency, peyote, mescalin, psilocybin, DMT (dimethylthryptamine), and LSD (dextrolycergic acid dimethylmide). The word psychedelic, meaning "mind manifesting"—from the Greek "psyche" (mind) and "delos" (minifest)—was first associated with the drugs by psychiatrist Humphrey Osmond, Director of the Bureau of Research in Neurology and Psychiatry in Princeton, N.J. Dr. Osmond, in a letter written to Aldous Huxley, versified: "To sink in Hell or soar angelic/Just take a pinch of psychedelic." It seems a more appropriate term for these chemicals than their medical counterpart, "hallucinogens," since hallucinations are rarely listed as one of the effects of the drugs. Architects report that perceptions as such are heightened and changed, but they are based on real—as against imagined—objects present in the physical environment.

It is not yet accurately known what these chemicals do to the brain. Since LSD, for example, completely disappears from the system 30 to 45 minutes after ingestion, the drug is thought to trigger the action of some other, as yet unidentified, chemical. The drugs alter the brain's chemistry, certainly, and they seem to inhibit the activity of another chemical, serotonin, that regulates the decoding processes of that part of the brain where raw, incoming sense data are interpreted and transformed into factual information about the environment.

A number of architects have added to the extensive evidence of the drugs' use as instruments for enhancing perception, for "training in visualization." They report that, under the psychedelic effect of the drugs, visual and auditory acuity (in addition to general awareness) are "revolutionized." Apparently, the taker has the sensation of seeing for the first time, as children must see before they learn labels

Reprinted from *Progressive Architecture* (August 1966), pp. 147–153, by permission of Reinhold Publishing Corp.

for their sense impressions of objects—directly, on contact. Colors seem to throb, textures vibrate, objects appear luminescent, everything is imbued with the glow of spring mornings. Aldous Huxley, one of the first to experiment with the perception-heightening effects of the drugs, which he described in his book, *The Doors of Perception,* even termed the experience as glimpsing the "morning of creation." Many say that the visual sensations are often accompanied by a sense of oneness with the universe and a disappearance of the feeling of being separated from other people and the physical environment. What is consistently reported is that the drug-taker remains acutely, totally, *conscious* throughout—not sleepily, drearily benumbed, as from too much alcohol. Indeed, the effects are termed by advocates as "consciousness-expanding."

Individuals are reported to derive from the experience with these chemicals what native endowment they bring to it: The more visually oriented one is, for example, the more likely one is to have a decidedly visual experience. In addition, architects have reported that, for the visually sensitive person, the effects of mescalin and LSD include an increased ability to visualize three-dimensionally, to see images vividly—in general, a heightened perception of spatial relations. Abstract thoughts apparently are transformed into visual images; words become irrelevant.

Moreover, one does not forget everything the next morning. Because it is a conscious experience thoughout, it is retained, and thus has been described as a learning experience.

LSD and Space Perception

Kyo Isumi, an architect practising in Saskatchewan, Canada, has described his own perceptual experience with LSD as follows:

> The space and the elements which define this space, the color, the texture, the forms, shades and shadows, the planes, the solids and voids, become points of reference and yet meaningful in themselves. . . . The elements of architectural design, as partially listed here, each attain visual significance in order and intensity to fit the mind's needs. . . . It heightened my ability to visualize in greater clarity the interrelationship of the elements of design, which are—to use the jargon of the architect—scale, proportion, color, texture, shade, and shadow. . . . In my case, the LSD experiences acted as a form of catalyst in the thinking process during the course of design. . . . My new awareness, and the subsequent accompanying phenomena of being able to experience simultaneously in series and in parallel the numerous perceptual effects of space and all its elements, would not have been achieved in almost an instantaneous fashion without the aid of LSD.

As Izumi's description makes clear, the quality, as well as the quantity, of visual perception is altered. Usually, physical objects and the environment are not seen as things in themselves, comprised of their own material, sitting within their own universe of weight, color, form, and texture. The preconceptions with which we habitually perceive objects—a chair as something to sit on, a lamp as something that throws light—are transcended, and objects are experienced as things in themselves, not merely as serving some particular function, but as colored, textured, seemingly alive *forms.* Architects report that the relevance of the psychedelic drugs should be apparent: A substance that enables man to increase his visual awareness, that heightens his ability to visualize three-dimensionally, might have serious and far-reaching applications to the practice of architecture, especially as buildings become more complex.

LSD as an Aid to Design

Kyo Izumi took LSD in 1957, when much of the research being done with it concerned its "psychotomimetic" effects—that is, the similarity of visual perception in schizophrenics and normal people experiencing the effects of LSD. The emotional experiences that accompany the perceptions differ, however, since normal people maintain their own consciousness and basic patterns of emotional response; the "mimetic" effects of LSD is that normal persons can *not* perceive the environment the way a schizophrenic does and psychologists believe that how and what one sees largely determines what one feels in response to that seeing. This is not to say, however, that the way one sees when using LSD as a psychotomimetic is the same as the way one sees when the drug is not being used for that purpose. In fact, that is apparently how some of the extraordinary properties of LSD were discovered; some people just did not begin to perceive schizophrenically. Instead, they felt they were "seeing for the first time."

In approaching the problem of designing a mental hospital Izumi knew that the mentally ill see the world differently than other people and that their altered perception influences their moods and feelings. LSD enabled him to enter their experiential world and thus to perceive the architectural environment as they do. The purpose of Izumi's experiment was to discover and then to avoid qualities of design that are confusing, terrifying, and psychically destructive for mentally ill people.

Besides this specific aid to Izumi in designing a mental hospital, LSD seems to have changed his attitude toward architecture generally:

> I no longer design for architects. I am now trying to design for human beings. . . . A most significant effect was on my concepts of aesthetics. Like most architects, I was seeing space as more of an aesthetic experience, without regard for what people would be doing in it. I now began to think of people living and working in these spaces. . . . I am much more conscious of spaces with relevance to the human being and in this sense critical of architectural spaces in which the human figure becomes an intrusion. In a similar way that some people see a 'halo' around their favorite subject, I am much more conscious of the 'territorial space' around a person that appears to move with them. . . . The acquisition of the sensitivity, and certainly the awareness of these phenomena to this intense degree, would not have occurred in such short order without the LSD experience.

LSD: The Dangers

One danger of LSD is its potency. One ounce contains 300,000 dosages of 100 micrograms—approximately the size of a grain of salt. Even when conditions are clinically right for its use, reactions to overdosage include extreme fear, panic, and sometimes a temporary psychosis. Perceptions and images reel through consciousness with an incomprehensible rapidity the mind cannot tolerate.

But the potency of the drug should not be confused with the drug itself. That is like saying that all driving is dangerous and that driving at 10 miles an hour is as dangerous as driving at 100 miles an hour. Furthermore, the reasons why a driver is in his car on a particular day have a lot to do with how dangerous his driving will be. If he is out for a thrill, he will be more dangerous than if he were out to demonstrate techniques of careful driving. And all of this has nothing to do with the car itself. The automobile is only a device, an instrument for getting from place to place, just as the psychedelic drugs are described by researchers as devices, tools for the exploration of the mind—a method for going from one level of perception to another, for experiencing the varied effects of a temporary alteration in brain chemistry.

A second danger of LSD (and the other psychedelic drugs) lies in the nature of the experience itself. As Osmond's verse indicates, it can be heaven or hell, and will depend, according to research findings, on three specific variables: the setting, the psychological "set" of the drug-user (his expectations, his reasons for taking the drug, his personality), and the qualities and expectations of the person supervising his use of the drug. That the outcome depends on these conditions has been amply documented. The experts apparently agree that the most dangerous situation occurs when the potent chemicals are used indiscriminately for thrills, binges, or on momentary whim. It is clear, however, that much more research is needed to determine exactly what effect the drugs will have under particular circumstances. So far, though, researchers report that, if the setting is comfortable, warm, and relaxing, the motivation of the person ingesting the drug is a serious one, and he is not psychotic (and the person with him is sympathetic and confident), the risk is minimal.

In spite of all the unknowns and uncertainties surrounding their use, the "hallucinogenic" drugs have reportedly been safely and constructively used in the treatment of psychoneuroses, frigidity, alcoholism, and even given to terminally ill cancer patients so that they can bear their pain and face death philosophically. Until Sandoz Pharamaceutical Company voluntarily stopped supplying LSD to investigators sanctioned by the National Institute of Health, some 54 research projects were being carried out (primarily into alcoholism psychoneurosis, and schizophrenia).

What would seem to emerge from the serious literature on the drugs is their unique, "midwife" quality. Dr. Robert E. Mogar, Associate Professor of Psychology at San Francisco State College, has commented, "Whether expanded awareness or increased insight accompany these unhabitual perceptions and altered frames of reference is *not* a function of the chemical agent." Apparently none of the effects of the drugs are simply spontaneous and general; results depend on how they are used and on whom. It would seem that architects, then, even though their visual abilities are high, might not experience the euphoria of imagery recounted by Huxley and others unless the situation is so structured and supervised that they can.

The Medical Evidence

To sum up the medical evidence concerning these chemicals, Dr. Sidney Cohen, Chief Psychiatrist at the Veterans Administration Hospital in Los Angeles, has stated: "Psychotic reactions lasting more than 48 hours after ingestion totaled less than two for each 1000 [mental] patients, and only two for each 2500 normal volunteers"—in *all* the clinical work done to date with LSD. C. C. Dahlberg, a prominent New York psychoanalyst, has used LSD for years in psychotherapy. He has said that he never gives it to a patient before three months of analysis have been completed, and that he has not yet had an unfavorable reaction. Finally, Dr. Mogar summarizes the results of 300 experiments using LSD as a therapeutic agent:

> Despite great diversity in the conduct of these studies, impressive improvement rates have been almost uniformly reported. . . . Based on findings with more than 1000 alcoholics, LSD was twice as effective as any other treatment program.

Mogar also believes that the possibility of positive bias in these reports is offset by their consistency and the divergent theoretical persuasions of the researchers.

In the context of the recent publicity about these drugs in the press generally, which has tended to stress the sensational and the more negative aspects of LSD, it is interesting to note a recent report of the Subcommittee on Narcotics Addiction (which, technically, has no business with the non-narcotic, non-addicting LSD). The subcommittee examined the records of 52 people who had taken the drug privately, without medical supervision, and who were admitted to the psychiatric division of Bellevue Hospital in New York City with "acute psychoses" induced by LSD, and found that 12 of the 52 had "underlying psychoses or schizoid personalities" before they took the drug, and "most of those with acute LSD psychoses recovered rapidly, 30 becoming oriented and normal in less than 48 hours. In an additional 10 patients, the psychoses were resolved in less than a week."

It would seem, then, from the available literature, that, for normal persons administered the drug in the proper setting, psychedelic drugs are not routes into madness. But, as yet, too little is known about how the drug actually works and what the long-term psychological and physical effects of its use are to make them available to the general public for self-experimentation. Approximately 5 per cent of the U.S. population is believed by psychiatrists to be predisposed to schizophrenia; an untold number in addition harbor psychotic inclinations. For these powerful and unpredictable drugs to get into such hands is dangerous both for them and for society.

LSD as an Aid to Creativity

Architects are apparently interested in the psychedelic drugs because of their perception-enhancing qualities, but Neill Smith, a San Francisco architect, is interested in them because of their effect on his ability to function creatively. He told *Progressive Architecture:*

I felt the effects of my two experiences with LSD to be positive and beneficial. . . . About the application of psychedelics in the field of architecture: It seems to me that the value of these drugs cannot be discussed apart from their effects on the total personality of the individual involved. My own experience effected changes in my thought processes and my abilities in dealing with three-dimensional imagery. But, even more importantly, there was a change in my approach to architecture through changes in personality structure and needs of my psyche. My whole approach to design has become far less concerned with conceptual structure and preconceived notions of form or ideal content. Instead, my interest has been on an increasingly more flexible, existential, or ontological design process. It is particularly in this respect that I think LSD and the other psychedelics seem to have the capability of enormously enhancing the human potential.

In observing myself and others who have taken LSD, DMT, and the other psychedelics with a constructive orientation, there seem to be two general effects on almost any level. One is the enhanced ability to function; the other is the greatly increased degree of personal and intellectual freedom that develops after taking the drugs.

Henrik Bull and Eric Clough, both California architects, took mescalin in creativity experiments carried out by the International Foundation for Advanced Study in Menlo Park, California. Like many of the research results reported, it was exploratory research that remains to be verified by more controlled studies; the results obtained are apparently in general obtainable only when the subjects are directed by specially trained persons. Henrik Bull commented:

"My experience during the session was an unbelievable increase in ability to concentrate and to make decisions. It was impossible to procrastinate, one of my favorite hobbies. Cobwebs, blocks, and binds disappeared. Anything was possible, but I was working on very real and rather right problems [during the session]. The designs were more free, but probably more from the standpoint of removing blocks in the consideration of what I felt the client might accept. Three designs were outlined in the three hours. All were accepted by the clients; one was tossed out after I saw that a better solution was possible. Perhaps this is the greatest long-term effect—a greater flexibility.

"There is definitely an enhancement of the ability to visualize, but my experience was that I became a better Henrik Bull, not Gaudí or Wright. I do feel that every architect should have the experience, to see what potential lies within himself. Beyond the usefulness, the experience was highly enjoyable and really quite fantastic."

Problem-solving Under LSD

Bull's point that he was not suddenly transformed into Wright or Gaudí is an important one, illustrating that these drugs do not work miracles, just as they are not yet believed to be destructive. Commenting in greater detail on his "session" in the International Foundation study of creativity and the psychedelic drugs, he continues:

. . . I had felt for a long time that my life was plagued with necessary but relatively unimportant detail work that was interfering with my creative work. The detail work was in competition with the design work, and both were suffering. Beyond that, I felt that my design efforts were often repeating old ideas and should be more free in spirit. These are the reasons I took mescalin. . . . [After the morning session of listening to music], I was looking forward to the opportunity to attempt some of the professional creative problems we had been told to bring with us. There were four of these, ranging from an extremely complex state college building with a program of 82 pages, to a rather simple vacation house. . . .

"The simplest problem was attacked first. Almost immediately, several relationships that had escaped my attention became apparent, and a solution to the spatial relationships followed soon after. I avoided looking at a watch throughout the session, but I would guess that 20 minutes had elapsed. Quite normally, I would stew and fret for weeks before coming to such a solution. Not to be misleading, on a simple problem the period at the end which is truly productive is often quite short under normal circumstances, but in any case a matter of hours. . . . Quite literally, I had only a head to think and a hand to make sketches and notes. . . . The first problem completed, I felt very exhilarated, and could not wait to get on to the next.

This was basically a site problem, locating a number of condominium houses on a very beautiful piece of property. The decisions came very quickly and I outlined a solution which pleased me in a very short time. In passing, I investigated the economic yield to my client for several similar solutions and decided on what I felt was the best one. Why not do a typical floor plan for one of the units? This, too, was accomplished without my usual number of false starts. . . .

[He began to work on a house for a client who had turned down several previous schemes]: This time, my approach to the problem was unrelated to all previous attempts, and I looked at the challenging site in a new way. I really believe the solution that resulted in a few minutes is better than any of those which preceded it. This is a job which has taken several hundred hours of time, and represents a great money loss for the office. Why had I never seen this solution before?

I should emphasize that the solution *could* have happened before. It belongs to the same family as my earlier work. The only real difference was that the solution I felt right about appeared in almost no time at all. . . .

The day had started at six in the morning and ended 22 hours later. It was probably the shortest and most enjoyable day in my life.

An Architect Describes His Experience in Full

Architect Eric Clough took part in the same study of creativity. He told *Progressive Architecture* of his two experiences with mescalin in detail. He pointed out some of the dangers as well as the benefits for him, which included a great improvement in his problem-solving capability. What follows is Clough's verbatim account:

After ingesting the drug [mescalin] the first time I took it, I lay down on the floor and began to melt into the environment. I felt as if I were a mass of protoplasmic jelly that was just creeping out into and infusing with everything around it. I felt some tension and wondered why—I'm generally relaxed—and I realized that, along with this melting of my general being, my ego was melting too. I visualized my ego as a head sticking up above the protoplasm, trying to preserve itself. Once I realized that and could laugh at myself—at my ego—it just went flop and away I went. The general feeling and the mental imagery that was involved in it had to do largely with a total involvement, physically and emotionally, with the world about me, and with life in general. I tried to think about what was happening and realized that I was trying to intellectualize about what was the most complete thinking process that I have ever experienced. I laughed again at how foolish we are sometimes; we think about thinking and we think about being when it's so simple and basic to just be.

That day, without thinking about it, I experienced deep inner knowledge of the philosophies that man has devised for himself through the centuries. I didn't any longer just intellectually understand philosophy, but I *knew* life and I *knew* that all the philosophies are essentially and integrally the same. I realized that man makes structures for himself—that is, constructs—which are all essentially paradoxically ridiculous, but at the same time are really necessary as ways of dealing with the world and ourselves.

I went from seeing myself as Professor, World's Foremost Authority, to a Zen master sitting on a mountain-top and seeing all the human constructs in a series of structures—abstract kind of geometric forms which interlapped and overlapped and stood on top and underneath. They all seemed to be the same thing and they all seemed to be very, very ridiculous. I felt that as a living thing, I was integrally a part of life, and, while I didn't ask for that particular state of being, neither could I accept any particular responsibility for it having happened, yet I was at the same time totally responsible for life itself because I was integrally involved in it.

One interesting thing about the psychedelic experience is the way in which these ideas, thoughts, feelings—whatever they might be called—come to one. Normally we use words as tools to form constructs, communicate, and to think with, but in the psychedelic experience there is really no thinking process involved. Thoughts are essentially mental images—very, very clear, and complete, and integral with being, so to speak—so that the thought-process, as we normally know it, doesn't really exist.

During the almost two years from the first to the second experience, I would say that my general ability to think in pictures, rather than in words was much enhanced. My ability to flow easily with life was enhanced, and therefore my creativity. There was less internal friction and a greater ability to focus on what I was doing, thinking, or designing. I don't think I learned anything new about design, but found it easier to explore possibilities in a freer way.

[The second session was the actual creativity experiment at the Foundation]. The problem I brought to the session was an art and cultural center on a site near the new University of California campus near Santa Cruz, California. Prior to the session, I thought about the project and discarded many different schemes. The day before the session, I had a basic construct in mind and an idea of a good solution for the problem. We were instructed to go into the session thinking about the fact that we were going to work on a particular project. There were three of us in the room that day: two physicists and myself, each working on his own project. We were told not to think about our projects as such during the morning but to be as open as we could.

That morning at 8:30, we talked for awhile, lay down, put on earphones and eyeblinders, and listened to stereo music for the bulk of the morning. My morning experience ended at 10:30 because I was anxious to get to work, but a program was set up so that we didn't work until noon. So I patiently waited until it was time to go to work. I took a technicolor dream trip through history: I found myself swinging through trees with a lot of other people, but we were all pretty much simian and we seemed to be enjoying ourselves. I could see the forest—or jungle—the flowers, the other 'pecple,' having a delightful experience, chattering back and forth in words I didn't understand but the mood seemed a very happy one. Immediately after that I was in a cave, with prehistoric paintings on the wall, people both clothed and unclothed sitting around a fire. I was eating a great chunk of raw meat, sort of braised meat. Particularly I noticed the environment we were in—the figure drawings on the cave wall. Immediately after that, I was in either an Incan or an Aztec village, wandering around through a market place that was the center of a large square, looking at the temple which was very huge and impressive, seeing the people in the market place, looking at their mode of dress—the gold ornaments the wealthy people were wearing, stopping and eating a piece of fruit at a stand; essentially living in and being a part of this beautiful city I was in. After that, I was in a formal ballroom, dressed in what looked like one of the old tintype photographs, talking to people with a very formal approach, feeling very formal inside and noticing the architecture of the huge ballroom, the big windows made up of small panels of glass, the clothing the people were wearing, the dancing. Then I was in an ice-cream parlor in the Roaring Twenties. Everybody was having a terrific time in the 23 Skidoo style, which somehow felt very superficial. Then I was in a modern city the likes of which I have never seen. It is best described as the "City of the Future"—the kind *Progessive Architecture* occasionally publishes as concepts for redevelopment. Everything was new, everything efficient, everything beautifully articulated.

I sat up at about 11:00 with the strong feeling that everything having to do with the history of architecture and everything having to do with leading all architects, all designers, myself, up to the cultural point we are at now with the ability to design based on experience and knowledge of the past—that all of this was fine, but any copying of or taking directly from any past age or any other culture was ludicrous, meaningless, and had no validity in a fresh design approach. With this feeling, the prior ideas I had had about my project were all gone; I found myself in an absolute void of idea and creative thought. It was about noon; the others were aroused from their eyeshades and earphones. We had some lunch, talked awhile, and then it was time to work.

I sat down with a sketch-pad and drew a square outline of the property, looked at it, and had absolutely no idea at all of what was appropriate to solve the problems. I must have looked at the paper for five or ten minutes with an absolute blank. And then, all of a sudden, with a total flash of an absolutely clear, completed project was the cultural center—designed, built, complete before my eyes. So complete that I could walk through it in my imagination, see the architectural detailing, see the insides of the shops, and so on. It was a totally complete, finished product. So I began to do the plot plan layout. I knew I had to have so many square feet of building, so many car parkings, knew the circulation patterns. I began to draw what I saw and everything fit precisely, and, although I had a scale ruler with me, I hardly had to use it, because everything seemed to be exactly as it should be and fitted exactly as it would if I were measuring it. I doodled figures around the edge of the sheet, trying to arrive at per sq. ft. estimates of construction cost, total value of project, potential monthly income. And all of these factors seemed to work too, so that the project had economic feasibility. As rapidly as I could, much faster than my hand would work, I tried to capture the essence of the building project, of the Center. I was almost certain that my total knowledge of it and how it was built wouldn't stay with me, and therefore I had to get symbols down on paper that would give me a key back in later. This was done in about an hour—the total process—and the project was completed.

While I felt I could certainly go on and do a great deal more work on the center, I instead had a lot of fun designing. I designed a little meditation house, for example, in the woods—in my head. I could see it just as completely as I could see the center. I designed a couple of mountain cabins, and I designed a residence that was larger than the cabins. I played with a piece of sculpture for a mailbox. This was all pure mental projection. I felt I had done my work for the day; in fact, the way I normally would work I had done something like four or five day's work of really good production in a matter of that hour-and-a-half or so. I spent the rest of the day enjoying and looking at the other people's mental wheels turning. They were sitting there deep in thought, working through very complex problems—one on light patterns and photons, and one on other things, just as complex, having to do with the neurological patterns of the human body.

The psychedelic materials seem to be 'facilitators', or perhaps 'focusers.' I think that what this experiment showed is that it's possible to use the materials to focus on anything, or to facilitate focusing on anything, that one may choose to do. So they could be used for designing, as I did, for scientific thinking, as others did, for psychotherapy, for explorations into telepathy perhaps—I don't know what the potentials are. I learned from being with the Institute twice that the setting is the vital part of the experiment with psychedelic materials. They open the unconscious completely, although it can still be tapped directly into a focus; but unless there *is* a focus, and unless there is a protective atmosphere, I think there is a great danger in having an experience that would be wide open to I don't know what: Some of the horrors of the unconscious, the losing of all structures that one functions with and not being able to replace them, or to replace them in a way that is antithetical to the society in which we live. I see a great danger in the misuse or the playing around with the psychedelic materials, but I'm tremendously enthusiastic about their potential. I want to say: All architects ought to have this experience. Maybe everybody ought to have this experience. But it would be sheer insanity to have mass distribution of the drugs and say to everybody, here, let's see what can be done.

Conjecturing about how the psychedelic experience enhanced my awareness and what it can do for the future: The project I designed isn't particularly unusual in architecture. Essentially, I had a problem to work out that needed a comfortable, warm architecture; it needed to have a feeling of culture, a feeling of artistry that wouldn't, as I see it, dominate so strongly that it would essentially destroy the integration of other people's arts into it. So, in the sense of using the psychedelic session for the creation of something totally new or even very different—that is something I wasn't involved in trying to do. What I was amazed by was the facility with which problem-solving was enhanced. Until the time of the session, it had been a fairly difficult problem; I hadn't been able to solve it in a way that I was happy with. The solution came so clearly and so completely and with no problems to readjust, that I think, for myself, the value was in that ability to problem-solve in such a complete, thorough, and rapid way. This quality has stayed with me. It was five months ago now. I am not functioning every day as I did on that day, but I've had the experience of sitting down in the morning and designing six houses in three hours—in rough, very crude sketch form. I have done a little bit of very free thinking and very free sketching on new forms and new shapes—things I hadn't attempted before—and I'm pleased with these too.

While people have said their experience doesn't stay with them, I think that somehow I learned something from it. I learned that whatever I was able to do that day was not because of the drug, but because the drug allowed me to function in a way that I was capable all along of functioning, without the usual frictions we encounter.

Perhaps the next step is to try and work out totally new concepts. Perhaps a whole new view of architecture could be developed. I'd like to see someone like the Institute put a group of people together in a problem-solving session where they were all working on the same project, for example. I believe that the psychedelics are a tool—like a key to open doors so that we can look at old things in new and open ways. This is what we are capable of all the time but we don't usually recognize the fact that we are.

The Wider Implications of LSD

The social and cultural implications of the psychedelic drugs have been widely commented upon. It is easy to speculate that 20th-Century Man, living in an age of scientific revolution that has overthrown in the span of a few decades the social and moral assumptions of several centuries—an age where theologians themselves are forced into anguished debates as to the very existence of God, and where the new technology is rapidly dehumanizing man—in such a context, the appeal of drugs that promise man a supposed ability to transcend the routine sense of self and environment are obvious. Whether these more mystical claims to self-discovery have any legitimate scientific base remains the job of steady, sober scientific study in the years ahead.

In terms of the limited aims of this article, the psychedelic drugs are of interest to the profession to the extent that they may be shown to facilitate creativity and problem-solving. The difficulty is that the nature of creativity itself, of talent, even of genius, although under scientific investigation for decades, still contains areas of mystery and speculation. Whether pharmacology can bring new weapons to bear in the war that psychologists and psychiatrists have been waging for so long is the interesting issue.

When one considers the enormous complexity of the brain as the ultimate instrument that classifies and interprets all the sense data the individual is exposed to, the problem becomes apparent. The brain receives one billion signals *per second*—many more than normally reach consciousness. There are between ten and thirteen billion brain cells, and each one is connected to 25,000 other cells. As yet, researchers have little knowledge of the chemical processes that occur among the cells. One of the great mysteries of the psychedelic drugs is whether or not anyone will be able to demonstrate that what an individual normally sees and experiences is more "real" than what is experienced with the aid of the drugs. They are repeatedly described as chemical agents that can somehow *open* the mind, allowing the free flow of sense data directly into consciousness, unimpeded by the intellectualizing, the categorizing according to preconceptions the individual normally resorts to. And yet this massive influx of sense data is experienced in a fully conscious state. Interestingly, from the descriptions of many who have taken the drug, the psychedelic experience seems to correspond to the world as it has been described by physicists—a world composed of minute, moving, bobbing particles of energy called electrons; everything is said to move and pulsate.

Another interesting aspect of the psychedelics is what several research psychologists have termed the similarity between the effects created by these chemicals and the sort of consciousness identified with creativity: The ability to become detached from everyday experience and become totally absorbed by deeper levels of awareness, coupled with the ability to abandon this detachment and return to normal levels of consciousness. A rather far-removed speculation in this respect that has been forwarded by some commentators is the fascinating possibility that in future years the psychedelic drugs may make accessible to the average man levels of consciousness and perception previously restricted only to the artist.

The consensus among the architects *Progressive Architecture* interviewed, several of whom we have quoted in these pages, seems to be that LSD, when administered under carefully controlled conditions, does enhance creativity to the extent that it vastly speeds up problem-solving, aids in visualizing three-dimensionally, and generally heightens perceptivity. The drug apparently cannot give an architect more talent than nature originally endowed him with, but it can make it more accessible. In a sense, Henrik Bull summed it up when he commented, "My experience was that I became a better Henrik Bull, not Gaudí or Wright."

47

The Peyote Way

J. S. Slotkin

Peyote (*Lophophora williamsi*) is a spineless cactus which grows in the northern half of Mexico and for a short distance north of the Texas border. It has attracted attention because it is used as a sacrament in religious rites conducted by Indians in the United States and Canada belonging to the Native American Church. The Peyote Religion or Peyote Way, as it is called by members, is the most widespread contemporary religion among the Indians, and is continually spreading to additional tribes.

From the viewpoint of almost all Peyotists, the religion is an Indian version of Christianity. White Christian theology, ethics, and eschatology have been adopted with modifications which make them more compatible with traditional Indian culture. The religion probably originated among the Kiowa and Comanche in Oklahoma about 1885.

The Peyote rite is an all-night ceremony, lasting approximately from sunset to sunrise, characteristically held in a Plains type tipi. Essentially the rite has four major elements: prayer, singing, eating the sacramental Peyote, and contemplation. The ritual is well defined, being divided into four periods: from sunset to midnight, from midnight to three o'clock, from three o'clock to dawn, and from dawn to morning. Four fixed songs sung by the rite leader, analogous to the fixed songs in the Catholic Mass, mark most of these divisions.

The rite within the tipi begins with the Starting Song; the midnight period is marked by the Midnight Water Song; there is no special song at three o'clock; at dawn there is the Morning Water Song, and the rite ends with the Quitting Song. At midnight sacred water is drunk again and a communion meal eaten.

Usually five people officiate at the rite. Four are men: the leader, often referred to as the Roadman because he leads the group along the Peyote Road (that is, the Peyotist way of life) to salvation; the drum chief who accompanies the leader when he sings; the cedar chief who is in charge of cedar incense; and the fire chief who maintains a ritual fire and acts as sergeant-at-arms. A close female relative of the leader, usually his wife, brings in, and prays over, the morning water.

In clockwise rotation, starting with the leader, each male participant sings a set of four solo songs; he is accompanied on a water drum by the man to his right. The singing continues from the time of the Starting Song to that of the Morning Water Song; the number of rounds of singing therefore depends upon the number of men

Reprinted from *Tomorrow*, IV, No. 3 (1955–56), 65–70, by permission of Mrs. Elizabeth J. Slotkin. and Garrett Publications.

present. On most occasions there are four rounds, so that each man sings a total of sixteen songs.

During the rite Peyote is taken in one of the following forms: the fresh whole plant except for roots (green Peyote), the dried top of the plant (Peyote button), or an infusion of the Peyote button in water (Peyote tea). Some people have no difficulty taking Peyote. But many find it bitter, inducing indigestion or nausea. A common complaint is, "It's hard to take Peyote."

The amount taken depends upon the individual, and the solemnity of the ritual occasion. There is great tribal variability in amount used, and accurate figures are virtually impossible to obtain. But in general one might say that under ordinary circumstances the bulk of the people take less than a dozen Peyotes. On the most serious occasions, such as rites held for someone mortally sick, those present take as much Peyote as they can; the capacity of most people seems to range from about four to forty Peyote buttons.

Peyotists have been organized into the Native American Church since 1918. These church groups run the gamut of comprehensiveness from the single local group on the one extreme, to the intertribal and international federation known as the Native American Church of North America, on the other extreme.

In a series of other publications I have discussed the early history of Peyotism ("Peyotism, 1521–1891," *American Anthropologist*, LVII [1955], pp. 202–30), presented an historical and generalized account of the religion (*The Peyote Religion: A Study in Indian-White Relations*, The Free Press, 1956) and given a detailed description of the Peyote Religion in a single tribe ("Menomini Peyotism," *Transactions of the American Philosophical Society*, XLII [1952], Part 4)—all from the viewpoint of a relatively detached anthropologist. The present essay is different. Here I concentrate on the contemporary uses of, and attitudes toward, sacramental Peyote, and write as a member and officer of the Native American Church of North America. Of course the presentation is mine, but I think substantially it represents the consensus of our membership.

Long ago God took pity on the Indian. (Opinions vary as to when this happened: when plants were created at the origin of the world, when Jesus lived, or after the white man had successfully invaded this continent.) So God created Peyote and put some of his power into it for the use of Indians. Therefore the Peyotist takes the sacramental Peyote to absorb God's power contained in it, in the same way that the white Christian takes the sacramental bread and wine.

Power is the English term used by Indians for the supernatural force called *mana* by the anthropologists; it is equivalent to the New Testament *pneuma*, translated as Holy Spirit or Holy Ghost. Power is needed to live. As a Crow Indian once remarked to me as we were strolling near a highway, man is like an auto; if the car loses its power it cannot go. Physically, power makes a person healthy, and safe when confronted by danger. Spiritually, power gives a person knowledge of how to behave successfully in everyday life, and what to make of one's life as a whole. The Peyotist obtains power from the sacramental Peyote.

Physically, Peyote is used as a divine healer and amulet.

For sick people Peyote is used in various ways. In a mild illness Peyote is taken as a home remedy. Thus when a man has a cold, he drinks hot Peyote tea and goes to bed. In more serious illnesses Peyote is taken during the Peyote rite. Such an illness is due not only to lack of sufficient power, but also to a foreign object within the body. Therefore a seriously sick person who takes Peyote usually vomits, thus expelling the foreign object which is the precipitating cause of the illness; then more Peyote is taken in order to obtain the amount of power needed for health.

In cases of severe illness, the rite itself is held for the purpose of healing the patient; it is often referred to as a doctoring meeting. In addition to having the sick person take Peyote, as in less desperate cases, everyone else present prays to God to give the patient extra power so he or she will recover.

Members may keep a Peyote button at home, or on their person, to protect them from danger. The latter is particularly true of men in the armed forces. The power within the Peyote wards off harm from anything in the area of its influence. In cases of great danger, as when a young man is about to leave for military service, a prayer meeting is held at which everyone present beseeches God to give the man extra power to avoid harm.

Spiritually, Peyote is used to obtain knowledge. This is known as learning from Peyote. Used properly, Peyote is an inexhaustible teacher. A stock statement is, "You can use Peyote all your life, but you'll never get to the end of what there is to be known from Peyote. Peyote is always teaching you something new." Many Peyotists say that the educated white man obtains his knowledge from books—particularly the Bible; while the uneducated Indian has to obtain his knowledge from Peyote. But the Indian's means of achieving knowledge is superior to that of the white man. The latter learns from books merely what other people have to say; the former learns from Peyote by direct experience.

A Comanche once said, "The white man talks *about* Jesus; we talk *to* Jesus." Thus the individual has a vividly direct experience of what he learns, qualitatively different from inference or hearsay. Therefore the Peyotist, epistemologically speaking, is an individualist and empiricist; he believes only what he himself has experienced.

A Peyotist maxim is, "The only way to find out about Peyote is to take it and learn from Peyote yourself." It may be interesting to know what others have to say; but all that really matters is what one has directly experienced—what he has learned himself from Peyote. This conception of salvation by knowledge, to be achieved by revelation (in this case, through Peyote) rather than through verbal or written learning, is a doctrine similar to that of early Middle Eastern Gnosticism.

The mere act of eating Peyote does not itself bring knowledge. The proper ritual behavior has to be observed before one is granted knowledge through Peyote. Physically, one must be clean, having bathed and put on clean clothes. Spiritually, one must put away all evil thought. Psychologically, one must be conscious of his personal inadequacy, humble, sincere in wanting to obtain the benefits of Peyote, and concentrate on it.

Peyote teaches in a variety of ways.

One common way in which Peyote teaches is by heightening the sensibility of the Peyotist, either in reference to himself or to others.

Heightened sensibility to oneself manifests itself as increased powers of introspection. One aspect of introspection is very important in Peyotism. During the rite a good deal of time is spent in self-evaluation. Finally the individual engages in silent or vocal prayer to God, confessing his sins, repenting, and promising to follow the Peyote Road (that is, the Peyotist ethic) more carefully in the future. If he has spiritual evil within him, Peyote makes him vomit, thus purging him of sin.

Heightened sensibility to others manifests itself as what might be called mental telepathy. One either feels that he knows what others are thinking, or feels that he either influences, or is influenced by, the thoughts of others. In this connection a frequent phenomenon is speaking in tongues, which results from the fact that people from different tribes participate in a rite together, each using his own language; Peyote teaches one the meaning of otherwise unknown languages.

For example, during the rite each male participant in succession sings solo four songs at a time. Recently a Winnebago sitting next to me sang a song with what I heard as a Fox text (Fox is an Algonquian language closely related to Menomini, the language I use in the rite), sung so clearly and distinctly I understood every word.

When he was through, I leaned over and asked, "How come you sang that song in Fox rather than Winnebago (a Siouan language unintelligible to me)?"

"I did sing it in Winnebago," he replied. The afternoon following the rite he sat down next to me and asked me to listen while he repeated the song; this time it was completely unintelligible to me because the effects of Peyote had worn off.

A second common way in which Peyote teaches is by means of revelation, called a vision. The vision is obtained because one has eaten enough Peyote under the proper ritual conditions to obtain the power needed to commune with the spirit world. The vision provides a direct experience (visual, auditory, or a combination of both) of God or some intermediary spirit, such as Jesus, Peyote Spirit (the personification of Peyote), or Waterbird.

The nature of the vision depends upon the personality and problems of the individual. The following are typical: He may be comforted by seeing or hearing some previously unexperienced item of Peyotist belief, or departed loved ones now in a happy existence. He may be guided on the one hand by being shown the way to solve some problem in daily life; on the other hand, he may be reproved for evil thoughts or deeds, and warned to repent.

A third way in which Peyote teaches is by means of mystical experience. This is relatively uncommon. It is limited to Peyotists of a certain personality type among the more knowledgeable members of the church; roughly speaking, they have what white people would call a mystical temperament. These Peyotists, in turn, rarely have visions, and tend to look upon them as distractions. The mystical experience may be said to consist in the harmony of all immediate experience with whatever the individual conceives to be the highest good.

Peyote has the remarkable property of helping one to have a mystical experience for an indefinite period of time, as opposed to most forms of mystical discipline under which the mystical experience commonly lasts for a matter of minutes. Actually, I have no idea of how long I could maintain such an experience with Peyote, for after about an hour or so it is invariably interrupted by some ritual detail I am required to perform.

What happens to the Peyotist phenomenologically that makes possible the extraordinary results I have described? It seems to depend on both the physiological and psychological effects of Peyote.

Physiologically, Peyote seems to have curative properties. Many times, after a variety of illnesses brought about by fieldwork conditions, I have left a Peyote meeting permanently well again.

Another physiological effect of Peyote is that it reduces the fatigue to an astonishing extent. For instance, I am not robust, but after taking Peyote I can participate in the rite with virtually no fatigue—a rite which requires me to sit on the ground, cross-legged, with no back rest, and without moving, for 10 to 14 hours at a stretch; all this in the absence of food and water.

Psychologically, Peyote increases one's sensitivity to relevant stimuli. This applies to both external and internal stimuli. Externally, for example, the ritual fire has more intense colors when I am under the influence of Peyote. Internally, I find it easier to introspect upon otherwise vague immediate experiences.

At the same time, Peyote decreases one's sensitivity to irrelevant external and internal stimuli. Very little concentration is needed for me to ignore distracting noises inside or outside the tipi. Similarly, extraneous internal sensations or ideas are easily ignored.

Thus, on one occasion I wrote in my field diary, "I could notice no internal sensations. If I paid very close attention, I could observe a vague and faint feeling that suggested that without Peyote my back would be sore from sitting up in one position all night; the same was true of my crossed legs. Also, my mouth might be dry, but I couldn't be sure."

The combination of such effects as absence of fatigue, heightened sensitivity to relevant stimuli, and lowered sensitivity to irrelevant stimuli, should make it easier to understand how the individual is disposed to learn from Peyote under especially created ritual conditions.

To any reader who becomes intrigued by Peyote, two warnings should be given. First, I have discussed the effects of Peyote on those who used it as a sacrament under ritual conditions. The described responses of white people to Peyote under experimental conditions are quite different; in fact, they tend to be psychologically traumatic. Second, Peyote is a sacrament in the Native American Church, which refuses to permit the presence of curiosity seekers at its rites, and vigorously opposes for sale or use of Peyote for nonsacramental purposes.

48

Report of the Peyote Experience of Crashing Thunder

Paul Radin

(Crashing Thunder is a Winnebago Indian in whose autobiography is described in detail his initiation to the peyote worship. Long persecuted by the guilt of having once fraudulently told his people that he had had a vision and of having made a shambles of his life through drunkenness, living with various women, and even through implication in a murder, Crashing Thunder sets out for a peyote meeting with some reluctance. In this first experience not too much happens except that he reports "I felt different from my normal self". Several further meetings follow, and then this one.)

When we arrived, the one who was to lead asked me to sit near him. There he placed me. He urged me to eat a lot of peyote, so I did. The leaders of the ceremony always placed the regalia in front of themselves; they also had a peyote placed there. The one this leader placed in front of himself this time, was a very small one. "Why

From "The Autobiography of a Winnebago Indian," by Paul Radin, University of California Publications in American Archaeology and Ethnology Vol. 16, No. 7; 1920. Reprinted by permission of The Regents of the University of California.

does he have a very small one there?" I thought to myself. I did not think much about it.

It was now late at night and I had eaten a lot of peyote and felt rather tired. I suffered considerably. After a while I looked at the peyote and there stood an eagle with outspread wings. It was as beautiful a sight as one could behold. Each of the feathers seemed to have a mark. The eagle stood looking at me. I looked around thinking that perhaps there was something the matter with my sight. Then I looked again and it was really there. I then looked in a different direction and it disappeared. Only the small peyote remained. I looked around at the other people but they all had their heads bowed and were singing. I was very much surprised.

Some time after this I saw a lion lying in the same place where I had seen the eagle. I watched it very closely. It was alive and looking at me. I looked at it very closely and when I turned my eyes away just the least little bit, it disappeared. "I suppose they all know this and I am just beginning to know of it," I thought. Then I saw a small person at the same place. He wore blue clothes and a shining brimmed cap. He had on a soldier's uniform. He was sitting on the arm of the person who was drumming, and he looked at every one. He was a little man, perfect in all proportions. Finally I lost sight of him. I was very much surprised indeed. I sat very quietly. "This is what it is," I thought, "this is what they all probably see and I am just beginning to find out."

Then I prayed to Earthmaker: "This, your ceremony, let me hereafter perform."

As I looked again, I saw a flag. I looked more carefully and I saw the house full of flags. They had the most beautiful marks on them. In the middle of the room there was a very large flag and it was a live one; it was moving. In the doorway there was another one not entirely visible. I had never seen anything so beautiful in all my life before.

Then again I prayed to Earthmaker. I bowed my head and closed my eyes and began to speak. I said many things that I would ordinarily never have spoken about. As I prayed, I was aware of something above me and there he was; Earthmaker to whom I was praying, he it was. That which is called the soul, that is it, that is what one calls Earthmaker. Now this is what I felt and saw. The one called Earthmaker is a spirit and that is what I felt and saw. All of us sitting there, we had all together one spirit or soul. At least that is what I learned. I instantly became the spirit and I was their spirit or soul. Whatever they thought of, I immediately knew it. I did not have to speak to them and get an answer to know what their thoughts had been. Then I thought of a certain place, far away, and immediately I was there; I was my thought.

I looked around and noticed how everything seemed about me, and when I opened my eyes I was myself in the body again. From this time on, I thought, thus I shall be. This is the way they are, and I am only just beginning to be that way. "All those that heed Earthmaker must be thus," I thought. "I would not need any more food," I thought, "for was I not my spirit? Nor would I have any more use of my body," I felt. "My corporeal affairs are over," I felt.

Then they stopped and left for it was just dawning. Then someone spoke to me. I did not answer for I thought they were just fooling and that they were all like myself, and that therefore it was unnecessary for me to talk to them. So when they spoke to me I only answered with a smile. "They are just saying this to me because they realize that I have just found out," I thought. That was why I did not answer. I did not speak to anyone until noon. Then I had to leave the house to perform one of nature's duties and someone followed me. It was my friend. He said, "My friend, what troubles you that makes you act as you do?" "Well, there's no need of your saying anything for you know it beforehand," I said.

Then I immediately got over my trance and again got into my normal condition so that he would have to speak to me before I knew his thoughts. I became like my former self. It became necessary for me to speak to him. . . .

Now since that time (of my conversion) no matter where I am I always think of this religion. I still remember it and I think I will remember it as long as I live. It is the only holy thing that I have been aware of in all my life.

After that whenever I heard of a peyote meeting, I went to it. However my thoughts were always fixed on women. "If I were married (legally) perhaps these thoughts will leave me," I thought. Whenever I went to a meeting now I tried to eat as many peyote as possible, for I was told that it was good to eat them. For that reason I ate them. As I sat there I would always pray to Earthmaker. Now these were my thoughts. If I were married, I thought as I sat there, I could then put all my thoughts on this ceremony. I sat with my eyes closed and was very quiet.

Suddenly I saw something. This was tied up. The rope with which this object was tied up was long. The object itself was running around and around in a circle. There was a pathway there in which it ought to go, but it was tied up and unable to get there. The road was an excellent one. Along its edge blue grass grew and on each side there grew many varieties of pretty flowers. Sweet-smelling flowers sprang up all along this road. Far off in the distance appeared a bright light. There a city was visible of a beauty indescribable by tongue. A cross was in full sight. The object that was tied up would always fall just short of reaching the road. It seemed to lack sufficient strength to break loose of what was holding it. Near it lay something which would have given it sufficient strength to break its fastenings, if it were only able to get hold of it.

I looked at what was so inextricably tied up and I saw that it was myself. I was forever thinking of women. "This is it with which I was tied," I thought. "Were I married, I would have strength enough to break my fastening and be able to travel in the good road," I thought. Then daylight came upon us and we stopped . . .

(He did marry, and "together we gave ourselves up at a peyote meeting. From that time on we have remained members of the peyote ceremony.")

On one occasion while at a meeting, I suffered great pain. My eyes were sore and I was thinking of many things. "Now I do nothing but pay attention to this ceremony, for it is good." Then I called the leader over to me and said to him, "My elder brother, hereafter only Earthmaker shall I regard as holy. I will make no more offerings of tobacco. I will not use any more tobacco. I will not smoke and I will not chew tobacco. I have no further interest in these. Earthmaker alone do I desire to serve. I will not take part in the Medicine Dance again. I give myself up to you. I intend to give myself up to Earthmaker's cause." Thus I spoke to him. "It is good younger brother," he said to me. Then he had me stand up and he prayed to Earthmaker. He asked Earthmaker to forgive me my sins . . .

Thus I go about telling everyone that this religion is good. Many other people at home said the same thing. Many, likewise, have joined this religion and are getting along nicely. . . . Before my conversion I went about in a pitiable condition, but now I am living happily, and my wife has a fine baby.

PART IV *America and the Social System*

America the complicated, too large to be comprehended, too varied to be labeled, won't stand still long enough to be studied. However, it is the one culture we have experienced and the one we must understand as fully as possible. By understanding our roots and cultural biases we can become more sensitive and realistic critics of our changing culture and other cultures as well.

After college I spent a year working and traveling in Europe. The most profound culture shocks came from realizing that certain assumptions I held about all mankind were true only for Americans. Everyone else is *not* just like us.

The first section looks at the historical fact of democracy as it has been observed throughout our history; the second considers the effects of various kinds of economic thinking; the third highlights new problems of affluence; and the last section looks into corporate problems as influences on America's cultural development.

Our national character is the sum of our ethical principals, our family life, our values and beliefs, our institutions, and a hundred other facets of our environment. The network of relationships is all-pervasive yet indistinct, all-inclusive yet not binding. A fish must be extremely aware of himself and his environment before he is capable of noticing that he is in water and that anything which affects the water affects him as well. Men, living in their own culture face an equally difficult task.

SECTION A *Perspectives on American Democracy*

The history of American national character appears to remain relatively constant: similar problems and solutions, and the same continuing differences between what we profess and how we behave. The labels change but the underlying flow remains the same.

Mrs. John Adams recalls a moment when Boston heard of the birth of this nation. De Tocqueville, a French nobleman, writes his impressions of America in the first twenty years after the Revolutionary War. Lord Bryce writes about America after the Civil War. C. Northcote Parkinson and Dorothy Lee both comment on our own era. All of them observe the same force, the same national character, changing but remaining recognizable through several generations. All of them find important strengths and serious faults with the American system.

In the final article Dorothy Lee questions the nature of freedom itself. What is this stuff that this nation is built on? What is liberty that we would die for it, fight for it, or even restrict it in the name of liberty itself?

Our system of government is a fundamental factor in the shaping of our attitudes and belief systems about the nature of man. To a lesser extent it also shapes our ideas about ourselves.

49

Reaction to the Proclamation of Independence

Mrs. John Adams (Abigail Adams)

Boston, 21 July, 1776.

Last Thursday, after hearing a very good sermon I went with the multitude into King Street to hear the Proclamation for Independence read and proclaimed. Some field pieces with the train were brought there. The troops appeared under arms, and all the inhabitants assembled there (the small-pox prevented many thousands from the country), when Colonel Crafts read from the balcony of the State House the proclamation. Great attention was given to every word. As soon as he was ended, the cry from the balcony was, "God save our American States." Then three cheers rent the air. The bells rang, the privateers fired, the forts and batteries, the cannon were discharged, the platoons followed and every face appeared joyful. Mr. Bowdoin then gave a sentiment, "Stability and perpetuity to American Independence." After Dinner, the King's Arms were taken down from the State House, and every vestige of him from every place in which it appeared, and burnt in King Street. Thus ends royal authority in this State. And all the people shall say Amen.

Reprinted from *Familiar Letters of John Adams and His Wife, Abigail Adams, During The Revolution,* Charles Francis Adams, editor, 1876, p. 204.

50

Unlimited Power of the Majority in the United States, and Its Consequences

Alexis de Tocqueville

Natural strength of the majority in democracies—Most of the American constitutions have increased this strength by artificial means—How this has been done—Pledged delegates—Moral power of the majority—Opinion as to its infallibility—Respect for its rights, how augmented in the United States.

The very essence of democratic government consists in the absolute sovereignty of the majority; for there is nothing in democratic states that is capable of resisting it. Most of the American constitutions have sought to increase this natural strength of the majority by artificial means.[1]

Of all political institutions, the legislature is the one that is most easily swayed by the will of the majority. The Americans determined that the members of the legislature should be elected by the people *directly*, and for a *very brief term*, in order to subject them, not only to the general convictions, but even to the daily passions, of their constituents. The members of both houses are taken from the same classes in society and nominated in the same manner; so that the movements of the legislative bodies are almost as rapid, and quite as irresistible, as those of a single assembly. It is to a legislature thus constituted that almost all the authority of the government has been entrusted.

At the same time that the law increased the strength of those authorities which of themselves were strong, it enfeebled more and more those which were naturally weak. It deprived the representatives of the executive power of all stability and independence; and by subjecting them completely to the caprices of the legislature, it robbed them of the slender influence that the nature of a democratic government might have allowed them to exercise. In several states the judicial power was also submitted to the election of the majority; and in all of them its existence was made to depend on the pleasure of the legislative authority, since the representatives were empowered annually to regulate the stipend of the judges.

Custom has done even more than law. A proceeding is becoming more and more general in the United States which will, in the end, do away with the guarantees of

From *Democracy in America,* by Alexis de Tocqueville, translated by Phillips Bradley. Copyright 1945 by Alfred A. Knopf, Inc. Reprinted by permission.

[1] We have seen, in examining the Federal Constitution, that the efforts of the legislators of the Union were directed against this absolute power. The consequence has been that the Federal government is more independent in its sphere than that of the states. But the Federal Government scarcely ever interferes in any but foreign affairs; and the governments of the states in reality direct society in America.

representative government: it frequently happens that the voters, in electing a delegate, point out a certain line of conduct to him and impose upon him certain positive obligations that he is pledged to fulfill. With the exception of the tumult, this comes to the same thing as if the majority itself held its deliberations in the marketplace.

Several particular circumstances combine to render the power of the majority in America not only preponderant, but irresistible. The moral authority of the majority is partly based upon the notion that there is more intelligence and wisdom in a number of men united than in a single individual, and that the number of the legislators is more important than their quality. The theory of equality is thus applied to the intellects of men; and human pride is thus assailed in its last retreat by a doctrine which the minority hesitate to admit, and to which they will but slowly assent. Like all other powers, and perhaps more than any other, the authority of the many requires the sanction of time in order to appear legitimate. At first it enforces obedience by constraint; and its laws are not *respected* until they have been long maintained.

The right of governing society, which the majority supposes itself to derive from its superior intelligence, was introduced into the United States by the first settlers; and this idea which of itself would be sufficient to create a free nation has now been amalgamated with the customs of the people and the minor incidents of social life.

The French under the old monarchy held it for a maxim that the king could do no wrong; and if he did do wrong, the blame was imputed to his advisers. This notion made obedience very easy; it enabled the subject to complain of the law without ceasing to love and honor the lawgiver. The Americans entertain the same opinion with respect to the majority.

The moral power of the majority is founded upon yet another principle, which is that the interests of the many are to be preferred to those of the few. It will readily be perceived that the respect here professed for the rights of the greater number must naturally increase or diminish according to the state of parties. When a nation is divided into several great irreconcilable interests, the privilege of the majority is often overlooked, because it is intolerable to comply with its demands.

If there existed in America a class of citizens whom the legislating majority sought to deprive of exclusive privileges which they had possessed for ages and to bring down from an elevated station to the level of the multitude, it is probable that the minority would be less ready to submit to its laws. But as the United States was colonized by men holding equal rank, there is as yet no natural or permanent disagreement between the interests of its different inhabitants.

There are communities in which the members of the minority can never hope to draw the majority over to their side, because they must then give up the very point that is at issue between them. Thus an aristocracy can never become a majority while it retains its exclusive privileges, and it cannot cede its privileges without ceasing to be an aristocracy.

In the United States, political questions cannot be taken up in so general and absolute a manner; and all parties are willing to recognize the rights of the majority, because they all hope at some time to be able to exercise them to their own advantage. The majority in that country, therefore, exercise a prodigious actual authority, and a power of opinion which is nearly as great; no obstacles exist which can impede or even retard its progress, so as to make it heed the complaints of those whom it crushes upon its path. This state of things is harmful in itself and dangerous for the future.

How the omnipotence of the majority increases, in America, the instability of legislation and administration inherent in democracy. The Americans increase the mutability of law that is inherent in a democracy by changing the legislature every year, and investing it with almost unbounded authority—The same effect is produced upon the administration—In America the pressure for social improvements is vastly greater, but less continuous, than in Europe.

I have already spoken of the natural defects of democratic institutions; each one of them increases in the same ratio as the power of the majority. To begin with the most evident of them all, the mutability of the laws is an evil inherent in a democratic government, because it is natural to democracies to raise new men to power. But this evil is more or less perceptible in proportion to the authority and the means of action which the legislature possesses.

In America the authority exercised by the legislatures is supreme; nothing prevents them from accomplishing their wishes with celerity and with irresistible power, and they are supplied with new representatives every year. That is to say, the circumstances which contribute most powerfully to democratic instability, and which admit of the free application of caprice to the most important objects, are here in full operation. Hence America is, at the present day, the country beyond all others where laws last the shortest time. Almost all the American constitutions have been amended within thirty years; there is therefore not one American state which has not modified the principles of its legislation in that time. As for the laws themselves, a single glance at the archives of the different states of the Union suffices to convince one that in America the activity of the legislator never slackens. Not that the American democracy is naturally less stable than any other, but it is allowed to follow, in the formation of the laws, the natural instability of its desires.[2]

The omnipotence of the majority and the rapid as well as absolute manner in which its decisions are executed in the United States not only render the law unstable, but exercise the same influence upon the execution of the law and the conduct of the administration. As the majority is the only power that it is important to court, all its projects are taken up with the greatest ardor; but no sooner is its attention distracted than all this ardor ceases; while in the free states of Europe, where the administration is at once independent and secure, the projects of the legislature continue to be executed even when its attention is directed to other objects.

In America certain improvements are prosecuted with much more zeal and activity than elsewhere; in Europe the same ends are promoted by much less social effort more continuously applied.

Some years ago several pious individuals undertook to ameliorate the condition of the prisons. The public were moved by their statements, and the reform of criminals became a popular undertaking. New prisons were built; and for the first time the idea of reforming as well as punishing the delinquent formed a part of prison discipline.

But this happy change, in which the public had taken so hearty an interest and which the simultaneous exertions of the citizens rendered irresistible, could not be completed in a moment. While the new penitentiaries were being erected and the will of the majority was hastening the work, the old prisons still existed and contained a great number of offenders. These jails became more unwholesome and corrupt in proportion as the new establishments were reformed and improved, forming a contrast

[2] The legislative acts promulgated by the state of Massachusetts alone from the year 1780 to the present time already fill three stout volumes; and it must not be forgotten that the collection to which I allude was revised in 1823, when many old laws which had fallen into disuse were omitted. The state of Massachusetts, which is not more populous than a department of France, may be considered as the most stable, the most consistent, and the most sagacious in its undertakings of the whole Union.

that may readily be understood. The majority was so eagerly employed in founding the new prisons that those which already existed were forgotten; and as the general attention was diverted to a novel object, the care which had hitherto been bestowed upon the others ceased. The salutary regulations of discipline were first relaxed and afterwards broken; so that in the immediate neighborhood of a prison that bore witness to the mild and enlightened spirit of our times, dungeons existed that reminded one of the barbarism of the Middle Ages.

> *Tyranny of the majority.* How the principle of the sovereignty of the people is to be understood—Impossibility of conceiving a mixed government—The sovereign power must exist somewhere—Precautions to be taken to control its action—These precautions have not been taken in the United States—Consequences.

I hold it to be an impious and detestable maxim that, politically speaking, the people have a right to do anything; and yet I have asserted that all authority originates in the will of the majority. Am I, then, in contradiction with myself?

A general law, which bears the name of justice, has been made and sanctioned, not only by a majority of this or that people, but by a majority of mankind. The rights of every people are therefore confined within the limits of what is just. A nation may be considered as a jury which is empowered to represent society at large and to apply justice, which is its law. Ought such a jury, which represents society, to have more power than the society itself whose laws it executes?

When I refuse to obey an unjust law, I do not contest the right of the majority to command, but I simply appeal from the sovereignty of the people to the sovereignty of mankind. Some have not feared to assert that a people can never outstep the boundaries of justice and reason in those affairs which are peculiarly its own; and that consequently full power may be given to the majority by which it is represented. But this is the language of a slave.

A majority taken collectively is only an individual, whose opinions, and frequently whose interests, are opposed to those of another individual, who is styled a minority. If it be admitted that a man possessing absolute power may misuse that power by wronging his adversaries, why should not a majority be liable to the same reproach? Men do not change their characters by uniting with one another; nor does their patience in the presence of obstacles increase with their strength.[3] For my own part, I cannot believe it; the power to do everything, which I should refuse to one of my equals, I will never grant to any number of them.

I do not think that, for the sake of preserving liberty, it is possible to combine several principles in the same government so as really to oppose them to one another. The form of government that is usually termed *mixed* has always appeared to me a mere chimera. Accurately speaking, there is no such thing as a *mixed government*, in the sense usually given to that word, because in all communities some one principle of action may be discovered which preponderates over the others. England in the last century, which has been especially cited as an example of this sort of government, was essentially an aristocratic state, although it comprised some great elements of democracy; for the laws and customs of the country were such that the aristocracy could not but preponderate in the long run and direct public affairs according to its own will. The error arose from seeing the interests of the nobles perpetually contending

[3] No one will assert that a people cannot forcibly wrong another people; but parties may be looked upon as lesser nations within a great one, and they are aliens to each other. If therefore, one admits that a nation can act tyrannically towards another nation, can it be denied that a party may do the same towards another party?

with those of the people, without considering the issue of the contest, which was really the important point. When a community actually has a mixed government—that is to say, when it is equally divided between adverse principles—it must either experience a revolution or fall into anarchy.

I am therefore of the opinion that social power superior to all others must always be placed somewhere; but I think that liberty is endangered when this power finds no obstacle which can retard its course and give it time to moderate its own vehemence.

Unlimited power is in itself a bad and dangerous thing. Human beings are not competent to exercise it with discretion. God alone can be omnipotent, because his wisdom and his justice are always equal to his power. There is no power on earth so worthy of honor in itself or clothed with rights so sacred that I would admit its uncontrolled and all-predominant authority. When I see that the right and the means of absolute command are conferred on any power whatever, be it called a people or a king, an aristocracy or a democracy, a monarchy or a republic, I say there is the germ of tyranny, and I seek to live elsewhere, under other laws.

In my opinion, the main evil of the present democratic institutions of the United States does not arise, as is often asserted in Europe, from their weakness, but from their irresistible strength. I am not so much alarmed at the excessive liberty which reigns in that country as at the inadequate securities which one finds there against tyranny.

When an individual or a party is wronged in the United States, to whom can he apply for redress? If to public opinion, public opinion constitutes the majority; if to the legislature, it represents the majority and implicitly obeys it; if to the executive power, it is appointed by the majority and serves as a passive tool in its hands. The public force consists of the majority under arms; the jury is the majority invested with the right of hearing judicial cases; and in certain states even the judges are elected by the majority. However iniquitous or absurd the measure of which you complain, you must submit to it as well as you can.[4]

[4] A striking instance of the excesses that may be occasioned by the despotism of the majority occurred at Baltimore during the War of 1812. At that time the war was very popular in Baltimore. A newspaper that had taken the other side excited, by its opposition, the indignation of the inhabitants. The mob assembled, broke the printing-presses, and attacked the house of the editors. The militia was called out, but did not obey the call; and the only means of saving the wretches who were threatened by the frenzy of the mob was to throw them into prison as common malefactors. But even this precaution was ineffectual; the mob collected again during the night; the magistrates again made a vain attempt to call out the militia; the prison was forced, one of the newspaper editors was killed upon the spot, and the others were left for dead. The guilty parties, when they were brought to trial, were acquitted by the jury.

I said one day to an inhabitant of Pennsylvania: "Be so good as to explain to me how it happens that in a state founded by Quakers, and celebrated for its toleration, free blacks are not allowed to exercise civil rights. They pay taxes; is it not fair that they should vote?"

"You insult us," replied my informant, "if you imagine that our legislators could have committed so gross an act of injustice and intolerance."

"Then the blacks possess the right of voting in this country?"

"Without doubt."

"How comes it, then, that at the polling-booth this morning I did not perceive a single Negro?"

"That is not the fault of the law. The Negroes have an undisputed right of voting, but they voluntarily abstain from making their appearance."

"A very pretty piece of modesty on their part!" rejoined I.

"Why, the truth is that they are not disinclined to vote, but they are afraid of being maltreated; in this country the law is sometimes unable to maintain its authority without the support of the majority. But in this case the majority entertains very strong prejudices against the blacks, and the magistrates are unable to protect them in the exercise of their legal rights."

"Then the majority claims the right not only of making the laws, but of breaking the laws it has made?"

If, on the other hand, a legislative power could be so constituted as to represent the majority without necessarily being the slave of its passions, an executive so as to retain a proper share of authority, and a judiciary so as to remain independent of the other two powers, a government would be formed which would still be democratic while incurring scarcely any risk of tyranny.

I do not say that there is a frequent use of tyranny in America at the present day; but I maintain that there is no sure barrier against it, and that the causes which mitigate the government there are to be found in the circumstances and the manners of the country more than in its laws.

> *Effects of the omnipotence of the majority upon the arbitrary authority of American public officers.* Liberty left by the American laws to public officers within a certain sphere—Their power.

A distinction must be drawn between tyranny and arbitrary power. Tyranny may be exercised by means of the law itself, and in that case it is not arbitrary; arbitrary power may be exercised for the public good in which case it is not tyrannical. Tyranny usually employs arbitrary means, but if necessary it can do without them.

In the United States the omnipotence of the majority, which is favorable to the legal despotism of the legislature, likewise favors the arbitrary authority of the magistrate. The majority has absolute power both to make the laws and to watch over their execution; and as it has equal authority over those who are in power and the community at large, it considers public officers as its passive agents and readily confides to them the task of carrying out its designs. The details of their office and the privileges that they are to enjoy are rarely defined beforehand. It treats them as a master does his servants, since they are always at work in his sight and he can direct or reprimand them at any instant.

In general, the American functionaries are far more independent within the sphere that is prescribed to them than the French civil officers. Sometimes, even, they are allowed by the popular authority to exceed those bounds; and as they are protected by the opinion and backed by the power of the majority, they dare do things that even a European, accustomed as he is to arbitrary power, is astonished at. By this means habits are formed in the heart of a free country which may some day prove fatal to its liberties.

> *Power exercised by the majority in America upon opinion.* In America, when the majority has once irrevocably decided a question, all discussion ceases—Reason for this—Moral power exercised by the majority upon opinion—Democratic republics have applied despotism to the minds of men.

It is in the examination of the exercise of thought in the United States that we clearly perceive how far the power of the majority surpasses all the powers with which we are acquainted in Europe. Thought is an invisible and subtle power that mocks all the efforts of tyranny. At the present time the most absolute monarchs in Europe cannot prevent certain opinions hostile to their authority from circulating in secret through their dominions and even in their courts. It is not so in America; as long as the majority is still undecided, discussion is carried on; but as soon as its decision is irrevocably pronounced, everyone is silent, and the friends as well as the opponents of the measure unite in assenting to its propriety. The reason for this is perfectly clear: no monarch is so absolute as to combine all the powers of society in his own hands and to conquer all opposition, as a majority is able to do, which has the right both of making and of executing the laws.

The authority of a king is physical and controls the actions of men without subduing their will. But the majority possesses a power that is physical and moral at the same time, which acts upon the will as much as upon the actions and represses not only all contest, but all controversy.

I know of no country in which there is so little independence of mind and real freedom of discussion as in America. In any constitutional state in Europe every sort of religious and political theory may be freely preached and disseminated; for there is no country in Europe so subdued by any single authority as not to protect the man who raises his voice in the cause of truth from the consequences of his hardihood. If he is unfortunate enough to live under an absolute government, the people are often on his side; if he inhabits a free country, he can, if necessary, find a shelter behind the throne. The aristocratic part of society supports him in some countries, and the democracy in others. But in a nation where democratic institutions exist, organized like those of the United States, there is but one authority, one element of strength and success, with nothing beyond it.

In America the majority raises formidable barriers around the liberty of opinion; within these barriers an author may write what he pleases, but woe to him if he goes beyond them. Not that he is in danger of an auto-da-fé, but he is exposed to continued obloquy and persecution. His political career is closed forever, since he has offended the only authority that is able to open it. Every sort of compensation, even that of celebrity, is refused to him. Before making public his opinions he thought he had sympathizers; now it seems to him that he has none any more since he has revealed himself to everyone; then those who blame him criticize loudly and those who think as he does keep quiet and move away without courage. He yields at length, overcome by the daily effort which he has to make, and subsides into silence, as if he felt remorse for having spoken the truth.

Fetters and headsmen were the coarse instruments that tyranny formerly employed; but the civilization of our age has perfected despotism itself, though it seemed to have nothing to learn. Monarchs had, so to speak, materialized oppression; the democratic republics of the present day have rendered it as entirely an affair of the mind as the will which it is intended to coerce. Under the absolute sway of one man the body was attacked in order to subdue the soul; but the soul escaped the blows which were directed against it and rose proudly superior. Such is not the course adopted by tyranny in democratic republics; there the body is left free, and the soul is enslaved. The master no longer says: "You shall think as I do or you shall die"; but he says: "You are free to think differently from me and to retain your life, your property, and all that you possess; but you are henceforth a stranger among your people. You may retain your civil rights, but they will be useless to you, for you will never be chosen by your fellow citizens if you solicit their votes; and they will affect to scorn you if you ask for their esteem. You will remain among men, but you will be deprived of the rights of mankind. Your fellow creatures will shun you like an impure being; and even those who believe in your innocence will abandon you, lest they should be shunned in their turn. Go in peace! I have given you your life, but it is an existence worse than death."

Absolute monarchies had dishonored despotism; let us beware lest democratic republics should reinstate it and render it less odious and degrading in the eyes of the many making it still more onerous to the few.

Works have been published in the proudest nations of the Old World expressly intended to censure the vices and the follies of the times: Labruyère inhabited the palace of Louis XIV when he composed his chapter upon the Great, and Molière criticized the courtiers in the plays that were acted before the court. But the ruling power in the United States is not to be made game of. The smallest reproach irritates its sensibility, and the slightest joke that has any foundation in truth renders it indignant;

from the forms of its language up to the solid virtues of its character, everything must be made the subject of encomium. No writer, whatever be his eminence, can escape paying this tribute of adulation to his fellow citizens. The majority lives in the perpetual utterance of self-applause, and there are certain truths which the Americans can learn only from strangers or from experience.

If America has not as yet had any great writers, the reason is given in these facts; there can be no literary genius without freedom of opinion, and freedom of opinion does not exist in America. The Inquisition has never been able to prevent a vast number of anti-religious books from circulating in Spain. The empire of the majority succeeds much better in the United States, since it actually removes any wish to publish them. Unbelievers are to be met with in America, but there is no public organ of infidelity. Attempts have been made by some governments to protect morality by prohibiting licentious books. In the United States no one is punished for this sort of books, but no one is induced to write them; not because all the citizens are immaculate in conduct, but because the majority of the community is decent and orderly.

In this case the use of power is unquestionably good; and I am discussing the nature of the power itself. This irresistible authority is a constant fact, and its judicious exercise is only an accident.

> *Effects of the tyranny of the majority upon the national character of the Americans—the courtier spirit in the United States.* Effects of the tyranny of the majority more sensibly felt hitherto on the manners than on the conduct of society—They check the development of great characters—Democratic republics, organized like the United States, infuse the courtier spirit into the mass of the people—Proofs of this spirit in the United States—Why there is more patriotism in the people than in those who govern in their name.

The tendencies that I have just mentioned are as yet but slightly perceptible in political society, but they already exercise an unfavorable influence upon the national character of the Americans. I attribute the small number of distinguished men in political life to the ever increasing despotism, of the majority in the United States.

When the American Revolution broke out, they arose in great numbers; for public opinion then served, not to tyrannize over, but to direct the exertions of individuals. Those celebrated men, sharing the agitation of mind common at that period, had a grandeur peculiar to themselves, which was reflected back upon the nation, but was by no means borrowed from it.

In absolute governments the great nobles who are nearest to the throne flatter the passions of the sovereign and voluntarily truckle to his caprices. But the mass of the nation does not degrade itself by servitude; it often submits from weakness, from habit, or from ignorance, and sometimes from loyalty. Some nations have been known to sacrifice their own desires to those of the sovereign with pleasure and pride, thus exhibiting a sort of independence of mind in the very act of submission. These nations are miserable, but they are not degraded. There is a great difference between doing what one does not approve, and feigning to approve what one does; the one is the weakness of a feeble person, the other befits the temper of a lackey.

In free countries, where everyone is more or less called upon to give his opinion on affairs of state, in democratic republics, where public life is incessantly mingled with domestic affairs, where the sovereign authority is accessible on every side, and where its attention can always be attracted by vociferation, more persons are to be met with who speculate upon its weaknesses and live upon ministering to its passions than in absolute monarchies. Not because men are naturally worse in these states than elsewhere, but the temptation is stronger and at the same time of easier access. The result is a more extensive debasement of character.

Democratic republics extend the practice of currying favor with the many and introduce it into all classes at once; this is the most serious reproach that can be addressed to them. This is especially true in democratic states organized like the American republics, where the power of the majority is so absolute and irresistible that one must give up one's rights as a citizen and almost abjure one's qualities as a man if one intends to stray from the track which it prescribes.

In that immense crowd which throngs the avenues to power in the United States, I found very few men who displayed that manly candor and masculine independence of opinion which frequently distinguished the Americans in former times, and which constitutes the leading feature in distinguished characters wherever they may be found. It seems at first sight as if all the minds of the Americans were formed upon one model, so accurately do they follow the same route. A stranger does, indeed, sometimes meet with Americans who dissent from the rigor of these formulas. with men who deplore the defects of the laws, the mutability and the ignorance of democracy, who even go so far as to observe the evil tendencies that impair the national character, and to point out such remedies as it might be possible to apply; but no one is there to hear them except yourself, and you, to whom these secret reflections are confided, are a stranger and a bird of passage. They are very ready to communicate truths which are useless to you, but they hold a different language in public.

If these lines are ever read in America, I am well assured of two things: in the first place, that all who peruse them will raise their voices to condemn me; and, in the second place, that many of them will acquit me at the bottom of their conscience.

I have heard of patriotism in the United States, and I have found true patriotism among the people, but never among the leaders of the people. This may be explained by analogy: despotism debases the oppressed much more than the oppressor: in absolute monarchies the king often has great virtues, but the courtiers are invariably servile. It is true that American courtiers do not say "Sire," or "Your Majesty," a distinction without a difference. They are forever talking of the natural intelligence of the people whom they serve; they do not debate the question which of the virtues of their master is pre-eminently worthy of admiration, for they assure him that he possesses all the virtues without having acquired them, or without caring to acquire them; they do not give him their daughters and their wives to be raised at his pleasure to the rank of his concubines; but by sacrificing their opinions they prostitute themselves. Moralists and philosophers in America are not obliged to conceal their opinions under the veil of allegory; but before they venture upon a harsh truth, they say: "We are aware that the people whom we are addressing are too superior to the weakness of human nature to lose the command of their temper for an instant. We should not hold this language if we were not speaking to men whom their virtues and their intelligence render more worthy of freedom than all the rest of the world." The sycophants of Louis XIV could not flatter more dexterously.

For my part, I am persuaded that in all governments, whatever their nature may be, servility will cower to force, and adulation will follow power. The only means of preventing men from degrading themselves is to invest no one with that unlimited authority which is the sure method of debasing them.

The greatest dangers of the American republics proceed from the omnipotence of the majority. Democratic republics liable to perish from a misuse of their power, and not from impotence—The governments of the American republics are more centralized and more energetic than those of the monarchies of Europe—Dangers resulting from this—Opinions of Madison and Jefferson upon this point.

Governments usually perish from impotence or from tyranny. In the former case, their power escapes from them; it is wrested from their grasp in the latter. Many observers who have witnessed the anarchy of democratic states have imagined that the government of these states was naturally weak and impotent. The truth is that when war is once begun between parties, the government loses its control over society. But I do not think that a democratic power is naturally without force or resources; say, rather, that it is almost always by the abuse of its force and the misemployment of its resources that it becomes a failure. Anarchy is almost always produced by its tyranny or its mistakes, but not by its want of strength.

It is important not to confuse stability with force, or the greatness of a thing with its duration. In democratic republics the power that directs[5] society is not stable, for it often changes hands and assumes a new direction. But whichever way it turns, its force is almost irresistible. The governments of the American republics appear to me to be as much centralized as those of the absolute monarchies of Europe, and more energetic than they are. I do not therefore, imagine that they will perish from weakness.[6]

If ever the free institutions of America are destroyed, that event may be attributed to the omnipotence of the majority, which may at some future time urge the minorities to desperation and oblige them to have recourse to physical force. Anarchy will then be the result, but it will have been brought about by despotism.

Mr. Madison expresses the same opinion in *The Federalist*, No. 51. "It is of great importance in a republic, not only to guard the society against the oppression of its rulers, but to guard one part of the society against the injustice of the other part. Justice is the end of government. It is the end of civil society. It ever has been, and ever will be, pursued until it be obtained, or until liberty be lost in the pursuit. In a society, under the forms of which the stronger faction can readily unite and oppress the weaker, anarchy may as truly be said to reign as in a state of nature, where the weaker individual is not secured against the violence of the stronger: and as, in the latter state, even the stronger individuals are prompted by the uncertainty of their condition to submit to a government which may protect the weak as well as themselves, so, in the former state, will the more powerful factions be gradually induced by a like motive to wish for a government which will protect all parties, the weaker as well as the more powerful. It can be little doubted, that, if the State of Rhode Island was separated from the Confederacy and left to itself, the insecurity of right under the popular form of government within such narrow limits would be displayed by such reiterated oppressions of the factious majorities, that some power altogether independent of the people would soon be called for by the voice of the very factions whose misrule had proved the necessity of it."

Jefferson also said: "The executive power in our government is not the only, perhaps not even the principal, object of my solicitude. The tyranny of the legislature is

[5] This power may be centralized in an assembly, in which case it will be strong without being stable; or it may be centralized in an individual, in which case it will be less strong, but more stable.

[6] I presume that it is scarcely necessary to remind the reader here as well as throughout this chapter, that I am speaking, not of the Federal government, but of the governments of the individual states, which the majority controls at its pleasure.

really the danger most to be feared, and will continue to be so for many years to come. The tyranny of the executive power will come in its turn, but at a more distant period."[7]

I am glad to cite the opinion of Jefferson upon this subject rather than that of any other, because I consider him the most powerful advocate democracy has ever had.

51

The Tyranny of the Majority

James Bryce

The expression "tyranny of the majority" is commonly used to denote any abuse by the majority of the powers which it enjoys in free countries under and through the law, and in all countries outside the law. Such abuse will not be tyrannous in the sense of being illegal, as men called a usurper like Dionysius of Syracuse or Louis Napoleon in France a tyrant, for in free countries whatever the majority chooses to do in the prescribed constitutional way will be legal. It will be tyrannous in the sense of the lines

> O it is excellent
> To have a giant's strength, but it is tyrannous
> To use it like a giant.

That is to say, tyranny consists in the wanton and improper use of strength by the stronger, in the use of it to do things which one equal would not attempt against another. A majority is tyrannical when it decides without hearing the minority, when it suppresses fair and temperate criticism on its own acts, when it insists on restraining men in matters where restraint is not required by the common interest, when it forces men to contribute money to objects which they disapprove, and which the common interset does not demand. The element of tyranny lies in the wantonness of the act, a wantonness springing from the sense of overwhelming power, or in the fact that it is a misuse for one purpose of power granted for another. It consists not in the form of the act, which may be perfectly legal, but in the spirit and temper it reveals, and in the sense of injustice and oppression which it evokes in the minority.

Philosophers have long since perceived that the same tendencies to a wanton abuse of power which exist in a despot or a ruling oligarchy may be expected in a democracy from the ruling majority, because they are tendencies incidental to human nature. The danger was felt and feared by the sages of 1787, and a passage in the *Federalist* (No. L.) dwells on the safeguards which the great size of a Federal

[7] *Letter from Jefferson to Madison*, March 15, 1789.

From James Bryce, *The American Commonwealth*, Louis M. Hacker, ed. (New York: G. P. Putnam's Sons), pp. 369–377.

republic and the diverse elements of which it will be composed, offer against the tendency of a majority to oppress a minority.

Since De Tocqueville dilated upon this as the capital fault of the American government and people, Europeans, already prepared to expect to find the tyranny of the majority a characteristic sin of democratic nations, have been accustomed to think of the United States as disgraced by it, and on the strength of this instance have predicted it as a necessary result of the growth of democracy in the Old World. It is therefore worth while to inquire what foundation exists for the reproach as addressed to the Americans of to-day.

We may look for signs of this tyranny in three quarters—firstly, in the legislation of Congress; secondly, in the constitutions and statutes of the States; thirdly, in the action of public opinion and sentiment outside the sphere of law.

The Federal Constitution, which has not only limited the competence of Congress, but hedged it round with many positive prohibitions, has closed some of the avenues by which a majority might proceed to abuse its powers. Freedom of speech, freedom of religion, opportunities for debate, are all amply secured. The power of taxation, and that of regulating commerce, might conceivably be used to oppress certain classes of persons, as, for instance, if a prohibitory duty were to be laid on certain articles which a minority desired and the majority condemned the use of. But nothing of the sort has been attempted. Whatever may be thought of the expediency of the present tariff, which no doubt favours one class, it cannot be said to oppress any class. In its political action, as, for instance, during the struggle over slavery, when for a while it refused to receive Abolitionist petitions, and even tried to prevent the transmission by mail of abolitionist matter, and again during and after the war in some of its reconstruction measures, the majority, under the pressure of excitement, exercised its powers harshly and unwisely. But such political action is hardly the kind of action to which the charge we are examining applies.

In the States, a majority of the citizens may act either directly in enacting (or amending) a constitution, or through their legislature by passing statutes. We might expect to find instances of abuse of power more in the former than in the latter class of cases, because though the legislature is habitually and the people of the State only intermittently active, the legislatures have now been surrounded by a host of constitutional limitations which a tyrannical majority would need some skill to evade. However, one discovers wonderfully little in the State Constitutions now in force of which a minority can complain. These instruments contain a great deal of ordinary law and administrative law. If the tendency to abuse legislative power to the injury of any class were general, instances of it could not fail to appear. One does not find them. There are some provisions strictly regulating corporations, and especially railroads and banks, which may perhaps be unwise, and which in limiting the modes of using capital apply rather to the rich than to the masses. But such provisions cannot be called wanton or oppressive.

The same remark applies to the ordinary statutes of the States, so far as I have been able to ascertain their character. They can rarely be used to repress opinion or its expression, because nearly all the State Constitutions contain ample guarantees for free speech, a free press, and the right of public meeting. For the same reason, they cannot encroach on the personal liberty of the citizen, nor on the full enjoyment of private property. In all such fundamentals the majority has prudently taken the possible abuse of its power out of the hands of the legislature.

When we come to minor matters, we are met by the difficulty of determining what is a legitimate exercise of legislative authority. Nowhere are men agreed as to the limits of State interference. Some few think that law ought not to restrict the sale of intoxicants at all; many more that it ought not to make the procuring of them, for purposes of pleasure, difficult or impossible. Others hold that the common welfare justifies prohibition. Some deem it unjust to tax a man, and especially an unmarried man, for the support of public schools, or at any rate of public schools other than elementary. To most Roman Catholics it seems unjust to refuse denominational schools a share of the funds raised by taxing, among other citizens, those who hold it a duty to send their children to schools in which their own faith is inculcated. Some think a law tyrannical which forbids a man to exclude others from ground which he keeps waste and barren, while others blame the law which permits a man to reserve, as they think tyrannically, large tracts of country for his own personal enjoyment. So, in the case of religion, any form of State establishment, or State endowment, or even State recognition, of a particular creed or religious body will by some be deemed an abuse, by others a proper and necessary use of State authority. Remembering such differences of opinion, all I can say is that even those who take the narrower view of State functions will find little to censure in the legislation of American States. They may blame the restriction or prohibition of the sale of intoxicants. They may think that the so-called "moral legislation" for securing the purity of literature, and for protecting the young against various temptations, attempts too much. They may question the expediency of the legislation intended for the benefit of workingmen. But there are few of these provisions which can fairly be called wanton or tyrannical, which display a spirit that ignores or tramples on the feelings or rights of a minority. The least defensible statutes are perhaps those which California has aimed at the Chinese (who are not technically a minority since they are not citizens at all), and those by which some Southern States have endeavored to accentuate the separation between whites and negroes, forbidding them to intermarry or to be taught in the same schools or colleges.

We come now to the third way in which a majority may tyrannize, *i.e.* by the imposition of purely social penalties, from mere disapproval up to insult, injury, and boycotting. The greatest of Athenian statesmen claimed for his countrymen that they set an example to the rest of Greece in that enlightened toleration which does not even visit with black looks those who hold unpopular opinions, or venture in anywise to differ from the prevailing sentiment. Such enlightenment is doubtless one of the latest fruits and crowns of a high civilization, and all the more to be admired when it is not the result of indifference, but co-exists with energetic action in the field of politics or religion or social reform.

If social persecution exists in the America of to-day, it is only in a few dark corners. One may travel all over the Northern and Western States, mingling with all classes and reading the newspapers, without hearing of it. As respects religion, so long as one does not openly affront the feelings of one's neighbors one may say what one likes, and go or not go to church. Doubtless a man, and still more a woman, will be better thought of, especially in a country-place or small town, if he or she is a church member and Sunday school teacher. But no one is made to suffer in mind, body, or estate for simply holding aloof from a religious or any other voluntary association. He would be more likely to suffer in an English village. Even in the South where a stricter standard of orthodoxy is maintained among the clergy of the Protestant bodies than in the North or West, a layman may think as he pleases. It is the same as regards social questions, and of course as regards politics. To boycott a man for his politics, or even to discourage his shop in the way not uncommon in some parts of rural England and Ireland, would excite indignation in America; as the attempts of some labour organizations to boycott firms resisting strikes have aroused strong displeasure. If in some parts of the South a man took to cultivating the friendship of negroes and organizing them in clubs, or if in parts of the West a man made himself the champion of the Indians, he might find his life become unpleasant, though one hears little of recent instances of the kind. In any part of the country he who should use his rights of property in a hard or unneighborly way; who, for instance, possessing a handsome park, with perhaps a waterfall or beautiful views over the country, should build a high wall round it and refuse all access, would be reprobated and sent to Coventry. I do not know of such cases; perhaps the fear of general disapproval prevents their arising.

In saying that there is no social persecution, I do not deny that in parts of the country, as, for instance, in the smaller towns of the West, there is too little allowance for differences of tastes and pursuits, too much disposition to expect every family to conform to the same standard of propriety, and follow the same habits of life. A person acting, however innocently, without regard to the beliefs and prejudices of his neighbours, would be talked about, and perhaps looked askance upon. Many a man used to the variety of London or Washington would feel the monotony of Western life, and the uniform application of its standards, irksome and even galling. But, so far as I could ascertain, he would have nothing specific to complain of. And these Western towns become every day more like the cities of the East. Taking the country all in all, it is hard to imagine more complete liberty than individuals or groups enjoy either to express and propagate their views, or to act as they please within the limits of the law, limits which, except as regards the sale of intoxicants, are drawn as widely as in Western Europe.

Forty or fifty years ago it was very different. Congress was then as now debarred from oppressive legislation. But in some Northern States the legislatures were not slow to deal harshly with persons or societies who ran counter to the dominant sentiment. The persecution of Miss Prudence Crandall, a benevolent Quakeress who had opened a school for negro children, by the legislature of Connecticut as well as by her own townsfolk, is a well-remembered instance. A good many rigidly Puritanic statutes stood unrepealed in New England, though not always put in force against the transgressor. In the South, laws of the utmost severity punished whosoever should by word or act assail the "peculiar institution." Even more tyrannical than the laws was the sentiment of the masses. In Boston a mob, a well-dressed mob, largely composed of the richer sort of people, hunted Garrison for his life through the streets because he was printing an Abolitionist journal; a mob in Illinois shot Elijah Lovejoy for the same offence; and as late as 1844 another Illinois crowd killed Joseph Smith, the Mormon prophet, who, whatever may be thought of his honesty or his doctrines, was as much entitled to the protection of the laws as any other citizen. In the South, as every one knows, there was a reign of terror as regards slavery. Any one suspected of Abolitionism might think himself lucky if he escaped with tar and feathers, and was not shot or flogged almost to death. This extreme sensitiveness was of course confined to a few burning questions; but the habit of repressing by law or without law obnoxious opinions was likely to spread, and did spread, at least in the South to other matters also. As regards thought and opinion generally over the Union, de Tocqueville declares..

Je ne connais pas de pays où il règne, en général, moins d'indépendance d'esprit et de véritable liberté de discussion qu'en Amérique. . . . La majorité trace un cercle formidable autour de la pensée. Au dedans de ces limites, l'ècrivain est libre, mais malheur à lui s'il ose en sortir! Ce n'est pas qu'il ait à craindre un auto-da-fè, mais il est en butte à des dégoûts de tout genre et à des persécutions de tous les jours. La carrière politique lui est fermée: il à offensé la seule puissance qui ait la faculté de l'ouvrir. On lui refuse tout, jusqu'à la gloire.*

He ascribes not only the want of great statesmen, but the low level of literature, learning, and thought, to this total absence of intellectual freedom.

It is hard for any one who knows the Northern States now to believe that this can have been a just description of them so lately as fifty-four years ago. Supposing, however, that it was a just description, how are we to explain the change to the absolute freedom and tolerance of to-day, when every man may sit under his own fig-tree and say and do (provided he does not drink) what he pleases, none making him afraid?

One is inclined to suspect that de Tocqueville, struck by the enormous power of general opinion, may have attributed too much of the submissiveness which he observed to the active coercion of the majority, and too little to that tendency of the minority to acquiescence which has been discussed in the last preceding chapter. Setting this aside, however, and assuming that the majority did in those days really tyrannize, several causes may be assigned for its having ceased to do so. One is the absence of violent passions. Slavery, the chief source of ferocity, was to the heated minds of the South a matter of life or death; Abolitionism seemed to many in the North a disloyal heresy, the necessary parent of disunion. Since the Civil War there has been no crisis calculated to tempt majorities to abuse their legal powers. Partisanship has for years past been more intense in Great Britain—not to say Ireland—and France than in America. When de Tocqueville saw the United States, the democratic spirit was in the heyday of its youthful strength, flushed with self-confidence, intoxicated with the exuberance of its own freedom. The first generation of statesmen whose authority had restrained the masses, had just quitted the stage. The anarchic teachings of Jefferson had borne fruit. Administration and legislation, hitherto left to the educated classes, had been seized by the rude hands of men of low social position and scanty knowledge. A reign of brutality and violence had set in over large regions of the country. Neither literature nor the universities exercised as yet any sensible power. The masses were so persuaded of their immense superiority to all other peoples, past as well as present, that they would listen to nothing but flattery, and their intolerance spread from politics into every other sphere. Our European philosopher may therefore have been correct in his description of the facts as he saw them: he erred in supposing them essential to a democratic government. As the nation grew, it purged away these faults of youth and inexperience, and the stern discipline of the Civil War taught it sobriety, and in giving it something to be really proud of, cleared away the fumes of empty self-conceit.

The years which have passed since the war have been years of immensely extended and popularized culture and enlightenment. Bigotry in religion and in everything else has been broken down. The old landmarks have been removed: the "latest results," as people call them, of European thought have become more familiar to the American masses than to the masses anywhere in Europe. At the same time, as all religious and socio-religious questions, except those which relate to education, are entirely disjoined from politics and the State, neither those who stand by the old

* I know of no country in which there is so little independence of mind and real freedom of discussion as in America. . . . The majority raises formidable barriers around the liberty of opinion; within those barriers an author may write what he pleases, but woe to him if he goes beyond them. Not that he is in danger of public execution, but he is exposed to continued obloquy and persecution. His political career is closed off, since he has offended the only authority that is able to open it. He is refused everything, even becoming a celebrity.

views nor those who embrace the new carry that bitterness into their controversies which is natural in countries where religious questions are also party questions, where the clergy are a privileged and salaried order, where the throne is held bound to defend the altar, and the workman is taught to believe that both are leagued against him. The influence of these causes will, it may be predicted, be permanent. Should passion again invade politics, or should the majority become convinced that its interests will be secured by overtaxing the few, one can imagine the tendency of fifty years ago reappearing in new forms. But in no imaginable future is there likely to be any attempt to repress either by law or by opinion the free exercise and expression of speculative thought on morals, on religion, and indeed on every matter not within the immediate range of current politics.

If the above account be correct, the tyranny of the majority is no longer a blemish on the American system, and the charges brought against democracy from the supposed example of America are groundless. As tyranny is one of those evils which tends to perpetuate itself, those who had been oppressed revenging themselves by becoming oppressors in their turn, the fact that a danger once dreaded has now disappeared is no small evidence of the recuperative forces of the American government, and the healthy tone of the American people.

52

Can Democracy Survive?

C. Northcote Parkinson

An unexpected sequel to the American occupation of Japan has been the growth of Japanese influence in America. Those who set out to teach the Japanese something about democracy have ended by learning from the Japanese something about architecture. This is but one reason among many for wondering afresh whether that original idea of a crusade for democracy had the sanction of common sense. Are we now quite so certain that democracy must everywhere prevail as not only the best but the final achievement of human wisdom as applied to politics? Does history reveal nothing but a series of experiments, each failing in turn but each bringing mankind a step nearer this, its ultimate goal?

History, in fact, reveals nothing of the kind. We learn from it that various forms of rule have tended to succeed one another in what might seem to have been a significant sequence, democracy showing a tendency to collapse in a chaos from which dictatorship offers the only escape. There is little in history to show that democracy is much more stable than any other form of rule. What history does show is that people have always inclined to regard their own form of government as perfect, or at any rate inevitable and eternal. Subjects of, say, a deified emperor have seldom supposed that any other form of rule was worth serious discussion. For most of them, at any period, talk of an alternative scheme would have seemed impracticable, blasphemous or merely crazy. Present advocates of democracy are apt in the same way to claim for that form of rule a universal validity which it would seem to derive neither from theory nor from fact. Representative democracy is a form of government which has a number of real advantages for some peoples at a certain stage in their development. To claim more than that, invoking some semireligious principle of human rights, is to assume just such an attitude as characterized the more pious inhabitants of dynastic Egypt. If we are to defend democracy in serious discussion, it must not be because it is sacred—few forms of rule have been anything else—but because it produces some demonstrably good result. If it is good, we should be able to explain why.

While a study of the past may warn us against accepting current beliefs merely because they are current, it throws only a doubtful light on the future. We can admittedly observe a sequence of political development in past civilizations; a recurring pattern in which monarchy has given place to aristocracy, aristocracy to democracy, and democracy to a dictatorship which has turned into monarchy again. Nor is there anything in the tempo of current history to suggest that what was once a phase in a recurring cycle should now be regarded as permanent. Were it possible to judge from political events considered in isolation, we might rather be tempted to assume that what happened before was likely to happen again. And indeed there is probably nothing in the present political scene—no movement, no investigation, no scandal or plot—for which past history affords no parallel. But the present age, which has so little to offer by way of political innovation, has much to offer in technical progress. The doubt is whether the political pattern can exactly repeat itself in an environment which has been so technically transformed. The argument from past experience may no longer hold good. Talk of technical achievement brings to mind the hydrogen bomb. But that is not so significant politically as other and less spectacular developments. Many of these might be instanced, and there are those who would maintain that a longer expectation of human life is the most important. But there are three other developments to which too little attention has been paid: developments respectively in psychology, communication and what is called "conventional" war.

To deal with psychology first, there was a time when the results of an election or plebiscite were given a sort of religious sanction. Victorian editors could announce that the people would oppose the Updrainville irrigation scheme, that the people had rightly demanded the construction of the Moose Canyon Bridge, or that the people had wisely chosen Mr. Clawhammer as governor. And while it may be doubted whether the will of the people had quite the force of revelation, there were many instances of the people proving right—the drainage scheme unworkable, the bridge vitally needed and Mr. Clawhammer a better man than his opponent. These side-whiskered men, leaning on their axes as they paused for thought, could arrive at the right decision. In a simply organized agricultural or pastoral society the relevant facts could be widely known. Today, in a more complex society, the mass psychologist has been able to dissect the voting process with disconcerting results. The will of the people breaks down under analysis, turning out to be ill-informed, emotional and liable to vary indeed from day to day; nor, incidentally, is there any close correlation between the views people express when approached individually and the views they express when collected in a group. Taken apart in this fashion, the will of the people turns out to be a myth. Voting is a more orderly process than rioting, but has only an even chance of producing the right answer. The Romans achieved the same result more cheaply by consulting the gods—whose guesses seem in general to have been no worse (or better) than their own. But the infallibility of the "general will" is a dogma that must remain where it belongs—in the last century; if not, indeed, in the last century but one.

As for communications, it must be remembered, first of all, that these have always determined the scale—and to some extent the nature—of political institutions. The earliest civilized states were each based on a river system as their means of communication, the length of the river determining the size of the state. Kingdoms based on the Nile, the Tigris or the Ganges could be relatively large; kingdoms based on the Tagus, the Mekong or the Scheldt had to be relatively small. The Romans and Chinese broke through these limits by building roads, but the river-system scale of political organization lingered on to a surprisingly recent period of history, determining the respective sizes of, say, Yorkshire, Virginia, Canada and Venezuela. A single government could stretch its authority only as far as it could reach, the amount of its influence being roughly proportionate to the distances involved.

Today the extent of a government's influence has been at once extended and intensified. Rail, road, telegraph, air and radio communications have made a distant supervision both effective and continuous. The river-system scale of political unit has become in some ways an anachronism; nor is there now the same need to establish a god-emperor (like Constantine or Stalin) whose shrine or effigy can represent him in places he will never visit. Today the Queen's voice, and even she herself, can come through the air; just as the President's personality can be projected by television or recorded on tape. Communication is no longer in the same sense a problem.

So, far from presenting any technical difficulty, communications now present the government, whatever its character, with almost limitless scope. By means of state-organized schools, newspapers, films, radio and television, a docile people can be taught practically anything—that all capitalists are wicked, that all Jews are criminals or that China does not exist. Techniques based on psychology and developed in advertising have already some remarkable achievements to their credit. Mass media of instruction would seem to have endless possibilities. So far the known results include the popular election, by enormous majorities, of both scoundrels and lunatics. There is nothing to prevent any government from building up for itself a dream world in which dramatized leaders with purely fictitious ability give the appearance of prosperity to lands of which the extent has been exaggerated, reporting triumphs over rival powers which have been invented for the purpose and boasting the success of improbable missions to other and imaginary planets. Past emperors of China built up such a dream world for themselves, but they lacked more than a fraction of the necessary equipment. The age of hallucination, of which Adolf Hitler was one of the earlier victims, has scarcely dawned. People will someday perhaps look back with wonder on a time when the camera was thought to matter less than the event it was supposed to record.

The world that has seen this revolution in the methods and speed of communication has also seen a transformation in the arts of war. From the time of the French Revolution to the time of the Russian Revolution land campaigns were mostly settled by massed infantry, national strength being roughly measured by the number of bayonets each nation could put in the field. It was also, and by no coincidence, the age in which the counting of votes had its greatest prestige. During World War II the massed-infantry attack went out of fashion, the strength of nations coming to be measured in quite other terms. Even if we ignore the possibilities of atomic warfare as something now probably obsolete, and even if we discount the possibilities of biological warfare, as something yet untried, the fact remains that numbers have come to matter less. The potential war strength of a country might be measured by the number of its scientists; it can no longer be measured by the mere number of its people. In general, democracy has best suited societies in which the equal value of votes has been reflected in the roughly equal value of the voters when armed for war. It has flourished less securely in societies where the decisive weapons—whether war chariots or cannon—have been in the hands of a few. For this reason it might be thought that the technical basis for democracy, in war as well as in peace, has by now been perceptibly weakened.

From facts such as these it would be natural to conclude that the days of democracy are over. The conclusion would be premature, however, for political systems do not evolve as rapidly as that. Where democracy exists, it may well survive for a further period; but there is good reason to question whether it is likely to take root in any soil to which it is new. With a less favorable climate, the transplanting becomes a less hopeful proposition and doubtfully worth the effort. What may flourish for a time in the atmosphere of the West has far more dubious prospects in the atmosphere of the East. For there the racial and religious background, the family, caste and clan relationships, the secret societies and fanaticisms, the prevailing illiteracy and ignorance make the voting process seem curiously irrelevant. There might be some point in the missionary effort if the technical progress of the age were moving in the same direction and at the same speed, but the East will feel the impact of improved communications long before it can absorb the lessons of nineteenth-century liberalism. If there was a time for that, the time is passing or has passed.

What, by contrast, are the prospects of democracy in the West? We have seen that it is there affected by technical developments which are mainly, if not entirely, adverse. Put in the simplest terms, it is now far easier for a government to tell the people what they are to believe than for the people to tell the government what it is to do. But that is not the whole story. In at least one important respect, democracy is being strengthened and it is important to see how this has come about—more especially in the United States.

The basic weakness of democracy has always been what the Greeks called "stasis,' or class war. Given political equality, the lower classes, which have always in times past been the more numerous, have sooner or later used their votes to despoil the rich. They have voted, in effect, for economic equality—that is, for socialism. The effect of this has always been disastrous, and more immediately disastrous for democracy. In the stresses and strains brought about by the legalized plunder there are bound to develop all sorts of treasons, stratagems and spoils. From the conflicts which have ensued, one man, usually a leader of the winning side, has emerged as dictator. Whatever the result of the battle, freedom has always been the first casualty. In the struggle between capital and labor both sides are impelled by exactly the same material motive, and both sides are guilty—as Gandhi pointed out—of exactly the same sin. Neither, of course, is concerned with the welfare of society as a whole.

In trying to transpose the Greek theory of class war into the terms of modern industry—which he very imperfectly understood—Karl Marx foretold a process by which the wealthy would become richer and fewer, the poor would become poorer and more numerous until the top-heavy absurdity of the situation would make revolution inevitable and irresistible. So would begin the rule of the proletariat, to last apparently forever; an odd conclusion for an admirer of Darwin to have reached. In the Marxist revolution the internal conflicts, as observable in the Greek and Roman city-states, have been neatly eliminated. These are only two classes, and the one had dwindled to a mere handful of people who can be hanged at leisure, after which event the unopposed remainder can live happily. Had Marx known anything about the working classes —a set of people with whom he had no social contact—he would have known that the problem is not quite so simple as that.

Quite apart, however, from any misconception that Marx may have had about the social equality existing between boiler riveters and bellhops, his account of the future has been completely falsified by events. There have been two Marxist revolutions on the large scale, both in countries almost entirely agricultural, while the industrial areas have developed, in the main, on lines of their own. Of this development the main feature has been the dwindling importance of the class which Marx expected to become supreme. His proletariat comprised for the most part the skilled workmen, the trade-unionists, of the mid-nineteenth century—the men who drove the locomotives or installed the plumbing, men who wore top hats on the way to church. That industrial society depended upon the skilled artisan was a truism of the period. The skilled artisan was the stanch supporter of Methodism and of labor politics—both anathemas to the gentry. He was a man who would do nothing for the really poor—insisting as he did upon the wage differential between himself and them—but the leader in all resistance to the capitalist. Trade-unionists of this type were so important in their day that few at first were to notice either their diminished status or their dwindling numbers. In twentieth-century industrialized societies it was not the proletariat that multiplied in growing poverty but a middle class that multiplied in growing wealth. The future lay not with the skilled artisan but with the qualified engineer on the one hand and the unskilled factory girl on the other. These were classes of people of whose existence Marx was only dimly aware. It is upon them, rather than upon the skilled artisan, that industry has come to rely.

A significant event in the development of western middle-class industrialism was the British General Strike of 1926. By all the accepted axioms of the day, a stoppage of railways—let alone all the other heavy industries—should have paralyzed the country. But the country was not paralyzed. It no longer depended upon railways. It also became suddenly apparent that the middle classes, which rallied against the trade-unions, were more numerous than the strikers. The strike failed and no subsequent labor victory at the polls could efface the impression that the middle classes had scored. The motorcar, which made them independent of the railways, was their symbol of victory. It was they, not the skilled artisans, who were to be the dominant group of the future. Marxism can appeal nowadays to such social groups in Australia as are psychologically still in the 1880's, but it long since died as a force in Britain; died with the discovery that the proletariat cannot be supreme and is not even particularly important.

The process by which the new urban middle class established itself in Britain was repeated, but with greater emphasis, in the United States. By a process of technical achievement, rehousing and education, the middle class came to outweigh the class above and outnumber the class below it. There are depressed classes in the United States, and there are people with a grievance against society; but they are swamped by the masses of people whose fear is that they will lose what they have—namely, a suburban home, garage, car, refrigerator, washing machine, television, telephone, supermarket and high school. That democracy in the United States should end in class war is now almost unthinkable, for the raw materials do not exist. People are more likely to choke themselves, as in Los Angeles, with the fumes of their own exhaust pipes. It is true that the whole picture could be drastically altered by an industrial depression, but the story, whatever happened, would not conform either to Greek theory or Marxist prediction.

If American democracy is a middle-class affair, firmly based on the long-term interests of a strong majority, it should not end in socialism nor should it collapse in chaos. The fact remains, however, that it is vulnerable in other ways. We have seen already that the whole machinery of persuasion is in the hands of any government that cares to use it. How great is the danger that such an influence may, in fact, be used? In attempting to judge the possibilities we must note, first of all, that the effect of mass education is to expose people more, not less, to propaganda. In theory a university or high-school graduate should be skeptical about what he reads and hears. But do American graduates criticize or do they merely conform? The man least vulnerable to propaganda is the illiterate peasant who possesses no radio. His views may be narrow but they are at least his own. Most vulnerable of all are the people who listen and believe. Are people of that kind tending to multiply? There are some grounds for thinking that they are.

Against the dangers of intensive propaganda the accepted remedy lies in the party system. People forced to hear both sides of every question are compelled, we are told, to decide for themselves. Those considering the merits of any presidential candidate will hear as much against as for him. In this there is an element of truth. The theory breaks down, however, whenever the two parties become too much alike. In the days when British Tories alternated in office with their Liberal opponents, the electorate had to choose, it was said, which of two wealthy cousins should introduce the same bill. Is there no danger of that in the United States? The extent of the danger is to be measured by the proportion of voters who do not bother to vote. In general the non-voting voter is unconvinced that it matters either way. A lack of public interest is normally the result of there being nothing to be interested in. If the crowd drifts away from the tennis match, it is usually taken as a comment upon the standard of play. There are those who believe that the great debate in the United States, at least as between the parties, is finished and that the voter's only concern is to defend his standard of living. For this theory there would seem to be some evidence. Some 62,027,000 valid votes were cast, for example, in the 1956 presidential election—a record figure but representing only 60.4 per cent of the theoretical maximum. To have had a few million less—to have had as few as 50 per cent of the voters participating—would have been a serious indictment of the whole system. With such a condemnation even remotely possible, the advocates of American democracy have cause to consider their case afresh.

One other weakness needs to be mentioned and it is this: there are too many people on the public payroll. This state of affairs could be denounced in the name of economy, but that is not to the present purpose. The question is how far this scheme for full employment is compatible with democracy. Let us take an extreme case and suppose that half the adult population were in public employment. This would mean that half the voters were employed under the direction of the party in power—dependent upon it for pay, security, privilege and promotion. Is that situation a proper basis for independent voting? Nor is the situation much improved if the roles were to be reversed, the voters blackmailing those by whom they are employed. "Give us double overtime," they will say, "or we shall vote you out of office." Situations are seldom quite as simple as that, but the final result either way would be a one-party system with one party controlling or controlled by the civil-service vote and that party perpetually in power. To this it may be objected that those on the public payroll are not so numerous as this. It may also be urged that civil servants are persons of the highest character who would never use any improper influence in wage negotiations. Arguments such as these are not without weight, but neither are they conclusive. For one thing, an election can be decided by a bloc far smaller than the one described. Given anything like equal strength as between parties, a mere 10 per cent of the voters, acting together, could easily tip the scale. In Great Britain those in public employment, some 6,000,000 out of a total population of 51,500,000 form a far higher proportion than that. As regards the high character of the people concerned, it must suffice to remark that the character of some of the earliest voting civil servants—those of ancient Athens—would not seem to have been high enough. Nor were English politicians of the period very happy about all the excisemen employed by George III. The crime of enlisting the civil service in the cause of a particular party (his own) was the very thing that people held against him. It may be that the descendants of the Athenians, mingled under the American flag with the descendants of the excisemen, have now a loftier moral tone than their ancestors could boast. But it is not, surely, an issue upon which the betting would be much more than even. It lacks, as an assumption, the rocklike solidity upon which the enlightened lawgiver would care to build.

To give democracy in its American form not an eternal validity but a new lease of life, there would seem to be a case for reform. The system needs reinforcing at the points where it is weak. For the specific weaknesses to which attention has been drawn, three remedies suggest themselves: the vote should be restricted to those who have earned it; the legislator should be freed from improper influence; the public revenue should be limited under the Constitution to a stated proportion of the national income. To take these points in order, we may conclude first that the voter's negligent attitude toward the ballot box derives from the fact that his vote was given him. It was not merely given him but thrust on him. He was implored to take it and begged to use it. He is pursued with the vote and can be fined in some democracies for failing to exercise it; from all of which anxiety the natural inference is that the vote must be worthless. Were every American citizen presented with a university degree at birth—a measure of economy for which there is much to be said—few would trouble to put "A.B." after their names; just as few bother to claim the war medals to which nearly the whole of their generation are entitled. For a thing to be valued it has to be specially earned. On this principle the vote might well be conceded, with obvious reluctance, to those whose title to it derived from blood, sweat and tears. It might be restricted, for example, to people over thirty who had passed a certain educational standard, who had done public service, who had paid taxes above a certain minimum and who should apply in writing (with fee enclosed) for their names to be placed on the electoral roll. Girls who prefer to remain aged twenty-nine would be very properly ruled out as immature. Men without military service would be ruled out as unpatriotic. People who misspelled their letter of application would be ruled out as illiterate. The vote would thus be confined to those who have taken some trouble and shown some interest, and would be instantly lost again if not exercised.

For this last stipulation to be enforced, however, the voter must clearly be given the means of voting against all the candidates. If every voting paper had not only the names of the real candidates but the further name of a fictitious Colonel Bogey, each vote for him would suggest "that no election be made until an adequate candidate presents himself." The world's politicians have so far managed to exclude Colonel Bogey from democratic constitutions. Failing his candidature, however, the municipal voters of São Paulo in Brazil recently elected Cacareco, a female rhinoceros—weighing 2400 pounds—to their city council. The popular support for Cacareco seems to have been overwhelming; nor could there be any objection to her on the score of nationality, she being a citizen of Brazil by birth. Her disqualification was based, no doubt, on some legal quibble; connected perhaps with her age—she is four and a half. To have been born in the zoo is no bar, surely, to the exercise of democratic rights. But politicians may fairly expect to find themselves opposed by other candidates whose claims are broadly similar. Nor will it be possible to exclude them all on some trivial technicality. With the world's zoological gardens so well supplied with popular personalities, qualified for the legislature by residence and age, there can be no doubt that their fuller representation is to be expected. A few heavy majorities for such candidates—a tortoise here, a reptile there—would be no bad thing in the annals of political science.

To explain the second point of proposed reform it becomes necessary to remind the reader that the English voter used to record his vote publicly on a "hustings" or platform set up for the purpose in the market place. He would sturdily march up the step and audibly declare his choice amid the applause of his friends and the rotten eggs hurled by his opponents. It was for long defended, and with some reason, as an opportunity for the display of the manly virtues. It was certainly that, but there were drawbacks to set against its advantages. When the practice was finally abolished it was not because voters were being fatally injured—often as this may have happened. It was not even because some of them had to be carried up the steps, collapsing thereafter in a drunken stupor—as many in fact did. It was simply and solely to prevent corruption. The secret ballot ended individual bribery overnight. The voter might accept the bribe, but there was no means of knowing that he would earn it or that he had not been equally bribed by the other side. Since then bribery has had to be collective, which is not as much as to deny that it exists.

What few have remarked, however, is that the arguments for secret voting at the poll are at least as unanswerable as applied to the legislature. It can be urged against it that voters have a right to know how their representatives have voted. The point, however, is a doubtful one at best. After all, the representative is not a delegate. He should vote according to his conscience and knowledge, not according to the wishes of people who were not present at the debate. And the people who, in practice, watch the House divide are not the voters but the party bosses, financial backers and mere thugs; all who might be in a position to threaten or reward. Under secret voting, it might be objected, the representative might sell his vote without fear of exposure. To some representatives no idea could be more attractive. But there would be no one to buy it. Who will purchase goods of which the delivery is uncertain and of which it cannot be known whether they have been delivered or not? "On my word of honor," says the representative, "I shall vote as we have agreed." But who cares about his word of honor? He is a crook or he would not be accepting the bribe; nor do we know that it is the only bribe he has taken. In any representative body a secret and a public vote will produce quite different results. Which result gives the better indication of what men really think? To add to the authority of a legislature, more especially as against the executive, a system of secret voting in the House is a first and decisive step.

Last of all comes the question of the public payroll. That socialism, or anything like socialism, is incompatible in the long run with democracy is tolerably obvious. What the remedy is to be is appreciably less obvious. It would be simple to propose an amendment to the Constitution by which the number of persons publicly employed should be limited to a certain proportion of the voting public. That, however, would hardly achieve the end in view. For the line is not so easy to draw. Those employed by a private corporation which is wholly or even mostly engaged on government contract, are hardly to be distinguished, for this purpose, from those whose public employment is direct. To preserve democracy in anything like its present form—still more, to revive its energies—the need is not so much to restrict the numbers on the payroll as to limit the total cost of administration. The problem is too large for discussion here—it might almost be the subject for a book—but there are grounds, surely, for concluding that the governmental share of the national income has increased, is increasing, is likely to increase still more—and ought to be drastically diminished.

The price of democracy, it has been said, is eternal vigilance. Is that a price the American public is willing to pay? There are forces today which tend to preserve democracy, the disappearance of the proletariat being the chief of these. There are forces which tend to swamp it, of which public extravagance is perhaps the most dangerous. But this much is certain: that the democracy which merely drifts, swayed this way and that by technical development and cyclical trend, is no longer dynamic and no longer even alive. It cannot be sustained, still less can it be improved, without constant effort and constant care. A written constitution is a life belt to which the exhausted can cling; it is not, in itself, an aid to further progress. In most countries the traffic police are not unreasonably suspicious of motor vehicles manufactured much before 1930. They demand some test of their roadworthiness before admitting them into the stream of modern traffic. For a machinery of government perfected in 1789 a test at least as stringent might well be devised; and it would be odd indeed if no overhaul was ever found to be advisable. It is one thing to say that what has lasted for 170 years must have been soundly designed in the first place. It is quite another to conclude that what has lasted so long with such trifling repair, can last, unadjusted, forever.

FURTHER READING

PARKINSON, C. NORTHCOTE. *The Evolution of Political Thought*. Boston: Houghton Mifflin Company, 1958.

PARKINSON, C. NORTHOTE. *The Law and the Profits*. Boston: Houghton Mifflin Company, 1960.

BARZUN, JACQUES. *The House of Intellect*. New York: Harper & Brothers, 1959.

KELLEY, STANLEY, JR. *Professional Public Relations and Political Power*. Baltimore: The Johns Hopkins Press, 1956.

53

What Kind of Freedom?

Dorothy Lee

In this essay I speak of the idea of freedom which is peculiar to American society; I am not concerned with the ultimate question of what freedom is. As a concept or as a recognized value, freedom is rarely if ever present in non-Western cultures; but the thing itself, freedom, is certainly often present and carefully implemented—as autonomy, or otherwise as a dimension of the self. In this country, on the other hand, we do have the notion of freedom, and an ideal image of ourselves as "free." Ours is the "land of the free," we are born "free and equal"; and certainly, when these phrases were originally used, *free* referred to something of value beyond price, worth fighting and dying for.

A few years ago, with this in mind, I proceeded to find out how we use the term *free* in the mid-twentieth century. I had been struck by the increasing use of the term "I have to" or "I gotta," and wanted to find out in what areas Americans still expressed a sense of freedom in their linguistic usage. After weeks of listening to conversations of college and high school students, and of reading novels, articles and plays, I came reluctantly to the conclusion that the term *free* was almost never used, except by people whose function it was to evoke or facilitate freedom, or to remind people about freedom, or to prod people into being concerned about it—that is, by people such as social scientists, politicians, psychoanalysts, and educators. Otherwise, the term *free* was not applied to the freedom of the self. When used at all, it was used occasionally to refer to freedom from entanglement, and more frequently, to free time and free objects, that is, objects which could be acquired or enjoyed without being paid for, such as free lectures or free cigars. *Free* here referred merely to a condition of the situation, a negative condition; to something that was not there. It referred to a welcome lack of requirement, to an absence of *have to.* I *do not have to* pay for the cigars, or for a ticket to attend the lecture; my time is free because I *do not have to* do anything now.

I found that the lack of requirement was welcome; yet it did not hold value. When I considered the attitude toward free objects, I discovered that to get a free ride, or to collect a large number of free samples, was perceived as a "break," or was a sign of one's ingenuity, but it did not enhance one's value; and a free cigar, however welcome and however good, held less value than the one for which a man *had* to pay a dollar. The violinist who charged and could get a high fee for his concert had more value than the one who offered to play "for free."

When it came to free time, it seemed, on

Reprinted from *The Humanist*, Yellow Springs, Ohio, No. 4, 1958, with permission of the American Humanist Association.

the face of it, that this was certainly valued. People are constantly trying to achieve it. The increasing use of automatic machines in the home, for example, is more than labor-saving; it also achieves time-saving. It provides more free time for the housewife. Yet it seems to me that free time is valued only as *freed* time—time freed from the schedules and requirements to which the rest of one's time is committed. I find that when people say, "I am free," they usually mean, "I have some uncommitted time." This is a statement of fact, neither good nor bad; but to say that one is free all the time is not acceptable as a mere statement. One has to go on and give an explanation or a justification for such freedom, so as to endow it with a validity which is certainly not self-evident. The person who has nothing that he *has to do,* the person who can do what he presumably merely wants to do all the time, seems to be suspect, or to be pitied; or he is someone to worry about. He is not automatically valued for having all his time free. Is he a playboy, or unemployed, or incompetent, or ill, or over age? Conversely, I hear people speaking proudly of all they *have to do*, whether they are referring to committed time, or to what they do during their "free time."

In addition, as in the case of free objects, the *free* in time appears to refer to a negative condition. In this case, free refers to emptiness; so that free time comes to be time to be filled. Our free time is "leisure" time, potentially passive and empty—and subject to boredom, unless we plan it carefully and fill it with activities. In fact, we have now a number of professions whose function it is to provide means and aid to people for the filling of empty time. And our increasing leisure is viewed with apprehension by many of our leaders. Our gerontologists have long been concerned over the increasing span of the age of leisure. More recently, our labor leaders have been worrying over the amount of leisure time which automation is bound to afford to the industrial workers. David Riesman, who was consulted about this looming problem, sees it not only as a case of having to fill empty time, but, more seriously, as a question of how to endow free-time activities with the value which is present in the non-free, "have-to" activities. As he sees it, even freed time—the free time of people whose time is otherwise regularly committed now, or has been committed in earlier years—is not highly valued. The freedom to choose does not contain value with which to endow the leisure-time activities which have been contrived to fill the free time.

Basic to all this is a conception of time and space which, if not peculiar to American culture, is certainly not common in non-Western thought. In Western thought —and I speak here of the view of the unsophisticated—space is empty and to be occupied with matter; time is empty and to be filled with activity. In both primitive and civilized non-Western cultures, on the other hand, free space and time have being and integrity. It was this conception of *nothingness* as *somethingness* that enabled the philosophers of India to perceive the integrity of non-being, to name the free space and give us the zero. In such societies, children are raised to listen to silence as well as sound. Luther Standing Bear, describing his childhood as an Oglalla Dakota in the eighteen-seventies, wrote: "[Children] . . . were taught to sit still and enjoy it. They were taught to use their organs of smell, to look when apparently there was nothing to see, and to listen intently when all seemingly was quiet. . . ." And Modupe, writing of his So-So childhood in French Guinea, says, "We learned that silences as well as sounds are significant in the forest and how to listen to the silences. . . . Deeply felt silences might be said to be the core of our Kofon religion. During these times, the nature within ourselves found unity with the nature of earth." In 1948, Virginia Lewisohn Kahn reported on the comfortable and not-empty silences of the Navaho women she visited—silences which at first disquieted her. The Wintu

Indians have a suffix to refer to alert non-activity, to a silent, non-mobile commitment to awareness; a suffix I have found impossible to translate because there is no equivalent concept in American culture.

In Japanese traditional culture, free time and space are perceived as the *ma*, the valid interval or meaningful pause. Such perception is basic to all experience, and specifically to what constitutes creativity and freedom in the framework of Japanese culture. This perception apparently persists, in spite of the adoption of Western culture and science. Even in 1958, Misako Miyamoto wrote of the Noh-plays: "The audience watches the play and catches the feeling through not only the action and words but also the intervals of the period of pauses. . . . There is a free creation in each person's mind . . . ; and the audience relates to this situation with free thinking." Of silent intervals in speech, she says, "Especially [in] the pauses in a tone of voice, I can feel the person's unique personality and his joy, sorrow or other complicated feelings." On listening to a robin in early spring: "It sang with pauses. . . . I could have time to think about the bird [in] the silent moment between one voice and others. . . . The pauses produced the effect of the relation between the bird and me." In *The Integrity of the Interval,* Emilio Lanier—reversing this process—tried in 1956 to explain to Japanese Rotarians what it means to perceive space and time as a Westerner: "Every aspect of Western life assert[s] with untiring iteration the *exclusive integrity* of things, objects. . . . The spaces between objects . . . are not perceived actually as integers at all. . . ."

I have taken this long excursion into other cultures to show how in these, free time, through being recognized as valid existence, can and does contain value. In our own culture it is perceived as the unallocated, the unscheduled, the nothing; and it cannot contain value, as it contains no being. In the minds of many who despair over juvenile delinquency, alcoholism and other social ills, it is regarded as the vacuum which (Western) Nature abhors. Why then have we in this country taken such a good word, a word which names our valued way of life, and applied it to an emptiness? Do we recognize only a freedom *from*?

I cannot answer the first question except upon the basis of speculation. I believe that freedom *from,* the condition of the situation, was at one time felt to be supremely necessary but has since been taken for granted. And, with the increasing emphasis on the individual, on the *self* as a focus and starting point, the *situation* has lost significance. The individual is no longer supremely interested in *what can be done,* but rather in *what I can do.* When Papashvily came from Russian Georgia to this country, he saw it as the land where Anything Can Happen. But when I came to the land of the free as a foreign student in the mid-twenties, my classmates were not phrasing it in that way; they sang: "*I* can do anything, anything, anything." Freedom is now expressed as capacity, as ability residing in the self; perhaps earned by the self through the acquisition of know-how or through training but not necessarily so. We do recognize a freedom *to,* but we do not refer to it in this way. To be free is vague, conditional and not the main point; what is vital is that I *can.* Our school teachers are fighting a losing battle when they try to teach their pupils to ask, "May I?" The *can*, emanating from the self, subsumes all other nuances of freedom; and after all, even if I am not "allowed to," I can still take matters in my own hands.

The *can*, nevertheless, refers to a personal capacity only. The emphasis has shifted from a passive potentiality in the situation to a vital capacity in the person. Yet this ability still has to be actualized, to be translated into doing or functioning. The situation may allow; the parents, the teachers, the supervisor may permit; but this is not enough. At one time leaders in the field of interpersonal relations held that unlimited freedom *from* would be conducive to freedom *for* or *to*. But recently this notion has been questioned. Educational leaders now consider that unbounded freedom is chaotic and frightening, and they advocate the setting of limits. But the limit, in American imagery, is something external; so we have seen the suggested limit as a surrounding boundary, a fence around the formless area of freedom.

But I believe that the trouble is not that the individual is frightened by unbounded freedom, but rather that the lack of structure leaves him inert. And the introduction of outer boundaries is no solution, within the American cultural framework. What incites the American individual to an answering engagement in the situation is definiteness, caliber, *within* the situation; a strong framework, "guts." Unstructured freedom, whether fenced in or not, is still namby-pamby. The limits must have the character of a skeleton. Randomness, the unplanned and unscheduled, are like the despised jellyfish, and perpetuate or evoke inertia. Modupe's silences, during which he became attuned to the rhythm of the earth, do not incite to an answering actualization of the capacity to do or feel.

This is why American leisure has to be filled with named games, organized recreation, labelled hobbies, planned activities. And this is why the *have to* is often paradoxically freeing.

There are questions raised beyond this: Does this version of freedom, with its dependence on the pre-planned and its main emphasis on the capacity of the self, engender creativity, originality, spontaneity? My own opinion is that it does not; that indefiniteness and randomness, the recognition of the pauses, are all essential to creativity. There is the further question as to whether capacity is automatically transformed into actualization, the *can* into *I do,* even in the presence of the structured. I answer this in terms of the American philosophy of the self as expressed, for example, in client-centered therapy: that the individual has to be enabled, and the function of the loving mother, of the trusting and trusted social environment, is to enable. And when enabling is present, it can also break through the meager confines of the American version of freedom, into the unsheltered spaces in between the defined projects and planned activities. But the discussion of these questions is beyond the scope of this article.

REFERENCES

RIESMAN, DAVID. "The Suburban Dislocation" in *Metropolis in Ferment*. The Annals of the American Academy of Political and Social Science. Vol. 314, November, 1957.

LEE, DOROTHY. "Freedom, Spontaneity and Limit in American Linguistic Usage" *Explorations* 4, 1955.

PRINCE MODUPE. *I Was a Savage*. Harcourt, Brace and Co., New York, 1957.

STANDING BEAR, LUTHER. *My People the Sioux*. Boston: Houghton Mifflin Co., 1928.

______. *Land of the Spotted Eagle*. Boston: Houghton Mifflin Co., 1932.

SECTION B *Social Factors in the Economic System*

There was a period in the fifties when the Russians did a little research on the effects of the classless structure they kept saying they were creating. They investigated the backgrounds of the college age and professional school population. They found (much to their ideological distaste) that the children of professionals, old-style enemies of the state, capitalists, etc., were most likely to have children in college. This was true in spite of numerous restrictions against children of these classes.

What went wrong? Nothing except that the children were part of a cycle that overshadowed the ideological changes that occurred in Russia during their youth.

The selections here look at some of the social factors that enter into the economic and educational system. The first article by A. M. Jordan is somewhat clumsy and heavy-handed. It offers very clear evidence, however, that the culture itself keeps the lower classes low. The effects of some kinds of childhood training are to limit capacity and possibility for advancement.

Parkinson's article, if it were not true, would be one of the funniest take-offs on conventional economics I have ever read. It is discussing a self-perpetuating aspect of modern economic existence. It poses strange visions of a future where no one will do the work but everyone will manage the paperwork of others. David C. McClelland in the final selection tells how to change other cultures.

Social scientists tend to ignore the economic forces operating on the social systems they study. By paying more attention to the economic variables, social science can become more accurate in its attempts to understand total human behavior.

54

Parental Occupations and Children's Intelligence Scores

A. M. Jordan

The effect of differing environments upon mental development is an age old problem of investigation. Can man by changing the conditions under which his off-spring are reared produce in them significant differences? Or does an individual of low potentialities merely neglect these surroundings rich in civilizing possibilities and react to those of the order which are suitable to the level of his inheritance? More specifically, in connection with our present study, do environments which differ widely among themselves produce in children mental changes differing in any substantial amount? The question then of whether the occupation of the parents, with its accompanying levels of leisure and refinement, influences the mental growth of children is one of general interest.

The Present Study

About 1200 school children were tested twice each year over a period of three years. The children all lived in one community and were located in Grades I to VII, inclusive. The intelligence tests used were: for Grades I and II, Pintner-Cunningham Primary Mental Tests and Dearborn Group Tests of Intelligence, Series I; for Grades III through VII, The National Intelligence Tests, Forms A and B.

In the first place, we find the children of professional workers far ahead of any other group in the *Genius level* for in this group appear 2.5 per cent of the total number while in most of the other groups there are no representatives at all. Three out of the 578 children of mill workers appear in this group or .5 percent. In the *very superior group* we find the children of mill workers, carpenters, and farmers below expectancy while the children of all the rest are above. The children of the professional men, salesmen, and machinists stand out clearly both above the other groups being studied as well as above theoretical expectancy. In the *superior group* only the IQ's of the children of salesmen, merchants, lumbermen, bankers and professional men are above theoretical expectancy. The rest are substantially below. The machinists', the carpenters', and the mill workers' children are not much more than 50 per cent of the expectancy. The farmers furnish a much larger per cent of the expected than they have at any previous level. Not a single group attains the theoretical expectancy in the *normal group*. The range is from 35.0 per cent to 57.1 per cent when 60 per cent is

This article originally appeared in the *Journal of Applied Psychology*, 1933, 17:103–19.

expected. We have noted more than the theoretical expectancy in several of the categories above normal but if we look carefully we shall find a much greater group among the dull, the borderline, and the feebleminded than might have been expected.

Let us consider in some detail these groups which fall below the normal group. In the dull group 23 per cent of the children of mill workers, 25 per cent of the children of carpenters, and 21 per cent of the children of farmers fall when fifteen per cent is the theoretical expectancy. Only in the professional group with 7.7 per cent are the results much different.

When we turn to the *borderline group* the lines are even more sharply drawn. The children of the mill workers, the carpenters, and the farmers fall into this group in large numbers. Around fifteen per cent among these children according to our tests fall in the borderline group. This percentage is three times as many as theoretical expectancy.

The *feebleminded,*—those who are unable to plan and who have no ability to criticise their own acts—are much more numerous than might be expected. In this group appears a very large number of children of mill workers and of farmers. Indeed far more than chance would allow. These two groups stand out above the others in the percentages furnished to the feebleminded group. If the children of mill workers alone are considered, since we have here such a large sampling, nearly four times as many fall in this group as appear in the column of theoretical expectancy. In brief, these two occupational groups, the mill workers and the farmers, furnish a very large percentage of feebleminded children, a much larger percentage than the average of other occupational groups.

Some insight into the cause of the very low scores earned by these children may be had by separating the IQ's into those earned on (a) language tests and on (b) non-language tests. Such a procedure has been carried through in Table 1.

In this table about the same theoretical expectancy is used as Woodrow used in "Brightness and Dullness in Children." In the first column we have the theoretical expectancy in percentages. In the second column appear the percentages calculated from the scores of Pintner-Cunningham and Dearborn; in the third column the results

TABLE 1. Percentage of Children of Mill Workers at Each Intelligence Level

YEAR / IQ	EXPECTANCY	1925 N103 NON-LANGUAGE	1925 N243 LANGUAGE	1922 (Jobe) LANGUAGE	AVERAGE LAST TWO
Genius (Above 139)	.1	0	1.2	0	.6
Very Superior (120–139)	2.4	6.8	.4	2.2	1.3
Superior (110–119)	15.0	16.5	5.3	3.7	4.5
Normal (90–109)	60.0	47.6	42.3	41.5	41.9
Dull (80–89)	15.0	16.5	22.6	20.6	21.6
Borderline (70–79)	5.0	8.7	16.0	19.5	17.8
Feebleminded (Below 70)	2.5	3.9	11.9	12.5	12.2

from a test involving written language (National Intelligence Test); and in the fourth the results of a language test (National Intelligence Test) given in another community by another investigator (Jobe, 1922). In comparing the non-language results with those of theoretical expectancy, children of mill workers have a slightly larger percentage of very superior (2.4 vs. 6.8), somewhat larger per cent of superior, a smaller percentage of normal, and a larger percentage of dull, borderline, and feebleminded. If we compare the language tests with theoretical cases we find both in 1922 and 1925 a smaller percentage of very superior, superior, and normal; a larger percentage of dull, a much larger percentage of borderline (5 vs. 16 or 19) and a much larger percentage of feebleminded (2.5 vs. about 12). In proportion as the tests depend upon language the children of mill villages suffer in comparison with theoretical expectancy.

Finally we see a combination of language and other environmental factors at work in Table 2. In these tables the median IQ's of each age for both the mill and non-mill are presented.

The children of textile workers show a decreasing IQ from year to year. If we consider the years from 6–13, ages in which the number of pupils represented is of substantial number, the median IQ drops from about 100 to 85. According to this table, in the ordinary environment the median child at year 6 would be amply able to hold his own in any school system in the country, but by the time this same child had reached the 13th year he would be definitely retarded and regarded as a dull child able only with assistance to carry on the work of the school. In part, to be sure, the difference between IQ's is accounted for by a change in tests after the second year and the sharp drop may be attributed to the language element appearing but even this language influence might be one of the clearest signs of an impoverished cultural background. With the non-mill group there are small decreases up to age 13 until the IQ that started at 100 is then only 92. The drop in IQ points from years 6–13 is in the case of children of mill workers 14.7 points; in the case of non-mill workers, 8.6 points. Two hypotheses might be offered in explanation of these rather curious phenomena. On the one hand, we might attribute the differences to a poverty stricken environment. Workers in cotton mills get very meager wages and these bring in their wake environments lacking in many cultural contacts found in other environments. This environmental lack is probably increased in the majority of cases by a failure on the part of the employees to own their homes. Then, too, many move around a very great deal and hence conditions are certainly not conducive to the development of desirable sorts of cultural contacts. Now these conditions prevent the children from developing as rapidly in reading, arithmetic, etc., as they would in some other communities and hence when a language test depending on a knowledge of reading and arithmetic is given, these children fall behind in a deplorable manner. The second hypothesis is that there really is a much larger number of feebleminded in the upper grades since the tests are very little dependent upon environmental factors. This hypothesis certainly does not ring true for how could children who were almost normal at seven

TABLE 2. Decrease of IQ's with Age

AGE	6	7	8	9	10	11	12	13
Number	41	77	71	65	53	71	62	54
Mill (Median IQ)	100	99	95	91	85	90	87	85
Number	70	123	117	107	108	95	101	90
Non-Mill (Median IQ)	101	103	100	94	92	94	94	92

years grow into feebleminded ones at 10 or 11? If there is one measure more constant than most others concerned with human beings that measure is the IQ. Furthermore, these language tests indicate a far larger per cent of definitely feebleminded children than common sense would indicate, for certainly there is no observable indication in mill children that as many as 12 per cent are feebleminded. These findings then are preposterous on their face and such an hypothesis is unsubstantiated. The first hypothesis seem to be the more plausible one.

In the present study a much larger percentage of children fall in the dull and feebleminded group than in the case of theoretical expectancy. Three lines of evidence which converge upon the same focus have been submitted in explanation of these phenomena.

(a) When we consider the median scores of children of mill workers, for example, we find that they decrease from about normal IQ's at year 6 to 85 at year 13.

(b) When the same children are tested with both language tests and non-language tests there are from 9–10 IQ points difference in favor of the non-language tests.

(c) When comparisons were made between language and non-language tests there were shown to be an impossible number of feebleminded present among the children of mill workers in the former test and a more reasonable number in the latter.

These three lines of evidence lead us to the conclusion that in those occupations represented largely by semi-skilled workers the poverty of the environment is so severe that children's scores on intelligence tests are definitely lowered so that children who began their work in school with normal capacities have dropped to the level of dullards by the time they have attained the age of thirteen.

55

Business Drive and National Achievement

David C. McClelland

What accounts for the rise in civilization? Not external resources (*i.e.*, markets, minerals, trade routes, or factories), but the entrepreneurial spirit which exploits those resources—a spirit found most often among businessmen.

Who is ultimately responsible for the pace of economic growth in poor countries today? Not the economic planners or the politicians, but the executives whose drive (or lack of it) will determine whether the goals of the planners are fulfilled.

Why is Russia developing so rapidly that —if it continues its present rate of growth— it will catch up economically with the most advanced country in the world, the United States, in 25 or 30 years? Not, as the U.S.S.R. claims, because of the superiority of its Communist system, but because—by hook or by crook—it has managed to develop a strong spirit of entrepreneurship among its executives.

How can foreign aid be most efficiently used to help poor countries develop rapidly? Not by simply handing money over to their politicians or budget makers, but by using it in ways that will select, encourage, and develop those of their business executives who have a vigorous entrepreneurial spirit or a strong drive for achievement. In other words: *invest in a man, not just in a plan.*

What may be astonishing about some of these remarks is that they come from a college professor, and not from the National Association of Manufacturers. They are not the defensive drum rattlings of an embattled capitalist but are my conclusions, based on nearly fifteen years of research, as a strictly academic psychologist, into the human motive that appears to be largely responsible for economic growth—research which has recently been summarized in my book, entitled *The Achieving Society.*[1]

Since I am an egghead from way back, nothing surprises me more than finding myself rescuing the businessman from the academic trash heap, dusting him off, and trying to give him the intellectual respectability that he has had a hard time maintaining for the last fifty years or so. For the fact is that the businessman has taken a beating, not just from the Marxists, who pictured him as a greedy capitalist, and the social critics, who held him responsible for the Great Depression of the 1930's, but even from himself, deep in his heart.

One of the queerest ironies of history, as John Kenneth Galbraith points out in *The Affluent Society,*[2] is that in a sense Marx won his case with his sworn enemies, the capitalists. Marx loudly asserted that they were selfish and interested only in profits. In the end many agreed. They accepted the Marxist materialistic view of history. The modern businessman, says Galbraith, "suspects that the moral crusade of reformers, do-gooders, liberal politicians, and public servants, all their noble protestations notwithstanding, are based ultimately on self-interest. 'What,' he inquires, 'is their gimmick?' "

If not only the Marxists, but Western economists, and even businessmen themselves, end up assuming that their main motive is self-interest and a quest for profit, it is small wonder that they have had a hard time holding their heads high in recent years.

But now the research I have done has come to the businessman's rescue by showing that everyone has been wrong, that it is *not* profit per se that makes the businessman tick but a strong desire for achievement, for doing a good job. Profit is simply one measure among several of how well the job has been done, but it is necessarily the goal itself.

The Achievement Goal

But what exactly does the psychologist mean by the "desire for achievement"? How does he measure it in individuals or in nations? How does he know that it is so important for economic growth? Is it more important for businessmen to have this desire than it is for politicians, bishops, or generals? These are the kinds of questions which are answered at great length and with as much scientific precision as possible in my book. Here we must be content with the general outline of the argument, and develop it particularly as it applies to businessmen.

[1] Princeton, D. Van Nostrand Co., Inc., 1961.
[2] Boston, Houghton Mifflin Company, 1958.

To begin with, psychologists try to find out what a man spends his time thinking and daydreaming about when he is not under presssure to think about anything in particular. What do his thoughts turn to when he is by himself or not engaged in a special job? Does he think about his family and friends, about relaxing and watching TV, about getting his superior off his back? Or does he spend his time thinking and planning how he can "sell" a particular customer, cut production costs, or invent a better steam trap or toothpaste tube?

If a man spends his time thinking about doing things better, the psychologist says he has a concern for achievement. In other words, he cares about achievement or he would not spend so much time thinking about it. If he spends his time thinking about family and friends, he has a concern for affiliation; if he speculates about who is boss, he has a concern for power, and so on. What differs in my approach from the one used by many psychologists is that my colleagues and I have not found it too helpful simply to *ask* a person about his motives, interests, and attitudes. Often he himself does not know very clearly what his basic concerns are—even more often he may be ashamed and cover some of them up. So what we do is to try and get a sample of his normal waking thoughts by asking him just to tell a few stories about some pictures.

STORIES WITHIN STORIES

Let us take a look at some typical stories written by U.S. business executives. These men were asked to look briefly at a picture—in this case, a man at a worktable with a small family photograph at one side—and to spend about five minutes writing out a story suggested by the picture. Here is a very characteristic story:

The engineer is at work on Saturday when it is quiet and he has taken time to do a little daydreaming. He is the father of the two children in the picture—the husband of the woman shown. He has a happy home life and is dreaming about some pleasant outing they have had. He is also looking forward to a repeat of the incident which is now giving him pleasure to think about. He plans on the following day, Sunday, to use the afternoon to take his family for a short trip.

Obviously, no achievement-related thoughts have come to the author's mind as he thinks about the scene in the picture. Instead, it suggests spending time pleasantly with his family. His thoughts run along *affiliative* lines. He thinks readily about interpersonal relationship and having fun with other people. This, as a matter of fact, is the most characteristic reaction to this particular picture. But now consider another story:

A successful industrial designer is at his "work bench" toying with a new idea. He is "talking it out" with his family in the picture. Someone in the family dropped a comment about a shortcoming in a household gadget, and the designer has just "seen" a commercial use of the idea. He has picked up ideas from his family before—he is "telling" his family what a good idea it is, and "confidentially" he is going to take them on a big vacation because "their" ideas was so good. The idea will be successful, and family pride and mutual admiration will be strengthened.

The author of this story maintains a strong interest in the family and in affiliative relationships, but has added an achievement theme. The family actually has helped him innovate—get a new idea that will be successful and obviously help him get ahead. Stories which contain references to good new ideas, such as a new product, an invention, or a unique accomplishment of any sort, are scored as reflecting a concern for achievement in the person who writes them. In sum, this man's mind tends to run most easily along the lines of accomplishing something or other. Finally, consider a third story:

The man is an engineer at a drafting board. The picture is of his family. He has a problem and is concentrating on it. It is merely an everyday occurrence—a problem which requires thought. How can he get that bridge to take the stress of possible high winds? He wants to arrive at a good solution of the problem by himself. He will discuss the problem with a few other engineers and make a decision which will be a correct one—he has the earmarks of competence.

The man who wrote this story—an assistant to a vice president, as a matter of fact—notices the family photograph, but that is all. His thoughts tend to focus on the problem that the engineer has to solve. In the scant five minutes allowed, he even thinks of a precise problem—how to build a bridge that will take the stress of possible high winds. He notes that the engineer wants to find a good solution by himself, that he goes and gets help from other experts and finally makes a correct decision. These all represent different aspects of a complete achievement sequence—defining the problem, wanting to solve it, thinking of means of solving it, thinking of difficulties that get in the way of solving it (either in one's self or in the environment), thinking of people who might help in solving it, and anticipating what would happen if one succeeded or failed.

Each of these different ideas about achievement gets a score of +1 in our scoring system so that the man in the last incident gets a score of +4 on the scale of concern or need for achievement (conventionally abbreviated to *n* Achievement). Similarly, the first man gets a score of −1 for his story since it is completely unrelated to achievement, and the second man a score of +2 because there are two ideas in it which are scorable as related to achievement.

Each man usually writes six stories and gets a score for the whole test. The coding of the stories for "achievement imagery" is so objective that two expert scorers working independently rarely disagree. In fact, it has recently been programed for a high-speed computer that does the scoring rapidly, with complete objectivity, and fairly high accuracy. What the score for an individual represents is the frequency with which he tends to think spontaneously in achievement terms when that is not clearly expected of him (since the instructions for the test urge him to relax and to think freely and rapidly).

THINKING MAKES IT SO

What are people good for who think like this all the time? It doesn't take much imagination to guess that they might make particularly good business executives. People who spend a lot of their time thinking about getting ahead, inventing new gadgets, defining problems that need to be solved, considering alternative means of solving them, and calling in experts for help should also be people who in real life *do* a lot of these things or at the very best are readier to do them when the occasion arises.

I recognize, of course, that this is an assumption that requires proof. But, as matters turned out, our research produced strong factual support. Look, for instance,

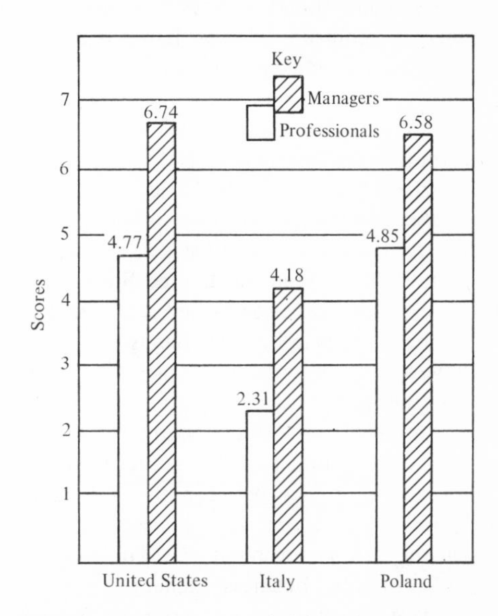

Exhibit I. Average *n* Achievement scores of managers and professionals in three countries

at Exhibit I. It shows that in three countries representing different levels and types of economic development, managers or executives scored considerably higher on the average in achievement thinking than did professionals or specialists of comparable education and background. Take the two democratic countries shown there:

In the United States the comparison was between matched pairs of unit managers and specialists of the same position level, age, educational background, and length of service in an electric appliance company. The managers spent more of their time in the test writing about achievement than the specialists did.

The same was true of middle-level executives from various companies in Italy when contrasted with students of law, medicine, and theology who were roughly of the same intelligence and social background.

In other words it takes a concern for achievement to be a manager in a foreign country like Italy, for instance, just as it does in the United States. It is worth noting in passing, however, that the level of achievement thinking among Italian managers is significantly lower than it is among American managers—which, as will be shown later, quite probably has something to do with the lower level and rate of economic development in Italy.

What about a Communist country? The figures for Poland are interesting because (1) the level of concern for achievement is about what it is in the United States, and (2) even in businesses owned and operated by the state, as in Poland, managers tend to have a higher concern for achievement than do other professionals.

Another even more striking result, not shown in Exhibit I, is the fact that there is *no real difference* between the average *n* Achievement score of managers working for the U.S. government (9.3) and those in U.S. private business generally (8.90). Apparently, a manager working for the Bureau of Ships in the Department of the Navy spends as much time thinking about achievement as his counterpart in Ford or Sears, Roebuck; government service does not weaken his entrepreneurial spirit. Whether he is able to be as effective as he might be in private business is another matter, not touched on here.

Careful quantitative studies of the prevalence of achievement concern among various types of executives also yield results in line with what one would expect. Thus, sales managers score higher than other types of managers do.

In general, more successful managers tend to score higher than do less successful managers (except in government service where promotion depends more on seniority). The picture is clear in small companies, where the president tends to score higher than his associates. In large companies, the picture is a little more complicated. Men in the lowest salary brackets (earning less than $20,000 a year) definitely have the lowest average *n* Achievement scores, while those in the next bracket up ($20,000 to $25,000 a year) have the highest average *n* Achievement level. Apparently an achievement concern helps one get out of the ranks of the lowest paid into a higher income bracket. But from there on, the trend fades. Men in the highest income brackets have a somewhat lower average concern for achievement, and apparently turn their thoughts to less achievement-oriented concerns. Possibly, these men are doing well enough to relax a little.

Businessmen and Achievement

Businessmen usually raise either one of two questions at this point:

(1) "Where can I get this test for *n* Achievement? It sounds like a good way of picking young executives!"

(2) "Why is this concern for achievement specific to being a success as a business manager? What about other types of achievement? Why isn't the entrepreneurial spirit necessary for success as an opera star,

a preacher, a great teacher, or a great scientist?"

The answer to the first question, unfortunately, is simple: no practicable marketable test for assessing achievement concern exists as yet. The method of measurement we have been using is too sensitive, too easily influenced by the social atmosphere surrounding the people who take the test, to give reliable individual results. Under carefully controlled conditions, it works adequately to distinguish large groups of people like managers versus professionals, but it is not yet useful for individual selection. What we have here is a theoretical, scientific "breakthrough," not a practicable working device.

The second question is harder to answer but it takes us further in the direction of understanding exactly what kind of a person it is who spends a lot of his time thinking about achievement. To begin with, the facts are clear: many important types of professionals (doctors, lawyers, priests, or research scientists) fail to score on the average as high as business executives, yet, clearly their work is in every sense as much of an achievement as the businessman's. How come?

Let us consider a particular case for a moment—that of the research scientist. Certainly his work represents an important achievement, for he is the one who often makes the breakthrough on which new technological and economic advances depend. Shouldn't he be thinking about defining a problem, doing a good job of solving it, getting help from experts, etc.?

Yet, when we tested a number of such scientists—including several outstanding Nobel prize winners—we found, somewhat to our surprise, that they were not unusually high in *n* Achievement but rather tended to be average. Then it occurred to us that having a very high concern for achievement might make a person unsuitable for being a research scientist. Why? Simply because in research a man must often work for what may become very long periods of time without any knowledge of how well he is doing. He may not even know if he is on the right track for as much as five or ten years. But a man with a high need for achievement likes to know quickly whether he is accomplishing anything and quite possibly would become frustrated by the lack of feedback in basic science as to whether he is getting anywhere. He would then more likely move into an area such as management where results are more tangible. On the other hand, the research scientist obviously needs *some* achievement concern, or he is not likely to want to engage in his occupation at all.

Characteristics of Achievers

Considerations like these focus attention on what there is about the job of being a business entrepreneur or executive that should make such a job peculiarly appropriate for a man with a high concern for achievement. Or, to put it the other way around, a person with high *n* Achievement has certain characteristics which enable him to work best in certain types of situations that are to his liking. An entrepreneurial job simply provides him with more opportunities for making use of his talents than do other jobs. Through careful empirical research, we know a great deal by now about the man with high *n* Achievement, and his characteristics do seem to fit him unusually well for being a business executive. Specifically:

1. *To begin with, he likes situations in which he takes personal responsibility for finding solutions to problems.* The reason is obvious. Otherwise, he could get little personal achievement satisfaction from the successful outcome. No gambler, he does not relish situations where the outcome depends not on his abilities and efforts but on chance or other factors beyond his control. For example:

Some business-school students in one study played a game in which they had to choose between two options, in each of which they had only one chance in three of succeeding. For one option they rolled a die and if it came up, say, a 1 or a 3 (out of six possibilities), they won. For the other option they had to work on a difficult business problem which they knew only one out of three people had been able to solve in the time allotted.

Under these conditions, the men with high *n* Achievement regularly chose to work on the business problem, even though they knew the odds of success were statistically the same as for rolling the die.

To men strong in achievement concern, the idea of winning by chance simply does not produce the same achievement satisfaction as winning by their own personal efforts. Obviously, such a concern for taking personal responsibility is useful in a business executive. He may not be faced very often with the alternative of rolling dice to determine the outcome of a decision, but there are many other ways open to avoid personal responsibility, such as passing the buck, or trying to get something else (or a committee) to take the responsibility for getting something done.

The famed self-confidence of a good executive (which actually is related to high achievement motivation) is also involved here. He thinks it can be done if *he* takes responsibility, and very often he is right because he has spent so much time thinking about how to do it that he does it better.

2. *Another characteristic of a man with a strong achievement concern is his tendency to set achievement goals and to take "calculated risks."* Again his strategy is well suited to his needs, for only by taking on moderately difficult tasks is he likely to get the achievement satisfaction he wants. If he takes on an easy or routine problem he will succeed but get very little satisfaction out of his success. If he takes on an extremely difficult problem, he is unlikely to get any satisfaction because he will not succeed. In between these two extremes, he stands the best chance of maximizing his sense of personal achievement.

The point can be made with the children's game of ring toss, some variant of which we have tried out at all ages to see how a person with high *n* Achievement approaches it. To illustrate:

The child is told that he scores when he succeeds in throwing a ring over a peg on the floor, but that he can stand anywhere he pleases. Obviously, if he stands next to the peg, he can score a ringer every time; but if he stands a long distance away, he will hardly ever get a ringer.

The curious fact is that the children with high concern for achievement quite consistently stand at moderate distances from the peg where they are most apt to get achievement satisfaction (or, to be more precise, where the decreasing probability-of-success curve crosses the increasing satisfaction-from-success curve). The ones with low *n* Achievement, on the other hand, distribute their choices of where to stand quite randomly over the entire distance. In other words, people with high *n* Achievement prefer a situation where there is a challenge, where there is some real risk of not succeeding, but not so great a risk that they might not overcome it by their own efforts.

Again, such a characteristic would seem to suit men unusually well for the role of business entrepreneur. The businessman is always in a position of taking calculated risks, of deciding how difficult a given decision will be to carry out. If he is too safe and conservative, and refuses to innovate, to invest enough in research or product development or advertising, he is likely to lose out to a more aggressive competitor. On the other hand, if he invests too much or overextends himself, he is also likely to lose out. Clearly, then, the business executive should be a man with a high concern for achievement who is used to setting moderate goals for himself and calculating carefully how much he can do successfully.

Therefore, we waste our time feeling sorry for the entrepreneur whose constant complaints are that he is overworking, that he has more problems than he knows how to deal with, that he is doomed to ulcers because of overwork, and so on. The bald truth is that if he has high *n* Achievement, he loves all those challenges he complains about. In fact, a careful study might well show that he creates most of them for himself. He may talk about quitting business and living on his investments, but if he did, he might then *really* get ulcers. The state of mind of being a little overextended is precisely the one he seeks, since overcoming difficulties gives him achievement satisfaction. His real problem is that of keeping the difficulties from getting *too* big for him, which explains in part why he talks so much about them because it is a nagging problem for him to keep at a level he can handle.

3. *The man who has a strong concern for achievement also wants concrete feedback as to how well he is doing.* Otherwise, how could he get any satisfaction out of what he had done? And business is almost unique in the amount of feedback it provides in the forms of sales, cost, production, and profit figures. It is really no accident that the symbol of the businessman in popular cartoons is a wall chart with a line on it going up or down. The businessman sooner or later knows how well he is doing; salesmen will often know their success from day to day. Furthermore, there is a concreteness in the knowledge of results which is missing from the kind of feedback professionals get.

Take, for example, the teacher as a representative professional. His job is to transmit certain attitudes and certain kinds of information to his students. He does get some degree of feedback as to how well he has done his job, but results are fairly imprecise and hardly concrete. His students, colleagues, and even his college's administration may indicate that they like his teaching, but he still has no real evidence that his students have *learned* anything from him. Many of his students do well on examinations, but he knows from past experience that they will forget most of that in a year or two. If he has high *n* Achievement and is really concerned about whether he has done his job well, he must be satisfied with sketchy, occasional evidence that his former pupils did absorb some of his ideas and attitudes. More likely, however, he is not a person with high *n* Achievement and is quite satisfied with the affection and recognition that he gets for his work which gratify other needs that he has.

The case of the true entrepreneur is different. Suppose he is a book publisher. He gets a manuscript and together with his editors decides that it is worth publication. At time of issuance, everyone is satisfied that he is launching a worth-while product. But then something devastatingly concrete happens—something far more definite than ever happens to a teacher—namely, those monthly sales figures.

Obviously not everyone likes to work in situations where the feedback is so concrete. It can prove him right, but it also can prove him wrong. Oddly enough, the person with high *n* Achievement has a compelling interest to know whether he was right or wrong. He thrives and is happier in this type of situation than he is in the professional situation.

Two further examples from our research may make the point clearer. Boys with high *n* Achievement tend to be good with their hands, to like working in a shop or with mechanical or electrical gadgets. What characterizes such play again is the concrete feedback it provides as to how well a person is doing. If he wires up an electric circuit and then throws the switch, the light either goes on or it does not. Knowledge of results is direct, immediate, and concrete. Boys with high *n* Achievement like this kind of situation, and while some may go on to become engineers, others often go into business where they can continue getting this kind of concrete feedback.

56

Parkinson's Law or the Rising Pyramid

C. Northcote Parkinson

Work expands so as to fill the time available for its completion. General recognition of this fact is shown in the proverbial phrase 'It is the busiest man who has time to spare.' Thus, an elderly lady of leisure can spend the entire day in writing and dispatching a postcard to her niece at Bognor Regis. An hour will be spent in finding the postcard, another in hunting for spectacles, half an hour in a search for the address, an hour and a quarter in composition, and twenty minutes in deciding whether or not to take an umbrella when going to the pillar box in the next street. The total effort that would occupy a busy man for three minutes all told may in this fashion leave another person prostrate after a day of doubt, anxiety, and toil.

Granted that work (and especially paperwork) is thus elastic in its demands on time, it is manifest that there need be little or no relationship between the work to be done and the size of the staff to which it may be assigned. A lack of real activity does not, of necessity, result in leisure. A lack of occupation is not necessarily revealed by a manifest idleness. The thing to be done swells in importance and complexity in a direct ratio with the time to be spent. This fact is widely recognized, but less attention has been paid to its wider implications, more especially in the field of public administration. Politicians and taxpayers have assumed (with occasional phases of doubt) that a rising total in the number of civil servants must reflect a growing volume of work to be done. Cynics, in questioning this belief, have imagined that the multiplication of officials must have left some of them idle or all of them able to work for shorter hours. But this is a matter in which faith and doubt seem equally misplaced. The fact is that the number of the officials and the quantity of the work are not related to each other at all. The rise in the total of those employed is governed by Parkinson's Law and would be much the same whether the volume of the work were to increase, diminish, or even disappear. The importance of Parkinson's Law lies in the fact that it is a law of growth based upon an analysis of the factors by which that growth is controlled.

The validity of this recently discovered law must rest mainly on statistical proofs, which will follow. Of more interest to the general reader is the explanation of the factors underlying the general tendency to which this law gives definition. Omitting technicalities (which are numerous) we may distinguish at the outset two motive forces. They can be represented for the present purpose by two almost axiomatic statements, thus: (1) 'An official wants to multiply subordinates, not rivals' and (2) 'Officials make work for each other.'

To comprehend Factor 1, we must picture a civil servant, called A, who finds himself overworked. Whether this overwork is real or imaginary is immaterial, but we should observe, in passing, that A's sensation (or illusion) might easily result from his own decreasing energy: a normal symptom of middle age. For this real or imagined overwork there are broadly speaking, three possible remedies. He may resign; he may ask to halve the work with a colleague called B; he may demand the assistance of two subordinates, to be called C and D. There is probably no instance, however, in history of A choosing any but the third alternative. By resignation, he would lose his pension rights. By having B appointed on his own level in the hierarchy, he would merely bring in a rival for promotion to W's vacancy when W (at long last) retires. So A would rather have C and D, junior men, below him. They will add to his consequence and, by dividing the work into two categories, as between C and D, he will have the merit of being the only man who comprehends them both. It is essential to realize at this point that C and D are, as it were, inseparable. To appoint C alone would have been impossible. Why? Because C, if by himself, would divide the work with A and so assume almost the equal status that has been refused in the first instance to B; a status the more emphasized if C is A's only possible successor. Subordinates must thus number two or more, each being thus kept in order by fear of the other's promotion. When C complains in turn of being overworked (as he certainly will) A will, with the concurrence of C, advise the appointment of two assistants to help C. But he can then avert internal friction only by advising the appointment of two more assistants to help D, whose position is much the same. With this recruitment of E, F, G, and H the promotion of A is now practically certain.

Seven officials are now doing what one did before. This is where Factor 2 comes into operation. For these seven make so much work for each other that all are fully occupied and A is actually working harder than ever. An incoming document may well come before each of them in turn. Official E decides that it falls within the province of F, who places a draft reply before C, who amends it drastically before consulting D, who asks G to deal with it. But G goes on leave at this point, handing the file over to H, who drafts a minute that is signed by D and returned to C, who revises his draft accordingly and lays the new version before A.

What does A do? He would have every excuse for signing the thing unread, for he has many other matters on his mind. Knowing now that he is to succeed W next year, he has to decide whether C or D should succeed to his own office. He had to agree to G's going on leave even if not yet strictly entitled to it. He is worried whether H should not have gone instead, for reasons of health. He has looked pale recently—partly but not solely because of his domestic troubles. Then there is the business of F's special increment of salary for the period of the conference and E's application for transfer to the Ministry of Pensions. A has heard that D is in love with a married typist and that G and F are no longer on speaking terms—no one seems to know why. So A might be tempted to sign C's draft and have done with it. But A is a conscientious man. Beset as he is with problems created by his colleagues for themselves and for him—created by the mere fact of these officials' existence—he is not the man to shirk his duty. He reads through the draft with care, deletes the fussy paragraphs added by C and H, and restores the thing to the form preferred in the first instance by the able (if quarrelsome) F. He corrects the English—none of these young men can write grammatically—and finally produces the same reply he would have written if officials C to H had never been born. Far more people have taken far longer to produce the same result. No one has been idle. All have done their best. And it is late evening before A finally quits his office and begins the return journey to Ealing. The last of the office lights are being turned off in the gathering dusk that marks the end of another day's administrative toil. Among the last to leave, A reflects with bowed shoulders and a wry smile that late hours, like grey hairs, are among the penalties of success.

From this description of the factors at work the student of political science will recognize that administrators are more or less bound to multiply. Nothing has yet been said, however, about the period of time likely to elapse between the date of A's appointment and the date from which we can calculate the pensionable service of H. Vast masses of statistical evidence have been collected and it is from a study of this data that Parkinson's Law has been deduced. Space will not allow of detailed analysis but the reader will be interested to know that research began in the Navy Estimates. These were chosen because the Admiralty's responsibilities are more easily measurable than those of, say, the Board of Trade. The question is merely one of numbers and tonnage. Here are some typical figures. The strength of the Navy in 1914 could be shown as 146,000 officers and men, 3249 dockyard officials and clerks, and 57,000 dockyard workmen. By 1928 there were only 100,000 officers and men and only 62,439 workmen, but the dockyard officials and clerks by then numbered 4558. As for warships, the strength in 1928 was a mere fraction of what it had been in 1914—fewer than 20 capital ships in commission as compared with 62. Over the same period the Admiralty officials had increased in number from 2000 to 3569, providing (as was remarked) 'a magnificent navy on land.' These figures are more clearly set forth in tabular form:

Admiralty Statistics

Classification	Year 1914	Year 1928	Increase or Decrease %
Capital ships in commission	62	20	−67.74
Officers and men in R.N.	146,000	100,000	−31.5
Dockyard workers	57,000	62,439	+ 9.54
Dockyard officials and clerks	3249	4558	+40.28
Admiralty officials	2000	3569	+78.45

The criticism voiced at the time centred on the ratio between the number of those available for fighting and those available only for administration. But that comparison is not to the present purpose. What we have to note is that the 2000 officials of 1914 had become the 3569 of 1928; and that this growth was unrelated to any possible increase in their work. The Navy during that period had diminished, in point of fact, by a third in men and two-thirds in ships. Nor, from 1922 onward, was its strength even expected to increase; for its total of ships (unlike its total of officials) was limited by the Washington Naval Agreement of that year. Here we have then a 78 per cent increase over a period of fourteen years; an average of 5.6 per cent increase a year on the earlier total. In fact, as we shall see, the rate of increase was not as regular as that. All we have to consider, at this stage, is the percentage rise over a given period.

Can this rise in the total number of civil servants be accounted for except on the assumption that such a total must always rise by a law governing its growth? It might be urged at this point that the period under discussion was one of rapid development in naval technique. The use of the flying machine was no longer confined to the eccentric. Electrical devices were being multiplied and elaborated. Submarines were tolerated if not approved. Engineer officers were beginning to be regarded as almost human. In so revolutionary an age we might expect that storekeepers would have more elaborate inventories to compile. We might not wonder to see more draughtsmen on the payroll, more designers, more technicians and scientists. But these, the dockyard officials, increased only by 40 per cent in number when the men of Whitehall increased their total by nearly 80 per cent. For every new foreman or electrical engineer at Portsmouth there had to be two more clerks at Charing Cross. From this we might be tempted to conclude, provisionally, that the rate of increase in administrative staff is likely to be double that of the technical staff at a time when the actually useful strength (in this case, of seamen) is being reduced by 21.5 per cent. It has been proved statistically, however, that this last percentage is irrelevant. The officials would have multiplied at the same rate had there been no actual seamen at all.

It would be interesting to follow the further progress by which the 8118 Admiralty staff of 1935 came to number 33,788 by 1954. But the staff of the Colonial Office affords a better field of study during a period of imperial decline. Admiralty statistics are complicated by factors (like the Fleet Air Arm) that makes comparison difficult as between one year and the next. The Colonial Office growth is more significant in that it is more purely administrative. Here the relevant statistics are as follows:

Colonial Office Statistics

YEAR	1935	1939	1943	1947	1954
Staff	372	450	817	1139	1661

Before showing what the rate of increase is, we must observe that the extent of this department's responsibilities was far from constant during these twenty years. The colonial territories were not much altered in area or population between 1935 and 1939. They were considerably diminished by 1943, certain areas being in enemy hands. They were increased again in 1947, but have since then shrunk steadily from year to year as successive colonies achieve self-government. It would be rational to suppose that these changes in the scope of Empire would be reflected in the size of its central administration. But a glance at the figures is enough to convince us that the staff totals represent nothing but so many stages in an inevitable increase. And this increase, although related to that observed in other departments, has nothing to do with the size—or even the existence—of the Empire. What are the percentages of increase? We must ignore, for this purpose, the rapid increase in staff which accompanied the diminution of responsibility during World War II. We should note rather, the peacetime rates of increase: over 5.24 per cent between 1935 and 1939, and 6.55 per cent between 1947 and 1954. This gives an average increase of 5.89 per cent each year, a percentage markedly similar to that already found in the Admiralty staff increase between 1914 and 1928.

Further and detailed statistical analysis of departmental staffs would be inappropriate in such a work as this. It is hoped, however, to reach a tentative conclusion regarding the time likely to elapse between a given official's first appointment and the later appointment of his two or more assistants.

Dealing with the problem of pure staff accumulation, all our researches so far completed point to an average increase of 5.75 per cent per year. This fact established, it now becomes possible to state Parkinson's Law in mathematical form: In any public administrative department not actually at war, the staff increase may be expected to follow this formula:

$$x = \frac{2k^m + l}{n}$$

where k is the number of staff seeking promotion through the appointment of subordinates; l represents the difference between the ages of appointment and retirement; m is the number of man-hours devoted to answering minutes within the department; and n is the number of effective units being administered, x will be the number of new staff required each year. Mathematicians will, of course, realize that to find the percentage increase they must multiply x by 100 and divide the total of the previous year (y), thus:

$$\frac{100\,(2k^m + l)}{yn}\%$$

And this figure will invariably prove to be between 5.17 per cent and 6.56 per cent, irrespective of any variation in the amount of work (if any) to be done.

The discovery of this formula and of the general principles upon which it is based has, of course, no political value. No attempt has been made to inquire whether departments *ought* to grow in size. Those who hold that this growth is essential to gain full employment are fully entitled to their opinion. Those who doubt the stability of an economy based upon reading each other's minutes are equally entitled to theirs. It would probably be premature to attempt at this stage any inquiry into the quantitative ratio that should exist between the administrators and the administered. Granted, however, that a maximum ratio exists, it should soon be possible to ascertain by formula how many years will elapse before that ratio, in any given community, will be reached. The forecasting of such a result will again have no political value. Nor can it be sufficiently emphasized that Parkinson's Law is a purely scientific discovery, inapplicable except in theory to the politics of the day. It is not the business of the botanist to eradicate the weeds. Enough for him if he can tell us just how fast they grow.

SECTION C *Perspectives on Affluence*

This section looks at some of the "fallout" of living in an affluent culture. Once the basic necessities of life are gained, what then? More leisure, more space, more education, more products, more invented and acquired needs, more of everything, including the problems associated with a different kind of living. The selections cover the problems caused by an affluent culture such as raising a child, national planning, and dealing with leisure. Also considered are the implications of creating a new class structure based on values which simply cannot exist without affluence.

The nature of work, the nature of education, and the nature of family life have all undergone enormous changes due to affluence. These changes are independent of the political system, religion, and economic beliefs. The Soviet Union has begun the cycle of affluence with the same startled and worried feelings that characterize our own culture. Germany, Japan, and the Scandinavian countries sometimes worry whether they are becoming too American. The problem is simply that they have become affluent and are undergoing social modifications similar to those of the United States.

In an affluent culture the need for working long hours diminishes, but the need to work long hours to obtain an education increases because the society is more complex and more information is necessary to achieve status in it. Thus students are working longer and harder today than was true a hundred years ago in order to move into positions where less work is required than ever before. It makes education sound like a good investment in leisure except that in many occupations the job is designed so that high prestige comes with working long hours. The irony is that now people at the top—professors, presidents of corporations, etc.—work evenings and weekends, while the "worker" fights successfully for a shorter and shorter work week.

There may come a time when education will be prized because it allows a person to work as much as he likes. There is no student union today that is confronting the school administration to ask for less education or shorter hours. Money and its fruit have turned some of our most central values topsy turvy.

57

Economic Abundance and the Formation of American Character

David M. Potter

To these questions, I believe, some highly explicit answers are possible. Let us therefore be entirely concrete. Let us consider the situation of a six-month-old American infant, who is not yet aware that he is a citizen, a taxpayer, and a consumer.

This individual is, to all appearances, just a very young specimen of *Homo sapiens,* with certain needs for protection, care, shelter, and nourishment which may be regarded as the universal biological needs of human infancy rather than specific cultural needs. It would be difficult to prove that the culture has as yet differentiated him from other infants, and, though he is an American, few would argue that he has acquired an American character. Yet abundance and the circumstances arising from abundance have already dictated a whole range of basic conditions which, from his birth, are constantly at work upon this child and which will contribute in the most intimate and basic way to the formation of his character.

To begin with, abundance has already revolutionized the typical mode of his nourishment by providing for him to be fed upon cow's milk rather than upon his mother's milk, taken from the bottle rather than from the breast. Abundance contributes vitally to this transformation, because bottle feeding requires fairly elaborate facilities of refrigeration, heating, sterilization, and temperature control, which only an advanced technology can offer and only an economy of abundance can make widely available. I will not attempt here to resolve the debated question as to the psychological effects, for both mother and child, of bottle feeding as contrasted with breast feeding in infant nurture. But it is clear that the changeover to bottle feeding has encroached somewhat upon the intimacy of the bond between mother and child. The nature of this bond is, of course, one of the most crucial factors in the formation of character. Bottle feeding also must tend to emphasize the separateness of the infant as an individual, and thus it makes, for the first time, a point which the entire culture reiterates constantly throughout the life of the average American. In addition to the psychic influences which may be involved in the manner of taking the food, it is also a matter of capital importance that the bottle-fed baby is, on the whole, better nourished than the breast-fed infant and therefore likely to grow more rapidly, to be more vigorous, and to suffer fewer ailments, with whatever effects these physical conditions may have upon his personality.

It may be argued also that abundance has provided a characteristic mode of housing for the infant and that this mode further emphasizes his separateness as an individual. In societies of scarcity, dwelling units are few and hard to come by, with the result that high proportions of newly married young people make their homes in the parental ménage, thus forming part of an "extended" family, as it is called. Moreover, scarcity provides a low ratio of rooms to individuals, with the consequence that whole families may expect as a matter of course to have but one room for sleeping, where children will go to bed in intimate propinquity to their parents. But abundance prescribes a different regime. By making it economically possible for newly married couples to maintain separate households of their own, it has almost destroyed the extended family as an institution in America and has ordained that the child shall be reared in a "nuclear" family, so-called, where his only intimate associates are his parents and his siblings, with even the latter far fewer now than in families of the past. The housing arrangements of this new-style family are suggested by census data for 1950. In that year there were 45,983,000 dwelling units to accommodate the 38,310,000 families in the United States, and, though the median number of persons in the dwelling unit was 3.1, the median number of rooms in the dwelling unit was 4.6. Eighty-four per cent of all dwelling units reported less than one person per room.[1] By providing the ordinary family with more than one room for sleeping, the economy thus produces a situation in which the child will sleep either in a room alone or in a room shared with his brothers or sisters. Even without allowing for the cases in which children may have separate rooms, these conditions mean that a very substantial percentage of children now sleep in a room alone, for, with the declining birth rate, we have reached a point at which an increasing proportion of families have one child or two children rather than the larger number which was at one time typical. For instance, in the most recent group of mothers who had completed their childbearing phase, according to the census, 19.5 percent had had one child and 23.4 had had two. Thus almost half of all families with offspring did not have more than two children throughout their duration. In the case of the first group, all the children were "only" children throughout their childhood, and in the second group half of the children were "only" children until the second child was born. To state this in another, and perhaps a more forcible, way, it has been shown that among American women who arrived at age thirty-four during the year 1949 and who had borne children up to that time, 26.7 per cent had borne only one child, and 34.5 per cent had borne only two.[2] If these tendencies persist, it would mean that, among families where there are children, hardly one in three will have more than two children.

The census has, of course, not got

[1] Data from United States Department of Commerce, *Census of Housing: 1950*, Vol. I, Part I (Washington: Government Printing Office, 1953), p. xxx. For purposes of enumeration kitchens were counted as rooms, but bathrooms, hallways, and pantries were not. Many dwelling units were, of course, occupied by single persons or others not falling under the definition of a family, but the number of households—43,468,000—was also less than the number of dwelling units.

[2] Clyde V. Kiser, "Fertility Trends in the United States," *Journal of the American Statistical Association*, XLVII (1952), 31–33. Figures given by Kiser, based on research by P. K. Whelpton, also include childless women; but my concern here is with the sibling relationships of children and not with the fertility of women, and I have therefore based my statements upon the record of women who have borne children rather than upon women of childbearing age. My statement has no way of allowing for half-brothers and sisters born of different mothers or for differentiating the number of children who survive from the number born.

around to finding out how the new-style family, in its new-style dwelling unit, adjusts the life-practice to the space situation. But it is significant that America's most widely circulated book on the care of infants advises that "it is preferable that he [the infant] not sleep in his parents' room after he is about 12 months old," offers the opinion that "it's fine for each [child] to have a room of his own, if that's possible," and makes the sweeping assertion that "it's a sensible rule not to take a child into the parents' bed for any reason."[3] It seems clear beyond dispute that the household space provided by the economy of abundance has been used to emphasize the separateness, the apartness, if not the isolation of the American child.

Not only the nourishment and housing, but also the clothing of the American infant are controlled by American abundance. For one of the most sweeping consequences of our abundance is that, in contrast to other peoples who keep their bodies warm primarily by wearing clothes, Americans keep their bodies warm primarily by a far more expensive and even wasteful method: namely, by heating the buildings in which they are sheltered. Every American who has been abroad knows how much lighter is the clothing—especially the underclothing—of Americans than of people in countries like England and France, where the winters are far less severe than ours, and every American who can remember the conditions of a few decades ago knows how much lighter our clothing is than that of our grandparents. These changes have occurred because clothing is no longer the principal device for securing warmth. The oil furnace has not only displaced the open fireplace; it has also displaced the woolen undergarment and the vest.

This is a matter of considerable significance for adults but of far greater importance to infants, for adults discipline themselves to wear warm garments, submitting, for instance, to woolen underwear more or less voluntarily. But the infant knows no such discipline, and his garments or bedclothes must be kept upon him by forcible means. Hence primitive people, living in outdoor conditions, swaddle the child most rigorously, virtually binding him into his clothes, and breaking him to them almost as a horse is broken to the harness. Civilized peoples mitigate the rigor but still use huge pins or clips to frustrate the baby's efforts to kick off the blankets and free his limbs. In a state of nature, cold means confinement and warmth means freedom, so far as young humans are concerned. But abundance has given the American infant physical freedom by giving him physical warmth in cold weather.

In this connection it may be surmised that abundance has also given him a permissive system of toilet training. If our forebears imposed such training upon the child we now wait for him to take the initiative in these matters himself, it is not wholly because the former held a grim Calvinistic doctrine of child-rearing that is philosophically contrary to ours. The fact was that the circumstances gave them little choice. A mother who was taking care of several babies, keeping them clean, making their clothes, washing their diapers in her own washtub, and doing this, as often as not, while another baby was on the way, had little choice but to hasten their fitness to toilet themselves. Today, on the contrary, the disposable diaper, the diaper service, and most of all the washing machine, not to mention the fact that one baby seldom presses upon the heels of another, make it far easier for the mother to indulge the child in a regime under which he will impose his own toilet controls in his own good time.

Thus the economy of plenty has influenced

[3] Benjamin Spock, *The Pocket Book of Baby and Child Care* (New York: Pocket Books, Inc., 1946), pp. 96–97.

the feeding of the infant, his regime, and the physical setting within which he lives. These material conditions alone might be regarded as having some bearing upon the formation of his character, but the impact of abundance by no means ends at this point. In so far as it has an influence in determining what specific individuals shall initiate the infant into the ways of man and shall provide him with his formative impressions of the meaning of being a person, it must be regarded as even more vital. When it influences the nature of the relationships between these individuals and the infant, it must be recognized as reaching to the very essence of the process of character formation.

The central figures in the dramatis personae of the American infant's universe are still his parents, and in this respect, of course, there is nothing peculiar either to the American child or to the child of abundance. But abundance has at least provided him with parents who are in certain respects unlike the parents of children born in other countries or born fifty years ago. To begin with, it has given him young parents, for the median age of fathers at the birth of the first child in American marriages (as of 1940) was 25.3 years, and the median age of mothers was 22.6 years. This median age was substantially lower than it had been in the United States in 1890 for both fathers and mothers. Moreover, as the size of families has been reduced and the wife no longer continues to bear a succession of children throughout the period of her fertility, the median age of mothers at the birth of the last child has declined from 32 years (1890) to 27 years (1940). The age of the parents at the birth of both the first child and the last child is far lower than in the case of couples in most European countries. There can be little doubt that abundance has caused this differential, in the case of the first-born by making it economically possible for a high proportion of the population to meet the expenses of homemaking at a fairly early age. In the case of the last-born, it would also appear that one major reason for the earlier cessation of child-bearing is a determination by parents to enjoy a high standard of living themselves and to limit their offspring to a number for whom they can maintain a similar standard.

By the very fact of their youth, these parents are more likely to remain alive until the child reaches maturity, thus giving him a better prospect of being reared by his own mother and father. This prospect is further reinforced by increases in the life-span, so that probably no child in history has ever enjoyed so strong a likelihood that his parents will survive to rear him. Abundance has produced this situation by providing optimum conditions for prolonging life. But, on the other hand, abundance has also contributed much to produce an economy in which the mother is no longer markedly dependent upon the father, and this change in the economic relation between the sexes has probably done much to remove obstacles to divorce. The results are all too familiar. During the decade 1940–49 there were 25.8 divorces for every 100 marriages in the United States, which ratio, if projected over a longer period, would mean that one marriage out of four would end in divorce. But our concern here is with a six-month-old child, and the problem is to know whether this factor of divorce involves childless couples predominantly or whether it is likely to touch him. The answer is indicated by the fact that, of all divorces granted in 1948, no less than 42 per cent were to couples with children under eighteen, and a very large proportion of these children were of much younger ages. Hence one might say that the economy of abundance has provided the child with younger parents who chose their role of parenthood deliberately and who are more likely than parents in the past to live until he is grown, but who are substantially less likely to preserve the unbroken family as the environment within which he shall be reared.

In addition to altering the characteristics of the child's parents, it has also altered the quantitative relationship between him and his parents. It has done this, first of all, by offering the father such lucrative opportunities through work outside the home that the old agricultural economy in which children worked alongside their fathers is now obsolete. Yet, on the other hand, the father's new employment gives so much more leisure than his former work that the child may, in fact, receive considerably more of his father's attention. But the most vital transformation is in the case of the mother. In the economy of scarcity which controlled the modes of life that were traditional for many centuries, an upper-class child was reared by a nurse, and all others were normally reared by their mothers. The scarcity economy could not support many nonproductive members, and these mothers, though not "employed," were most decidedly hard workers, busily engaged in cooking, washing, sewing, weaving, preserving, caring for the hen-house, the garden, and perhaps the cow, and in general carrying on the domestic economy of a large family. Somehow they also attended to the needs of a numerous brood of children, but the mother was in no sense a full-time attendant upon any one child. Today, however, the economy of abundance very nearly exempts a very large number of mothers from the requirement of economic productivity in order that they may give an unprecedented share of their time to the care of the one or two young children who are now the usual number in an American family. Within the home, the wide range of labor-saving devices and the assignment of many functions, such as laundering, to service industries have produced this result. Outside the home, employment of women in the labor force has steadily increased, but the incidence of employment falls upon unmarried women, wives without children, and wives with grown children. In fact, married women without children are two and one-half times as likely to be employed as those with children. Thus what amounts to a new dispensation has been established for the child. If he belongs to the upper class, his mother has replaced his nurse as his full-time attendant. The differences in character formation that might result from this change alone could easily be immense. To mention but one possibility, the presence of the nurse must inevitably have made the child somewhat aware of his class status, whereas the presence of the mother would be less likely to have this effect. If the child does not belong to the upper class, mother and child now impinge upon each other in a relationship whose intensity is of an entirely different magnitude from that which prevailed in the past. The mother has fewer physical distractions in the care of the child, but she is more likely to be restive in her maternal role because it takes her away from attractive employment with which it cannot be reconciled.

If abundance has thus altered the relationship of the child with his parent, it has even more drastically altered the rest of his social milieu, for it has changed the identity of the rest of the personnel who induct him into human society. In the extended family of the past, a great array of kinspeople filled his cosmos and guided him to maturity. By nature, he particularly needed association with children of his own age (his "peers," as they are called), and he particularly responded to the values asserted by these peers. Such peers were very often his brothers and sisters, and, since they were all members of his own family, all came under parental control. This is to say that, in a sense, the parents controlled the peer group, and the peer group controlled the child. The point is worth making because we frequently encounter the assertion that parental control of the child has been replaced by peer-group control; but it is arguable that what is really the case is that children were always deeply influenced by the peer group and that parents have now lost their former measure of control over this group, since it is no longer a familial group. Today the nursery school replaces the large family as a peer group, and the social associations, even of young children, undergo the same shift from focused contact with family to diffused contact with a miscellany of people, which John Galsworthy depicted for grown people in three novels of the *Forsyte Saga*. Again, the effects upon character may very well be extensive.

Abundance, then, has played a critical part in revolutionizing both the physical circumstances and the human associations which surround the American infant and child. These changes alone would warrant the hypothesis that abundance has profoundly affected the formation of character for such a child. But to extend this inquiry one step further, it may be worth while to consider how these altered conditions actually impinge upon the individual. Here, of course, is an almost unlimited field for investigation, and I shall only attempt to indicate certain crucial points at which abundance projects conditions that are basic in the life of the child.

One of these points concerns the cohesive force which holds the family together. The family is the one institution which touches all members of society most intimately, and it is perhaps the only social institution which touches young children directly. The sources from which the family draws its strength are, therefore, of basic importance. In the past, these sources were, it would seem, primarily economic. For agrarian society, marriage distinctively involved a division of labor. Where economic opportunity was narrowly restricted, the necessity for considering economic ways and means in connection with marriage led to the arrangement of matches by parents and to the institution of the dowry. The emotional bonds of affection, while always important, were not deemed paramount, and the ideal of romantic love played little or no part in the lives of ordinary people. Where it existed at all, it was as an upper-class luxury. (The very term "courtship" implies this upper-class orientation.) This must inevitably have meant that the partners in the majority of marriages demanded less from one another emotionally than do the partners of romantic love and that the emotional factor was less important to the stability of the marriage. Abundance, however, has played its part in changing this picture. On the American frontier, where capital for dowries was as rare as opportunity for prosperous marriage was plentiful, the dowry became obsolete. Later still, when abundance began to diminish the economic duties imposed upon the housewife, the function of marriage as a division of labor ceased to seem paramount, and the romantic or emotional factor assumed increasing importance. Abundance brought the luxury of romantic love within the reach of all, and, as it did so, emotional harmony became the principal criterion of success in a marriage, while lack of such harmony became a major threat to the existence of the marriage. The statistics of divorce give us a measure of the loss of durability in marriage, but they give us no measure of the factors of instability in the marriages which endure and no measure of the increased focus upon emotional satisfactions in such marriages. The children of enduring marriages, as well as the children of divorce, must inevitably feel the impact of this increased emphasis upon emotional factors, must inevitably sense the difference in the foundations of the institutions which holds their universe in place.

In the rearing of a child, it would be difficult to imagine any factors more vital than the distinction between a permissive and an authoritarian regime or more vital than the age at which economic responsibility is imposed. In both these matters the modern American child lives under a very different dispensation from children in the past. We commonly think of these changes as results of our more enlightened or progressive or humanitarian ideas. We may even think of them as results of developments in the specific field of child psychology, as if the changes were simply a matter of our understanding these matters better than our grandparents. But the fact is that the authoritarian discipline of the child, within the authoritarian family, was but an aspect of the authoritarian social system that was linked with the economy of scarcity. Such a regime could never have been significantly relaxed within the family so long as it remained diagnostic in the society. Nor could it have remained unmodified within the family, once society began to abandon it in other spheres.

Inevitably, the qualities which the parents inculcate in a child will depend upon the roles which they occupy themselves. For the ordinary man the economy of scarcity has offered one role, as Simon N. Patten observed many years ago, and the economy of abundance has offered another. Abundance offers "work calling urgently for workmen"; scarcity found the "worker seeking humbly any kind of toil."[4] As a suppliant to his superiors, the worker under scarcity accepted the principle of authority; he accepted his own subordination and the obligation to cultivate the qualities appropriate to his subordination, such as submissiveness, obedience, and deference. Such a man naturally transferred the principle of authority into his own family and, through this principle, instilled into his children the qualities appropriate to people of their kind—submissiveness, obedience, and deference. Many copybook maxims still exist to remind us of the firmness of childhood discipline, while the difference between European and American children—one of the most clearly recognizable of all national differences—serves to emphasize the extent to which Americans have now departed from this firmness.

This new and far more permissive attitude toward children has arisen, significantly, in an economy of abundance, where work has called urgently for the workman. In this situation, no longer a suppliant, the workman found submissiveness no longer a necessity and therefore no longer a virtue. The principle of authority lost some of its majesty, and he was less likely to regard it as the only true criterion of domestic order. In short, he ceased to impose it upon his children. Finding that the most valuable trait in himself was a capacity for independent decision and self-reliant conduct in dealing with the diverse opportunities which abundance offered him, he tended to encourage this quality in his children. The irresponsibility of childhood still called for a measure of authority on one side and obedience on the other, but this became a means to an end and not an end in itself. On the whole, permissive training, to develop independent ability, even though it involves a certain sacrifice of obedience and discipline, is the characteristic mode of child-rearing in the one country which most distinctly enjoys an economy of abundance. Here, in a concrete way, one finds something approaching proof for Gerth and Mills's suggestion that the relation of father and child may have its importance not as a primary factor but rather as a "replica of the power relations of society."

If scarcity required men to "seek humbly any kind of toil," it seldom permitted women to seek employment outside the home at all. Consequently, the woman was economically dependent upon, and, accordingly, subordinate to, her husband or her father. Her subordination reinforced the principle of authority within the home. But the same transition which altered the role of the male worker has altered her status as well, for abundance "calling urgently for workmen" makes no distinctions of gender, and, by extending economic independence to women, has enabled them to assume the role of partners rather than of subordinates within the family. Once the relation of voluntarism and equality is introduced between husband and wife, it is, of course, far

[4] Simon Nelson Patten, *The New Basis of Civilization* (New York: Macmillan Co., 1907), pp. 187–88. I am indebted to Arthur Schlesinger, Jr., for calling my attention to Patten's important observations on this subject.

more readily extended to the relation between parent and child.

If abundance has fostered a more permissive regime for the child, amid circumstances of democratic equality within the family, it has no less certainly altered the entire process of imposing economic responsibility upon the child, hence the process of preparing the child for such responsibility. In the economy of scarcity, as I have remarked above, society could not afford to support any substantial quota of nonproductive members. Consequently, the child went to work when he was as yet young. He attended primary school for a much shorter school year than the child of today; only a minority attended high school; and only the favored few attended college. Even during the brief years of schooling, the child worked, in the home, on the farm, or even in the factory. But today the economy of abundance can afford to maintain a substantial proportion of the population in nonproductive status, and it assigns this role, sometimes against their will, to its younger and its elder members. It protracts the years of schooling, and it defers responsibilities for an unusually long span. It even enforces laws setting minimal ages for leaving school, for going to work, for consenting to sexual intercourse, or for marrying. It extends the jurisdiction of juvenile courts to the eighteenth or the twentieth year of age.

Such exemption from economic responsibility might seem to imply a long and blissful youth free from strain for the child. But the delays in reaching economic maturity are not matched by comparable delays in other phases of growing up. On the contrary, there are many respects in which the child matures earlier. Physically, the child at the lower social level will actually arrive at adolescence a year or so younger than his counterpart a generation ago, because of improvement in standards of health and nutrition.[5] Culturally, the child is made aware of the allurements of sex at an earlier age, partly by his familiarity with the movies, television, and popular magazines, and partly by the practice of "dating" in the early teens. By the standards of his peer group, he is encouraged to demand expensive and mature recreations, similar to those of adults, at a fairly early age. By reason of the desire of his parents that he should excel in the mobility race and give proof during his youth of the qualities which will make him a winner in later life, he is exposed to the stimuli of competition before he leaves the nursery. Thus there is a kind of imbalance between the postponement of responsibility and the quickening of social maturity which may have contributed to make American adolescence a more difficult age than human biology alone would cause it to be. Here, again, there are broad implications for the formation of character, and here, again, abundance is at work on both sides of the equation, for it contributes as much to the hastening of social maturity as it does to the prolongation of economic immaturity.

Some of these aspects of the rearing of children in the United States are as distinctively American, when compared with other countries, as any Yankee traits that have ever been attributed to the American people. In the multiplicity which always complicates social analysis, such aspects of child-rearing might be linked with a number of factors in American life. But one of the more evident and more significant links, it would seem certain, is with the factor of abundance. Such a tie is especially pertinent in this discussion, where the intention of the whole book has been to relate the study of character, as the historian would approach it, to the same subject as it is viewed by the behavioral scientist. In this chapter, especially, the attempt has been made to throw a bridge between the general historical force

[5] Alfred C. Kinsey, *et al., Sexual Behavior in the Human Male* (Philadelphia: W. B. Saunders Co., 1948), p. 397.

of economic abundance and the specific behavioral pattern of people's lives. Historical forces are too often considered only in their public and over-all effects, while private lives are interpreted without sufficient reference to the historical determinants which shape them. But no major force at work in society can possibly make itself felt at one of these levels without also having its impact at the other level. In view of this fact, the study of national character should not stand apart, as it has in the past, from the study of the process of character formation in the individual. In view of this fact, also, the effect of economic abundance is especially pertinent. For economic abundance is a factor whose presence and whose force may be clearly and precisely recognized in the most personal and intimate phases of the development of personality in the child. Yet, at the same time, the presence and the force of this factor are recognizable with equal certainty in the whole broad, general range of American experience, American ideals, and American institutions. At both levels, it has exercised a pervasive influence in the shaping of the American character.

58

Labor, Leisure, and the New Class

John K. Galbraith

In a society of high and increasing affluence there are three plausible tendencies as regards toil. As the production of goods comes to seem less urgent, and as individuals are less urgently in need of income for the purchase of goods, they will work fewer hours or days in the week. Or they will work less hard. Or, as a final possibility, it may be that fewer people will work all the time.

In the last century a drastic decline has occurred in the work week. In 1850 it is estimated to have averaged just under seventy hours, the equivalent of seven ten-hour days a week or roughly six at from six in the morning to six at night. A hundred years later the average was 40.0 hours or five eight-hour days.

This decline reflects a tacit but unmistakable acceptance of the declining marginal urgency of goods. There is no other explanation. However, such is the hold of production on our minds that this explanation is rarely offered. The importance and rewards of leisure are urged, almost never the importance of goods. Or, since production per hour has been increasing as the work week has declined, it is said that we are able to reduce the work because more is produced in less time. No mention is made of the fact that even more would be produced in more time. Or, finally, the decline is related to the feeling that steps must be taken to share the available work as productivity per worker rises. This also implies that the marginal urgency of production is low or negligible, but again the point remains unmade.

A reduction in the work week is an exceedingly plausible reaction to the declining marginal urgency of product. Over the span of man's history, although a phenomenal amount of education, persuasion, indoctrination, and incantation have been devoted to the effort, ordinary people have never been quite persuaded that toil is as agreeable as its alternatives. Thus to take increased well-being partly in the form of more goods and partly in the form of more leisure is unquestionably rational. In addition, the institution of overtime enables the worker to go far to adjust work and income to his own taste and requirements. It breaks with the barbarous uniformity of the weekly wage with its assumption that all families have the same tastes, needs, and requirements. Few things enlarge the liberty of the individual more substantially than to grant him a measure of control over the amount of his income.

Unfortunately in the conventional wisdom the reduction in hours has emerged as the only legitimate response to increasing affluence. This is at least partly because the issue has never been faced in terms of the increasing unimportance of goods. Accordingly, though we have attributed value to leisure, a ban still lies on other courses which seem to be more directly in conflict with established attitudes on productive efficiency. In a society rationally concerned with its own happiness these alternatives have a strong claim to consideration.

II

The first of these is that work can be made easier and more pleasant.

The present-day industrial establishment is a great distance removed from that of the last century or even of twenty-five years ago. This improvement has been the result of a variety of forces—government standards and factory inspection; general technological and architectural advance; the fact that productivity could be often increased by substituting machine power for heavy or repetitive manual labor; the need to compete for a labor force; and union intervention to improve working conditions in addition to wages and hours.

However, except where the improvement contributed to increased productivity, the effort to make work more pleasant has had to support a large burden of proof. It was permissible to seek the elimination of hazardous, unsanitary, unhealthful, or otherwise objectionable conditions of work. The speed-up might be resisted—to a point. But the test was not what was agreeable but what was unhealthful or, at a minimum, excessively fatiguing. The trend toward increased leisure is not reprehensible, but we resist vigorously the notion that a man should work less hard while on the job. Here older attitudes are involved. We are gravely suspicious of any tendency to expend less than the maximum effort, for this has long been a prime economic virtue.

In strict logic there is as much to be said for making work pleasant and agreeable as for shortening hours. On the whole it is probably as important for a wage earner to have pleasant working conditions as a pleasant home. To a degree, he can escape the latter but not the former—though no doubt the line between an agreeable tempo and what is flagrant featherbedding is difficult to draw. Moreover, it is a commonplace on the industrial scene that the dreariest and most burdensome tasks, requiring as they do a minimum of thought and skill, frequently have the largest numbers of takers. The solution to this problem lies, as we shall see presently, in drying up the supply of crude manpower at the bottom of the ladder. Nonetheless the basic point remains: the case for more leisure is not stronger on purely *prima facie* grounds than the case for making labortime itself more agreeable. The test, it is worth repeating, is not the effect on productivity. It is not seriously argued that the shorter work week increases productivity—that men produce more in fewer hours than they would in more. Rather it is whether fewer hours are always to be preferred to more but more pleasant ones.

III

The third of the obvious possibilities with increasing affluence is for fewer people to work. This tendency has also been operating for many years although in a remarkably diverse form. Since 1890, when one boy in four and one girl in ten between the ages of ten and fifteen were gainfully employed, large numbers of juveniles have been retired from the labor force and their number now is negligible. At the same time a large number of women have been added. In 1890 19.5 percent of the female population ten years and over was in the labor force and by 1953 this proportion had risen to 29.7 percent. However, this change reflects in considerable measure the shift of tasks—food preparation, clothing manufacture, even child-rearing—out of the home. Women who previously performed them have gone along to other work. The woman who takes charge of a day nursery has joined the labor force, as have the women whose children she cares for.

For seventy-five years the proportion of the male population in the labor force has been constant at around seventy-five percent of those over ten years of age. There are a smaller percentage of the very young and of those over sixty-five, but this has been offset by the increase in population in the ages between twenty and sixty-five where the proportion of workers to the total is very high.

With diminishing marginal urgency of goods it is logical that the first to be spared should be old and young. We have yet, however, to view this tendency consistently and comprehensively. We are able to dispense with the labor of those who have reached retiring age because the goods they add are a low order of urgency, whereas a poor society must extract the last ounce of labor effort from all. But we have ordinarily subjected those who retire to a drastic reduction in income and living standards. Obviously, if the retirement can be afforded because the product is no longer urgent, a satisfactory—meaning for most purposes the customary—living standard can be accorded to the retired employee for the same reason. Similarly we have excluded youngsters from the labor market, partly on the ground that labor at too early an age is unduly painful and injurious to health, and partly to make way for educational opportunity. But while we have felt it possible to dispense with the goods that the youngsters produce, we have yet to provide them, at least in full and satisfactory measure, with the education that their exemption from labor was designed to make possible. If we are affluent enough to dispense with the product of juvenile labor, it again follows that we are affluent enough to provide the education that takes its place.

In addition to releasing the old and young, it may be that we need not use all of the labor force at all times. . . If the marginal urgency of goods is low, then so is the urgency of employing the last man or the last million men in the labor force. By allowing ourselves such slack, in turn, we reduce the standards of economic performance to a level more nearly consonant with the controls available for its management. And in so widening the band of what is deemed tolerable performance lies our best hope of minimizing the threat of inflation with its further and persistent threat to social balance.

Such a step requires much more adequate provision than now for those who are temporarily unemployed. . . . Such measures are possible and, indeed, have a vital stabilizing effect. And again such compensation accords with the logic of the situation. If our need for production is of such a low order of urgency that we can afford some unemployment in the interest of stability—

a proposition, incidentally, of impeccably conservative antecedents—then we can afford to give those who are unemployed the goods that enable them to sustain their accustomed standard of living. If we don't need what the employed do not make, we can obviously afford them what they customarily eat and wear.

IV

However, the greatest prospect that we face—indeed what must now be counted one of the central economic goals of our society—is to eliminate toil as a required economic institution. This is not a utopian vision. We are already well on the way. Only an extraordinarily elaborate exercise in social camouflage has kept us from seeing what has been happening.

Nearly all societies at nearly all times have had a leisure class—a class of persons who were exempt from toil. In modern times and especially in the United States the leisure class, at least in any identifiable phenomenon, has disappeared. To be idle is no longer considered rewarding or even entirely respectable.

But we have barely noticed that the leisure class has been replaced by another and much larger class to which work has none of the older connotation of pain, fatigue, or other mental or physical discomfort. We have failed to appreciate the emergence of this New Class, as it may be simply called, largely as the result of one of the oldest and most effective obfuscations in the field of social science. This is the effort to assert that all work—physical, mental, artistic, or managerial—is essentially the same.

This effort to proclaim the grand homogeneity of work has commanded, for different reasons, the support of remarkably numerous and diverse groups. To economists it has seemed a harmless and, indeed, an indispensable simplification. It has enabled them to deal homogeneously with all of the different kinds of productive effort and to elaborate a general theory of wages applying to all who receive an income for services. Doubts have arisen from time to time, but they have been suppressed or considered to concern special cases. The identity of all classes of labor is one thing on which capitalist and communist doctrine wholly agree. The president of the corporation is pleased to think that his handsomely appointed office is the scene of the same kind of toil as the assembly line and that only the greater demands in talent and intensity justify his wage differential. The Communist officeholder cannot afford to have it supposed that his labor differs in any significant respect from that of the comrade at the lathe or on the collective farm with whom he is ideologically one. In both societies it serves the democratic conscience of the more favored groups to identify themselves with those who do hard physical labor. A lurking sense of guilt over a more pleasant, agreeable, and remunerative life can often be assuaged by the observation "I am a worker too" or, more audaciously, by the statement that "mental labor is far more taxing than physical labor." Since the man who does physical labor is intellectually disqualified from comparing his toil with that of the brainworker, the proposition is uniquely unassailable.

In fact the differences in what labor means to different people could not be greater. For some, and probably a majority, it remains a stint to be performed. It may be preferable, especially in the context of social attitudes toward production, to doing nothing. Nevertheless it is fatiguing or monotonous or, at a minimum, a source of no particular pleasure. The reward rests not in the task but in the pay.

For others work, as it continues to be called, is an entirely different matter. It is taken for granted that it will be enjoyable. If it is not, this is a source of deep dissatisfaction or frustration. No one regards it as remarkable that the advertising man, tycoon, poet, or professor who suddenly finds his work unrewarding should seek the counsel of a psychiatrist. One insults the business executive or the scientist by suggesting that his principal motivation in life is the pay he receives. Pay is not unimportant. Among other things it is a prime index of prestige. Prestige—the respect, regard, and esteem of others—is in turn one of the more important sources of satisfaction associated with this kind of work. But, in general, those who do this kind of work expect to contribute their best regardless of compensation. They would be disturbed by any suggestion to the contrary.

Such is the labor of the New Class. No aristocrat ever contemplated the loss of feudal privileges with more sorrow than a member of this class would regard his descent into ordinary labor where the reward was only the pay. In the years following World War II a certain number of grade school teachers left their posts for substantially higher paid factory work. The action made headlines because it represented an unprecedented desertion of an occupation which was assumed to confer the dignity of the New Class. The college professor, who is more securely a member of the New Class than the schoolteacher, would never contemplate such a change even as an exercise in eccentricity and no matter how inadequate he might consider his income.

In keeping with all past class behavior, the New Class seeks energetically to perpetuate itself. Offspring are not expected to plan their lives in order to make a large amount of money. (Those who go into business are something of an exception at least partly because income, in business, is uniquely an index of prestige.) But from their earliest years the children are carefully indoctrinated in the importance of finding an occupation from which they will derive satisfaction—one which will involve not toil but enjoyment. One of the principal sources of sorrow and frustration in the New Class is the son who fails to make the grade—who drops down into some tedious and unrewarding occupation. The individual who meets with this misfortune—the son of the surgeon who becomes a garage hand—is regarded by the community with pity not unmixed with horror. But the New Class has considerable protective powers. The son of the surgeon rarely does become a garage hand. However inadequate, he can usually manage to survive, perhaps somewhat exiguously, on the edge of his caste. And even if, as a salesman or an investment counselor, he finds little pleasure in his work, he will be expected to assert the contrary in order to affirm his membership in the New Class.

V

The New Class is not exclusive. While virtually no one leaves it, thousands join it every year. Overwhelmingly the qualification is education. Any individual whose adolescent situation is such that sufficient time and money is invested in his preparation, and who has at least the talents to carry him through the formal academic routine, can be a member. There is a hierarchy within the class. The son of the factory worker who becomes an electrical engineer is on the lower edge; his son who does graduate work and becomes a university physicist moves to the higher echelons; but opportunity for education is, in either case, the open sesame.

There can be little question that in the last hundred years, and even in the last few decades, the New Class has increased enormously in size. In early nineteenth century England or the United States, excluding the leisure class and considering the New Class as a group that lived on what it has carefully called earned income, it consisted only of a handful of educators and clerics, with, in addition, a trifling number of writers, journalists, and artists. In the United States of the eighteen-fifties it could not have numbered more than a few thousand individuals. Now the number whose primary identification is with their job, rather than the income it returns, is undoubtedly in the millions.

Some of the attractiveness of membership in the New Class, to be sure, derives from a vicarious feeling of superiority—another manifestation of class attitudes. However, membership in the class unquestionably has other and more important rewards. Exemption from manual toil; escape from boredom and confining and severe routine; the chance to spend one's life in clean and physically comfortable surroundings; and some opportunity for applying one's thoughts to the day's work, are regarded as unimportant only by those who take them completely for granted. For these reasons it has been possible to expand the New Class greatly without visibly reducing its attractiveness.

This being so, there is every reason to conclude that the further and rapid expansion of this class should be a major, and perhaps next to peaceful survival itself, *the* major social goal of the society. Since education is the operative factor in expanding the class, investment in education, assessed qualitatively as well as quantitatively, becomes very close to being the basic index of social progress. It enables people to realize a dominant aspiration. It is an internally consistent course of development.

Recent experience has shown that the demand for individuals in the occupations generally identified with the New Class increases much more proportionately with increased income and well-being. Were the expansion of the New Class a deliberate objective of the society this, with its emphasis on education and its ultimate effect on intellectual, literary, cultural, and artistic demands, would greatly broaden the opportunities for membership. At the same time the shrinking in the number of those who engage in work *qua* work is something to be regarded not alone with equanimity but with positive approval. For one of the inevitable outlets for the intellectual energies and inventiveness of the New Class will be in finding substitutes for routine and repetitive manual labor. To the extent that such labor is made scarce and more expensive, this tendency will, of course, be accelerated. To minimize the number of people doing such work is the counterpart of the goal of expanding the New Class.

It is a measure of how little we need worry about the danger from reducing the number of people engaged in work *qua* work that, as matters now stand, our concern is not that we will have too few available for toil but too many. We worry lest such technical advances as automation, an already realized dividend of the expansion of the New Class, will proceed so rapidly as to leave a surplus of those who still work. This, indeed, could be the greater danger.

VI

I venture to suggest that the unprofessional reader will find rather reasonable and rational the ideas here offered. Why should men struggle to maximize income when the price is many dull and dark hours of labor? Why especially should they do so as goods become more plentiful and less urgent? Why should they not seek instead to maximize the rewards of all the hours of their days? And since this is the plain and obvious aspiration of a great and growing number of the most perceptive people, why should it not be the central goal of the society? And now to complete the case, we have a design for progress. It is education or, more broadly, investment in human as distinct from material capital.

But in the more sophisticated levels of the conventional wisdom, including, regrettably, some professional economists, any such goal will seem exceedingly undesirable. The production of material goods, urgent or otherwise, is the accepted measure of our progress. Investment in material capital is our basic engine of progress.

Both this product and the means for increasing it are measurable and tangible. What is measurable is better. To talk of transferring increasing numbers of people from lives spent mostly in classical toil to lives which, for the most part, are spent pleasantly has less quantitative precision. Since investment in individuals, unlike investment in a blast furnace, provides a product that can be neither seen nor valued, it is inferior. And here the conventional wisdom unleashes its epithet of last resort. Since these achievements are not easily measured, as a goal they are "fuzzy." This is widely deemed to be a fatal condemnation. The precise, to be sure, is usually the old and familiar. Because it is old and familiar it has been defined and measured. Thus does insistence on precision become another of the tautological devices by which the conventional wisdom protects itself. Nor should one doubt its power.

Yet anyone who finds this analysis and these proposals sensible should not be entirely discouraged. We are here in one of the contexts where circumstance has marched far beyond the conventional wisdom. We have seen how general are the efforts to join the New Class and how rapid is its expansion. We are not here establishing a new economic and social goal but identifying one that is already widely if but tacitly accepted. In this situation the conventional wisdom cannot resist indefinitely. The economist of impeccable credentials in the conventional wisdom, who believes that there is no goal in life of comparable urgency with the maximization of total and individual real income, would never think of applying such a standard to himself. In his own life he is an exponent of all the aspirations of the New Class. He educates and indoctrinates his children with but one thing in mind. It is not that they should maximize their income. This is abhorrent. He wants above all that they will have an occupation that is interesting and rewarding. On this he hopes, indeed, that they will take their learned parent as their model.

59

Planning in the Welfare State

Gunnar Myrdal

In the last half century, the state, in all the rich countries in the Western world, has become a democratic "Welfare State," with fairly explicit commitments to the broad goals of economic development, full employment, equality of opportunity for the young, social security, and protected minimum standards as regards not only income, but nutrition, housing, health, and education for people of all regions and social groups. The Welfare State is nowhere, as yet, an accomplishment; it is continually in the process of coming into being. . . . In all countries, even in those where the building of the Welfare State is most advanced, the architects are continually laboring with the tasks of simplification, coordination, rationalization and achievement of efficiency. Indeed, this planning becomes pressing as the edifice of the Welfare State rises. . . .

The historical and casual order has been that acts of intervention in the play of market forces came first, and that planning then became a necessity. In a process of cumulative causation, the secular increase in the volume of intervention has been spurred on by the sequence of violent international crises since World War I, the increasing rationality of people's attitudes, the democratization of political power, and the growth of provincial and municipal self-government and of large-scale enterprises and interest organizations in all markets. Thus, as public and private intervention became more frequent and more far-reaching and closely related to the other constituents of this mighty process of social change, so there arose situations of growing complexity, contradiction, and confusion. With ever greater impact, the need for a rationalizing coordination of them all was pressed upon the state as the central organ for the public will.

Coordination leads to planning or, rather it *is* planning, as this term has come to be understood in the Western world. Coordination of measures of intervention implies a reconsideration of them all from the point of view of how they combine to serve the development goals of the entire national community, as these goals become determined by the political process that provides the basis for power. The need for this coordination arose because the individual acts of intervention, the total volume of which was growing, had not been considered in this way when they were initiated originally.

As the state is increasingly involved in coordinating and regulating the national economy, it becomes compelled to make short-term and long-term forecasts, and to try to modify its policies for commerce, finance, development, and social reform in the light of what these forecasts show. A very much improved basis of statistical and other information is also becoming available to the governments. This coordination of policies, and their continued modification in order to remain appropriate in the setting of factual trends revealed by the forecasts, does not take the shape of a rigid, all-embracing plan. Nevertheless, it constitutes a steadily developing approach to planning, which tends to become firmer and more embracing as present tendencies work themselves out.

As regards the activities of the big enterprises and the organizations in the infrastructure beneath the formal constitutional structure, it is, of course, clear at the outset that they were not from the beginning part of a rationally coordinated national plan. They regularly represented special interests, not the general and common interests of the nation. But, as a matter of fact, the lack of coordination is equally apparent in public policies as they were initially motivated and decided upon. The history of economic policies in every country, as regards, for instance, tariffs and taxes, gives abundant proof of this thesis.

There is further proof in the records of how the huge structures for primary and higher education and for public health were built up, and also in the big redistributional reforms, such as the social security schemes and other measures for the care of the sick, the disabled, the unemployed, the aged, and the children. All these complexes of economic and social intervention, as they now exist, have been the end product of a long process of piecemeal, gradually induced changes, which in the different fields have been pressed forward, at first as independent and unrelated policy measures, motivated on their own merits or undertaken in response to group pressures.

It is, for instance, remarkable that the social security schemes, which are becoming increasingly expensive, were initially supported only by arguments of social justice and welfare for specified groups of people in need; and such arguments remained predominant for a long time. When the opponents of these schemes, who argued all the time that they would ruin the economy of the country, were again and again proved wrong, this was largely the result of the effect of these reforms in raising the productivity of the mass of the people—an effect which had never played an important part in their motivation. As considerations of these wider effects and interrelations gradually come to the fore in public discussion, the explanation is mainly that these policy measures have by now become so numerous and important, and that they re-direct the distribution of such a very large portion of the national product, that they simply must be coordinated with one another, and with the development of the entire national economy. Thus we arrive at planning in the modern sense.

Public intervention in the field of housing and construction of new houses, affords another example. Since the scanty and diffuse beginnings of a few decades ago, it has been increasing tremendously in all Western countries. The state now finds itself responsible for influencing decisively—directly through its legislation and administration and that of the provincial and municipal authorities, or indirectly through the organizations in the infrastructure that operate under the state's indulgence and sanction—the conditions under which people can find houses to live in, and under which some people can make it a business to provide homes. This involved complex of intervention concerns the level of rents, the availability and price of building and mortgage credits, the conditions on the several labor markets and the markets for building materials, and, indeed, every aspect of the entire economic process by which houses are built, owned or rented, and inhabited. The future number and the age composition of families and other factors determining both human need and effective demand for housing, must be predicted and allowed for, as must the effects of building activity upon trends of general business activity, in the short and long run. The latter effects are so important that the level of building activity has to be watched carefully, even from the point of view of general economic policy. As the cities grow, and as more public investment becomes involved in preparing for such growth, town planning becomes ever more necessary, as does the general public preoccupation with planning and directing the location of industry.

In the same way, the rapid development of higher and professional education now absorbs so much money, and concerns so many young people in all these countries, that it is gradually becoming realized that this activity cannot continue as an independent process of dispersed public policies. Instead, it has to be planned carefully on the basis of calculations of future demand for, and supply of, labor trained in different ways. This necessarily involves a forecast and a plan for the whole national economy. Again, the converse also applies; no long-range forecast or plan for the national economy can any longer be made without including policies for education and training. . . .

In a sense, the biggest commitment to economic planning in the Welfare State of the Western countries is that they are all now pledged to preserving "full employment," though the definition, as well as the form, of the commitment varies. The political process by which governments have gradually reached this situation illuminates this trend towards planning.

Not many decades ago the periodic appearance of mass unemployment was accepted as a more or less natural consequence of necessary market adjustments to changing business conditions, about which not much could be done. As, however, the political power of the workers increased in the process of democratization, and as the social conscience became more alert to the sufferings of the unemployed and their families—two changes which, of course, are closely related—measures of financial aid to the unemployed were instituted in one country after another.

At first, these policy measures were all of a compensatory nature, aimed merely at providing the unemployed workers with some of the incomes they had lost by becoming unemployed. It was the symptom, not the cause, of unemployment that was being dealt with. Unemployment insurance, which now forms an integral part of the social security system in all Western countries, represents the consummation of this line of social policy. But soon the demand was raised that the state should take positive measures in order to create additional work opportunities for the unemployed. In the twenties, and still more during the Great Depression, public works policies spread in all Western countries. At the same time, the workers began to press for full wages even in these public works.

These developments represented only steps towards demanding that the state should so direct all its financial and economic policies as to create demand for labor sufficient to liquidate mass unemployment and to keep the national economy uninterruptedly in high gear. Economic theory now responded to the ideological needs of the time by placing the responsibility for economic depressions and unemployment on an imbalance between aggregate demand and supply, opening up a rational way for the state to raise investment and production and to create employment simply by raising its expenditure while keeping down taxation. . . .

After World War II we have all become accustomed to much bigger budgets and also to taking huge budget deficits less seriously. The expansionist theory of spending one's way out of a depression is now on the way to becoming orthodox, even in the more conservative sections of the business world. It has, as yet, not been put to much of a test, however, as first the urgent reconstruction needs and the pent-up demands immediately after the war, and later the immense armament expenditures and other financial consequences of the cold war, have contributed in mighty fashion to sustain total demand. Inflation and not deflation has been the continuous worry. But, whatever the explanation, it is in any case a fact that on the whole all the Western countries have enjoyed full employment, not only during but also after the war. . . . It is safe to predict that in none of the Western countries will a period of severe unemployment ever again be tolerated by the people.

In a sense, this determination to preserve full employment is the crowning accomplishment of the democratic Welfare State. It is generally understood and accepted that this implies a preparedness to use even radical policy measures, when needed, in order to keep the entire labor force employed, and also that this assumes a most careful watch on the entire economic development and a planned coordination of all economic policies.

60

The Unity of Work and Leisure

C. Wright Mills

During the course of a recent study, I came upon a man who was doing three things at once, or rather who was having three things done to him at once. With one eye and an ear, he looked at and listened to a baseball game on TV. With his other ear he listened to jump music on the radio beside his chair. With his other eye and both hands he thumbed a brightly colored magazine.

He was not drunk, although he was somewhat out of health by several years of overeating. He was not sick, although he did complain of worrying a good deal and, now that he had reached forty, of a vague bodily discomfort. He said that he was not tired, but still, on week ends, he was pretty much beat. He only worked eight hours a day, five days a week, but with the traffic and all it took him about an hour each way to and from work, which, after all, made 10 hours a day.

Then, too, his work was too petty to be interesting but too complex to be routine, and, although he had rather a good job, it had no personal significance to him whatsoever.

The year before he had bought a garden machine that did everything—and a truly huge amount of seed. But after the first season, the thing was hard to start and he had found out that it would not weed between the rows. Yes, he had a camera—didn't everyone?—but he had taken about everything there was to take around him, and when they had not come out like those in the picture magazines, even though his was a very expensive camera, he had become discouraged. His wife, he said, was playing bridge with the girls, in order, he said, smilingly, to get some relief from his being in the house all week end. Yes, she had tried to paint for a while, but she couldn't learn to draw and did not actually enjoy doing those abstractions.

Talking with this man, one could see that he was not unintelligent but that he was rather in a muddle about public affairs, snatching impatiently and haphazardly at the easy, emphatic conclusions. And as for his private life, one could see that although he was not aware of being unhappy, still the ground tone of his life experience was the state of sluggish distraction in which I had found him that Sunday afternoon.

I

I do not know if this man represents the Average Middle Class American, but I do suppose that his condition is less exceptional than that of the fortunate and talented people whom we have heard this afternoon describing what they and other Americans at leisure do. For most of our

Reprinted from *Power, Politics and People: The Collected Essays of C. Wright Mills,* by permission of Oxford University Press and the estate of C. Wright Mills.

speakers—in fact or as ideal—have two things in common which set them off as a tiny minority in the United States population: their leisure and their work form a unity. And they are capable of genuine individuality.

For such people, leisure does not exist as a special problem in separate realm. Their life-work is an independent sphere of self-cultivating action which requires and contains what others call leisure.

Apart from mere animal rest, the problem of leisure does not arise in a society or for an individual until work has been split from life. For if our work allows us to express our true interests and to facilitate their more skillful expression, then our leisure is not escape, or recuperation, or that tired frenzy by which we strive for the animated glee we call fun.

Today many people have to trivialize their true interests into "hobbies," which are socially considered as unserious pastimes rather than the center of their real existence. But only by a craftsmanlike style of life can the split domains of work and leisure become unified; and only by such self-cultivation can the everyday life become a medium for genuine culture. The deeper problems of leisure, and of the cultural content of leisure time, can be solved only when lesiure and work are easy companions rather than tense opposites.

II

The most significant fact about work and play in modern times is that as the hours organized by work have decreased, the remaining hours have been intensively organized for commercial purposes. As the machinery of production has destroyed work as independent, meaningful action, it has given many people more free time. But now the machinery of amusement is destroying the freedom of this time.

The mere chronological fact of more time on our hands is a necessary condition for the cultivation of individuality, but by no means guarantees it. As people have more time on their hands, most of it is taken away from them by the debilitating quality of their work, by the pace of their everyday routine, and by the ever-present media of mass distraction.

The mass production of distraction is now as much a part of the American way of life as the mass production of automobiles. In fact, the values that make up this way of life are more and more the values of an ethic of leisure. For, as work declines in meaning and gives no inner direction or center, leisure becomes the end of life itself, and the leisure ethic swallows up all values, including those of work.

III

The most important questions to ask of any sphere of society are: What kinds of men and women does it tend to create? What personal styles of life does it inculcate and reinforce?

When we ask these questions seriously we have to answer: Of course there is a minority that uses leisure for self-cultivation. I do not know whether that minority is getting smaller, standing still, or becoming larger. But the deeper point perhaps is that genuine self-cultivation—like genuine art—tends to be cut off from the major routines of American life. It is not a part of the average texture of everyday life in America.

When it does occur it is among a fortunate minority or it is an episode. And this minority is not counted among those whom we celebrate.

Those we celebrate are the jabbering, aimless, lightwitted heroes of popular culture. Here are the cheerful illiterates at whose easy, empty chatter we chuckle. Here are the taut, mammary girls we so loudly admire as images of the female. Here are the athletes who have broken really important statistical records.

These personnel of the machinery of amusement are character-forming influences of the first order. By their pervasive distribution among the young, and by the absence of alternatives, such homey clowns, erotic ladies and statistical athletes become the models of the adolescent's world of leisure. Where in America today can those who are coming into new leisure-time look for models of self-cultivation rather than of distraction and mere pastime?

IV

All the ugly clamor of the radio, which has now been visualized on television, has become so much a part of the texture of our daily life that we do not truly experience it any more. It is good that we do not, else we should all become blathering idiots. But for this protection we pay a price: we become blasé. Our eyes and ears and feelings and imaginations withdraw in panic lest they be shattered. And this happens to us so early that we do not know that it is happening. By our trained inattention, we thus blunt our capacity for liberating experience as we block off those experiences that would stultify us.

But what leisure—genuine leisure—ought to do is relax our attention so that we come to know better our true selves and our capacities for creative experience. Beyond animal rest, which is both necessary and for many today quite difficult to get, genuine leisure allows and encourages our development of greater and truer individuality. Leisure ought to be what work ought to be, and what neither of them usually is: a sphere of independent action.

But more than that: genuine leisure, especially today, requires periods of genuine privacy. For without privacy, there is no chance to discover, to create, and to reinforce our individuality. And it is the lack of privacy—one must say, the fear of privacy—which places most of our nonworking time at the disposal of these forces of modern society that would stereotype our tastes and lower the level of our enjoyment.

V

We ought to judge the quality and level of our personal culture by the best that has been achieved anywhere and any time, and we ought to go further than that: with our material equipment, and the more ample time it might make available, we ought to project our ideals even higher than the best mankind has ever achieved. Were we to do this, seriously and imaginatively, we would see that our choice is between genuine leisure, which enlarges the feeling and reason, and spurious leisure, which blunts the very capacity for truly personal experience.

The first thing to be said about this choice is that most Americans never get to make it. They have grown up in a leisure pattern of distraction and sloth, and they do not really know the world of self-cultivation.

The second thing to be said is that this is not due to any inherent mediocrity of taste and capacity on their part.

There is, of course, a widespread idea, often and carefully repeated, that on the market for leisure, the consumers determine the products, that people get childish fare because that is what they really want. We should not be misled by this naive and mistaken "democracy of taste," in the name of which merchants of amusement reinforce the prevailing low levels of experience in America. What a man does with his leisure is determined by the leisure experiences that are most readily available to him, and by his sensibilities and tastes. But what has happened is this:

As the hours of nonwork have increased, the mass means of communication and entertainment have trained the sensibilities and tastes of a generation or more of Americans. For levels of sensibility are, in fact, largely acquired, by atmosphere and by training.

Moreover, these means of entertainment have become so continuously and so unavoidably available that the effort involved to cultivate and to gratify individual tastes is simply too great to be widely expected. In order really to allow a choice between genuine leisure and the spurious leisure that now prevails, the commercial producers who now hold the field would at least temporarily have to be put out of business.

VI

It has not been my purpose this afternoon to give angry, confident answers to the so-called problems of leisure in America. For surely, in our situation, it is more fruitful to ask the right questions than to provide the half answers now available to us.

What I have asked is whether, properly conceived, there is any special problem of leisure?

For is not any life worth living as life in which both work and leisure are but phases of one meaningful whole, a life which is largely composed of truly independent domains of experience, a life in which the mass means of distraction are not felt to be necessary?

The so-called problem of leisure, in short, is the problem of how we can heighten the qualities of experience in all areas of American life to such an extent that there will be no problem of leisure.

SECTION D *Perspectives on Management*

Two great institutions override our culture. One is education, the other is business. In the preceding section, John K. Galbraith suggested that it is part of the morality of the "New Class" to teach their children not to go into business. Oddly enough, this has not been what is occurring. Rather business has gone into fields coveted by the members of the "New Class." Social organizations, charitable trusts, educational ventures, and a host of other enterprises are run as if they were large corporations. Government service, which is often referred to as public service, repeatedly utilizes the ideas and techniques of large corporate enterprise.

Business is full of people trying to understand and motivate other people to do a good job and thereby have a full and meaningful daily existence. The three selections in this section look at different phases of this aspect of business. Edmund P. Learned's article describes simple situations and suggests simple solutions. Notice that the real problems are all interpersonal, none deal with business as business. Learned suggests that participative management—decisions arising from within the group—is more productive in many cases than rules applied from the top. This is the case *even* when those on the top have more information and skill.

Maier and Zerfoss present simulations of role-playing in business that are involving, easy to play, and easy to understand. Theirs is the kind of research that actually benefits the experimental subject.

The third selection shakes up traditional ideas on profit and loss, balance sheets, and the like. Abraham Maslow suggests that this area needs to be recast to fit a healthy society. It is part of the problem of industry to integrate itself into a fully meaningful life instead of being that part of life in which one performs "work" (something unpleasant) in order to have leisure (something pleasant).

61

Problems of a New Business Executive

Edmund P. Learned

The arrival of a new executive in an established organization is usually an event of considerable importance—both to the man appointed and to the company he joins. What is the impact upon the administrative relationships already existing? How can the outsider find his place and become fully effective in the executive structure? How should he conduct himself to achieve that end? And how far should he be helped by his superiors or others to make his adjustment to the new situation?

These are questions that deserve answers. They represent problems which not only occur frequently in business but are vastly more important in their total impact upon an organization than the frequency of their occurrence would indicate. They afford subtle, yet very real, tests of executive skill, both for the new man and for the organization which he joins.

To a large extent the answers to these questions depend on still more fundamental questions as to the executive attitudes and assumptions which characterize the existing administration of the company or which the newcomer brings with him. The attitudes administrators reveal in their day-to-day work and the assumptions administrators make or appear to make regarding people and events always have much to do with the effectiveness, efficiency, and morale of the organization. Indeed, there is some evidence that they are often controlling. In the circumstances surrounding the introduction of a new executive they are particularly likely to be critical.

The purpose of this article, however, is not to come to complete and generalized conclusions about the problems of a new executive. Rather, it is to look at some specific business situations that have raised questions along this line, *primarily for the sake of the questions themselves.* If we find some clues to workable suggestions in the process, so much the better.

The situations or "cases" which we shall consider are three in number. (All three cases are disguised to protect sources; all names are fictitious, and dates have been shifted slightly, but the situations themselves are maintained.) The first case, drawn from the Dashman Company, follows upon the introduction of a new central vice president in charge of purchasing into a large manufacturing company characterized by decentralization of management functions. The other two cases are from the Dixie Company—a manufacturer of electrical equipment largely dependent for its success upon the work of specialists in electronics, electrical engineering, and pure

Reprinted from the *Harvard Business Review*, July-August 1966. By permission of the Publishers.

The original article was printed in the Harvard Business Review in May 1949. It was reprinted in 1966 with the section "Retrospective Comments" added to the article.

physics—one centering on the problems a new product-development manager faces as he seeks acceptance by the top management team of which he is supposed to be a member and by the other departments with which he has to work, and the other describing the behavior of a new chief engineer who must organize a new department and make it useful.

Inasmuch as the purpose and the content of this article may differ somewhat from the usual pattern, several explanatory remarks are in order before we proceed to the substance of the individual cases and to the detailed questions they raise. First of all, the use of cases is not a device whereby I try to inflict *my* answers on you. Nor are the cases merely examples of occurrences which illustrate some point I want to talk about. Rather, they are facts such as almost anyone in a business organization observes firsthand. I hope the article will be a fact-exploring adventure which you and I can share together.

Fact exploring of this kind can be exciting, and I only ask that together we try to observe the reactions and interactions of the people and events unfolded in the three cases, and note the values attached by different participants to the behavior of other people in the situations. I sincerely urge you to reach your own conclusions about the meaning of the events described, and to accept or discard—as you please—such tentative interpretations as I make.

Because an article of this sort cannot reproduce the whole case, it is possible that my selection of data, despite care to make it a fair representation, may prejudice your conclusions. But in any event it is not our purpose to judge a man's total capacity on so limited a sample of his executive behavior as is revealed in these cases. We are more interested in grasping the significance of his behavior and attitudes for his organization and in gauging their effect on the people concerned. The hope is that our discussion of the facts will contribute to an understanding of people in organizations and suggest measures for minimizing the frictions which inevitably occur among people who have a job to do together.

Dashman Company

The Dashman Company was a large manufacturer of many types of equipment for the armed forces of the United States. The purchasing procedures of its 20 plants—all located in the Middle West—had never been completely coordinated. The head office of the company, in fact, had encouraged each of the plant managers to operate with his staff as an independent unit in most matters. Late in 1940, when it began to appear that the company would face increasing difficulty in securing certain essential raw materials, Mr. Manson, the company's president, appointed an experienced purchasing executive, a Mr. Post, to assume a new vice presidency in charge of purchasing.

One of Post's first decisions was to begin the immediate centralization of the company's purchasing procedures. He decided that he would require each of the executives who handled purchasing in the individual plants to clear all purchase contracts in excess of $10,000 with his office. He felt that if the head office was to accomplish coordination helpful to each plant and to the whole company, he should be notified that the contracts were being prepared at least a week before they were to be signed. He talked his proposal over with the president, who presented it to the board of directors. The board approved the plan.

Although the company made purchases throughout the year, the beginning of its peak buying season was only three weeks away at the time this new plan was adopted. Post prepared a letter to be sent to the 20 purchasing executives of the company. The letter follows:

Dear ________:

The board of directors of our company has recently authorized a change in our purchasing procedures. Hereafter, each of the purchasing executives in the several plants of the company will notify the vice president in charge of purchasing of all contracts in excess of $10,000 which they are negotiating at least a week in advance of the date on which they are to be signed.

I am sure you will understand that this step is necessary to coordinate the purchasing requirements of the company in these times when we are facing increasing difficulty in securing essential supplies. This procedure should give us in the central office the information we need to see that each plant secures the optimum supply of materials. In this way the interests of each plant and of the company as a whole will best be served.

Yours very truly,

Post showed the letter to an assistant and invited his comments. The assistant suggested that since Post had not met more than a few of the purchasing executives, he might like to visit all of them and take the matter up with each of them personally. Post dismissed the idea at once because, as he said, he had so many things to do at the head office that he could not get away for a trip. Consequently, he had the letters sent out over his signature.

During the two following weeks replies came in from all except a few plants. Although several executives wrote at greater length, the following reply was typical:

Dear Mr. Post:

Your recent communication in regard to notifying the head office a week in advance of our intention to sign contracts has been received. This suggestion seems a most practical one. We want to assure you that you can count on our cooperation.

Yours very truly,

During the next six weeks the head office received no notices from any plant that contracts were being negotiated. Executives in other departments who made frequent trips to the plants reported that the plants were busy and the usual routines for that time of year were being followed.

Looking behind the formal acquiescence of the plants, can you see difficulty in the plant managers' accepting Post's move as a part of the standing company policy? Had they expressed a need for centralization of purchasing procedures? Did they realize that such a need existed? Did such a need in fact exist? Or why did Post receive formal replies which were never followed up by the kind of action he wanted? Was this request ignored merely because of the imminence of the peak buying season?

The attitude of the plant managers seems significant. The very simple decision to rearrange procurement procedures and policies in order to make ready for a special war emergency in plenty of time may have been the act of a forward-looking president, but it may also have been a bombshell for his organization. The plants were the doers, and they were relatively autonomous. Suddenly one of the bastions of their independence—the freedom to act independently in purchasing—came under attack from the home office. Without prior consultation the home office assumed the responsibility for policy and operation in this area. The plant managers may have been uncertain about what their future relationship to their own purchasing agents was to be. The plants had experienced no need for the new position. If any of them had been stymied in their jobs and had already been brought face-to-face with the need for help in the higher echelon of management, they surely would have welcomed the chance occasioned by the letter to lay their problems before Post. They presented nothing to him.

What about Post's assumptions? He may have assumed that the president and the board understood his purchasing problems when they approved his plan. Perhaps they did not. He may have thought that the approval of his plan by the board gave him effective authority to put it through, that a statement of that authority would result in obedience. Apparently, he further assumed that the interest of each plant would be the same as the interest of the company as a whole. He did not seem disturbed by the possibility that a one-way communication in a letter at this stage of acquaintance with the organization might not be so good as a two-way communication made possible by a personal conference. He underestimated the task of getting started. He sent out instructions with a minimum of explanation.

In replying to his assistant's suggestion that he go into the field, Post assumed—if we may presume to put it in words for him —that "what I think is important actually *is* important." Is this an attitude of arrogance, or is it solely an indication that he had many things to do? Whatever the answer, the effect on the receiving end of the communication is fairly clear.

Post may have assumed also that a major break in the continuity of the decentralization policy would be understood correctly by plant managers without explanation. No matter what Post's assumptions were, a serious breakdown of communication occurred in the actual situation. The plant managers and the plant purchasing agents had, as a whole, not indicated actual acceptance of any of the functions which Post, with the concurrence of his superiors, had laid down for himself.

Examination of Post's actions presents additional assumptions that may have prompted his ineffectual behavior and reveals certain of his underlying attitudes. This list may be unkind and perhaps unfair, but it is suggestive of some of the reasons he did not get better results.

Post behaved as if he thought he knew what the purchasing problems of this company were and would be. He did not ask for the opinions of experienced subordinates who had been in full charge of the purchasing function in their respective plants. Post assumed that he had the right answers for these problems, that a dollar dragnet would bring them to his attention for solution, and that his new subordinates in the plant had nothing to contribute either to the statement of problems or to their solutions. *In other words, he thought he needed no help.*

Furthermore, Post acted as if he believed that subordinates would accept his authority and follow his instructions; that purchasing agents and plant managers would have the same conception of Post's job that Post had; that a week's warning on contracts of $10,000 or more was enough notice to make him useful to the purchasing agents. Or Post may have assumed that all purchasing agents worthy of their hire would know that a week's notice was only a way of getting background information to the new boss: that they would immediately supply the information in order to help the new executive.

This type of behavior reveals an attitude of self-importance and a failure on Post's part to recognize that men of top stature and responsibility have pride in their work and want an opportunity to show their capacity in the company. It also demonstrates his complete lack of comprehension of the major change in policy involved in the new relationships.

Dixie Company I

Starting years ago as a small business, the Dixie Company had prospered because of the reliability and dependability of its products. The management had grown up with the company. The corporation, ably supported by its own director of research, had benefited by the technical revolution. Like its competitors, the company had grown rapidly during the 1930's and spurted ahead during the war period.

The top management organization consisted of Mr. Eaton, the president; the vice president in charge of sales; the vice president in charge of production; and the treasurer, who also was a vice president. The rapid growth in business had increased the burden of coordinating the major departments. The top officials were unable to initiate and follow up all the necessary research on market potentials, manufacturing costs, or margins involved in appraising fully the desirability of adding a new item to the company lines. Nor could they devote the requisite time and energy to the multitude of administrative details involved in expediting a product through all steps of experimental design, fullscale production and promotion, up to the time when the product could be considered firmly established in the company's manufacturing and marketing departments.

Product development at Dixie was complicated by continuous pressure from the sales department to gain an initial competitive advantage by being the first to make a new item available. This eagerness was countered by the cautious insistence of the research staff that a thorough, time-consuming experimental job be completed first. To resolve such conflicts and to deal with all the related problems the management decided to establish a new "product development" department.

To head the new department the Dixie top management chose a highly successful line executive from a company in another industry, Mr. Gardner by name, who had extensive experience in market research, sales promotion, and product development. Gardner's department was to report to the president, and was to carry the responsibility for coordinating the development of products. But Gardner was not made a vice president of the company.

In his initial interview, the president explained Gardner's duties to him as follows:

> Your principal function will be to coordinate and expedite all the phases of the business related to these new products. When a product proposal gets to the point of putting money into plant facilities, we of the Management Committee want to turn to you for a balanced appraisal from a top management point of view regarding the project. It is not your job to originate projects, but to study them on our behalf from the standpoint of scientific basis, stages of experimental development, end uses, market surveys, competition, plant investment, profit margins, and the like. You will be coordinating the work of the staff and line departments on product developments until a project is approved. After a product is authorized, you will expedite its development, manufacture, and sale until it is going commercially.
>
> Your activities will cut across the work of all departments, but you will not absorb their responsibilities. You will take authority and responsibility on behalf of the top management for getting a project through. You will examine the basic problems, fix responsibility for their solution or for recommendations, coordinate the work of all agencies, and do this without upsetting the organization. Your work may be resented by some who fail to see at first the function you are performing and feel that you are encroaching on their responsibilities, but we'll solve those difficulties when we come to them.

The new product development manager needed to reflect upon the president's directive. In order to assess his assumptions and attitudes we too should try to interpret Eaton's directive. What does the job involve? What does Eaton mean by "coordinate," "expedite," "appraisal from a top management point of view," "not your job to originate or . . . absorb . . . responsibilities [of other departments]"? What does he mean by: "You will take authority and responsibility on behalf of the top management for getting a project through. You will examine the basic problems, fix responsibility for their solution or for recommendations, coordinate the work of all agencies, and do this without upsetting the organization"?

The new job is obviously a tough one, requiring the highest degree of administrative, as opposed to technical, skill. If administration is primarily the process of getting work done through the integration of many hands, then Gardner's mission is primarily administrative. He must fit together the work of others with respect to policies, products, facilities, procedures, investments, inventories, training, and devise schedules so paced that profitable products are manufactured to meet present and potential market demands.

Questions which Gardner might have asked himself when he undertook this particular assignment are: Do members of the top management committee have a common understanding about the functions of the new department? How will I find out? Do I make product policy or preside over its making? With whom will I work, and on what? How many of the vice presidents and department heads are informed about the purpose of the new department and its relationship to their duties? How can they contribute to the success of the company's program? How can I fit together the work of others without doing the original work?

Note that Gardner was instructed by the president only in general terms. He was left to make his own way over uncharted territory in which many conflicts would have to be brought into balance with or without the consent of the department heads accustomed to operating without a product development department. When numerous people have overlapping interests in a project, different opinions among them may retard cooperation. The depth of feeling and the extent of departmental loyalty may make resolution of conflicts difficult.

Another danger which Gardner had to guard against was his own background as a line executive. He was accustomed to making final decisions. It is not easy for a man to shift from a position of authority for making policies into a pattern of leading a group to joint recommendations or decisions. Gardner could find it difficult to refrain from giving orders to the expert heads of departments who knew more about their own jobs than he did. When such department heads desire to make their contributions to the company their own way, and when seniority has given them ideas about their importance and status in the company, a newcomer is likely to have trouble if he does not give weight to their points of view. As a former line executive now leading a group, Gardner might well be required to equip himself with a new set of administrative practices made appropriate by the combination of logic and sentiment in the new situation.

Let us examine some of Gardner's first moves. He began at once to organize and staff his own department. Making use of the company's organization manual department, he prepared a complete list of his functions for publication in the manual. Without ado he announced by this means that he would, among other things, *correlate and direct* all matters related to the establishment of new products by the company, *survey and analyze* sales possibilities and *determine* sales potentials, make *initial sales* of new products before relinquishing them to the sales department, *steer* new products through the company, and *integrate* the efforts of all company departments concerned with new products. Gardner decided, furthermore, that it was desirable to work out product policies for classes of products before taking up any product within a class.

During the months devoted to these activities, other departments complained to top management that Gardner had taken action without clearing it with them. Gardner himself believed that he could not make progress in his job until a fully detailed list of procedures—equivalent to the functions already published—could be worked out and put into force by the management. Six months after his appointment he had by no means achieved companywide acceptance of himself and his department, and the development of new products was no more under control than before.

Did Gardner's first moves contribute to his lack of success? The forthright phrasing of his departmental functions in the organization manual prior to much actual work on specific projects with other departments could easily have led to misunderstandings which might not always be stated. The phrase "*correlate and direct* . . . the establishment of new products" could easily cause a loyal subordinate of the production or sales vice president to say: "The new guy thinks he's the whole cheese. My boss made this company. We got along before he arrived, and we can get along after he leaves. We'll see how far he gets in *directing*."

Some of Gardner's other phrases could well have raised departmental eyebrows. "Determining sales potential" could properly be a function of the marketing department rather than the work of a coordinator. Gardner may have ignored existing routines in the organization and the ambitions of people in various departments.

Gardner made no genuine effort to obtain the assistance of other major department heads in formulating the list of functions for the new department. He was unaware that these other department heads might consider the new department as overlapping their activities. These departments had been "in business" many, many years; they had established routines of doing work; and in all probability the senior heads of these departments expected the newcomer to seek their advice and cooperation. Gardner made no effort to understand the activities of these departments and their relationship to his office but, instead, worked relatively alone in listing his own department's functions. He may have made trouble without knowing it and created resistance to what others felt as usurpation when that was not intended.

Why, we may ask, did Gardner insist on formulating policies before handling particular cases cooperatively with other departments? Will a general policy determine the best way to handle an individual product, or should the "best" way to handle particular products eventually build up a general policy? Should one work from the abstract policy to the detailed application, or should one experiment with specific cases in order to formulate a broad, overall policy? Gardner followed his own logic to the limit and thereby disturbed other executives who were devoted to their particular logics and routine patterns of doing things. His adherence to his own views on procedures and on methods of getting things done left him essentially helpless. His pet ideas of administration did him no good.

Gardner's attitudes toward other people were a genuine handicap. He conveyed a sense of authority and position and did not reveal an attitude of humility which inspires cooperation. His *early* quest for authoritative policies, procedures, and clear definitions of functions, though easy to understand, may not be well founded in experience. The attitude which he took toward his fellow executives seems to have had a very substantial bearing on their reaction to him and on their willingness to cooperate wholeheartedly in determining and carrying out company policy with respect to coordination of product developments.

Dixie Company II

Contrasting assumptions and attitudes were held by a new chief engineer in the Dixie Company. His approach was quite different from that of Gardner. These differences reveal the significance of assumptions and attitudes to management accomplishments.

As a result of the growth of the company, the management decided to enlarge and reorganize its engineering activities. The new chief engineer, a Mr. Kirkland, had to merge the electrical engineers, formerly responsible to the director of research, with four other engineering departments, which previously had reported individually to the vice president in charge of production. These four were the industrial engineering group, the mechanical engineers, the construction engineers, and the maintenance engineers. One man had headed two of these departments. Two more men had headed the other two. All three men and their organizations were assigned to the new chief engineer. The problem was further complicated by the fact that the electrical engineers had not wanted to join the department; their transfer had also been opposed by the director of research. Each engineering group was impressed by its contribution to the company, but the electrical engineers plainly regarded themselves as the élite.

When Kirkland was employed as chief engineer, the president gave him very broad, general instructions. He was to avoid duplication of effort, to improve the previous lack of coordination and poor allocation of work. Eaton said, "We want to accomplish changes by evolution rather than by revolution. We can't be sure of each step toward our ultimate goal, and to freeze a procedure or policy before it is seasoned would be bad business."

What is the significance of the president's behavior in assigning both Gardner and Kirkland to their jobs with high-level blessings but general and possibly vague directives? Was Eaton deliberately requiring his new executives to demonstrate their mettle by undertaking themselves the concrete definition of their responsibilities and obtaining acceptance thereto from their working colleagues?

Whatever the president's design in giving both Gardner and Kirkland broad areas of responsibility, his behavior in doing so is not at all unusual. Its consequence, at least for these two new men, was a freedom from the handicap of specific instructions which might have prejudiced their developing sound working relationships in the process of solving the problems which would soon come into their purview. However, a company may run a very considerable risk that the new men will not make smooth adjustments to the organization. True, as a hard-boiled way of developing executives the method used by the president may be wholly satisfactory. The man who can make the adjustment himself is likely to be better than the one who needs assistance. On the other hand, such tactics can lead to serious disruption of activities and much frustration on the part of all executives involved in cooperative work and adjustment.

With the stated purpose of creating a competent organization, the chief engineer physically consolidated all the engineering functions. The newly merged departments moved into a new building. Minor problems of adjustment to the new space setup appeared at once. The head of the industrial engineering group, whom Kirkland placed in charge of laying out the new offices, planned to avoid the use of cubicles for individual engineers. Although the use of glassed-in space was common in other company office buildings, he thought it a waste of limited room and, in addition, believed that more work could be accomplished in the engineering group without such obstacles to informal communication.

The electrical engineers had enjoyed unusually good office space in the research building; the loss of those physical comforts had been one of their objections to the consolidation of the engineering departments. After a discussion of several weeks and in spite of his inability to give enclosed offices to other engineers, the head of the industrial engineers gave the electrical engineers the office arrangements they desired. Kirkland did not question or overrule this decision.

Do you agree with the apparent assumption of Kirkland that physical consolidation would encourage interaction among the engineering groups? What is the hazard implicit in deferring to the electrical engineers' assumed superiority and tacitly allowing them to acquire offices denied to the other engineers? Was the head of the industrial engineers astute in his decision to recognize the sentiments of the electrical engineers and give them enclosed space, or insensitive to the impact of this decision on the other engineering groups? What steps should Kirkland have taken to minimize this impact?

Kirkland set out to complete unification by developing and promoting departmental and professional pride, by establishing yardsticks for appraisal of results, by providing incentives for outstanding work, and by personally and forcefully presenting the point of view of the combined engineering groups in all top management discussions which involved engineering functions. He held numerous dinner meetings at a downtown hotel, at which all engineering employees were present, and he discussed departmental engineering issues with the groups at this time. He made daily effort to become acquainted with all the engineers, with the plant and its procedures, with the key men in the research department and in the factory; and he dealt personally with situations which caused confusion and conflict.

What is the significance of these various moves by Kirkland? How are they different from Gardner's? Was Kirkland proceeding on the assumption that his job was to lead, not to direct, to review suggestions and not necessarily originate them, and to bring about a meeting of minds both within and without the department? He seems to have assumed that his subordinates were technically capable of contributing to the company and that his job was primarily to give them a chance to do so. If a defect in the organization temporarily prevented them from so contributing, it was their joint task to find a way to break the jam. Perhaps he assumed, as well, that his men wanted as much as he to be productive and efficient. He gave individuals opportunities for personal development and recognition and enabled them to preserve their individuality while working within a group.

Kirkland arranged frequent joint conferences with his four subordinate engineering heads. He discussed the problems that arose in their work, and together the men reviewed the areas in which inefficiency and disagreement had arisen in the past. They attempted to formulate the best procedures to follow in the future. He took all four men completely into his confidence with respect to departmental problems and proved himself receptive to the ideas and opinions of other engineers. Outside the department he followed up faithfully the decisions reached in departmental conferences. He required his group leaders to help clarify the interrelationships between the engineering groups. He made it clear that the achievement of all the engineers would be recognized and made the basis for promotion, and he tried to get to know the engineers personally.

Kirkland seems to have assumed that collaborative effort on statements of policy and procedure would yield better results than individually conceived directives of the chief. He betrayed a genuine humility in the presence of his subordinates, and he showed a willingness to listen to and accept their contributions toward the objectives of the group. Perhaps he knew the effect on morale of such an attitude. He seems to have been aware that genuine interest by supervisors in subordinates has a positive effect on the individual and on the organization.

In addition to the problem of merging the engineering groups, Kirkland faced immediately the need for proper division of responsibilities for experimental production among the engineering, production, and research departments. There had long been a question in the company regarding the responsibility for experimental production. When should the production department and the engineering group take over from the research department? Kirkland and the director of research spent a considerable time together in the experimental laboratory and factory discussing ways and means of translating new products into full-scale factory production. When a specific issue arose in a day's work, the subordinate engineers and the subordinate research physicists brought it to the joint attention of the two chiefs who, if possible, tried to formulate a plan from the one event that might be applicable to future situations. Both men realized that the research group had the assigned responsibility of development until products were being smoothly produced in the factory and that the engineering groups were obligated to furnish services required by the research men in carrying out their jobs.

Conflicts between engineering and research could easily have arisen from differences in the backgrounds and basic interests of the groups concerned. Instead of trying, as Gardner did, to resolve the differences in advance in terms of abstract policies and to mark out clearly defined areas for each department, Kirkland and the director of research built from particular situations toward general rules. The two men focused their attention on getting particular jobs done, allowing the problem being solved to determine the specific responsibilities and rules for each group. The two men worked perhaps on the assumption that by solving together particular difficulties their groups might better understand the place that each deserved in the whole. Thus, final lists of functions and responsibilities growing out of this type of relationship could be based on experience rather than theory.

* * *

We have been exploring the actions of three new executives, all presumably intelligent men. Many questions have come to mind, which perhaps have seemed quite obvious. But they apparently were not uniformly asked by the men concerned. We, as readers, have had the advantage of simplification and objectivity. That is why it can do no harm, and why rather it may be of much help, to become conscious of the kind of questions which need to be asked in these or similar circumstances. Once he is conscious of the problems involved, and of their significant relation to underlying attitudes and assumptions, the intelligent executive is far on his way to achieving desirable solutions.

It is in the same spirit that the following questions, by this time also quite obvious, are made explicit by way of conclusion:

Can there be any doubt in your mind that Kirkland is a more successful executive than either Gardner or Post? What do you think is the basis of his success? Is it the difference in the assumptions he makes regarding other people? Is it a difference in the attitude which he takes throughout—in speaking, in writing, and in behavior?

Does it seem desirable to take an interest in other people or groups with whom one must work? Is it wise to take account of their status in the organization and of their attitudes toward oneself and toward each other? Does it seem important to consider the assumptions upon which they appear to be working, as well as to consider one's own?

Does the comparative study of these cases give *you* any clues as to how executives, department heads, or staff groups like to be treated? Do these accounts of others' experiences give you any insight into the ways of developing cooperative efforts between people and departments?

RETROSPECTIVE COMMENTARY

Any claim which "Problems of a New Executive" may have to be regarded as a classic is surely based on the universality of the case situations it presents and on the enduring significance of the issues and concepts it poses.

Drawn mainly from three cases developed for a then relatively new course, Administrative Practices (sometimes known as Human Relations), the article also includes a number of specific questions. The latter are all derived from questions raised or observations made in class by the mature and experienced executives who had studied and discussed these cases as participants in several Harvard Business School Advanced Management Programs.

Universality

Certainly, at the time this article was originally prepared from these materials, the universality of the three situations it describes was amply demonstrated. Nearly every man in the class, whether he had been a "new" executive anywhere or not, had personally shared in experiences akin to those described in these three cases.

Thus, whether they were on the giving or the receiving end, many individuals—like

Post in the Dashman case—had seen instructions for change followed by acquiescence only at the lip-service level, or one-way written communication resulting in inaction or misunderstanding. They had watched as a deaf ear was turned to the adviser who might suggest that an executive act only after exchanging ideas with the people on whom he would have to rely to implement his plans. They had heard the plea of urgency advanced for going full-steam ahead on undiscussed proposals, and they had seen experts thinking only in terms of their particular specialties, with little or no understanding of how their plans might look from the vantage point of others.

Or, like Gardner in Dixie I, many individuals had at some time been given very general job assignments, the details of which the men were left to fill in for themselves. Some had been plunged into new situations, with no briefing on relevant company history and no introduction to the personalities and personal values that might be involved. Many had experienced difficulties in moving from a line to a staff position, or from an operating assignment to one where activities were mainly planning and/or working with and through other people.

Some of these mature executive-students could also recall executive behavior like that of Kirkland in Dixie II. They had seen complex problems attacked on a joint-effort basis, where a leader, without abdicating, had shown himself responsive to spokesmen for subgroups seeking to protect values to which they attached deep meaning.

This list of archetypal situations in one or another of these three cases might be indefinitely extended, but the point to be emphasized here is the *intensity* of response to the cases on the part of executives themselves, both in the classroom and as readers of the HBR article. Indeed, it is only after executives have empathetically explored the many parallels stored in their own personal experiences that they become ready and willing to turn to the complex issues and concepts raised by these three cases themselves.

Were the same cases to be analyzed today, I believe their universality would be found to have withstood the test of time. Assuredly, there would be some difference. Thanks in part to the widespread training in human relations, not only in the classroom and the laboratory, but also through publications such as HBR, there are probably relatively few high-ranking executives today who would fall as innocently into error as did Post and Gardner. Hopefully, many more participants' recollections might involve leadership like Kirkland's. But I have no doubts that these classic cases would still evoke strong identification from readers with one or another of the acting or acted-on figures in the episodes described. (This point is one to which I shall return following the case, in some comments on the efficacy of cases as a means of teaching concepts in human relations.)

Significance

As previously stated, many significant issues and concepts are embodied in these three cases, including:

- Whether authority inheres in the position, or whether it has to be won and how.
- The relative efficacy of one-way, two-way man-to-man, or group communication.
- Resistance to change, and techniques by which it may be lessened.
- The role of the change agent.
- Specialization and the extent to which it may impose blinkers on understanding.
- Competence in technical and in human matters and the circumstances under which one or the other seems most essential.
- An autocratic versus a participative style of leadership.

These are but a few of the issues suggested by these cases. They are issues on which every executive will have many occasions to ponder as he rises or grows in stature.

To complete this list of issues and concepts, or to discuss all those already mentioned, is clearly beyond the scope of this note. Space can, however, be spared for discussing one or two of these ideas, and I would like to comment briefly on the role of the change agent and on participative leadership.

Change Agent. At least one individual in these cases exemplifies the role of the change agent—that is, one who facilitates rather than actually effects the introduction of change. The best example is the unnamed assistant to Post, who suggests that the latter consult with other managers before sending out his directive on wartime purchasing procedures. When Post dismisses this idea on grounds of time involved, the assistant is reported as making no reply. Thus, although the insight of the agent is such as to facilitate change, his behavior here is far from aggressive. He seems to be acting on the assumption—if I may borrow a phrase from my valued colleague the late Professor Charles I. Gragg—that "learners learn, but teachers cannot teach." In other words, this assistant is planting a seed, but is leaving the growth thereof in Post's mind to be nurtured by subsequent events.

Many will agree with the essential wisdom of this relatively passive kind of teaching. Others will wonder whether something more positive cannot be done and if so what. Being an activist by nature, I feel one further step might have been open to the change agent here and to others who might elsewhere find themselves in a like situation. It is a step that has sometimes worked for me when acting as a business consultant. This additional step is not so much to fight the "wrong" move on the part of an executive as to go on record with a very explicit prediction as to what the outcome of it is likely to be. When borne out, forecasts of this kind have a catalytic effect—that is, they ensure and expedite learning by attaching a lesson to the outcome of events even before the events themselves had had time to transpire.

Participative Leadership. All three cases in this article have something to say about the participative style of leadership: to Post (in a 1940 situation) it seems an unimportant notion, one for which he has no time. Gardner (five years later) is aware of the style, but, in his behavior, participation has the hollow ring of a mere formality or manipulative technique. For Kirkland, however, participation seems to be the most productive way of getting high-level strategy decisions translated into workable policies that will be accepted and implemented.

Since this article was written, a great deal of research has been done on styles of leadership, including the participative style. Results, it must be stressed, have not always been in its favor—especially where the populations studied have been relatively low-ranking or engaged in primarily routine work.

As a consequence of these and other findings, some researchers now suggest that participation may be the most effective style *only* for certain kinds of situations—e.g., for certain types of industrial technologies, or for certain types of functional departments, or for certain types of individuals. (Some leading exponents of these three different possibilities are, respectively, Professor Joan Woodward, formerly of the Tavistock Institute of Human Relations; and my two colleagues, Professors Paul Lawrence and Abraham Zaleznik.)

In contrast, some analysts continue to feel that participation is *always* the most effective style. They explain the not infrequent contrary findings as arising from our inability, using present control techniques, to measure *all* of the costs associated with an authoritarian style over a long enough period of time. (A leading exponent of this point of view is Professor Rensis Likert, Director of the Institute for Social Research at the University of Michigan.)

My own position is that findings inimical to wholesale endorsement of participation must be given some credit; at the same time, I would stress that these findings do nothing to diminish the case for a participative style at the highest levels of management in large and complex organizations. Here the problems are simply too many and too big to permit autocratic rule. An authoritarian style could neither elicit inputs from all the different levels and functional managers whose creative potential must be tapped nor inspire commitment among those diverse, often hostile, elements to overall organizational goals.

In short, *although some situations may not be suited to participation, others—including the most challenging ones—require it.* Though some people may not be able to adapt to it and use it, others can. These others are the ones who must be identified and developed as leaders for our largest and most complex organizations. When one considers what a large proportion of our gross national product is accounted for by organizations of this kind, the social importance of participation is all the greater.

Questions

Having discussed the role of the change agent and the participative style, I may at this point not inappropriately interject a few related comments on the use of questions in the text of "Problems of a New Executive."

Why use questions instead of stating conclusions to be drawn? Because questions invite the reader or the listener to think and interpret for himself. In *questions* there can be no hint of the voice of formal authority —no element of the sage's "Behold what I see." Questions neither limit nor define. They take into account the fact that in a given episode each observer may find for himself the meaning or the lesson most pertinent to *him.*

In short, questions are appropriate for both the teacher who feels there are very real limits to what teaching can accomplish and the would-be practitioner—as well as theoretical proponent—of the participative style in interpersonal relations.

Cases

Readers who have followed, in HBR or elsewhere, trends in human relations training will expect a word to be added on the use of cases as a teaching vehicle in this field. Cases have come under fire for dealing with the "there and then" rather than the "here and now." It has been urged that reading about others does not impart skills which the individual can transfer to his own work situation. In place of cases, then, some have urged reliance on sensitivity training through the T-group or its more recent offshoot, the Managerial Grid (HBR November–December 1964, p. 133).

The argument against cases has not, of course, displaced them from school curricula. And why? In part, I think, because a really effective case can have the universality claimed for the three cases on which this original article was based. And, having this universal quality, cases can evoke not just interest but strong and positive *identification* with the people and events that they describe.

When this identification takes place (as I have argued above that it did here), cases are no longer "there and then"; they are "here and now." For each individual, they are himself and his own situation. As such, some cases will prove to be both long-lived and highly effective as vehicles for increasing reader skills in the vital field of human relations.

62

Training Supervisors—The Use of Human Problems

Norman R. F. Maier and Lester F. Zerfoss

Human-relations skills are difficult to learn merely through reading or by hearing lectures. To be effective, training in the skills must be accompanied by attitude and feeling changes. A supervisor who does not respect his employees will have difficulty in practicing effective methods because his approaches will not hide his basic attitude. It is because skills and attitudes are so interdependent in personnel work that training methods must incorporate both.

One of the important approaches in the improvement of supervisors is that of increasing their employees' participation in the solving of some of the day-to-day job problems. Many employees are distrustful of changes in the job, and there frequently is a feeling that the supervisor plays favorites and discriminates against others. Techniques of selling employees on changes that affect them, and the usual procedures designed to develop fair practices, usually fail to solve these attitudinal problems (Coch and French, 1948; Lewin, 1947). It is exactly in these areas that employee participation seems to be most valuable and for which the group decision method (Bradford and Lippitt, 1945; Lewin, 1947; Lewin, *et al.,* 1939; Maier, 1948) (in which the supervisor shares his problem with his group) has been developed.

However, there is great deal of resistance on the part of supervisors to sharing work problems with their groups because they feel they are giving up something in the process (Maier, 1949). In order to overcome this resistance, new types of training methods are needed. These new methods require that the supervisors learn through participation because they, like rank and file employees, also shy away from changes that affect them.

Discussion meetings (Coch and French, 1948; Maier, 1948, 1949) and roleplaying procedures (Bavelas, 1947; Bradford and Lippitt, 1945; Lippitt, *et al.,* 1947) are two of the best participation training methods. However, their nature is such as to limit their uses in small groups. In training large groups, it has been necessary to confine one's procedures to lectures, visual aids, movies, and demonstrations. None of these approaches permits active participation and practice. An audience-participation technique, recently developed by Donald Phillips (1948), has received a high degree

Reprinted from Norman R. F. Maier and Lester F. Zerfoss, "MRP: A Technique for Training Large Groups of Supervisors and Its Potential Use in Social Research," *Human Relations,* Vol. 5 (Ann Arbor: The University of Michigan, Research Center for Group Dynamics, 1952), pp. 177–186, by permission of the publisher.

of acceptance in industry. It is one of the first methods to permit small group discussions within the general framework of an audience situation. The procedure, often referred to as "Phillips 66," accomplishes general participation by dividing the audience into committees of six, each of which holds a discussion for six minutes on some specific question previously put to them. The major limitation of the Phillips 66 method is that the subject matter to be used for discussion is limited in scope, and it can only be adapted to certain types of situations.

Recently, we have tested a procedure at The Detroit Edison Company which combines the role-playing approach with Phillips 66, and which may be described as Multiple Role Playing (MRP). This method permits role-playing to be carried out in such a manner that all members of a large audience can participate. The purpose of the technique is to give each member of an audience a first-hand experience in the group decision method. It permits the training of supervisors in skills of leading discussions and at the same time gives them an experience of the way things appear to employees, by finding themselves placed in the employee's position. Training supervisors to use group decision requires that they develop: (1) confidence in the way employees behave when given an opportunity to solve job problems, and (2) skill in putting a problem to the group. The MRP method serves in both of these capacities. The experiences obtained in these group discussions give the participants an opportunity to discover that the way employees behave depends greatly upon the kind of situation the supervisor creates. Thus, both the attitude of the supervisor and his skill in leading the discussion directly determine the outcome of the conference. Participants who function as employees see the errors that the supervisor makes and discover how their own reactions are influenced by the situation he creates. Participants who serve as supervisors can discover how conflicts in groups become resolved and find ways to help the process along. All can experience some of the emotional loadings that attach themselves to matters of prestige and fair play. The few participants who function as observers can discover how lifelike a role-playing process might become, and they can observe how the discussion process leads to attitude changes. As an observer, a person can have a disinterested attitude and objectively evaluate the process.

In repeating this method, different persons can function as observers, supervisors, and employees and thus gain a variety of experiences from these exchanges in function.

In order to make the group decision experience a success with untrained leaders, it is important that the problem be so structured that the leader is likely to do a good job and that the group will readily participate in the discussion. To accomplish good discussion leadership, the problem used for our demonstration was one for which the supervisor is unlikely to have a ready-made solution. In having no preferred solution himself, he is inclined to act permissively, and thus encourage free and frank discussion instead of imposing or selling his own views. To produce a lively discussion, the problem that is used must be one which creates a conflict in attitudes. In order to solve the problem, these attitudes have to become reconciled.

The work situation described in this article is based on an actual case in industry and raises the type of problem that a crew can solve more satisfactorily than a supervisor. As such, it readily lends itself to a group decision rather than an autocratic decision which is imposed on the crew by the supervisor. In the real-life situation, the foreman had a new truck to distribute. He realized that his decision would not meet with approval since each man would feel he had a claim. He therefore put the problem to the crew. The crew solved the problem in such a way that there was a general exchange of trucks so that each man got a different truck, and at the same time the poorest truck was discarded. Everyone was satisfied with the solution.

In setting up this problem for role-playing, we have given each participant a personal attitude so that a typical set of lifelike conflicts would be created. This is the usual procedure in role-playing. The deviation from the usual procedure is that the same roles are simultaneously played by many groups, each without the guidance of a trainer. This absence of specific guidance during the role-playing process makes standardization more essential and requires the use of clear-cut problems. However, we find that these limitations are not serious.

Setting Up the Role-Playing Procedure

1. The first step in the procedure is for the trainer or the person in charge of the meeting to request the audience to divide itself into groups of six, with three persons in one row turning around to meet with three persons directly behind them. Assistants can be an aid to help persons in odd seats join others in making up these groups. By arranging the seating rows in multiples of three, the task of organizing the groups is simplified. (In our situation, the seats themselves could be turned around and thus made for more comfort.)

Since the number of persons required in a group is six, there may be a remainder of from one to five persons. Each of those extra persons is asked to join one of the discussion groups and serve as an observer.

2. When the audience has been divided into groups, the trainer announces that each group will receive a set of instructions. The persons who pass out the material will hand these instructions to one member of each group. This member will play the part of Walt Marshall, the foreman of a crew of repairmen. The other five members of the group will be repairmen who report to Walt Marshall. The foreman is to keep this material until instructed further. In the meantime, he may look over the top page, labeled "Walt Marshall—Foreman of the Repair Crew."

3. The trainer then asks the crew members of all groups to give their attention while he reads them their instructions.

General Instructions for Crew:

You are repairmen for a large company and drive to various locations in the city to do your work. Each of you drives a small truck, and you take pride in keeping it looking good. You have a possessive feeling about your trucks and like to keep them in good running order. Naturally, you like to have new trucks, too, because a new truck gives you a feeling of pride.

Here are some facts about the trucks and the men in the crew who report to Walt Marshall, the supervisor for repairs:

George—17 years with the company, has a 2-year-old Ford truck.
Bill—11 years with the company, has a 5-year-old Dodge truck.
John—10 years with the company, has a 4-year-old Ford truck.
Charlie—5 years with the company, has a 3-year-old Ford truck.
Hank—3 years with the company, has a 5-year-old Chevrolet truck.

Most of you do all of your driving in the city, but John and Charlie cover the jobs in the suburbs.

In acting your part in role-playing, accept the facts as given as well as assume the attitude supplied in your specific role. From this point on let your feelings develop in accordance with the events that transpire in the role-playing process. When facts or events arise which are not covered by the roles, make up things which are consistent with the way it might be in a real-life situation.

The names of the five men, years of service, age, and make of truck should then be placed on an easel chart or blackboard so that ready reference to them can be made.

4. The foreman is then asked to pass out the material he has been given, which consists of six sets of instructions, one for each person in the group. He should keep

the top set for himself and pass out one set of instructions, beginning on his left, to each of his five crewmen. The sequence of the instructions should be George, Bill, John, Charlie, and Hank so that the seating order corresponds to the order of seniority as listed on the easel.

The content of the specific instructions for each member of the group is as follows:

Walt Marshall—Foreman of Repair Crew

You are the foreman of a crew of repairmen, each of whom drives a small service truck to and from his various jobs. Every so often you get a new truck to exchange for an old one, and you have the problem of deciding to which of your men you should give the new truck. Often there are hard feelings because each man seems to feel he is entitled to the new truck; so you have a tough time being fair. As a matter of fact, it usually turns out that whatever you decide, most of the men consider wrong. You now have to face the issue again because a new truck has just been allocated to you for distribution. The new truck is a Chevrolet.

Here are some brief facts about your situation:

George—17 years with the company, has a two-year-old Ford truck.
Bill—11 years with the company, has a five-year-old Dodge truck.
John—10 years with the company, has a four-year-old Ford truck.
Charlie—5 years with the company, has a three-year-old Ford truck.
Hank—3 years with the company, has a five-year-old Chevrolet truck.

All of the men do city driving, making fairly short trips, except for John and Charlie who cover the suburbs.

In order to handle this problem you have decided to put the decision up to the men themselves. You will tell them about the new truck and will put the problem in terms of what would be the most fair way to distribute the truck. Avoid taking a position yourself because you want to do what the men think is most fair.

George: When a new Chevrolet truck becomes available, you think you should get it because you have most seniority and don't like your present truck. Your own car is a Chevrolet, and you prefer a Chevrolet truck such as you drove before you got the Ford.

Bill: You feel you deserve a new truck. Your present truck is old, and since the senior man has a fairly new truck, you should get the next one. You have taken excellent care of your present Dodge and have kept it looking like new. A man deserves to be rewarded if he treats a company truck like his own.

John: You have to do more driving than most of the other men because you work in the suburbs. You have a fairly old truck and feel you should have a new one because you do so much driving.

Charlie: The heater in your present truck is inadequate. Since Hank backed into the door of your truck, it has never been repaired to fit right. The door lets in too much cold air, and you attribute your frequent colds to this. You want a warm truck since you have a good deal of driving to do. As long as it has good tires, brakes, and is comfortable you don't care about its make.

Hank: You have the poorest truck in the crew. It is five years old, and before you got it, it had been in a bad wreck. It has never been good, and you've put up with it for three years. It's about time you got a good truck to drive, and you feel the next one should be yours. You have a good accident record. The only accident you had was when you sprung the door of Charlie's truck when he opened it as you backed out of the garage. You hope the new truck is a Ford since you prefer to drive one.

Members are asked to study their roles until they have a feeling for them. It is perhaps necessary to caution them not to show their roles to each other, but to put them aside when they have finished with them.

5. When everyone is ready, the trainer gives the signal for the foreman to take the responsibility of starting their meetings. Each foreman should assume that he has

called his men together and that he is seated with them to discuss a problem.

6. Less than half an hour is adequate for most groups to solve the problem. (If the leader and his assistants observe the groups, they can pretty well judge when most of the groups have reached a solution). Before interrupting the discussion, it is desirable to announce from the floor that three more minutes will be allowed the groups to settle on some arrangement.

7. At the end of the three-minute period, the members are asked to break off their discussions and join in the analysis of the results.

Analyzing the Results

The extent of the analysis need not be confined to the points discussed below, but the analysis should cover the following points:

1. Determination of the number of groups arriving at a solution. (In obtaining this figure, only the foreman should vote.)

2. Determination of the number of men who are satisfied with the solution. (In this case, only the repairmen of crews which reached a solution should raise their hands.) This figure is important because it indicates the degree of satisfaction obtained from the procedure. The chairman may ask how this degree of acceptance compares with what would have been obtained if the foreman had supplied the solution.

3. Determination of number of crews which discarded Hank's truck. (In this case only the foremen should raise their hands.) The proportion of the number of times that Hank's truck was discarded to the number of groups becomes a measure of the quality of the solution. The fear that men might fail to discard the poorest truck would constitute one of the reasons why a foreman might hesitate to put such a problem to them. If the proportion of crews discarding the poorest truck is very large, it indicates that the danger of not having the poorest truck discarded is more imagined than real.

4. Determination of the number of crews in which the new truck went to various members of the crew. (In this case only the foreman should vote on the five alternatives.) This analysis brings out the variety of solutions obtained and shows that the same problem with the same roles produces different solutions. Under such circumstances it becomes clear that a company could not work out a policy that would be satisfying to all crews.

This analysis might also be followed by questions such as, "In how many cases did George use his seniority and make a strong demand for the new truck?" "How often did he get it when he was that kind of a George?" "How often did George get the new truck when he did not throw his seniority around?" Such questions frequently reveal that George is more likely to get the new truck when he is a reasonable person and is considerate of men with less service than when he is demanding.

5. Determination of the number of crews in which

(a) All men obtained a different truck.

(b) Four men obtained a different truck.

(c) Three men obtained a different truck.

(d) Two men obtained a different truck.

(e) No exchange in old trucks were made and only the man receiving the new truck benefited.

(Only the foreman should vote on these alternatives.) This analysis gives an idea of the extent to which all men were given consideration. If time is taken to analyze these data, it might be found that the foreman's conduct of the meeting determined the number of men who benefited by the addition of a new truck to the crew.

Following the analysis of the crews, the persons serving as observers should be asked to give their evaluations of the discussion meetings they observed. Their report may include: (a) the way the foreman put the problem, (b) the extent to which he hampered the discussion, (c) the extent to which he imposed his own ideas, and (d) evaluation of things he did which helped things along. These reports not only involve the observers in the procedure, but add supplementary material on the different approaches various foremen may have used.

Some Sample Results

We have tested the case in three audiences. In one of these, 17 groups were formed and in 14 of these, all persons were satisfied with the solution they had reached. A total of 5 individuals out of 102 were dissatisfied with the solutions of their groups. In the second group tested, 6 groups were used and 2 persons (in two different groups) out of 42 were dissatisfied. In the third audience, 19 out of 21 groups had time to reach a decision and only one person in each of two groups was dissatisfied. If we combine our groups, we find that 42 out of 44 groups reached a decision and only 9 out of 220 repairmen (4.1 per cent) were dissatisfied.

In each of three tests of the method, all persons participating readily agreed that anything approaching the degree of satisfaction shown could not have been obtained if supervisors had supplied the solution.

In 41 out of the 42 groups, Hank's truck (the poorest one) was eliminated. This result clearly shows that the group decisions were in accordance with the interests of good management. Thus the fear that group decisions might lead to poor-quality decisions was not supported.

The new truck went to George, the senior man, in 20 of the 42 groups. In 16 cases out of 28, he got it when he did not insist on it because of his seniority, and in 4 cases out of 10, he got it by defending his rank. Thus George gained most when he acted least in his own selfish interests.

A great variety of solutions developed in these groups. The new truck went to each of the individuals in one group or another; the frequency being in the order of George, John, Hank, Bill, and Charlie. In most instances there was a general exchange of trucks. All men got a different truck in 4 groups; 4 men got a different truck in 10 groups; 3 men in 16 groups; 2 in 8 groups; and only 1 got a different truck (the new one) in 4 groups.

From descriptions of the discussion process, there seemed to be a trend in which the general exchange of trucks was greatest when the leader was permissive. The first part of the discussion develops a conflict of interests, and if the leader is permissive at this stage, the idea of exchanging trucks develops. Many men who played the part of the supervisor were surprised at this development because most of them went into the discussion with the idea of getting the new truck assigned to some particular individual and getting the rest of the group to agree on who was most needy. It is this emphasis on the leader's part which prevents the general exchange which usually develops out of the free discussion. Thus the idea that all can profit when the crew gets a new truck emerges as a new idea, and it is a group product.

General Evaluation

The technique of MRP has some distinct advantages over ordinary role-playing. When many groups of persons engage in role-playing at the same time, the process is facilitated since all of them enter into it without the embarrassment that comes from feeling that they are being observed. Thus groups which have never experienced role-playing quickly get the spirit of the procedure and go into the process in a natural and interested manner. The feeling that the situation is unreal and artificial, which nonparticipants frequently report, is eliminated because all become involved. Because this method reduces self-consciousness, it is particularly helpful for initiating role-playing techniques in supervisory training.

A second value that emerges is the fact that real-live data is obtained from the subsequent analysis. A single role-playing case raises questions which have to do with the fact that a certain individual determined the outcome and so the result may not be typical. In being able to draw upon various groups, one is able to make comparisons and generalizations which could not be made without a rich background of experience. The idea that solutions are tailored to fit a particular group of personalities is clearly brought home by the fact that solutions vary even when the problem and the roles are identical.

Thus we find that in the process of attempting to induce into a large group some of the benefits of small group discussion and role-playing, we not only succeeded in achieving some of these advantages, but captured some entirely new ones.

The MRP method can be used for all types of role-playing which are so effective for attitude change and the development of skills. One must however structure the roles so as to conform to the purpose of the training and the experience of the participants. Thus if one wishes to emphasize (a) leadership skills in putting a problem to a group, (b) discussion-leading skills, (c) sensitivity to the feelings of others, (d) ways for dealing with hostile persons, (e) skills to upgrade the quality of decisions, and (f) methods to cause a group to feel responsible for reaching decisions acceptable to all, one must design role-playing situations which will highlight these performance areas.

Uses of MRP in Social Research

MRP also can be used as a tool to evaluate various kinds of leadership approaches, as well as to measure the effect of different kinds of participants on the outcome of a discussion. For example, the leaders of half of the groups may receive instructions which differ from those supplied by the other half. These differences may be as follows:

(a) Encourage disagreement in your group vs. discourage disagreement in your group;
(b) Suggest possible solutions to your group vs. be careful not to suggest any solutions yourself;
(c) Try to sell a particular solution that seems fair to you vs. be careful not to show any preference for any solution suggested; and,
(d) Have your group explore a variety of solutions before selling on any one idea vs. hurry the group along so that leisurely exploration of many ideas is discouraged.

The effect of different kinds of participants can be tested by making the roles slightly different for two sets of groups. For example, (a) George can be asked to insist on getting the truck in one set and asked to help out Hank's case in the other; (b) one set of groups might be so instructed that they form two cliques, whereas the other set of groups are not so instructed; and (c) one set of groups may have one member who is asked to play the part of a conciliatory individual, whereas in the other set of groups the same individual may be requested to play the part of a belligerent person.

By comparing the outcomes of two sets of groups with similarly instructed leaders and the differences obtained with differently instructed leaders working with similarly instructed groups, one can demonstrate the importance of the injected differences.

The use of the observer can also be expanded by having one or two such persons in each group. (The purpose of two observers is to see to what extent different persons vary in what they see in the same situation. With experience these differences rapidly decline.)

The observers' reports are of particular value in pointing up how each person's remarks has an effect on the behavior of others. Their comments would tend to sensitize participants to important details in the discussion process, and the reports of skilled observers would become a valuable training aid to participants. The use of observers would be of special value in the training of individuals who meet repeatedly in conferences.

REFERENCES

1. Bavelas, A. "Role-playing and Management Training." *Sociatry*, 1947, *1*, 183–191.
2. Bradford, L. P., and Lippitt, R. "Building a Democratic Work Group." Personnel, 1945, *22*, 2–13.
3. Coch, L., and French, J. R. P., Jr. "Overcoming Resistance to Change." *Human Relations*, 1948, Vol. I, No. 2, 512–532.
4. Lewin, K. "Group Decision and Social Change." pp. 330–344 in *Readings in Social Psychology* (ed. by T. M. Newcomb and E. L. Hartley), New York, Henry Holt and Co., 1947.
5. Lewin, K., Lippitt, R., and White, R. K. "Patterns of Aggressive Behaviour in Experimentally Created Social Climates." *J. Soc. Psychol.*, 1939, *11*, 271–299.
6. Lippitt, R., Bradford, L. P., and Benne, K. D. "Sociodramatic Clarification of Leader and Group Roles." *Sociatry*, 1947, *1*, 82–91.
7. Maier, N. R. F. "A human relations program for supervision." *Indust. and Labor Rel. Rev.*, 1948, *1*, 443–464.
8. Maier, N. R. F. "Improving Supervision through Training." pp. 27–32 in *Psychology of Labour-management Relations* (ed. by A. Kornhauser), Indust. Relations Research Assn., Champaign, Ill., 1949.
9. Phillips, J. D. "Report on Discussion 66." *Adult Educ. Jour.*, 1948, *7*, 181–182.

63

Memorandum on the Redefinition of Profit, Taxes, Costs, Money, Economics, etc.

Abraham H. Maslow

The redefining of the concept "profit" necessarily involves the redefining of the concept "cost". Also it requires the redefining of the concept "price." Maybe I can approach the whole business from a different angle altogether, that is, from the angle of the critique of classical economic theory. In the textbooks I've seen, this is based almost entirely on an obsolete motivation theory of lower basic needs exclusively (leaving out higher needs and metaneeds); furthermore it assumes that these can be phrased in interchangeable terms, which in turn implies that any

Reprinted with permission from Maslow, *Eupsychian Management: A Journal* (Homewood, Ill.: Richard D. Irwin, Inc., and the Dorsey Press), pp. 205–216.

accounting deals entirely with objects or qualities or characteristics that can be phrased in terms of money and therefore put into a money accounting balance sheet.

But all this is today absolute nonsense. This is true only because we now know so much more about the higher basic needs and also the metaneeds beyond them (which will be far more important motivators in the affluent, automated society). One way of showing this is to stress the fact that money no longer is a very important motivation. There are now many people in our society who cannot be won away to another job by offering more money unless it is a *huge* increase in money. Or say it still another way. Suppose that money becomes unimportant because everybody has enough, or anybody can get enough rather easily in order to satisfy his basic needs. As labor of any kind gets higher and higher priced it becomes possible to earn a minimum subsistence with less and less work. Anybody who really wants to be a hobo can rather easily be one these days. It's very easy to earn what used to be called "a living." (The trouble is when most people talk about earning a living these days they really mean earning an automobile, a fine house, landscaped garden, and so on and so on).

If this is so, as it indeed seems to be, there are many people who cannot be won away from their present jobs except by offering all sorts of higher need and metaneed satisfactions. Furthermore, many people are influenced more by nonmonetary than by monetary considerations. For instance, I pointed out to Andy Kay that when anybody offered me a job I tried to put some rough money value on all sorts of intangibles, like for instance, giving up a friend, or beautiful surroundings, or giving up warm relationships at my place of work, or the simple fact of familiarity with everything and everybody, or going to the trouble of moving from one city to another, or even such things as having to learn my way around a new city. I have asked myself how much money is it worth to me to give up my friendship with my best friends. At my time of life it is difficult to develop this kind of intimacy in a short period of time. Is my best friend worth $1,000 a year or $500 a year or $5,000 or what? Anyway, it's quite clear that he is worth *something* which I had better take into account. If, for instance, I arbitrarily assign a value of $1,000 a year to having an intimate friend (which is certainly a modest figure), then this new job which has been offered at a raise, of let's say $2,000 or $3,000, or $4,000 a year simply is not what it looked like at first. I may actually be losing value, or dollar value, if I take into account all these other higher need intangibles which nobody puts into the contract nor on the balance sheet, but which are nevertheless very, very real to any sensible person.

But something of the same sort is true of industry. Why should a necessary and valuable person stay in a job rather than move to another one? Well, is it not that he likes the house he lives in or that he has a pleasant boss to work with or pleasant colleagues or that the secretary that he works with is cheerful rather than surly or that the janitors are obliging rather than nasty or even such a thing as that the place is attractive or beautiful rather than ugly? Certainly the questions of climate and weather and education for the children, etc. are all taken into account by any sensible person.

The old concept of taxes is that they are like the fees which the robber barons arbitrarily imposed, or which some group of bandits squeezed out of passersby under threat of military oppression. The "protection money" which the gangsters used to impose in Chicago is very close to this original meaning of the word "tax." The word today still carries some of this connotation, that of arbitrary, greedy people who are demanding some money for which they return nothing, just simply because they're in a position of power, and you have to grind your teeth and give in. But, under good circumstances and under eupsychian theoretical conditions, taxes are a very different kind of thing and must be seen in a very different way, that is, as payment for necessary services at a bargain rate, because otherwise the healthy long-term enterprise would have to replace all of these services on a private basis, which would cost a great deal more. This is true for water, police services, medical services, fire services, general sanitation services and the like. Practically all of these represent terrific bargains, and the taxes for them should be considered to be part of the necessary costs of any long-term enterprise, an indispensable *sine qua non* of enterprise. This is also as true or almost as true for the huge chunk of local taxes which goes for education and schools in general. From this point of view of an enterprise, this can be seen as preparation by the community of skilled workers and managers of all kinds. If the community did not teach reading, writing, and arithmetic, then the enterprise itself would have to do this. If there were no school system, then this would have to be created by the enterprise itself. So this, too, is a great bargain.

(Of course this all assumes enlightened managerial policy in which the more developed the human being is, the more evolved, the more fully grown, the better for the enterprise. Under Theory X conditions the opposite would be true, because authoritarianism rests upon ignorance and fear rather than upon enlightenment, autonomy, and courage).

Sooner or later we will have to deal with the questions of higher-need economics and of metaneed economics in a serious theoretical way. I cannot foresee how many modifications of economic theory and practice would be needed because of this, but certainly some can be seen now. One is this; in a prosperous society and under fairly good conditions and with fairly good people, the lowest creature needs would be taken care of very easily; it would take rather little money to be able to barely eat and sleep and have shelter and so on. Perhaps it will even be cheaper to give them away. Then as we rise higher in the hierarchy of basic needs, we find that money gets to be less and less important in buying them. Of the highest needs we can say that they come free or almost free. Or to say it another way, the higher need satisfactions of belongingness, of love and friendliness and affection, of respect given, and of possibility of building self-respect—all these are largely outside the money economy altogether; e.g., they can be given to the poorest family just so long as it is well organized.

These higher needs are precisely what enlightened management policy points itself toward. That is to say, enlightened management policy may be *defined* as an attempt to satisfy the higher needs in the work situation, in a nonmonetary way, that is, to have the work situation give intrinsically higher need satisfaction (rather than to give the money and expect the money to buy these satisfactions outside the work situation). We can go pretty far with this because it's actually possible to distinguish between Theory X management and Theory Y management simply on this basis; that is, Theory X is a theory of motivation which implies all the lower needs and Theory Y is a more inclusive and more scientific and realistic theory of motivation because it includes the higher needs and considers them to be factors in the work situation and in the economic situation. Or to say it still another way, authoritarian economies or Theory X economics and managerial policy proceed on the assumption that there are no instinctoid higher basic needs. (Since there is so much evidence that there are such needs, Theory X is not only distasteful in a democratic society on moral principles, but it is also scientifically false). (I think the high and low grumble experiment [see below] will prove that metaneeds are also part of the economic situation or the work situation and of managerial Theory X. That is, we may turn out to have a lower-need economics, a higher-need economics, and also a metaneed economics, in a kind of hierarchy of prepotency). I wish Walter Weisskopf could be permitted to teach others about these points as he has taught me.[1]

The trouble is how to put these on the balance sheet, how to put them into the accounting system, how to give them weight in the actual calculation of salary for a particular man or of the worth to the organization of the personality development of the people in it, for instance. Try to put it this way, for one example: if a particular man who is twenty-five years old is working in an organization at a particular level X which is not terribly good, and then for some reason goes into psychotherapy for a long period of time and becomes a better person and as a result comes out able to work at a higher level Y, then it is very clear that attaining this higher level of efficiency in productivity and managerial skill cost him a great deal of money. Is this part of his "wealth"? Where in his accounting system does this gain get written down? (The same question is true for higher education of any other kind).

Still another question here: assuming that in one factory Theory X prevails and in another factory Theory Y prevails, and that naturally the latter one is better for the personal growth of any individual in it, how can this gain be put into the accounting system? Certainly it all costs some money. The cost of training enlightened managers is greater than the cost of training unenlightened managers. How shall this gain be represented in a numerical fashion in the balance sheet? Certainly it must be considered some kind of fringe benefit, that is to say a nonmoney benefit, and any sensible man, of course, would realize that this was a benefit, an economic benefit, a higher-need economic benefit, even though it would be hard to put into numerical terms or monetary terms.

Another question: the fact that an enlightened factory undoubtedly will be discovered to make all sorts of differences not only in the intrinsic work situation, that is, by way of turning out better products and so on, but also in helping its people to become better citizens, better husbands, better wives, etc., etc. This is an asset or a benefit to the population at large in exactly the same way that a schoolhouse is or college or hospital or a therapeutic institute. That is, how could an accounting system build into itself the benefits that an enterprise gives to the community? Certainly, even in the money economy, this makes a certain amount of sense, because this costs a certain amount of money to the enterprise, e.g., for education within the company, for enlightened services of various sorts, for education in the broadest sense, etc.

Sometime in the future we will have to deal with more subtle aspects of long-term, enlightened management, democratic holistic society economics, in at least this sense: A healthy business assumes all sorts of things that we haven't yet spoken about. For instance, it really assumes a kind of an open and free market, perhaps we can use the word "open competition" here. It is better for the long-term health of an enterprise that it be able to compete, that there be rival factories turning out similar products which can be compared with each other, that other factories keep on pressing for improvement, etc. This is in contrast with, let's say, the Franco-Spain situation in which a monopoly is arbitrarily given to some relative, who thereafter, for instance, will produce all the matches in Spain or all the automobiles or whatever it may be. What happens inevitably in the monopoly situation of this sort, since there is no pressure to keep up quality or certainly none to improve, is that everything will most likely deteriorate steadily. The people involved must inevitably become cynical

[1] W. Weisskopf, *The Psychology of Economics* (Chicago: University of Chicago Press, 1955); also "Economic Growth and Human Well-Being," *Manas,* August 21, 1963, *16,* 1–8.

as they realize that they are crooks and liars and evil people in general who have been forced into an evil situation. They will almost inevitably tax the helpless population, i.e., set a higher price on the products than they would be worth in an open market, and furthermore, since the product itself will most likely deteriorate, the enterprise will certainly not be healthy.

To use a slightly different parallel a child who is brought up in a germ-free environment, is carefully protected against all bacteria and viruses and so on, loses entirely, sooner or later, the ability to resist disease. That is to say, he must thereafter, for the rest of his life be artificially protected because he cannot protect himself. By contrast, the child who is permitted to take his own chances and to live in the world of dangers and is only ordinarily and reasonably protected against the dangers will, because he gets these dangers in small doses, build up antibodies and resistances so that he can walk freely through all the germs and viruses thereafter for the rest of his life without fear and without getting disease. I think this is indication enough that some new theory of competition or of free market or of free enterprise in this sense will have to be worked out. It should be kept separate from cold war talk, or political talk of any kind, because precisely the same thing is true of any other kind of social or economic system. That is, a healthy enterprise in the socialistic economy would depend upon the same conditions of exposure to stress, exposure to competition that would be required in a capitalistic economy. That is to say, this is not simply a political economic or moral consideration; it follows very simply from the intrinsic necessities of an enterprise which is to last for a couple of centuries, and which is to remain alive homeostatically and also to grow. A good boxer needs a good sparring partner or he will deteriorate.

Furthermore, if we assumed, as I think it could be demonstrated that we *must*, that rationality, truth, honesty, and justice in this free market, in this free competition of similar products, should prevail in order to keep up the health of all the enterprises and of all the people in these enterprises and of the society in general, then it is very desirable (and perhaps even theoretically necessary), that cream be able to rise to the top of the milk. The best product should be bought, the best man should be rewarded more. Interfering factors which befuddle this triumph of virtue, justice, truth, and efficiency, etc., should be kept to an absolute minimum or should approach zero as a limit. Here I'm talking about the salesman's winning smiles, personal loyalties, favoring your relatives, or fake advertising which stresses the wrong thing (like the beautiful design of a car on the outside without regard to the lousy motor inside).

If all these things can be demonstrated to be true for the healthy enterprise and the healthy system of enterprises, i.e., society, then many things will follow. And one of these things is that the consumer, the buyer, the customer must be assumed to be rational, that is, that he will want the best product for his purposes. This means also to think that he will look for factual information, examine specifications, read the labels, get indignant over being swindled instead of taking it for granted, and shudder with disgust when he meets a crook or liar and thereafter stay away from him, etc., etc. Now, all these qualities are characteristics of higher psychological health, growth toward self-actualization. Therefore, any determinant that increases the health of a particular person, making him therefore not only a better manager or better worker or better citizen but also a better consumer, must be considered to be good for the health of any particular enterprise, even though in a tiny, tiny way. Anything that will enable the consumers to select out on the basis of facts and of truly good workmanship, etc., is good for everybody else or everything else in the whole society, including the single, long-termed enlightened enterprise. Therefore, the enlightened factory which helps people to grow is thereby helping every other factory in the whole society in principle. And, in principle at least, this should be valued by all the other factories, just as anything else should be valued that turns out better, more realistic, "higher" customers. Now the question is, can this somehow be put on the balance sheet: can an accounting system take account of fringe benefits to other factories from having an efficient, enlightened scientific factory setup.

Another way to try to say these various things is to start with the conception of the "good customer in eupsychia or the eupsychian customer." Everything that has preceded and everything in the management literature rests on assuming that the customer is rational, prefers good quality, will choose the better product for the purpose, will choose the lesser price if quality is equal, will not be seduced by irrelevancies, will prefer virtue and truth and justice and so on, and will get indignant or insulted or disgusted or angry when someone tries to swindle him. This assumption is also necessary because the main basis upon which enlightened management policy so far rests is that productivity is improved both in quantity and quality. *But* what good will it do to turn out a better product at a cheaper price if betterness and cheapness mean nothing to the consumer? That is, if he cares less about these than about other things which are irrelevant, then the whole argument for more efficient factories, managers, and supervisors falls to the ground entirely. If people like being fooled, if they like being swindled, if they prefer being seduced, if they prefer being bribed, then enlightened management is bad, rather than good for economic survival. Therefore, the theory of the good and efficient factory has an absolute prerequisite, the good and rational customer armed with good taste and with righteous indignation. It is only when people value honesty that honesty pays. It is only when people value good quality that good quality pays. It is only when people get righteously indignant over being swindled, that people will tend to stop swindling. If swindling pays, then it will *not* stop. The definition of the good society is one in which virtue pays. I can now add a slight variation on this; you cannot have a good society *unless* virtue pays. But here we get very close to the whole subject of metaneeds, and also of the synergy theory, which in turn is a by-product of B-psychology—the B-psychology of ideal conditions where dichotomies are resolved and transcended. (Put all this together with the other memorandum on the good eupsychian salesman and the good eupsychian customer and stress that a "good customer" is both a necessity and a virtuous, desirable person, because he wishes the system to work. As soon as he stops caring, the whole system will collapse).

Observe that much of the difficulty in the conception of profit, taxes, costs, and so on, can be seen to come from the professionalization of the accountants as a group. They are the ones who force upon the industrial situation the concern with numbers, with exchangeable money, with tangibles rather than intangibles, with exactness, with predictability, with control, with law and order generally, etc. Andy Kay pointed out that the accountants have the lowest vocabulary scores of any of the professional groups. I added that the psychiatrists think of them as being the most obsessional of any group. From what I know of them, they also attract to the schools of accounting those who are number bound, those who are interested in small details, those who are tradition bound, and the like.

In the colleges and the universities, with all their educational policies and intellectual goals, the accountant types and other obsessional types somehow manage to force an overemphasis upon the interchangeability of credits, of grades, of diplomas, of degrees, of scores, and of arithmetizing the whole of the educational venture, even though this is entirely alien and antagonistic to it. Clearly, in this same way the new kind of industry and enterprise philosophy will certainly need a different type of accounting, and, therefore, probably a different accountant character structure.

So much of this accountant's philosophy of life ultimately boils down to a mistrust of self. These are the people who will make budgets for their households, put certain sums of money in one bottle or another bottle or another envelope or whatever and not touch it. These are the people who earmark funds for particular purposes. These are the people who will not touch their savings which are drawing 4 percent interest and prefer instead to borrow money at 12 percent interest, just because it is their habit or philosophy to "not touch your savings ever." These can be considered to be people who fool themselves, in a way like the ones who arbitrarily set their alarm clocks ten minutes ahead so as to fool themselves into getting a little more sleep, but not too much sleep, etc. The whole thing is ludicrous because, of course, they know that the alarm clock is set ten minutes ahead. This is a little like the mild form of pathology that we see in the confusion of daylight savings time. Instead of passing laws to make offices open an hour earlier in the summertime, everybody has to fool himself by making believe he is getting up at the same hour by changing the clock time.

This is all the opposite of the creative personality. The creative person trusts himself sufficiently to face a new problem or a new situation without any preparation, to improvise a solution in the new situation. The more obsessional person tends to classify the whole of the future, to prepare for every contingency, to have schedules and plans which he will not break, and the like. Some obsessionals make themselves a promise about the future and then stick to it through thick or thin. For instance, if they have planned to go to a party or a picnic or a trip on a certain date, they will do it even if they have broken a leg or even though they feel very depressed or unhappy or whatever. It's as if they cannot change their minds, as if this throws them into anxiety, into a panic. Of course, this kind of scheduling of the future, of geometrizing the future, of making everything arithmetical, exact, predictable, controllable and so on, this is all a big set of defenses against the anxiety which comes to such people from having to meet something unexpected, something they're not prepared for. It's as if they want to avoid getting into any situation without being prepared for it in advance. They can't improvise. They don't trust themselves to find the solution on the spur of the moment.

For such people, for such accountants, the giving up of careful controls and checks is going to be an anxiety-producing situation. They must know everything that is going on at all times, even if it's trivial or unimportant, and even if it involves mistrusting other people. Probably also, this accounts for the tendency in our accounting systems to deal only with tangibles and only with qualities or characteristics that can be translated into money exchange. Obsessional people in general tend to mistrust emotions, chaos of any kind, unpredictability of any kind, human nature in general. I am reminded here of the parallel between the accountant's necessity for having everything down in numbers, and those authoritarian organizational theorists who have to have all the human and interpersonal relationships in any organization reducible to a chart on the wall with simple lines and simple geometric form.

Statistics, schedules and other external cues can serve as a substitute for the lack of inner voices and certainties. The person who is decisive because he *knows* experientially is the one who can use these external aids in a healthy way.

PART V *Perspectives on the Future*

There is a lot of talk these days about whether there will be a future. All the authors here assume there will be one.

Buckminister Fuller, whose designs may already have given future architecture its shape, suggests a variety of major changes in the educational structure. Fuller is unique among futurists in that he never makes a prediction about a technological revolution until he has invented the process he is describing. This makes him one of the most conservative forecasters in terms of technology. The implications of his inventions, however, are as sweeping and socially significant as those of his less conservative colleagues.

Richard Bolt suggests that the next step in the development of devices to augment human intellect will be closer links connecting man and machine. This interactive process is already underway and promises to change our ideas about machines as radically as Fuller's work changes our ideas about space and education. The article by Ralph Ezios describes another current research breakthrough, the autoregulation of physical and emotional states by self-teaching procedures.

The procedures for changing our internal states at will are probably the most revolutionary of all the ideas considered in this book. A group of researchers has opened up to view and to control the inner workings of the psyche and the body, processes that had been called autonomic—i.e., incapable of voluntary control. Man is suddenly capable of greater freedom through improved self-control. Conversely, he can be easily and more fully controlled than ever before.

The final article by Kahn and Wiener is a look at a series of possible futures. Their lists are based on extensive and rigorous studies of trends in a host of different areas.

We are part of a culture committed to widespread technological change. Change in one segment of a culture brings changes to other parts of the culture; some are intentional, many are accidental. The future of social science may lie in learning to predict and modify the social and psychological effects of technology with the same skill and rapidity presently done by technology alone.

64

Education Automation

R. Buckminister Fuller

I have talked to you about solving problems by design competence instead of by political reform. It is possible to get one-to-one correspondence of action and reaction without political revolution, warfare, and reform. I find it possible today with very short electromagnetic waves to make small reflectors by which modulated signals can be beamed. After World War II, we began to beam our TV messages from city to city. One reason television didn't get going before World War II was because of the difficulty in distributing signals over long distances from central sources on long waves or mildly short waves. We were working on coaxial cables between cities, but during the war we found new short ranges of electromagnetic frequencies. We worked practically with very much higher frequencies, very much shorter wave lengths. We found that we could beam these short waves from city to city. Television programs are brought into the small city now by beam from a few big cities and then *rebroadcast* locally to the home sets. That is the existing TV distribution pattern. My invention finds it is now possible to utilize the local TV masts in any community in a new way. Going up to, say, two hundred, three hundred, or four hundred feet and looking down on a community you see the houses individually in the middle of their respective land plots. Therefore, with a few high masts having a number of tiny masers, lasers, or reflectors, each beam aimed accurately at a specific house, the entire community could be directly "hooked up" by beams, instead of being broadcast to. This means a great energy saving, for less than 1 per cent of the omnidirectionally *broadcast* pattern ever hits a receiving antenna. The beaming makes for very sharp, clear, frequency-modulated signals.

In the beaming system, you also have a reflector at the house that picks up the signal. It corresponds directly to the one on the mast and is aimed right back to the specific beaming cup on the mast from which it is receiving. This means that with beam casting you are able to send individual messages to each of those houses. There is a direct, fixed, wireless connection, an actual direct linkage to individuals; and it works in both directions. Therefore, the receiving individual can beam back, "I don't like it." He may and can say "yes" or "no." This "yes" or "no" is the basis of a binary mathematical system, and immediately brings in the "language" of the modern electronic computers. With two-way TV, constant referendum of democracy will be manifest, and democracy will become the most practical form of industrial and space-age government by all people, for all people.

It will be possible not only for an individual to say, "I don't like it," on his two-way TV but he can also beam-dial (without having to know mathematics), "I want number so and so." It is also possible with this kind of two-way TV linkage with individuals' homes to send out many different programs simultaneously; in fact, as many as there are two way beamed-up receiving sets and programs. It would be possible to have large central storages of documentaries —great libraries. A child could call for a special program information locally over the TV set.

With two-way TV we will develop selecting dials for the children which will not be primarily an alphabetical but a visual *species* and *chronological category* selecting device with secondary alphabetical subdivisions. The child will be able to call up any kind of information he wants about any subject and get his latest authoritative TV documentary, the production of which I have already described to you. The answers to his questions and probings will be *the best information* that man has available up to that minute in history.

All this will bring a profound change in education. We will stop training individuals to be "teachers," when all that most young girl "education" students really want to know is how they are going to earn a living in case they don't get married. Much of the educational system today is aimed at answering: "How am I going to survive? How am I going to get a job? I must earn a living." That is the priority item under which we are working all the time—the idea of *having to earn a living*. That problem of "how are we going to earn a living?" is going to go out the historical window, forever, in the next decade, and education is going to be disembarrassed of the unseen "practical" priority bogeyman. Education will then be concerned primarily with exploring to discover not only more about the universe and its history but about what the universe is trying to do, about why man is part of it, and about how can, and may man best function in universal evolution.

Automation is with us. There is no question about it. Automation was inevitable to intellect. Intellect was found to differentiate out experience continually and to articulate and develop new tools to do physically repeated tasks. Man is now no longer *essential* as a worker in the fabulously complex industrial equation. Marx's *worker* is soon to become utterly obsolete. Automation is coming in Russia just as it is here. The word *worker* describing man as a muscle-and-reflex machine will not have its current 1961 meaning a decade hence. Therefore, if man is no longer essential as a worker we ask: "How can he live? How does he acquire the money or credits with which to purchase what he needs or what he wants that is available beyond immediate needs?" At the present time we are making all kinds of economic pretenses at covering up this overwhelming automation problem because we don't realize adequately the larger significance of the truly fundamental change that is taking place in respect to man-in-universe. As automation advanced man began to create secondary or nonproductive jobs to make himself look busy so that he could rationalize a necessity for himself by virtue of which he could "earn" his living. Take all of our bankers, for example. They are all fixtures; these men don't have anything to do that a counting machine couldn't do; a punch button box would suffice. They have no basic banking authority whatsoever today. They do not loan you their own wealth. They loan you your own wealth. But man has a sense of vanity and has to invent these things that make him look important.

I am trying to keep at the realities with you. Approximately total automation is coming. Men will be essential to the industrial equation but not as workers. People are going to be utterly essential as consumers—what I call *regenerative consumers*, however, not just swill pails.

The vast industrial complex undertakings and associated capital investments are today so enormous and take so long to inaugurate that they require concomitantly rapid regenerative economics to support them. The enterprise must pay off very rapidly in order to be able to refund itself and obtain the economic advantage to inaugurate solution of the next task with still higher technical advantage. In that regenerative cycle of events, the more consumers there are the more the costs are divided and the lower the individual prices. The higher the frequency of the consuming the more quickly the capital cost can be refunded, and the sooner the system is ready for the next wave of better technology. So man is essential to the industrial equation as a consumer—as a regenerative consumer, a critical consumer, a man who tasting wants to taste better and who viewing realizes what he views can be accomplished more efficiently and more interestingly. The consumer thus becomes a highly critical regenerative function, requiring an educational system that fosters the consumer's regenerative capacity and capability.

At present, world economics is such that Russia and China work under an integrated socialist planning in competition with our literally disorganized economic world (for our anti-trust laws will not permit organization on a comprehensive basis). The Communists have high efficiency advantage because of their authoritarianism. We have very little centralized authority, save in "defense." The Communists now have the industrial equation, too, in large scale, and soon complete automation will be with them. They are very much aware of the fact that the more customers there are, the more successful the operation will be, because the unit costs are progressively lower. This is why the Soviets were historically lucky in getting China as customers. They would like also to have, exclusively, India and Africa as customers. If Russia acquires the most customers, we will not be able to compete. They will always have the lower costs on any given level of technology. We are going to have to meet this possibility and meet it vigorously, swiftly, and intelligently. Within the next decade, if we survive at all as an organized set of crossbreeding men on the American continent it will be because we will have suddenly developed a completely new attitude on all these matters. In case you are apprehensive that social and political economics are to be so laggard as to impede your advanced educational programming, it is well to remember that the comprehensive world economics are going to force vast economic reforms of industries and nations, which incidentally will require utter modernization of the educational processes in order to be able to compete and survive.

Every time we educate a man, we as educators have a regenerative experience, and we ought to learn from that experience how to do it much better the next time. The more educated our population the more effective it becomes as an integral of regenerative consumer individuals. We are going to have to invest in our whole population to accelerate its consumer regeneration. We are going to be completely unemployed as muscle-working machines. *We as economic society are going to have to pay our whole population to go to school and pay it to stay at school.* That is, we are going to have to put our whole population into the educational process and get *everybody* realistically literate in many directions. Quite clearly, *the new political word* is going to be *investment*. It is not going to be *dole*, or socialism, or the idea of people hanging around in bread lines. The new popular *regenerative investment* idea is actually that of making people more familiar with the patterns of the universe, that is, with what man has learned about universe to date, and that of getting everybody inter-communicative at ever higher levels of literacy. People are then going to stay in the education process. They are going to populate ever increasing numbers of research laboratories and universities.

As we now disemploy men as muscle and reflex machines, the one area where employment is gaining abnormally fast is the research and development area. Research and development are a part of the educational process itself. We are going to have to invest in our people and make available to them participation in the great educational process of research and development in order to learn more. When we learn more, we are able to do more with our given opportunities. We can rate federally paid-for education as a high return, mutual benefit investment. When we plant a seed and give it the opportunity to grow its fruits pay us back many fold. Man is going to "improve" rapidly in the same way by new federally underwritten educational "seeding" by new tools and processes.

Our educational processes are in fact the upcoming major world industry. This is *it*; this is the essence of today's educational facilities meeting. You are caught in that new educational upward draughting process. The cost of education will be funded regeneratively right out of earnings of the technology, the industrial equation, because we can only afford to reinvest continually in humanity's ability to go back and turn out a better job. As a result of the new educational processes our consuming costs will be progressively lower as we also gain ever higher performance per units of invested resources, which means that our wealth actually will be increasing at all times rather than "exhausted by spending." It is the "capability" wealth that really counts. It is very good that there is an international competitive system now operating, otherwise men would tend to stagnate, particularly in large group undertakings. They would otherwise be afraid to venture in this great intellectual integrity regeneration.

I would say, then, that you are faced with a future in which education is going to be number one amongst the great world industries, within which will flourish an educational machine technology that will provide tools such as the individually selected and articulated two-way TV and an intercontinentally net-worked, documentaries call-up system, operative over any home two-way TV set.

The new educational technology will probably provide also an invention of mine called the Geoscope—a large two-hundred-foot diameter (or more) lightweight geodesic sphere hung hoveringly at one hundred feet above mid-campus by approximately invisible cables from three remote masts. This giant sphere is a miniature earth. Its entire exterior and interior surfaces will be covered with closely-packed electric bulbs, each with variable intensity controls. The lighting of the bulbs is scanningly controlled through an electronic computer. The number of the bulbs and their minimum distance of one hundred feet from viewing eyes, either at the center of the sphere or on the ground outside and below the sphere, will produce the visual effect and resolution of a fine-screen halftone cut or that of an excellent television tube picture. The two-hundred-foot geoscope will cost about fifteen million dollars. It will make possible communication of phenomena that are not at present communicable to man's conceptual understanding. There are many motion patterns such as those of the hands of the clock or of the solar system planets or of the molecules of gas in a pneumatic ball or of atoms or the earth's annual weather that cannot be seen or comprehended by the human eye and brain relay and are therefore inadequately comprehended and dealt with by the human mind.

The Geoscope may be illuminated to picture the earth and the motion of its complete cloud-cover history for years run off on its surface in minutes so that man may comprehend the cyclic patterning and predict. The complete census-by-census of world population history changes could be run off in minutes, giving a clear picture of the demological patterning and its clear trending. The total history of transportation and of world resource discovery, development, distribution, and redistribution could become comprehendible to the human mind, which would thus be able to forecast and plan in vastly greater magnitude than heretofore. The consequences of various world plans could be computed and projected. All world data would be dynamically viewable and picturable and relayable by radio to all the world, so that common consideration in a most educated manner of all world problems by all world people would become a practical event.

The universities are going to be wonderful places. Scholars will stay there for a long, long time—the rest of their lives—while they are developing more and more knowledge about the whole experience of man. All men will be going around the world in due process as everyday routine search and exploration, and the world experiencing patterning will be everywhere—all students from everywhere all over the world. That is all part of the new pattern that is rushing upon us. We will accelerate as rapidly into "yesterday" through archaeology as we do into "tomorrow." Archaeology both on land and under the seas will flourish equally with astronautics.

65

Man–Machine Partnership

Richard H. Bolt

. . . Computers were designed to calculate mathematical relations among numbers and perform logical operations using symbols. In the modern world, unless a worker is engaged in manipulation of physical materials he is engaged almost totally in manipulation of symbols. Further, computers for the most part have been used to carry out long and tedious but conceptually simple manipulations. The design of high-speed digital computers endows them with an extraordinary ability to perform mathematical and logical manipulations in amounts and at speeds that completely over-shadow man's ability in these respects.

When man thinks and reasons, however, he generally uses words, sentences, and language that do not behave neatly like numbers. Further, the manipulations man performs on linguistic information usually are more subtle and complex than mathematical calculations. Here we are drawing two quite different distinctions between computation of the sort usually done on today's computers and cognition of the sort we shall be able to do in tomorrow's partnership. Today we use mostly numbers;

Reprinted from *Toward Better Utilization of Scientific and Engineering Talent,* Publication 1191, Committee on Utilization of Scientific and Engineering Manpower, National Academy of Sciences—National Research Council, Washington, D.C., 1964.

tomorrow we shall use not only numbers but also words—verbal abstractions. Today we perform mostly simply, routine operations; tomorrow we shall perform not only simple operations but also operations that are more complex than any that today's computer systems and programs can handle.

The more important distinction, probably, is the one that concerns complexity. Advancing from numerical to linguistic communication will not be an easy step, but the reward is simply the one we gain from learning a foreign language: now we can communicate where before we could not. Once we have achieved linguistic communication with the machine, however, we then can develop an ever-expanding ability to handle complex processes of thought, and we can apply this ability to all spheres of intellectual endeavor, which, of course, involves a combination of two faculties, memory and association.

The sort of new complexity we can tackle, if we "take a machine into partnership" instead of simply using it from time to time as a one-shot computer, can be explained with the help of an analogy. Solving a problem is like making a journey. There are two distinctly different ways in which we can make a journey—say, from Boston to San Francisco. We can get into an automobile and set off along the highway, following at every intersection the direction-signs that were already in place before this particular journey began. This procedure, of course, depends upon the existence of an elaborate road network and system of signs which exploit and codify the experience of our predecessors, and, to that extent, the element of discovery is taken out of the journey.

At the other extreme, we may travel as the pioneers did, working our way westward toward a goal whose nature is known beforehand only in the most general terms (the Pacific Ocean). In this case, we have no set procedure or highway system: we must make our way from point to point, resetting our course whenever we crest a ridge and come in sight of the next stretch of countryside before us. In such a journey, we are continually being faced with the need to make fresh decisions as we go along, and it is—in the nature of the case—impossible to specify beforehand a detailed set of instructions that will guarantee successful and efficient completion of the journey.

There are two correspondingly different kinds of intellectual problems. There are those in which we can specify explicitly beforehand all the intellectual steps that must be taken if the problem is to be followed successfully through to its solution; and there are those in which, once again, we have to make our way from point to point, repeatedly taking new intellectual decisions in the light of things that are discovered only as we go along. Solving the first, simple, straightforward kind of problem is a standardized and routine operation. All intellectual work involving an element of discovery is of the second, more complex kind, and involves the making of decisions repeatedly and in succession, as the investigation proceeds. Each great discovery made in science, for example, may be viewed as a decision made at an important crossroad.

It is this sort of complexity with which the new generation of machine-aids to cognition is enabling us to deal. The first generation of computing machines was programmed and used largely for routine and standardized operations, comparable to a journey by highway along a route entirely predetermined. Hitherto, that is, machines have been used mainly for "batch processing," in which a completely determinate set of instructions is laid down at the beginning of computation, and there is no opportunity to vary the manner in which the machine deals with the input data in the course of its operation. Although variations are allowed for in some commercial operations, in which the program selects different branches depending upon the inputs received, even in this case all contingencies must be specified in advance.

In order to tackle the more complex kind

of intellectual problem, in which we proceed from point to point, making fresh decisions as we go along, we must develop new ways of working with machines, so as to open up the possibility of repeated interactions between the machine and the user in the course of any particular operation. We must replace batch-processing with a more flexible partnership between man and machine, thereby providing for a sequence of decisions to be taken on route. We mean decisions among *unforeseen* alternatives.

The advantages of this new kind of procedure can be explained easily enough by extending our analogy. There are only two ways we can, in advance, lay down precise instructions for making the automobile journey from Boston to San Francisco: (1) by specifying explicitly, before the journey begins, which road is to be taken at every single intersection along the way, or (2) by requiring that at every intersection all the alternative routes are to be explored, one after another. We can follow the first procedure only if all the essentially creative work of exploration and mapping has been done already; the second procedure will no doubt be effective in the long-enough run, but it may be intolerably wasteful, and we shall most likely end up by surveying a great part of the United States before we actually reach the Pacific.[1]

Yet these are, in effect, the only alternatives batch-processing offers us. We can either instruct the computer beforehand precisely how it is to proceed at every step (and this may involve guessing the answers to a lot of difficult questions, about which reliable information would turn up only in the course of solving the problem under investigation), or else we can set the machine to explore every single possibility as it turns up (and this, once again, is a highly wasteful procedure).

The new style of procedures for machine-aided inquiry, involving repeated interaction between the user and the machine, opens up a whole new degree of freedom in the solution of complex intellectual problems, and permits one to escape from the limitations of batch-processing. But we can gain the advantages of a "repeated interaction" only if we can resolve a major economic problem that such interaction poses.

An investigator who was in a position to monopolize a high-grade computing machine could, no doubt, break down any inquiry into a sequence of small steps, and proceed from point to point by orthodox methods—as it were, stopping his car at every intersection to consult his map afresh. But such a use of a computer would in practice be unacceptable: the machine would be effectively used for only a few milliseconds at a time, and would lie inactive after each step for minutes or even hours. An apparatus costing millions of dollars would thus be utilized for only a very small fraction of the time.

If we are to make repeated-interaction procedures economic, we must develop techniques by which *many independent users* or *teams of users* can operate in partnership with a single central machine *at one and the same time*. In a word, the price of repeated-interaction procedures is the development of a "multiple-access" computer. This is the new technical step upon which all machine-aided cognition, as contrasted with simple computing, fundamentally depends.

Progress in Machine Capabilities

The step required has been taken: during the past three years, time-sharing operation of computers has moved from concept, to laboratory demonstration, to prototype

[1] Whether this second procedure is too wasteful depends, of course, on the speed and cost of the computer used. Also, economy can be increased by programming the machine to remember its successes and failures as it proceeds over any route it has seen before, or to recognize general features of the "map" that may have been described in the program.

systems being used simultaneously by many users.

Time-sharing in itself is not a new art: it is used extensively, for example, in telephone switching networks. What is new is the capability to provide man-machine partnership simultaneously to several users of one computer. Especially relevant is the multiple access to the computer's memory, as is reflected in the expression *memory-sharing* now coming into use. The key step has been the development of special programs that control the access to the computer.

An example of a large, multiple-access system now operating is the Project MAC system at the Massachusetts Institute of Technology. This system includes some 40 Teletypewriters (Model 35), which have access to an IBM 7094 computer in Project MAC and also to another computer of the same type located in the M.I.T. Computation Center. Placed in offices and laboratories throughout the campus, these Teletypewriters offer access to the system simply by dialing through the M.I.T. telephone exchange. Professors and students in many departments are using the system to carry on research on such diverse topics as solving mathematical equations, proving theorems, designing mechanical structures and systems, and making decisions in industrial management.

The system is connected to the TELEX network of the Western Union Company, and within months will be connected to the TWX network of the American Telephone and Telegraph Company. Access thereby offered to persons throughout the United States and in Europe enables the carrying out of several experiments, to provide experience in long-distance operation of time-sharing systems for machine-aided cognition. Already one scientist in Europe has used the system at M.I.T. through a trans-Atlantic Telephone connection.

How many other time-sharing computers are in operation now? Perhaps five or ten, but the number is uncertain because experiments with new uses of computers are springing up faster than news about them can get around.

Most of the progress achieved thus far has come from the development of new programs for the computers. Some of the advances have appeared in the form of new devices, such as visual displays, that help give man an easier, more natural way of interacting with the computer. Not many changes specifically to aid machine-aided cognition have as yet shown up in the design and construction of the basic computer itself, although more such changes will find their way into computers in the future. Perhaps more relevant is the change in the balance among types of "hardware" used; proportionately more of it will be input-output equipment used in linking man and machine.

Advances made in computer programs, now usually called the "software," have been aimed at serving functions of several kinds. One function, mentioned earlier in this paper, is the provision of new language that enables the user to communicate more easily with the machine. Another function is the rapid switching needed to provide multiple access; any one user is hooked in for only a very short interval at a time, but the intervals recur so often that the user, in effect, has continuous access to the computer. Other programs manage the handling of data stored in the computer, call up bodies of information as needed, or assist a programmer in preparing still more programs.

Let us now look, in somewhat more detail, at a few representative systems (perhaps we should say sub-systems) that have been put together to serve man-machine cognition in certain ways. Although for the most part these systems are experimental ones, they already have led to practical results through use in activities such as planning, engineering design, research, and teaching.

First we mention two systems, developed independently, that link a computer to a designer engaged in planning. *Sketchpad*, developed at M.I.T.'s Lincoln Laboratory, puts before the designer a cathode-ray screen, like the face of a television set, flanked by a set of control buttons. With a light-senstive pointer or "light pen" in one hand, the designer sketches a diagram, which may, for example, represent a small machine part or a complete office building. With the other hand on the control panel, he gives the computer the additional information needed to interpret the meaning of the lines he is sketching. The computer can help the designer in a number of ways: it can rotate the figure, change its size, display different cross sections, or combine it with other pieces drawn previously.

In doing its work, *Sketchpad* can put individual pieces together to form an assembly; combine several such assemblies together as sub-assemblies to form a higher assembly; and so on, until the entire structure is put together. Eventually the designer completes his first rough sketch. At this point the computer, using specific dimensions and scales specified by the user, takes over and produces on the screen an accurately scaled drawing with all relevant dimensions indicated. Then the designer can continue to interact with the computer in order to modify and improve his design.

Coplanner, a somewhat different system, is being developed by my colleagues for use in architectural planning. In designing a new hospital, for example, the architect might start by giving the system some relevant statistical data concerning operations in a number of existing hospitals, such as the number of patients served per day, the number of trips that doctors make between various parts of the hospital, and the flow of visitor traffic.

On its screen, *Coplanner* can display the data in any of several forms, such as graphs, tables, or bar charts. With the use of a light pen, the designer can modify the statistical distributions to make them apply more specifically to the particular hospital under consideration, or to project future requirements. Then the designer sketches a possible plan of the hospital, and instructs the computer, using the statistical data, to evaluate the hopital layout in terms of objective design criteria, such as communications efficiency, delays in serving patients, the number of doctors and support personnel needed, and so on. Working together, *Coplanner* simulates the assumed operations in the hospital and the designer modifies the layout, back and forth, until a suitable plan emerges.

Next we cite the use of computer-based systems in engineering design. New roads being built in Sweden, Norway, Finland, and Germany have been designed by engineers interacting with programmed aids developed by AB Nordisk ADB and the Swedish Board of Roads. Aids provided include computer-made movies that let you see "from the driver's seat" what it would be like to drive along roads you have designed. Recently this movie technique has received further development at the Bell Telephone Laboratories.

Stress, a computer program for use in the analysis of structures, is being developed in the Civil Engineering Department at M.I.T. *Stress* converses with the engineer in his own language; helps him analyze a large variety of structures; and carries on a dialogue resulting in successive modifications and improvements to the original design concept.

Machine-aided cognition is starting to play a role in fundamental research. At Thompson Ramo Wooldridge (now Bunker-Ramo), Culler and Fried have developed a system to help the scientist carry out mathematical computations. Seated at a console that includes display scopes and keyboards, the user develops his mathematics on a symbolic level, using any new symbols and operations he may need in exploring the mathematical problem at hand. When he embarks, the scientist may have no clear-cut idea as to how he can solve the problem. At any point along the road, he can ask the machine to display the partial results found up to that point.

Then the scientist may continue to follow the route he has chosen or he may go back and try another approach. In actual use, this system has enabled the solution of some complex, previously unsolved problems in contemporary physics.

As we can see, some of these systems resemble a fast, tireless laboratory assistant with an unlimited memory. And some of the systems being conceived or demonstrated promise to bring truly revolutionary capabilities to bear upon intellectual tasks carried out by planners, managers, physicians, lawyers, educators, writers, scientists, and engineers.

Although very large (and costly) computers serve as the central processors of information for many of the systems being developed, some of the new aids to cognition, such as *Coplanner*, operate in connection with small or medium sized computers. Each size has its advantages and disadvantages, which are being studied in several different organizations using computers of different size and kind. Larger machines can more readily provide multiple access by users in large numbers, and this more widespread use can help in defraying the high costs associated with the development of the auxiliary equipment and with the complex programs needed. Smaller machines, on the other hand, can be set up more cheaply and quickly to explore new approaches in early stages of conception; and can be enlarged later. As we have already noted, the future will see the evolution of computers specially adapted, in size, speed, and all other characteristics, to the special needs of machine-aided cognition.

Future Impacts upon Utilization of Manpower

We turn now to speculations based upon the evidence sketched in preceding sections and elaborated in many publications including those cited in the references. We try to visualize ways in which machine-aided cognition in future decades may affect the utilization of manpower, particularly scientists and engineers. Any or all of the impacts suggested could occur, but we shall not try to guess which ones will prove to be the more important or when the impacts will show up. Some of the impacts will be felt as benefits; others, as difficulties to be overcome. All the impacts will compel us from time to time to reassess the patterns of utilization.

Machine-aided cognition will increase the effective *supply* of manpower in research and, at the same time, will increase the *demand* for such manpower. The research scientist or engineer working in partnership with the machine will be able to carry out a given intellectual task in less time than he would take working alone. Parts of his task automated, and thus speeded, will include searching the literature for information relevant to his research problem, checking the information for reliability and consistency, combining the information with new facts that he (in partnership) has found, plotting graphs and combining graphical data from several sources, and recording all the results. Helping the man carry out these relatively routine chores will not be the most significant contributions the machine will make, but it will save him a great deal of time. The time thus saved converts into an increase in the effective supply of research manpower.

What seems quite likely, in view of the motivational nature of highly creative people, is that the man will go on and do more research, make additional discoveries, and uncover yet more problems that merit research. He will increase the *demand* for more research personnel and for more assistants to help investigators work on the new problems.

More significantly, machine-aided cognition will give men some fresh *capabilities*, beyond those they possess when working alone: notably, in the study of complex processes, involving enormous numbers of variables and interrelationships. To return to our analogy of a cross-country journey, such extremely complex processes present one with many "crossroads," points at which one must make choices among alternatives that could not be foreseen except in the vicinity of the new choice-point. In such cases, man-machine partnership, with its continuous, on-line interaction, will bring its greatest rewards, and the analytical power of this partnership will gain in strength as we discover how the responsibilities may most effectively be divided between the man and the machine.

As a result, the ways in which scientists and engineers tackle their work will be greatly changed. The relative amounts of time they spend on different tasks, the kinds of problems they attack, the patterns of machine-aided collaboration among different persons: the whole *pattern of endeavor* in science and technology will be altered by revolutionary new equipments and environments.

Here the main effect will be an indirect one: machine-aided cognition amplifies the role of automation, such as machine tools, and the automation then replaces skilled and semi-skilled labor in large numbers. For example, certain systems, such as aircraft, already are being designed in part through the use of computers and automated instruments, which are replacing rooms full of draftsmen and months of routine handwork in the shop. In many cases, too, simulation based on the use of computer-based models enables one to dispense with the making and testing of large-scale, physical models of the system. Thus the net impact upon the pattern of endeavor will be a shift away from the more routine tasks and toward the more creative ones. . . .

These new capabilities will, of course, carry with them grave responsibilities, and the moral issues so raised may be as difficult in their own way as those highlighted by the development of nuclear weapons. By his very nature, man will continue to expand his intellectual horizons and venture into the unknown. His new power to control nature will increase his power to control and to encroach upon the privacy of his fellow man. Every such new intellectual advance will carry with it a moral responsibility to use the new powers wisely. This applies to the development of machine-aided cognition as much as to any other new development. Man cannot resolve this issue of possible abuse of his new powers simply by preventing their development; instead, he must learn to live with these powers, to use them properly and so to grow in wisdom and moral sense.

The new man-machine partnership will increase the rate at which scientific and technical information accumulates, and thereby will create added demands for *storage, dissemination, and retrieval of information.* At the same time, systems for man-machine cognition will automatically —we might say necessarily—contain the seeds of solution for the problems associated with the "information explosion."

Through linkage among all the machine systems involved, all recorded information, including the contents of all libraries, will become accessible to all users, no matter where they are. The word "accessible" here refers to the full power of the system to search, check, correlate, and display all relevant information to the human user. The system would, of course, contain such aids to information retrieval as automated card catalogues, aids to bibliographic search, display and print-out capabilities, and all the other appurtenances of the automated library of the future.

Two particular possibilities merit comment here. First, through the use of associative memory, the system will retrieve items of information related to a specified topic but expressed in different ways—specialized jargons—used by workers in different fields. The computer memory is organized in such a way as to associate all items that resemble each other in specified, substantive respects no matter how they are put into language. Second, the system will seek out the user instead of waiting to be consulted. If Scientist A is interested in a certain topic, the information system will recognize the relevance of a new contribution reported by Scientist B, and will relay it directly to Scientist A. Both of these new capabilities, associating similar items and initiating the dissemination of new information, will also find valuable uses outside of science—for example in business management, in which decision makers often require up-to-date information from many unrelated sources.

Improving our ability to retrieve information, in the several ways mentioned, might alone justify all the investments of men and dollars now being made or contemplated in the development of man-machine systems to aid cognitive processes. But again we must emphasize that these relatively "mechanical" gains, speeding and expanding the search for information, are not the contributions that will in the long run be most significant for man's progress. Even more significant will be the creation of entirely new capabilities to deal with complex problems and those that enlarge our conceptual outlooks. . . .

66

Implications of Physiological Feedback Training

Ralph Ezios

In a much-cited passage, Weston LaBarre explicates his idea of *evolution-by-prosthesis* in the following way:

> With human hands, the old-style evolution by body adaptation is obsolete. All previous animals had been subject to the *autoplastic* evolution of their self-substance, committing their bodies to experimental adaptations in a blind genetic gamble for survival. The stakes in this game were high: life or death. Man's evolution, on the other hand, is through *alloplastic* experiments with objects outside his own body and is concerned only with the products of his hands, brains, and eyes—and not with his body itself. (1954, p. 90).

As LaBarre implies, man's technological evolution so far has allowed him to gain better and better discrimination of, control over, and ability to communicate about all manner of events and processes in his environment.

Included in the ever increasing comprehension of the environment, with concommitant ability to manipulate it, through science man has come to learn more about all organisms' internal events and processes.

Printed by permission. The author acknowledges the invaluable assistance of Barbara B. Brown, Eleanor Criswell, Lester Fehmi, Elmer Green, Joseph Hart, Joe Kamiya, Hugh Macdonald, David Nowlis, and Robert Ornstein.

However, man's ability to discriminate, control and communicate about his own personal internal events and processes has never been markedly aided by technological development, and thus the prosthetic evolution has primarily had its effect on man's external environment and only indirectly has it effected him internally. Men have dreamed however of prosthetic devices which would expand their awareness and facility with their interiors. For example in *Mr. Tomkins Inside Himself* (Gamow and Ycas, 1967) the central character has the technological capacity to shrink himself to the size of a blood cell and then inject himself into his own body, so that he can observe various phenomena of modern biology going on inside his heart, cortex, sexual organs, and so on.

Physiological feedback training is exciting in this context because it is a small beginning in expanding and changing the direction of *evolution-by-prosthesis* and for the first time making it possible for an individual man to use technology to come to know himself better. The basic mechanism employed in feedback training is an electronic system which amplifies and informs the person as to the on-going activity of a selected physiological process, thereby aiding the person in discriminating the presence of events or stages in the process, thereby enabling him to gain some degree of voluntary control over this process, and also allowing him to develop a degree of sophistication in communicating about the process previously out of his scope. Although it could be argued that the mirror and the bathroom scale are considerably earlier instruments designed to give personal feedback on intrapersonal processes, the type of feedback is useful primarily in monitoring internal processes only indirectly as they effect externally apparent aspects of a person using them.

Now that the basic technique has been pioneered by Kamiya (1962) and Brown (1968), a number of psychologists have independently taken up the study of physiological feedback training. In discussions with each other we have been surprised at how many times various potential applications of the basic technique have occurred to us separately in our various laboratories. Consequently we have gathered together the following list of potential applications of the technique, in the hopes that these ideas will stimulate further research interest in the basic technique, that our report will be helpful for students in learning more about it, and that we may prove helpful in providing some sort of jumping-off-place for others to go further with our ideas. Thus we list below some of our ideas about potential applications of the technique to basic research, therapy, entertainment and education.

Basic Research in Psychology

Recently mathematical techniques have been developed for describing internal representations, and the relationship between these internal representations and their corresponding external objects (Shepard and Chipman, 1969). So far the technique has only been applied to internal representations of external objects, but there would seem to be no barrier to using the technique to study internal representations of internal events. It is hoped, for example, that Shepard's technique (see also Shepard, 1962) could be applied to scaled reports on the mental activity associated with EEG alpha generation or alpha suppression (Nowlis & Macdonald, 1969). Perhaps even more promising would be the possibility of applying the Shepard and Chipman procedure to subjective reports on a number of concurrent physiological processes. Green (1969) for example now has a technique for simultaneously giving EEG, EMG, and skin temperature feedback. And Macdonald, at Stanford, has developed a feedback system capable of giving wave-analog, envelope-analog, or on-off auditory feedback that has been used successfully in teaching discrimination and control over heart rate, skin temperature, EMG, EEG, vasodilation and GSR. Using such electronic systems in a laboratory, the mathematical model to be derived could be of the relations between the internal representations of the processes in question, and the isomorphism could be studied with the relations between the processes themselves as recorded on the polygraph. For example, rather than be asked to describe the experience of EEG alpha per se, a subject could be asked whether it was more similar to lowering EMG or lowering skin temperature. With many physiological parameters, a model could be built up of the subjective proximities of the various parameters, and it certainly would be interesting to compare such a subjective model with an objectively derived model of actual tendencies for the various parameters to vary conjointly or independently.

The above considerations point to a need for a more adequate theory of the relationship between awareness and internal somatic events. We have definitely felt this need. Three alternatives are currently vying for our favor, and hopefully some of the basic and applied research problems that we will enumerate here, plus others using feedback training as an investigatory tool, will lead to a selection between, or, more likely, a synthesis of the various points of view. One perspective, implicitly advanced in the paper on feedback training by Stoyva and Kamiya (1968) is that awareness and the physiological processes are overlapping and to some extent identical. That is, a person generating regular alpha is, while the alpha is present, in an "alpha state," strongly predisposing him to certain subjective feelings (e.g., pleasure and relaxation) and certain behaviors (e.g., wanting to generate more alpha). The second perspective, advanced by Shepard and Chipman for the study of internal representations of external events and revised by us only slightly so as to be applicable to internal events, posits that the internal events themselves are not identical or even isomorphic with internal representations of them, but that the internal representations can best be brought to the fore and made the object of research by looking into their relations with each other. Finally there is a third perspective, best described as the *evolution-by-prosthesis* argument turned inward, which assumes that awareness and internal physiological processes are basically separate, although affected by one another, and that feedback training can simply be a tool of awareness, for developing the same skills in discrimination, control and verbalization of one's somatic world that earlier technological advancement has led to for one's external environment. The first position lends itself to model building based on subjective report concerning single physiological processes, the second to the Shepard proximity analysis technique, and the third to standard psychophysical scaling techniques, designed to study the threshold and just noticeable differences in the awareness of one's own physiological processes. Whatever theoretical position wins the day, a positive result will be reconceptualization of the presently unsatisfactory term *introspection.*

Finally, another application of feedback training technique to basic research is illustrated in the work of Dr. David Kahn. In Kahn's procedure a reinforcer is controlled by activity in a particular physiological site, generally a single motor unit in the hand, and the subject, because of dummy electrodes, lack of explanation, and the extreme specificity of the site monitored, has no idea of the relationship between the site activity and the appearance or disappearance of the reinforcer.

Kahn uses essentially two different experimental paradigms. In the first subjects are given a complete explanation of the procedure. When highly experienced with the technique they can then imitate a wide variety of rhythmic patterns with the firings and resting periods of the particular site selected. But these same subjects cannot explain how they do it, nor can they identify for Kahn any phenomenological associations of their ability to control the site activity. In the other paradigm, naive subjects are given no explanation of the procedure, and even though they have no awareness of what they are doing, they learn to lengthen the duration of exposure to tachistoscopic pictures through changes in the site activity. When told later the appearance of the picture had been associated with some physiological process, and asked to guess which one, subjects are as likely to pick one of the dummy electrodes as the electrode for the site in question.

In this type of feedback procedure, the focus of attention is on the reinforcer rather than the internal event. Kahn's technique is particularly promising for the study of implicit preference, for finding out about what people value when they don't realise their values or preferences are being tested. However, similarities are present between this technique and the Kamiya-Brown feedback technique as far as research applications go. For example, it would certainly be interesting to study the isomorphism between a model derived of a person's explicit value structure and his implicit value structure. In an experimental way it would appear to be possible to objectify non-conscious preferences and compare them with preferences expressed with awareness of the fact of making the choice.

It would also be interesting to investigate the degree to which non-conscious preferences could be altered by giving the subject awareness of what he was doing. For example, would a puritanical type who has non-consciously learned to evoke tachistoscopic pictures with sexual material in them than choose to inhibit the picture after learning what he was doing? Would he be able to?

Clearly some of the basic research applications of the feedback technique are closly tied to problems in diagnosis and treatment. The dividing line is not clear, but let us now move on to some applications that are still researchable, but more straightforwardly oriented toward the therapeutic.

Therapeutic Applications: Biomedical and Psychological

Hart (in press) points out that feedback training tends to obscure somewhat the normal expert-patient relationship in therapy. Feedback devices allow a patient to know himself better, while allowing him to develop his own attitudes about what he finds out.

The development of inexpensive and portable devices to give feedback opens up a number of therapeutic possibilities. One may begin by considering some applications in the field of psychosomatic medicine. For example, Shapiro, et al. (1969) have shown that people can learn to lower their blood pressure. Thus patients with high blood pressure could be given small portable devices for checking themselves regularly against high blood pressure. If the blood pressure were unusually high, they could then employ techniques that they had previously learned to lower it, and could make sure that they had succeeded by checking themselves against the portable device. This procedure either could be used at bedside in the hospital, or the device could be rented or purchased to be used in the patients' regular daily life. Thus the physiological consequences of states of mind engendered by environments or actions which the patient would be likely to encounter could be better comprehended, thereby allowing the patient to get insight into the psychological component of his particular illness, and even providing an opportunity to learn to control the symptomotology after developing this insight. While the patient should not be led to overly high expectations during his illness, the ability to use such devices could well be morale boosting to the patient who otherwise feels he has no hand in combatting his own illness, and that his fate is in the hands of the experts alone.

Many variations on the theme exist. A portable device for monitoring psychogalvanic skin response is already in production. Similarly a device that has been built by Hugh Macdonald with integrated circuitry capable of giving feedback on EEG, EMG, heart rate, skin temperature, vasoconstriction, and GSR could be mass produced for sale at very low prices. Patients with irregular EEGs predisposing to epilepsy, who get headaches or backaches from tense muscles, who have irregular heart beats at times, or who have any relevant physiological irregularities which vary with their psychological state might find these devices helpful. It would even seem in the realm of possibility to build small, inexpensive devices for feed-back concerning stomach acidity, of potential use to patients with ulcers. Or feedback devices could be developed to allow a patient to listen to his intestinal functioning, to aid in proper digestive actions. Miller (1969) has shown that control over intestinal and digestive functioning can be developed very rapidly in animals.

A number of alternatives exist as to the type of feedback that would be given in these portable devices. In one potential type, most useful as a portable constant monitor, a physiological process would be monitored and the patient would receive a signal only if the process should cross a criterion indicating it was moving in an unfavorable direction (blood pressure too high, stomach acidity too high, heart becoming irregular, etc.) In another approach, most useful as a portable means for learning or regaining control, the feedback would be more analogous to the full process. Tiny variations in the physiological parameter would be brought to the attention of the patient and the patient could then engage in mental activities which would help to bring out desirable functioning.

In the area of psychiatry and clinical psychology such devices could also possibly be used with patients who had no specific somatic complaints. Because it is now possible to simultaneously monitor overt behavior, covert moods, and physiological processes in the natural setting (Nowlis & Cohen, 1968) procedures could be developed whereby both patient and therapist could develop more understanding of the covert moods and physiological patterns of behavior accompanying exposure to various aspects of the patients' environment. Then the patient could choose internal events which he would like to have occur more regularly, or more voluntarily, in his daily life and could begin a program of training, first at some training facility, then attempting to produce the pattern in the desired situation in his natural setting. Such procedures could increase the number of patients that a therapist could see, decrease the cost of psychotherapy, and decrease the problems associated with therapists' perceiving and dealing with patients from a single value system. In this type of therapy program, patients would have an unusual degree of freedom to choose their own goals, experiment with implementing and modifying the goals as they progressed in therapy, and test the results of the therapy in a very direct way against their actual life situation.

Another psychotherapeutic use of feedback technology could be in sensitivity training. Two people could use the feedback devices mutually in a number of meaningful ways. For example, one person could learn to help a naive person to reach certain physiological states. The naive person would receive no feedback, but the other person would behave in various ways to attempt to deliberately bring about various states in the first person. Or two people could observe the effect of various kinds of behavior on each other. Or, again, two people could together attempt to control a feedback loop designed to cue them only when both were in the same desired physiological state.

Furthermore, whole groups can learn to control certain feedback devices together.

For example, the portable device previously mentioned designed by Buryl Payne, now available commercially to be used in giving visual and auditory feedback as to GSR, can easily be used by a large group holding hands, with two people in the group each holding one electrode instead of each other's hand. Groups could then attempt to together learn to increase and decrease their GSR, either alone or while being exposed to various stimuli. This kind of learning situation might be quite useful to certain groups. For example, any group of people who have to work together under conditions of high stress might want to learn to keep their GSR low, first alone, and then while exposed to stress provoking messages. Presumably, each individual would be learning not only to keep his own responses low, but would also be learning ways to help his fellow team members stay relaxed.

More basic research needs to be done on understanding physiological relaxation. Most of the physiological processes which have been successfully conditioned in our various laboratories are apparently influencable by relaxation; that is, subjects learning to generate more alpha rhythm in their electroencephalogram, or lower muscle tension in their electromyogram, or lower heart rate, or warmer skin temperature, or larger vasodilation, or lower galvanic skin responsivity all tend to say that there is an element of relaxation involved in moving the process in that direction. Interestingly, our early findings also tend to agree that a subject who, through relaxation, has learned to influence one of these processes is not necessarily making any change in the other processes apparently influencable by relaxation—for which the subject has not been given feedback. In fact, the processes appear to be remarkably independent in spite of the similar reports of relaxation. However, because relaxation is clearly involved in some way in the learning of each, one wonders if feedback training could in any way be used as a substitute for relaxant and tranquilizing drugs with patients suffering from anxiety symptoms, especially if the patients were trained to relax by multiple physiological criteria.

In our laboratories we know of at least one case of anxiety that has been treated with EMG and EEG feedback. Doctors had prescribed doses of tranquilizing drugs so heavy that the patient could barely operate in her normal setting. The patient now has successfully learned her EMG low and the alpha component of her EEG high, even while sitting in postures similar to the ones she must sit in during her normal daily routine. Anxiety and tension has been reduced markedly enough, so that the patient now uses much lower amounts of tranquilizers, as recommended by her independent physician. EMG may be a particularly promising process to work with for such therapeutic benefits (see also Stoyva, 1969), but it may be that several processes monitored simultaneously could give the most effective relaxation training of all.

Those of us who have had experience in teaching relaxation to subjects through hypnosis, autogenic training, the Jacobson relaxation method, or other systems all feel that subjects can learn the same degree of deep relaxation which otherwise might take months of training after only a few sessions, perhaps two or three hours, of feedback training.

More directly in the area of psychopharmacology, another clinical use could be in the area of studying the interaction of various levels of a given physiological process with the effects of pharmacological agents. For example pharmacological research could be aided by human or animal subjects who had learned to shift to many different levels of functioning so that the effects of the drug could be evaluated more precisely at specific levels over fairly long periods of time. This would be preferable to the present method of letting subjects simply fluctuate without controlling their physiological processes in any way. It could become easier to identify certain dangers in the way in which a drug could interact with a person's physiological changes. Also, it might be that certain desirable drug effects could be potentiated by administering them to a subject who would then keep himself in a certain state. For example a psychoactive drug might have a particularly positive effect in a subject maintaining a high amount of alpha in his EEG. Or a pain reducing drug might be especially effective when a patient also was showing vasodilation. Thus smaller doses of drugs might be used, and their effects predicted more carefully, in suitable patients who had learned to control appropriate physiological processes.

Entertainment and Aesthetics

There are at least two, rather different, applications of feedback technique to entertainment, one of the Kahn procedure, the other of the Kamiya-Brown procedure. Both applications however are based on the same general strategy, namely that the feedback signal itself need not be just a tone or a light, but can be slides of paintings of fine art, a motion picture, recorded music, or any of a large number of aesthetically pleasing stimulations.

The Kahn technique could be used in the study of aesthetic preference. When subjects do not realise they are making the choice, what kind of aesthetic stimuli do they actually choose to have prolonged for their enjoyment? If a film for example were brought into focus by activity in a single motor unit in the hand, but dissolved by cessation of activity, and a subject had various dummy electrodes on and had incomplete understanding of the situation (as in the Kahn experiment), would the subject involuntarily "choose" to watch certain films and "choose" to dissolve others. Or in the study of architecture or interior design, what pictures of living arrangements would be preferred and which dissolved. Again, if TV or magazine advertisements were the stimuli, which would be accepted and which dissolved? In marketing and advertising there is probably an important psychological distinction between what people say they like, and what in fact they feel a real tendency to choose. This is the only method that we know of that could give objective data about both factors independently.

It has been called to our attention that there are now multi-media environment systems available, where as many as 12 film or slide projectors are controlled simultaneously and as many as 5 tracks of sounds. It could be both entertaining and instructive to have such a presentation controlled by a number of on-going physiological processes in a single individual, entertaining because of the person's sense of being intimately linked with the presentation, and instructive because in the past one of the most difficult aspects of psychophysiology to grasp has been the simultaneous intervariability of many physiological parameters.

Another potentially entertaining and instructive situation would be to have two or three people control with their physiological processes various aspects of the multi-media presentation. The people at first would just enjoy watching and hearing the patterns they were producing, and then could begin to test the effects of various kinds of interaction with each other on the blendings and discordances of the displays.

Education

In most of our laboratories the most easily obtained subjects have been college students. We have all been impressed with the intense enthusiasm that some of these subjects have developed for feedback training. Some have offered to shave off their hair if it would be helpful in attaching the electrodes (a totally unnecessary step incidentally); others have asked if we would be willing to continue running them as subjects if they would pay us to do it.

The remarkable interest in feedback training, unprecedented in the other kinds of psychological research that we have done, has also been apparent among professional people in psychology, particularly in the younger members of the field. Plans to form a "feedback society" of people in the field were met with unusual enthusiasm, and there are now over 100 professionals on a potential society mailing list (a marked increase over the six on the list last year), many of them planning to attend the first meetings of the proposed society in September.

What explains this interest? Part of it is that very meaningful questions are being asked about human beings, questions which are fascinating to laymen and professional, and to people from eastern and western cultural backgrounds alike. Part of it is the pleasure both experimenter and subject can feel in research which does not need to include deceit or manipulation on the part of the experimenter. And part of the interest may be because of an increasing desire on the part of young people to explore and come to know the internal world as well as the external.

We ourselves have felt this interest in exploring our own internal process. Thus one of us, like his subjects, has learned to control to at least some extent his EEG, EMG, vasodilation, GSR, heart rate, and skin temperature. The most fascinating and pleasurable experience for this experimenter was in the brief time he spent working on the skin temperature of his hands. Within ten minutes the person could warm or cool his hands, deliberately altering the direction on command when another of us signalled with a click from a nearby instrument room, the click signaling "go in the opposite direction." The experimenter could alternately cool and warm his hands even when the clicks came as rapidly as one a second. The process involved was one the experimenter had lived with all his life but had never had any insight into or voluntary control over until the ten minute feedback practice period. It was almost like discovering a new frontier, still needing to be charted and explored although close to us for millennia.

Some feel that oriental meditators are among the very few people who have developed sophisticated perceptual skills for internal processes. Such considerations might be useful in explaining why one aspect of the feedback training technique has been of particular fascination to many lay people (e.g., Luce and Segal, 1966) and professionals alike. This aspect is the potential application of feedback training to the western practice of eastern meditation. A number of independent studies done in India and Japan (e.g., Anand, 1961; Kasamatsu and Hirai, 1962) agree that there are physiological patterns which are strongly related to deep meditation, particularly in the EEG, and EMG. The alpha rhythm is markedly increased in both yogic and zen meditation, and is generated over areas of the cortex normally not involved in alpha production. Meanwhile, the EMG tends to fall to very low levels.

By this time some yogis and zen monks have actually had the opportunity to try feedback training, and to listen to themselves as they meditate. They have tended to agree with westerner's speculations that such devices might be useful in teaching people the elementaries of meditation. In other words, westerners could overcome handicaps of cross-cultural translations and busy schedules in imitating the physiological patterns of expert meditators, thereby perhaps learning the basic state of mind for at least the beginning stages of meditation. Subjects can learn to control their EEG to a measurable extent after only a brief period of practice (Nowlis & Kamiya, 1968; Nowlis & Macdonald, 1969). EMG control, depending on the muscle used, is also not difficult to achieve. Thus a student with either a portable feedback device similar to that designed by Macdonald, or with a central training facility available, for example at his college health service, could learn to meditate in a state of mind similar to that of a zen monk or a yogi.

Thus feedback devices and feedback training may be helpful in providing people with a chance to explore the internal, and in a socially constructive way. Perhaps because western society and western education are so oriented to discrimination and control of external events, the opposite abilities, perhaps providing some relief from practice of the others, are highly prized among the younger generation. Certainly feedback training is less dangerous and more constructive than drug use, or "dropping out," alternatives which attract large numbers of bright and potentially highly valuable young members of our society (H. H. Nowlis, 1968).

Thus our first hope is that feedback training will be valuable in education because through it students could learn to discriminate internal processes potentially affecting their physical health and psychological well-being, and, in addition, would be provided with a meaningful alternative to taking drugs or dropping out of school to "expand" their internal awareness.

Other applications to education are possible. For example, educational psychologists might want to determine if certain controllable physiological states lead to maximum receptivity in learning. If so, probably depending on the type of learning task, a student could deliberately bring out a favorable internal state before involving himself with his work. Particularly, on days of high academic stress, a student could imitate the covert behavior patterns, during studying and/or breaks, of students who had shown themselves especially capable of handling such stressful days (Nowlis & Cohen, 1968).

Where Do We stand?

Although results on feedback training have so far consistently yielded encouraging results, we have no idea at present of what the limits are. Results with animals have demonstrated some particularly complex processes can be rapidly brought under control, such as blood flow in one ear lobe, blood flow in the stomach lining, peristalsis, and kidney functioning (see review by Miller, 1969). There is no doubt that EEG activity can be controlled by animals and humans (Kamiya, 1962; Olds, 1963; Bundzen, 1965; Dewan, 1966; Mulholland, 1967; Hart, 1967; Sterman & Wrywicka, 1967; Carmona, 1967; Sterman and Howe, 1969; Fox, 1969). Heart rate can clearly be controlled by humans (see review by Murray & Katkin, 1968), and blood pressure can be lowered (Shapiro et al., 1969). Similarly, with humans, GSR, EMG, skin temperature, and vasodilation are controllable (Green, 1969; Stoyva, 1969).

In one experiment, subjects were allowed to gain insight into the effect of various types of mental activity on their EEG for a practice period of 15 minutes, observing the effects on a feedback tone keyed to their EEG alpha. After this short practice period, 16 out of 16 were able to show some ability to control the feedback tone, that is when instructed to keep the tone on for 2 minutes they did so more than when instructed to keep the tone off for the same period of time (Nowlis & Kamiya, 1969). In another similar experiment, 28 out of 32 subjects were able to show evidence of control after only seven minutes practice and 31 out of 32 showed control after 12 minutes of practice (Nowlis & Macdonald, 1969). The subjects used in these experiments knew nothing about EEG alpha beforehand and were not aware of the reports of other subjects as to mental activity associated with control.

Limitations

Although there is clearly promise in the area, the dynamics of the types of control acquired are poorly understood; there are many thorny theoretical problems to be solved; and there are important issues of methodology, especially with human subjects, involving experimental control procedures, baseline recordings, and other things which have not been well worked out.

Also, we know little about possible aversive effects of feedback training. In the Stanford laboratory over 100 subjects have been given at least one session with their EEG feedback, and about 50 have come in for experiments involving large numbers of sessions. Generally good communications have been developed with these subjects and they have been encouraged to talk about any possible aftereffects of their training experiences, even though neurologists have assured us there is little need for concern here. Two incidents have occurred which temporarily worried us. In the first, a girl who had been in for ten sessions with us had a small cardiovascular accident in her cortex 8 weeks after her last session, causing some temporary paralysis on one side. She was given three days of intensive neurological testing at the Stanford Medical School, and the neurologists there then felt that the cause of the problem was birth control pills, which she had just begun using. They assured us the problem had not been the result of the feedback training. In the second, a girl who had 3 training sessions missed a fourth appointment two weeks after the third because of dizzy spells. An intensive phsychiatric interview revealed that there were stress factors present at the time which most likely explained the problem, and again it was felt that there was no relation to the feedback training. The first girl's problem did clear up with abstinence from birth control pills, and it seems most likely the second girls problem will clear up on reduction of her anxiety provoking current situation. Since we know of no other cases with any type of feedback training where any kind of aversive consequences occurred, there is no evidence at present that such training could have harmful consequences.

A good deal of basic research and theory building still needs to be done. Hopefully, the proposed feedback society will be helpful in encouraging communication and areas of specialization in the field.

Concluding Remarks

The feedback training technique lends itself easily to speculation, and we are sure there are many applications beyond what we have mentioned here. When inexpensive portable feedback devices are commercially available, for example, we are sure people will think of many creative uses. We have only mentioned our more straight forward and practical ideas. Much more speculative thinking has gone along the lines of (1) could a feedback device be built to cue a woman as to her time of ovulation, (2) could feedback devices be used to get two or more people into very similar states, thus allowing demonstration of mental telepathy and other phenomena of parapsychology, (3) could feedback devices be helpful in the training of creative artists, training the artists to bring out internal states appropriate to various types of aesthetic productions, (4) could such devices be used in controlling artificial limbs, so that voluntary physiological changes would change the position of the limb, (5) could awareness of various muscle activities through EMG feedback be useful to athletes, etc. It is hard to stop thinking of uses once you begin trying it.

BIBLIOGRAPHY

ANAND, B. K., CHHINA, G. S. & SINGH, B. Some aspects of electroencephalographic studies in Yogis. *Electroencephalography and Clinical Neurophysiology,* 1961, *13,* 452–456.

BASMAJIAN, J. V. Control and training of individual motor units. *Science*. 1963, *141*, 440–441.

BRENER, J., KLEINMAN, R. A., & GOESLIN, W. J. The effects of different exposures to augmented sensory feedback on the control of heart rate. *Psychophysiology*, 1969, *5*, 510–516.

BROWN, B. B. Awareness of EEG-subjective activity relationships detected within a closed feedback system. Presented to the Society for Psychophysiological Research, October, 1968.

BROWN, B. B. Recognition of aspects of consciousness through association with EEG alpha activity represented by a light signal. *Psychophysiology*, 1970, *6*, 442–452.

BUNDZEN, P. V. Autoregulation of functional state of the brain: An investigation using photostimulation with feedback. *Federation Proceedings Translation Supplement*, 1966, *25*, T551-T554. (Originally from *Fiziologicheskii Zhurnal SSSR* imeni I. M. Sechenova, 1965, *51*, 936.)

CARMONA, A. B. Trial and error learning of the voltage of the cortical EEG activity. Yale University, doctoral dissertation, 1967.

DEWAN, E. Communication by voluntary control of the electroencephalogram. *Proceedings of the Symposium on Biomedical Engineering*, Marquette University, June, 1966.

Engel, B. T. & Hansen, S. P. Operant conditioning of heart rate slowing. *Psychophysiology*, 1966, *3*, 176–187.

ENGEL, B. T. & CHISM, R. A. Operant conditioning of heart rate speeding. *Psychophysiology*, 1967, *3*, 418–426.

FETZ, E. E. Operant conditioning of cortical unit activity. *Science*, 1969, *163*, 955–958.

FOX, S. S. & RUDELL, A. P. Operant controlled neural event: Formal and systematic approach to electrical coding of behavior in brain. *Science*, 1968, *162*, 1299–1302.

GAMOW, G. & YCAS, M. *Mr. Tompkins Inside Himself: Adventures in the New Biology*. New York: The Viking Press, 1967.

GREEN, E. E. Autoregulation of hand temperature and of electromyographic responses. In L. FEHMI (Chm.) Autoregulation of electrophysiological processes. Symposium presented at the Second Annual Winter Conference on Brain Research. Snowmass-at-Aspen, Colorado, January, 1969.

GREEN, E. E., WALTERS, E. D., GREEN, A. M., & MURPHY, G. Feedback technique for deep relaxation. *Psychophysiology*, 1969, *5*, 371–377.

HART, J. T. Autocontrol of EEG alpha. Paper delivered to the Society for Psychophysiological Research. San Diego, October, 1967.

HART, J. T. Beyond psychotherapy: A programmatic essay on the applied psychology of the future. Chapter 34 in Hart, J. T. and Tomlinson, T. M. (eds.), *New Directions in Client-Centered Psychotherapy*. Houghton-Mifflin Co., 1970.

KAMIYA, J. Conditional discrimination of the EEG alpha rhythm in humans. Paper presented at the Western Psychological Association, San Francisco, 1962.

KAMIYA, J. Operant control of the EEG alpha rhythm and some of its reported effects on consciousness. In Tart, C. T. (Ed.) *Altered States of Consciousness*. New York: Wiley and Sons, 1969.

KASAMATSU, A. & HIRAI, T. An electroencephalographic study on the Zen meditation (Zazen). *Folia Psychatrica et Neurologica*, 1966, *20*, 315–336.

KUPRIANOVICH, L. The process of instruction during sleep can be regulated. Technika-Molodezhi, 1965, no. 11, 26–28. Cited by Mulholland, T. in Feedback electroencephalography, *Activitas Nervosa Superior*, 1968, *10*, 410–438.

LABARRE, W. *The Human Animal*. Chicago: University of Chicago Press, 1954.

LUCE, G. G. & SEGAL, J. *Sleep,* Chap. 11, "Unconscious Learning," pp. 263–287. New York: Lancer, 1966.

MILLER, N. E. Learning of visceral and glandular responses. *Science,* 1969, *163*, 434–445.

MULHOLLAND, T. The concept of attention and the electroencephalographic alpha rhythm. Paper read at National Physical Laboratory on "The concept of attention in neurophysiology," Teddington, England, October, 1967. To be published in the proceedings.

MURRAY, E. N. & KATKIN, E. S. Comment on two recent reports of operant heart rate conditioning. *Psychophysiology,* 1968, *5*, 192–195.

NOWLIS, D. P. & COHEN, A. Y. Mood-reports and the college natural setting: A day in the lives of three roommates under academic pressure. *Psychological Reports,* 1968, *23*, 551–566.

NOWLIS, D. P. & KAMIYA, J. The control of electroencephalographic alpha rhythms through auditory feedback and the associated mental activity. *Psychophysiology,* 1970, *6*, 476–484.

NOWLIS, D. P. & MACDONALD, H. Progress toward a model of mental activity associated with voluntary control of EEG alpha. In L. Fehmi (Chm.) Autoregulation of electrophysiological processes. Symposium presented at the Second Annual Winter Conference on Brain Research. Snowmass-at-Aspen, Colorado, January, 1969.

NOWLIS, D. P. & MACDONALD H. Rapidly developed control of EEG alpha rhythms through feedback training with reports of associated mental activities. Unpublished.

NOWLIS, H. H. *Drugs on the College Campus.* New York: Doubleday, 1968.

OLDS, J. Mechanisms of instrumental conditioning. In R. Hernandez-Peon (Ed.). The physiological basis of mental activity. *EEG and Clinical Neurophysiology,* Suppl. 24, 1963, 219–234.

OLDS, J. & OLDS, M. E. Interference and learning systems. In J. F. Delafresnaye (Ed.). *Brain Mechanisms and Learning.* Springfield, Ill.: C. C. Thomas, 1961. Pp. 153–187.

SHAPIRO, D., TURSKY, B., GERSHON, E., & STERN, M. Effects of feedback and reinforcement on the control of human systolic blood pressure. *Science,* 1969, *163*, 588–590.

SHEPARD, R. N. The analysis of proximities: Multidimensional scaling with an unknown distance function. I & II. *Psychometrika,* 1962, *27*, 125–140; 219–246.

SHEPARD, R. N. & CHIPMAN, S. A revised concept of isomorphism and a technique for the study of internal representations. Unpublished manuscript, Stanford and Harvard Universities, April, 1969.

STERMAN, M. B. & WYRWICKA, W. EEG correlates of sleep: Evidence for separate forebrain substrates. *Brain Research*, 1967, *6*, 143–163.

STERMAN, M. B. & HOWE, R. EEG correlates of behavioral inhibition. In L. Fehmi (Chm.) Autoregulation of electrophysiological processes. Symposium presented at the Second Annual Winter Conference on Brain Research. Snowmass-at-Aspen, Colorado, January, 1969.

STOYVA, J. & KAMIYA, J. Electrophysiological studies of dreaming as the prototype of a new strategy in the study of consciousness. *Psychological Review,* 1968, *75*, 192–205.

STOYVA, J. Can electrophysiological studies of dreaming be used as a paradigm for other research in psychophysiological relationships? In E. Hartmann (Ed.), *Sleep and Dreaming,* International Psychiatry Clinics, Quarterly Monograph Series, Little-Brown, 1969.

WYRWICKA, W. & STERMAN, M. B. Instrumental conditioning of sensorimotor cortex EEG spindles in the waking cat. *Physiology and Behavior,* 1968, *3*, 703–707.

67

Inventions—Likely and Less Likely for the Last Third of the Twentieth Century

Herman Kahn and Anthony J. Wiener

One Hundred Technical Innovations Very Likely in the Last Third of the Twentieth Century

1. Multiple applications of lasers and masers for sensing, measuring, communication, cutting, heating, welding, power transmission, illumination, destructive (defensive), and other purposes
2. Extreme high-strength and/or high-temperature structural materials
3. New or improved superperformance fabrics (papers, fibers, and plastics)
4. New or improved materials for equipment and appliances (plastics, glasses, alloys, ceramics, intermetallics, and cermets)
5. New airborne vehicles (ground-effect machines, VTOL and STOL, superhelicopters, giant and/or supersonic jets)
6. Extensive commerical application of shaped-charge explosives
7. More reliable and longer-range weather forecasting
8. Intensive and/or extensive expansion of tropical agriculture and forestry
9. New sources of power for fixed installations (e.g., magnetohydrodynamic, thermionic and thermoelectric, and radioactivity)
10. New sources of power for ground transportation (storage battery, fuel cell, propulsion [or support] by electromagnetic fields, jet engine, turbine, and the like)
11. Extensive and intensive worldwide use of high altitude cameras for mapping, prospecting, census, land use, and geological investigations
12. New methods of water transportation (such as large submarines, flexible and special purpose "container ships," or more extensive use of large automated single-purpose bulk cargo ships)
13. Major reduction in hereditary and congenital defects
14. Extensive use of cyborg techniques (mechanical aids or substitutes for human organs, senses, limbs, or other components)

15. New techniques for preserving or improving the environment
16. Relatively effective appetite and weight control
17. New techniques and institutions for adult education
18. New and useful plant animal species
19. Human "hibernation" for short periods (hours or days) for medical purposes
20. Inexpensive design and procurement of "one of a kind" items through use of computerized analysis and automated production
21. Controlled and/or supereffective relaxation and sleep
22. More sophisticated architectural engineering (e.g., geodesic domes, "fancy" stressed shells, pressurized skins, and esoteric materials)
23. New or improved uses of the oceans (mining, extraction of minerals, controlled "farming," source of energy, and the like)
24. Three-dimensional photography, illustrations, movies, and television
25. Automated or more mechanized housekeeping and home maintenance
26. Widespread use of nuclear reactors for power
27. Use of nuclear explosives for excavation and mining, generation of power, temperature–high-pressure environments, and/or as a source of neutrons or other radiation
28. General use of automation and cybernation in management and production
29. Extensive and intensive centralization (or automatic interconnection) of current and past personal business information in high-speed data processors
30. Other new and possibly pervasive techniques for surveillance, monitoring, and control of individuals and organizations
31. Some control of weather and/or climate
32. Other (permanent or temporary) changes—or experiments—with the overall environment (e.g., the "permanent" increase in C-14 and temporary creation of other radioactivity by nuclear explosions, the increasing generation of CO_2 in the atmosphere, projects Starfire, West Ford, and Storm Fury)
33. New and more reliable "educational" and propaganda techniques for affecting human behavior—public and private
34. Practical use of direct electronic communication with and stimulation of the brain
35. Human hibernation for relatively extensive periods (months to years)
36. Cheap and widely available central war weapon systems
37. New and relatively effective counterinsurgency techniques (and perhaps also insurgency techniques)
38. New techniques for very cheap, convenient, and reliable birth control
39. New, more varied, and more reliable drugs for control of fatigue, relaxation, alertness, mood, personality, perceptions, fantasies, and other psychobiological states
40. Capability to choose the sex of unborn children
41. Improved capability to "change" sex of children and/or adults
42. Other genetic control and/or influence over the "basic constitution" of an individual
43. New techniques and institutions for the education of children
44. General and substantial increase in life expectancy, postponement of aging, and limited rejuvenation
45. Generally acceptable and competitive synthetic foods and beverages (e.g., carbohydrates, fats, proteins, enzymes,

vitamins, coffee, tea, cocoa, and alcoholic liquor)

46. "High quality" medical care for undeveloped areas (e.g., use of medical aides and technicians, referral hospitals, broad spectrum antibiotics, and artificial blood plasma)
47. Design and extensive use of responsive and supercontrolled environments for private and public use (for pleasurable, educational, and vocational purposes)
48. Physically nonharmful methods of overindulging
49. Simple techniques for extensive and "permanent" cosmetological changes (features, "figures," perhaps complexion and even skin color, and even physique)
50. More extensive use of transplantation of human organs
51. Permanent manned satellite and lunar installations—interplanetary travel
52. Application of space life systems or similar techniques to terrestrial installations
53. Permanent inhabited undersea installations and perhaps even colonies
54. Automated grocery and department stores
55. Extensive use of robots and machines "slaved" to humans
56. New uses of underground "tunnels" for private and public transportation and other purposes
57. Automated universal (real time) credit, audit and banking systems
58. Chemical methods for improving memory and learning
59. Greater use of underground buildings
60. New and improved materials and equipment for buildings and interiors (e.g., variable transmission glass, heating and cooling by thermoelectric effect, and electroluminescent and phosphorescent lighting)
61. Widespread use of cryogenics
62. Improved chemical control of some mental illnesses and some aspects of senility
63. Mechanical and chemical methods for improving human analytical ability more or less directly
64. Inexpensive and rapid techniques for making tunnels and underground cavities in earth and/or rock
65. Major improvements in earth moving and construction equipment generally
66. New techniques for keeping physically fit and/or acquiring physical skills
67. Commercial extraction of oil from shale
68. Recoverable boosters for economic space launching
69. Individual flying platforms
70. Simple inexpensive home video recording and playing
71. Inexpensive high-capacity, worldwide regional, and local (home and business) communication (perhaps using satellites, lasers, and light pipes)
72. Practical home and business use of "wired" video communication for both telephone and TV (possibly including retrieval of taped material from libraries or other sources) and rapid transmission and reception of facsimiles (possibly including news, library materials, commerical announcements, instantaneous mail delivery, other printouts, and so on)
73. Practical large-scale desalinization
74. Pervasive business use of computers for the storage, processing, and retrieval of information
75. Shared time (public and interconnected?) computers generally available to home and business on a metered basis.
76. Other widespread use of computers for intellectual and professional assistance (translation, teaching, literature search, medical diagnosis, traffic control, crime detection, computation, design, analysis and to some degree as intellectual collaborator generally)

77. General availability of inexpensive transuranic and other esoteric elements
78. Space defence systems
79. Inexpensive and reasonably effective ground-based BMD
80. Very low-cost buldings for home and business use
81. Personal "pagers" (perhaps even two-way pocket phones) and other personal electronic equipment for communication, computing, and data processing program
82. Direct broadcasts from satellites to home receivers
83. Inexpensive (less than $20), long lasting, very small battery operated TV receivers
84. Home computers to "run" household and communicate with outside world
85. Maintenance-free, longlife electronic and other equipment
86. Home education via video and computerized and programmed learning
87. Stimulated and planned and perhaps programmed dreams
88. Inexpensive (less than one cent a page) rapid high-quality black and white reproduction; followed by color and high-detailed photography reproduction—perhaps for home as well as office use
89. Widespread use of improved fluid amplifiers
90. Conference TV (both closed circuit and public communication system)
91. Flexible penology without necessarily using prisons (by use of modern methods of surveillance, monitoring, and control)
92. Common use of (longlived?) individual power source for lights, appliances, and machines
93. Inexpensive worldwide transportation of humans and cargo
94. Inexpensive road-free (and facility-free) transportation
95. New methods for rapid language teaching
96. Extensive genetic control for plants and animals
97. New biological and chemical methods to identify, trace, incapacitate, or annoy people for police and military uses
98. New and possibly very simple methods for lethal biological and chemical warfare
99. Artificial moons and other methods for lighting large areas at night
100. Extensive use of "biological processes" in the extraction and processing of minerals

The following are areas in which technological success by the year 2000 seems substantially less likely (even money bets, give or take a factor of five), but where, if it occurred, it would be quite important, are these:

Some Less Likely But Important Possibilities

1. "True" artificial intelligence
2. Practical use of sustained fusion to produce neutrons and/or energy
3. Artificial growth of new limbs and organs (either in situ or for later transplantation)
4. Room temperature superconductors
5. Major use of rockets for commercial or private transportation (either terrestrial or extraterrestrial)
6. Effective chemical or biological treatment for most mental illnesses
7. Almost complete control of marginal changes in heredity
8. Suspended animation (for years or centuries)
9. Practical materials with nearly "theoretical limit" strength
10. Conversion of mammals (humans?) to fluid breathers
11. Direct input into human memory banks